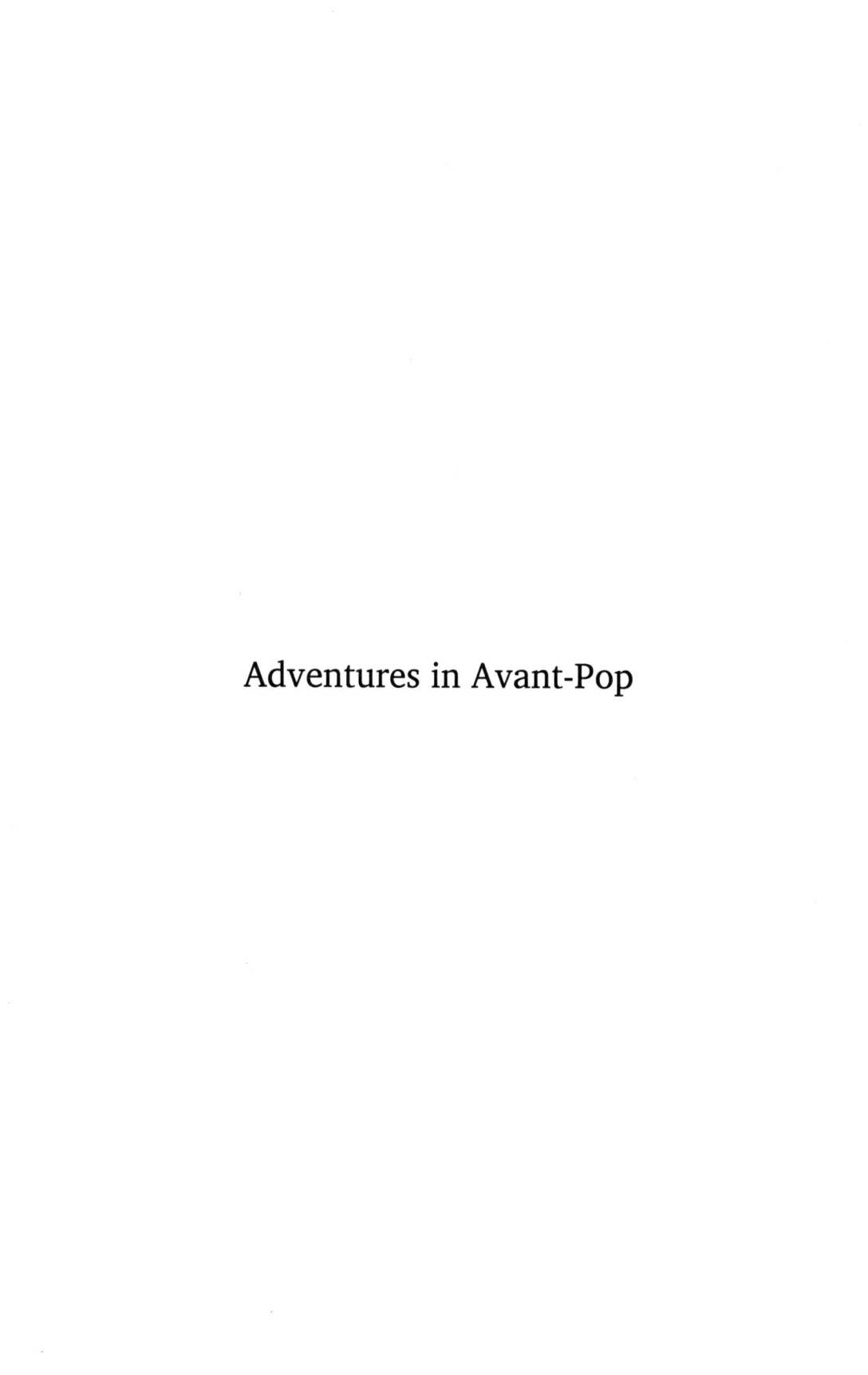

Adventures in Avant-Pop

Adventures in Avant-Pop

Bob Mielke

(Version 1.0)

Naciketas Press
715 E. McPherson
Kirksville, Missouri 63501
2013

Copyright ©2013 by Bob Mielke

All rights reserved. No portion of this publication may be duplicated in any way without the expressed written consent of the publisher, except in the form of brief excerpts or quotations for review purposes.

ISBN   978-1-936135-02-8 (1-936135-02-7)

Library of Congress Control Number: 2013949222

Published by:
Naciketas Press
715 E. McPherson
Kirksville, Missouri 63501

Available at:
Naciketas Press
715 E. McPherson
Kirksville, Missouri, 63501
Phone: (660) 665-0273
http://www.naciketas-press.com
Email: ndelmoni@gmail.com

Lovingly dedicated to the memory and achievements of Lester Bangs:
"There will never be another one like you."

Contents

Introduction: Building a Mystery   ix
    Works Cited xx

Adventures in Avant-Pop   5

The Three Musical Faces of Yoko Ono   7
    Approaching Yoko 7
    Plastic Ono Abjection 9
    Sisters 0 Sisters 18
    Season of Glass 30
    Dragon Lady Beats 36
    P. S. Forever Young Yoko! 43
    P. P. S. Yoko's Last Laugh 47
    Works Cited 47
    Works Consulted 48

Frank Zappa's Big Note   53
    "Hello, Frank Zappa ... ": The Project/Object, Conceptual Continuity
       and Other Bedevilments for the Young Sophisticate 53
    Don't Shoot the Messenger?: Zappa and/or Feminism 61
    "Would y'all like some more-a?": A Tentative Listening Guide 69
       Instructions for Use 69
       The Guide Itself 70
    Strictly Genteel 122
    Works Cited 122
    Works Consulted 123
    Appendix: Ranked Titles by Genre and Thematic Mix Tape Suggestions 124

Neil Young: Prisoner of Avant-Pop — 133
- Phenomenology Continued: Crazy Horse — 137
- Neil Young's Masks — 140
- Journeys Through The Ditch — 177
- Neil in the 1990s — 203
- From "Let's Roll" to "Let's Impeach The President": Neil Young's Conceptual Politics for the New Millennium — 206
- "We Left Our Tracks In The Sound:" Neil Young's First Last Statement — 231
- The Archives: Neil's Ultimate Avant-Pop Gesture — 236
- P.S.: Forever Young! — 238
- Works Cited — 253
- Appendix: The Bonnaroo Letter — 254

Joni Mitchell's Musical Hejira — 265
- Joni's Special Sauce — 267
- *Blue* — 272
- Joni's Journeys Through The Ditch — 279
  - *The Hissing of Summer Lawns* — 279
  - *Hejira* — 284
  - *Don Juan's Reckless Daughter* — 291
  - *Mingus* — 296
  - *Dog Eat Dog* — 300
- The Persistence of Joni — 305
- Works Cited — 309

We Travel Ra's Spaceways — 313
- Cosmo Sun Connection to the Alter-Destiny — 313
- But Is It Jazz? — 318
- But Is It Avant-Pop? — 321
- Where Is Sun Ra Coming From, Besides Saturn? — 326
- Was Sun Ra From Saturn? — 330
- Some Omniversal Listening Suggestions — 338
- The Chicago Years (1948 - 1960) — 340
- The New York Years (1961-1968) — 342
- The Philadelphia Years and the Arkestra on World Tour (1968-1992) — 349
  - Studio Work (1968-1970) — 349
  - First European and African Tours (1970-71) — 351
  - Stateside Live Appearances, Studio Work, and a Jaunt to Paris (1970-71) — 353
  - Back in Europe (1976) — 360
  - The Late Seventies: Outburst of Productivity — 360
  - The 1980s — 366

CONTENTS vii

    Final Recordings, or, Sun Ra Leaves Earth 371
    Posthumous Discoveries and Tributes 373
        Discoveries 373
        Tributes 385
    Why Sun Ra Matters 389
    Works Cited 396
    Appendix: Musical Highlights from The Complete Detroit Jazz Center
        Residency, December 26, 1980 - January 1, 1981 398

James Brown: Funky Surrealism, Surrealist Funk   417
    Soul Power: James Brown's Contributions to Soul Music 425
    Papa's Brand New Bag 429
    Brother Rapp 434
    Starch Surrealism: Let a Man Come In and Do the Popcorn 435
    He's Real 438
    Works Cited 441

Who's Afraid of Sigmund Snopek III?   447
    Location Is Everything 447
    Progressive Snopek 451
    Virginia Woolf 452
    Trinity Seas Seize Sees 456
    Nobody to Dream 461
    Roy Rogers Meets Albert Einstein 466
    "We're Setting Sights upon the Eighties" 469
    Thinking Out Loud 469
    First Band On The Moon 473
    WisconsInsane 477
    Elephant 480
    Beer 484
    Sigmund Snopek Meets Santa Claus 489
    Works Cited 492
    Appendix: the Sigmund Snopek Interview 493

Index   519

Introduction: Building a Mystery

This book is, on one level at least, a fan's notes on fifty years of listening to music—albeit it is focused on seven figures who have especially mattered to me over those years. I am fully aware of the risks associated with a project like this. Popular culture studies, especially aimed at a general audience (vs., say, the academic rigors of the Birmingham School), can smack of self-indulgent, narcissistic chat. Furthermore, the more politically inclined on the left tend to disparage insufficiently Marxist and overly aesthetic considerations of popular material. Such writing, they argue, merely reaffirms the bourgeois status quo. I know now from reading *Uncovering the Sixties*, Abe Peck's history of the underground press, that such charges were levied at rock journalism from its inception. Music as a handmaiden of revolution was not completely to be trusted. Since popular music itself was also not to be trusted, it has never been, for some, a worthy subject of critical attention.

Ambivalences about music go back to the very beginnings of western consciousness, of course. On the one hand, we have stories that affirm music's power: Joshua tumbling down the walls of Jericho in the Old Testament, Orpheus' many accomplishments in Greek mythology. On the other, we have Plato's nervous determinations in *The Republic* regarding what kind of musical modes ought to be allowed in an ideal state, lest the wrong kind of music corrupt the populace. The long shadow of these concerns reaches to the Frankfurt School of sociology in the twentieth century: Teodor Adorno fretting about jazz, Walter Benjamin concerned about the loss of "aura" in the technologically reproduced artifact. Some of us can still remember the Parents Music Resource Center (PMRC) in the eighties, a conglomeration of congressional wives who eventually got content labels onto the packaging of new releases. More of us can remember ongoing controversies about rap lyrics.

The first (safe) assumption of this book is that music does matter. Although birds and humpback whales remind us we do not have a species monopoly on music, music is a human universal. Every culture produces it, even ones who occasionally ban it for religious reasons. Music augments our feelings of contact with the sacred, ranging from voodoo drumming to Gregorian chant. Politicians are also keenly aware of its importance. I'm not just thinking of all that Nazi marching music Joseph Goebbels commissioned for Hitler rallies. I am reminded how Bill Clinton set the tone for his administration with Fleetwood Mac's "Don't Stop (Thinking About Tomorrow);" and, more ominously, how Dubya appropriated an edited version of the Who's "Won't Get Fooled Again" on the eve of his non-election (leaving out the lines "Meet the new boss / same as the old boss").

A corollary to this first assumption is that music is worth talking about and studying. Perhaps my eight years of studying with the Jesuits is showing here in part. St. Ignatius Loyola considered it axiomatic that one can "find God in all things." All of the universe manifests the goodness of the divine if we know how to look closely enough. A more secular humanist way to rephrase this would be to consider that everything in the world has value, certainly including popular music. If you have any doubts about this claim, check out the writings of Lester Bangs—the rock critic this book is dedicated to. Bangs raised the writing of popular music criticism to literary art, all the while burnishing the jewel of his musical subject matter so we could hear what he was hearing. His passion, lightly worn erudition, and clarity far surpass the efforts of more rewarded and honored academic critics in the humanities. (The only way the rest of us can write about music is to not obsess about coming up to his extraordinary standards, a stance he would approve of: such anxieties lead to bad imitation.)[1]

My third assumption is that music can be approached from across disciplinary lines, that interdisciplinary writing is doable and valuable—even if the writer is not technically an expert in the disciplines at hand. This is a less safe assumption: at my university, I still have colleagues who believe that you need a doctorate in every field you wish to say something meaningful about. We have an interdisciplinary seminar requirement for all majors; in the initial phases of its development, credentials were closely examined lest dilettantes got a crack at teaching these courses.

I come from another place entirely. Several decades of membership in the Society for Values in Higher Education, an interdisciplinary think tank, has enabled me to have meaningful conversations across the disciplines and shown me that non-experts can have a valuable outside perspective on the discursive formations that constitute various areas of study. Environmental, nuclear and foreign policy issues, for example, are far too important to be left exclusively in the hands of a trained elite who have been socialized to think inside a particular box. But the same even goes for aesthetic issues as well. I have a colleague from Kashmir, trained to appreciate Indian classical music, who never took seriously folk "wedding bands" from that region until I explained to her how

Introduction: Building a Mystery xi

much they impressed the American jazz world and why.

These attitudes and proclivities of mind were thoroughly reinforced by my fourteen summers (1986-1999) spent teaching American Foundations, a team-taught interdisciplinary summer course in American studies based out of the Reynolda House Museum of American Art on the campus. The music faculty showed us all how to talk about music in a non-technical fashion, a kind of careful "listening by ear" that helped us account for what we were hearing formally and expressively in the music at hand. This method is the way I will be describing in greater depth some of the pieces discussed below. More importantly, American Foundations confirmed that interdisciplinary approaches to culture can be interesting and illuminating. So, for me, a book on popular music by someone who has received no advanced training in the field became possible.

It's not that I utterly lack credentials for undertaking this project beyond all this exposure to interdisciplinary discussion. I bring to this project a considerable background in American studies and critical theory—and 50 years of reverential appreciation of this music. I have been a disk jockey in four separate venues; I have even been in a certifiably avant-pop band in my own right: I played theremin synthesizer, sundry reed instruments and a series of drainpipes tuned to an octave which I played with an amplified electric vibrator! And my music archive is conveniently huge.

Yet my final assumption is that, when all is said and done, music remains a mysterious miracle. There is a limit to what one can write about it (even if, unlike me, one is an expert). To some extent, all writers on music are writing listening guides; and at some point, we are all reduced to pointing our fingers at something sublimely ineffable and saying "listen! listen!" If these words make you want to go out and hear this music—or make you re-listen more carefully if you already have it lying around—I will have succeeded.

My study on William Dean Howells entitled *The Riddle of the Painful Earth*, promised that it was the first part of a trilogy on social activism. The remaining two parts were to be *Tickling the Dragon's Tail: American Nuclear Culture* (a look at same with photographer-collaborator James Crnkovich; since completed but still unpublished and ever-mutating as a project) and a projected book offering a Nietzschean genealogy of ideas about war and peace from Sun Tzu through Von Clausewitz and Herman Kahn to the visionary ends of history in Bernardo Bertolucci's films *1900* and *The Last Emperor*. I have temporarily abandoned this project. Initially, this was because of ongoing delays in the publication of the nuclear culture book. Then I began to think the Nietzschean book was somewhat self-evident except for the Bertolucci part (which I would still like to write someday): strategists on war and peace tend to be dialectical and paradoxical to begin with. They deconstruct themselves before a reader can do it!

Plan B was to write a biography of Yoko Ono, a figure I have long been fascinated by. I gave up this earlier effort for what I consider to be ethical reasons: I found as a biographer that I did not have an unconditional love for my subject. I discovered that I liked Yoko's art, but not her life. In addition, I was daunted by questions of access needed to do such a biography while based in rural Missouri. The decision to just consider Yoko Ono's music became the germ for this book. Fortunately, a biography of Ono was published in 2004: *Woman: The Incredible Life of Yoko Ono* by Alan Clayson (with Barb Jungr and Robb Johnson).[2]

I then decided to look at seven representative careers in music, including Yoko Ono's, that bridged the hypothetical divide between popular music and avant-garde composition in varying degrees. These figures range from ones that may barely strike readers as avant-garde (James Brown, Neil Young) to others that hardly seem popular (Yoko Ono, Sun Ra, Sigmund Snopek III). All seven do blur this hypothetical and contested line between high and low culture, however, in varying degrees. In addition, all seven have had careers spanning more than several decades.

Even by these minimal criteria, the artists chosen are not meant to be privileged over many other people I could have discussed using the same criteria: Lou Reed, John Cale, the Grateful Dead and all its members broadly considered, Robert Fripp, Brian Eno, Patti Smith, Kate Bush, Prince / The Artist, Lester Bowie, David Bowie, Captain Beefheart, David Byrne and Polly Jean Harvey, just off the top of my head, would have been equally suitable for inclusion.

Given those I have chosen, however, a new trilogy is emerging from my computer. (You'd think I'd learn to be cautious as a prophet after my previous experience!) My book on nuclear culture, coupled with this book and a planned work on American Catholicism will form a trilogy triply unified as critical autobiography (my three formative influences were the cold war, music and Catholicism), oblique sixties reflections / memoirs, and cases in American studies.

The impetus behind this particular book, though, transcends these issues of memory, history and nationality. One larger historical context I wish to evoke emerges from considerations of *Rabelais and His World* by Mikhail Bakhtin and *Highbrow/Lowbrow: The Emergence of Cultural Hierarchy in America* by Lawrence W. Levine. Both of these books document quasi-utopian moments in cultural history when the laughing voice of the people was audible in conjunction with serious art, when culture was less stratified. Bakhtin concentrates on the middle ages and Francois Rabelais' preservation of this festive folk culture in *Gargantua and Pantagruel*, a work that puzzles the modern reader because of its very freedom and ease in transgressing ostensible proprieties. Medieval and early modern culture had safety valves: festivals, fairs, carnival, feasts of fools where culture could go topsy-turvy in a liberating way. Such entertainments

Introduction: Building a Mystery xiii

both critiqued and renewed the culture by a kind of collective purgation. As modernity and enlightenment crept into Europe, Bakhtin argues, the subversive quality of these rituals became muted into mere tourist spectacle. The belly laugh of popular ridicule became rarefied into polite irony. Culture became incrementally more stratified.

Lawrence Levine notes a second chance for high / low erosion that occurred in Jacksonian-era America, when the voice of the people was again empowered. We see an example of this American high / low cultural blurring and fusion in Mark Twain's *Adventures of Huckleberry Finn*. You will recall the curious performances of the Duke and the Dauphin, offering both the Royal Nonesuch and odd cuttings from Shakespeare. Levine in fact shows that Shakespeare proved highly adaptable in this new country. He was a popular favorite appropriated for all sorts of purposes in diverse manners of presentation. Samuel Clemens is not making this stuff up! Even opera was universally popular then: Jenny Lind, the "Swedish Nightingale," was a pop star in her day (see Levine 89). Walt Whitman's writings also attest to the catholicity of post-Jacksonian America.

As Levine notes, this began to change around mid-century. Culture became "sacralized;" temples like the first opera houses and concert halls were built to it. The actual music became more important than the performance (110). In a parallel fashion, the Bard was viewed as a text one had to be faithful to. Public performance became less exuberant; audiences became less rowdy. High culture was a serious matter, a sign that America was joining European civilization. Popular culture became more marginalized and devalued: the sentimental song was confined to the beer hall or the family parlor.

Levine sensed in the epilogue to his 1988 book that things were loosening up a little again in the present moment. My book takes that suspicion as a point of departure. I am most interested here in how people's musics such as jazz and rock and roll became capable of high art, even avant-garde gestures. Those intersections will comprise the bulk of this book. But let me remind the reader that these cross-fertilizations did not occur in a vacuum. The sixties were all about eroding high / low cultural distinctions—fuelled by solvents as diverse as LSD and the "happening," mass performance art which spread from Black Mountain College in rural North Carolina to New York and beyond. A typical iconic moment would be Ken Kesey and his Merry Pranksters entertaining the Hells Angels motorcycle gang at his compound in La Honda. This psychedelic event was also attended by poet Allen Ginsberg and gonzo journalist Hunter S. Thompson. They both wrote about it, as did journalist Tom Wolfe in his *Electric Kool-Aid Acid Test*. This kind of cultural cross-fertilization was a frequent occurrence then; it was the fertile soil from which an avant-pop sensibility could emerge. This is one reason why the sixties proved to be important for all seven of my representative figures.

That was then; this is now. Once again our culture seems highly stratified and fragmented. Subcultures receive their own narrowcasts without much interaction with others: the worlds of NASCAR and the WWF might overlap a little, but neither will have much truck with Lincoln Center. The only serious blurring of high / low distinctions I see these days, pathetically enough, can be discerned in the diverse audience base of voyeurs who eavesdropped in on *The Osbournes* reality show and its legion of successors. It's come down to this, I fear. Or the post 9 / 11 displaying of the flag—which is too diffuse a gesture to unify a culture very much, I'd submit. This book, then, is an homage to a relatively recent moment that made some interesting cultural moves possible for a time.

* * *

We can consider another historical narrative to place these artists in besides the tale we have just told using Bakhtin and Levine. For avant-pop is not only the result of a populist eruption into high culture, but also a reflection of the current definitional crisis in aesthetics: foundational uncertainty as to what is art, literature, music in general (let alone where such should be placed with regard to genres and subgenres). Let me explain.

This genre crisis doesn't impact most consumers of popular culture in a practical way. If you go to our local Hastings to buy the latest CD by the White Stripes, your only genre dilemma regards the issue of whether they will be filed under "independent / alternative" or "rock" (indie-alt that's achieved sufficient mainstreaming, e.g. REM or U2). If you went instead to a Tower Records, a Streetside or a Sam Goody's, you wouldn't even have this minor problem: these chains collapse the distinction Hastings makes. And on Amazon.com, yes, all popular music is pretty much lumped together (with classical a separate consideration).

The minor genre problem, with major implications, has to do with your ears. You would think that you could identify a genre by listening to an actual recording, but you can't in many cases—especially with the artists I will be discussing. Try this experiment I have used on several occasions. Play for any audience these five tracks and ask the listeners to identify what genre they would be located in at a music store:

1. "Dream Song of the River" by Sigmund Snopek III (*Nobody to Dream*)

2. "Atlantis" by Sun Ra (*Atlantis*)

3. "N-Lite" by Frank Zappa (*Civilization Phaze III*)

4. "Toilet Piece / Unknown" by Yoko Ono (*Fly*)

Introduction: Building a Mystery

5. "4'33"" by John Cage, covered by Frank Zappa (*A Chance Operation: The John Cage Tribute*).

I would be very surprised if your listeners could guess the genre-labeling of more than one of these compositions. (The answer key would be, respectively: rock, jazz, rock, rock, rock. But what they would be actually hearing would be, respectively, a string quartet; atonal electronic improvisation; a classical synclavier composition; a toilet flushing; and unintentional sound [so-called, if incorrectly, "silence"].) Music is processed on the basis of expectations, as opposed to actual content. It turns out anything goes, and thereby hangs another narrative.

This historical narrative is presented by philosopher and aesthetician Arthur Danto in his 1997 tome *After the End of Art: Contemporary Art and the Pale of History*. Danto argues that western art is dead, although it naturally continues to be produced (art is dead; long live art!). He even has a date for its demise (in 1964) and a place where it died (the Stable Gallery on East 7th street in Manhattan) (Danto 35). 1 want to extend his argument to suggest that western music has also perished, although it continues to be written and performed. Music also died in New York City, a bit earlier: on August 29, 1952. What on earth are Arthur Danto and I talking about?

Arthur Danto roughly divides western art into three major phases. Initially, he says, it underwent a quest for certain ultimate universal ideals and goals largely shared by its practitioners and loosely described under the rubric of representation or mimesis. In other words: pictures that look like landscapes, people, fruit in a bowl; sculpture that replicates the human form. Some people and even cultures were more accomplished at this than others (as resources relating to perspective developed), but everyone was more or less attempting the same goal (broad strokes, I concede) (cf. Danto 29).

But, as many have noted, the aesthetic quest changed after the invention of photography in the nineteenth century. Painting was no longer needed in the service of mimesis: a photograph could do it better (although it has been noted that portraits are superior to photographs since they observe the subject over time). According to Danto, the response to these new developments was the modernist Age of Manifestos (Danto 29-30). Art explored many approaches during this new phase—not just issues of mimesis—and art theorists defended its particular practice in writing to the exclusion of other approaches, creating the aesthetic philosophical prose of the manifesto. Many manifestos were written by actual practitioners of the plastic arts (Marinetti's Futurist manifesto, Andre Breton's Surrealist manifestos); others were penned by art critics (Roger Fry's writings in the Bloomsbury Group, Clement Greenberg's promotion of the abstract expressionists in New York). These writings argued for what was valid and invalid art after representation itself ceased to be a criterion.

So what happened at the Stable Gallery in 1964? Round up the usual suspects: Andy Warhol displayed painted Brillo boxes (I have to tell my students these days that Brillo was a cleaning pad) indistinguishable from real Brillo boxes. Even Marcel Duchamp's "Fountain," a "readymade" sculpture displaying a urinal, had the decency to turn the urinal on its side (as replicated at the recent Whitney centennial show, thereby answering the age-old philosophical conundrum: what's the difference between art and life? 90 degrees!). But Andy's Brillo boxes looked just like, well, Brillo boxes. After he got away with this, clearly *anything* could be art—and is if we are so persuaded. (Admittedly, this question was first raised by some aspects of dadaism; the power of the Warhol Brillo box is the sheer banality of its radical gesture).

O brave new world! The good news is that art after the death of art (as a stable philosophical category) is now inclusive, multicultural, pluralistic. The bad news is that we have no current lodestar to guide our collective tastes by other than critical, aesthetic and (especially) curatorial will-to-power. My favorite anecdote to illustrate this odd state of affairs is a sculpture I saw a few years ago at the Walker Art Museum in Minneapolis. It was a "sculpture" of a made-up bed (mixed media); that is to say, it WAS a made-up bed in the gallery (replete with pillows, blankets and sheets). I forget the name of the artist who did it, but I am haunted by the title of the work: "Untitled." All the uncanny power of the art was in that label—and the fact that the bed was in an art gallery.

I would argue that parallel developments have occurred in western music (and many other fields, but that is a long, separate story we need not go into here). In music, the ultimate ideals and values associated with the first phase were concerned with harmony and consonance. One telling illustration of these concerns can be indicated by the discouragement of the dissonant "diabolus" chord in the middle ages. At that time, dissonance was associated with the devil himself!

The move from harmonic ideals to music's Age of Manifestos is a much more complex narrative, since mechanical reproduction was too late a development to be a technological game-changer as photography was for the visual arts: the musical transition had already occurred. One almost has to look at composers on a case-by- case basis to see hoow approaches shifted. Here are some reasons for this new music based on non-traditional approaches to harmony and consonance:

1. A simple interest in copying aesthetic innovations in painting. After pictorial impressionism, we had musical impressionism from fellow Europeans Claude Debussy and Maurice Ravel. (The literary impressionism of Stephen Crane and Joseph Conrad came even later.) Different media, same approach: what and how the eye sees.

Introduction: Building a Mystery xvii

2. The impact of modernity in general. The resources of the old ways had been exhausted; time to innovate for innovation's sake.

3. More specifically, an interest in capturing the sounds of the new industrial technologies. Cultural studies scholar Michael Jarrett has been working on a massive book about the musical impact of the sounds of the railroad. When I labored in a factory, the machines not coincidentally sounded like passages from Stravinsky's *Rite of Spring*. George Antheil caused his Paris riot (a la Stravinsky) by running an airplane engine onstage at the premiere of *Ballet Mecanique*.

4. An attempt to democratize musical sounds. In *The Book of Laughter and Forgetting*, Milan Kundera tells an evocative fable about how Arnold Schoenberg's twelve-tone row serial composition technique overthrew the monarchy of being dominated by a particular key. This may be more than just a witty fable. American composer Charles Ives was interested in capturing certain sounds he enjoyed that were not conventionally melodic (e.g., a passionate drunk singing off-key in a church choir). His bandleader dad's sonic experiments, like having two marching bands pass each other playing in different keys, were also influential. The new "classical" music was unquestionably more inclusive.

5. The fruits of imperialism and colonialism. The different scales, rhythms and approaches of conquered cultures (Asian, African, Middle Eastern, Native American) all had an impact on the music of the late nineteenth and early twentieth centuries comparable to the effect African art had on painters like Picasso. Before ethnographic field recordings, there was travel—and immigration by the colonized to the centers of Europe.

All of these developments were in full bloom before the dissemination of mechanical reproduction of sound via the phonograph. So I would submit the record only accelerated the process (especially regarding the last two points in the series). What it did do varied by genre. In classical music, as Teodor Adorno lamented, it led to a cult of certain conductors (e.g., Arturo Toscanini) and certain performers (Enrico Caruso). A similar result happened in popular music when the microphone made possible more subdued singing ("crooning"). Enter Bing Crosby, Frank Sinatra and the deluge. (Why they disliked rock and roll music: no need to sing that loud anymore!).

In folk and blues, records unquestionably slowed down—but did not halt—the mutations of the folk process for those who could hear a recorded version of a tune. Jazz undoubtedly benefitted the most by recording technology: nonce improvisations could be captured for posterity and given the same permanence as classical music (before recording via the musical score). Indeed, jazz scholars transcribe these recorded solos to learn their craft.

In any case, composers such as Schoenberg, Ives and Harry Partch (to name but a few) wrote important theoretical treatises with the force of manifestos in this era paralleling Danto's paradigm for the visual arts. Then, on August 29, 1952, pianist David Tudor premiered (I dodge temporarily one metaphysical bullet by this verb choice) John Cage's 4'33"—the only classical piece in my personal piano repertoire at this point. The piece consists of three movements (I. 30"; II. 2'23"; III. 1'40") and the instruction to the pianist "Tacet." Don't strike the keyboard; let it remain silent (literally from the Latin). Here was music indistinguishable from the ambient noise of the concert hall (or wherever it was performed). Don't call it silence: there is no such thing. John Cage found this out while visiting Bell laboratory's anechoic chamber, a soundproof environment. Cage told the technicians that the room was flawed, since he could hear a low rumbling sound and a high whine. They explained to him that nothing was wrong with the room: the low rumbling sound was the noise made by his blood flowing and the high whine was his central nervous system. In other words, we as humans can never hear total silence; we are wedded to sound inexorably if we have the capacity to hear. This revelation led Cage towards 4'33."

After this blast of unintentional sound heard round the world, anything could potentially be music as long as it was framed as such. As with the plastic arts, the fallout has been a great diversity of possibilities: the avant-pop hybridities considered herein, world beats, songs in the key of Z, you name it. And again, the critical will-to-power sorting it out as opposed to the standards and strictures of treatises on harmony. This is another story about how this book and its subjects came to be possible.

And yes, this tome is also a listening guide distilling over fifty years of paying attention to this music for those less committed to it, but curious about it. I offer my informed, if non-specialist, opinions. As philosopher David Hume among others has suggested, there is nothing mysterious about taste: it's just a matter of exposure and informed judgment. I tell my film students that the first film they see will be the best one they ever saw; when they see two, they can and will prefer one over the other. So it goes with all the arts. The reason why most rock journalism is so weak in campus media is because the average budding rock writer doesn't have a sufficient listening repertoire for comparisons. Whatever my faults, this is certainly not one of them. I've heard a lot of music!

I want to thank the late jazz trumpeter Lester Bowie and actor Owen Wilson for my title. Bowie called one of his Brass Fantasy albums *Avant-Pop*; Owen Wilson invoked the term during a cocktail party scene in the otherwise undistinguished film *Permanent Midnight*. (I suppose I should be really thanking the screenwriter here.) I want to thank John and Jim Blasky for initially exposing me to the music of Neil Young many years ago. I owe a similar debt of grat-

Introduction: Building a Mystery

itude to Judith Markowski for encouraging me to listen more closely to Joni Mitchell—and for personally introducing me to Sigmund Snopek at the Jabberwocky nightclub in Milwaukee. The late Greg Bovee was kind enough to tape a series of Sun Ra concerts for me at Milwaukee's Jazz Gallery.

And speaking of Sigmund Snopek, I want to especially thank him for his willingness to talk to me, mail me unreleased recordings and help make the chapter concerning him as accurate as possible. I am always a bit daunted when I have the rare privilege of showing a living artist what I have to say about them as a critic, especially an artist like Snopek whom I have followed for four decades with the greatest admiration. He couldn't have been more helpful or enthusiastic about this project. I especially appreciated his giving me lots of leash with regards to my interpretation of his works, confining his corrections to factual matters (even though I'm sure he would disagree with some of my opinions).

The 2002 Crosby, Stills, Nash & Young St. Louis / Columbia / Kirksville honor roll of avant-pop depravity includes Arnie (since deceased), Alanna and Amy Preussner, Rod Taylor, Marc Rice, the also late and much-missed Karl Kopitske, Ruth Ann Gagnon, Mary Hurley, Jen Creer, Dereck Daschke and Lisa Glaubitz—and apparently some strippers in East St. Louis I took a pass on. I also want to extend to Marc my appreciation for letting me sit in on his Rock Generation junior interdisciplinary seminar, which helped me get many ideas for this book.

I have been similarly abetted by the teaching staff of American Foundations at Reynolda House and Wake Forest University. Special thanks are extended to Louis Goldstein, Gloria Fitzgibbons, Nick Bragg and Barbara Millhouse. At Truman, this book was facilitated by sabbatical years in 2001-2002 and 2012-2013: I thank Heinz Woehlk, Gary Gordon, Jack Magruder, Cole Woodcox, Priscilla Riggle, and Troy Paino for this opportunity.

I wish to thank especially Neal and Betsy Delmonico for helping me get this book out to the public. I also thank Jenny Jalack, Emily Murdock, Matt Felzke and Sam Politte (scanner/editors extraordinaire); Joyce Schmitz, Marie Delaney and Kathy Bulen (the helpful secretaries for Truman's English and Linguistics Department). Dr. Masahiro Hara graciously translated some of Yoko Ono's Japanese lyrics for me. And where would I be without Ben Ogden, my expert computer wrangler? And thanks to Ashley Butner, who helped me when Ben was unavailable.

Many other friends and family (you know who you are) got me through this project. Much of this book has been a result of prolonged conversations about popular music with Arnie Preussner, Rod Taylor, Marc Rice, Bill McKemy, Marty Erickson, Mr. Peabody, Royce Kallerud, Jane Donovan, James Crnkovich, the late Ken Watson and Jan Wilson. Thanks to all of these for insights, challenges and feedback.

Last, but certainly not least, my feline honor roll of support: the once and future Heidi (as in Wendy Wasserstein's play), Sylvia (Plath), Michael (Field), Merlin, Cleo / Cookie, and the late, great Top Cat and Yusef (Komunyakaa). Their unconditional love was and is the wind beneath my wings.

May you all keep on rocking in the free world!

Works Cited

Bakhtin, Mikhail. *Rabelais and His World.* Trans. Helene Iswolsky. Bloomington: Indiana University Press, 1984.
Bangs, Lester. *Psychotic Reactions and Carburetor Dung.* Ed. Greil Marcus. New York: Vintage, 1988.
Danto, Arthur C. *After the End of Art: Contemporary Art and the Pale of History.* Princeton: Princeton University Press, 1997.
Levine, Lawrence W. *Highbrow/Lowbrow: The Emergence of Cultural Hierarchy in America.* Cambridge: Harvard University Press, 1988.
Miles, Barry. *Zappa: A Biography.* New York: Grove Press, 2004.

Notes

[1] These three pieces show Lester Bangs at the very top of his game: "Of Pop, Pies and Fun: A Program of Mass Liberation in the Form of a Stooges Review, or, Who's the Fool?"(31-52); "The Clash" (224-259); and "Review of Peter Guralnick's *Lost Highway: Journeys & Arrivals of American Musicians* (318-336).
[2] Chrome Dreams from Surrey, UK.

Ironically, "Chrome Dreams" is the title of a discarded Neil Young release from the 1970s. In 2007, he issued a "sequel" called *Chrome Dreams II*—obviously a modest dig at his record label for thwarting his original intentions.

This coincidence reminds me of a more interesting issue: the cross-fertilization of the careers of these seven figures. One connection is obvious: the long friendship and occasional collaborations between Neil Young and Joni Mitchell. Or Sun Ra opening for James Brown at the Ann Arbor Blues Festival one year. The richest linkages, however, are with Frank Zappa. Yoko Ono performed with him (in the company of John Lennon) at the Fillmore East in June of 1971.

Even more surprisingly, a recent Zappa biography reveals that Joni Mitchell was a girlfriend of Motorhead Sherwood, one of the original Mothers of Invention. At this time, she lived with Motorhead and Zappa at a crash pad in Laurel Canyon, working on the songs for her first album (Miles 139). This connection might explain why Joni also sat in with Zappa and the Mothers at the Fillmore

East in November 1970. At this venue she shocked her fans in attendance by reciting a poem which began "Penelope wants to fuck the sea" over the band's improvisations. Then she sang "Duke of Earl" with the group (Miles 204-5). (Like Zappa, Mitchell is a fan of doo-wop.) To some extent, these folks are all simpatico!

Adventures in Avant-Pop

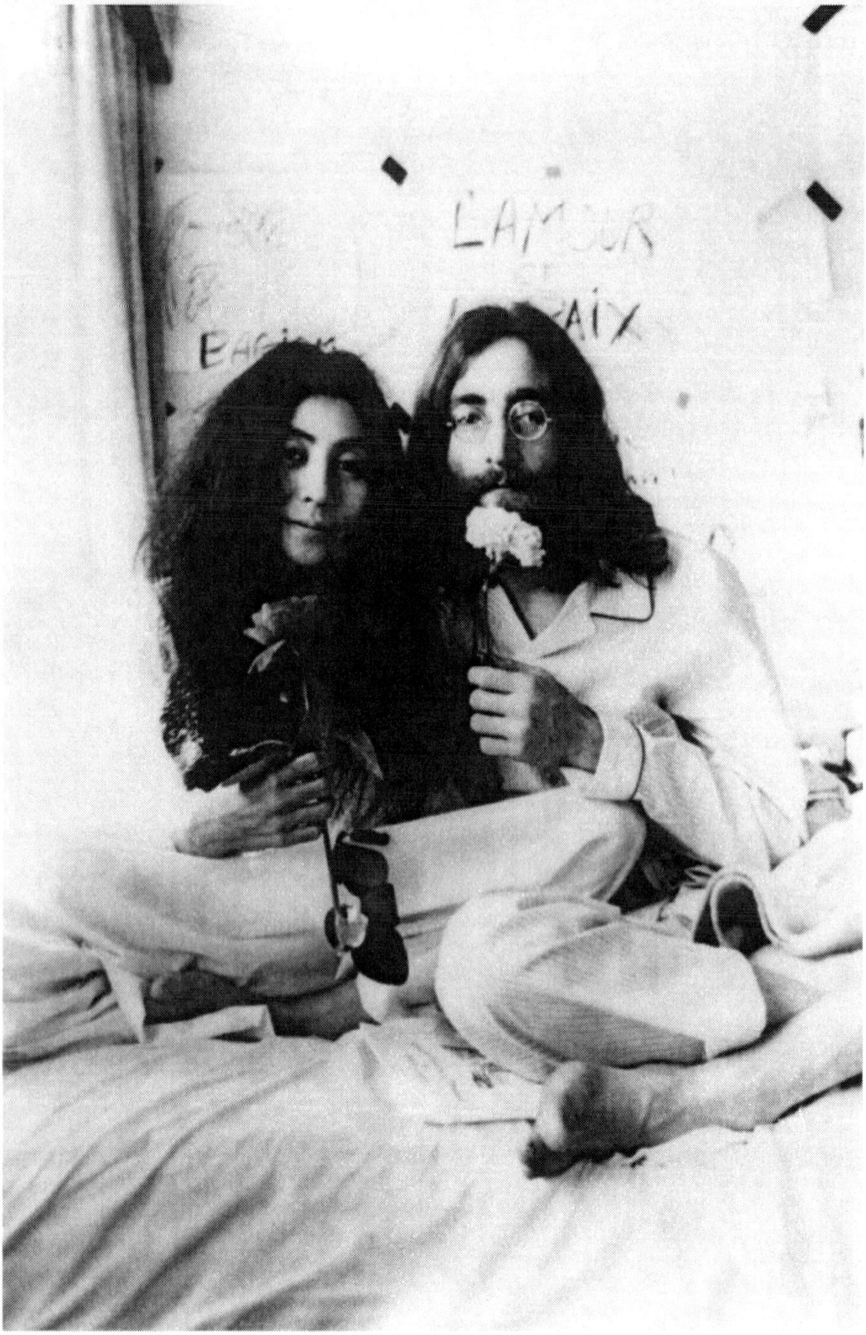
L'AMOUR

on the Beatles' Christmas records for their fan club?) and some sampling of pre-recorded sound. More auspiciously, you first hear on this record a tenuous example of Yoko's approach to vocalization and John's discovery of the great freedom Yoko gave him as a guitarist to improvise and create extended sonic sculptures of indeterminate length, a liberation denied him as a guitarist for a pop band. This experimental playing, as it improved, would eventually cast a long shadow into the future for bands like Sonic Youth even as Yoko's vocalizing would come to impress artists such as the B-52s and Diamanda Galas.

Needless to say, the rock critics were not amused. The couple's full nudity on the sleeve didn't help matters any, either. Lacking the musical referents on display in the piece, there was no possibility of any appreciation of the disk: it ended up being exhibit A of John's drug-induced insanity. "Revolution 9" on the *White Album*, arguably more of a John and Yoko piece than a Beatles piece, is far more successful simply because it's not unfinished: the splices that form the sound collage took a great deal of time. *Two Virgins* suffers from its impromptu nature: John and Yoko hadn't really learned to jam yet.

Yoko's second collaboration with John, May 1969's *Unfinished Music No. 2: Life With The Lions*, is a whole other story. Although the second side is a mix of homages to Cage ("Two Minutes Silence" and "Radio Play") and reality art in response to Yoko's hospital stay and miscarriage from the previous November ("No Bed For Beatle John," "Baby's Heartbeat"), side one contains the first aural masterpiece of Yoko's first musical phase: "Cambridge 1969," recorded live at Lady Mitchell Hall on March 2, 1969. This 26:28 full-frontal assault on the listener not only sounds fresh today; it sounds threatening. The shock of the new experienced at its premiere is almost impossible to imagine. Art this intense sends most listeners scurrying into defensive rationalizations and dismissals.

How to describe this sonic artifact? Imagine an Indian *rāga*, in about three movements with a long string-vocal duet before the percussion arrives— then amplify it! To be more formally descriptive, musical events happen in the piece like this: it begins with Yoko vocalizing and John experimenting with guitar feedback. At 7:42 on your CD counter, John's playing changes from long swells to short bursts reminiscent of a diesel horn, evoking rock music's rich reliance on train sounds. At 16:17 (note the rough shifts initially around the 8 minute mark), John Stevens comes in on percussion. As the piece winds to a close, it gets busier and busier (much like a raga). At 18:12, John reprises the diesel horn guitar and Stevens comes in on high-hat cymbals. At 22:16, John Tchicai comes in on sax, playing a brooding melody line while Yoko's vocalizing switches from sustained screams to staccato bursts; at 24:00, his playing switches to a more honking riff reminiscent of Albert Ayler. Then a mysterious sound like the plucking of strings from inside a piano intrudes (24:34). From 25:49 to the fadeout, only the saxophone keeps playing a kind of demented carnival strut, again very reminiscent of Ayler. The sonic barrage fades.

When I first heard this music after its initial release, I hated it. At the time, a freshman in high school, I had no context for appreciating it. I remember melting the lp down and turning it into a decorative ashtray (literally). I would have to pay collector's prices at a record convention in the early 1980s to reacquire it. But I did this for several reasons. It had stuck in my head all these years as a kind of art in extremis; furthermore, I had been exposed by my housemate to a lot of avant-garde jazz over the years. I suspected that the composition was better than I thought—and a lot more structured and crafted than met a first listen.

I didn't find a way to account for its power—or indeed the power of Yoko's first phase as a recording artist through her release of *Fly* in 1971—until I read Julia Kristeva's treatise on *Abjection, Powers of Horror* (1980, translated 1982). Kristeva's project is basically to rewrite Freud to account more for the importance of the mother in identity formation. Instead of the Oedipal moment as the arrival of the paternal, she considers it as part of the loss of the maternal body for the infant that begins with the severance of the umbilical cord and proceeds through weaning and the alienation from the mother as a suitable object of desire for the infant libido. Cut off from the maternal, our initial linkage is now reconfigured as taboo, even monstrous and threatening. Hence when boundaries slip between self and world in a manner evocative of our lost connection with the maternal, regressive pleasure is mixed with revulsion and fear. This is the experience of abjection (4, 9, 13, 38).

Kristeva applies her model to writers such as James Joyce, Antonin Artaud and Louis-Ferdinand Celine, but it finds expression in music as well as literature. A colleague of mine once tried to explain abjection to a theory class by talking about the moment in deep blues singing when the singer stops reciting lyrics and begins to moan. This slurring between words and subvocalization is an erosion of boundaries—at its most threatening "[t]he abject confronts us ... with those fragile states where man strays on the territories of *animal*" (Kristeva 12; her italics). This is precisely where Yoko's project takes us: if you don't believe me, play "Cambridge 1969" to a dog or a cat. Every such animal I've exposed this piece to responds as if there's another animal in the speakers.

Yoko's own explanation of her singing seems congenial to Kristeva's agenda:

> What I was trying to attain was a sound that almost doesn't come out. Before I speak I stutter in my mind, and then my cultured self tries to correct that stutter into a clean sentence ... and I wanted to deal with those sounds of people's fears and stuttering ... and of darkness, like a child's fear that someone is behind him, but he can't speak and communicate this ... .

Or:

> The older you get, the more frustrated you feel. And it gets to a point where you don't have time to utter a lot of intellectual bullshit. If you were drowning you wouldn't say: "I'd like to be helped because I have just a moment to live." You'd say "Help!" but if you were more desperate you'd say "Eioghhh" or something like that. And the desperation of life is really life itself, the core of life, what's really driving us forth. (Palmer for both)

Yoko Ono's early recordings are not pretty (as if art needed to be): they are testaments to fear, darkness, stuttering. They are literally monstrous. Psychoanalytically, they scream for a lost mother (Arthur Janov's primal scream therapy before the couple ever read him or worked with him), a narcissistic wound that can never be healed, a lack that can never be filled. John Lennon approached her technique in such works of his as "Cold Turkey" and "Mother" (after Janov). But "Cambridge 1969" sustains this for over 26 minutes. Sympathetic commentators like Robert Palmer have noted how this pain had both personal and historical causes. John and Yoko both had painful relationships with their biological mothers: Julia Lennon was mostly absent until her death when John was seventeen years old (whence his being raised by Aunt Mimi); Isoko Ono was present but aloof. (This cycled into their own problems with Julian, Kyoko and Sean.) Both artists have primal memories of World War II as well: Yoko experienced Curtis LeMay's firebombing of Tokyo; John remembered the blitz as it hit Liverpool shipping. Add into this psychic stew the inward journeys of psychedelics and meditation and the palpably felt chaos when the summer of love went sour into the Vietnam debacle, worldwide political upheaval, assassinations and violence. The result is a fertile loam for an extreme music of abjection and agony. Sensitive cultural registers that they were, that is precisely what Yoko and John gave the world in their groundbreaking avant-pop performances.

Even Yoko seemed to back off from the extremity of "Cambridge 1969" in her next major public performance at a Toronto Rock 'n Roll Revival concert on September 13, 1969. Instead of "instrumental" vocalizing, she threw in a few words: "Don't Worry Kyoko" and "John, John (Let's Hope For Peace)." But only a little bit: as D. A. Pennebaker's documentary film demonstrates, this festival was the most subversive context imaginable for Yoko's music.

For what Yoko and John did, by letting Yoko end the show with these two pieces, was in fact a critical act: her performance was contextualized as the culmination of rock and roll. Pennebaker's film *Sweet Toronto* makes this clear. It begins with Bo Diddley promising to take us "back to 1955" with his trademark riffing on "Hey Bo Diddley." He is followed by a song each from Jerry

Lee Lewis, Chuck Berry and Little Richard—a fair canon of rock's fifties past, especially since Lewis invokes Elvis by playing "Hound Dog." And, just as T. S. Eliot suggests in "Tradition and the Individual Talent," upon rewatching the tape we notice how rock's future (Ono) changes rock's past. These older figures scream and vocalize non-lyrical content (especially Little Richard). Their performances have a strongly narcissistic dimension: Yoko singing about John and Kyoko is anticipated by Bo Diddley singing about ... Bo Diddley!

When the Plastic Ono Band with Eric Clapton hit the stage, there is no doubt that the "Rock and Roll Revival" is shifting into the present tense. John opens with a Carl Perkins number the Beatles never did (on record at least by then), "Blue Suede Shoes" (also evoking Elvis). Yoko removes herself from the proceedings by climbing into a bag onstage. For the next two songs, "Money" and "Dizzy Miss Lizzie" (covered but not written by the Beatles), she is out of the bag but silent. Lennon's songlist continues to follow strict chronological order by performing "Yer Blues" from the *White Album* next. Yoko begins her background vocalizing here, as if to mark historically when she entered the rock-and-roll continuum. John's only fiddling with the chronology comes when he plays "Cold Turkey," a brand-new song, before "Give Peace a Chance"—no doubt to punctuate his political agenda.

With John's admonition that "Now Yoko's going to do her thing all over you," the Plastic Ono Band makes a case for rock's potential future with her two amazing performances that both extend and demolish the tradition. "Don't Worry Kyoko" still has a strong rhythmic backbone from Clapton and Lennon's playing and the rhythm section of Klaus Voorman on bass and Alan White on drums. But "John, John (Let's Hope For Peace)" gives an indelible record in sound and vision of how radical these early performances were (if only we had a video of "Cambridge 1969"). As Yoko vocalizes, John moves from simple guitar feedback to playing the whole physical guitar (plucking the bridge, moving toggle switches and plugs on the amp). The performance gets more visually choreographic as he swings his guitar against the amp and around in a circle. Clapton even begins experimenting with a bottleneck slide. Yoko's extended vocalizations turn to staccato birdlike cries; the guitarists lay their instruments against the amplifiers. John dances behind Yoko like a wild man, and then imitates a swooping bird much like the lovers' moves on the bow of the Titanic in the James Cameron film. Then all leave the stage with megawatts of pure feedback juice drenching the audience, recalling Ono's original plan to have a band consisting merely of music-making machines or players in plastic boxes on a stage—the genesis of the name "Plastic Ono Band." It must have felt like *götterdämmerung* that day in Toronto, and several light years from Bo Diddley's opening. Yoko gives a challenging performance to consider now; what would a 1969 audience at a rock and roll revival concert have made of it?

John's agenda for the gig was exposing Yoko to the music that influenced him, but the result was an unprecedented if barely noticed fusion of classic rock and roll and the avant-garde. Like any good conceptual artist, Yoko's performance raises interesting questions: is she performing rock and roll? How multicultural is it as a musical medium? Can people of Asian descent "own" it as much as those of African or European descent? How will they inflect it differently? Why? Can rock accommodate high art gestures of an avant-garde nature (vs., say, the romantic art rock of then-contemporary bands like the Moody Blues)? She offers a provocation which different viewers and listeners will come to different conclusions about.

The next interesting musical work from Yoko is 1970's *Yoko Ono/Plastic Ono Band* release. The preceding *Wedding Album* is more reality art/concept art/documentary than conventional music with its love side (John and Yoko reciting each other's names) and its peace side (a press conference at a bed-in) on the lp accompanied by a treasure trove of elaborate production goodies: a cardboard piece of cake, a photo album, a copy of the marriage license. *Yoko Ono/Plastic Ono Band*, the indispensable companion recording to the much more famed *John Lennon/Plastic Ono Band*, on the other hand marks the first moment when Yoko's work received critical comprehension and appreciation (for instance as reviewed in *Rolling Stone*). *Cashbox* favorably compared her voice to a Moog synthesizer, and *Record Mirror* aptly described the recording as "human electronic music" (*Yoko Ono/Plastic Ono Band* CD liner notes).

The first song on the album, "Why" features Ringo Starr's best drumming ever as well as stellar guitar from John (except for the jazz cut "AOS," the same players grace the two Plastic Ono Band albums. Its companion, the slower "Why Not," has the same brooding rhythmic intensity as John's album. Its conclusion with train sounds calls to mind the diesel guitar of "Cambridge 1969." Yoko seems quite aware conceptually of the relationship of rock and roll to train sound, a connection most amply explored in the work of Michael Jarrett. By punctuating this connection through *musique concrete*, she in effect realizes synaesthetic effects: her sounds become (train) sculptural. Neil Young later achieved similar results on his "Southern Pacific" off *Re.Ac.Tor*; indeed, you can hear this effect on earlier tunes such as "Rock Island Line" or symphonic works by George Gershwin or Arthur Honegger. The relevance of all these intertextual linkages is that Ono is aware of, and dialoguing with, a tradition in rock music. She is catching on to new terrain with great authority.

If one believes her liner notes on *Onobox*, "Greenfield Morning I Pushed An Empty Baby Carriage All Over The City" begins with uncredited sitar work from George Harrison (making this 3/4 of a Beatles recording!) before proceeding to more stately rock beats and the "earplay" of bird sounds complementing her vocalizations. There is an oft-overlooked confessional element to even these more abstract vocalizations. Just as her repeated "don't worry" injunctions scattered throughout this phase of her work are telegrams to estranged daughter Kyoko, this piece seems to be about her miscarriages—an attempt to contain her grief both through Eastern perspectives (the sitar) and the continuity of nature (bird song). As such, it introduces elements that will achieve greater exfoliation in the next two phases of her career. "Greenfield Morning" is Yoko Ono's work in microcosm: it is a sound sculpture "earplay" with abject vocalization, feminist confessionalism and an exploration of the grieving process. All in 5:38. Of course, one has to hear a lot more Yoko to appreciate this![2]

"AOS" on the flipside of the lp is a jazz departure with Ornette Coleman, Charlie Haden and other great players. Yoko's voice works equally well in this more austere setting. She seems to simulate sex (with cries of "not yet") before running through an ever expanding vocabulary of staccato shrieks, coughing sounds and varied vocal dynamics. "Touch Me" returns to the rock setting and seems to be composed in movements with different tempos separated by a sound resembling crackling paper and/or a scratchy record. "Paper Shoes" closes the record with more *musique concrete* train sounds segueing into rain and thunder, vocalizing over Ringo's tribal drumming and "don't worry" final injunctions. The original lp's injunction on the label to "play in the dark" emphasizes this music's status as a kind of sound sculpture for the imagination. It still sounds adventurous and fresh today. Yoko Ono clearly knows what she's doing here, and it's an incredibly ambitious agenda: a fusion of avant-garde concepts and beats with pop music—and an early gesture towards a multicultural world music. Long before David Byrne, there was Yoko Ono. But who was listening? Only a few of us in the dark ... .

Fly, her follow-up recording of 1971, is even more ambitious and amazing. It's a double album, for starters. Yoko, in fact, made more recordings in the 1970s than John did! The album begins with "Midsummer New York," a real rocker finding Yoko confident enough to imitate Elvis. Its lyrics of seeming junk withdrawal and its intensity remind us that Yoko, like the Velvet Underground, is grounded in New York. The next track, "Mind Train," offers more railroad sound sculpture and a possible reference to Amiri Baraka's play *Dutchman* with its lyric "thought of killing that man." I think Yoko is channelling Baraka's Lula here with revisionist intent, emphasizing her power and beauty as well as her terror. Side two reveals how much variety Yoko can provide within these basic choices: "Mind Holes" is a beautiful acoustic guitar piece reminiscent of many tapes John and Yoko did together at the time that have been added as CD bonus tracks (e.g., "The South Wind" on the *Yoko Ono/Plastic Ono Band* reissue); "Mrs. Lennon" is a brooding ballad (no screaming) close in feel to John's solo work on piano; "Don't Worry Kyoko" and "Hirake (Open Your Box)" are rockers; "O'Wind (Body Is The Scar of Your Mind) features Indian instrumentation which reinforces that subcontinent's contributions to Ono's vocal style.

The third side of the lp contains three collaborations with Joe Jones and the Tone Deaf Music Company, a fellow Fluxus artist who built his own instruments (in the grand tradition of Harry Partch and oh so many others). In fact, Joe Jones built instruments that basically played themselves once you turned them on with a switch or lever. My favorites of these are "Don't Count The Waves," where form nicely fits function (repetition with variation in both performance and subject) and "You" which resembles in its conclusion the quiet introspection of Jimi Hendrix's "Moon, Turn The Tide ... gently gently away" from *Electric Ladyland*. The album closes with the title cut, a soundtrack to her eponymous film that features her attempt to sound like a darting fly—another sound sculpture in short. This long track is followed by one of two sound pieces on the lp which are like her Grapefruit instruction poem koans, "Telephone Piece" (the other is "Toilet Piece / Unknown"). The reissued Mike Douglas shows which John and Yoko co-hosted, roughly contemporaneous with *Fly*, demonstrate this whimsy best.

Yoko's next lp (with John again this time in co-billing), *Sometime in New York City* (1972) marks the end of this phase of Yoko's music until she revived it in the nineties with CDs such as *Rising* and benefit vocal performances with Thurston Moore of Sonic Youth. In fact, on the first studio disk, the only extended vocalization occurs on the last track, "We're All Water." Songs like "Sisters 0 Sisters" mark Ono's move to straightforward lyrical commentary and a more conventional if more accessible approach to the music itself, more pop than avant-garde. The newspaper graphics underline the immediacy of the communication: Yoko and John were issuing broadside ballads for the revolution. For the moment, the vocalizing was counter-revolutionary. On the second "Live Jam" lp, however, it is given its last exposure for awhile. One side is the Plastic Ono Supergroup doing a 1969 Christmas benefit with players such as Eric Clapton, Keith Moon, George Harrison, Billy Preston and Bobby Keys. Their extended reading of "Don't Worry Kyoko" is a real piledriver, especially with the added horn section and Moon's drumming. The muddy mix only hints at what this must have sounded like in performance.

The other jam side with the Mothers of Invention documents a near-perfect pairing up of Yoko with Frank Zappa's band. Her vocalizations find a call-and-response from the Phlorescent Leech and Eddie (Mark Volman and Howard Kaylan of the 1971 Mothers); Zappa finds a bottomless bag of his own melodies to counterpoint Yoko's work ("King Kong," "Sharleena"). The final feedback freakout first heard in Toronto (variously titled "AU" or "A Small Eternity With Yoko Ono") resembles Zappa's own closing freakout piece "Weasels Ripped My Flesh" and gets added charge from Don Preston on Mini-Moog. There are two mixes of this historic collaboration: John, Yoko and Phil Spector's on *Sometime in New York City* and Frank Zappa's later mix on *Playground Psychotics*, a 1992 compilation of the Flo and Eddie band. The former is muddier but bigger-sounding, foregrounding Yoko's vocals and overdubbing Klaus Voorman on bass for a more rock feel; Zappa's is crisper, cleaner and more egalitarian musically. You can hear good playing on it that John, Yoko and Phil preferred to bury for greater simplicity and impact. Both versions have their virtues, I think. Either's final "don't worry" marks the end of Yoko Ono's season of abjection for a few decades.

The importance of this work might best be gauged by citing Marxist cultural critic Frederic Jameson's observation that postmodern global culture is obsessed with the beautiful (in a strict aesthetic sense) and has abandoned the quest for the sublime that characterized heroic modernist art in the earlier half of the century (124-133). He offers as evidence in this essay ("Transformations of the Image in Postmodernity") and elsewhere trends in film, painting and architecture. Pop music would work equally well, I'm sure. The problem then becomes: how can we access the sublime in late capitalism? Are we condemned to beautiful surfaces which are too much with us at every turn? Yoko's discovery, I would argue, is that we can approach the sublime under the monstrous guise of the abject. After all, as Edmund Burke once said, the sublime is "danger at a distance." It is not pleasing to the eye (or ear); it is an aesthetic of awe, terror, force. When I listen to Yoko's recordings of this era, that is ultimately what I hear. One would not want it necessarily as a steady aural diet, but it provides a needed alternative to sonic bathos old and new. This is real "classic rock" which radio programmers pretend doesn't exist—so they can turn the history of the nineteen sixties into an innocuous myth.

Sisters O Sisters

If Yoko Ono's sole contribution to global feminism was the coinage of the phrase "Woman is the nigger of the world" (which John converted into a pop lyric), she would deserve a place in the history books chronicling the woman's movement. Fortunately, she has done—and continues to do—a lot more. In the amazingly productive year of 1973, Yoko finished three albums (four disks!) while John had his notorious "lost weekend" in Los Angeles with May Pang, Harry Nilsson, Ringo Starr, Keith Moon, Phil Spector—to name only a few of the cast of thousands fuelled by a variety of drugs and fortified brandy Alexanders. (Ringo taught his compatriots to order a sidecar extra shot of brandy and add it to the drink, making a potent beverage even more so—with disastrous results for John, who was both a lightweight as a tippler and a mean drunk [Goldman 490].) Two of the albums were released that year: *Approximately Infinite Universe* (a double album with the Elephant's Memory Band lineup also featured on *Sometime in New York City*, a rough quasi-garage-band that had worked with David Peel) and *Feeling the Space* (with top-drawer New York studio musicians such as David Spinozza, Jim Keltner and Michael Brecker). A third, *A Story* (also with the studio players of *Feeling the Space*) was withheld from release until the *Onobox* came out in 1992. John, although estranged, managed to play on the first two (released) recordings, and accompanied Yoko at a feminist conference in Cambridge, Massachusetts in June of 1973 (she also attended a women's conference in Chicago in the fall of 1973) (Giuliano 55). The Cambridge conference provided a showcase for these new songs, as did a few New York club venues such as Kenny's Castaways (Goldman 468).

The genesis of this remarkable new material was both global and personal. Clearly, emergent second-wave feminism was giving a sensitive artist like Yoko Ono a chance to raise her consciousness and address the anger she had been repressing as a woman in the then almost totally patriarchal world of rock music and culture. More specifically, John Lennon was beginning to make sexual advances towards other women in front of her, as he responded in various self-destructive and perverse ways to the pressures of the Nixon administration's attempts to deport him (Giuliano 55). Yoko was angry, and developing a voice to articulate that anger. As French feminist Helene Cixous would write a few years later:

> Woman must write herself: must write about women and bring women to writing, from which they have been driven away as violently as from their bodies—for the same reason, by the same law, with the same fatal goal. Woman must put herself into the text—as into the world and into history—by her own movement. (in Adams 309)

Yoko, surprisingly enough, may have been the first woman to bring this project to rock music! This is no small achievement. Before Yoko's early seventies work, there were strong women in rock (Grace Slick comes to mind immediately). But women's rock had a certain victimized quality to it, a lack of real empowerment—be it the blues of Janis Joplin or the folk-angst of Laura Nyro or Joni Mitchell (at this time).[3] Yoko's work preceded stronger voices such as Patti Smith's, let alone Yoko's true inheritors: the strong confessional anger of everyone from Sheryl Crow and Alanis Morissette to punks like the Au Pairs and the Slits to Ani DiFranco, Babes in Toyland, L7, Hole, Lydia Lunch, Liz Phair, Polly Jean Harvey, Sinead O'Connor and so many others too numerous to mention. Yoko Ono was the mother of them all, the first woman lyricist to put the central concerns of feminism into the rock song.

Overall, the music of this phase in her work is accessible, straightahead jazz and blues-tinged rock, eschewing overall the abject screaming of the earlier phase of her musical career. It was meant to reach a broad audience, to be a kind of aural agitprop. Because of the more unusual timbre of Yoko's voice (and, implicitly, racism?) and no doubt the radical content of many of the songs, however, this work received virtually no airplay. Certainly not in the midwestern urban markets I was listening to at the time, even ones with "progressive" formats. Yoko was tacitly blackballed. I never heard this music over the airwaves, in fact, until a campus radio show played it in March of 2001! That's how long it took radio in the Midwest to catch up with this phase of Yoko's career.

No artist operates in a vacuum, even an innovator like Yoko. On the liner notes to *Feeling the Space*, she makes a telling remark about her influences: "in my mind I'm a singing Sylvia Plath, half her head out of the gas stove still looking for a pencil to write her last beauty." One of the keys to the lyric writing of this portion of Yoko's career is its intertextual awareness of the poetry of such women confessionalists as Plath, Anne Sexton (who herself was performing with a rock band at her readings during this time) and Adrienne Rich. I wouldn't call the numerous parallels in content which I shall briefly illustrate a question of influence so much as one of resonance or shared common ground. But it is significant that the kind of writing Yoko was doing did exist in contemporary poetry; Yoko's genius was to adapt its concerns to the pop lyric. (And, make no mistake, this phase of her career was primarily lyric-driven: session guitarist David Spinozza recalls seeing only lyrics with chords jotted above them when he showed up for the sessions [Goldman 453].) She had to be aware of these literary models, not only because of her direct reference to Sylvia Plath but because of the ambient culture of the feminist conferences she was attending.

A few examples should suffice to indicate what are in fact a host of parallel thematic lines. Sylvia Plath is the most obvious point of connection in many respects, beginning with Yoko's direct allusion to Plath. Moreover, Yoko might have seen a certain rough parallel between her life and Sylvia's. Both attended one of the Seven Sisters (Ono, Sarah Lawrence; Plath, Smith) and married an Englishman who was also an artist. Both had passionate, public romances; both were betrayed and abandoned—or so it would look like to Yoko in 1973. (Despite the revisionist accounts, most biographies suggest that Lennon left her. Only later was the narrative constructed that she kicked him out.)

Lyrically, Ono and Plath share a few significant tropes. In Plath's *juvenilia*, for example, she has a recurrent image of riding in a death car:

> In the first dream I was driving
> down the dark in a black hearse
> with many men until I crashed
> a light, and right away a raving
> woman followed us and rushed
> to halt our car in headlong course.' ("The Dream")
>
> ... Death comes in a casual steel car, yet

We vaunt our days in neon and scorn the dark. ("Sonnet: To Time")
(Plath 310, 311)

Yoko deploys a very similar image in "Coffin Car" from *Feeling the Space*:

Coffin car
She's riding a coffin car
Wives showing tears for the first time
Husbands taking their hats off for the first time
Crushing their handkerchiefs, rubbing their nose
Telling each other how good she is

Half the world is dead anyway
The other half is asleep
And life is killing her
Telling her to join the dead

So every day
She likes to ride a coffin car ...

This mysterious parallel imagery has been linked in Yoko's case to both Jackie Kennedy and fantasies/premonitions of noble widowhood on Yoko's part (Goldman 453). The Plath poems are from the fifties, however (perhaps even earlier), suggesting other archetypes at work—for starters, a passive deathly embrace of automotive technology in ways that anticipate a writer like J. G. Ballard (*Crash*)? An update of death as a charioteer or of the demon lover (cf. Emily Dickinson's "Because I Could Not Stop For Death" or Joyce Carol Oates's "Where Are You Going, Where Have You Been?")? As with much poetry, parallels come more readily than meanings.

Ono and Plath also share an interest in witches as a symbol of feminine power, not surprising at their historical moment. Plath's breakthrough "Poem for a Birthday" (1959) has a section entitled "Witch Burning":

In the marketplace they are piling the dry sticks.
A thicket of shadows is a poor coat. I inhabit
The wax image of myself, a doll's body.
Sickness begins here: I am a dartboard for witches.
Only the devil can eat the devil out.
In the month of red leaves I climb to a bed of fire ...

... My ankles brighten. Brightness ascends my thighs.
I am lost, I am lost, in the robes of all this light. (135-6)

Yoko and John visited sites associated with the Salem, Massachusetts, witch trials on the way back from the Cambridge conference, which resulted in two

Ono lyrics, "Woman of Salem" and "Yes, I'm a Witch." As with Plath's poem, both lyrics involve identification with the witch, although the more defiant later song refuses the promised flames:

> I'm not gonna die for you
> You might as well face the truth
> I'm gonna stick around for quite awhile ...
>
> It's gonna change, sweetie legs
> So don't try to make cock-pecked people out of us.

Also like Plath, Yoko uses humorous invective, babytalk and what French feminist Luce Irigiray calls "mimicry," a usurpation of the voice of patriarchy for subversive purposes. Perhaps regrettably, weight becomes a way to target patriarchy. Plath writes of "Uncle, pants factory Fatso, millionaire" while Ono sings of a "potbelly rocker" in the eponymous song (Plath 230). Where Plath has "Ich, ich, ich, ich" and "gobbledygoo" in her famous poem "Daddy" (223), Yoko has similar wordplay in such songs as the aforementioned "Potbelly Rocker" ("Rocksuck doo doo / With a big fat choo choo / Don't be a coo coo") and "Catman" ("Wetter cake wetter cake baker's boy / Make me a cake that's sweet as your toy"). Plath's poem "The Applicant" (221-2) ventriloquizes the voice of patriarchy setting a man up with an ideal wife, while Ono's "Men Men Men" has her doing a Marilyn Monroe imitation (!) and dishing out condescending requests mirroring typical demands on women:

> Your lips are not there for voicing opinions
> Your eyes are there for us to look into
> I want you to take your rightful position ...
>
> Pardon me, honeycum
> Your hair piece's slipping.

And finally, Yoko Ono shares with both Sylvia Plath and Anne Sexton an interest in suicide in these lyrics; as with them, in counterpoint with the more exuberant, sardonic and mythic material:

> Age 39 looking over from a hotel window
> Wondering if one should jump off or go to sleep
> People tell you up is better than down
> But they never tell you which is up and which is down ...
>
> Age 39 feeling pretty suicidal
> The weight gets heavier when you've bled thirty years
> Show me your blood John
> And I'll show you mine

> They say it's running even when we're asleep
>
> ... If I ever die, please- go to my daughter
> And tell her that she used to haunt me in my dreams
> (That's saying a lot for a neurotic like me)
>
> Age 39 looking over from my hotel window
> Trying to tackle away with heart of clay
> The weight gets lighter when there's nowhere to turn
> God's little dandruff floating in the air ("Looking Over From My Hotel Window")

As Anne Sexton observed in her poem "Wanting to Die," "suicides have a special language / Like carpenters they want to know which tools / They never ask why build" (Sexton 142). Although Yoko has not as yet joined Plath and Sexton in their ultimate gestures (and is hardly likely to at this point), she was looking into a similar abyss in 1973.

Anne Sexton also shares with both Plath and Ono a fascination with witches. Sexton's poem "Her Kind" identifies the speaker with a "possessed witch:"

> I have ridden in your cart, driver,
> waved my nude arms at villages going by,
> learning the last bright routes, survivor
> where your flames still bite my thigh
> and my ribs crack where your wheels wind.
> A woman like that is not ashamed to die.
> I have been her kind. (15-16)

Sexton also shares a few tropes more exclusively with Yoko. Both women confront drug dependency rather explicitly. For example, consider Anne Sexton's poem "The Addict:"

> Sleepmonger,
> deathmonger,
> with capsules in my palms each night,
> eight at a time from sweet pharmaceutical bottles
> I make arrangements for a pint-sized journey.
> I am the queen of this condition.
> I'm an expert on making the trip
> and now they say I'm an addict.
> Now they ask why.
> Why!
>
> Don't they know
> that I promised to die!

> I'm keeping in practice.
> I'm merely staying in shape.
> The pills are a mother, but better,
> every color and as good as sour balls.
> I'm on a diet from death.
>
> Yes, I admit
> it has gotten to be a bit of a habit—
> blows eight at a time, socked in the eye,
> hauled away by the pink, the orange,
> the green and the white goodnights.
> I'm becoming something of a chemical
> mixture.
> That's it! ... (165)

Yoko (and John's) drug dependencies are alluded to as explicitly in Yoko's solo work as in Lennon songs such as "Cold Turkey" and "Happiness Is A Warm Gun." On *Approximately Infinite Universe*, Yoko included a song about their drug connection called "Peter the Dealer" which alludes to heroin, cocaine and orange sunshine LSD among other things:

> We were waiting for peter the dealer
> He comes in the evening when we're fussing in bed
> He says good morning here's your breakfast and give us plates of stone
> Takes a pint of blood from each of us to give to the poor
> We count the windows in the cities and tell each other
> Yes, life is a helluva lot of waiting time ...
>
> We were waiting for peter the blower
> He comes in when we're fixing snow on rock
> Gives us orange juice laced with sunshine and spring
> And takes a heart each from us to give the world
> We count the memories that are lost and tell each other
> Yes, life is a helluva lot of waiting time ...

Both writers also have an iconic image of woman as runner, a vision of urgency. Anne Sexton's poem "The Play" begins with an image of running for one's life:

> I am the only actor.
> It is difficult for one woman
> to act out a whole play.
> The play is my life,

my solo act.
My running after the hands
and never catching up.
(The hands are out of sight—
that is, offstage.)
All I am doing onstage is running,
running to keep up,
but never making it. (440)

Compare this imagery with the lyrics to the title song from *Feeling the Space*:

I came out of the darkness
Into the house
The lights were left on
But nobody around
Feeling the room
Feeling the space
Suddenly I noticed that it wasn't spring anymore

Run, run, run, run
Run through your life
Run, run, run, run
Run for your life (2 times)

The importance of this image for Yoko is evident in her decision to entitle the third CD of *Onobox*, the one devoted primarily to material from *Feeling the Space*, "Run, Run, Run." Her feminist iconography of running women, addicts, witches and would-be suicides presents a gallery of images of women far more resonant with then-contemporary confessional poetry than standard pop lyric fare. As in her earlier, more musicologically (vs. lyrically) avant-garde phase, she was trying to get rock to grow up, sensing its importance. As she once said in an interview, she thought rock lyrics like those of the Beatles were silly—until she thought of them as surrealist poems. Regarding "Yellow Submarine," for example:

> Yellow was the color of light ... and the yellow submarine—the unconscious mind—was moving under water, which was emotion. And we all live in that submarine. What a beautiful concept. This surrealist poetry was being played on radio and phonographs around the world to millions of people of all ages. Musically, the beat and chords of pop and rock felt too simplistic. I finally got it when I was sitting in on the Beatles' recording sessions. That simple beat was the heartbeat of the Universe. (qtd. in Munroe 60)

Yoko Ono's lyrical resonances with Adrienne Rich—by any measure the third major confessional woman poet during this part of Yoko's career—are the most tenuous. Unlike Plath, Sexton and Ono, Rich discovered during this time that lesbianism was for her the most important way of being a feminist, being truly woman-centered:

> *I am the lover and the loved,*
> *home and wanderer, she who splits*
> *firewood and she who knocks, a stranger*
> *in the storm,* two women, eye to eye
> measuring each other's spirit, each other's
> limitless desire,
>   a whole new poetry beginning here.
> (from "Transcendental Etude," Rich 268)

Yoko did not downplay the importance of lesbianism for feminism, but she gave it somewhat mixed reviews in her 1971 article in the *New York Times* entitled "The Feminization of Society:"

> The major change in the contemporary woman's revolution is the issue of lesbianism. Lesbianism to many was a means to express rebellion toward the existing society through sexual freedom. It helped women realize that they didn't necessarily have to rely on men for relationships. They had an alternative to spending 90% of their lives waiting for, finding and living for men. But if the alternative of that was to find a woman who replaced the man in her life, so she could build her life around another female or females, it wasn't very liberating. (reprinted in liner notes for *Approximately Infinite Universe*)

Although she is careful to qualify her conclusion ("But if ... "), Yoko nonetheless seems limited to perceiving the feminist embrace of lesbianism as simply substituting another woman in the patriarchal position where man once stood, a rather myopic negation of lesbianism's potential as a source for new kinds of loving and interacting not merely doomed to replay man/woman as butch/femme.

Having said all that, there are a few predictable ways in which Yoko and Adrienne Rich converge. Rich also embraces the witch as an icon of feminine solidarity. For example, in her 1974 poem "From an Old House in America:" "Hanged as witches, sold as breeding-wenches / my sisters leave me" (Rich 215). Rich also echoes Ono's preference for survival rather than suffering or martyrdom noted previously in the lyrics cited for "Yes, I'm a Witch:"

> Well, that's finished. The woman who cherished
> her suffering is dead. I am her descendant.
> I love the scar-tissue she handed on to me,
> but I want to go on from here with you
> fighting the temptation to make a career of pain. (from "Twenty-One
>   Love Poems," Rich 240)

Although no one seemed to notice at the time, Yoko Ono's work in the early seventies was in lyrical dialogue with emerging feminist poetics. As these few examples attest, she was not working in a vacuum from an interdisciplinary standpoint (and Yoko herself jumps media with ease and proficiency!). Only from the strict standpoint of the world of pop music did these recordings seem ignorably anomolous.

With the hindsight of nearly thirty years, the contemporary listener can revisit this music's pleasures and potencies via the *Onobox* and Rykodisk's reverent reissues. Many people I have exposed these tracks to are astonished that Yoko made recordings like this, since she has been frozen in time as the mad screamer. I think the best song on *Approximately Infinite Universe* is "What a Bastard the World Is." It is an extraordinarily complex lyric for a pop song. The song begins with a confessional dramatic monologue about an abusive relationship accompanied by a brooding and haunting piano (although the liner notes credit Adam Ippolito, the phrasing sounds remarkably like Lennon's playing on "Imagine" and "Mrs. Lennon," leading me to believe it's really John on this track). The story of a woman abandoned by her man was based on "a girlfriend of a musician ... crying one night in the studio," although the press was quick to misread it as being about John ("New York Rock," *Onobox* liner notes). The narrator moves from hurt, anger, and rage to strident rejection and militancy, while the music gets more anthemic and pronounced:

> You know half the world is occupied by you pigs
> I can always get another pig like you
> You've heard of Female Liberation
> Well that's for me ...
> Are you listening, you jerk, you pig, you bastard
> You scum of the earth, you good for nothin'.

But then, she suddenly begs "Don't go / Please don't go / I didn't mean it, I'm just in pain." In other words, the song refuses the happy ending of feminism triumphant in favor of a far more nuanced, realistic (rare in rock lyrics) portrayal of limited and compromised rebellion. (Tellingly, the reprisal of the title chorus shifts from the man being a bastard to the world being the bastard—at best an acknowledgment of male victimization by patriarchy, but psychologically a seeming denial of his culpability for his misbehavior.) The final verses shift to the third person, observing the character and eventually drawing some general conclusions about the state of feminism in the early seventies:

> Female lib is nice for Joan of Arc
> But it's a long, long way for Terry and Jill
> Most of us were taught not to shout our will
> Few of us are encouraged to get a job for skill
> And all of us live under the mercy of male society
> Thinking that their want is our need.

"I Have a Woman Inside My Soul" is also quite amazing, a bluesy and somber tune with some fine saxophone breaks from Stan Bronstein. Its unusual subject is a kind of secret self within the self, for Yoko an inner woman who gives her cryptic and unexplained visions. That it's a woman seems an interesting revision of Jung's tendency to cross-gender inner voices (animus for women, anima for men). Yoko's psychic delvings seem to yield bitter premonitory results here:

> I see a tombstone inside my soul
> It's old and mossy covered in dead leaves
> It stands with an engraving on its surface
> But I don't know what it reads
>
> I wish I knew what it reads
> I wish I knew what it says
> I wish I knew what it says to me
> I wish I knew what it means to me.

Although John Lennon was cremated, the song has an eerie intimation of mortality in it.

On a more whimsical note, there's "I Felt Like Smashing My Face in a Clear Glass Window." This dramatic monologue about a disgruntled teen is done in a bizarre retro fifties style, with chugging staccato rhythms reminiscent of Coasters-era instrumentation. The lyrics catalogue typical dissatisfactions in a slangy, off-hand way: "Daddy's always smelling like he's pickled in booze." The climax in the middle eight stems from the narrator's discovery that both President Nixon and Mick Jagger wear makeup "just like my Mommy's." Eventually, the parents break up and leave the protagonist in the frustrated state where s/he (gender unknown) contemplates the ominous actions of the title, settling for more minor vandalism against phone boxes, station wagons and churchyards. As with "What a Bastard the World Is," the emotional attitudes are complex, ambiguous and dialectical here. The song is largely humorous, but its imagery is staggeringly violent and menacing. It's as if Yoko converted the mood of the then-current film *A Clockwork Orange* into a 5:07 pop song. As such, it's a tour de force.

Sean Ono Lennon has said that "Death of Samantha" is a thinly veiled account of Yoko's discovery of John sexually betraying her (Giuliano 55). Appropriately, it is very bluesy with fine guitar breaks from Wayne Gabriel. The narrator is a "cool chick" to the outside world, hiding her angst over an unspecified event which Sean's explanation serves to illuminate convincingly:

> A friend lent me shades
> So I could hide my eyes that day
> It was a snowy day and the shades have seen
> A lot of things I didn't want to know myself.
>
> It was like an accident
> Part of growing up, people tell me
> But something inside me
> Something inside me
> Died that day.

The observed details and the mood of the song incline one to see it as a confessional lyric despite the distancing gesture of naming the song's main character "Samantha." (An allusion to the cool witch Samantha Stevens on the television show *Bewitched*? Probably not.)

I have already alluded to some other important songs on *Approximately Infinite Universe*. "Looking Over From My Hotel Window," her melancholy ballad about aging and suicidal thoughts, also has piano accompaniment very reminiscent of *Imagine*-era Lennon playing. The lyrics give a clear indication of what she thought of her notoriety and wealth: "People say stardust and goldust [sic] are it / But they never tell you it chokes you just as sawdust does." "Catman (The Rosies Are Coming)" is another retro rocker, replaying the donnybrook of the sexes as an underground cartoonish battle between "Catman" and the "Rosies." Given Lennon's fondness for cats, an autobiographical approach to the lyrics is tempting.

Instrumentally, there's some great signature Lennon work on "Move On Fast," alternating between bluesy riffing on the verses and a sound on the chorus reminiscent of his playing for the Beatles around the time of the "Paperback Writer / Rain" single. "Yangyang," a satiric portrait of an executive wheeler and dealer (Allen Klein in all likelihood), has musical jokes such as a use of the medieval diabolus chord progression once censored by the church and a klezmer-like clarinet break from Stan Bronstein. The simple ditty "Waiting for the Sunrise" has cheery and breezy flute work that helps make this the most upbeat song on the double album.

Feeling the Space is almost as good an effort, with standout tracks such as "Men, Men, Men" where Yoko does her Irigirayan mimicry of Marilyn Monroe by way of Tokyo Rose (with even a dash of an Elvis impersonation a la "Midsummer New York" quoting the melody line from "Heartbreak Hotel"). "Woman Power" is a feminist anthemic rocker like Yoko's best work on *Sometime in New York City*. "If Only," a bluesy slow song, continues the thematics of "Death of Samantha" addressing an emotional wound that refuses to heal:

> I cut my finger when you left the room
> The wound has healed long since then
> But the finger keeps bleeding, keeps bleeding
> For reasons unknown to me.

The playing is consistently polished, given the session's all-star line-up of New York studio greats David Spinozza and the Brecker brothers. Arthur Jenkins contributes some great conga work on "Woman of Salem."

The unreleased *A Story* continues along similar thematic and musical lines with the released material. "Will You Touch Me" finds Yoko again in a cabaret mood (one actually has enough of this kind of material in her work for an EP!). "Winter Friend" is a confessional ballad about a man telling her decades ago how he slit his arm and mailed his blood to an ex-girlfriend: "When I heard the story, I'd heard it like a car accident / That I would never be in myself." Needless to say, the narrator learns otherwise.

In addition to all this material in English, Yoko Ono released a feminist anthem in Japan in 1972, "Joseijoi Banzai" (roughly translatable as "Women Rise Up and Charge Forward"). This recording also used the Elephant's Memory Band. Her intense year and a half of solo productivity (for the sessions on *A Story* extended into 1974) had left a sizable body of pop music with a clearly articulated feminist sensibility. Yoko's life took another surprising turn when she had a reconciliation with John Lennon after he played Madison Square Garden on Thanksgiving (November 28) of 1974 as a surprise guest at an Elton John concert. Yoko showed up backstage, and the Lost Weekend was over (Coleman 448). Over the next five years, Yoko would become a businesswoman, an art collector, a mother again. But not until 1980 would she again compose music.

Season of Glass

The 1980 album *Double Fantasy*, which marked the public return of John and Yoko as a musical couple, has always had a conflicted status for the admirers of each or both of the duo. If Albert Goldman's biography is to be believed (and that, unfortunately, is always a big if), the genesis for the album was John's trip to Bermuda, where he got pumped up on reggae music and wanted to do a funky album with the Caribbean sound. Yoko was an interloper, wanting to throw in her songs and evolving the album into a collaborative "heart play" (644-5). Goldman concedes with other biographers that John's chance hearing of the B-52s' "Rock Lobster," which sounded like it was influenced by Yoko, suggested that this might be a good idea (645). The only repeated evidence that supports this historical reading is the notoriously lost "I'm Losing You" jam at the Hit Factory with members of Cheap Trick that Yoko vetoed (and disappeared?), but which Jack Douglas, the co-producer, played on headphones for the actual studio musicians on the album to inspire them (663).

A kinder and more accurate reading is to look at what they actually accomplished, not what they didn't do. As Lennon suggests on the interview record called *Heart Play* (issued posthumously), *Double Fantasy* evolved from an "ear play" (a play for the ears like an oldtime radio drama done as a musical) to a "heart play" because it's about a relationship—and happily "ear" is in "heart." They sequenced the songs cinematically; John keeps calling it a "movie." In fact, they realized that the 22 songs which they recorded should be split into two ear movies; *Milk and Honey* was a sketch of what that second film would have looked like. *Double Fantasy* makes the most sense if listened to in this manner. Its musical negotiations reflect the compromises resultant from being in a working romantic relationship. The album starts out positive and assertive ("[Just Like] Starting Over," "Kiss Kiss Kiss," "Cleanup Time"), then hits a trouble spot in the marriage ("Give Me Something," "I'm Losing You," "I'm Moving On"). Yoko's accusations of being "phony" in this last song weirdly and coincidentally echo Mark David Chapman's obsession with Lennon's phoniness as a wealthy person singing about imagining no possessions: creepy synchronicity. And indeed, the premonitory elements of the album make it less than a joyous listening experience. In preparing her songs for *Onobox* from this period, Yoko described the compilation work as "hell" (*Onobox*).

Musically, Yoko risked more abject performance than she had in her second feminist phase. There are screams and orgasmic moans in "Kiss Kiss Kiss" and musical chortles in "I'm Moving On." By this time, the pro-New Wave rock reviewers preferred Yoko's work on the disk. John's final versions seemed more conservative than his previous solo work ("Starting Over" almost imitates Elvis), whereas "Kiss Kiss Kiss" was a danceclub hit in its extended version.

But back to our storyline in the heart play ... . The marital crisis is resolved by thoughts of the joys of parenthood ("Beautiful Boy"). The second side begins with Lennon's best contribution to the album, the haunting ballad of disengagement "Watching the Wheels." Nothing but affirmation and resolution follow. We get cabaret Yoko again in the campy "Yes, I'm Your Angel" replete with sound effects of a carriage pulling up to an elegant hotel ballroom, presumably at their favorite New York hotel (the Plaza). The melody line is courtesy of Eddie Cantor's "Makin' Whoopee," resulting in a 1984 court settlement (Goldman 655). Another fine Lennon song follows: "Woman," a paean to feminine power and an apology for masculine shortcomings. Yoko tellingly offers the counterpoint "Beautiful Boys"—John is a boy while she is a woman. Then a final trilogy of affirmation: "Dear Yoko," "Every Man Has a Woman Who Loves Him" (with a great melody line), "Hard Times Are Over."

As I have already suggested, perhaps our real ambivalence about the album is that it is too joyous a production for the abyss it precedes, leaving us only premonitory shivers of John's traumatic death. In its 2000 reissue, Yoko vastly improved the album by adding "Help Me To Help Myself," a Lennon demo which begins "Well I tried so hard to stay alive [not "settle down" as on the lyric booklet!] / But the angel of destruction keeps on / Houndin' me all around" and Yoko's greatest and most successful pop song, "Walking On Thin Ice." Lennon predicted that it would be Yoko's first "number one," and thought it was better than anything on *Double Fantasy* (*Onobox*, Goldman 683). It does have a deeper engagement and honesty than anything on the album. It is rawer, edgier, more biting and honest from Lennon's whipsaw guitar work to Yoko's bleak parable of

> ... a girl
> Who tried to walk across the lake
> 'Course it was winter and all this was ice
> That's a hell of a thing to do, you know
> They say this lake is as big as the ocean
> I wonder if she knew about it?

All this within an essentially late disco format, and with Yoko making near-vomiting noises at one point on the recording. The feel is that of Polish director Krystof Kieslowski's very ominous tale of thin ice in the first commandment of the *Decalogue*. Unfortunately, the song proved to be much more of its time than the album that preceded it; its presence on the reissue makes sense. For the double fantasy ended in a nightmare of global grief when Lennon was shot to death on December 8, 1980, holding the mix tapes of "Walking on Thin Ice." We knew then where that puking sound was coming from, and 1980 saw a replay of the worst mass traumas of the 1960's, one last charismatic leader gunned down. Yoko Ono turned her grief into musical art, a gesture she has felt compelled to explain on several occasions:

> I seriously thought maybe I should quit making the album [*Season of Glass*] because, as some people had advised me, "It was not the time."
>
> But the question was, when would it be the time? I thought of all the people in the world whose voices were choking and cracking

for many reasons. I could sing for them. I could call it a 'choke' or 'crackle.' Well, wasn't that what the critics had been saying about me for all these years anyway? That gave me a laugh, and it became easier. (*Season of Glass*, original liner notes)

There is a story about a composer who went to his mother's funeral and though he was very upset about the loss, he could not help noticing that his sister was crying off key. It was a story to indicate how inhuman a composer can get in his professionalism. Listening back to these tracks, I don't know how I made them at the time when I was in sheer pain. But I also think it helped me to get through the hard times to just think about being on key. (*Onobox*, liner notes for "No, No, No")

This last phase of Yoko Ono's musical career can be helpfully construed, by her own admission, as using music to recover from a trauma. For this reason, I think it is helpful to look at how recovery from trauma works from a standard source such as Harvard psychiatrist Judith Herman's *Trauma and Recovery*. Recovery from a trauma occurs in roughly three overlapping stages. First, there is a need to establish safety, to get away from the threatening forces associated with the trauma. Then there is the work of "remembrance and mourning" for one's experience. Finally, there is the process of "reconnection with ordinary life" (155). This is not a simple, linear development; it is more like "running a marathon" (174).

To elaborate more on the especially germane second stage, one's remembrances are often a "highly emotional, contradictory, and fragmented" mixture of "truth-telling and secrecy" resultant from conflicting motives of revelation and protective self-concealment (1). Herman refers to these initial formulations as a kind of raw "prenarrative" (175). Such prenarratives often obsess on questions like "Why?" and "Why me?" (178). Why did this horrible thing happen to me? The exploration of the past during the second stage can lead to an experience of "frozen time; the descent into mourning feels like a surrender to tears that are endless" (195). Yoko Ono's musical output from 1981 to 2001 is illuminated by this basic model in ways that I hope to demonstrate. The importance of her achievement, again, is that by making these recordings she was showing rock and roll another way to grow up. One need only contrast Ono's work in this phase with the classic teenage death songs of the fifties and sixties ("Tell Laura I Love Her," "Leader of the Pack")—or even with more advanced attempts such as Dion's "Abraham, Martin and John" about the deaths of Lincoln, King. and the Kennedy brothers. Yoko by contrast produced a series of heart plays about the grieving process with *Season of Glass*, *It's Alright (I See Rainbows)*, *Starpeace* and *Rising* that fearlessly turned her life experiences into art. As with her previous phases, she was an innovator who influenced later work. Lou Reed's album *Magic and Loss* explores similar psychological territory which she unquestionably broke ground on. Not surprisingly, these songs are mainly centered on issues of remembrance and mourning. Her concerns with safety are, in effect, pre-musical and expressed more in her liner notes about her trepidations in dealing with the public:

> From '81 to '83, it was as though Sean and I were standing in a snowfield surrounded by human wolves, who claimed themselves "close friends" and meanwhile raped and desecrated John's body in front of our eyes. We saw beautiful rainbows behind the black forest and people calling us with love from the distance, but there was no way to let them know what was happening. And Sean and I decided to call the rainbow to us by sharing our song with you. (liner notes to *Milk and Honey*)

> ... [T]here was a bomb scare and Sean and I were warned to move into a hotel and to stay away from the studio. I wrote the song IT'S ALRIGHT when we were cooped up in the hotel room—as a prayer. Finally, I went to the studio despite the warning. I couldn't hide all my life. (*Onobox*, liner notes for "No, No, No")

The "prenarrative" quality of her earliest recordings after John's death is best illustrated by the song "No, No, No." Yoko's commentary on the song is quite informative:

> NO, NO, NO was how I felt through the first couple of months. John was dead. I was alive. But John's side of the bed was still warm when I came back from the hospital. My side was cold. I was shivering. It was as if John were still alive. I wanted somebody to hold me. In my mind, I was saying please, hold me. I wanted to stop shivering. I was saying please, don't hold me. My body still remembered my husband's warmth. My mind was like a shattered glass, the sharp points split in tangents. I made myself impossible for anybody to hold me. When I wrote the song, I juxtaposed the atonal and minor chords, which suited the woman who felt like she was wearing a pair of mismatched shoes. In the recording, I used real gun shots and sirens. It was not a tea party. A musician came to me and said he could make a siren effect with the guitar, using two of my atonal chords. "It's better to keep the song a musical experience," he said. He played the chords. I didn't like it. It was too beautiful. It lacked the urgency I was feeling. No, it had to be the real siren. Now I knew what "Music Concrete" had meant. (*Onobox*, liner notes for "No, No, No")

This narrative is both self-contradictory (hold me ... don't hold me) and contradictory (the song clearly uses a guitar for the siren effect, not a real siren, despite Yoko's claims). The fragmentation is augmented when one considers how oddly this explanation fits the song. In his essay for the *Onobox*, Robert Palmer trusts his instincts and calls the song "the most forthright and penetrating account of sexual revulsion in the history of popular music." The atonal bits are a kind of Irigirayan "mimicry" of a striptease before sex ("Let me take my pants off / No, no, no ((yes, yes, yes))") culminating in "Don't do it, I can't do it / I'm seeing broken glass when we do it."[4] The lyrics in the minor key portions are about abandoned promises. Yoko's liner notes suggest that this song is about her reaction to proffered intimacy after Lennon's death, which would lead most informed listeners to link the lyrics to Sam Havadtoy, Ono's more-or-less constant companion after John's death from 1981 to 2001 (and the anti-John in his utter absence from Yoko's public dealings). They broke up, by the way, because they admitted "she was still with Lennon" (Carver 131-2). But any sense of the complexities of her relationship with John suggests that it could be about him as well. The song is about both or either. It is ambiguous in its referents. Although its powerful emotions are clearly communicated, its cognitive content both conceals and reveals, hides and tells. "No, No, No" is traumatic prenarrative memory work.

"I Don't Know Why," also from *Season of Glass*, addresses dramatically the archetypal question of the trauma victim: why? At one point, Yoko bursts into rage: "You bastards / Hate us, hate me / We had everything, you—." She was originally going to end this song with "half an hour of screaming and swearing," later changing her mind in the studio (*Onobox*, liner notes for "No, No, No").

Finally, the sense of "frozen time" pervades this material, especially the slower songs and ballads from *Season of Glass* ("Mindweaver," "Silver Horse," "Dogtown," "Toyboat") and the repetitive and ritualistic chants on *It's Alright* ("Let the Tears Dry," "Dream Love," "I See Rainbows"). Yoko has commented on this quality of the latter album especially:

> In a way, the *It's Alright* time was much more difficult for me as a woman, as a person, than when I had made *Season of Glass*. Life went on. I had to walk and talk normally, when I knew that somewhere inside me there was a clock that had stopped in '80. (*Onobox*, liner notes for "No, No, No")

Yoko Ono's reconnection with everyday life is adumbrated in *It's Alright's* second side which addresses an incrementally larger audience (Yoko herself and Sean on "It's Alright" and "Wake Up" moving to the larger world on "Let the Tears Dry" and "I See Rainbows"). *Starpeace* in 1985 finds her fully re-engaged with the world, protesting SDI and the Reagan years in "Hell in Paradise" and interacting with an all-star cast of funky world musicians (including Shankar and Sly and Robbie). She even toured the world in 1986, performing a passionate version of "Imagine" that is a bonus track on the *Starpeace* CD.

Ten years later she returned to the studio with IMA, her son Sean's band, to produce arguably her best music yet (if no formal innovation from her previous work).[5] *Rising* brings to some closure her fifteen year engagement with the grieving and recovery process with her song "Goodbye, My Love: It's time to say goodbye." And Yoko had come full circle: she could now work with her more abject vocalese surrounded by musicians who knew exactly what she was trying to do. John Lennon and Yoko Ono had virtually invented a new musical universe blending rock with the avant-garde along certain lines; now the world had finally caught up with Yoko. Although not universally admired, she was understood by a critical mass of appreciative listeners. The *Rising Mixes* compilation showed how her music could be deftly interpreted by diverse artists such as Tricky, Ween and Thurston Moore of Sonic Youth. Combined with her amazing touring retrospective in the visual arts, *YES*, and its sympathetic and informative catalogue, the times seemed most propitious for Yoko. She was thoroughly ensconced in a canon which tried for decades to exclude her musically and artistically. Even a new Dar Williams song "I Won't Be Your Yoko Ono," upon close listening, was very much pro-Yoko. (in her liner notes, Williams said that at her undergraduate college, Wesleyan—given its love for experimental music and ethnomusicology—"*Double Fantasy* was called, by some, a 'Yoko Ono album with special guests ... '" [*The Green World*].)

Dragon Lady Beats

Yoko Ono's 2001 release, *Blueprint For A Sunrise*, offered—even more than *Rising*—a synthesis of all three aspects of Yoko's work, a kind of summation. The cover features Yoko's face juxtaposed over a portrait of the empress dowager of China "who became the first 'Dragon Lady,' a name coined for her by the British Press at the time, fueling Britain's then colonialism" (liner notes). At age 68, Ono was comfortable with an ironic embrace of the hurtful iconography the world press used to saddle her with. Yes, I'm a dragon lady! What are you going to do about it? The world had few terrors left for Yoko.

The purest replication of Yoko's earlier abject vocalese can be found on the live track "Mulberry." This is no coincidence, since it was originally recorded in the studio with John in 1968 (it is a bonus track on the *Life With The Lions* CD reissue). Yoko's introduction to the song explains how she composed it as a child during World War II when she went out at night to pick mulberries for the family to eat. She sang the song on the way home to appease the ghosts which she believed lurked throughout the countryside.[6] Sean stands in for his father on guitar, replicating the rapid experimental plucking. The live audience goes wild at the end of the song with far more enthusiasm than the baby boomers ever mustered for Yoko. Other tracks ("Soul Got Out Of The Box," "Rising II") have passages of vocalese interspersed with the feminist lyric writing. The new version of "Rising" is also an extended live track; Yoko's alternation of English and Japanese lyrics recalls the border writing of Gloria Anzaldua: she is completely accessible only to those who can cross her ethnic and linguistic borders.

Much of the lyric content of the songs contained herein is unabashedly feminist: portraits of battered women ("I Want You To Remember Me"), ecofeminist outrage at the rape of the earth ("Is This What We Do") and chants for empowerment ("It's Time For Action"). Yoko explains her intent in the liner notes:

> I recently did an art show—Herstory—in Berlin. A young woman journalist started an interview by saying that she thought it was interesting that I would bring back such an old theme in 2001. "Feminism is an old issue now, isn't it? Women do not have to wave flags anymore. That was the sixties." But I know women who are powerful, intelligent members of their communities who still live in fear because of the position they are put in as women in our society. To some extent, all of us women are living in fear, quietly exercising a caution known only to us, all the time, pretending to be sprightly and strong.
>
> Sometimes, I wake up in the middle of the night hearing thousands of women screaming. Other times just one woman seems to try to talk through me.

Yoko Ono puts out the same message she did in the early seventies because she still sees it as relevant. Tell a battered woman we're living in a post-feminist age!

In keeping with the closure of "Goodbye, My Love" on *Rising*, there is really only one song on *Blueprint For A Sunrise* seemingly about John Lennon, the wistful and relective "I Remember Everything" ("In the morning I miss your eyes / In the evening I miss your thighs"). After 21 years, John can be remembered fondly—and the loss remains. But Yoko's place in the culture is far more rich and extensive now. She is not just—and should never have been perceived as just—John Lennon's widow.

In 2007, she released two surprising new works: *Yes, I'm A Witch* and *Open Your Box*. The former recording is a set of "collaborations" with other musicians using Yoko's vocal tracks as a basis for their own instrumental settings;

the latter CD contains dance club remixes of Yoko's original recordings. *Yes, I'm A Witch* seems to have a more overt narrative structure than *Open Your Box*, although both have a logic to their sequencing that makes them more heart plays than any of her other recent releases.

After an introductory version of a portion of the title song, the listener is drawn in by some fairly accessible tracks, both musically and lyrically. "Kiss Kiss Kiss" (from *Double Fantasy*) as used by Peaches has good beats and staccato synthesized handclaps to ensure its danceability. "O'Oh" (from *A Story*) slows things down with its country slide guitar effects provided by Shitake Monkey, but its closely observed snapshot of the New York cityscape is also rather user-friendly.

Yoko's first subversive move is a new version of "Every Man Has A Woman Who Loves Him (also from *Double Fantasy*) called "Everyman Everywoman." The new vocal lines, either re-recorded or edited from the original, reiterate "every man has a man who loves him" and "every woman has a woman who loves her." Thus the heteronormative angle of the original is supplanted by a gay anthem, taking the song a long way from its original context and moving Ono far beyond her earlier hesitations about same-sex relationships. The collaborating band, Blow Up, also add lots of sixties twang guitar (think of Johnny Rivers doing "Secret Agent Man"). The auditory result is both retro and cutting-edge, a true avant-pop gesture which you can dance to!

This ear-opener is followed by Le Tigre's deep bass beat version of "Sisters 0 Sisters" (from *Sometime in New York City*) which results in making the song a far more militant feminist anthem, a rallying cry. Then Porcupine Tree slows things down with an acoustic blues rendering of "Death of Samantha" (from *Approximately Infinite Universe*). Their version brings out even more the melancholy of the lyric of betrayal and serves as a good thematic complement to the previous song. Yoko's feminist lyric writing has always addressed both the problems of patriarchy and the possibility of something beyond it (her blueprint for a sunrise?).

The next standout track is "Nobody Sees Me Like You Do" (from *Season of Glass*). The Apples in Stereo, as befits their Beatlesque name and approach, take these vocal lines about John's unique appreciation of Yoko and give them an uncanny setting which combines the Phil Spector wall of sound approach with overt touches from Beatles recordings: Ringo-influenced drumming and Moog synthesizer programmed to sound like Paul's playing on "Maxwell's Silver Hammer." Church bells also chime throughout the piece, evoking the bell effects used by John in "Mother" (Big Ben) and "Starting Over" (a little Chinese bell). The sense conveyed by the song is that John is best symbolized now by a church bell as he transcendentally "sees" Yoko from beyond his mortal coil. This phat production packs a metaphysical wallop in addition to showing us what might have resulted if Yoko really had been allowed to become the fifth

Beatle!

The Polyphonic Spree work a similar reinterpretive mojo on "You And I" (from *Starpeace*) by adding flute and turning the song into poppy candy psychedelia *à la* something like The Small Faces' "Itchycoo Park." This upbeat blast is followed rather jarringly by a reworking of "Walking On Thin Ice" from Jason Pierce (of the neo-psychedelic British band Spiritualized). When I first heard this agonizing arrangement, replete with elementary synthesized drumbeat, turgid chain gang percussion, and explosive guitar crescendoes contrasting with Yoko's unadorned lyric phrases, I thought it was the only dud on the album. Coming back to it after a year of computer problems that delayed this writing, I now realize that agony was precisely the intended effect. After the preceding Beatle-influenced idylls, we get the rupture of this song so associated with John's death. Jason Pierce, in effect, takes it back from its peculiar status as a club track and restores it to its original haunting and dolorous context. As such, it's a move I can respect—and a disruption solidly in the spirit of Yoko Ono.

Appropriately enough, this mood shift is sustained by Antony (of Antony and the Johnsons) in the next track, a reworking of "Toyboat" from the postassassination *Season of Glass*. Antony's operatic quaver and association with older artists such as Lou Reed and Leonard Cohen (in the concert documentary *I'm Your Man*) have given him rare crossover transgenerational credibility not seen since U2. His sublime additions to Yoko's crooning make this collaboration a little bit of pop perfection, albeit with a melancholy edge.

The Flaming Lips manage to make "Cambridge 1969" even more extreme, albeit in a shorter time frame, by adding heavy beats, organ and orchestral flourishes to loops of Yoko's screaming and John Tchicai's saxophone playing. The results are very danceable, which is why this is the most adventurous track: only extremely unusual ears could hear the original, thoroughly discussed above, and hear possibilities for a dance track.

The CD ends, symbolically enough, with three songs by way of closure. First, a reworking of "I'm Moving On" by The Sleepy Jackson. They seem to be paying homage to John Cage (and Yoko's homages to Cage in cuts like "Radio Play" from *Life With The Lions*): much dial changing and radio noise occurs, pulling in some choral work very reminiscent of (sampled from?) Brian Wilson's *Smile*. An extended ending with synthesizer whooshes might have been a good place to stop ... .

But wait, there's more! Hank Shocklee reprises "Yes, I'm A Witch" with a repeated sample of one lyric line: "I'm not gonna die for you." In context, not just an homage to Yoko as survivor, but the audio equivalent of her throwing off the cape *à la* James Brown: the show's not over yet. The CD ends on a softer note with an acoustic rendering (with big strings) of "Shiranakatta (I Didn't Know)" from *Approximately Infinite Universe* by Craig Armstrong. The intimate setting matches the inclusiveness of the song (sung in English, French and Japanese). At the end of the recording, an engineer gets the last word by acknowledging "That was beautiful."

As you can gather, *Yes, I'm A Witch* is an interesting project: a reinvention of Yoko Ono for a new generation of listeners who do not carry all the baggage which earlier listeners lug around regarding her. The Elvis estate made a small move in this direction with their approved techno remix of "A Little Less Conversation." But Yoko has carried this to a whole other level. With a few exceptions (e.g., "Walking On Thin Ice"), most listeners—including this one—might actually prefer these new versions to the original recordings: they are denser, more fully realized, more interesting—better settings for Yoko's neglected jewels. I am reminded of filmmaker John Waters' comment: why do they remake good movies instead of remaking bad ones and fixing them? Yoko's earlier efforts were just fine, but they were not widely appreciated. And, let's face it, the Elephant's Memory Band made Crazy Horse look like professional studio players! So this was a wise aesthetic decision. And don't worry: Yoko Ono is never in danger of really selling out! These gestures only move her a few inches towards the mainstream anywhere outside of lower Manhattan.

Open Your Box carries this rethinking of her canon to the next level with overt dance club remixes. The sequencing here is less narratival—and after all, it's pretty old school to even consider such things in the age of downloads and custom mixes—but one could safely generalize that the tracks go from the more accessible to the more adventurous. But the ultimate audience for the CD is a dance club, so it's the choice of the DJ as to what gets played off this (which is why there are three separate remixes of "Walking On Thin Ice," Yoko's signature club track). After three very danceable openers (including the first "Walking" remix, a "Tribute Mix" by Felix Da Housecat which manages to get its groove on even more than the original), the first challenge to the listener is an ominous and paranoid reworking of "Hell In Paradise" off *Starpeace*. Yoko contributes new, whispered vocals to complement the menacing synthesizer work. This song reminds us that the state of things has gotten even worse than it was in the Reagan era that inspired the original.

The second "Walking" remix (a very synthesizer-heavy treatment by the Pet Shop Boys) again segues into a *Season of Glass* remix. As on the previous CD, the death of Lennon is a kind of emotional center to the selection. Sapphirecut's "I Don't Know Why" is a real tour de force—although this is an odd track to dance to, to say the least. Sapphirecut gets the strongest effect by juxtaposing the sung line "You left me without words" with Yoko's rant: "You bastards! Hate us! Hate me! We had everything!" The sadness and the anger combined give the track an eerie, ritualistic feel; it re-conceives the death of John Lennon as a kind of dismemberment of Orpheus.

Orange Factory's "Yang Yang" (originally off *Approximately Infinite Universe*) shifts the mood by running Yoko's original vocals through a vocoder to make her voice sound deeper and more masculine. Given that this song is about the masculine principle out of control, it's a good choice. Lyric lines like "'I own you, I own you, so give us a song" again suggest that the specific masculine principle evoked here might be Allen Klein, John and Yoko's manager at the time.

After Orange Factory's overtly erotic "Club Mix" of "Open Your Box" (from *Fly*), replete with orgasmic moaning and a judicious editing of the original lyrics ("open your box ... legs ... thighs ... skirts" but not "factories ... prisons ... parliaments"), the CD closes with two standout tracks: a third epic-length reworking of "Walking" by Danny Tenaglia (the aptly named "Walked Across The Lake Mix") and ... "Give Peace A Chance!" This last is absolutely amazing. Yoko speaks the lines accompanied by John's electronically processed voice (which fades in and cuts off abruptly, as if he originally spoke the line backwards and then the tape was reversed—an effect David Lynch likes to use, though here not the actual case). DJ Dan adds in heavy beats and big phat square waves on the synthesizer building to a huge crescendo. The result is a populist antiwar anthem re-envisioned as a club track! Some purists might object to this move, but I'd submit these are better messages to hear in the background than most club cuts. Like Bootsy Collins once said, "free your ass and your mind will follow!"

Then, in 2009, Yoko pulled off her boldest musical career move yet: forty years after its inception, she reformed the Plastic Ono Band and put out a CD. Yoko has always been concerned with timing, astrological and otherwise. Perhaps she felt empowered by the warm reception of the remixes and dance tracks by a new generation of listeners; perhaps she thought it was a good idea given the rampant Beatlemania resultant from the *Beatles Rock Band* game and the reissue of the entire Beatles catalogue in pristine digitally cleaned-up formats (and she must have gotten quite a chunk of change from that!). In any case, we got to hear *Between My Head and the Sky*.

The sticker on the CD describes the release: "A career-defining album, Yoko is at the top of her game in the prime of her life ... ." Unusual words, to say the least, to describe a recording made by a woman born on February 18th, 1933! You can be "in the prime of [your] life" at age 76 (her age when she recorded this)? This CD qualifies her for the Guinness Book of World Records: the oldest performer to release a new rock recording (as opposed to rock and roll, *pace* Chuck Berry, etc.). And the record jobbers have to decide whether to file it under rock or alternative/indie—because it's edgy at times! The miracle continued when she showed up on the late-night talk shows performing material from the album with her young band wearing a low-cut top and a miniskirt, the ultimate rock and roll survivor (and damn good looking for her age). Why didn't she get a cover on the AARP magazine? Answer: Yoko still scares people!

So much for the marvels of the media event. What about the actual music? Is she "at the top of her game?" I don't think so, but it's a very solid album that showcases Yoko in all her varied approaches. I don't think it would convert many people to her music—and once you get past the dramatic opening, there are even some New Age sonic *longeurs* (although there is a demographic for that sound in abundance). But here's the interesting thing: listen to this album back to back with Sir Paul McCartney's studio release from the same time, *Memory Almost Full,* and ask yourself: which is more interesting musically and conceptually? I'd submit that Yoko would get your vote hands down, thereby making her the liveliest extender of the Beatles legacy (irony duly noted).

I invoke Paul's CD deliberately, for both releases have a lot to do with encroaching mortality. Yoko's CD opens with another dynamic driving train song featuring energetic vocalese, "Waiting for the D Train" (get it?). The recording's loose conceptual structure is a kind of summing up and settling of accounts while anticipating that last ride. Addressing the youngsters (and the young at heart), Yoko includes a whimsical children's song ("Ask the Elephant"). For the first time, John Lennon's ghost seems utterly absent from the lyric proceedings. But we do have several love songs arguably directed at his successor, Sam Havadtoy: "Memory of Footsteps" with its noirish saxophone thanks someone "for being here and now;" "I'm Going Away Smiling" praises a man who gave her "true" love when she "was all black and blue." And a number of the songs have strong environmental themes: "Healing," "Feel the Sand," "Higa Noboru" ("The Sun Rises" would be the translation).

Musically, we get a wide range of dynamics and timbres, from dance beats ("Waiting for the D Train," "The Sun Is Down") to a rock drone *à la* "Tomorrow Never Knows" ("Calling"), vocalese electronica ("Moving Mountains"), quasi-jazz ("Memory of Footsteps," "Hashire, Hashire" ["Run, Run"]) and New Age acoustic meditations ("Healing," "Feel the Sand"). The recording climaxes with three tracks that come even closer to German art songs / lieder than Joni Mitchell's work in this line, mystic jewels set with subdued cello (courtesy of the phenomenal Erik Friedlander) and shimmering yet crystalline piano (Sean Lennon and/or Yuka Honda): "Un un. To" (an onomatopoeia for a groan in Japanese), "I'm Going Away Smiling" and ""Higa Noboru." I believe these three selections are Yoko "at the top of her game"; and yet, paradoxically (and thus typically?), it's a game Yoko never played before in her long career. After all the angst, a gift of unadulterated beauty. So yes, when all is said and done, an amazing album. Yoko's description of life in "Un un. To" somehow applies to herself as well:

> Don't ever give up on life
> Life can be so beautiful

Especially after you spent a lot of years with it
Because then life becomes like a lover
You have been close to
You know him so well
And yet every day he gives you a surprise

Between My Head and the Sky provides grand closure to an astonishing career—and yet I wouldn't be surprised if she still isn't finished! As the song titles indicate, Yoko is singing in both English and Japanese (but mostly in English); all lyrics are printed in both languages. Her musicians are also from both east and west, building a sonic bridge of connection to unify Yoko's complex life. I am reminded of the compelling late work of poets like William Butler Yeats, W. H. Auden and Stephen Spender. Yoko has nothing to prove; she certainly doesn't need the money. On this recording she sings like the birds do—because they can. Perhaps the final track on the CD, "I'm Alive," a final piece of audio conceptual art, gives us the main point of this exercise. Over random industrial percussive sounds, Yoko speaks to us directly: "It's me. I'm alive." Yoko, 2010.

Thus today we find Yoko Ono as mainstreamed as she could ever hope for. Even the press tries to be fair to her—although it's so hard for them! A June 20, 2005 review of a London concert in the *Guardian* concedes that she's "become a respected survivor" whose music is "contrary and reliably perplexing."

By contrast, it is almost refreshing to see Yoko Ono excluded utterly from the reissued feminist history *Unsung: A History of Women In American Music*. Laurie Anderson is on the cover (not Amy Beach), but not one citation to Yoko can be found in the book, despite even her more "classical" recent avant-garde montage pieces such as "Georgia Stone" (for the John Cage tribute CD *A Chance Operation*) and "A Blueprint For The Sunrise" (for the *YES* catalogue). A great American aesthetic iconoclast like Yoko, kindred spirit to Gertrude Stein and Georgia O'Keeffe, would probably be amused by the snub. She has repeatedly suggested in interviews how resistance to her work has strengthened it. To give her the last word: "the essence of what I [am]—with warts and all [—is ...] me saying to the world I love you ... and up yours!" (*Onobox*, liner notes for *A Story*).

P. S. Forever Young Yoko!

The problem with my grand conclusion above is that Yoko Ono is a living, active artist who doesn't especially believe in closure—or at least that one grand gesture such as reforming the Plastic Ono Band might suffice. In the fall of 2012 we find an even more adventuresome release from her: *Yokokimthurs-*

ton, a collaboration on Chimera records with Kim Gordon and Thurston Moore, former members of the art noise band Sonic Youth. Since this band liked to explore sonic sculptures and textures in the grand tradition of John Lennon's experimental guitar playing with Yoko (or of electronic composer Karlheinz Stockhausen, for that matter), they prove to be perfect folks for Yoko to work with.

The result is Yoko's most experimental work since the late 1960's. Because her voice is in such paradoxically pristine condition, upon hearing the first track "I Missed You Listening" one might think that this was recorded around the same time as "Cambridge 1969" off *Life with the Lions*, her first solo *Plastic Ono Band* release, or *Fly*. Nothing has changed: she uses her voice as an instrument; my cats still think there's an animal trapped in my stereo speakers; crescendos and diminuendos of sound undulate like a tempest-tossed musical ocean. An occasional vocal phrase emerges from the overall abject vocalese: "listening." Over forty years down the road, she's still a little ahead of her time. (Your grandkids might like this music more than you do.)

On this outing, you can't dance in any conventional sense to this music—and you could never do the dishes to Yoko really ... . You have to listen to this music attentively. It has its real pleasures. My best analogy for the aesthetic joys of this avant-pop would be to describe this CD as six abstract expressionist recordings, paintings for your CD player. Or six modern primitives displaying full-body tattoos. (For this is pretty raw sound.) It may even strike you as a musical prank, an art joke. That's okay too: a subtle humor pervades Yoko Ono's entire body of work—something she learned from Marcel Duchamp and her Fluxus movement cohorts (including John Cage).

Two of the six pieces recapture the vocalese and feedback-drenched guitar jams Yoko executed with John in the late sixties: the aforementioned opener and "Let's Get There" (both aptly titled). But there are some interesting new developments as well. The other four tracks have a strong theatrical element. All three musicians sing—and recite—on two of them. On the other two Yoko gives us one-woman dramaturgy. I'm reminded of how the Art Ensemble of Chicago would blend theater and music in performance (or Sun Ra's Arkestra on occasion for that matter). The combination of recitation and noise even can remind one of some of the Velvet Underground's experiments along these lines ("The Gift," "Murder Mystery"), making this a very New York album. The upshot is that this is both a new direction for Yoko and her compatriots and part of a discernible avant-pop tradition.

Finally, I'd describe the verbal content of two of these four pieces as, by genre and theme, psychomachia. (The other two are respectively a dramatic monologue and a dialogue.) This obscure term refers to a few works in the middle ages that staged debates between contending aspects of the mind or psyche: the virtues and the vices, the mental and the somatic. My strongest evidence for this can be found on "Mirror Mirror," a straight-up revisitation of Snow White with Yoko whimsically cast as the evil queen (she likes villain roles which let her mimic and transcend her detractors). But other aspects have come down the pike since the brothers Grimm: psychoanalysis in general and French Freudian Jacques Lacan's Mirror Stage in particular (the stage in child development when the infant recognizes its image in the mirror and projects onto it an ideal Other). Yoko (or her character) explores her paradoxes, as the tape recorder fumbles and clicks on and off, in a musical equivalent of an onanistic (Ononistic?) talking cure: "I'm an intrinsically nervous person.... I'm nervous every day ... At the same time I'm an extremely relaxed person ... I love being daring ... I'm a staggeringly emotional person ... I'm a staggering perfectionist ... Listen up, Yoko [this is still her voice] ... Don't always be a perfectionist ... Sometimes it's good to roll in the mud ..." She finally asks the mirror who's the "ugliest" and the "smallest of them all?" All this with lovely muted electric guitar strumming for accompaniment.

Even though there are three voices on "Running the Risk," I lean towards one confused and complicated psyche interacting with itself (there's legitimate room for disagreement). The dominant theme is for "big fish" to take risks (a gloss on this project?): "The biggest fish faces the littlest risk ... Face the risk of being laughed at ... The biggest fish is attacked ... Swimming in the universe ... The biggest fish runs the risk." Gordon and Moore contribute random dada phrases reminiscent of the stream of consciousness: "GOPs abandoned babies ... secrets from a phallus ... stroking so tenderly." Both of these pieces are a kind of performed self-given pep talk.

"I Never Told You, Did I?" is a dramatic monologue concerning secrets and regrets about their concealment. The recitation alternates between whispers and moans. The results are very dramatic, but mysterious. We're invited to project our own backstory here, I think.

Yokokimthurston concludes with the fifteen minute mini-epic "Early in the Morning." The piece begins very quietly with coughing vocal noises and guitar manipulations worthy of vintage Pink Floyd (e.g., "Echoes" off *Meddle*). The drama builds as Yoko pleads "I'm not ready to go, no, no, no" against a sinister invitation from another voice to "come on in ... my town house." At the intense climax, the instrumental noise overwhelms while Yoko pleads "Don't" and even unleashes some banshee wail screams for *auld lang syne*. All in all, a generous pour of the most tantalizingly evocative and crystalline avant-pop. Big fun for open ears that certifies Yoko Ono as the most avant-garde elder of the tribe, a relentless explorer.

Another fortuitous event for Yoko in the fall of 2012 was the publication of *Reaching Out with No Hands: Reconsidering Yoko Ono* by cultural critic and performance artist Lisa Carver (from a publisher out of my hometown Milwaukee, no less). This tome is the book-length study of Yoko I wanted to write initially but couldn't because of my ambivalences about her. Carver elegantly solved this problem by boldly confronting the ambivalences head on:

> Ono has made a career and a life out of doing exactly what she was not supposed to do, and not being what she was supposed to be. And when she does tell us what to do, it's the undoable. Because if you cannot do that, what else might you not do? The possibilities of the impossible are endless! [Cf. Sun Ra's project below] ...
>
> So ... if I love her so much, why does this little old lady still make me so uncomfortable?...
>
> ... Yoko Ono is the ultimate feminist. She isn't fighting for women's rights per se, but she expresses herself doggedly and with a single-minded purpose of art for art's sake, truth for truth's sake, and doesn't seem to care what anyone thinks about her as a woman, just like male artists do and we don't think anything of it. She's an artist, not a woman artist. Her life—and those of the people around her—is a tool. She uses incredibly personal autobiographical details in her work, yet she doesn't seem to feel any need for perfect factual order, or to worry about anyone's feelings. That quality is neither feminine nor masculine. It's genius, which is always disturbing when peered at too closely, but more so when it's housed in the body of a female, who should be maternal, who is supposed to be fuckable, agreeable, likable.
>
> That is the ultimate feminism: Yoko Ono doesn't need us to like her. She doesn't care.
>
> Then sometimes I think she does care.
>
> Oh, Yoko Ono, you trouble me so. (19, 23-4)

A small taste of a brilliant little book which anyone interested in Yoko should check out. It covers everything: the visual art, the films, the instruction poems and the music. And Lisa Carver complements this chapter nicely. Whereas I have tried to look for thematic patterns of interest in Yoko's music, Carver emphasizes the elusiveness of her work, how it resists containment or categorization. Both approaches are valid for Ono—and arguably for any artist. I think of that half-full water glass on the cover of *Season of Glass*. For me, the conceptual glass is half-full; for Lisa Carver, it's half empty. Both observations are accurate.

P. P. S. Yoko's Last Laugh

A final irony: as this book goes to press in October 2013, Yoko Ono has released a new recording with the reformed Plastic Ono Band called *Take Me to the Land of Hell*. I don't have time to do it justice yet given the deadlines (as opposed to subsequent printings of this book), but it is easily the best musical work she's done since *Fly*—and possibly ever. So if you're intrigued by Yoko, you need to listen to it. In fact, one could readily show how far rock has come by listening to this release after a revisiting of Elvis Presley's Sun Sessions.

After some driving rockers with abject vocalese like "Cheshire Cat Cry," she revisits her relationship with John Lennon in a series of haunting *lieder*. The title track is especially gorgeous with its muted piano and cello setting. In interviews she has noted that "the Land of Hell" refers to her days with John when the couple were vilified by the press. The lyrics themselves reveal more metaphysical implications as well. They envision a reunion beyond the grave, in hell, like Dante's Paolo and Francesca. No rock artist has ever produced a recording of such pristine beauty at the age of eighty. It's as if everyone else has left the field and Yoko is alone doing a victory lap. The photos in the CD booklet of her in the recording studio convey an unstoppable energy, visual proof that she's a force of nature.

Works Cited

Adams, Hazard & Leroy Searle. *Critical Theory Since 1965*. Tallahassee: Florida State University Press, 1986.

Carver, Lisa. *Reaching Out with No Hands: Reconsidering Yoko Ono*. Milwaukee: Backbeat Books, 2012.

Goldman, Albert. *The Lives of John Lennon*. New York: William Morrow & Company, Inc., 1988.

Giuilano, Geoffrey. *Lennon in America: Based in Part on the Lost Lennon Diaries 1971-1980*. New York: Cooper Square Press, 2000.

Herman, Judith Lewis. *Trauma and Recovery*. New York: Basic Books, 1992.

Jameson, Frederic. *The Cultural Turn: Selected Writings on the Postmodern, 1983-1999*. New York: Verso, 1998.

Kristeva, Julia. *Powers of Horror: An Essay on Abjection*. Trans. Leon S. Roudiez. New York: Columbia University Press, 1982.

Lennon, John. *Skywriting By Word of Mouth and other writings, including The Ballad of John and Yoko*. 1986. New York: Harper Perennial, rpt.1996.

Munroe, Alexandra with Jon Hendricks. *YES YOKO ONO*. New York: Japan Society and Harry N. Abrams, Inc., 2000.

Ono, Yoko. *Approximately Infinite Universe*. Apple SVBB 3369.1973.

——. and the Plastic Ono Band. *Between My Head And The Sky*. Chimera Music 1. 2009.
——. *Blueprint For A Sunrise*. Capitol CDP 7243 5 36035 2 6. 2001.
——. *A Blueprint For The Sunrise*. With YES book. 2000.
—— and John Lennon. *Double Fantasy: A Heart Play*. Geffen Records K99131.1980. Reissued as Capitol CDP 7243 5 28739 2 0. 2000.
——. *Feeling the Space*. Apple SW 3412.1973.
——. *Fly*. Apple SVBB 3380.1971.
——. "Georgia Stone." On *A Chance Operation: The John Cage Tribute*. Koch 3-7238-2 Y6x2. 1993.
——. *Grapefruit*. New York: Simon and Schuster, 1970.
—— and John Lennon. *Heart Play: Unfinished Dialogue*. Polydor 817-238-Y1.1983.
——. *It's Alright (I See Rainbows)*. Polydor PD 1- 6364.1982.
—— and John Lennon. *Milk and Honey*. Polydor 817-2381 -Y1. 1984.
——. *Onobox*. Rykodisk 10224/29.1992.
——. *Open Your Box*. Astralwerks ASW 88710 094638871026. 2007.
—— and John Lennon. *The Plastic Ono Band—Live Peace in Toronto*. Apple SW 3362.1969.
—— with IMA. *Rising*. Capitol CDP 7243 8 35817 2 6.1995.
—— with IMA. *Rising Mixes*. Capitol CDP 7243 8 37268 0 6.1996.
——. *Season of Glass*. Geffen Records GHS 2004.1981.
—— and John Lennon. *Sometime in New York City*. Apple SVBB 3392.1972.
——. *Starpeace*. Polydor 827 530-1. 1985.
—— and John Lennon. *Unfinished Music No. 1: Two Virgins*. Apple T5001. 1968.
—— and John Lennon. *Unfinished Music No. 2: Life With The Lions*. Zapple ST 3357.1969.
—— and John Lennon. *Wedding Album*. Apple SMAX 3367.1969.
——. *Yes, I'm A Witch*. Astralwerks ASW 79287 094637928721. 2007.
——. *Yoko Ono/ Plastic Ono Band*. Apple SW 3373.1970.
Palmer, Robert. "On Thin Ice: the Music of Yoko Ono." Essay in *Onobox*.
Pennebaker, D. A., director. *Sweet Toronto*. 1969.
Plath, Sylvia. *The Collected Poems*. Ed. Ted Hughes. New York: Harper Perennial, 1992.
Rich, Adrienne. *The Fact of a Doorframe: Poems Selected and New 1950-1984*. New York: W. W. Norton & Company, 1984.
Sexton, Anne. *The Complete Poems*. New York: Houghton Mifflin, 1999.
Williams, Dar. *The Green World*. Razor & Tie 7930182856-2. 2000.
Zappa, Frank. *Playground Psychotics*. Barking Pumpkin Records D2 74244.1992.

Works Consulted

Works Consulted

Ammer, Christine. *Unsung: A History of Women in American Music.* Portland, Oregon: Amadeus Press, 2001.

Clayson, Allen with Barb Jungr and Robb Johnson. *Woman: The Incredible Life of Yoko Ono.* Surrey, UK: Chrome Dreams, 2004.

Coleman, Ray. *Lennon.* 1984. New York: McGraw-Hill, rpt. 1986.

DiLello, Richard. *The Longest Cocktail Party.* New York: Playboy, 1981.

Gaar, Gillian. *She's a Rebel: The History of Women in Rock & Roll.* Seattle: Seal Press, 1992.

Lennon, John. *In His Own Write and A Spaniard in the Works.* New York: New American Library, 1967.

O'Dair, Barbara, ed. *Trouble Girls: The Rolling Stone Book of Women in Rock.* New York: Random House, 1997.

Ono, Yoko. *In The Guests Go In To Supper.* Santa Fe: Burning Books, 1986.

———. *Instruction Paintings.* New York: Weatherhill, 1995.

Rosen, Robert. *Nowhere Man: The Final Days of John Lennon.* No place of publication listed: Soft Skull Press, Inc., 2000.

Sheff, David. *The Playboy Interviews with John Lennon & Yoko Ono.* Ed. G. Barry Golson. New York: Berkley, 1982.

Somach, Denny and Ken Sharp. *Meet the Beatles ... Again!* Havertown, PA: Musicom International Publishing, 1996.

Notes

[1] I have some pretty distinguished company agreeing with me. Consider John Lennon's remarks about England's response to the couple in his autobiographical prose in *Skywriting By Word of Mouth*:

> Having been brought up in the genteel poverty of a lower-middle-class environment, I should not have been surprised by the outpouring of race-hatred and anti-female malice to which we were subjected in that bastion of democracy, Great Britain ... . What a riot! One of "our boys" leaving his Anglo-Saxon (whatever that is) hearth and home and taking up with a bloody Jap to boot! Doesn't he know about *The Bridge on the River Kwai*? Doesn't he remember Pearl Harbour! ... The racism and sexism were overt. I was ashamed of Britain. (15)

[2] On the other hand, to complicate my reading I would quote one of Yoko's instruction poems from *Grapefruit*, "City Piece:" "Walk all over the city with an empty baby carriage." This piece was written in the winter of 1961, well before any of the miscarriages with Lennon (although not perhaps before other confessional sources for this poem that may be relevant, memories which could be evoked by her public traumas with John). Nonetheless, I maintain this track is not just an illustration of the *Grapefruit* piece. The other reading works for me as a listener—all by way of acknowledging there is complexity and indeed aesthetic overdetermination in this deceptively simple recording. It's *Grapefruit* AND the three phases of her musical career... and no doubt much else besides.

[3] Upon reflection, Aretha Franklin is Ono's clearest predecessor with a song like "Respect"—arguably the first feminist pop song to get any mass audience.

[4] This lyric helps explain why the album is entitled *Season of Glass*. Also note the half-empty, half-filled glass of water next to Lennon's bloody spectacles on the cover. When Geffen records objected to the image, Yoko responded "I'm not changing the cover. This is what John is now" (*Onobox*, liner notes for "No, No, No").

[5] And her longest work ever on *Rising Mixes*. The brooding vocal jam with IMA called "Franklin Summer," after a series of biomorphic sketches Yoko has been working on recently, is 30:02 in length.

[6] Recall her previously cited statement in the Palmer essay, where she describes this kind of singing being designed "to deal with those sounds of people's fears and stuttering ... and of darkness, like a child's feeling that someone is behind him, but he can't speak and communicate this ... ." Her remarks here sound like a direct gloss on "Mulberry."

Frank Zappa's Big Note

"Hello, Frank Zappa ... ": The Project/Object, Conceptual Continuity and Other Bedevilments for the Young Sophisticate

I feel the need to approach the monumental output of Frank Zappa in a very different fashion than we have used in discussing Yoko Ono's music. Obviously, it is an immense corpus: even an expeditious run through the canon would take over six hundred pages, as Ben Watson's wonderful *Negative Dialectics of Poodle Play* attests. (And Ben did not get to discuss fully later releases such as

Civilization Phaze III and *The Lost Episodes*.) As Zappa commented once to an interviewer about his work:

> It is a heck of a thing to comprehend. It's a miracle if anybody can follow all of it, because that would mean that they would have had to have done a lot of research to find out what all those lyrics mean, and/or have listened to a wide variety of different ethnic music and classical music and different kinds of blues stuff that I've listened to throughout my life. (qtd. in Watson 92)

As a result, most interviews with Zappa proved to be an exercise in futility. Unless the interviewer was a highly intelligent and thorough fan, the legwork necessary to ask Zappa appropriate questions did not occur. The best one could hope for would be that Frank would hijack the interview and insert helpful statements that might pass by the touch of an editor in relatively untrammelled form.

I am a pretty thorough fan, to situate my discourse. Although I never got into the loop of tape-trading, I have purchased every official release of Zappa since I first acquired *Freak Out!* in the fall of 1968, a year and a half after its initial release. I am the kind of fan Frank used to deny existed, one that kept up with him throughout his career and never left because I felt betrayed by some shift of direction. Although he baffled me plenty, he never alienated me—and always intrigued me! My claim to fame might be a one-credit course I taught at Truman State University in the fall of 1991 on Zappa (as part of freshman orientation, the poor dears). The kind folks at Barfko-Swill (his corporate headquarters / distributors) relayed the news to Frank; I hope it gave him cause for some amusement. I have no idea if I am the first academic to devote a course to Zappa; I hope so for the record books (but doubt it, actually). I also saw Frank Zappa in concert five or six times, depending upon how you're counting: a 1971 show in Milwaukee with the Flo and Eddie lineup (not listed in Greg Russo); May 11, 1973, Milwaukee Arena (again) with the Jean-Luc Ponty lineup; April 23, 1974, Riverside Theater in Milwaukee (2 shows, not one as in Russo) with the Napoleon Murphy Brock version; May 11 (Chicago) and May 13 (St. Louis), 1975, with the Captain Beefheart ensemble. I made crude cassette recordings of the 1973 and 1974 shows.

Although one can address Zappa's music chronologically (as Watson and Russo among others more or less do), I plan to take to heart the full implications of the project/object and its conceptual continuity. In other words, Zappa's music is a big ripple in the time/space continuum, the elephant the visually differently abled guys of fable grab ahold of in various places and attempt to describe—capturing only pieces of it. (Since it's Frank, we should substitute a giant poodle for the elephant!) I want to talk about the big picture here and give

Frank Zappa's Big Note 55

what Frederic Jameson would call a "cognitive map" for the project/object. There will be chronological discussion inevitably, but my focus will be more of a spatial nature, the shape of this thing. Armed with this general knowledge, I would simply encourage the reader to find a CD store that does returns and has a listening booth. With such a facility, one can work through the canon! I think it's all good (although I will offer a tentative "listening guide"). With a canon of this complexity, one hesitates to play tastemaker. My favorite Zappa track today will not be my favorite one tomorrow—let alone yours.

What is the beloved project/object, oft referred to in interviews and other writing by and about Frank Zappa? Put simply, it is a sense he had that his work was a whole as well as a bunch of individual accomplishments in music, film and writing—that it interlinked and played off itself in synchronistic ways regardless of when it was produced; in short, that it had self-reflexive and/or intertextual elements that added up when one started listening/watching/reading. This does not mean that his work has a carefully articulated deep structure, that there is some sort of secret key or secret message one can decode by consuming all of it—or that it was tending towards or achieved a kind of ultimate closure. It was not a modernist, totalized project like T.S. Eliot's *Four Quartets* (achieved) or Ezra Pound's *Cantos* (arguably, a totalized plan that broke down and mutated into something closer to Zappa's work). Rather, through conceptual continuity, Zappa attempted to grasp an emergent whole in his work which he was simultaneously designing and revising. This glimpsed "whole" is the project/object. Its lack of closure or totality invites us to historicize it as postmodern, which is an apt descriptor for many other reasons as well (such as its obliteration of taste levels and genre boundaries).

Let me provide a series of potentially illuminating analogues. From literature, I'd mention the writings of William S. Burroughs. In the "Atrophied Preface" to *Naked Lunch*, Burroughs asserts that "You can cut into Naked Lunch at any intersection point" (203). In other words, its obsessions, techniques, characters and stories keep recurring: one can hop aboard the text at any point. Similarly in Zappa, does it matter whether one first encounters the poodle in "Dirty Love" off *Over-Nite Sensation*, "Stinkfoot" from *Apostrophe* or "Cheepnis" from *Roxy and Elsewhere* (to name only a few of its appearances)?

On a more mundane level, Zappa's universe resembles that of authors such as Thomas Hardy, William Faulkner and Louise Erdrich in that it creates a geography (Southern California, especially the greater Los Angeles area) and a set of recurrent characters (often based on real people, in fact often real people in the groups or close to them.): Potato-Headed Bobby, Jeff Simmons, Kenny and Ronnie, Ruben and the Jets, Uncle Meat, Minnesota Tishman, L. Ron Hoover. As one gets further into the work, one gets to know these people better and better—and to get a real sense of place from the Zappa landscape.

Musical parallels to the project/object would include, jocoseriously, Neil Young's work (on the *Year of the Horse* CD, he responds to a complaint that "they all sound the same" by saying "it's all one song"). More relevantly, I would invoke Richard Wagner. Wagner's way of using the musical leitmotif, phrases that evoke dramatic incident or character within an opera, are extended by Zappa throughout all his recorded output. For example, a romantic snatch of melody from his early film soundtrack *The World's Greatest Sinner* recurs in both *Lumpy Gravy* and "Mother People" from *We're Only In It For The Money* . Zappa is equally fond of appropriating other composers' riffs. He is notoriously fond of quoting Richard Berry's "Louie, Louie" and Stravinsky, for example. (My favorite example of the latter is the doo-wop version of the opening bars of *Rite of Spring* on the fade-out of "Fountain of Love" on *Cruising With Ruben And The Jets*.) And, yes, as in Wagner, the leitmotifs have thematic resonance. The film snatch connotes a kind of utopian gesture not -to-be-trusted in the contexts it is juxtaposed with, "Louie, Louie" obviously (but affectionately) connotes dumbness (e.g., opening of "Plastic People" on *Absolutely Free*); *Rite of Spring* quotations suggest fertility and sex (not exactly rocket science here, eh?). Such conceptual continuity provides a useful shorthand for the composer, who can telegraph emotions and ideas to the listener efficiently. For these to work, one need not even know the explicit reference; with Zappa, the message is always first and foremost in the notes themselves.

Using the visual arts, we might compare the project/object to an enormous mixed-media collage (for it includes music, film and literature). Ben Watson compares it to Fredric Jameson's notion of "rubbish-epic" (invoked to describe Wyndham Lewis' prose) (103). This works for me, because Zappa is working on an epic scale—and he is careful to include a diverse range of thematic material, never just the niceties of conventional lyric material (unless ironically).

Perhaps the best analogy for Zappa's project comes from structuralist anthropology. Like Claude Levi-Strauss's anthropologist, Zappa is a *bricoleur*, an assembler of material culture and detritus into a larger structure. Technically speaking, however, Zappa is closer to a sociologist than an anthropologist. He is interested in group behaviors and character types mostly within his own culture: the pachuco, the disco afficianados, the leather crowd, groupies, touring rock musicians, politicians, etc. When I taught my course on Zappa, I subdivided it into music, sociology and politics. I think all are equally important entries into Zappa's universe. From as early as the founding of the Bizarre label in 1968, Zappa identified himself as an armchair sociologist. The sleeve for the label accurately promised that he would "present musical and sociological material which the important record companies would probably not allow you to hear." The sociological content is obvious on such early Bizarre/Straight releases as *An Evening With Wild Man Fischer* (an acappella singer who sold songs on Sunset Strip for a dime), *Permanent Damage* by the GTOs (Girls Together Outrageously, among other cited acronyms—they were groupies!), Alice Cooper's *Pretties For You and Easy Action* (Until they hooked up with Bob Ezrin—the Canadian producer who midwifed their breakthrough single "I'm Eighteen"—they were more of a freak show than a musical act.), and even Captain Beefheart's *Trout Mask Replica*. Let us not forget that this last avant-garde masterpiece was produced by musicians kept in near-cult conditions by Don Van Vliet. They all lived together, and he used elementary conditioning techniques to keep them all on edge and highly trained. So much so that most of the double album was recorded in four and one half hours when they finally booked a studio (*Grow Fins* 59). Zappa's own work with the Mothers took a decided turn for the sociological with *Uncle Meat* (recorded in 1968, released in 1969), the lyrics for which contained "a random series of syllables, dreams, neuroses & private jokes that nobody except the members of the band ever laugh at," a mere foretaste of the fullblown sociological project the Mothers would become when Mark Volman (the Phlorescent Leech) and Howard Kaylan (Eddie) joined (from the Turtles). This incarnation of the band relentlessly outed the sexual arcana of the touring rock band for several years. But Zappa was always really a *bricoleur*, from his earliest album *Freak Out!*. This album carefully notes song origins in the sayings of the original Suzy Creamcheese, Pamela Zarubica: "'You Didn't Try To Call Me' was written to describe a situation in which Pamela Zarubica found herself last spring ('Wowie Zowie' is what she says when she's not grouchy ... who would guess it could inspire a song?)."

And, yes, the project/object has its own materialist metaphysic as well, the concept of the "Big Note" first introduced in dialogue on *Lumpy Gravy*: "Everything in the universe is made of one element, which is a note—a single note. Atoms are really vibrations, you know, which are extensions of THE BIG NOTE. Everything's one note, everything ... ." Zappa's project/object draws an analogy similar to modernist conceptions of the artist developed by Flaubert and James Joyce (the artist paring his fingernails outside of his creation like a deity in *A Portrait of the Artist as a Young Man*). To wit, the Big Note : the material universe : Zappa : Zappa's project/object. It is all an emanation from its creator.

Lest things get too heavy, we must remind ourselves that Zappa's sole purpose as an artist was repeatedly stated as "to entertain his listeners," which he correctly deemed was a noble enough goal for a musician (Russo 167). As such, all metaphysical webspinning Zappa might introduce was also subject to parody. This was a man who did not take himself too seriously, despite his dedication to getting the sound sculptures he wanted as exactly right as possible. And he really did not take the world, especially these United States, too seriously. I agree with Ben Watson that he intuited (without reading a word of Guy DeBord or the Situationists) that America has become the Society of the

Spectacle (Watson xix-xxi). He designed his art to create a counter-spectacle which both provided a simulacrum of the main deal (so we could see it better) and an implicit critique of its excesses. Frank has explained this crucial point better:

> Perhaps the most unique aspect of the Mothers' work is the *conceptual continuity of the group's output macrostructure*. There is, and always has been, a conscious control of thematic and structural elements flowing through each album, live performance and interview.
>
> Do you know about Earth Works? Imagine the decades and the pile of stuff on them subjected to *extensive long-range conceptual landscape modification*. Houses. Offices. People live there and work there. Imagine that you could be living there and working there and not even know it. Whether you can imagine it or not, that's what the deal is ... .
>
> The illusion of freedom will continue as long as it's profitable to continue the illusion. At the point where the illusion becomes too expensive to maintain they will just take down the scenery, they will pull back the curtains, they will move the tables and chairs out of the way, and you will see the brick wall at the back of the theatre ... .
>
> What we sound like is more than what we sound like. We are part of the *project/object*. The *project/object* (maybe you like *event/organism* better) incorporates any available visual medium, consciousness of all participants (including audience), all perceptual differences, God (as energy), The Big Note (as universal basic building material), and other things. We make a special art in an environment hostile to dreamers. (qtd. in Watson 217-8)

That's what's the deal he's dealing in, according to this reputed memo sent to Warner Brothers executives in 1971 and reprinted in the *International Times* (Watson 216). Think Thomas Pynchon at his most paranoid (he's a Zappa fan, too, quoting the liner notes to *Ruben and the Jets* in the introduction to *Slow Learner*), or Phillip K. Dick. Think even of *The Matrix*. Or consider the claymation of Bruce Bickford, much admired by Zappa and utilized in his films and videos (especially *Baby Snakes*). Bruce animates a simulational hell-world very close in spirit to the kind of place described in the above quotation. And yes, think of the insights of the Frankfurt School of Sociology on the culture industry (as Ben Watson reminds us). With his clever eye, Frank Zappa was seeing the same thing as these folks from very early on in his career. (Check out "Who Are The Brain Police?" on *Freak Out!*.) Zappa's playful and joyous (but never chaotic) project/object is both a parodic emulation of and a counterforce poised against the sinister dreck of now nearly universal corporate-sanctioned "art" polluting airwaves, broadcasts and theaters near you! Got that? Frank Zappa offers us an unusual alternative: excellence!

This memo charts a basic direction which Zappa's career took (a brief nod to chronology here as promised). After his apprentice work at Studio Z in Cucamonga, he formed the Mothers of Invention as a satiric group taking stands on large public issues as well as performing unusual music (*Freak Out!*, *Absolutely Free*, *We're Only In It For The Money*). Beginning with *Lumpy Gravy* and *Uncle Meat*, he began to turn more toward the in-jokes of the band, the private codes of the group he participated in (a development never abandoned, as the endless "Hi-Ho Silver!" jokes on the 12 CD live set, *You Can't Do That On Stage Anymore*, demonstrate). By *Over-Nite Sensation* in 1973, Zappa's writing trafficked in personal surrealism. These three phases in his work are cumulative. After 1973, his output contained social criticism AND sociological observation AND personal surrealism. But I agree with Ben Watson that *Lumpy Gravy/Uncle Meat* and *Over-Nite Sensation* are watershed releases. (Not that these transitions were unanticipated: we have already noticed sociological interests on *Freak Out!*; surrealism goes at least back to *Absolutely Free*'s "Duke of Prunes.")

The project/object is accessible to all who wish to engage it. It is not hermetic (although it can seem that way to the uninitiated; I would not recommend that anyone start listening to Zappa's music with *Thing-Fish*, for example: not for beginners!). To borrow from Teodor Adorno's aesthetic theory, it is "autonomous" art. It stands on its own, and we have to approach it on its own terms. Most pop music, by contrast, is what Adorno would call "affirmative." It mirrors back our pre-existing tastes and desires. It requires no work of us; it is user-friendly; we can listen to it while we do the dishes or make love. Although Zappa will provide parodic moments resembling such affirmative music (e.g., *Cruising With Ruben And The Jets*), his output is mostly not usable as background music: it has a way of commanding your aural attention.

The other recently deceased figure in American culture that comes to mind when I think of Frank Zappa is the director Stanley Kubrick. Both men were auteurs communicating a personal vision; both were "control freaks" that nonetheless allowed room for collaborators to improvise (Zappa with all of his musicians; Kubrick with actors he trusted such as Peter Sellers, Jack Nicholson and Lee Ermey); both were supposedly cold and unemotional; but were warm family men, both were abidingly self-referential in their art; both were committed to aesthetic excellence and had to bend the system to get what they wanted from it (Kubrick got a better deal from Warner Brothers, though, and hence got along much better with them); both are arguably a major portion of America's cultural legacy to the latter twentieth century (along with other luminaries such as John Cage, Sun Ra, Thomas Pynchon and Robert Rauschenberg).[1]

Zappa's contribution, the project/object, consists of several main elements—as his memo implies. Most obviously, it employs every musical technique discernible. Beginning with his dual adolescent interests in rhythm and blues and Edgard Varese, Zappa came to employ an encyclopedic variety of compositional techniques from the classical world: serial composition, sprechgesang (music that imitates the rhythms of the human voice), polyphony, atonality, etc.—and an exhaustive variety of popular genres: blues, disco, sea chanties, even country and western. (There are enough Zappa "country" tunes to fill an album in their own right!) At the end of his life, Zappa became fascinated with the Chieftains (a well-known traditional Irish group) and Tuvan throat singers from the former Soviet Union; he recorded and arranged for both. Musicological web sites devoted to Zappa have noted that he employs all available techniques, but resists easy categorization by the use of any. In other words, it is hard to tell based on technique whether you're listening to a Zappa composition. (I would submit the best indicators are melodic and rhythmic complexity—"Oh No" has alternating bars of 3/4 and 4/4 time, for example—and, on the other hand, fragments of lush romanticism. Zappa is never as austere as most academic avant-garde classicists.)

Secondly, the project/object displays a sociological interest in what's happening around the composer on several levels. For starters, as aforementioned, material from the members of the band, family and other co-workers (potentially overlapping categories!). This goes all the way back to "Wowie Zowie," but attains great elaboration in a song like "Let's Make the Water Turn Black" from *We're Only In It For The Money*. It turns out that this song's surreal references to saving nose effluvia on a window and to growing creatures in a jar are all straight information about two brothers, Kenny and Ronnie Williams (see Zappa with Occhiogrosso 85-7). Another level would be observations regarding society at large, especially new sociological types: the freak ("Hungry Freaks, Daddy"), the hippie ("Who Needs The Peace Corps?"), the disco dancer ("Disco Boy," "Dancin' Fool"), the S & M fetishist ("Mudd Club"), and so forth. Such material includes not only Zappa's observations, but his honest engagement with his real reactions to these discoveries (cf. British writer J. G. Ballard, who confronts car crashes and even nuclear holocaust as sites of desire as well as fear). Needless to say, this dimension of the project/object consistently alienated some folks.

Don't Shoot the Messenger?: Zappa and/or Feminism

Even as astute a Zappa critic as Ben Watson gets into some trouble over this dimension of the project/object; that is to say, he got a bit more offended than he might have needed to if he kept digging. I think he would agree with me overall, though, that Frank Zappa is a materialist and a realist (as well as a surrealist), not an idealist with regard to human contact by any gender. (There is romantic idealism in his work, however, in the utopianism of his lovelier melodies. He includes that element sonically; he just won't write lyrics about it. This avoidance is part of his care to not work overmined dimensions of popular music: by refusing to write "straight" love songs, he avoids the overwhelming conventionality of the popular song!)[2] Zappa's commentary on gender is closely observed, universally sardonic and critically realistic. It leaves to others the chance to tell us what we'd like to hear and believe.

Before we look at actual cases, it must be said that the biographical realities of Zappa's gender politics, like Kubrick's (who also got in trouble over *Lolita, A Clockwork Orange* and *Eyes Wide Shut*), are that he was a devoted husband and father to four kids (two women and two men). Even more telling is a moment in his film *Uncle Meat*. The editor of the film, Phyllis Altenhaus (later Smith), is asked to become an actor. She consents, so much so that she is given top billing in the credits! Zappa asks her to do a shower scene with Don Preston (as Uncle Meat) where he will rub hamburger on her. She does not want to do it in the nude. Zappa nudges her a little (after all, nudity in a shower scene is a pretty typical arrangement!), but she stands her ground. As a result, Zappa works around her with a contrived bit involving some special clothes that Uncle Meat wants her to wear in the shower. Phyllis does a clothed shower scene! I don't think that one can watch this sequence without getting the sense that Zappa basically respects women and their wishes, that he is far from the leering pig of some of his lyrics.

The key to those lyrics, of course, is that they are almost entirely dramatic monologues. After a few early songs on *Freak Out!* ("I Ain't Got No Heart," "How Could I Be Such A Fool," "Anyway The Wind Blows," and "I'm Not Satisfied"), Zappa completely abandoned the lyric verse (personal expression) in favor of dramatic and even epic material. The narrative personae in all the offensive Zappa sex songs can thusly no more be pinned on him than we can try Robert Browning for the Duke's crimes in "My Last Duchess." (For instance, "Duke of Prunes" on *Absolutely Free* is sung by this surreal figure [Browning on acid?]: "I see your lovely beans / and in that magic go-kart / I bite your neck.") This tends to get lost in the shuffle, of course, because we are not used to rock writing that works in this fashion. That's why we call them lyrics, in fact:

we assume they are operating in a reliably lyrical fashion. We BELIEVE Elvis Presley, Bob Dylan, Joni Mitchell, Neil Young, John Lennon, Yoko Ono—even when they're singing somebody else's lyrics, they're selling the authenticity of the song. Zappa's project is 180 degrees from this approach. He may be mocking or observing or ventriloquizing a position, but he consistently eschews raw emotion: for him, that's a private affair. Like Browning, Yeats and Eliot, he'd rather wear a mask. My invocation of these names suggests that this is acceptable modernist practice, although less employed in the pop song. (Which is not to say that "authentic" expression is not a performance: the John and Yoko media creation was performative, as previously noted. Zappa would duly observe this and be suspicious of it.)

The first lyric that has drawn criticism from friends of feminism (and I consider myself more than that, actually) is "Harry, You're A Beast" from *We're Only In It For The Money*. Our voice-of-God social commentator/narrator observes:

> I'm gonna tell you the way it is
> And I'm not gonna be kind or easy
> Your whole attitude stinks, I say
> And the life you lead is completely empty
> You paint your head
> Your mind is dead
> You don't even know what I just said
> THAT'S YOU: AMERICAN
> WOMANHOOD!
> You're phony on top
> Phony underneath
> You lay in bed & grit your teeth ... .

Ben Watson does defend this particular lyric on the grounds that it is an "exposure" of the fact that "the lifestyle of rock stars is not conducive to respect for women," a kind of preview of the rock sociology of the Flo and Eddie years (117). I would add a few other perspectives. *We're Only It For The Money* as an album modulates between social commentary and a suspicion of rock's pretensions to do just that. Hence, the tone of the text is unstable: is it a jeremiad or a mock-jeremiad from our unreliable rock star pundit? But even granted its possible utter seriousness, it has several other redemptive contexts: the song continues with Harry forcing sex from Madge ("MADGE ... I COULDN'T HELP IT ... I ... DOGGONE IT!"). Hence, the rhetoric of the speaker ("You lay in bed & grit your teeth") is his rationale for marital rape, behavior which is mocked and critiqued but certainly not endorsed by the song. (By the way, if we make the reasonable assumption that Harry is speaking the opening lines, we can conclude that it is NOT a rock star, but a suburban husband speaking. Or is it Frank Zappa ventriliquizing a rock star ventriloquizing a suburban husband?) Furthermore, this song links up with the preceding song "Mom & Dad" as a critique of familial situations that led to the unfocused youth rebellion of the sixties (as Dave Marsh notes, Zappa criticizes the kids, but he criticizes the parents more [in Kostelantz 53]). It also leads into the following song, "What's The Ugliest Part Of Your Body?," with its critique of American post-Puritan body shame and ugly-mindedness ("your mind" is the answer to the question). Indeed, it anticipates "Honey, Don't You Want A Man Like Me?" from *Zappa In New York*, a much more focused and closely observed portrayal of the dysfunctionality of American gender communication. And finally, what is in these lyrics that isn't in the writings of Betty Friedan (*The Feminine Mystique*) or Germaine Greer (*The Female Eunuch*)? Zappa is noticing the same things about the construction of femininity that feminists also observed.

Finding misogyny in the lyrics of the Mothers during the Flo and Eddie era (Mark Volman and Howard Kaylan of The Turtles, natch) might seem like shooting fish in a barrel, but I think Zappa's detractors have been too quick to judge. Recall that Zappa produced a rock band composed of groupies, the GTOs, before the Mothers sang about groupies to a large extent. ("Motherly Love" on *Freak Out* is an exception.) The larger dimensions of the project/object thusly provide a more balanced view (and the GTOs are significant participants in the film *200 Motels*, one of the major showcases for this material). Secondly, the Flo and Eddie groupie routine was insufficiently gender-stable to be straight-up misogyny. Mark Volman played the groupie always, sometimes in drag (as in the film). The crossgendered nature of the performance put everything in camp quotation marks; if anything, the ludic routine risked silliness more than offense (especially when seen in performance as opposed to being merely heard on vinyl). And again, the musical notes don't lie: a song like "Shove It Right In" off *200 Motels* exudes beauty, poignancy and sympathy for the woman venturing forth for sexual adventures—just as "What Will This Morning Bring Me This Evening" (in the film, but not on the soundtrack) does for the male rock star. It is no accident that *200 Motels* ends with Zappa's parodic AND serious version of Beethoven's "Ode to Joy," "Strictly Genteel." Its haunting benedictions for "every poor soul who's adrift in a storm" (among many others) create the same kind of complicated emotional registers as the final song of the German woman in Kubrick's *Paths of Glory*. We may be suspicious, but we are also moved by human solidarity. Zappa's lyrics may undercut the expressive emotions of his music, but the music of *200 Motels* betrays a universal tolerance and appreciation of the characters depicted in the film.

The Kaylan-Zappa collaboration on *Just Another Band From L. A.* entitled "Magdalena" provides an extreme example of how far this configuration of the band pushed the envelope. Based on an actual case of a father molesting his daughter, Kaylan turns it into jokes about Canada and the effects of working in a maple syrup factory. Its observation of the primacy of "father-daughter eroticism ... at the heart of conservative morality," as Watson suggests, links it with similar project/object moments as "Brown Shoes Don't Make It" (off *Absolutely Free* and *Tinsel Town Rebellion*)—and indeed with Nabakov's *Lolita* and many sitcom subtexts (Watson 194). Kaylan and Zappa's lyrics empower the girl more: she tells him to "go eat shit" and runs down the hall, forcing him to persuade her to the sex act as opposed to forcing it. But lines like "I thought to myself 'my god, I gave my sperm to this thing'" make for pretty conflicted post-feminist listening.

Surprisingly, Ben Watson rolls with even this phase of the career as well, but he momentarily parts company with Zappa over the notorious lyric of "The Illinois Enema Bandit" first heard on the originally unreleased *Lather* and the released *Zappa In New York* (1977) :

> His stock response 'I satirize stupid women, but I satirize stupid men too' is repeated by sidemen like Chad Wackerman and is really no answer at all. Zappa has no qualms about indulging the full-blown sexism encouraged by being part of a group of male rock musicians on tour, and such incomprehension of the woman's point of view is amply demonstrated by 'The Legend of the Illinois Enema Bandit.' If Zappa was likely to be raped himself, it would not be a song he would sing. On the other hand, when he claims that he is only making social documentary, the accuracy of his observations and the fact that he presents an absent moral centre come to his defence. (Watson 322)

"The Illinois Enema Bandit" is carefully explained in the liner notes. It is a song based on the true story of Michael Kenyon, who terrorized coeds at the University of Illinois for ten years by giving enemas to his robbery victims. Watson's equation of a forced enema to rape is understandable because Kenyon was a stranger (otherwise many of us were raped by our parents!). Zappa also notes that the song's "final courtroom verse is a parody of traditional blues mythology where some girl has got to have her man go free, no matter what he's been accused of" (liner notes, *Zappa In New York*). In general, the song is a parody of songs celebrating the outlaw. (Only a few years previously Bob Dylan recorded a bunch of them on the *Pat Garrett and Billy the Kid* soundtrack.) For all this song's tastelessness (and Zappa has never seen a taste barrier he didn't want to knock over, with the exception arguably of his final illness), it provides a *reductio ad absurdum* of the admiration and fear we have for outlaws in late twentieth-century America. The Bandit is mocked, not endorsed: it's not like Zappa fans went out and committed copycat crimes here.

Admittedly, Zappa seems to be fascinated by the enema as a kind of primal scene here with allegorical implications. The parentally administered enema is one of the first symbolic incursions of one's body space by authority; any later enema recalls this scenario. Furthermore, Zappa's lyrics beginning around this time became fascinated with the anus as a site of negotiated power in addition to the genitals (see also "Bobby Brown" and "Dong Work For Yuda," to name but two). In other words, Frank was becoming more polymorphously perverse lyrically, first noticed (again!) by Watson (322). The allegorical politics of the bandit were emphasized more by jazz artist Henry Threadgill, who composed a "Salute to the Enema Bandit" and defended him to Nat Hentoff:

> Richard Nixon was on his list, by the way, but he got caught before he got to Nixon. Why did he do it? He said he did it because people were full of shit. They didn't make him serve much time in prison. He had to do community work, and he had to see a psychiatrist. Why did I write a piece about him? I thought he had something important to say. He was making a statement at that time, in the 1970s. When America was going backwards after the increase in freedom and honesty in the 1960s. (qtd. in Watson 321-2)

As Frank's lyric goes, "it must be just what they all needs." A tough listen for non-fans, "The Illinois Enema Bandit" remains a favorite for many fans—an example of Zappa pushing one aspect of his work very far.

Let me mention a few other problematic test cases in the project/object. "The Torture Never Stops" off *Zoot Allures* (1976) has been described by critics as an "audio snuff movie" (in Watson 299). It portrays a torture chamber in surrealist and cartoonish wording (a "room where the giant fire-puffer works," for example), then proceeds to have a female victim (portrayed by Gail Zappa and another woman) scream in such a way as to blur pain and pleasure, both in arch quotation marks. Too unsettling to be as popular as the Enema Bandit, the song nonetheless works as a critical descriptor of actual patriarchal practice in totalitarian regimes and a limit case of sadomasochistic sexuality (previously explored in *Bongo Fury*'s "Carolina Hard-Core Ecstasy" [1975]). The ultimate fantasy of the torturer is that his victim "enjoys" it; but even more problematically and profoundly, this blurring of categories can be passed onto the victim. Susan Brownmiller's feminist work over the years has made similar observations. And, of course, Zappa's scenario is resonant not only with feminist critiques of power, but also sundry political situations. In 1976, Zappa is already noting the clandestine activities of the regimes which the U.S. supported for geopolitically strategic expedience. The surrealism keeps it universal and fresh, but Iran's Savak police provide the best referent for the song at its time of composition. (Unfortunately, it seems more prophetic of the experiences of Sister Dianna Ortiz in Guatemala during the senior Bush administration.)

Then again, Ben Watson also argues that this song is a musical riposte to disco, especially the heavy breathing of Donna Summer's collaborations with Giorgio Moroder (in Kostelantz 158). For a few years in the mid-seventies, the torture never stopped! And finally, it returns to the primal scene of Zappa's bust in 1964 for preparing a "party tape" at Studio Z in Cucamonga for an undercover member of the vice squad. The ersatz moaning on the tape has been sporadically reappropriated as art object on recordings as early as *Freak Out!* (on "The Return of the Son of Monster Magnet") through *Over-Nite Sensation* ("Dinah Moe Humm") until its apotheosis here.

"Bobby Brown" off *Sheik Yerbouti* (1979) contains Zappa's busiest transgressive lyric writing. It is a ballad about a date rapist who eventually gets castrated by a lesbian and becomes a homosexual interested in sadomasochism and water sports—all in the length of a top-forty single! The lyrics were no problem for European airplay, where it became a huge club hit. Since it is a tale of feminine revenge, it has not drawn as much ire as songs like "The Illinois Enema Bandit" (which it is certainly as humorous as). This tune reveals an important principle for how Zappa responded to intelligent criticism of his writing: rather than retract, he'd respond by equal-opportunity satire directed at a complementary subject position: if "The Illinois Enema Bandit" showed a "rapist" released, "Bobby Brown" shows a rapist punished. (The best example of this approach is Zappa countering "Jewish Princess" off *Sheik Yerbout!* with "Catholic Girls" on *Joe's Garage*.)

Then there's "Pick Me, I'm Clean" off *Tinsel Town Rebellion* (1981), a tale of a young international woman from impoverished circumstances trying to connect with the band. Ben Watson believes this song "orchestrates the band members' underlying hostility in a way that seems callous and jaded compared to Flo & Eddie's hysterical enthusiasm," but concedes the "utopian freedom" of the music itself (387). I'd suggest that such a dialectic is redemptive. The beauty of the melody dignifies and sympathizes with the character which the lyrics disparage (e.g. "I'm learning English / I can say 'thank you' / Pick me, I'm clean"). Zappa has captured here the poignancy of a poor European trying to latch onto a shot at prosperity through wealthier and more vulgar Americans, an update of a classic Henry James plotline and a striking kind of inverted colonialism. It's an interesting situation, and a beautiful song.

"Jumbo Go Away" off *You Are What You Is* (1981) is the only Zappa song that "really upsets" Ben Watson (549). It depicts a band member driving off a woman he is tired of; it has not only sexist humor in it, but a threat of violence: "Jumbo better get back / Or your eye will get black / When I give you a smack." Zappa's defense to Watson, expectedly, was "That's a true story ... . Guy's name is Denny Walley [a member of the band at the time], it happened" (Watson 549). Zappa's lyric writing has charted the increasing chill in the air of band groupie interactions, as a matter of some historical and (yes) sociological interest. From the Flo and Eddie lyrics through "Pick Me, I'm Clean" to "Jumbo Go Away," we see a noticeable deterioration of affairs. Arguably, this is Zappa's whole point for the exercise—information for future students of the history of everyday life, "a record for future generations that during this part of the 20th century there actually were people who did not think or act like the plasticized caricatures that will survive to represent us in TV reruns or 'Real World' history books" (liner notes, *Uncle Meat* video box).

And finally, there is the overwhelmingly transgressive *Thing-Fish* (1984), Zappa's parodic anti-Broadway play (the recording describes itself as an "original cast recording"). It does its job so well that one senses Zappa backing off from such material, relatively speaking, for the remainder of his career: he had virtually exhausted this dimension of the project/object. *Thing-Fish* has something to offend everyone along lines of gender, sexuality and ethnicity. Its monumental (but often humorous) negativity is best seen as a passionate counter-formation to the treacly affirmation of the spectacular Broadway show. As Watson cleverly notes, "It works like a great eruption of pus, akin to picking an extremely unpleasant boil, which Broadway does indeed represent." Zappa himself responded appreciatively to Watson when this line was read to him (435, 550). One also senses that the formations of the project/object work along the lines of Saussurean semiotics: Zappa's art tries to detect missing counter-formulations and supply them, just as the present tense of a verb arrays itself contrastively with past and future tenses. *Thing-Fish* is what it is because it's trying to be a spectacle that is "Not Broadway."

As such, one might compare the way *Thing-Fish* functions semiotically within the grammar of the Broadway musical with Zappa's original interest in working with excluded musics in his career—race records and avant-garde classical music: "I composed a composite, gap-filling product to plug most of the gaps between so-called serious music and so-called popular music" working from those two outside extremes of very lowbrow and very highbrow (qtd. in Watson xxix). As Watson repeatedly asserts, Frank Zappa—in good post-dadaist fashion—mistrusted any musical institutions. (It's hard to believe that Frank never read Louis Althusser's definition of Ideological State Apparati.) Both classical and pop music have rules which Zappa was determined to break. It is no accident that in *The Real Frank Zappa Book* he offered scathing critical "anthropologies" of both the symphony orchestra and the rock and roll band. He especially deflates the pretensions of the contemporary orchestra, which sticks to overplayed crowd-pleasers as opposed to trying to learn difficult new music (like the stuff he was composing): "Why is that any better than a bunch of guys in a bar band jamming on 'Louie Louie' or 'Midnight Hour?'" (186). *Thing-Fish* does in microcosm what his entire career does in macrocosm: it offers a great refusal and a sublime negation of the way things are done here and now in American culture. The problematics of Zappa's gender representations must also be seen ultimately in this light. He is resisting the social construction of gender in his writing because he is ultimately resisting social constructions of ANYTHING per se. He has a particular axe to grind as a composer in this regard: "A composer is as useful to a person in a jogging suit as a dinosaur turd in the middle of his runway" (Zappa, *Them Or Us* 11). He once decribed America to an Australian interviewer as caught up in a "Peruvian work ethic" [obviously the view from Los Angeles!] and an obsession with body image:

> Right now this society cares about its stomach in terms of whether it's flat, how much is in it, and its nose, and beyond that nothing else matters. No art, no music, no drama, no sculpture, no painting, and who could give a shit? ... .
>
> The problem with the system is that it's the illusion that something is happening. I resent the illusion that something is happening when it's really not. You think you're in control of your existence? You think your vote matters? You think that these promises are ever going to occur? Face the facts. The fucking oil companies have got you by the balls. And if it ain't the oil company it's the guy that makes soybeans, and soybean products, or it's the plastics guy ... .
>
> But I'm just a musician. (Gritter 317-8)

"All that's left anymore is business," he says elsewhere in this interview (316). No wonder that the serious Zappa scholars have to keep name-checking Karl Marx, Walter Benjamin, Teodor Adorno and Louis Althusser. Although Zappa was a firm believer in small entrepeneurship—and his Barfko-Swill company lives on after his death—his teeth-grinding hatred for big business matches the most melancholy moments in Marxist thought. A self-described "practical conservative," Zappa could also be called a utopian capitalist: on a modest scale, the system can work (Zappa, *Real Frank Zappa Book* 315). Nigey Lennon is onto something when she depicts him as an essentially Victorian individual in a twentieth-century world (55). Besides espousing such classic Victorian values as abstemiousness, Zappa had the work ethic of Thomas Carlyle, the faith in small-business craftsmanship of William Morris, the obsession with technology of Henry Adams, the critical gender consciousness of Thomas Hardy. Hardy shocked his audience as much as Zappa shocked his. Both men possessed a keen critical eye.

Frank Zappa had an unerring instinct for America's biggest hangups: religion, sex, money and race—the first three courtesy of our long Puritan hangover, the last a nasty inheritance from less congenial aspects of the Enlightenment organization of reality. These four problems taint our national culture, and the "art" it produces. Zappa felt these forces upon him from the get-go: the hassles he received for being in an interracial band, the Studio Z bust, right up through his testimony before the U. S. Congress about the activities of the Parents' Music Resource Center in 1985. The fix is on, friends, which is why I'm writing this little book. With the exceptions of Neil Young, Joni Mitchell and James Brown, college radio stations are the only places that will even occasionally play the music discussed in these chapters over the airwaves. Business and sex and religion and race warp our national culture, supremely in places like Disneyland or Branson, Missouri. But a quick stroll past the cineplex, through the corporate bookstore chain, or across the radio dial or cable remote will confirm Zappa's most paranoid statements. It's all cheese, as he expressed in a rejected *Newsweek* column that ended up in the gatefold of *You Are What You Is*:

> The Quality *Of Our Lives* (if we think of this matter in terms of "How *much* of what we *individually* consider to be *Beautiful* are we able to experience every day?" [)] seems an irrelevant matter, now that all decisions regarding the creation and distribution of Works of Art must first pass *under the limbo bar* (a/k/a "The Bottom Line"), along with things like *Taste* and *The Public Interest*, all tied like a tin can to the wagging tail of the sacred *Prime Rate Poodle*. The aforementioned *festering poot* is coming your way at a theatre or drive-in near you. It wakes you up every morning as it droozles out of your digital clock radio. ("Say Cheese ... ," *You Are What You Is*)

Given this dilemma, anxiety about Zappa's gender representations seems akin to not liking what's on the screen in a burning theater. Fortunately, music is nonetheless "THE BEST" (as Mary proclaims in "Packard Goose" on *Joe's Garage*)—at least as it was practiced by Frank Zappa.

"Would y'all like some more-a?": A Tentative Listening Guide

Instructions for Use

This section of the chapter is a result of a felt need among many music lovers, relayed to me as a Zappa aficionado, for some listening tips. With an output as mammoth as Frank's, even the sympathetic would-be listener is daunted. I have the advantage of growing up with him for over forty years, and absorbing the music as it came out. I have heard it all, and have some definite opinions about it! Whence this guide: unlike most published reviews of the discography, this is not chronological. It is unabashedly (and subjectively) a matter of taste. I have "ranked" in descending order Frank Zappa's music according to some balanced considerations of accessibility and quality. In other words, the first things which I mention should knock your socks off. As you proceed down the list, you will be exposed to music more hard-core Zappaphiles enjoy.

But a few caveats:

1) It's all good. Zappa was always striving for excellence, so the lowest-ranked musical item on this list is still well worth your attention. I would only submit that it might not be where I'd start if I were you.

2) Since I'm not you, feel free to experiment with the list in subversive ways. If you're underwhelmend by my top picks, start at the bottom and move up—or from the middle number, alternating towards either end. Which use best matches your response to the music? In effect, I'm inviting you to calibrate yourself with my tastes however best you can.

I not only provide a ranking, but some gesture towards identifying genres of these releases. I have settled upon rock, rock instrumental, jazz, classical and Synclavier. But these are crude labels. Rock especially proves a catch-all, since most of Zappa's rock recordings have strong jazz (and classical) elements. I reserve the other categories for overtly non-rock gestures. All I will claim is that I am being more precise than your local CD emporium, which throws everything/almost everything the man did in the rock bin.

After ranking Zappa's own releases, I will then list in similar descending fashion Zappa's work as a producer and collaborator with other artists—and some tribute recordings.

In the appendix, I will relist my rankings by genre (vs. the initial jumble), inviting you again to subvert them to maximally approximate your own taste. I will also provide some mix tape suggestions for creating collections of Zappa music related to love songs (probably this should be in quotation marks), dental hygiene, country and western stylings, and poodles. (Your collections may be more focused than the posthumous compilations *Strictly Commercial* and *Have I Offended Someone?*)

The Guide Itself

1) *Frank Zappa Plays The Music of Frank Zappa: A Memorial Tribute* (rock instrumental, 1996). This is a very efficient introduction to Zappa's amazing guitar pyrotechnics, compositional density and, yes, soul power. It's typically not in the stores: you have to call 1-888-922-7873 or order online from www.zappa.com. But it's well worth this modest effort. The CD consists of live and instrumental versions of Zappa's best guitar instrumentals according to his family (and Zappa himself: he referred to

these as his "signature pieces" [*FZ Plays FZ*, liner notes])—and I readily agree. These would be (in ascending order for me) "Zoot Allures," "Black Napkins" and "Watermelon in Easter Hay." This last number makes me run out of superlatives. The family and I think it is his best solo. The back melody alone ("Amazing Grace" played backwards) is hauntingly melancholy and a masterpiece in its own right, but the lead he overlays on it is incredibly poignant and powerful. The guitar tone is pristine. Not since Bach himself has a musician crawled so far into the mind of God. If "Watermelon in Easter Hay" doesn't do it for you proceed to the classical and Synclavier rankings in the appendix: you don't like Zappa's amplified music!

This CD also includes "Merely a Blues in A," which is a good glimpse into what a fine blues player Zappa could be—as well as a glimpse of Frank's own musical roots in the stylings of Guitar Slim, Slim Harpo and Johnny Guitar Watson.

2) *You Can't Do That On Stage Anymore, Volume 2: The Helsinki Concert* (rock, 1988). This is a complete recording of a 1974 concert in Finland. Although the 12 CD official live collection is directed overall at a serious fan base, this volume is highly accessible to the novice listener (as I have discovered in field tests). This concert not only showcases the sheer variety and virtuosity of Frank Zappa in performance, but features what conceptually might have been his best band. He certainly worked with some more technically proficient players, but he never had a band with more fire and funk. This band could have held its own on a double bill with either Parliament or Chick Corea in an electric mode.

It features three Zappa hall-of-fame players: jazz keyboardist George Duke, classically trained percussionist Ruth Underwood and vocal madman Napoleon Murphy Brock (who could also play gut-bucket sax and a mean flute). Arguably, Duke is the glue that held this group together, being equally comfortable with its technical playing and its more funky proclivities. He might be the "secret sauce" here. Zappa himself, bassist Tom Fowler and drummer Chester Thompson are, of course, also far more than adequate. But Frank's mixture of musical freedom and control are here almost in perfect balance. He knows that he can safely let out the leash on this ensemble with fantastic results.

The music, of course, is spectacular. These disks contain the definitive version of his Von Daniken send-up "Inca Roads" (in fact he used the guitar solo from this concert in its studio version), another one of Frank's loveliest compositions. Beautiful tracks from *Roxy & Elsewhere* such as "Village of the Sun," "Echidna's Arf (Of You)," "Don't You Ever Wash That

Thing?" and "Pygmy Twylyte" are given more uptempo arrangements, since the band is more comfortable with the scores. They're wonderful on that album, but even better here. Napoleon Murphy Brock leads off a gorgeous cover of the old Mothers' "Idiot Bastard Son." "Dupree's Paradise," another dense Zappa composition (about late-night low-lifes at the after-hours hangouts) gets a 24 minute reading with plenty of good soloing opportunities. "Building A Girl" showcases the audio results of Zappa's use of hand signals to conduct the band in spontaneous avant-garde compositions. And there is a fair introduction throughout to the tomfoolery that goes with a Zappa concert, his Spike Jones side. But things don't get too sleazy: the band is always on better behavior when there are women in it. I guess I must prefer that arrangement.

3) *We're Only In It For The Money* (rock, 1968). The only Zappa album *Rolling Stone* lists among its 100 greatest rock recordings. Oh well; they're missing a lot. But this is certainly the best work the original lineup of the Mothers of Invention ever accomplished. Not only does it visually parody *Sergeant Pepper's Lonely Hearts Club Band*, it surpasses it musically, ideologically and conceptually (as John Lennon himself more or less implied in the post-Beatles *Rolling Stone* interviews when he praised Zappa's genius). The pop writing is catchier than the Beatles ("It's His Voice On The Radio" aka "Lonely Little Girl"), the psychedelia more psychedelic despite Frank's abstinence ("Nasal Retentive Calliope Music") and the avant-gardisms more avant-garde (the concluding song "The Chrome Plated Megaphone of Destiny" makes "A Day in the Life" look like Pat Boone).

Ideologically, it criticizes the emergent counterculture which the Beatles had initially endorsed (and helped to create). Since the album was actually recorded only a few months after the release of *Sergeant Pepper*, Frank is being fairly prescient here. His lyrics predict the trivial commercialization of hippie culture ("Who Needs The Peace Corps?"), the murder of the innocents ("Mom & Dad," which eerily anticipates the Kent State shootings) and even mass incarceration of the counterculture ("Concentration Moon," "The Chrome Plated Megaphone of Destiny"). If he was a bit paranoid on this last, he was accurate about the fact that such detention camps were being planned in anticipation of civil disorder. (See, for instance, the tip of the iceberg in the extensive police training shown in Haskell Wexler's film *Medium Cool*—and Wexler later worked with Frank on *Uncle Meat*. Or Thomas Pynchon's novel *Vineland*. Much of this planning remains classified, but a sensitive register like Zappa's could pick it up in the general conversation.) Unlike the 1967 version of the Beatles, Frank Zappa didn't think the establishment would surrender its power willingly when given a better cultural alternative. It wasn't "getting better all the time" for him!

Conceptually, the song cycle moves from counterculture commercialization through individual incarceration and murder towards genocidal apocalypse with some interesting autobiographical asides (Ronnie and Kenny's booger and fart saga in "Let's Make The Water Turn Black") and some fingerpointing satire ("Harry, You're A Beast," "The Idiot Bastard Son"). Although cultural studies academics such as Sheila Whitely claim to find an order in *Sergeant Pepper*, Lennon always denied it was more than a loose bunch of songs unified by the thin English bandstand frame (Whitely, chapter 3; Lennon and Ono 207). I'd submit the Zappa album takes you on a more noticeable journey, and it's a satisfyingly heady mixture of power pop and avant-gardism all the way. Ironically for a psychedelic teetotaller like Frank, it may well be the best psychedelic album ever—and was used as such by a bevy of listeners when it first appeared.

4) *Lumpy Money: an FZ audio documentary project / object* (2008 [recorded 1967]). If you can afford it, this deluxe audio documentary presentation of *We're Only In It For The Money* is also worth acquiring. You will not get the stereo mix of the original album, but a mono 1968 mix and a 1984 remix with new drum, bass and guitar parts in places where Zappa thought the original playing could be improved (a controversial move with frequently defensible results). On the 1984 version, you can finally hear what the wife is saying in "Harry, You're A Beast" ("don't come in me / in me") and appreciate how the speaker separation in "Flower Punk" contrasts an idealistic speeded-up voiceover (left speaker) with money-grubbing plans for how to spend the "royalty check" (right speaker)—and much more. The instrumental build tracks that showcase partial instrumentation before other material gets added (like vocals) feature much pop loveliness on the various versions of "Lonely Little Girl" and a great sax solo on "Who Needs The Peace Corps?"

With this version, the much more lowly ranked *Lumpy Gravy* (see below #68) gets a big boost, as it should. The original version for Capitol Records (legally suppressed by MGM) is entirely instrumental, shorter and much more accessible to the novice listener. For the first time, it is available here along with an unreleased 1984 remix that also improves upon the piece (odd opening vocals singing the words to "Go Down, Moses" to a different melody) and other odd tidbits. An even more interesting piece from the Capitol sessions is (for me) "How Did That Get In Here?"—the results of a February 1967 recording, preceding the March *Lumpy Gravy* work, which Frank first edited as a selfcontained piece, but later pulled material from for incorporation into the latter construct of *Lumpy Gravy*. As a lovely jazz / classical hybrid, the earlier version eminently stands on its own.

This new project/object forces one to confront two related questions: other than for chronological considerations, why did Frank Zappa consider these works to be ultimately one (a critical truism repeated here in the liner notes by David Fricke which no one ever bothers to convince me about)? And why did Frank Zappa (in 1971 at least, in an interview on disc three) and Gail Zappa (liner notes, 2008) deem *Lumpy Gravy* their favorite Zappa album? In other words, what am I missing here?

The linkage, I guess, is specifically compositional (orchestral overlaps between the two works and the similarity between "The Chrome Plated Megaphone Of Destiny" and some of the Varese-inflected moments on *Lumpy Gravy*) and sociological (the Ronnie and Kenny songs on *Money* resemble some of the vocal material recorded inside the piano for *Lumpy Gravy*). But I'd submit a bigger reason for the linkage is that this is the moment when Zappa fully realized his theory of the Big Note (see above) and that all his work could be a related, integrated whole of some sort. So he would be especially inclined to notice and enforce such a connection at the moment of discovery.

And since working on *Lumpy Gravy* facilitated the discovery, it would be a personal favorite album of his. Gail Zappa praises it for similar reasons in her liner notes, saying that it "at once defin[ed] Frank Zappa and his approach on entering Earth's atmosphere." I admit as much below when I rank it as a stand-alone project, but I keep that lower ranking for it because, as noted, I do not think it is as accessible a point of entry for novice listeners (as opposed to the versions on this edition): *Lumpy Gravy* is a great breakthrough for the composer, thoroughly appreciated by his wife, which will take the rest of you longer to appreciate. But don't take my word for it: check it out for yourself. (Curiosity is always a powerful revisionist motivator.)

One last thought: I suspect Frank loved *Lumpy Gravy* also because it was his first serious and extended solo orchestral project as a composer / conductor. In a 1969 interview on disc three, he talks about using John Cage's aleatoric methods in editing some of the final results, an avant-garde gesture showing his self-identification with the cutting edge of twentieth-century classical composition. And he worked apart from the Mothers of Invention with professional studio players. That had to have been empowering and liberating for him musically. As a result, I think he downplayed the brilliance of his companion work *We're Only In*

It For The Money. In a 1969 interview on disc three, he talks about using John Cage's aleatoric methods in editing some of the final results, an avant-garde gesture showing his self-identification with the cutting edge of twentieth-century classical composition. And he worked apart from the Mothers of Invention My ranking here is based on exposing a wide variety of people to both albums, and I stand by it with all these qualifications and admissions (which the audio documentary thoroughly calls into play).

5) *Ship Arriving Too Late To Save A Drowning Witch* (rock, 1982). This magnificent recording is known best for Moon Unit and Frank's chart-topping teen satire "Valley Girl," but there are at least two even more incredible tunes on it: "No Not Now" (a demented country-inflected ballad which raises the Phil Spector wall-of-sound approach to hebephrenic intensity) and "Teen-age Prostitute" (which features the operatic voice of Lisa Popeil—along with Thana Harris, the best female vocalist Frank ever worked with; I think his music was consistently enriched by such collaborations). Add in Bob Harris' wild falsetto work on "I Come From Nowhere" and the compositional density of "Drowning Witch" and "Envelopes," spectacular playing from Tommy Mars on keyboards and Steve Vai on "impossible guitar parts," and the genial presence of Ike Willis on rhythm guitar and vocals. The result is another near-perfect recording. Much good is to come further down this list, but these first five are "desert island discs." They will tell you if you might like Zappa's rock work—or if you agree with my assessment of it (or if a subversive use of this ranking would prove more fruitful for you).

6) *Mothermania: The Best of the Mothers* (rock, 1969). This compilation is here on a technicality. It contains all the best songs from *Absolutely Free* (# 7 below), plus better remixes of songs from *Freak Out!* and *We're Only In It For The Money* (including the uncensored versions of "Mother People" and "It Can't Happen Here"). This is the only compilation of "greatest hits" Zappa authorized until near the end of his life, and he did a fabulous job. Even though it is derived only from his first three recordings with the Mothers of Invention, its revisioning of the material made it highly collectable for discerning ears.

I am not ranking here the other compilation CDs of almost entirely preexisting material: *Strictly Commercial* (his most accessible music and/or tunes that got radio play), *Have I Offended Someone?* (Zappa's most transgressive lyrics) or *Understanding America* (some of his most pointed social commentary). These no doubt have a reason to exist and a larger audience than what I'm writing about here. But, as with Sun Ra, this is too vast an output of work to be distilled into anthologies except in these rather artificial ways. (Perhaps I'm contradicting myself, since I have mix tape suggestions in the appendix. But I would submit mine are along more off-beat lines.) The power in the music overall is its dizzying variety, which gets slightly lost in these thematic collections. As a hardcore Zappa fan, I don't really need these releases. But, hey, you might find them an easier point of entry to him than this guide. Fair enough.

7) *Absolutely Free* (rock, 1967). Frank's second album with the original Mothers of Invention saw a quantum leap in compositional complexity from the magnificent if cruder *Freak Out!*. Like the Beatles, Zappa was writing and recording material his band couldn't yet play live. "Brown Shoes Don't Make It," the masterpiece of the album, only showed up in live repertoire in the early 1980s. Here it's pure studio wizardry delivering this twisted tale of the bourgeois male's redirection of libidinal energy from his wife to his daughter (among other things). As such, it's also a breakthrough mix of aesthetic beauty AND transgression, a combination that would prove to be the hallmark of some of Zappa's best lyrics. "The Duke of Prunes" is a durably lovely melody that goes back to Frank's orchestral score for a western film his high school English teacher made (*Run Home Slow*). The added lyrics are full-blown surrealism: I've always pictured the Duke of Prunes in his "magic go-cart" as a kind of Ed "Big Daddy" Roth custom car monster, especially since he "bite[s] the neck" of his would-be duchess. How can you resist a song that quotes both the Supremes ("Baby Love") and Igor Stravinsky (the ever-popular "Rite of Spring")? "Call Any Vegetable" is another surreal standard. All three of these tracks are on *Mothermania*, by the way.

8) *Sleep Dirt* (jazz, 1979—but get the CD reissue from 1991). This is an example of a debatable genre call, as this album rocks hard enough at times ("Filthy Habits," "The Ocean Is The Ultimate Solution") to qualify for rock instrumental. But it is jazz, nonetheless, in the sense that Chick Corea's electric band or Herbie Hancock are jazz. But as often happens when Zappa forays into more respected genres, he leaves his competition in the dust. Corea and Hancock sound pretty tame next to the playing on the aforementioned tracks, fuelled by the passion and fury of Terry Bozzio, for my money Zappa's all-time best drummer (although Chad Wackerman and Vinnie Coliauta have mundo chops as well).

This album originally was issued by Warner Brothers during a contract dispute without Frank's final approval of the tape. For the CD release, he radically changed and improved an already fine album by adding Thana Harris' exquisite vocals to "Flambay" (demented cocktail jazz),

"Spider of Destiny" and "Time Is Money." These three songs are sung by Drakma, Queen of Cosmic Greed, to her giant spider consort Hunchentoot in Zappa's projected science-fiction opera also called *Hunchentoot*. (You can get the libretto for this unfinished work in *Them Or Us: The Book* from the Zappa online store.) The feel for the project is very close to that of the Zsa Zsa Gabor grade-Z masterpiece of cheapness, *Queen of Outer Space* (which he duly alludes to in the script [180]). But even if you don't know the plot, these demented arias stand on their own (and may inspire you to check out Thana Harris' other recordings and memoir *Under the Same Moon*).

Completing this near-perfect CD are the title track, a rare chance to hear Zappa play acoustic guitar, and a strutting big-band number ("Regyptian Strut") originally written for the Grand Wazoo ensemble.

9) *Broadway the Hard Way* (rock, 1989). This last primarily vocal album from Zappa's last rock outfit shows that he just kept getting better over time. Eight years of Ronald Reagan and company generate a high level of satiric writing, as you might expect. (He also takes a swipe at the Reverend Jesse Jackson in "Rhymin' Man.") But the reason I rank this so highly has more to do with "Any Kind of Pain," Zappa's last (and possibly best) fusion of a lush melody with harsh lyrics—in this case, about the re-sexualization of the American businesswoman through the "power suit." In *Thing-Fish*, Harry-as-a-boy describes potential erogenous contact with this icon as like "fucking a slightly more voluptuous version of somebody's father" (*Them Or Us: The Book* 307). Fortunately, you need not accede to Frank's gender politics to appreciate the music. Also noteworthy are a big band rendition of the standard "Stolen Moments," followed by a guest appearance from Sting performing the controversial Police classic "Murder By Numbers."

10) *Roxy & Elsewhere* (rock, 1974). As with the Helsinki concert (#2 above), this is ranked highly because it is such a well-rounded introduction to everything Zappa does, and because it features arguably his best overall ensemble. I like the Helsinki show better for its greater length and superior "tightness," but there are some songs on here you can't get on that other recording, most notably the intense hyper-be-bop of the "Be-Bop Tango (Of The Old Jazzmen's Church)," a standout showcase for keyboardist George Duke. This piece can be lumped in with other works like "The Black Page" (in all its numberings): not only is it insanely difficult to play, but Zappa liked to get audience members onstage and have them try to dance to it! The results were never strictly ballroom ... .

11) *One Size Fits All* (rock, 1975). More timeless art from Zappa, Duke, Brock

and Ruth Underwood. One of the best studio albums Zappa ever produced. Consistently beautiful writing and playing (especially on "Inca Roads," "Florentine Pogen," "Andy" and "Sofa"). "San Ber'dino" is the hardest rocking tune Zappa ever composed. Like "Village of the Sun," it's tapping into autobiography (his brief stint in tank C of the San Bernadino jail for audio pornography). The presentation is also roots-oriented, featuring both Frank's adolescent guitar idol Johnny "Guitar" Watson and his adolescent friend Captain Beefheart (for contract reasons, playing harmonica under the name of "Bloodshot Rollin' Red"). Another superb introduction to the range of Frank's sonic territory.

12) *Tinseltown Rebellion* (rock, 1981). This is the band that could play "Brown Shoes Don't Make It" live—and much more besides. "Pick Me, I'm Clean" is another memorable mix of beautiful melody and harsh lyrics (if more sympathetic to its subject than Zappa is given credit for; see above); as you may gather, I think this approach produced consistently excellent results for Frank. "Easy Meat" has a keyboard break from Tommy Mars with a romantic classical feel. "Peaches and Regalia" from *Hot Rats* is given a Gary Numan / Devo reading in "Peaches Ill." To say nothing of "The Blue Light," an early (and fantastic) example of sprechstimme / "meltdown," two terms (the former technical, the latter the band's) for the later Zappa practice of playing exactly to the rhythms and pitches of everyday speech. The lyrics to "The Blue Light" are memorably strange, even by the arduous standards of the Zappa catalogue:

> The seepage, the sewage, the rubbers, the napkins,
> Your ethos, your pathos,
> Your flag pole, your port hole,
> Your language.

13) *Joe's Garage* (rock, 1979). Zappa described this rock opera as "a really cheap kind of high school play" or an illustrated anti-drug lecture about the evils of music (*Joe's Garage*, liner notes). At times the piece does seem to revel in its cheapness, most notably in its Felliniesque concluding romp ("A Little Green Rosetta") and in Frank's narration as the "Central Scrutinizer." But there is some fabulous music here, including the original context for "Watermelon in Easter Hay." I also love a guilty pleasure like "Catholic Girls," the operatic "Why Does It Hurt When I Pee?," the plaintive reggae ballad "Lucille Has Messed My Mind Up" (reworked from its original appearance on a Jeff Simmons solo album of the same name), the similarly unctuous robo-ballad "Sy Borg" and the underrated manifesto "Packard Goose." The band is consistently polished, and production values are superb except when deliberately cheesy for comic effect.

14) *Bongo Fury* (rock, 1975). This mostly live recording commemorates the brief period when Captain Beefheart played with the Mothers. His finest work appears on the opener "Debra Kadabra," which assaults the listener with dense imagery and cheesy music (including a Mexican horror film score) worthy of the best stuff on the Captain's *Trout Mask Replica*. But I'm also a big fan of another beautiful "romantic" anti-ballad, "Carolina Hard-Core Ecstasy," which has fun tilting at the Who both lyrically and musically (it quotes "I Can't Explain"). "Advance Romance" is big fun as well, with the usual high-quality vocalizing from Napoleon Murphy Brock and the reappearance of "Potato-Head Bobby" from "San Ber'dino."

15) *You Are What You Is* (rock, 1981). A mixed collection which has moments of real genius. I especially like the Halloween anthem "Goblin Girl," which concludes by layering musical motif on top of musical motif (including the riff from the previous song "Doreen")—kind of like Phil Spector meeting Charles Ives. "Teen-age Wind" is similarly intertextual and complex. Plus guilty pleasures abound, from Jimmy Carl Black's twisted country ballad "Harder Than Your Husband" through the sexual tourism of "Mudd Club" to the Saturday Night Live tribute ditty "Conehead."

16) *Sheik Yerbouti* (rock, 1979). Another superbly produced collection that features standout players such as guitarist Adrian Belew and drummer Terry Bozzio. The best songwriting can be found in the anti-drug vision "City of Tiny Lites," the savage putdown "Yo' Mama" and the irrepressible comic tale of "Bobby Brown." But those who remember the seventies will also like the piss-takes on Peter Frampton ("I Have Been In You"), Bob Dylan ("Flakes"), disco ("Dancin' Fool") and punk rock ("I'm So Cute" and "Tryin' To Grow A Chin," the latter of which eerily predicts the deaths of Sid and Nancy). "Rubber Shirt" is Zappa's second use of xenochronicity, the tape juxtaposition of separate solos to create seeming musical interplay. And "Rat Tomago" is one of Frank's heaviest and dirtiest guitar solos. Overall a better album than *You Are What You Is*, I rank it lower only because the latter hits higher peaks at times. *Sheik Yerbouti* offers more even quality throughout.

17) *The Making of Freak Out! : An FZ Audio Documentary* (4 and 2 disc versions) (rock, 1966). If you can afford it, get the expanded versions of the release with build-up tracks, overdubs, interviews, alternate takes, remixes and other rarities. (if you have beaucoup cash, get both audio documentaries—since there are a few things on the abbreviated two-disc version not included on the four-disc release.) In my film classes, I ask students to watch a film just for its editing, camera work, mise-en-scene or soundtrack. Similarly, one reason why Zappa's music repays extensive

re-listening is that he builds so much beautiful musical information in the mix through multi-tracking (and little sonic in-jokes via the "eyebrows" of chosen genre expression/parody). With this audio documentary you can hear all this stuff: who knew there was such lovely piano work in "Go Cry On Somebody Else's Shoulder" (in a cocktail vein) or on "Who Are The Brain Police?" (in counterpoint to the melody)? Or that one could hear the plucking of strings inside a piano a la composer Henry Cowell (check out "The Banshee") in "Return Of The Son Of Monster Magnet"? Both documentaries include a generous booklet; the four-disc version has the historic L.A. map of Freak Out hotspots that you could mail in for in 1966 when the album first came out. Appropriately for this book, the Zappa family has expanded the original list of "people [who] have contributed materially in many ways to make the music what it is" to now include Sun Ra and Yoko Ono! Once again, mysterious linkages emerge.

18) *Freak Out!* (rock, 1966). This ranking of Frank's first album acknowledges both that he did accomplish better things later (as he always was careful to point out) and that this is an album of both historical and musical importance. This was the first double album of rock music ever released, and it may be the first rock "concept" album. Paul McCartney has stressed its importance, along with the Beach Boys' *Pet Sounds*, for paving the way to *Sergeant Pepper*. Frank Zappa amazingly emerges full-blown here. His double embrace of doo-wop and rhythm and blues with avant-garde classical music (especially Stravinsky, Varese, Schoenberg and Webern) produces this unique music which is simultaneously complex and raw. The beauty that was soon to arrive with "The Duke of Prunes" and "Lonely Little Girl" is not here yet; the gut-bucket rawness of this album is not afraid to be harsh, even ugly. It remains extremely challenging if rewarding listening.

Zappa once provided instructions for use sending the listener immediately to the freak-out on side four (or the last track on the CD), "The Return of the Son of Monster Magnet" (with its first movement, "Ritual Dance of the Child-Killer," whipping up Dionysian violence a la Stravinsky's *Rite of Spring*): "if you live through the 12 minutes 37 seconds [sic] proceed ... " (*Beat the Boots! Scrapbook* 17). Almost as far-out is the demented barbershop-quartet of "Help, I'm a Rock." And let's not forget "Who Are The Brain Police?," a paranoid vision worthy of Phillip K. Dick and the Frankfurt School that remains the scariest song ever crafted as a potential pop record. Frank even backed off from the abyss this thing teeters on for 3:22. This is a stunning debut for Zappa and his band.

19) *Zoot Allures* (rock, 1976). This is the closest Zappa ever came to a big seventies arena-rock record with solid chops and teen appeal. Tellingly, it contains the other two of his signature guitar solos ("Black Napkins" and the title track). "Friendly Little Finger" is the first application of xenochronicity, creating a fictitious interplay between Frank, Terry Bozzio and Ruth Underwood. "Disco Boy" provides more toe-tapping satire; "The Torture never Stops" and "Ms. Pinky" (named after a sex doll) are queasier fare. The signature instrumentals are why I place this release as high as it is.

20) *Road Tapes Venue #1: Kerrisdale Arena, Vancouver B.C., 25 August 1968* (rock / classical 2012 [recorded 1968]). Simply put, as far as the music goes, this is the best live recording of the early version of the Mothers of Invention I've ever heard. As with the Carnegie Hall Flo and Eddie material, I suspect that it was not released in Frank's lifetime because it was on mono tape. And no doubt Vaultmeister Joe Travers had to do a lot of manipulations with current technologies to get it sounding this spiffy—and even he can't fix an apparent reel change or tape break during "Trouble Every Day."

You get to hear rare live versions of material from *Freak Out!* (besides "Trouble Every Day," "Help, I'm a Rock" and "Hungry Freaks, Daddy") and extended instrumental renditions of "The Orange County Lumber Truck," "Let's Make the Water Turn Black," "Harry, You're a Beast," "Oh No," "Holiday in Berlin Full Blown," "Pound for a Brown," "Sleeping in a Jar" and "King Kong" (this last even features Zappa explaining to his audience its programmatic features: the drums are the "lewd, pulsating jungle rhythms" on Skull Island, for example).

But the most amazing moment in the show—a transition which exposes Zappa's agenda in microcosm—is a segue from the dispensable doo wop of the hitherto unreleased original "Oh, In the Sky" to an encore performance of the beginning of Edgard Varese's "Octandre." (Perversely but appropriately, this makes the release the highest ranked "classical" one in the appendix.) The music itself is stellar: one of the most challenging composers of the past century performed on amplified rock instruments. But the obvious reverence and admiration one hears between the notes is also overwhelming. Here is a young musician wanting to get it right for his greatest sonic mentor. It's astonishing that we had to wait so long to hear this. And I can only imagine how great that all-Varese program conducted by Zappa might be (unless the classical musicians weren't as equipped to play the material as these Mothers were).

A further irony is that Zappa joked to the audience before playing "Octandre" that this "special encore" was designed to drive audiences away and make them really want the concert to end. But this Canadian audience loved the Varese rendition and clamored for a second encore, giving us a rare glimpse of Frank respecting an audience: "... an unprecedented response for the bullshit that we do ... . You appear to like what we do. That's nice."

21) *QuAUDIOPHILIAc* (rock and jazz, 2004 [recorded 1970-1978]). This audio DVD release from the vaults contains an assortment of quadraphonic mixes Zappa did in the seventies when "four-way" stereo was all the rage: not only rock and jazz, but even a little classical ("Naval Aviation in Art?"). Half the tracks are previously unreleased in any form. The long, slow exploration of Chunga's Revenge ("Chunga Basement") is very interesting, but I rank this offering so highly because of one track: the quad remix of "Waka / Jawaka." Compared to the vinyl and CD versions of this song, this presentation allows you to hear almost twice as much music because of the spectacular separation of instruments in the mix. I am especially fond of Don Preston's endlessly inventive Mini-Moog soloing, which is comparatively buried in other recordings. As rendered here, this is perhaps Zappa's finest composition and studio performance in a jazz vein: as the title promises, a real treat for the ears.

22) *Philly '76* (rock, 2009 [recorded 1976]). This double CD features a very rare line-up of the Mothers: Terry Bozzio on drums, Patrick O'Hearn on bass, Ray White on rhythm guitar, Eddie Jobson on violin and keyboards and the hitherto unheard in recorded form Bianca Odin on keyboards and vocals. As I've noted elsewhere, the band always sounds better to my ears when there are women in it. This is no exception. Bianca Odin brings soul and sass to the show lifting it to some sublime heights.

The whole concert is fantastically memorable, but there are definite highlights—frequently provided by Odin. For example, she delivers a gospel-inflected version of "You Didn't Try to Call Me" which reveals possibilities for the song unheard in its previous incarnations. This show also has the definitive rendition of the mostly instrumental "Black Napkins," which is saying a lot. Bianca's vocalizations bring out the sorrow of the melody in a way oddly akin to Clare Torry's stellar work on "The Great Gig in the Sky" off Pink Floyd's *Dark Side of the Moon*. Who'd have thought? As if that weren't enough, Eddie Jobson's violin solo soars and Frank takes his time with a mellow, slow and bluesy guitar exploration that builds to an epic climax for nineteen minutes of musical nirvana. I prefer this version even to Dweezil's favorite off the Halloween audio DVD.

There is also a generous selection of songs rarely performed live from

Chunga's Revenge and *200 Motels* (e.g., "Rudy Wants to Buy Yez a Drink" and "Daddy, Daddy, Daddy') and a nonce cover of the politically incorrect doo wop classic "Stranded in the Jungle" (cannibal savages putting a guy in a pot) as part of a four-song encore. We see early glimmerings of Zappa's persona as avuncular emcee for a younger generation of fans: "Think of me as an older, more sinister Dick Clark." And finally, an unlikely country and western partial interpretation of "Dinah-Moe Humm" takes it beyond its often cliched run-through. Great band, great concert. One wonders why they never went into the studio. Maybe Frank thought (correctly) that this live document would suffice.

23) *Hot Rats: Waka / Jawaka* (jazz, 1972). Recorded when Frank was convalescing from an attack by a demented fan, this album showcases two of the loveliest jazz instrumentals he ever composed, "Big Swifty" and (especially) the title track.George Duke and Don Preston give amazing solos on the keyboards; Sal Marquez plays a mean trumpet. There are also two vocal tracks, including the eclectic "It Just Might Be A One-Shot Deal," which even features Jeff Simmons on Hawaiian slack-key guitar and country session man "Sneaky Pete" on a pedal steel guitar—unusual timbres for Zappa.

24) *Carnegie Hall* (rock, 2011 [recorded 1971]). This is the definitive audio statement of the Flo and Eddie era of the band (respectively Mark Volman and Howard Kaylan, those two potty-mouthed and funny ex-members of the Turtles), one so sweeping that it has forced me to reevaluate that ensemble on this list and rank it higher than I originally thought they deserved. At the time they existed, this band seemed like the greatest thing since sliced bread to Zappa aficionados. As the dust settled, I came to agree with Frank himself that he certainly led better groups after this line-up. This band had the highest schtick factor: they were easily the most verbal incarnation of the Mothers, doing musical comedy that ended up being both a sociological study of life on the road and a kind of surrealist comic light opera hearkening back to Gilbert and Sullivan (but amplified) and anticipating the rock surrealism of the *Overnite Sensation* era. And, not incidentally, mocking the long progressive rock compositions favored by bands in that historical moment.

Why is this recording a game-changer? Because with four disks documenting two shows on October 11, 1971 at Carnegie Hall (the only time Frank Zappa played the venue), it's all conveniently here: all the material from *Just Another Band From L.A.* done much better, some of the best of *Chunga's Revenge, 200 Motels* and *Fillmore East, June 1971* (also superior because the band knows the material better, just like the Helsinki show surpasses the Roxy recordings). And we get a fair amount of earlier covers, including my favorite boogie version of "Who Are The Brain Police?" available until this release only on the bootleg *Disconnected Synapses*. Plus instrumental workouts galore. These latter two features were kept to a minimum on the original releases from this era, which reduced (unfairly, perhaps) *Just Another Band From L.A.* and *Fillmore East* to musical comedy albums. On this release by contrast you get the group in all its variety, glory and skill. As a bonus, you even get 26 minutes of the Persuasions, the a cappella opening act long associated with Zappa (and Joni Mitchell to a lesser extent). At the time they were even on Straight, one of his record labels.

So why didn't he release this amazing music in his lifetime? I can think of a number of reasons. First of all, the recordings were in mono, not stereo—a deal breaker at the time. (But they've been enhanced brilliantly by Vaultmeister Joe Travers.) But back then the audio quality would have been limited by the technologies available. Secondly, this release clocks in at over four hours total. It would have been a financially prohibitive undertaking to put all that out on vinyl. And finally, too much of this material was already recently released (albeit in less spiffy renditions). A time lag was needed lest this album be seen as economic exploitation (cf. the delay in putting out the Helsinki concert).

Better late than never! Now you can hear what might be the best concert performed by this band. I'll steer you to a few of the many highlights of these epic shows. In general, I'd mention Aynsley Dunbar's drumming throughout. Although I prefer Terry Bozzio, this set makes a strong case for Dunbar being the second-best drummer that Frank ever worked with. These are devilishly difficult compositions, and he holds the band together at all times like sonic Superglue—and he cooks!

Another sweeping observation that I already mentioned above is that these are the best versions of material mostly released previously (by now, not necessarily in 1971). "Peaches En Regalia" has better vocal harmonizing than on the Fillmore version; the "Shove It Right In" suite from *200 Motels* allows one to hear the vocals more clearly, which highlights the exquisite tension between the nuanced if explicit lyrics and the gorgeous melody. We get the aforementioned monster version of "Brain Police" and a premiere of the twenty-minute full version of the "Divan" composition, sung in German (and later available only in pieces on *One Size Fits All* and bootlegs). This piece offers one of the several moments in the show where it seems that Frank Zappa perfectly belongs at Carnegie Hall.

But the absolute highlight of the concert, and of this band's recordings, is the nearly fifty minute long version of "Billy the Mountain" (about twenty minutes longer than any previous release available). Is it an allegory about the counterculture? (Were we the "mountain ... you don't want to fuck with" that destroys various authority figures?) Is it a satire of progressive rock? Is it an update of Gilbert and Sullivan? Is it a series of in-jokes that contribute to the conceptual continuity of the Zappa universe? Is it postmodern intertextuality galore? (I just caught the "Help me!" reference to the original movie version of *The Fly* on this my umpteenth hearing.) All this and more: here it becomes a venue for fierce musical solos as well. The melodies and motifs will stay in your head for weeks! I especially like a new section whereStudebaker Hoch has to give "the code" which becomes an elaborate mnemonic tongue-twister that inspires the audience to burst into applause. For some of my readers, this might well be where they calibrate their taste in Zappa. But with all those words, it's not much by way of background music by even the remotest of chances. You have to listen to this one—and you'll be glad you did.

25) *FZ:OZ* (rock, 2002 [recorded 1976]). This is the first release of the VAULT-ernative series, a collection of nearly complete single concert shows. The January 20, 1976 concert occurred in Sydney, Australia with a rare stripped-down, five-piece lineup: Zappa on guitar; Napoleon Murphy Brock on sax; Terry Bozzio on drums; Andre Lewis on keyboards; and Mothers veteran Roy Estrada on bass. They get a lot of sound out of those five instruments, making this a really compelling event. The highlights include great Spanish-inflected guitar work (think "Bolero") on the then-new instrumental "Filthy Habits," a funky block from *Freak Out!* featuring Brock channeling James Brown, exquisite and stately readings of the signature instrumentals "Black Napkins" and "Zoot Allures" (the former has both spectacular guitar and keyboard solos; the latter includes wah-wah exploration very similar to "Ship Ahoy" on *Shut Up 'N Play Yer Guitar*). "Chunga's Revenge" lets Brock explore the higher registers of his tenor saxophone. Rarities include additional lyrics to "Lonely Little Girl" (from *We're Only In It For The Money*), a more elaborate explanation to the Australian audience about "The Illinois Enema Bandit" (just what the world needed) and two versions (one in rehearsal) of "Kaiser Rolls," a nonce track of urban observation (a la "Pygmy Twylyte" and "Advance Romance"). The only reason I rank this splendid workout lower than the studio *Zoot Allures* release is the absence of "Disco Boy," delightful cosmic stupidity which can be found there but not here. But what is here is very, very good!

26) *Joe's Menage* (rock, 2008 [recorded 1975]). This is an excerpt of a November 1, 1975 concert at the College of William and Mary in Williamsburg,

Virginia. The lineup of players is quite unusual, especially with Norma Jean Bell on alto sax and vocals: an African-American woman member of the Mothers whom I never heard of / heard in any other context. Her name does not even appear in Barry Miles or Ben Watson, two of the most thorough chroniclers of Zappa. For whatever reason, despite the quality of her playing, her stint with the band must have been extremely brief. The other members are Napoleon Murphy Brock, Andre Lewis (keyboards), Terry Bozzio and veteran Roy Estrada on bass. This outfit is thus a transition between the *Bongo Fury* group with Captain Beefheart and the band we hear on *FZ:OZ*. Sound quality is a little raw, since this comes from a crude cassette dub which Frank gave to a Danish fan (the master recording has not yet been found in the vault). But it is an official release tweaked for listenability as best Joe Travers could. The music is delightful, fortunately: an early version of "Illinois Enema Bandit" with a good guitar solo and Virginia jokes ("for lovers AND perverts") because some of the audience knew who Michael Kenyon was; a funky wah-wah solo on the also new "Carolina Hard-Core Ecstasy;" soulful Brock vocals on "Lonely Little Girl" from the *We're Only In It For The Money* set that surpass even the Australian concert; a fine keyboard solo on "Take Your Clothes Off When You Dance" from same (done in a reggae beat). Zappa uses "Chunga's Revenge" to give the band a chance for a round of solos, highlighted by Bozzio's always hyperactive drumming, Lewis playing a melodica (a rare "baby synthesizer") and Frank taking a self-proclaimed "rhythm guitar solo" (well-played, but refusing to make lead moves). A solid exploration of "Zoot Allures" closes the tape, CD and concert (although one suspects there was an encore). The magic and energy are on the recording—even the distortion works in this driving context, a serendipitous addition to Zappa's body of released recorded work emergent from a gift to a European admirer of the music.

27) *Hammersmith Odeon* (rock, 2010 [recorded 1978]). Three hours of live highlights culled from four London shows courtesy of the band that gave us *Sheik Yerbouti* and the bedrock foundation for the film *Baby Snakes*: Terry Bozzio on drums, Patrick O'Hearn on bass, versatile guitar slinger Adrian Belew (who gets Frank to stretch even more), two keyboardists (Peter Wolf and Tommy Mars), plus Ed Mann on percussion. Although the sound quality here is excellent for a live show, it's not as pristine as *Sheik Yerbouti*. And if you're familiar with the other two releases mentioned above, there may not be much in the way of surprises.

Probably the most interesting inclusions are the band's re-workings of old Mothers of Invention jazz standards like "Pound for a Brown," "The Little House I Used to Live In" and "King Kong." The twenty-minute "Pound for a Brown" is especially strange: after some jazzy keyboard breaks, we get a spacey freak out, cries of "Hail Caesar!" and a mixture of fake Roman army marching music and oriental dancing melodies. (I'd love to see the visuals for all this.) And there are some shared backstories for band classics of this era like "I Have Been in You" and "Bobby Brown." The former is especially hilarious: Frank recreates the fantasy seduction of a fan in "a real teenage bedroom"—described in Proustian detail—by an archetypal pop star, a Barry White styled goof narrative, while the band backs him up with mellow soul vamping. (On a related note, you can make out the zany lyrics for "Disco Boy" better than on the studio version: "You never go doody / That's what you think.") Zappa scholar Ben Watson, much cited in this chapter, even makes a cameo under the name of "Eric Dolphy" (a fairly obscure jazz reference) in an audience participation dance to "The Black Page #2" (see Watson 335 for the confession).

28) *Lather* (rock/ jazz/ classical, 1996). This mammoth collection was planned as a four lp release in 1977, but was tied up legally by Warner Brothers in a nasty contract dispute which put Frank's career on hold for several years. He responded by giving the album away over the public airwaves on the Burbank-Pasadena station KROQ (Watson 311). Bootleggers eventually put it out, and then Rykodisc finally gave it a posthumous legitimate release on CD. Most of its wide-ranging material ended up on many other albums, often in different versions. The power of the original concept as envisioned here was its breathtaking display of Zappa's sheer range over genres: big-band jazz is juxtaposed with arena rock and even some classical material. The result is an unparalleled introduction to the variety of Zappa's projects—which are nonetheless unified by the way his sensibility manages to hop genres successfully. No matter what the setting, it's all Frank Zappa.

If you want to hear what the *Sleep Dirt* material sounds like without the Thana Harris vocals (and it's still pretty interesting), here's your chance.

29) *Zappa in New York* (rock, 1978). Like *Lather*, this release showcases the notorious "Illinois Enema Bandit" discussed above. Its concluding courtroom scene has a sly nod to Johnny "Guitar" Watson's hit song "Gangster of Love" (less ethically referenced by Steve Miller). In fact, except for two tracks, every cut on here is also on *Lather*. But since they're consistently of high quality—from Zappa's recasting of the Faust legend and/or Stravinsky's *Soldier's Tale* in "Titties and Beer" to the instrumental splendors of "I Promise Not To Come In Your Mouth" (entitled "Lather" on that album), "The Black Page" and "The Purple Lagoon"—I place this immediately after the more deluxe release of *Lather*. Zappa has another great

band here: standby hall-of-famers such as Ruth Underwood, Terry Bozzio and Ray White are augmented by top-drawer New York session hornmen like the Brecker brothers, Lou Marini and Ronnie Cuber.

30) *Unmitigated Audacity*e (rock, 1991 [recorded 1974]). A bootleg, this one from the lovely George Duke and Napoleon Murphy Brock era (with Don Preston also on synthesizer). I include this because this band did lots of reworkings of early material from *Freak Out!* and *We're Only In It For The Money* which never showed up in legitimate release ("Hungry Freaks, Daddy," "Wowie Zowie," "Let's Make The Water Turn Black," etc.). Zappa knew he could get this band to match the records better than the original performing Mothers. These medleys are striking, especially when juxtaposed with "Dupree's Paradise" and "Camarillo Brillo." It's hard to believe one ensemble can deliver all this so well. Slight overlap with the Helsinki show and *Roxy & Elsewhere*, but you won't mind.

31) *Freaks and Motherfu*#@%!* (rock, 1991 [recorded 1970]). Another Flo-and-Eddie era bootleg, this one distinguished by the vocal version of the old Mothers classic "Holiday in Berlin." It offers a compelling historical window into European radical student movements' attempts to co-opt Frank for their own purposes; as such, it is important listening. The rest of the concert is fine, too, replete with a live "Concentration Moon" and a Dr. John pastiche (he was in the Mothers for about five minutes, by the way).

32) *Disconnected Synapses* (rock, 1992 [recorded 1970]). Another Flo-and-Eddie era bootleg, this used to be the only way to obtain the brilliantly subversive yet still menacing Canned Heat boogie vamp version of "Who Are The Brain Police?" (until the *Carnegie Hall* release). The live rendition of "Penis Dimension" (the title says it all) from *200 Motels* is also a definitive workout.

33) *Everything Is Healing Nicely* (classical, 1999). Another release you have to get from Zappa's store directly. Despite Todd Yvega's modest liner notes suggesting that this is more of an "audio documentary" of Zappa's work with the Ensemble Modern than "polished music," I actually prefer it to the nonetheless wonderful *Yellow Shark* concert. What makes for sloppier classical playing makes for funkier Zappa music. Several cases in point: 1) the readings from *PFIQ* (*Piercing Fans International Quarterly*) in "Master Ringo" and "Wonderful Tattoo!" are funnier than anything on *The Yellow Shark*; and 2) "Amnerika Goes Home" is a harder piece than anything on the live concert disc, because of its insane use of "hocketing" (having instruments spread a melody from instrument to instrument). Since it's

also one of his saddest and loveliest later compositions, I prefer this imperfect performance to the Synclavier splendor on *Civilization Phaze III*. This document proves Zappa worked with classical musicians in a very Zappaesque manner (once he found some disciplined enough to learn his stuff), stretching them and making them improvise. This was Frank's last "group," it turned out—and one of his very best.

34) *Boulez Conducts Zappa: The Perfect Stranger* (Synclavier / classical, 1984). Good, but not as good as the Ensemble Modern. Pierre Boulez was an ideal choice to conduct Zappa's chamber works. His work with smaller ensembles on his own pieces such as *Le Marteau sans Maitre* reminds the listener of the solid stream of rhythmic and tone color experimentation in European classicism since Varese and Webern. Since Frank's classical writing is solidly in this tradition, Boulez would be a kindred spirit—and he already had an ensemble, the Ensemble Intercontemporain, to learn it. The devil was in the details, however; once again (recurrent bad luck for Zappa) the players were underrehearsed for this difficult music—so these are arguably as much recorded rehearsals as the previous release. What makes this a fabulous recording is thus not the three Boulez pieces (the title is misleading), but the four Synclavier tracks provided by Zappa— especially "The Girl In the Magnesium Dress" (composed from "digital dust," the odd noises and ambience you get along with intended sampling input) and "Jonestown," Zappa's most powerful indictment of humanity's religious inclinations composed in response to the Peoples' Temple mass suicide in Guyana on November 18, 1978. "Jonestown" is as close as Zappa ever got in his classical work to "Who Are The Brain Police?" Well worth a close listen with big ears.

35) *200 Motels* (classical/ rock, 1971). This first release of Zappa's symphonic writing for a large orchestra—not counting the bootleg of the same name documenting his collaboration with Zubin Mehta and the Los Angeles Philharmonic—is also a film soundtrack. My musical focus prohibits my elaboration of what a fantastic film this is for the dedicated Zappa observer—or even a film lover! (Hint: most reviewers missed its relationship with German expressionist cinema overall, and *The Cabinet of Dr. Caligari* in particular. A viewing of these two films back to back is quite revealing.)[3]

The music here is splendid as well, both in its classical and rock modes. Symphonically, the overture is lush and the "difficult" intimate stuff is leavened by sopranos having to sing lines like "Munchkins get me hot." "Strictly Genteel" is as close as Zappa gets to Beethoven's "Ode to Joy," ironic AND sincere. Of the rock bits, the best writing and playing is on the groupie suite ("She Painted Up Her Face / Half A Dozen Provocative Squats / Shove It Right In"). Another highlight from the Phlorescent Leech and Eddie version of the group.

36) *Just Another Band From L.A.* (rock, 1972). More Flo and Eddie, this time peaking with the extremely transgressive incest ballad "Magdalena"—a real pleasure, if a guilty one. The soaring vocals of Volman and Kaylan make it all work. The epic comic rock opera" "Billy the Mountain" is crucial for conceptual continuity, at least. Billy, his wife Ethel (a tree) and Studebaker Hoch are recurring characters in the storybook aspect of the Zappa universe. Weirdly enough, the topical references aren't so dated: Crosby, Stills, Nash and Young are still around, as are Joni Mitchell and Howard Johnson's. Studebaker Hoch's method of transport is still hilarious to me (the key here is visualizing the lyrics), almost as good as Bill Cosby's "Chicken Heart" routine. Perhaps a better genre tag for this record would be "rock/comedy."

37) *Swiss Cheese/Fire!* (rock, 1992 [recorded 1971]). A bootleg commemorating the Montreux, Switzerland show where the venue burned down (the same tour where a crazed and jealous fan pushed Frank into the orchestra pit at a London performance, his unluckiest tour ever). The "Zanti Serenade" introduction is the best tune-up you'll ever hear (love those old-timey synthesizers). The rest is more vintage Flo-and-Eddie, tailored to a Swiss audience (fondue and St. Bernard jokes). The "Sofa" routine appears here in full Germanic glory for more conceptual continuity.

38) *Playground Psychotics* (rock, 1992). Veering close to "social anthropology," as Zappa suggests in the liner notes, this collection combines more rock antics of the Flo-and-Eddie Mothers with substantial audio verite field recordings of life on the road. You have to be patient to get to the good stuff, like a crisper and more democratic mix of the John Lennon and Yoko Ono collaboration with Zappa. (Tellingly, you can't hear Flo and Eddie singing "put Yoko in a scumbag" on the version John and Yoko released on *Sometime in New York City* .)

39) *You Can't Do That On Stage Anymore, Volume 6* (rock, 1992). This last volume of his mammoth retrospective on the live bands provides suitable closure to the project and abundant audio pleasure. The first CD in the set is a relentless compilation of the sexual dimensions of the Zappa project, the demystifying of all things glandular. Even if you've made it this far through the canon, there might be some rough listening (example: the band playing behind recordings of women attaining / faking orgasm on "Tracy Is A Snob" and "Emperor of Ohio"—shades of Studio Z in Cucamonga!). But even here there are delights such as "The Poodle Lecture"

Frank Zappa's Big Note 91

from the film *Baby Snakes*, a riff on Peter Frampton and the record business in "Is That Guy Kidding Or What?" (also from the aforementioned film), a discourse on blow-up dolls and Finnish porn magazines (the best women in them "looked like Grace Slick") in "Lonely Person Devices," and even more Flo-and-Eddie band hijinx in "The M.O.I. Anti-Smut Loyalty Oath."

But it's the second disc that will really thrill your ears; he tries to leave on a high note. Standout tracks include the other superb vocal of Lisa Popeil ("Lisa's Life Story"), a duet with L. Shankar on "Thirteen" in a very tough time signature, and—by way of a grand finale to it all—"Strictly Genteel" from the 1981 Halloween show at the Palladium. That rock band outplays the full symphonic version from *200 Motels*. Quite impressive, to say the least. But these are only highlights; the second disc is pure audio baklava.

40) *You Can't Do That On Stage Anymore, Volume 4* (rock, 1991). Another one of the better parts of the set. "Montana" from *Over-Nite Sensation* (see below) features a Zappa guitar solo far surpassing the original. "Let's Move To Cleveland" offers a tenor sax solo from the legendary Archie Shepp. The 1984 version of "The Black Page" hits those Conlon-Nancarrow-paced notes with spectacular accuracy. We also got a version of "Take Me Out To The Ball Game" replete with a faked audio baseball game and Captain Beefheart's original bluesy approach to "The Torture Never Stops."

The second disc has a fine version of the Steve Vai showcase, "Stevie's Spanking," with Zappa and Vai trading solos. There's some goofing around from both the original Mothers ("Tiny Sick Tears") and the George Duke era ("Smell My Beard" and "The Booger Man")—followed by another fine reading of "Carolina Hard Core Ecstasy" and a closing six-song tribute to doo wop done with some reverence and fidelity.

41) *Piquantique* (jazz, 1991 [recorded 1973]). This is a bootleg from a television special in Stockholm. Although the personnel overlaps with the Helsinki concert era, Brock is not in the band (and jazz violinist Jean-Luc Ponty is). These slight adjustments make the group an electric jazz band, especially given the selections on the bootleg (not the complete concert). "Rdnzl" features a spectacular Bruce Fowler trombone solo; "Dupree's Paradise" and "Father O'Blivion" both feature great work from Ponty. Despite Zappa's displeasure with the conclusion of the latter piece (he makes the band play it again), this is a fine set.

42) *Greasy Love Songs* (rock, 2010 [recorded mostly in the late sixties]). This is the third FZ audio documentary project/object, in this case centering on the Ruben and the Jets material that became his fifth album. Since

it has all of the original songs from the next entry below, plus bonus tracks, this is clearly the one to get if you have a little more spare cash. A further incentive is that this CD contains the original 1968 vinyl stereo mix, which most Zappa listeners prefer to the reworked mix for the Old Masters collection in the early 1980s. (I like both and have both, but the earlier one was much harder to obtain until this release came out.)

What are the new gems here? There's an acoustic guitar version of "Jelly Roll Gum Drop" with even higher processed vocals and a longer version of "No. No. No." with a drum and piano intro. The longer version of "Stuff Up the Cracks" features a slow-burn closing guitar solo which is satisfying, but not as intense as the take that made it onto the original record. "Serious Fan Mail" is a spoken word track culled from a college lecture q and a and a radio interview about this doo wop project. We learn that since the first pressing did not directly mention the Mothers of Invention, it got top 40 radio play and a significant amount of fan mail from folks who thought Ruben and the Jets were a new, real band.

Perhaps the highlight of the bonus material is a pre-*Burnt Weeny Sandwich* cover of the doo wop chestnut "Valerie." This version features some of the most spectacular Zappa vocalizing I've ever heard. He starts out quite sincere in approach before faking some crying moves in homage to the genre, becoming more and more absurd as he gets accompanied by backing vocals that sound like actual shrieks. There's nothing quite like this in his entire catalogue; I can see why it was deemed too strange even for *Cruising With Ruben & The Jets*.

We also get a third version of "Jelly Roll Gum Drop," the 45 rpm single variant with more pop punch in the mix and a bigger drum sound; a live reading by Zappa on air of the hilarious "Story of Ruben & The Jets" on the album's liner notes (he gets more and more of a pachuco accent as he reads!); and an ultra-rare "Love Of My Life" from the early sixties Studio Z Cucamonga days that features a female vocalist named Mary Gonzales sharing singing duty with future Mother Ray Collins. All this and new liner notes from Cheech Marin of Cheech and Chong!

43) *Cruising With Ruben & The Jets* (rock, 1968). Initially greeted with bafflement by early Mothers fans (where's the psychedelic freak-out?), this pastiche of doo wop has aged like a fine cabernet. In the clear CD mix, you can really appreciate how profoundly stupid, funny and brilliant this all is. Zappa's "low grumbles" alone are worth the price of admission. How the guy who cracked up doing the Central Scrutinizer voice could lay down these vocal tracks without busting a gut is beyond me. My favorite example of "cretin simplicity" (all previous quotes are from the

liner notes) is "Fountain of Love," originally recorded at Studio Z as a "straight" song co-written with Ray Collins. Zappa's vocal rumblings are drop-dead funny, but then you add on the single-entendre lyrics, a spoken-word middle and concluding vocal harmonizing on the opening melody from Stravinsky's *Rite of Spring*. The result is one amazing song.

And there are plenty more where that came from. The Mothers' mostly deadpan delivery means you can listen to this when you're craving either doo wop or a belly laugh. It's pastiche, not parody. They're too close to this material to merely lampoon it; they're paying homage to it, but with a big twinkle in their eye!

44) *The Yellow Shark* (classical, 1993).Sadly, this was the last release of his that Frank lived to see come out. But it proved to be a strong conclusion to a brilliant career. The Ensemble Modern proved to be the grail attained for Frank, classical musicians who could play as well as his rock groups and who would take the time needed to learn his difficult scores. More than one listener has found in some of these recordings (especially "Times Beach" II and III) a melancholy and even a quiet rage directed more at those who pollute our planet for profit than at his illness (although arguably, he related the two in his mind: consider *Civilization Phaze III*'s concluding plane spraying pesticide). "Pentagon Afternoon" out-Vareses Varese by deploying not only sirens but toy rayguns (a nod to the Gipper?). And this band plays the bejesus out of earlier rock and Synclavier compositions such as "Be-Bop Tango" and "G-Spot Tornado." This last sounds like a demented jig, as Ben Watson has observed, linking a final gesture with his admiration for the Chieftains (530).

45) *Civilization Phaze III* (Synclavier/ classical, 1994). This is the first posthumous release. An extension from the *Lumpy Gravy* dialogues inside a piano, this has some updating with new characters (including actor Michael Rappoport and daughter Moon). I found the Synclavier extravaganza "N-Lite" to not match the rapturous description it received from visitors to the Zappa home who heard it in a more expanded multi-channel format rather than the stereo mix. (It's still quite amazing, but I wish I could have heard the version that made listeners declare it the best thing he ever did.) Which leaves other good things: another version of the haunting "Amnerika," the Nancarrow speed of "Buffalo Voice," and the spectacular conclusion of "Beat The Reaper" and "Waffenspiel." The former is a dance mocking America's obsession with youth preservation and immortality through exercise and diet faddism; the latter is Zappa's last great prank: an audio verite recording that subtly fades into the ambient sounds of your actual living space. With one gesture, Zappa deconstructs

the art / life dualism. Given his (and our) approaching mortality, a comforting thought.

46) *Feeding the Monkies at Ma Maison* (classical / Synclavier, 2011 [recorded 1986]. As Todd Yvega (Zappa's computer programming assistant at the time) points out in the liner notes, these pieces are the "missing link" (pun intended, I'm sure) between the Synclavier work on *Jazz From Hell* and *Civilization Phaze III*. I rank it closer to the latter because it sounds more akin to that more mature and thus superior composition (and works in the same longer forms). Frank was learning how to play this alien toy quite superbly. And, in fact, two of the five compositions here are longer versions of works that showed up on *Civilization Phaze III*.

In the liner notes, Gail Zappa lumps all non-rock band Zappa under the category of "Jazz From Hell" as opposed to jazz, classical, Synclavier as I do. Her argument is that we should honor his term. I get her point, but I'm sticking to my guns with regard to my classification schema. For example, it's very hard for me to think of the *Francesco Zappa* baroque album as "jazz" in any way (i.e., no improvisation or even a simulacrum of same).

But what of the actual music here? Like much of Zappa's classical and Synclavier work, it bears a significant family resemblance to the late electronic pieces of Edgard Varese and the speeded-up piano rolls of Conlon Nancarrow. Like most Varese, it is percussion-driven. (Before Frank played guitar, he was a drummer.) It is austere with moments of hard-earned sonic beauty. After all, Zappa also liked Anton Webern.

But the Synclavier gave him resources Varese could scarcely have dreamed of. Unlike the Moog and its cousins, the Synclavier is a near-perfect mimic of any musical instrument's timbre, an extremely advanced synthesizer. On the hitherto unreleased title composition (a major showcase at over twenty minutes), you'll swear you're hearing an acoustic guitar, vibes, drums of various sorts—but it's all an electronic keyboard hooked up to a computer. "Feeding the Monkies at Ma Maison" might also be program music if you have the imagination to visualize those simians.

The next three tracks are longer versions of previously released material: "Buffalo Voice" and "Secular Humanism" end up in a more compressed manner on *Civilization Phaze III*; "Worms from Hell" is a longer version of the title music for the 1987 video *Video from Hell*. The first two pieces electronically process daughter Moon's voice in interesting ways; her laughter on "Secular Humanism" is especially uncanny. "Worms from Hell" is intense and driving. One of its motifs reminds me a little of the original *Twilight Zone* theme. (For what it's worth, this piece got the biggest reaction from my cats.)

And finally, we have another premiere, "Samba Funk," which also makes for exquisite listening. Its title is somewhat misleading: there might be a samba buried in the piece, but it's not very funky by the standards of, say, James Brown. Irony is no doubt afoot here.

The beauty and value of this music overall is that one is hard-pressed to think of a musician who explored the resources of the Synclavier more thoroughly and better than Frank Zappa. A parallel case would be Sun Ra's relentless investigation of what a Moog can do as a vehicle for soloing (as opposed to Walter / Wendy Carlos' multi-tracking of that instrument). Perhaps these recordings will inspire someone to pick up the torch and revisit this powerful compositional tool.

47) *Make A Jazz Noise Here* (jazz/rock, 1991). This double compact disc showcases the instrumental prowess of Zappa's last touring band, which was a rather large ensemble. You're basically hearing expanded and statelier versions of Zappa standards such as "Black Napkins," "The Black Page," "Alien Orifice," "Cruising For Burgers" and "Strictly Genteel." But there are a few new originals that augment the power of the collection: "When Yuppies Go To Hell" uses the Synclavier with the live band to get collage effects similar to earlier Mothers material—a solid reminder that Zappa never abandoned earlier aesthetics in his growth as a composer. "Star Wars Won't Work" (still a timely tune!) makes a political point primarily without words (something Zappa wished his listeners could notice more readily, as he would rather play certain ideas than spell them out lyrically). By just using sound effects, tape looping and some ominous guitar playing, he expresses extreme skepticism about technology. The scat vocals on the fadeout assuring us "it's a piece of shit ... it's just an expensive bunch of nothing" are a gilding of the instrumental lily.

Most editions also have brief covers of the Royal March from Stravinsky's *Soldier's Tale* and the theme from Bartok's third piano concerto, two of Zappa's favorite pieces of music. (Copyright issues caused them to be pulled in some countries initially [Russo 146]).

48) *Trance-Fusion* (rock instrumental, 2006 [originally mixed in 1993]). This collection of guitar solos from the late seventies and eighties is not only one of the last projects Frank Zappa more or less finished before his untimely demise in December, 1993; it is arguably the most musically important posthumous release. For the simple fact of the matter is that Zappa kept improving as a guitarist. Thus, this third collection of solos naturally features his best playing. Another advantage it has over its predecessors is its comparative brevity. Being only one carefully chosen disc

(running a little over an hour in playing time), it does not exhaust the listener. What higher tribute can be paid to a guitarist than the fact that an hour of just a series of solos is so eminently listenable and captivating? Who else in rock could put out such a release? Certainly the Jimi Hendrix estate; possibly John McLaughlin. But not many ... .

Enumerating highlights here is quite subjective, but I think the selections build in quality to make the second half of the set the most impressive (although the opening read on the standard "Chunga's Revenge"—the only track available in other versions—is a noteworthy exception). "Scratch and Sniff" showcases his ability to bend the notes; this extravaganza is then followed by the amplified *rāga* runs of the title track and the lovely, upbeat "Gorgo." "For Guiseppe Franco" moves from a slower exploration to some blistering speed accompanied by exquisite drum moves from Chad Wackerman. "After Dinner Smoker" is a spacey blues riff which mutates into the psychedelic electronica of "Light Is All That Matters." Appropriate closure is provided by the electric blues blast and high notes of "Bavarian Sunset." But it's all stellar playing and a reminder that we shall not see the likes of Frank on rock guitar again.

49) *Guitar* (rock instrumental, 1988). This is the second of two collections of Zappa solos released in his lifetime. Both are very good, but this one shows how accomplished he eventually got at creating his "air sculptures," as he liked to call them. What is astonishing about these solos is that they are spontaneous compositions. He is doing this without a net, as it were, aided only by the alertness of his accompanists. The results seem almost telepathic at times, as he duly noted in interview (Swenson 48). Consider for example the astonishing interplay with the rhythm section on "Move It Or Park It" and "Do Not Try This At Home." There are more uses of sound to make political commentary in his ugly instrumental "Republicans." A few tracks experiment with combining melodies: "In-A-Gadda-Stravinsky" juxtaposes the Iron Butterfly psychedelic workhorse "In-AGadda-Da-Vida" with our old friend *The Rite of Spring*; "It Ain't Necessarily The Saint James Infirmary" combines "It Ain't Necessarily So" with the blues standard "Saint James Infirmary."

An amazing album, all told. The only reason I've ranked it so low is that I question its ease of accessibility. One has to be pretty hard-core to listen to it all in one sitting. It's so dense and complex that it will wear your ears out! And it refuses, as does almost all of Frank's work, to serve as background music. You can't put this on at most parties; it is NOT dance music. You have to give it fairly undivided attention to appreciate it. These are not soothing sounds for sophisticates, but tough and angular compositions for electric guitar: Charles Ives with a big amplifier. Almost worth getting to know in gradual doses, a track from this placed on a mix tape will overshadow most of its neighbors. Again, audio baklava.

50) *Over-Nite Sensation* (rock, 1973). One of Frank's best-selling albums, this record was a watershed move into primarily surrealist whimsy instead of political commentary—at least for a while. (Only "I'm The Slime" here continues his attack on the culture industry in an overt fashion.) "Montana" has aged best here, with its juxtaposition of an Aaron Copland classical cowboy feel and bizarre lyrics about dental floss and pygmy ponies. "Camarillo Brillo" and "Dinah-Moe Humm" became staples in performance; most Zappa fans got tired of them, and maybe that was the point: the absurd ennui of sexual pursuit? "Dirty Love" has good poodle continuity; "Zomby Woof" is another fine monster song.

The playing on the album is redemptively tight (this is, after all, almost the Helsinki band—no Brock yet). And the production values are excellent. But there's an uncanniness here that won't go away. The artist/audience relationship with Zappa has always had an element of sadomasochism in it. With *Freak Out!*, it was obvious. This release seems to give the teenage listener everything they might want in a pop release (and many a bong was fired up to celebrate that fact), but there's a lingering sting to the project that gives a dicey complexity to it. Arguably, this album is Zappa's response to the co-optation of the counterculture, the arrival of corporate control of the rock industry (now a real industry), and the lyrical pretensions of prog-rockers like Yes. All this was part of the ambience of the early 1970s. This is Frank Zappa's *Dark Side of the Moon*. It seems lighter, but it's really much, much darker than the Pink Floyd (because of its more sardonic approach).[4] A fascinating album, but not as user-friendly as it might seem at first listen.

51) *Them Or Us* (rock, 1984). This release is a fascinating hodge-podge of great stuff from several different bands. The first side of the vinyl record was a kind of history lesson, going from doo wop (a cover of "The Closer You Are") through roots rock ("In France" with Johnny "Guitar" Watson) to Zappa's own past (a new version of "Sharleena"). More guitar wizardry follows with "Truck Driver Divorce" (a vocal blend of country and western and "meltdown," followed by an amazing xenochronicitous solo) and "Stevie's Spanking" (this time with Steve Vai and Dweezil Zappa trading solos). Thana Harris and her husband Bob contribute some backup vocals on "Baby, Take Your Teeth Out;" Bob takes lead on another aria from *Hunchentoot*, "The Planet of My Dreams." The album concludes with "Be In My Video," a palpable swipe at MTV and David Bowie's *Let's Dance* ("led dance de blude agin"), and a first cover of the Allman Brothers'

"Whipping Post." Good stuff.

52) *Uncle Meat* (rock/ jazz, 1969). Some of the best music of the earlier Mothers, borne out by the omnipresence of "Dog Breath," "Uncle Meat," "Cruising For Burgers" and "King Kong" as concert favorites throughout Zappa's career. The version of "Dog Breath" here, with speeded-up vocals and a massive forty-track instrumental interlude, is the definitive one. I also have always liked the underappreciated "Project X," which features a first (but not last) taste of Zappa on acoustic guitar. This album constitutes a turn from social commentary to band sociology with respect to its lyrics.

53) *Frank Zappa Meets The Mothers Of Prevention* (Synclavier/ rock, 1985). The standout piece here is "Porn Wars," a Synclavier composition skewering the senate hearings on record labelling which Zappa testified at. A cry *de profundis* on many levels lamenting the utter stupidity of American politics as currently practiced, this piece has an edge and a power unheard in Zappa's work since *We're Only In It For The Money*. Its intensity also reminds me of Penderecki's "Threnody for the Victims of Hiroshima" (a composer Frank admired). The remaining Synclavier and band pieces are quite good, especially "Alien Orifice" and "What's New in Baltimore?" (great solo). "We're Turning Again" trashed the sixties nostalgia harder than any punk band dared; as such, not for everyone.

54) *Weasels Ripped My Flesh* (rock/ jazz, 1970). This sampler suggests what Frank might have had in mind for his planned mammoth retrospective on the earlier Mothers of Invention after he disbanded them. Side one of the record highlights Don ("Sugar Cane") Harris on violin covering Little Richard's "Directly From My Heart to You." Most of the best material is on side two. "Eric Dolphy Memorial Barbecue" shows just how close the polyrhythms of the Mothers could come to free jazz levels. "My Guitar Wants to Kill Your Mama" mockingly literalizes the menace of rock culture. "Oh No" remains one of Frank's loveliest compositions, and the segued follow-up ("The Orange County Lumber Truck") wasn't too shabby, either. The concluding title track is amazingly abrasive and aptly named, a reminder that Zappa doesn't always want to play nicely for his audiences.

55) *Burnt Weeny Sandwich* (rock/ jazz, 1970). More archival Mothers, in either jazz instrumental or doo wop mode. Sugar Cane Harris' work on "Little House I Used To Live In" is again exceptional, but the real highlight is the instrumental version of "Holiday In Berlin, Full Blown" followed by the extraordinarily lovely piano solo by Ian Underwood, "Aybe Sea"—a

marvel of controlled dynamics and subtlety. Some of the best notes the earlier Mothers ever hit.

56) *Wazoo* (jazz, 2007 [recorded 1972]). A two-CD selection from the last concert of the Grand Wazoo band played in Boston on September 24, 1972. This 20-piece ensemble was the largest group Zappa ever toured with (followed by his 12-member 1988 touring band and the 10-piece Petit Wazoo that immediately supplanted the Grand Wazoo). He simply contacted the top session players of Los Angeles to see who was available. Because of the expense, this outfit only played eight concerts in the United States and Europe in the space of less than a month. By any indication (with rehearsal time factored in), a costly and extravagant gesture for a rock musician—especially since he decided against releasing this concert recording in his lifetime.

The music is fabulous, if not as much a compositional revelation as the Petit Wazoo's much rarer song selections. Everything here has turned up elsewhere, more or less, albeit in altered form ("The Adventures of Greggary Peccary" is here an instrumental with extended soloing). I rank this as high as I do because it's a splendid treat to hear these compositions given cadillac arrangements with top-notch professional players (this version of "Big Swifty" blows the studio version on *Waka / Jawaka* out of the proverbial lake). Not too surprisingly, this band gets its best effects when Frank lets out the leash a bit. In addition to the solos on "Greggary Peccary," there is a "Boston version" of "Approximate": an experimental composition that determines rhythm but gives the players a range of about 20 pitches to play in (thereby generating unpredictable levels of consonance / dissonance). The result herein is a very rich listening experience with funky bassoon action, wild old-timey synthesizer whooping from Ian Underwood and exquisite percussion work from Ruth Underwood. In this case, more is more.

57) *London Symphony Orchestra Volumes I and II* (classical, 1995 [originally issued in 1983 and 1987]). Most Zappa listeners like these recordings better than Frank himself did. He thought the orchestra was underrehearsed and sloppy, reserving special contempt for the trumpet section who got boozed up before "Strictly Genteel." Their marred playing resulted in much studio labor to compensate—with ultimate failure, in Zappa's opinion. As such, he thought these releases were recorded rehearsals.

Granting all that, there is some gorgeous music here. "Sad Jane" gives the first indication of the deep melancholia of Zappa's classical writing, very evident from his work with the Ensemble Modern. "Bogus Pomp" is an interesting and witty reworking of the *200 Motels* music. The other stuff makes for very rigorous listening; he wears his oft-listed European influences on his sleeve. And yet, it is unmistakably Zappa. The digital audio work is breathtaking; he actually creates synthetic room dynamics which change within the pieces. Recommended headphone listening.

58) *The Dub Room Special!* (rock, 2007 [recorded 1974 and 1981, mixed by Frank in 1982). This is the soundtrack to a 1985 video release which combined footage from a never-released 1974 television special (called *A Token Of His Extreme*) with a few numbers from a 1981 Halloween concert at the Palladium (the entire concert, mostly showcasing material from *You Are What You Is*, came out on Honker home DVD in 2007 under the title *The Torture Never Stops*). So it's that great Helsinki concert era band—with George Duke, Napoleon Murphy Brock and Ruth Underwood—augmented with some 1981 Steve Vai stuff ("Stevie's Spanking"). That being said, the only goodies here not well covered elsewhere are a variation on Zappa and Brock's "Room Service" rock touring routine and a somewhat more extended reading of "Cosmik Debris" with tasty sax and guitar solos. If you see this before more highly ranked recordings of this band, grab it. Otherwise, this is for collectors and completists.

59) *Does Humor Belong In Music?* (rock, 1986). Originally released in Europe only, this showcases the 1984 touring band. An epic version of "Let's Move To Cleveland" is a hands-down highlight, with great solos from Alan Zavod (keyboards), Chad Wackerman (tuned drums) and F. Z. (lowdown dirty guitar). If you've made it this far, you just might want their cover of the dirty doo-wop ditty "Cock-suckers' Ball."

60) *Halloween* (rock, 2003 [recorded 1978]. If you have a Dolby 5.1 or DTS 5.1 home theater setup, you'll probably want to ignore my lower ranking of this effort and immediately grab this audio DVD (with a few video bonus tracks). The production on this conversion from a planned quadrophonic release is utterly superb. But we are talking about the music here. From that standpoint, you'd be listening to this for one, admittedly stellar, track: a seventeen minute closing medley of two great instrumentals, "The Black Page" and "The Deathless Horsie." Dweezil Zappa admits that his dad's extended exploration of the former is "about as far as Frank ever went" (DVD liner notes). And L. Shankar's electric violin exchange with Zappa is more than impressive. So this may be the best Zappa solo ever: it's certainly one of the best. So why haven't I ranked this Vaulternative release higher? Because it's a live Palladium show from the band's annual Halloween New York stint. These shows were definitely more fun to be at than to revisit through mechanical reproduction (unless they're an

audio souvenir of a show you actually attended). Most of the rest of the set list is the usual assortment of crowd pleasers, rendered competently but unexceptionally enough: "Dancin' Fool," "Stink-Foot," "Dinah-Moe Humm," "Camarillo Brillo," "Conehead" (this last admittedly also elevated by Shankar). So run to get this if you have an advanced system; otherwise, you're buying it for one sublime track other versions approach.

61) *You Can't Do That On Stage Anymore, Volume I* (rock, 1988). A miscellaneous collection, to be sure, intent on showcasing the sheer variety of live material in the vault. Lots of solid versions of the canon, but I especially like the previously unreleased "Babbette" (more poodle bidness from Napoleon Murphy Brock) and an epic version of "Don't Eat The Yellow Snow" replete with poetry readings from the audience. The sofa routine is shorter than on *Swiss Cheese / Fire!*, but the audio quality is better.

62) *At The Circus* (rock, 1992 [recorded 1970, 1978]). Most of this bootleg is from a 1978 German television special. Memorable guilty pleasures abound, most stemming from drummer Vinnie Colaiuta's obsession with a seal call attached to his percussion kit. Whereas Frank kept citing Ike Willis' Lone Ranger obsession as a source of stupid band humor, I think seal calls interrupting "Easy Meat" are the height of memorable and risible band strangeness. Thus, "Seal Call Fusion Music" is an apotheosis/nadir of sorts. You also get Frank's interesting anti-drug declaration "I'm On Duty" (doody?) and a tasty version of "Conehead."

63) *Shut Up 'N Play Yer Guitar* (rock instrumental, 1981). More exquisite sculpting in time with Frank's soloing. It's all good, but a few highlights include "While You Were Out" (a lovely acoustic solo with pick-ups), "Treacherous Cretins" (full-band reggae with Warren Cucurullo on sitar), "Canarsie" (exotic middle eastern feel, and more sitar), "Ship Ahoy" (stratocaster abuse), "Pink Napkins" (a more sinuous version of "Black Napkins"), "Return of The Son of Shut Up 'n Play Yer Guitar" (amazingly fast runs), "Stucco Homes" (more killer acoustic work) and "Canard du Jour" (a lovely duet with Jean-Luc Ponty featuring Zappa on bouzouki). As with *Guitar*, you can get overwhelmed by the density of it all. But taken in measured doses or mixed in with other stuff, it works great. (I guess what I'm talking about here is the audio equivalent of "museum fatigue"—a risk in general with an oeuvre as massive as Frank's.)

64) *Finer Moments* (jazz / classical, 2012 [recorded 1967-1972]). Since this is likely to be the last Zappa release to come out before this book is published (his 94th [!] official one as opposed to bootlegs), a few global

comments may be in order before a brief listing of this compilation's highlights.

Although prophecy is always dangerous, I think it's safe to assume nearly twenty years after his death that Vaultmeister Joe Travers will not find an unreleased Holy Grail of Frank's work superior to the better stuff that he did release. (Zappa's conduction of Edgard Varese's work remains an interesting exception to the above; it would provide an important missing piece to the Project / Object.) Frank Zappa, like all of the artists discussed here with the possible exceptions of Neil Young and Sun Ra, did not bury his best canvases. He tried to put out the best music he could find from his extensive recordings. (Indeed this prophecy was risky—and wrong. A few months after writing this, I discovered some big exceptions to this rule. Frank did not release some superb performances if they were only on mono tape [*Carnegie Hall; Road Tapes Venue #1*].)

The impulse that compelled him to compile this assortment of tracks for future release in 1972—but never put out in his own lifetime—can best be understood as emanating from a wish to archive the old incarnations of the Mothers of Invention, a band he had some deep ambivalences about. On the one hand, they made the big, sassy splash that put him on the map. They were an entertaining bar band with serious musical chops that could capitalize on the anything-goes moment of summer-of-love psychedelia by adding lots of musical freak outs, improvisation and theatrics to delight stoned-out hippies while sneaking in some interesting music. That Frank Zappa was an astute armchair sociologist deeply interested in the Los Angeles freak scene and groupies didn't hurt either. In those initially more unguarded days, Zappa and the Mothers had their very own subculture: a state of affairs which made possible projects such as the *Uncle Meat* film and soundtrack album for the then-uncompleted movie.

But on the other hand, they were much sloppier and excessive players (with a few possible exceptions like Ian Underwood) than any of his later, more carefully auditioned ensembles. Zappa could get the earlier bands to do what he wanted in the studio, but live they were all over the place (even if delightfully and entertainingly so). This is why the survivors of this band, who tour as the Grandmothers, are essentially a nostalgia act that have made no further cultural impact on the history of avant-pop. They resented his breaking up the band—in effect, handing them their pink slips—but he saw he could no longer grow with them as an artist. (Neil Young made similar tough decisions over the years).

Thus *Finer Moments*, a successful attempt to salvage some decent performances from these earlier outfits. Although low on this ranking, as I often say, any other band might consider this an immense achievement. Frank Zappa's music sets the bar quite high. So what do we have here?

The first disc of the double set opens with four selections from the epic Mothers stand at the Royal Albert Hall which has graced a few other earlier releases. Highlights include a decent Zappa guitar solo ("Sleazette") and Ian Underwood vamping on themes from Mozart's Piano Sonata in B Flat while the band dances (good music, but alas no visuals except for one still photo in the booklet). The other standout track here is "Uncle Rhebus," a 1969 jazz medley of themes from the *Uncle Meat* era augmented by the dual drumming of Art Tripp and Jimmy Carl Black. I think this is also on *The Ark* bootleg (#82 below), but the sound quality is much higher here to expected good effect.

After some gratuitous snorking nose noises, disc two showcases "Enigmas 1 Thru 5," a Zappa composition for solo percussion performed by Art Tripp. This work clearly exhibits the profound influence of Edgard Varese on Zappa (again). "Pumped and Waxed" is Zappa's solo exploration of what some kind of Moog synthesizer can do (in his famous basement). The next two tracks capture the rarish moment in the band when later Little Feat member Lowell George was a member doing free jazz wildness utterly unlike his later more commercial output. The latter track, "Squeeze it. Squeeze it. Squeeze it." also incorporates Roy Estrada's sex tape moaning falsetto, a recurrent treat / provocation whenever he happened to be in the group. The last long jazz workout, "The Subcutaneous Peril," is probably the best piece assembled here—as such, a fitting conclusion to the constructed set. A solid 1971 line-up (Zappa, Ian Underwood and Don Preston on keyboards, Aynsley Dunbar on drums) playing a distinguished venue (Carnegie Hall) equals jazz magic. After Preston's stellar Moog solo, Dunbar cuts loose on the skins, which is in turn followed by Frank who moves his solo into a loping boogie as good as anything in the *Chunga's Revenge* era. Finer moments indeed—and we're not through yet with these rankings!

65) *The Man From Utopia* (rock, 1983). This release showcases Zappa's experimentation with sprechstimme / "meltdown." With Steve Vai, he had a guitarist who could follow the twisting intricacies of speech rhythms. These talents are on full display in "The Dangerous Kitchen," "The Radio Is Broken" and "The Jazz Discharge Party Hats." Perhaps more to be admired than embraced, they are at least worthy of musical respect—and, like later Schoenberg, it kinda grows on you. As one might expect, this band could play astounding instrumentals ("Tink Walks Amok," "Moggio," "We Are Not Alone"). Plus, there's the radio-friendly standard "Cocaine Decisions."

66) *Baby Snakes* (rock, 1983). This is the partial soundtrack of the film of the same name (it omits some of the best playing, which occurs during the extended encore). I list it because of its fine versions of "The Black Page #2," "Disco Boy" and "Punky's Whips" (Terry Bozzio's homoerotic psychodrama about the glam-metal band Angel). But check out the film as well. This recording does not exhaust the musical pleasures of the actual movie. This is a fine version of the band with Adrian Belew, Tommy Mars, Terry Bozzio and even veteran Mother Roy Estrada.

67) *one shot deal* (rock, 2008 [recorded between 1972 and 1981]). This unpretentious little offering bridges two mysterious "build reels" (sequences Zappa intended for a future release) with three extended guitar showcases. One of these, "Occam's Razor," became "On the Bus" on *Joe's Garage* in truncated form; another, "The Illinois Enema Bandit," is from *The Torture Never Stops*, the 1981 Halloween Palladium concert available on DVD. Another track, "Rollo," is available in another mix on *QuAUDIOPHILIAc*. So only six out of nine cuts here are completely new. I rank it as highly as I do primarily because of "Australian Yellow Snow," a 1973 performance of his prog-rock epic piss take. This version is so wonderful because it preceded the studio release. The audience is genuinely enjoying the song because it's brand-new, not the concert staple it eventually became. And Frank does an additional routine while spelling out "mar-juh-ren" (sic) that he had also performed a month earlier in Milwaukee. This is not just nostalgia on my part; it really adds to the humor of the song. I also value this CD as a good all-around introduction to the oeuvre (nice variety).

68) *Jazz From Hell* (Synclavier / jazz, 1986). If you had any doubts about the grammy awards, consider that this won for "best instrumental rock record." Zappa doubted that the committee had even listened to it (Watson 472). What this really is can best be compared with *trompe l'oeil* painting (like that of William Harnett or John Frederick Peto). Zappa fools the ear by making jazz instrumentals on the Synclavier (except for "St. Etienne," the one non-electronic track). So all the interplay and "jamming" is synthetic, a mere simulacrum of jazz. What would tip most listeners off to this is the Nancarrowesque pacing—faster than most human musicians can play (although the Ensemble Modern could encore with "G-Spot Tornado" from this release!). Just as Conlon Nancarrow got his effects on player piano rolls, Zappa can get any pace he wants on the Synclavier.

Amidst this electronic frenzy, there is some real compositional loveliness, especially in the complex and surreal melody (because of the shifting timbres) of "Night School" and the spunk of the aforementioned "G-Spot Tornado."

69) *Hot Rats* (jazz, 1969). It may seem perverse to rank this crowd-pleaser so low on my list. English fans, for example, tend to consider this his best (because least self-indulgent?) release. Don't get me wrong—it is a wonderful record inaugurating a new kind of electric jazz more interesting than most of what passed for fusion. And the players are solid: Sugar Cane Harris on violin, Ian Underwood on keyboards and reeds, Captain Beefheart on guest vocals for "Willie The Pimp." I just think this was a beginning for Frank; he got much better at this on subsequent releases. You may well rank it higher personally, especially if you don't like seal calls or enema bandits as much as I do.

70) *Studio Tan* (rock, 1978). This is also a wonderful record, ranked lower only because everything on it is also on the expanded release *Lather*. So no need to buy both unless you're very German. But each track here is a winner: the faux nostalgia of "Let Me Take You to the Beach," the classical adventures of "Revised Music For Guitar And Low Budget Orchestra," the instrumental splendor of "REDUNZL" and the conceptual continuity / homage to Stravinsky's *Soldier's Tale* of "Greggary Peccary."

71) *Imaginary Diseases* (jazz, 2005 [recorded 1972]). This recording offers up one of the rarest Zappa outfits, the Petit Wazoo jazz band (which toured as the Mothers, but is known among insiders by the former monicker): no keyboards, five horns, one woodwind player, two guitars, bass and drums. None of the compositions on this release appeared elsewhere in Zappa's lifetime ("Rollo" shows up in another version on *QuAUDIOPHIL-IAc*). So this is about as collectable as it gets—and it's a great band. The most important piece historically is "Father O'Blivion," a sixteen-minute workout that ended up being recycled in numerous other works ("Be-bop Tango," "Greggary Peccary"). The most enjoyable selections are "Been to Kansas City in A Minor" (straight funky blues), "D.C. Boogie" (the result of the audience "voting" how they want the song to end) and "Montreal" (sparkling guitar tone on the solo). But it's all very good. Zappa mixed it in the seventies, but never got around to releasing it to a fan base which understandably clamored for it.

72) *Orchestral Favorites* (classical, 1979). Same *Lather* situation as the previous entry, except for two additional tracks: "Strictly Genteel" and "Bogus Pomp," both reworkings of *200 Motels* material. A smaller ensemble than the London Symphony Orchestra, but arguably better played. "Naval Aviation In Art" is a minimalist masterpiece, as close as Zappa got to Anton Webern.

73) *The Grand Wazoo* (jazz, 1972). Another popular fave I'm low-balling. Solid big-band jazz, great players (George Duke on keyboards, Sal Marquez on trumpet, etc.). The aggregate just sounds a little more unwieldy than, say, the 1988 big band. But it's pretty good, and better than that at times. "Eat That Question," for example, has a keyboard riff that puts *Tarkus*-era Emerson, Lake and Palmer out to dry.

74) *Lumpy Gravy* (classical [with spoken word], 1967). More hubris on my part ranking Zappa's first solo outing so low. I do it strictly on account of accessibility. I don't know if this would make you an instant Zappa fan. It is where conceptual continuity begins. Zappa's theories about the Big Note and the simultaneity of time when seen beyond linear clock perception are first glimpsed here amidst classical, rock, and even surf instrumental sonic tidbits. This recording will become more important to you as you keep listening to Zappa: he's very metaphysically and sociologically generous here. (Note this recording's much higher ranking as part of the *Lumpy Money* box set.)

75) *Buffalo* (rock, 2007 [recorded 1980]). This double concert VAULTernative CD documents the beginning of Frank Zappa's last decade of live touring with a rock band. He had younger players and a much younger audience who seemed to be attending the shows for a sexual rite of passage (could your date endure all of Zappa's dirty jokes?) as much as for a chance to perform obsequies in front of the aural shrine of the greatest living guitar god. By these criteria, this October 25, 1980 show in Buffalo, New York, was ideally suited for such sociocultural purposes—a suspicion verified by the incredible enthusiasm of the crowd. The unquestionable musical highlight here is the presence in the band of Steve Vai (on "stunt guitar"), one of the few guitarists who could keep up with the maestro (Adrian Belew also comes to mind). You can usually tell when Steve's soloing by his grungier and crunchier tone—but both could deliver note clusters with a speed and clarity most guitar heroes can only dream of. So the two trade solos of consistently high interest with some regularity here on "Pick Me, I'm Clean," "City Of Tiny Lites," "Easy Meat," "The Torture Never Stops"" (here given an epic 23 minute workout with multiple band solos) and "Andy." And that's why this is a great listen. Everything else is available in abundance in other places except for "The 'Real World' Thematic Extrapolations," a funny and closely observed sociological rap by Zappa about the disco dating scene. (One can imagine social historians mining this material in future centuries!)

76) *You Can't Do That On Stage Anymore, Volume 5* (rock, 1992). The first disc of this set showcases the early Mothers (1965-1969). Zappa's liner notes

convey typical amused skepticism about "those collectors who still believe that the only 'good' material was performed by those early line-ups." But Zappa puts his best foot forward by scrupulously editing the excerpts from live performance. As bootlegs further down the list show, these early bands were much more long-winded musically than later ensembles. With the audio only, you're not getting the theatrics that sustained an otherwise more repetitive performance. As a result, judicious editing is the best way to showcase this material. Highlights include the experimentalism of "Chocolate Halvah," another accompaniment to a sex tape ("Right There"), a musical approximation of cat sounds good enough to get actual cats to respond ("Meow"), a very well-recorded drum / percussion duel amongst Zappa, Jimmy Carl Black and Arthur Tripp ("FZ/ JCB Drum Duet") and Lowell George's imitation of a German immigration official ("German Lunch"). This last anticipates the mirrored situation on *The Yellow Shark* of "Welcome to the United States."

The second disc showcases the 1982 band. There are some overlaps with other close versions of this material, but some new treats as well: a witty depiction of English sexual mores ("Dead Girls of London"), great bass guitar work from Scott Thunes on "City of Tiny Lites" and a very solid rendering of "A Pound For A Brown (On The Bus)" showcasing both a scat shuffle and fine work from Ed Mann on xylophone.

I rank this release as low as I do because of the comparative difficulty of the first disc for the novice listener.

77) *Conceptual Continuity* (rock, 1992 [recorded 1977]). This bootleg features one of the smallest and rarest of Zappa. line-ups: Zappa, Terry Bozzio on drums, Eddie Jobson on keyboards, Patrick O' Hearn on bass and Ray White on rhythm guitar and vocals. But they're all great players, and they get a big sound out. The result is about as close as Frank ever got to classic arena rock. The banter with the Detroit audience is consistently amusing, the solos are blistering and Ray White's soulful vocal on "City of Tiny Lights" sets a standard.

78) *Our Man In Nirvana* (rock, 1992 [recorded 1968]). The best of the early Mothers bootlegs, because of the delightful presence of Wild Man Fischer with the band. He not only tells us "The Wild Man Fischer Story" from his own lp (see below); he performs an otherwise unavailable rarity ("I'm The Meany"). Again, the interaction with the audience is good. Musical highlights include a cover of the rhythm and blues classic "Bacon Fat" and a version of "King Kong" with a fine guitar solo and a solid (if a bit repetitive) rhythmic groove.

79) *The Best Band You Never Heard In Your Life* (rock, 1991). Why so low? Remember, it's the best band you "never" heard, not "ever" heard! They are better than that, of course. It's the 1988 touring ensemble, big and highly accomplished. One could argue that these are the most technically finished versions of songs from *One Size Fits All* such as "Florentine Pogen," "Andy" and "Inca Roads"—to say nothing of their sublime reading of "The Eric Dolphy Memorial Barbecue" from *Weasels Ripped My Flesh*, which few of Frank's bands could dream of attempting live. Or their ease with everything from Ravel ("Bolero") to Led Zeppelin ("Stairway To Heaven"). I guess I prefer the fire and sass of earlier bands. This one seems too subservient to Frank, no doubt because of its unwieldy size. Sure, there's some humor (a "Lonesome Cowboy Burt" rewritten for Jimmy Swaggart), but it doesn't fly off the rails as it does with the seventies vocal bands. I like the more raggedy versions of these songs; you may like these more polished ones.

In any case, "A Few Moments With Brother A. West" remains a highlight—a fake preacher so realistic audiences booed him.

80) *Ahead Of Their Time* (rock, 1993). This release documents a 1968 Mothers concert at the Royal Festival Hall in London. The first half is a musical play which allegorizes tensions between traditional classical music, twentieth century experimentalism and pop music—highly relevant themes for Frank's project. It's funny, interesting and even prophetic: "Agency Man" seems to anticipate a synthetic Presidential candidate like Ronald Reagan (who reads the cue cards of his backers). The second half of the disc is a "fair" (Zappa's accurate evaluation) Mothers concert. Ranked this low because of its unsuitability for novice listeners who may not tolerate its dadaistic indulgences.

81) *You Can't Do That On Stage Anymore, Volume 3* (rock, 1989). I rank this volume of the stage retrospective lowest because, again paradoxically, of the musical perfection of the 1984 band which predominates on it. I like when they do their own material: an insanely complex live "Drowning Witch" or "Nig Biz," a critique of the music business' exploitation of rhythm and blues (and beyond) musicians. And there is plenty more where that came from on this collection. But their covers seem a little too slick and clever compared to other versions. Cases in point: "Bamboozled By Love" (which interpolates "Owner Of A Lonely Heart" by Yes) and "Advance Romance (1984)." These renditions are incredibly tight, but maybe that's not the whole point with this music. Feel free to disagree.

82) *Tenga Na Minchia Tanta* (rock 1992 [recorded 1971]). Another bootleg

from the Flo and Eddie era. I rank this fairly low because almost everything on it is available elsewhere in better renditions. The exception is a rare live version of "What Will This Morning Bring Me This Evening?," the bookend to "What Will This Evening Bring Me This Morning?" (naturally). This song is in the film of *200 Motels*, but not the soundtrack. Since it's a lovely tune, this is a convenient way to acquire it.

83) *Francesco Zappa* (Synclavier / classical 1984). This is as good a place as any to insert this atypical recording. Looking in Grove's dictionary of music to see what had been written about Frank (if anything), the Zappa clan discovered a baroque composer of almost the same name. Since Francesco had never been recorded, Frank decided to check his manuscripts out (conveniently at the Bancroft Library at Berkeley)—then program them into his Synclavier. These sonatas are quite accessible and listenable, especially if you like baroque music (and don't insist it be played on traditional instruments). I rank them low only because they are a misleading indication of the nature of Zappa's overall musical project (granted that it allows for anarchy). And, more importantly, since he is strictly "covering" his relative, this is the only recording he made where you don't get to hear any compositions by Frank Zappa. David Ocker acknowledges in the liner notes that this is as close as Frank gets to easy listening: "You can enjoy it with dinner, or just listen along the next time you feel the urge to wear a powdered wig." Is this Frank's *Barry Lyndon*? (If so, Kubrick is more subversive in this round.)

84) *Thing-Fish* (rock, 1984). This release offers a dilemma complementary to that of *Francesco Zappa*. It is 100% Frank, uncut, so much so that all but the most committed Zappaphile will be driven off by it. As Zappa has argued, *Thing-Fish* is "a major work" (Watson 550). But it is not for those easily offended. It parodies a Broadway musical (the record claims to be an "original cast recording"). The plot involves biologically altered convicts who become the "mammy nuns" (an odd mix of nun, Aunt Jemima, potato head and duck beak), an Evil Prince, two Broadway theatergoers who become part of the show in a big way, and a conspiracy theory about AIDS. This last is only one of several pet theories Zappa trots out, another notorious one being that the resexualization of the businesswoman will drive men into homosexuality. And the Mammy Nuns speak in an invented language close in spirit to the dialogue on *Amos and Andy* (riffing on Kingfish, of course).

The good news is that the production values are high and the script is an equal-opportunity offender. (Perhaps also an equal-opportunity amuser: most listeners are bound to find something risible about this, given its relentless absurdity.) In fact, this is a testimony as to How Far Zappa Will Go. But since it's a play, you really have to listen to it all the way through (3 albums, 2 cds). It can't easily be excerpted without losing its full effect. And some of the music is recycled old stuff with the new invented language ("The 'Torchum' Never Stops"). It ends up being Zappa for special occasions. But I'd like to meet an individual who was turned on to Frank by way of this!

85) *Fillmore East, June 1971* (rock, 1971). I never thought I would rate this classic Flo-and-Eddie recording so low. As a teenager, I thought it was Zappa's finest hour. Let's just say you can wear this one out. It is a comedy album, and the groupie routine will overstay its welcome. The music takes more of a backseat here than on other recordings by this band, and I don't think that's ultimately a good thing. Still, it is opera for the people—and "Tears Began To Fall" is a great song.

86) *Chunga's Revenge* (rock, 1970). More excess from Flo and Eddie, albeit of a usually more musical nature ("Would You Go All The Way?," "Rudy Wants To Buy Yez A Drink"). "Sharleena" makes its first humble appearance here as well. This collection is good for conceptual continuity, as it looks back to *Hot Rats* ("Twenty Small Cigars") and forward to *200 Motels*. But I think there's some really tedious stuff here ("The Nancy & Mary Music"—although George Duke's parody of John Mayall's vocalizing on "Room to Move" was funny at the time), as well as some brilliant work (the title track, which became one of Frank's signature instrumentals). Too much of a hodge-podge for all but the diehards.

87) *Apostrophe* (rock, 1974). More iconoclasm on my part, since this sold a lot of copies in its day. As Ben Watson has noted, it addresses a specific situation: the pomposity of progressive rock in the seventies (in Kostelantz 174). Zappa's pre-punk response was to come up with the most intricate music imaginable linked to the most inane lyrics: rock operettas about eskimos and pancake breakfasts. When I saw him preview this material in concert in 1973, he interrupted the "Don't Eat The Yellow Snow" sequence during the "lonely trudging" bit to remark upon how "stupid" the song was (my personal bootleg cassette)—a typical statement. He's right: it IS stupid—and clever. But it's musical satire addressing a pretty specific environment: the world of Yes, Gentle Giant and the like. Like the Sex Pistols and the music on *Over-Nite Sensation*, it assaults the audience and confronts it with its consumer stupidity.

As such, I don't think it's aged well—although its dadaism arguably makes it timeless. If it were a little less obscene (what's Father O'Blivion doing to the pancakes?), it could almost be Frank's children's record. As with

Fillmore East, June 1971, there are too many words here—except for the title instrumental with just Jack Bruce on bass and Jim Gordon on drums (where Frank out-Creams Cream with a power jam).

88) *'Tis The Season To Be Jelly* (rock, 1991 [recorded 1967]). This bootleg showcases the early Mothers doing a lot of wild covers (Stravinsky's "Petroushka," "Bristol Stomp," "Baby Love," "Blue Suede Shoes," "Hound Dog," even a bit of Tchaikovsky's Sixth Symphony). More amusing than sublime, overall. There are also some rare live versions of material from *Freak Out!*: "You Didn't Try To Call Me" and a version of "It Can't Happen Here" adapted for a Swedish setting. "King Kong" begins in a mellow jazz reading, then proceeds to lots of keyboard work from Don Preston and/or Ian Underwood before concluding with a "freak out" typical of this band in performance. Mainly of archival interest.

89) *The Ark* (rock, 1991 [recorded 1969]). This bootleg begins with a version of "Big Leg Emma" quoting "Charade," then proceeds to showcase some melodies from *200 Motels* ("Some Ballet Music"). The version of "My Guitar" from *Weasels Ripped My Flesh* stretches out nicely. The record concludes with a long medley of "Uncle Meat / King Kong" that has its moments (a fine drum/percussion break and a stirring conclusion), but also some langoruous bits. For the committed listener.

90) *The Lost Episodes* (rock, 1996). An unabashedly archival project for fans who want to get behind the music. Ronnie and Kenny confirm that there was a window covered in boogers. There is a lot of Studio Z and early Mothers material (even a sea chanty, "The Handsome Cabin Boy"). Captain Beefheart makes some welcome appearances ("Lost In A Whirlpool," "Tiger Roach," "I'm A Band Leader," "The Grand Wazoo"). Musical highlights are some early readings of "RDNZL" and "Inca Roads" and a marvellous extended version of "Sharleena" (featuring Sugar Cane Harris) that far surpasses the rendition on *Chunga's Revenge*.

91) *Joe's Domage* (jazz, 2004 [recorded 1972]). This Joe Travers VAULTernative release documents a rehearsal of the jazz outfit that would play on *Waka / Jawaka* and *The Grand Wazoo* (while Zappa was wheelchair bound recovering from injuries inflicted on him by the deranged concertgoer who pushed him into the orchestra pit in London). As such, it would be of interest only to the most committed collector of the music. What gives it some additional caché is that it contains a fascinating vocal version of "The Grand Wazoo" entitled "Think It Over." This is a rare Zappa pastiche of New Age religion—as opposed to his more typical satiric approach. In other words, the lyrics are both funny and fairly good spiritual doctrine:

> If something gets in your way,
> Just *THINK IT* Over ... ...
> And, it will fall down
> It will fall down ...
> Everything that gets in your way ain't real ...
> It ain't real, so
> *What's the deal?* (liner notes)

When set to the catchy jazz melody, this really grooves. Which leaves us to wonder why Frank ultimately abandoned this version. Perhaps because it was too close to actual eastern and New Age thought, and Zappa wanted to mock gurus, not be a guru?

The big lesson of this CD is the reason why Zappa's jazz projects never got that far out (into, say, extended free jazz improvisation). His jazz compositions were so complex and intricate that it was all the players could do to learn them as written (they were thoroughly scored). So when they were allowed to cut loose, the solos tend to be basic riffs in a given key to avoid losing the larger thread of the piece. Paradoxically, Zappa's rock players had more room to move. You can hear all this for yourself in the meticulous (detractors would say obsessive) rehearsal process revealed here. I prefer to think of Frank Zappa as a platonist trying to realize a perfect performance rather than a control freak. But to be one is to be accused of being the other. This recording contains the evidence for you to draw your own conclusions. If you have any doubts that he was a musician's musician, hearing this will lay your doubts to rest.

92) *Mystery Disc* (rock, 1998). More archival material, originally included in the first two *Old Masters* releases of Zappa's earliest recordings which he reissued in the mid-1980s. More Studio Z and Beefheart ("Metal Man Has Won His Wings"); lots of Mothers noodling and clowning. The best material overlaps with *Ahead Of Their Time* and even *The Lost Episodes*. For the completist.

93) *Joe's Corsage* (rock, 2004 [recorded late 1964-1965]). The first of vault-meister Joe Travers' archival projects, this documents the pre-*Freak Out!* Mothers of Invention. Its crisp production beguiles the ear, and Zappa's interviews interspersed throughout are illuminating (his interest in sea chanteys accounts for an odd live cover of "The Handsome Cabin Boy"). There are other tidbits here: folk-rock jangly guitars on "Motherly Love" and "Any Way The Wind Blows," "I Ain't Got No Heart" as a shuffle boogie. But yes, this is primarily of historical interest and a disc for the completist. So not a priority unless / until you're a diehard fan.

94) *As An Am* (rock, 1991 [recorded 1981]). A good bootleg of the 1981 band, taken from their second set of the Palladium Halloween concert. Ranked low for reasons of redundancy—you can get this stuff elsewhere in abundance. The only rarity is "Young & Monde," the melody of "Let's Move To Cleveland" with different lyrics. There is a funky version of "Sharleena" with driving drums, and a good solo on "Black Page."

95) *Anyway The Wind Blows* (rock, 1991 [recorded 1979]). More redundancy with a release such as *Tinseltown Rebellion*. The band is great, but you can hear them in better reproduction elsewhere. The transition from "Dead Girls Of London" to "I Ain't Got No Heart" is inspired.

96) *Saarbrucken 1979* [sic] (rock, 1991 [recorded 1978]) Yet more bootleg redundancy. Vinnie Colaiuta works in some seal calls (especially appropriate for "Nanook Rubs It"). "Village of the Sun" leads into some fine extended jamming; "Pound For A Brown" is given a very jazzy reading with good keyboard soloing from Tommy Mars.

97) *Electric Aunt Jemima* (rock, 1992 [recorded 1968]). Long drum-based instrumental jamming on early Mothers melodies. Raw and wearisome. Frank's countenance of this bootleg release serves full notice on the very real limitations of his earlier bands in concert. Point taken!

98) *Joe's Xmasage* (rock, 2005 [recorded ca. 1963]). This VAULTernative CD contains a generous selection of Zappa's personal comedic and musical projects from the days when he worked for and eventually ran Pal Recording Studio / Studio Z in Cucamonga (California, naturally). Both Zappa's biographers (e.g., Barry Miles) and the family (widow Gail Zappa's liner notes herein) suggest that his eventual bust for making a bogus sex tape to sell to an undercover vice squad officer, leading to a brief stint in Tank C in the San Bernadino jail, was a kind of primal scene for the composer resulting in a career-long obsession with foisting sexual material on his listeners to rectify the puritanical mindset that led to his traumatic incarceration. As such, this material is certainly of historical interest. But, obviously, not of much merit for the uncommitted listener. You can hear a pre-Mothers power trio (a la Cream) live, some electronic noodling for a planned science fiction film and the earliest poodle reference in the oeuvre ("The Purse"). And more tellingly, you can detect a note of condescension towards his audience before he even really earned it ("The Uncle Frankie Show")—or is he just parodying the tone of kiddie show hosts? Listen, and decide.

99) *"Congress Shall Make No Law..."* (spoken word / Synclavier, 2010 [recorded mostly 1985-6]). This release is pretty much for the committed Zappa-

phile, but I still would rather hear the dulcet tones of Frank's voice than some of the Cucamonga recordings listed below. This recording preserves the bulk of his testimony in the mid-eighties before a U.S. Senate committee and the Maryland legislature, along with a few additional interviews, all to fight the Parents' Music Resource Center (PMRC) in their attempt to label musical recordings—a result of Tipper Gore's catching her daughter listening to Prince's "Darling Nikki" off the *Purple Rain* soundtrack. Zappa won only a partial victory here, by the way. There aren't labels for drugs and alcohol, sex, violence or the occult (as Frank point out, that last is especially ominous: does it cover "astrology"... "yoga"... "the rosary" or "Kaballah"?). But the recording industry caved in and puts to this day "Parental Advisory: Explicit Content" warning labels on CDs (which result in some retailers refusing to carry such products, as Zappa feared).

The CD is mostly spoken word with a little Synclavier music, mostly at the end ("Reagan at Bittberg some more"). There is also the "burp art" of Jade Teta (vocalizing words and phrases while she belches). The booklet included gives a generous archive of both the PMRC's mailings (know your enemy) and all of Zappa's writings on the subject (including a four-page letter to President Reagan). As such, this package is invaluable for anyone researching the PMRC.

The most interesting thing I learned from this package is Zappa's take on country music. There was no interest in Congress about labeling country music (as opposed to rock and rap) even though, as Frank wrote in his longer statement to Congress on September 19, 1985,

> ... inside those Country albums with the American flags, the big trucks and the atomic pompadours there lurks a fascinating variety of songs about sex, violence, alcohol and THE DEVIL, recorded in a way that lets you hear EVERY WORD, sung for you by people who have been to prison and are PROUD OF IT. [Block capitals are Zappa's]

Given this, he argues that the PMRC's secret agenda is an "affirmative action program" for the Gores' home state of Tennessee. His cogent argument might even be why he wrote some more country music at this time ("Truck Driver Divorce"), since one angle he explores is the challenge of labeling multi-genre recordings: if there's a country song on a Zappa album, wouldn't that make it exempt from a warning sticker?

In an interview he also points out how the Grammy awards are rigged. Their charter statement claims that it's solely on the basis of "artistic merit"—not sales. Zappa explains that this is impossible given the sheer number of recordings issued per year which the awards committees would have to listen to, preferably more than once, to judge fairly.

Other highlights of the recording include his crossfire with Al Gore, where Frank unquestionably triumphs so thoroughly he gets chastised by the next senator at the hearing for his "boorish" remarks. And there's a surreal moment when Paula Hawkins of Florida criticizes him for not being more hands-on in buying his children toys. Bottom line: this is a comedy album. The comedy is provided both by Zappa's extraordinary wit and the utter lameness of these elected officials. (If only we had a Frank Zappa in our era of the Tea Party.)

100) *Rare Meat: Early Productions of Frank Zappa* (rock, 1983). This material is available in a number of releases: besides this version, I've also seen a CD entitled *Cucamonga*. It's a selection of his Studio Z productions for other clients, although he also plays the odd guitar lick for these bands. You can see where he learned how to make goblin giggles for "Goblin Girl" by listening to the "Jeepers" records he made for a horror movie host. There was a very steep learning curve between these efforts and *Freak Out!*.

These recordings are the collected works of Frank Zappa. Let me also alert you, again in ranked form, to some of the productions which he oversaw and a few of the better tribute recordings.

A) *Trout Mask Replica* by Captain Beefheart and His Magic Band (rock, 1969). Unquestionably the greatest sessions Zappa ever produced of somebody else's music (although the Mothers provide the instrumental backup for "The Blimp"). Much ink has been spilled over this truly unique amalgam of Chicago blues, free jazz and full-tilt surrealism. Beefheart's finest hour: an album of unrelenting strangeness that seems to obey its own internal logic. Proof positive that Frank as a producer enhanced other musicians' visions rather than imposing his own on them.

B) *The Zappa Album* by Ensemble Ambrosius (classical, 2000). For my money, the best of the many Zappa tribute recordings that continue to come out. This Finnish ensemble covers Zappa compositions on baroque instruments — and it works, because they know how to groove! Had Frank lived to hear this, I think he would have concurred that they're almost as good as the Ensemble Modern (in fact, with regard to swinging, maybe better). Their versions of Synclavier compositions such as "Night School" and "Alien Orifice" bring out textures and complexities which comparatively overwhelm on the electronic versions. Their "Black Page #2" is incredibly dynamic, as is their "Echidna's Arf (of You)." The fake "art" vocals on "The Idiot Bastard Son" are hilarious. They clearly love this music, and it shows. The power and passion shine through, and then you occasionally recall you're listening to a baroque ensemble!

C) *Touch Me There* by Shankar (rock, 1979). I rank this so highly because Shankar is arguably the best musician Zappa ever produced an album for (yeah, I prefer him as a violinist to Jean-Luc Ponty). I first heard a later recording of Shankar's, *Out To Lunch*, coming into Washington, D.C., at night on Radio Pacifica. His *rāga*-inflected jazz seemed to capture the rhythms of the passing cars and metro trains: I was instantly hooked. This is an earlier effort working in shorter forms with occasional lyrics, which is why I roughly label it rock—even though Shankar's music, like Zappa's, defies pigeonholing.

The many highlights include "Dead Girls of London," a Zappa lyric lamenting the repressed nature of Londoners of the female persuasion (a sociological observation I regrettably must confirm by my own experiences) abetted by a blistering violin solo. Zappa's own bands would later perform this item as well. "Touch Me There" with its French vocalist sets up an interestingly sensual contrast. The words Frank provides to accompany the seductive violin work are as close as he ever got to Barry White! "No More Mr. Nice Girl" is a compositional collaboration between the two (Zappa sings on "Dead Girls," but never plays on the album); its big band vamps hearken back to "Waka / Jawaka" and "The Grand Wazoo." "Darlene" features fast *rāga* runs and Simon Phillips' drums emulating the tabla. When Shankar boasts on "Knee-Deep In Heaters" that he "will play you anything," you'd best believe him: he can, will and does! Shankar got even better than this over time, but it remains a highly remarkable and listenable effort—proof yet again that Frank has a great ear for extraordinary musicianship (and a first glimpse of the world music interests that would dominate his last days).

D) *Ensemble Modern Plays Frank Zappa: Greggery Peccary and Other Persuasions* by Ensemble Modern (classical, 2004 [recorded 2002]). This third recording of the Ensemble Modern playing Zappa (following actual collaboration with him on *The Yellow Shark* and *Everything Is Healing Nicely*) maintains the same energetic and faithful standards of the previous efforts — largely because of the technical support of the Zappa estate. Todd Yvega transformed Synclavier electronic compositions into playable scores; Harry Andronis gave the recordings "eyebrows" (so it wouldn't be a soulless technical run-through); Gail Zappa even wrote the extensive program notes, thereby making this almost an official release. So it's fun stuff and well worth a listen—I'm probably perverse in slightly preferring the Ensemble Ambrosius. Maybe it's because these pieces don't sound THAT different from Zappa's versions (which is actually a huge compliment, but recall that Ensemble Modern were the most technically gifted musicians Frank ever had the privilege of working with). The relentless percussive drive of "Night School," the Stravinsky-esque futurism of "Put A Motor In Yourself" (from *Civilization Phaze III*), the wacky musical in-jokes and satire of the title track are all here. Operatically trained singer Omar Ebrahim does a good job emulating the special pig's vocals (achieved on Zappa's version by speeding up his own voice). There's even a bonus track (from *200 Motels*), a real rarity on a classical release! But as even Gail laments in the liner notes, no electric guitar on "Peaches En Regalia." Frank has left the building. The optimal purpose of this recording would be to introduce more staid classical listeners suspicious of Zappa's music to its legitimate place in the repertoire. For the rest of us, the kick is in hearing the seemingly unplayable played extremely well—the classical equivalent of a bitchin' Zappa guitar solo. And isn't that enough?

E) *An Evening With Wild Man Fischer* by Wild Man Fischer (rock, 1968). Frank's best sociological production. Larry Fischer is a street musician on the L. A. strip. Frank recorded him a cappella, and with accompaniment from several of the Mothers (including Zappa himself on guitar). Some of the a cappella work is studio; some in the form of field recordings on the strip. Larry is both an extreme outsider (he was committed to back-to-back mental institutions in the early to mid-sixties) and a pop star wanna-be. His songs are both infectious and bizarre, often at the same time. This album, along with *Trout Mask Replica*, offers a kind of limit case for how experimental artists could be while still getting recorded. At times, this becomes very hard to listen to—psychodrama, actually ("Larry Under Pressure"). The results are oddly moving and certainly memorable.

F) *King Kong* by Jean-Luc Ponty (jazz, 1970). A fine jazz album offering a transition between Frank's own *Hot Rats* and the 1973-4 versions of the Mothers (George Duke is very much in evidence here). Zappa only plays guitar on a Ponty composition, but he arranges all the tracks on the album (and all the rest are Zappa compositions, including the premiere of "Music For Electric Violin And Low Budget Orchestra"). The version of "America Drinks And Goes Home" has more musical humor than the one on *Absolutely Free*: its conclusion emulates drunks racing to the bathroom.

G) *Lucille Has Messed My Mind Up* by Jeff Simmons (rock, 1969). This interesting psychedelic blues gem by former bassist and rhythm guitar player for the Mothers, Simmons (recorded before he joined the group), was co-produced by Zappa under the whimsical pseudonym La Marr Bruister (with Chris Huston). Its chief claim to fame is the appearance of two songs that would later appear on Zappa albums: the title track (on *Joe's Garage, Act 1*) and "Wonderful Wino" (on *Zoot Allures*). Zappa plays guitar on both here—and on the bluesy "Raye" as well. "Lucille" is an especially compelling cut: besides Zappa's guitar, it has great vocals from Simmons, sax from Ian Underwood and compelling rock and roll piano (i.e., in the style of Fats Domino). It's a completely different reading than the reggae-inflected version on *Joe's Garage*. This should have been a pop hit, but the fates are fickle. There are other treats on the album as well: the jazz lounge of "Aqueous Humore" and the intriguingly dense "Conversation With A Recluse" (its intricate transitions and rapid pace suggest either compositional help from Zappa or a strong indication why Simmons was asked to join the Mothers). Reissued by Collectors' Choice music, this will no longer cost you triple digit dollars to obtain.

H) *Grow Fins* by Captain Beefheart and His Magic Band (rock, 1999). Included on this list because of one spectacular track from Australian radio, "Orange Claw Hammer." This 1975 recording features Zappa accompanying Beefheart on acoustic guitar (on *Trout Mask Replica*, the song is a cappella). The result is a cross between a sea chanty and a Dylan song like "It's A Hard Rain's A-Gonna Fall." This box set also features the house "field recordings" of *Trout Mask Replica* done before the Captain asked Frank to move the band into a studio.

I) *Jefferson Airplane Loves You* by Jefferson Airplane (rock, 1992). Included here because of one 1968 recording, "Would You Like A Snack?" (no deep relation to the *200 Motels* ditty). This curious little "art song" features Grace Slick singing and playing piano with the Mothers of Invention. The improvisation, co-written by Zappa and Slick, has lyrics that could be about either hemophilia or menstruation ("help a bleeder ... give her a snack"); if the latter, this might be a rare feminist moment for Frank.

Although brief, this offers an intriguing glimpse into what might have happened if Zappa had had the time to produce *After Bathing At Baxter's* for the Airplane. And "A Small Package Of Value Will Be Coming To You Shortly" off that album seems somewhat indebted to Frank for its sonic experimentation after you hear this track.

J) *Good Singin' Good Playin'* by Grand Funk Railroad (rock, 1976). Here's a production by Zappa that many folks are not aware of. Populist boogie rock meets Frank? He was a complicated guy ... . The album offers a compelling song cycle of lyrics moving from a breakup ("Just Couldn't Wait") through pain ("Miss My Baby") to redemption and renewal ("Release Your Love," "Goin' For The Pastor"). In addition to crisp production values, Zappa contributes a blistering lead solo on "Out To Get You" and vocal wackiness on "Rubberneck" (the latter on the 1999 CD reissue only). Frank aside, "Crossfire" is a greatly emotional up-tempo ballad that deserved more attention than the disco era gave it. Frank could have produced a hit album here; the stars just weren't in the proper alignment.

K) *Permanent Damage* by the GTO's (rock, 1969). Another more sociologically oriented production by Zappa, this time of a band of groupie vocalists. Turning groupies into a girl group is an interestingly empowering notion: putting the backstage crowd on center stage, making them the rock goddesses. Lots of rockers were willing to help out, including Jeff Beck, Rod Stewart, Lowell George and Davy Jones of the Monkees (not all credited on the sleeve). The singing has a glee club feel to it (i.e., not professionally trained), but is nonetheless charming. The lyrics offer many insights into groupie interests and obsessions. "Do Me In Once & I'll Be Sad, Do Me In Twice & I'll Know Better (Circular Circulation)" has a hook that has stayed in my craw for over thirty years—and a fine vocal from Miss Pamela (aka Pamela Des Barres).

L) *Frankly A Cappella: The Persuasions Sing Zappa* by the Persuasions (rock, 2000). Another one of the better tribute releases, showing that Frank's music works even when rendered (almost entirely) a cappella. You would expect an early song like "Anyway The Wind Blows" to work well, with its close ties to Frank's own pre-Mothers doo wop writing with Ray Collins (most noteworthily, of "Memories of El Monte" for the Penguins). But surprisingly, later material comes off great as well, because of the rhthymic and chordal inventiveness of the group ("Hot Plate Heaven At The Green Hotel," "You Are What You Is," "Find Her Finer"). "Tears Begin To Fall" takes on an elegiac tone by dint of its concluding position. A sincere gesture from a band with soul to burn.

M) *Take Your Clothes Off When You Dance* by The Ed Palermo Big Band (jazz, 2006 [recorded 2005]). This recording features big band arrangements of Frank Zappa material by Ed Palermo. As with Ensemble Ambrosius, you're hearing different sonic approaches—since they are not just playing Grand Wazoo arrangements but also performing their own adaptations of works not scored for big band. Great players doing fine solos off compelling charts provides an entry for regular jazz fans into the Zappa canon. Highlights include Emedin Rivera's Brazilian percussion effects on the title track, a melancholy and subtle "Sleep Dirt," a funky "Gumbo Variations," a suitable medley of "Mom and Dad" and "Oh No" (replete with vocals) and a punchy version of "Moggio." You can feel the love for the music here.

N) *Prophetic Attitude: Le Concert Impromptu & Bossini Play Frank Zappa* by Le Concert Impromptu and Bossini (classical, 1997). A well-meaning tribute recording from a French ensemble that suffers only in comparison with the Ensembles Modern and Ambrosius. This disc is less rocking than these other classical groups—its sound is thinner (relatively), less busy, less textured. It sounds more like so-called "classical musicians" playing rock than musicians willing to translate Zappa's emotions and nuances (which he called "eyebrows") into another musical medium. The playlist is easier on this recording as well. Nevertheless, I mention it for several reasons. Some of their covers are pleasant: "Cleetus Awreetus-Awrightus" is nicely jaunty; "Peaches En Regalia" bops. But more importantly, there are two Zappa compositions only available here: the brief "Wind Quintet" (very complex and fast), and the less remarkable "Number 6." Completists will be interested as a result.

O) *The Nova Convention* by various artists (spoken word [primarily], 1979). This tribute to William S. Burroughs includes Frank reading "The Talking Asshole" section of *Naked Lunch*. Besides its intrinsic interest, there are conceptual continuity issues. Zappa borrows Burroughs' references to UDT (undifferentiated tissue) in the storyline for *The Grand Wazoo*.

P) *For Real* by Ruben and the Jets (rock, 1973). Zappa produced this band which emulated and extended his Ruben and the Jets pachuco persona on the Mothers release. It is not a pastiche, however; these guys ARE "for real." They sound pretty good too, as they should: their personnel overlaps with Zappa's own bands (Tony Duran on guitars, Motorhead Sherwood on saxophone). Zappa wrote one song for them ("If I Could Only Be Your Love Again") and arranged several, in addition to producing everything. Highlights include their cover of "Dedicated To The One I Love" and a fine FM-friendly Duran tune ("Show Me The Way To Your Heart"). Another Zappa mainstream effort unfairly cursed by the radio gods.

Q) *A Chance Operation: The John Cage Tribute* by various artists (classical [primarily], 1993. Zappa gets the plum assignment of playing Cage's breakthrough "4'33"." A rare example of Frank on solo piano. If you don't know about this piece, I won't spoil it for you.[5] Suffice it to say, you will detect its influence on "Waffenspiel" from *Civilization Phaze III*.

R) *Sandy's Album Is Here At Last!* by Sandy Hurvitz (rock, 1967). Actually, this music would be better described as piano-based jazz folk. One listen and you will realize that the far more successful Laura Nyro was not operating in a vacuum. This album presciently antedates the female singer-songwriter boom by about a year. Its presence on this list is far more problematic, as the only remaining Zappa connection is his picture on a television set on the cover proclaiming the title in a word balloon. Turns out he intended to produce the session, but Sandy walked out of the studio over a disagreement with Frank about the production of "Arch Godliness of Purplefull Magic," resulting in his turning over the reins to new Mother Ian Underwood. As Hurvitz ruefully observes in the liner notes, "[i]t was one of a list of really wise things I've done in the course of my career."

For Sandy at the time was an actual member of the Mothers of Invention at Zappa's behest. She filled in for Don Preston when he was ill at one of the Garrick Theater shows in New York and ended up doing vocal duets with Ray Collins and other theatrical bits for the performance art / music hybrid that was the band at this time. Frank gave her the name "Uncle Meat" until she objected to it, the beginning of an increasing strain in their relationship. She lasted as a Mother through their first brief European tour in the fall of 1967, followed by the eruption in the studio and her departure. Historically, Sandy was the first artist Frank signed to his new Bizarre label (in 1967).

So this recording has everything Bizarre but Frank himself (except for the cover pic) because of the rift: a Cal Schenkel cover design (then her boyfriend), Herb Cohen production supervision, Dick Kunc engineering and Ian Underwood standing in for Frank in the booth. Certainly it's of more historical interest than anything else—both Zappa's history and the history of the sixties. The lyrical optimism of "Many Different Things" ("There are many different worlds in this world / where I hope you get to go") provides a veritable time capsule of that year and that season: I can almost smell the patchouli incense! But couldn't we use a little time travel back to that era (even if we weren't born yet)? On three tracks she has the jazz legend-to-be Eddie Gomez on bass; on "The Sun" Ian Underwood contributes a lovely sax solo (he provided them for other tracks, then deleted them for a more stripped-down feel). But it's Frank's spirit that is most interesting here: this would have been an even more surprising choice for an act to produce than Grand Funk if they had gotten along. Oh well. One can only hope that Joe Travers finds in the vaults for our delectation the backing track of "Arch Godliness of Purplefull Magic" that the Mothers, including Zappa, played on (the fight happened before she added her vocals). Perhaps it was fate, since the lyrics were a straight-up lament about a guy not wanting to drop acid with her! Oh, and here's the punchline: Sandy Hurvitz changed her name to Essra Mohawk, under which *nom de plume* she still enjoys an enormous cult following!

Strictly Genteel

Well, that's it. Been swell having you with us tonight, folks. Frank Zappa once said in an interview: "I would say that my entire life has been one massive failure" (Kostelantz 218)—a self-evaluation others of our artists will also make (e.g., Sun Ra). A corollary to his frequent claim that stupidity was the "basic building block of the universe," one is tempted to reject the claim. If Zappa's career was a failure, what would success look like?

But let us tarry seriously with his remark. In context, he is suggesting that he would have done it all even better if he could have—that the music in his head was always compromised by the economic, human and technical means at his disposal to realize it for a listener. Frank Zappa was a musical platonist, in short. He was always striving for musical goals almost beyond human possibility. With the Synclavier, the Ensemble Modern, and some moments with some of the rock bands, he had a pisgah view of that watermelon in easter hay he sought: the creation of perfect music in a flawed world. In this respect, Frank was not unlike his mentor Edgard Varese, who also longed for a technology to realize his ideals. Surely such a sonic adventurer as Frank Zappa will never be forgotten as long as there are beings around who can process his creations. If Samuel Beckett left a "stain upon the silence" of the cosmos, Frank Zappa left us a lot of beautiful and interesting notes—and some memorable dada theater. And more, more, more ... . There is really so much more to say, but I'll leave that to you after you hear and see this material.

Works Cited

Beefheart, Captain, and His Magic Band. *Grow Fins: Rarities [1965-1982]*. Revenant 210. Liner notes by John "Drumbo" French.

Burroughs, William S. *Naked Lunch*. 1959; rpt. New York: Grove Press, 1992.

Gritter, Headley. *Rock 'N' Roll Asylum: Conversations With The Madmen of Music*. New York: Delilah, 1984.

Kostelantz, Richard, ed. *The Frank Zappa Companion: Four Decades of Commentary*. New York: Schirmer Books, 1997.

Lennon, Nigey. *Being Frank: My Time With Frank Zappa*. Los Angeles: California Classics Books, 1995.

Russo, Greg. *Cosmik Debris: The Collected History and Improvisations of Frank Zappa*. Revised edition. Floral Park, NY: Crossfire Publications, 1999.

Sheff, David. *The Playboy Interviews with John Lennon & Yoko Ono*. Ed. G. Barry Golson. New York: Berkley, 1982.

Swenson, John. "Frank Zappa: The Interview." *Guitar World*. March 1982, pp. 35,49,72-3.

Watson, Ben. *Frank Zappa: The Negative Dialectics of Poodle Play*. New York: St. Martin's, 1993.

Whitely, Sheila. *The Space Between the Notes: Rock and the Counterculture*. New York: Routledge, 1992.

Zappa, Frank. *Beat The Boots! Limited Edition Box Set #2*. Rhino, 1992. Scrapbook.

——. *Cruising With Ruben & The Jets*. Rykodisc RCD 10063. 1968, reissued 1985. Liner notes by Frank Zappa.

——. *Frank Zappa Plays The Music Of Frank Zappa: A Memorial Tribute*. UMRK 02. 1996. Liner notes by Dweezil Zappa.

——. *Freak Out!* Verve V-5005-2. 1966. Liner notes by Frank Zappa.

——. *The Real Frank Zappa Book*. With Peter Occhiogrosso. New York: Poseidon Press, 1989.

——. *Them Or Us: The Book*. Los Angeles.- Frank Zappa, 1984.

——. *Uncle Meat*. Bizarre 2024. 1969. Liner notes by Frank Zappa.

——, dir. *Uncle Meat: The Mothers Of Invention Movie*. MPI 4002. 1987. Box notes by Frank Zappa.

——. *You Are What You Is*. Barking Pumpkin PW2 37537. 1981. Liner notes by Frank Zappa.

——. *Zappa In New York*. Discreet 2D 2290. 1978. Liner notes by Frank Zappa.

I am not listing the complete discography in detail here, as it can be found in the body of the chapter. Obsessives should consult Greg Russo for complete, if occasionally inaccurate, information. Ben Watson is almost as helpful and arguably more reliable.

Works Consulted

Des Barres, Pamela. *I'm With The Band: Confessions of a Groupie*. New York: Jove Books, 1988.

Harris, Suzannah (Thana). *Under the Same Moon: My Life with Frank Zappa, Steve Vai, Bob Harris, and a community of other artistic souls*. Revised edition. New Castle, CO: Mastahna Publishing, 1999.

Menn, Donn, ed. *Zappa!* (From the publishers of Keyboard and Guitar Player). 1992.

Walley, David. *No Commercial Potential: The Saga of Frank Zappa & The Mothers of Invention*. New York: E. P. Dutton & Co., 1972.

Appendix: Ranked Titles by Genre and Thematic Mix Tape Suggestions

I. Ranked Titles by Genre

  a) Rock Instrumental
     1. *Frank Zappa Plays The Music of Frank Zappa: A Memorial Tribute*
     2. *Trance-Fusion*
     3. *Guitar*
     4. *Shut Up 'N Play Yer Guitar*

  b) Rock
     1. *You Can't Do That On Stage Anymore, Volume 2: The Helsinki Concert*
     2. *We're Only In It For The Money*
     3. *Lumpy Money*
     4. *Ship Arriving Too Late To Save A Drowning Witch*
     5. *Mothermania: The Best of the Mothers*
     6. *Absolutely Free*
     7. *Broadway the Hard Way*
     8. *Roxy & Elsewhere*
     9. *One Size Fits All*
     10. *Tinseltown Rebellion*
     11. *Joe's Garage*
     12. *Bongo Fury*
     13. *You Are What You Is*
     14. *Sheik Yerbouti*
     15. *The Making of Freak Out!: An FZ Audio Documentary*
     16. *Freak Out!*
     17. *Zoot Allures*
     18. *Road Tapes Venue #1: Kerrisdale Arena, Vancouver B.C., 25 August 1968*
     19. *QuAUDIOPHILIAc*
     20. *Philly '76*
     21. *Carnegie Hall*
     22. *FZ:OZ*
     23. *Joe's Menage*

Works Consulted

24. *Hammersmith Odeon*
25. *Lather*
26. *Zappa in New York*
27. *Unmitigated Audacity*
28. *Freaks and Motherfu*#@%!*
29. *Disconnected Synapses*
30. *200 Motels*
31. *Just Another Band From L. A.*
32. *Swiss Cheese/ Fire!*
33. *Playground Psychotics*
34. *You Can't Do That On Stage Anymore, Volume 6*
35. *You Can't Do That On Stage Anymore, Volume 4*
36. *Greasy Love Songs*
37. *Cruising With Ruben & The Jets*
38. *Make A Jazz Noise Here*
39. *Over-Nite Sensation*
40. *Them Or Us*
41. *Uncle Meat*
42. *Frank Zappa Meets The Mothers Of Prevention*
43. *Weasels Ripped My Flesh*
44. *Burnt Weeny Sandwich*
45. *The Dub Room Special!*
46. *Does Humor Belong In Music?*
47. *Halloween*
48. *You Can't Do That On Stage Anymore, Volume 1*
49. *At The Circus*
50. *The Man From Utopia*
51. *Baby Snakes*
52. *one shot deal*
53. *Studio Tan*
54. *Buffalo*
55. *You Can't Do That On Stage Anymore, Volume 5*
56. *Conceptual Continuity*
57. *Our Man In Nirvana*
58. *The Best Band You Never Heard In Your Life*
59. *Ahead Of Their Time*

60. *You Can't Do That On Stage Anymore, Volume 3*
61. *Tenga Na Minchia Tanta*
62. *Thing-Fish*
63. *Fillmore East, June 1971*
64. *Chunga's Revenge*
65. *Apostrophe*
66. *'Tis The Season To Be Jelly*
67. *The Ark*
68. *The Lost Episodes*
69. *Mystery Disc*
70. *Joe's Corsage*
71. *As An Am*
72. *Anyway The Wind Blows*
73. *Saarbrucken 1979*
74. *Electric Aunt Jemima*
75. *Joe's Xmasage*
76. *Rare Meat*

c) Jazz

1. *Sleep Dirt*
2. *QuAUDIOPHILIAc*
3. *Hot Rats: Waka / Jawaka*
4. *Lather*
5. *Piquantique*
6. *Make A Jazz Noise Here*
7. *Uncle Meat*
8. *Weasels Ripped My Flesh*
9. *Burnt Weeny Sandwich*
10. *Wazoo*
11. *Finer Moments*
12. *Jazz From Hell*
13. *Hot Rats*
14. *Imaginary Diseases*
15. *The Grand Wazoo*
16. *Joe's Domage*

d) Classical

1. *Everything Is Healing Nicely*

Works Consulted

2. *Boulez Conducts Zappa: The Perfect Stranger*
3. *200 Motels*
4. *The Yellow Shark*
5. *Civilization Phaze III*
6. *Feeding the Monkeys at Ma Maison*
7. *London Symphony Orchestra Volumes I and II*
8. *Finer Moments*
9. *Orchestral Favorites*
10. *Lumpy Gravy*
11. *Francesco Zappa*

e) Synclavier

1. *Boulez Conducts Zappa: The Perfect Stranger*
2. *Civilization Phaze III*
3. *Frank Zappa Meets The Mothers Of Prevention*
4. *Jazz From Hell*
5. *Francesco Zappa*
6. *"Congress Shall Make No Law ... "*

II. Thematic Mix Tape Suggestions

a) For Lovers Only

1. "It's His Voice On The Radio (Lonely Little Girl)"—*We're Only In It For The Money*
2. "The Duke of Prunes"—*Absolutely Free*
3. "Brown Shoes Don't Make It" —*Absolutely Free*
4. "Pick Me, I'm Clean"—*Tinseltown Rebellion*
5. "Sy Borg"—*Joe's Garage*
6. "Flambay"—*Sleep Dirt*
7. "No Not Now"—*Ship Arriving Too Late To Save A Drowning Witch*
8. "Shove It Right In"—*200 Motels*
9. "Magdalena"—*Just Another Band From L. A.*
10. "Oh No"—*Weasels Ripped My Flesh*
11. "Carolina Hard-Core Ecstasy"—*Bongo Fury*
12. "Lucille Has Messed My Mind Up"—*Joe's Garage*
13. "Any Kind Of Pain"—*Broadway the Hard Way*

b) Zappa Country

1. "Harder Than Your Husband"—*You Are What You Is*
2. "No Not Now"—*Ship Arriving Too Late To Save A Drowning Witch*
3. "Lonesome Cowboy Burt"—*200 Motels*
4. "It Just Might Be A One-Shot Deal"—*Hot Rats: Waka / Jawaka*
5. "Truck Driver Divorce"—*Them Or Us*
6. "Ring Of Fire"—*The Best Band You Never Heard In Your Life*
7. "Dinah-Moe Humm," —*Philly '76*

c) Dental Hygiene Dilemmas

1. "I'm Stealing The Towels / Dental Hygiene Dilemma / Does This Kind Of Life Look Interesting To You?"—*200 Motels*
2. "Baby, Take Your Teeth Out"—*Them Or Us*
3. "The Talking Asshole"—*The Nova Convention*
4. "Montana"—*Over-Nite Sensation*
5. "Charlie's Enormous Mouth"—*You Are What You Is*

d) Poodle Play (apologies to Ben Watson)

1. "The Purse"—*Joe's Xmasage*
2. "The Poodle Lecture"—*You Can't Do That On Stage Anymore, Volume 6*
3. "Dirty Love"—*Over-Nite Sensation*
4. "Evelyn, A Modified Dog"—*One Size Fits All*
5. "Dog Breath Variations"—*Uncle Meat*
6. "Dog Breath"—*Uncle Meat*
7. "Babbette"—*You Can't Do That On Stage Anymore, Volume 1*
8. "Stink-Foot"—*Apostrophe*
9. "Cheepnis"—*Roxy and Elsewhere*; *You Can't Do That On Stage Anymore, Volume 2*
10. "Stink-Foot," —*Philly '76*
11. "The Poodle Lecture," —*Philly '76*
12. "Dirty Love," —*Philly '76*

Notes

[1] 1. Frank Zappa himself seemed to have a significant admiration for Stanley Kubrick, especially *2001: A Space Odyssey*. He was careful to include a black monolith in *200 Motels*, and he throws a number of overt intertextual references to *2001* into the storyline of *Them Or Us: The Book*. For example, "We see an

exact duplication of the escape-pod scene from '*2001*' ... " or "CUT TO: The interior of the same bedroom that the '*2001*' astronaut found himself in at the end of the psychedelic optical sequence" (182).

[2]I wrote these remarks before finding these remarkable comments by Zappa in interview to the same effect:

> It's quite a challenge to reach somebody emotionally without using words that have literal connections. To perform expressively on an instrument, I have respect for that. To get to the level of performance where you are no longer thinking about operating a piece of machinery and can just project something emotional through the machinery, that is worthy of respect. Writing a song about why somebody left you, that's stupid ... .
>
> What I think of as the emotional content of music is probably a lot different than what you think of. Since I write music I know what the techniques are. If I wanted to write something that would make you weep, I could do it. There's ways to do it. It's a cheap shot.

He proceeds to elaborate how, for example, playing a lot of B notes in the key of A minor will produce "that little twinge" in the listener (in Kostelantz 216-7). This is not to deny, as Zappa takes care to explain, that he conveys powerful emotions through his music. Only that he eschews "cheap shots" to make you simply sad. He seems more moved by Bela Bartok's *Third Piano Concerto*, if we can trust Nigey Lennon (103), than one guesses he would be by the likes of Samuel Barber, Benjamin Britten or Henryk Gorecki. For what it's worth, I will vouch that Zappa's music has never intrinsically made me tear up, although it has often moved me.

For example, when I searched for a musical correlation to the intense emotion of anguish I felt after the terrorist acts of September 11, 2001, I reached for "Oh No" and "Trouble Coming Every Day" from the Zappa ouevre. They were, in effect, fast relief. Had I been capable of more reflection, I think I would have found solace also from some works on *The Yellow Shark* and parts of *Civilization Phase III*. But the works that really gave me comfort were, in ascending order, Mahler's 3rd (*mysterioso* movement), Samuel Barber's "Knoxville: Summer of 1915" and Henryk Gorecki's *Symphony No. 3* ("Symphony of Sorrowful Songs")—these last two both exquisitely rendered by soprano Dawn Upshaw. Had I (again) been more reflective, I would also have listened to Arnold Schoenberg's "A Survivor From Warsaw" and Krystof Penderecki's "Threnody for the Victims of Hiroshima."

I guess my point is that there are no right answers here when it comes to this vital dimension of music. Beyond the love song and its banalities, there are no real "cheap shots" in music—if they give you what you need when you need it. Evaluation of aesthetic legitimacy is a luxury the non-grieving have. The untimely death of Frank Zappa spared him from having to confront the events those who lived beyond him long enough have to process, but I think he would have risen to the occasion. His fondness at the end of his life for the Chieftains and the tantalizing emotional depth of late Zappa compostions suggest he was learning how to convey the deepest emotional registers with the consummate skill of our greatest classical composers. Like Stanley Kubrick (or Schoenberg, for that matter), Zappa gets an undeservedly bad rap for being cold and clinical. That's not what I hear in those billions of notes, his sonic valentine to a crazy world. This footnote needs to be dated: September 14, 2001.

[3] I am indebted to Hillary Enslinger for this observation.

[4] It dawned on me that I should unpack this peculiar claim! Sheila Whitely, in her interesting book *The Space Between the Notes*, makes the observation in her final chapter that *The Dark Side of the Moon* is a kind of book-end to *Sergeant Pepper* and the psychedelic / counterculture project (104). Whereas the Beatles were somewhat hopeful about the prospects of the new consciousness, Pink Floyd—a far spacier group initially—came up with a song cycle using psychedelic production to address issues of workaholism ("On the Run"), mutability ("Time"), mortality ("The Great Gig in the Sky"), materialism ("Money"), power ("Us and Them") and madness ("Brain Damage"). Not only does the amazing psychedelic journey not allow you to evade existential issues, it ultimately heightens your awareness of them. And with the corporate management of the counterculture, anything oppositional about a band like the Floyd is exiled to "the dark side of the moon:" the underground has become the invisible (insofar as it still exists). It's all between the lines now.

I would submit that Zappa makes a parallel set of moves on *Over-Nite Sensation*. The opener "Camarillo Brillo" addresses the reduction of the counterculture to a set of accessories for room decoration. The album's obsession with sexual themes provides an earthy existentialism as well. "I'm the Slime" addresses the creeping one-dimensional fascism that has replaced the hippie dream of utopia; "Fifty-Fifty" is about the ultimate ineffectuality of the culture industry for making oppositional pronouncements, a swearing off (for the moment) of the grand statement. And "Montana" is Zappa's metaphoric parallel to the dark side of the moon; he no longer resides where he once did. What he represents is way out on the margins; he is also invisible, "plucking the old dental floss."

Similar turns can be found in a number of lyricists of this era, most notably Bob Dylan in his move from *Blonde on Blonde* to *John Wesley Harding*: "Don't go mistaking paradise / For that house on down the road" ("The Ballad of Frankie Lee and Judas Priest").

[5] For example, if you're the kind of reader who skips introductions to books!

Neil Young: Prisoner of Avant-Pop

Upon casual consideration, it might seem peculiar to be discussing the career of Neil Young in tandem with those of Yoko Ono and Frank Zappa. Neil's music, overall, is far more commercial and accessible than either of the latter artists. And yet I wish to suggest that Young truly is an avant-gardist of pop music on several major counts.

First, because of who he is— his phenomenology, if you will. The voice of Neil Young itself is one of the most unusual in rock music. His mother Rassy once observed: "Everybody said that Neil couldn't sing except me ... I said 'It's an interesting key but if that's your key, who cares'" (Einarson 76). Even though the rough voice of Bob Dylan was accepted ultimately as a vocal option, Neil's voice presented further challenges that many listeners still have not accepted. It is a banshee wail at times, almost a falsetto, that seems to force the listener into an intimate relationship with the lyric or even the abject moaning (again, in a Kristevan sense); a voice of secrets revealed and raw pain uncovered, a confessional voice, the opposite of showmanship in any conventional sense. It is the naked rock and roll voice, heard only rarely: Elvis Presley's *Sun Sessions*, Bob Dylan's "I'm Not There" from the basement tapes (now available on the soundtrack CD for the film of that name), John Lennon on the *Plastic Ono Band* solo recording ... maybe even bluesman Pat Hare singing "I'm Gonna Murder My Baby" before he gets around to doing it. But Neil's voice is usually in this hallowed ground other artists only occasionally reach at moments of peak intensity. Like Frank Sinatra (in a very different way), Neil Young's voice always hits the ground running ... but running scared. (And certainly Roy Orbison sounds like a precursor in some ways.) Neil's voice is well suited for murder ballads ("Down by the River"), gothic paranoia ("Don't Let It Bring You Down"), Blakean songs of childhood innocence ("I Am A Child") and political jeremiads ("Ohio"). Its time of day is twilight or dawn, its season autumn, its book something by Ray Bradbury (*The October Country* or *Something Wicked This Way Comes*); its mode of transport a railroad. It is a campfire voice, which is why Neil occasionally records it beside a crackling fire ("Soldier," "Will to Love"). At times it's a queer voice ("Philadelphia"), a genderfuck voice: "If I hadn't of been a woman / I guess I'd never have been caught" ("The Last Trip to Tulsa"). Its region is North Ontario, when all is said and done—for its apotheosis is the song "Helpless." It can haunt you like all these things and places.

Then Neil adds instruments to it: a chopping, axe-wielding version of acoustic guitar ("Dance, Dance, Dance," "Heart of Gold"), harmonica so intense that it can sound like he's chewing the instrument ("Ambulance Blues"), piano that sounds like thinking out loud ("Borrowed Tune") or just honky tonkin' ("Speakin' Out"). And like Zappa, Neil is one of the greatest post-Hendrix electric guitarists. His signature black Les Paul enables him to get a tone color and distortion that leads to majestic air sculpture orbits for his Blakean electric jams of experience. Without any of Zappa's metric complexity, Neil manages through sheer emotional force and volume to produce lengthy and even repetitive solos that are nonetheless compelling to hear again and again: "Down by the River," "Cowgirl in the Sand," "Southern Man," "Cortez the Killer," "Like a Hurricane," "Love to Burn," "Love and Only Love."

In addition to Neil's phenomenology, there are his many masks (already alluded to). Neil Young is every bit as protean a figure as David Bowie; he just doesn't spend as much on the costumes! There are the songs of innocence sung in a childlike way—from "Sugar Mountain" and "I Am A Child" through

"Philadelphia" to "Daddy Went Walkin' " and "Red Sun." This confessional style hearkens back to an era when the listening audience hung on every word of their singer / songwriter faves—when one had to look for guidance in turbulent times to the relevant troubadours. Whence the importance of Crosby, Stills, Nash and Young's one moment of glory on the album *Déjà Vu*: for a few months, they had a generation in the palm of their collective hand.

Or there is "political" Neil: a master of ambiguity inviting audience projection into the song of their own values. Neil Young himself, as we shall see, is always "lefting and then righting / it's not a crime, you know" ("Are You Ready for the Country?"). And Native American Neil, the "Hollywood Indian" of the Buffalo Springfield days. No doubt possessed of a drop of Native American blood on his father's side, Neil nonetheless messes with ethnicity as he does with gender. At times, he traffics in a mythic essentialism conjuring up a "homeland" he's never seen: "Broken Arrow," "Cortez the Killer," "Pocahontas," "Like an Inca," "Inca Queen."

A less thought of, but equally prevalent mask, is Neil the proto-Goth folkie. Before Joy Division, Neil had been writing some of the gloomiest songs available in a pop format: "The Old Laughing Lady," "Don't Let It Bring You Down," "Harvest," "Tired Eyes," "Revolution Blues," "On the Beach," "Ambulance Blues." (And after them, for that matter—"Misfits," "The Great Divide.") All of these masks (and there are others besides, like the country rocker and the gentleman farmer) can recur at any time in the career. Unlike Bowie, Neil never lays any of these permanently to rest. They can be invoked at any time if so desired. These are Neil's synchronic options.

One way that Neil expresses his various personae is through the bands he chooses to work with, especially his more durable compatriots such as Crazy Horse and Crosby, Stills, Nash, and Young (CSN & Y). Certain personae become more viable with certain accompanists. For example, Crazy Horse lack the generational clout of CSN & Y and are thus not typically Neil's preferred venue for political lyrics—a big exception here would be *Greendale*. (In fact, these choices affect Young's phenomenological presence as well: when he wants to sound especially ragged and raw, Crazy Horse are the natural choice.)

Finally, in addition to Neil's phenomenology and synchronic masks, there is his diachronic behavior, the history of his career. On the liner notes to *Decade*, Neil talked about wanting to drive said career into the "ditch" to see the more interesting people on the margins. More dramatically, he has also claimed he's "someone who's always tried systematically to destroy the very basis of my record-buying public ... that's what keeps me alive" (Petridis back cover). Neil may be perhaps too revered and canonized at this point to pull it off: his nineties work with Pearl Jam, his raw instrumental soundtrack for Jim Jarmusch's *Dead Man* and even his CD of pure feedback (*Arc*) didn't seem to upset the fan base too much. *Sleeps With Angels* (1994) will be considered as a special case here. For it raises an interesting theoretical question, hinted at by its black Reprise label echoing the label for *Tonight's The Night*, regarding the status of a repeated avant-garde gesture. Can you make the same transgressive move twice, as this CD does by mourning Kurt Cobain and David Briggs as he once did Danny Whitten and Bruce Berry? (And form fits function here, since the songs repeat melodies from other songs; the entire CD is about repetition on some level.) But he did thoroughly run his career into the ditch twice previously, creating some of his most challenging and rewarding work.

In the early seventies, Neil followed up the commercial smash *Harvest* with an obscure experimental film (*Journey Through the Past*) and a series of increasingly morose confessional recordings engaging the heroin deaths of friends Danny Whitten (guitarist for Crazy Horse) and Bruce Berry (roadie), the breakup of his relationship with Carrie Snodgress, and the general malaise of the death of the sixties and the Watergate scandal: *Time Fades Away, Tonight's The Night, On The Beach*. During this era, Neil even participated in the one musical project of his that was so underground that it has never seen the light of day (except for a few bootleg cassettes). In the summer of 1977, Young played with ex-members of Moby Grape in the Santa Cruz area. Their band, called the Ducks (because of a jocoserious symbolic attempt to lift an environmental curse off the place resultant from a surfer running over some ducks [Downing 136]), remains the stuff of legends. For after all, there are few more radical gestures an artist with mass appeal can do than hide his light under a bushel by narrowcasting his art deliberately under the most ephemeral of circumstances. The Ducks were not a money-making proposition—especially after the house he rented got burglarized (Downing 137). After this self-imposed eclipse, Neil readily resurrected himself with other work such as *Zuma* (with Crazy Horse), *Comes A Time* and *Rust Never Sleeps* (also with Crazy Horse).

In the early 1980s, Neil headed for the ditch again after signing with Geffen records. *Trans* (1982) emulated Kraftwerk and concealed the Neil Voice through vocoders. His next album, *Everybody's Rockin'* (1983) offered Neil as a rockabilly sleazoid in a gesture of high postmodern pastiche. By the time Neil offered David Geffen a third album of serious if slightly skewed country and western stylings, *Old Ways* (eventually released in 1985), Geffen was suing Young for three million dollars. The charges? Hold onto your hat: Neil's product was neither "commercial" nor "characteristic of Neil Young" (Downing 175). Neil Young had ceased to be Neil Young; or more to the point, Neil Young had ceased to be "Neil Young" (TM). As with the previous *Tonight's The Night* and the subsequent *Sleeps With Angels*, Neil seemed to be using his career to raise theoretical issues about authenticity and simulation. (Since at least "Mr. Soul" with the Buffalo Springfield, Neil's lyrics have been intrigued by and concerned with how fame turns one into a double of oneself, "the event of the season.")

Neil Young: Prisoner of Avant-Pop 137

As with the dip in the seventies, Neil slowly turned things around. On the legal front, he calmed Geffen down with an obvious squelch:

> I told them the longer you sue me for making country music, the longer I'm going to play country music forever. And then you won't be able to sue me anymore because country music will be what I always do, so it won't be uncharacteristic anymore, hahaha. So stop telling me what to do or I'll turn into George Jones. (Petridis 35-6)

Musically, he returned to rock, eventually back with Crazy Horse (*Life*, 1987), blues (*This Note's For You*, 1988) and a "characteristic," semi-confessional, recognizable "Neil Young" album (*Freedom*, 1989). His fan base was reassured, but he had spent most of the decade problematizing who he was—or even that he was—in ways David Bowie could only dream of.

I will spend the rest of this chapter elaborating upon and illustrating these broad claims about Neil Young's work. Unlike the efforts of Frank Zappa, Neil's work has received little theoretical attention—as opposed to biography and discography. So these remarks will hopefully break some ground for later folks. More problematically, my concentration on what makes Neil Young an avant-pop musician underemphasizes some of Neil's very best work which is lovely, but not necessarily avant-garde: his Buffalo-Springfield-era psychedelia, which extended the studio experimentation of the Beatles ("Expecting to Fly," "Broken Arrow"); his foray into punk (*Rust Never Sleeps*); beautiful consolidations of his most accessible country-folk such as *Comes A Time* and *Harvest Moon*. The psychedelia and punk are too belated to be on the cutting edge (although paradoxically, the 1973 tour of Europe covering material from *Tonight's The Night* became a major influence on punk—even as Crazy Horse inspired garage and grunge stylings); the latter country-folk is too mainstream for these purposes. Fortunately, that still leaves a lot to talk about.

Phenomenology Continued: Crazy Horse

When Neil Young's second solo album (*Everybody Knows This Is Nowhere*) was released in May of 1969, a new rock sound was created. This new sound was a culmination of a trajectory that Young had been charting since his early work in Canada. The sound Crazy Horse produced, especially in the extended tracks "Down by the River" and "Cowgirl in the Sand," was a fierce flurry of guitar interplay, staccato single-note guitar solo bursts, open-tuned power chords, whammy bar and tremolo abuse: hard rocking minimalism vs. virtuosity, "garage folk" (Downing 50). Although Neil's love of distortion devices for his guitar owed something to Jimi Hendrix's experimentalism, the Crazy Horse sound was antipodal to the kind of extended jamming other sixties musicians were doing (e.g., Cream and their many imitators). Neil's music was about raw emotion and persistence—not control, speed, precision.

He got there after a long musical journey that began in Winnipeg, Canada, with a series of guitar-based instrumental bands (the Jades, the Squires). Like the Beatles, Neil Young was especially enamored of Hank Marvin's British instrumental group, the Shadows—backup players for skiffle king Cliff Richard (Einarson 64). Even as Zappa's ethnic marginality led him to atypically explore rhythm and blues race records most white teenagers would be scared to slap on the turntable, Neil's Canadian environment gave him access to both English and American popular culture: skiffle, country, folk, r & b, rock and roll. Neil's first approximation of the Crazy Horse sound was with the Squires in the fall of 1964 at clubs in Fort William (later to become Thunder Bay). The band performed traditional folk material with amplification:

> "It was different from anything else I did before or after," [Neil] said. "It was minor key, folk, punk, rock kind of thing. We did 'Clementine' and 'She'll Be Coming Round The Mountain.' We changed them totally with rock 'n' roll arrangements." (Petridis 4)

Folk singer Stephen Stills was impressed when he ran into this band in Fort William while touring with the Company:

> Neil was playing folk rock before anybody else ... . He had his big Gretsch, a rock 'n' roll band that had just turned from playing "Louie, Louie" to playing the popular folk songs of the day with electric guitar, drums, and bass. It was a funny band because they could go right from "Cotton Fields" to "Farmer John." (Einarson 120)

A glance at the date of these Squires suggests that, unbeknownst to the world at large, Neil Young may have played folk rock before the Byrds or Bob Dylan. But it was at some bar in Canada: no tapes were rolling, no record executives were listening. Then, in the summer of 1965, Neil's hearse "Mort" broke down in Blind River (as related with an incorrect date in "Long May You Run") (Einarson 129-130). He missed a Squires gig as a result, moved to Toronto, and would have to wait a few years to get back to a version of that unusual sound which he had pioneered.

The next landmark on the way to the Crazy Horse sound was actually the Buffalo Springfield. As with the Squires, this is more of a matter of reportage than any kind of recoverable audio document (although there is an excerpt of their last live performance on the Archives). By the time Neil Young went to Los Angeles in the spring of 1966, he had other ambitions and other musics he wanted to fuse with his previous syntheses: the power pop of the Beatles, the rawness of the Rolling Stones, the lyrical complexity of Bob Dylan. You can hear these influences on the modest amount of studio recording the band did. What we cannot hear so readily is their live sound. Neil Young and Stephen Stills pioneered the extended rhythm / lead guitar duel, trading off fiery riffs with passion and power. By November of 1967, music reporters would duly note that not only could the live Buffalo Springfield play Stills' song "Bluebird" for half an hour, but that their live musicianship surpassed that of the other bands on the bill: Cream extenders Blue Cheer and the Grateful Dead! Buffalo Springfield were the headliners at this concert, by the way (*Buffalo Springfield Box Set* 70, 56-7).

Some of the closest approximations to the live Buffalo Springfield sound that we have, of course, are the guitar duels between Stills and Young on *Four Way Street* by Crosby, Stills, Nash and Young—to say nothing of countless bootlegs which feature fierce CSNY workouts on "Down by the River." Imagine these solos played wilder, louder and faster and you can get a Pisgah view of what the live Springfield must have accomplished. Or, even better, try to get hold of a live bootleg of the Stills-Young Band on tour in 1976. This band played driving, solo-laden versions of old Springfield classics ("For What It's Worth," "Mr. Soul") and stretched out on Neil songs that CSNY featured live ("Southern Man," "Cowgirl in the Sand"). They even breathed new life into "Suite: Judy Blue Eyes" by playing it electric. Stills claimed "the spirit of Buffalo Springfield is back!" (Petridis 25). Unfortunately, none of that energy translated into the lethargic studio album this band released (*Long May You Run*); but the live performances may be as close a glimpse as we have available of the live Buffalo Springfield.

As that earlier band disintegrated, Neil Young met the much rawer Rockets in the greater Los Angeles area. Their sound, hinted at on their eponymous *White Whale* debut recording, proved to be the final click of the combination lock—from the Squires through Buffalo Springfield to the Rockets—that would release the Crazy Horse sound. Bassist Billy Talbot has observed, "Listen to 'Let Me Go' on the Rockets' album and you can hear the birth of 'Down by the River'"(Downing 48). He's right: this Danny Whitten composition features raucous and repetitive soloing, heavily distorted guitars (sounding like a buzz saw or bird screeches at times). There were three guitarists in the band alongside a bass guitarist (Whitten and the two Whitsell brothers, Leon and George)—a comparable line-up to the Springfield's triple threat of Stills, Young and Richard Furay. But this recording is much wilder than anything the latter band ever recorded. It's only a 3:47 track, but live jamming with Neil readily enabled them to stretch even in the studio. Neil Young took the Rockets' drummer (Ralph Molina), bass player (Billy Talbot) and one of the guitarists (Danny Whitten, the best writer); he left behind the violinist (except for one track on

Everybody Knows This Is Nowhere) and the other two guitarists (who wrote all the weaker stuff on side two of the eponymous debut). Thus Crazy Horse and its sound were born.

Although I don't quite agree with Neil's joke on *The Year of the Horse* CD that "it's all the same song," there is a remarkable consistency to the output of this outfit—excepting a dip in the 1980s with *Re.Ac.Tor* and (to a much lesser extent) *Life*. These will receive some consideration when we look at Neil's avant-gardism diachronically. But I want to simply note here that Crazy Horse is the yang to the yin of Neil's acoustic voice and presence duly noted at the beginning of this chapter. In 1969, Neil assisted at the creation of a great new thing, a rock sound that has reverberated down the ages into such unlikely offshoots as the Sex Pistols, Nirvana and Pearl Jam. Crazy Horse are not only the longest surviving garage band (where are the Premiers now?); they lived to make Neil the Godfather of both punk and grunge. These are the same claims justifiably made for Iggy Pop and his band the Stooges. Both Crazy Horse and the Stooges released their debut albums in 1969. Both drew critical interest, but were seen as aberrations from the mainstream. Who could have suspected that these two far-flung, eccentric streams would converge in the formation of several subsequent rock subgenres? (And what of the future? Surely Britney Spears isn't the last word!)

Neil Young's Masks

The earliest persona which Neil Young created in his lyric writing is the childlike innocent on the verge of experience, a mask I have been constantly thinking of in terms of William Blake's *Songs of Innocence and Experience*. While I see no evidence that Neil read Blake, we do know he was a reader of complex poetry: at a February 27, 1971 London Festival Hall concert, he said his song "The Bridge" was in response to Hart Crane (*Neil Young London 1971* bootleg). But he needn't have read Blake to have echoed his approach. Both figures are drenched in the romantic sensibility that privileges childhood and nature over adulthood and civilization. Autobiographically, the separation and subsequent divorce of Young's parents in 1960 provided a clear psychic watershed between an idyllic childhood and a troubled coming of age. Young has mined this rich contrastive vein for fifty years and counting, beginning with his first clear expression of it in 1964 on the verge of his nineteenth birthday. The resultant composition, "Sugar Mountain," is the earliest Neil Young song that he still features on a regular basis in concert. His first major work, it translates issues of transition and maturity away from autobiographical parental separation (to be confronted somewhat later, beginning with "Don't Be Denied" in 1973); in the song, "your mother and your dad" are together. Rather, it is about being exiled from "Sugar Mountain" when you turn twenty "though you're thinking that you're leaving there too soon" (Einarson 101). Some Canadian friends have told me that Sugar Mountain is a kind of teen club with an upper age limit, but I don't think this reading is necessary or inevitable. As with Blake's lyrics of innocence, the power of the song is its universality. Who hasn't worried about growing up and leaving childish ways behind?

After "Sugar Mountain," the deluge regarding this type of Young lyric! I will not attempt to list every appearance of this persona, but will rather cull a few lyric highlights. An obvious early example would be his last tune with the Buffalo Springfield, "I Am A Child."[1] The song matches a simple, beguiling melody with lyrics that capture childhood innocence without being too cloying:

> I am a child, I last awhile.
> You can't conceive of the pleasure in my smile.
> You hold my hand, rough up my hair.
> It's lots of fun to have you there.
>
> I gave to you, now you give to me.
> I'd like to know what you've learned.
> The sky is blue and so is the sea.
> What is the color, when black is burned?
> What is the color?
>
> You are a man, you understand.
> You pick me up and you lay me down again.
> You make the rules, you say what's fair.
> It's lots of fun to have you there. ("I Am A Child," 1968)

The song's subversive power lies in its acute psychological detail. The child's one question ("What is the color, when black is burned?") raises not only a paradox (if things change color when they burn, where can black go?), but evokes issues of mortality (black's color symbolism: what is our fate beyond death?) and even racism. Black people were being burned in the south; as such, this song obliquely anticipates "Southern Man" and "Alabama." Given the aporia of the child's question, his assertion to the adult that "you make the rules, you say what's fair" seems undercut by gentle irony. Adults are not all-knowing, as this song illustrates. The child-narrator has a premature awareness that society is a mere convention, a social contract of made-up rules. The truth about things is elusive—for adults as well as for children. The final line of the verses ("It's lots of fun to have you there") has the child accepting his part of this social contract—for very pragmatic reasons, undoubtedly. But the lyrics reveal a double fragility: not only of the ephemeral state of childhood itself, but of the "rules" and conventions of everyday life—apt reflections that come more easily to a child of divorce. "I Am A Child" remains one of Neil's most

Blakean lyrics, fit to be put alongside the latter's "The Chimney Sweeper" from the *Songs of Innocence*.

"Helpless" (1970) is arguably an even more archetypal song of innocence, one of Neil's all-time most popular lyrics. In the drunken frenzy of the 1973 "Tonight's The Night" tour, he would joke about how its chorus was potentially endless: you could keep singing "helpless, helpless, helpless" till the cows came home or all your demons were exorcized (*Speakin' Out* bootleg). The "town in north Ontario" alluded to is often attributed to his childhood home of Omemee, when his parents were together and all was right with the world (Einarson 22). But he needn't name it: the vagueness allows the listener to project their favorite power spot in nature into it. And furthermore, half-sister Astrid points out in her memoir that "Omemee is not in North Ontario; it's more South, actually, about seventy-five miles north east of Toronto" (16). (She speculates it might refer to Fort William instead.) The imagery is beautiful yet simple ("Yellow moon on the rise / Big birds flying across the sky, / Throwing shadows on our eyes"). The only puzzling line refers to "Blue, blue windows behind the stars"—perhaps a purely visionary moment hinting at a higher neoplatonic reality? A world behind the sensible world with "windows [looking in on it] behind the stars?" Pretty obscure for a pop hit! The melody, simple instrumentation and repetition reinforce the literally timeless feel of the tune: it gives us a small piece of eternity. Composed in a turbulent era, it offers musical comfort food. (As with most of James Taylor's work: not surprisingly, the two collaborated from time to time.)

None of Neil's subsequent songs of innocence attained quite this level of popularity, although a few came close ("Powderfinger," "Philadelphia"). "There's A World" off *Harvest* (1972) offers a typical case in point:

> There's a world you're living in
> No one else has your part
> All God's children in the wind
> Take it in and blow hard

Perhaps too universal a sentiment, rendered overly sententious by its orchestral accompaniment. "Soldier," off the much less successful *Journey Through The Past* film soundtrack, works better with its eerie juxtaposition of a combat soldier and Jesus Christ both having eyes that "shine like the sun": a comment on the ability to see beyond life to avoid the fear of death. Yet the narrator concludes the verses by saying "I wonder why." It is more of a song of doubt than belief, ultimately. And unlike "There's A World," the musical setting is incredibly simple audio verite: a piano beside a roaring fire. Oddly, it works.

Neil's other fireside composition, "The Will to Love" (from *American Stars 'N Bars*, recorded in 1976) is a much stranger affair, perhaps an equal illustration of Neil doing Dylan as Neil doing Blake. The storyline of the song concerns a fish swimming upstream to mate, driven by the "will to love." The unusual subject matter is matched by the oddly distorted vocal, the striking instrumentation and playing (vibes, strange piano improvisations and runs) ... and, yes, that crackling fire again. "Love Is A Rose" from this same era ought to also be mentioned because of its resonance with one of Blake's most memorable images ("The Sick Rose").

"Powderfinger" (1978) may seem too historically detailed to be part of this persona, but a closer examination of the lyrics reveals that the conflict described in the song cannot be pinned down chronologically (although its "feel" seems nineteenth century). It captures a supremely dramatic moment of transition from innocence to experience, a young man taking up a gun to defend his family from mysterious invaders. He is unsuccessful, being seriously outgunned:

> ... I saw black and my face splashed in the sky ...
> Just think of me as one you never figured
> Would fade away so young
> With so much left undone
> Remember me to my love, I know I'll miss her

The naivete of the narrator comes across more clearly in the bootlegged acoustic readings of the song (*Chrome Dreams*, for example) than in the searing Crazy Horse performances.

The next major instance of this persona is in the 1994 film soundtrack to *Philadelphia*. Neil's eponymous ballad concerns the moment in childhood when one discovers one's sexual identity. In the film, it plays to home movies of the childhood of the deceased protagonist (played by Tom Hanks). A rare instance of Neil dropping his typically heterosexual stance (cf. "The Last Trip to Tulsa," "The Bridge"), this song displays real sensitivity and sympathy despite the ideologically problematic dimensions of the project: mainstreaming AIDS and even gayness by packing the film with heterosexuals like Hanks, Young and Springsteen. It's still a powerful tune.

"My Heart," the opening track from *Sleeps With Angels* (1994 as well), exhibits another wide-eyed lyric about love ("I don't know what love can do"). The accompaniment of tack piano and marimba perfectly sets the jewel here. And most recently, *Silver and Gold* (2000) has brought Neil almost full circle to contemplating his Canadian childhood and the separation of his parents in songs such as "Red Sun" and "Daddy Went Walkin'." The concert video / DVD that he released showcases their power far better than the CD. Not only does Neil have a double vision on the songs from being both a son and a father, but he performs them with a gentleness and simplicity that is actually breathtaking. In his mid-fifties, he seemed closer than ever to the sunnier side of Sugar Mountain, in as easy contact with his inner child as any romantic poet.

Finally, there are also any number of Young compositions which approach these songs of innocence, but are more simple than actually childlike. These lyrics address more adult issues in a manner reminiscent of, but not equatable with, the songs discussed above. Such a list would certainly include the following in chronological order: "Till the Morning Comes" (*After The Gold Rush*), "Love in Mind" and "The Bridge" (*Time Fades Away*), "Midnight on the Bay" and "Ocean Girl" (*Long May You Run*), "You and Me" (*Harvest Moon*) and "Out of Control" (*Looking Forward*).

Another early persona developed by Neil Young is the Native American one. This image originated in the days of the Buffalo Springfield, when Neil wore Comanche jackets and posed as a "Hollywood Indian." He perpetuated this iconography by naming his new backing band Crazy Horse and by placing cigar store Indian carvings on stage at his shows.[2] More importantly, a few key songs establish this voice—starting with "Broken Arrow" (1967) off the second Buffalo Springfield album. Although this song offers little more to us than the image of a "brown-skinned / Indian on the banks that were crowded and narrow [who] / Held a broken arrow" (a symbol of ending conflict, perhaps offered as an olive branch to Canadian friend and Squires bandmate Ken Koblun, to whom the song was dedicated [Einarson 197]). Nonetheless, it anticipates more elaborate subsequent developments.

Most of these later songs concentrate on Mesoamerican cultures, especially the Aztecs and the Incas. The most famous of these is "Cortez the Killer" (from *Zuma*, 1975). The lyrics draw a contrast between the Spanish conquistador Cortez and an extremely idealized, nay mythic, court of Montezuma:

> He came dancing across the water
> With his galleons and guns
> Looking for the new world
> And that palace in the sun.
>
> On the shore lay Montezuma
> With his coca leaves [!] and pearls
> In his halls he often wandered
> With the secrets of the worlds.

Even Aztec human sacrifice is given legitimation from a multicultural perspective: "They offered life in sacrifice / So that others could go on."

The power of the song derives not only from the extraordinarily brooding guitar soloing of Crazy Horse, but also from a surprise ending which reveals the narrator to be an inadvertent time traveler exiled from this Aztec utopia and the woman he loved. Such a move is reminiscent of Dylan's final verse of "Black Diamond Bay" from his album *Desire*, a kind of narrative jump cut:

> And I know she's living there
> And she loves me to this day
> I still can't remember when
> Or how I lost my way.

The song's lush romanticism seems to undermine the force of its anti-imperialist allegory—is it about Cortez or a lost ancient love? Certainly Generalissimo Franco got some of the former message, albeit in a perhaps skewed manner: the song was banned in Spain (*Decade* liner notes).

Another complex use of this persona occurs in "Pocahontas" (1977), a lovely melody with adventurous lyrics. As with "Cortez the Killer," it posits a pre-European Native American utopia:

> Aurora borealis
> The icy sky at night
> Paddles cut the water
> In a long and hurried flight
> From the white man to the fields of green
> And the homeland we've never seen

Again, contact brings atrocity as Karl Himmel's tribal drumming kicks in to accompany the acoustic guitar:

> They killed us in our teepee
> And they cut our women down
> They might have left some babies
> Cryin' on the ground ...
> They massacred the buffalo ...

And, also as in "Cortez the Killer," the lost utopia gets feminized and eroticized:

> I wish I was a trapper
> I would give a thousand pelts
> To sleep with Pocahontas
> And find out what she felt
> In the mornin' on the fields of green
> In the homeland we've never seen

In this case, though, the anachronistic shock ending involves not the narrator's being thrust into the future, but the future being thrust into the past:

> And maybe Marlon Brando
> Will be there by the fire

> We'll sit and talk of Hollywood
> And the good things there for hire
> And the Astrodome and the first teepee
> Marlon Brando, Pocahontas and me ...

Young got the inspiration for this song after watching Sasheen Littlefeather pick up Brando's Oscar for *The Godfather* (Downing 146). But, as I have tried to suggest, it ends up not only being about much more, but also a replay with variations of the mythic terrain first elaborated upon in "Cortez the Killer." Although the latter is the more astonishing musical event as played by Crazy Horse, "Pocahontas" is tonally richer by daring to juxtapose comedy with historical tragedy. This double-edged coding of mood characterizes not only Neil's Native American persona at this time, but his work at large. (An excellent illustration would be the film *Human Highway*, his "nuclear comedy" [Long 103].) In fact, scholars like me have argued that this ambiguity is one defining indicator of whatever postmodernism was: consider other films such as *Blue Velvet* and *River's Edge*; it was no coincidence that Dennis Hopper worked on *Human Highway*. As with Crazy Horse a decade earlier, Neil Young was far ahead of the curve: by the late 1970s, he had more in common with punk and new wave than he did with band mates Crosby, Stills and Nash. "Pocahontas" displays this readily and marvelously.

Trans (1982) will merit consideration below as a challenging career moment in its own right, but let me focus on just the persona of its closing track, "Like an Inca." By now, the position of these songs is a foregone conclusion:

> Well I wish I was an Aztec
> Or a runner in Peru
> I would build such beautiful buildings
> To house the chosen few
> Like an Inca from Peru

The differences here are a reference to lost Atlantis (also featured in the Stills-Young band's song "Evening Coconut") and an explicit, post-Reagan nuclear vision of imminent destruction:

> The Gypsy told my fortune
> She said that nothin' showed
>
> Who put the bomb
> On the sacred altar?

This last imagery seems derived from the bomb-worshipping post-nuclear mutants in *Beneath the Planet of the Apes*, but it could just be an accurate observation regarding what Robert Jay Lifton called "nuclearism," a kind of sacralization of the bomb (87-99). In Young's own career, this song dovetails nicely with the apocalyptic stance taken in his under-seen film *Human Highway*. Although Neil may have romanticized economic deregulation under Reagan (see Heatley 139, for example), he had no illusions about the nuclear buildup's implied teleology.

Finally, his last major Native American statement seems to be "Inca Queen" off *Life* (1987) with Crazy Horse. Again, acoustic guitars and a lilting melody set the mood:

> Once there was an Inca queen
> She gazed at her sundial
> All around her workers carried
> Golden idols to her smile
>
> She spoke of silver from the sky
> And many floating safety boats
> To pick them up when they would fly
> Far above their dreams and hopes

The imagery borrows liberally from Erich von Daniken: the Incan culture seems to be in contact with extraterrestrial craft ("silver from the sky," cf. the "silver spaceships" in "After the Gold Rush").

The tale continues with the building of a "mountain city;" then the goddess manifests. To the strains of tropical bird song, more tribal drumming and rhythmic chanting, we learn that the "Inca queen has, Inca queen has, Inca queen has come." No grand message here, just another idyll for "the homeland we've never seen."

I will also mention a few songs that flirt with this persona without engaging it at length, both off the showcase album for this imagery (*Rust Never Sleeps*). The surreal (see below) "Ride My Llama" promises to ride him "from Peru to Texarkana"—a not-so-oblique Incan allusion. And "Sail Away" begins opining "I could live inside a teepee."

The Native American community has been typically guarded about what they make of all this; but it is safe to say that Neil Young is not the only person with some Native American ancestry to idealize the pre-contact era. And Neil puts his money where his mouth is by performing benefits for Native American causes—for example, the Red Wind Foundation that raises money for Native American housing construction (Long 69).

A third early mask Neil Young learned to wear was that of the vatic and surreal troubadour—a conscious emulation of Bob Dylan at his most complex. Neil sensed that there was "more to the picture / than meets the eye" ("My My, Hey Hey"), that a mysterious enough persona could sell the most obscure of lyrics to an eager audience. This kind of performance creates obvious problems for the critic. With these songs, the goal should not be explication necessarily. Like good modern poetry, the origin of these lyrics ranges from a clear perception communicated for an audience that's just not getting it through a private meaning one cannot really expect more than a few to get to inspired wordplay and pure surrealist imagery.

Let me illustrate with a classic and early example of all this, the second verse of "Broken Arrow" (1967):

> Eighteen years of American dream
> He saw that his brother had sworn on the wall
> He hung up his eyelids and ran down the hall
> His mother had told him a trip was a fall
> And don't mention babies at all
> Did you see him?

This verse is one of three word-pictures the song creates; it is preceded by a verse about rock stardom and followed by a strange wedding scene (cf. the much later "Misfits" from *Old Ways* to be considered below). The unifying image from the chorus is the "Indian on the banks" holding the broken arrow symbolizing concluded conflict. I have listened to this song countless times without really getting cozy with its meanings. The first line of the second verse is clear enough: this protagonist is an eighteen-year-old American male (which would make him eligible for the Vietnam draft in 1967, by the way). His "brother had sworn on the wall"? Arguably graffiti with cuss words—probably countercultural, perhaps antiwar. I've always assumed (and here we get into some weird reader-response shit) that it was an older brother (you should be of age to swear?). But there is really nothing in the song to tell me this: it could certainly be a younger brother. And it need not even be a nuclear family! It could be a hippie "brother," although the "mother" reference two lines down makes it seem more plausibly a conventional domestic scenario.

The fun really starts with "hung up his eyelids and ran down the hall." My easiest reading of this is as a reference to LSD. Hanging up one's eyelids could allude to the dilated pupils of the LSD user. This interpretation also gives me an appropriate intertext with the young man walking "on down the hall" toward an oedipal confrontation in "The End" by the Doors (who shared the bill with the Buffalo Springfield at the Whiskey in May and June 1966 well before this song was written [Long 15]). The Doors connection and the LSD hypothesis make the next line fall into place more as a revisitation of the Morrison scenario. Mom could be giving the son either an anti-drug message ("a trip was a fall"), an anti-Vietnam message (don't take that trip—a far less plausible reading) or even (a la Morrison) an oedipal warning, especially if you hear—as I do—a Klang association allowing the auditor to hear "a trip was a

BALL" instead of the intended lyric. This last devious reading does the most to explain the final line of the verse. Although babies could be unmentionable in general to a conservative mother contemplating the ways of the counterculture, a baby produced by taking a trip down the hall and balling your mother would be most transgressive and not to be mentioned. The last line could (again, very implausibly) be the mother reassuring the son she is on contraception ("don't mention babies" because you don't have to).

As you can see, this verse is a kind of Rorschach test which enables the listener to project many potential readings within a certain semantic limitation of possibility (you can't read any old thing into the song; as Stanley Fish likes to say, meaning is neither fixed nor arbitrary). We know the verse is addressing countercultural and family issues; on a deeper level, it is engaging Vietnam and incest; ultimately perhaps, it is confronting taboo death (Vietnam) and taboo sex (Oedipus and Jocasta), thanatos and eros, the two great Freudian drives. Not bad for a guy who quit school after the tenth grade.

But wait: there's more. Since the song is dedicated to Ken Koblun, it might have purely private significance for Ken which we can only overhear but not accurately interpret. (Cf. T. S. Eliot assuring us *The Waste Land* was only a piece of "rhythmical grumbling.") Who can know for sure?

I am inclined to spare you similar elaborations of this type of Neil Young mask as opposed to a partial listing of tunes that work the same way. Trust me that you can play similar interpretive games with them, and you will get very interesting results! Such a partial and chronological listing of the most obvious examples would include "The Last Trip to Tulsa" (1968; some more accessible allusions to his folk-singing career in Toronto), "After the Gold Rush" (1970; science fiction and environmental elements, but pretty damn obscure!), "Ambulance Blues" (1974; also has Canadian biographical elements to ground it somewhat), "Evening Coconut" (1976; on bootleg only; Atlantis and UFOs), "Goin' Back" (1978; a mysterious primal vision to be discussed below in another context), "Thrasher" (1979; perhaps an allegory about CSN & Y); "Sedan Delivery" (1979; a punk sound with very cryptic lyrics), "Ride My Llama" (1979; spacemen, dope and Incans), "The Old Homestead" (1980; an experiment with verse drama [assigned dialogue parts] also about CSN & Y arguably; the rider imagery echoes fantasy sequences from his first film *Journey Through The Past*), "Lost In Space" (1980; more verse drama; "marine munchkin" sped-up voices, an "infinity board" one should not draw on, and other head-scratching strangeness); "Grey Riders" (1984, *A Treasure*; more imagery reminiscent of *Journey Through The Past*), "Misfits" (1985; a "Broken Arrow" style surreal triptych with space stations and "see-through hookers;" an odd song to include on an ostensibly country-and-western outing), "Crime in the City (Sixty to Zero Part 1)" (1989; a surreal epic about a failed bank heist, the quest for a "perfect track" in a recording studio, a corrupt cop and a fireman-convict who "keeps getting younger;" even longer in live performance than in its studio version) and "Music Arcade" (1996; the "TV sky" may be an allusion to the opening sentence of William Gibson's cyberpunk masterpiece *Neuromancer*;[3] overall, a mellower and more accessible example of this persona). Give these a listen, and hit the chat rooms with your readings. Because these songs all work melodically and musically (good playing and good singing), the listener doesn't mind their surrealism and obscurity. Something seems to be happening; we just don't seem to be continuously in on it!

The previous masks are arguably derivative of other figures (or at least not original with Young)—i.e., William Blake, Black Elk, Bob Dylan. The next mask Neil begins to wear, the proto-gothic gloom rocker, seems much more of an original idea. This is not to say that it lacks antecedents, most notably in the murder ballad subgenre of traditional music. The Louvin Brothers' song "Knoxville Girl" out-creeps anything Neil accomplished in this vein. And there has always been an element of this is in the teen death songs ("Tell Laura I Love Her," "Leader of the Pack"). Literarily, one thinks of Ray Bradbury's moody atmospheres; as noted above, I think Neil comes up with music that feels remarkably like Bradbury in a gothic vein.

Having said all that, I think Neil Young is an original here—largely because he returns to this material after the first notorious new wave of serial killers and mass murderers (Ed Gein, Richard Speck). An important subset of these proto-goth songs creates a spooky urban male stalker with potential violence on his mind. The clear origin of this figure can be found in "The Loner" off his first eponymous solo album (1968). The title sounds like a book Albert Camus intended to write, and the lyrics do not disappoint:

> If you see him on the subway he'll be down at the end of the car
> Watching you move until he knows who you are
> When you get off at your station alone he'll know that you are.
>
> Know when you see him
> Nothing can free him
> Step aside, open wide
> It's the loner.

The countryish instrumental break that follows the chorus, in its incongruity, only adds to the chills. When Crazy Horse played this on the 1978 tour, Frank Sampedro did an incredible harmony line for the riff that gave it even more force and terror (see, for example, *Live Rust* [1979]).

"The Old Laughing Lady" off the same album also adds *chiaroscuro* with its tale of a feminized figure of death coming to take away various characters ("pretty Peggy," "the drunkard of the village"). The understated vocals add to the eeriness, augmented by the powerful soul backup of the likes of Merry Clayton. By the time we get to the "fever on the freeway [that] blacks out the night," we're well into the Twilight Zone. The slow vamping fade on the electric piano offers a final disturbing conclusion.

Although *Everybody Knows This Is Nowhere* has a bonafide murder ballad ("Down by the River"), it doesn't really create the feel of these two earlier songs. Perhaps this is because of the exuberant playing on it; perhaps it's because of Neil's typically ambiguous waffling about whether in fact it is a murder ballad. At one point, he claimed it was a metaphorical tale about the end of a relationship: "[t]here's no real murder in it" (Downing 51). On the other hand, when on tour with the International Harvesters in 1984, he would introduce the song as a tale about "a man who let the dark side get control of him one night" (Long 145). (He knew country audiences have fewer issues with a good murder ballad!) So these issues make our next major example "Don't Let It Bring You Down" (1970). And who could disagree here? As Alex Petridis has remarked, it's "gloriously doom-laden" (62). So much so that *Four Way Street* finds him joking with the audience to alleviate the gloom: "Here's a new song guaranteed to bring you right down. It's called 'Don't Let It Bring You Down.'" The song itself, with sparse instrumental backing, paints a series of gloomy word-pictures of "red lights flashing in the windows in the rain" while "the sirens moan," an "old man lying by the side of the road," and other urban atmospheres indicative of "castles burning." Perhaps this is also a song of innocence, since it has a wide-eyed quality of wonder at the urban goings-on. Too unfocused in theory to work, it succeeds because of the sheer conviction of its delivery—and remains one of Neil's most-loved songs (brilliantly covered by Annie Lennox, among others).

Even the cheery bestseller *Harvest* (1972) has its gothic moments: the title track has a "mother in so much pain ... screamin' in the rain" (rain is almost always an indicator of gothic doings for Neil!) and a "black face in a lonely place." This imagery seems to be a cross of vintage film noir *mise-en-scène* and moody civil rights agitprop such as the film of *Black Like Me*. "The Needle and the Damage Done" seems at least as much about relishing gloom as it is an anti-drug lyric. After all, "every junkie's like a setting sun" is an extremely ambiguous simile implying glory as well as closure.

Neil's subsequent embrace of the ditch in the next four consecutive albums yields nearly relentlessly gothic fare (to be considered more below), but I would single out as exceptional examples of same "Vampire Blues" (what's more gothic than a vampire?), "Revolution Blues" (a dramatic monologue of a Laurel Canyon massacre in the persona of Charles Manson), "On the Beach" (with its striking imagery of alienation: "I need a crowd of people / But I can't face them day to day;" "I went to the radio interview / I was standing alone at the microphone") and "Tired Eyes" (a narrative of a failed drug deal with remarkable imagery ["bullet holes in the mirrors"]). "Revolution Blues" seems especially outside the purview of what people stereotype a Neil Young song to be and do, but it exists—with its fierce and raw electric soloing and lyrics like "I hear that Laurel Canyon is full of famous stars / But I hate them worse than lepers and I'll kill them in their cars." It was especially striking in 1974 to hear CSN & Y perform this song.

After the goth orgy of *On the Beach* and *Tonight's the Night*, Neil put this persona away for awhile. Not until 1985 did it resurface, in the unlikeliest of contexts: the otherwise solidly country album *Old Ways*. "Misfits" has some more neutral imagery (a "new space station / Living Kennedy's dream"), but its second verse features an asthmatic hooker having an attack in a Texas hotel lobby for whom "there is no hope" ultimately. And its third verse describes a modern cowboy "drinkin' whiskey all day" beside a canyon "where only misfits can go." Even the space station frame is less than cheery, since Houston tells them "'the sky is falling / do you know what that means?'" Doana Cooper's chilling background vocals add pathos and terror to these ultimately apocalyptic hard-luck stories. Despite the strings and the Waylon Jennings vocals, this seems much in the vein of "Don't Let It Bring You Down"—updated for the Reagan era and its military build-up.

Neil's next effort, the much undervalued *Landing On Water* (1986; to be discussed at greater length below) shows us that "Misfits" was not a fluke. "Violent Side" and "Touch the Night" both feature imagery of urban paranoia. "Violent Side" contrasts an extremely atypical arrangement of heavy synthesizers, including drum machines, and a bouncy pop melody with lyrics like these:

> Electric light shining on your block
> Sayin' to everyone
> The power is on
> While your alarm
> Set up for safety
> Keeps out invaders
> Who come
> But still can't control
> Control the violent side.

The relationship between music and text makes for very unsettling listening in this arrangement, as opposed to the harder-edged live versions Neil did with Crazy Horse at the Catalyst Club in Santa Cruz (February 1984; bootlegged).

"Touch the Night" is a more complex song, a narrative of a man walking away from the "tangled steel" of a car wreck "without a scratch" thinking of a woman who (we discover in the second verse) "walked away / And left him standing all alone." We are left to draw our own conclusions here, but there seems to be an implication that the breakup and the wreck are related—perhaps even that the wreck was a suicide attempt (or accidental suicide attempt). The promise in the chorus that "ev'ry one will touch the night" is a promise that we will all encounter similar abysses in life. This is the only track from *Landing On Water* with a pronounced guitar riff, but its edge is ironized and muted by an unusual background vocal accompaniment from the San Francisco Boys Choir. As with "Violent Side," the tempering of the force of the song only makes it gloomier. It's as if Neil is implying this is too much to handle unless he sweetens the mix. This approach goes back to his first solo album ("The Loner" and "The Old Laughing Lady"); indeed, this is the first recording he made since that release unaffiliated in any way with an accompanying band. No wonder this second purely solo effort (with accompanying musicians but no named group as such) oddly echoes it both in musical strategy and in an especially gothic feel.

After this release, Neil Young more or less abandoned this persona (outgrew it?). Significant exceptions would include "Dreamin' Man" off *Harvest Moon* (1992) and—to a much lesser extent—"The Great Divide" from *Silver and Gold* (2000). "Dreamin' Man" works as a spoiler on *Harvest Moon* the way "Misfits" did on *Old Ways*. If you're not paying attention, its beautiful arrangement just slips the lyrics past you. But its subject is a homeless stalker of a woman:

> I see your curves and I
> Feel your vibrations
> You dressed in black and white
> You lost in the mall

In a kind of self-criticism of the romantic primitivism of songs like "Cortez the Killer," Neil has his protagonist blame the culture for his significant interpersonal problems:

> Another time or place
> Another civilization
> Would really make this life
> Feel so complete

Which is not to say that this criticism could not be potentially valid ... . But Neil crafts this character as such a soft-spoken wack-job that we are invited to regard him as an unreliable, if sympathetic, character—a far cry from the narrator of "Cortez the Killer."

"The Great Divide" merits notice only because it is the only gloomy moment on a fairly upbeat release. Neil introduced this composition in concert as an "emotional geography" song (*Silver and Gold* video). Its opening stanza, if rather murky semantically, is unquestionably downbeat:

> In the canyons of the Great Divide
> Familiar places we can run and hide
> Are filled with strangers
> Walking in our houses alone.
> In the Great Divide
> Nothin' to decide
> No one else to care for or love
> In the Great Divide
> You won't fit in too well.

Is this a divorce song (the division of property and the estrangement of affections)? A song of marital turmoil and crisis stopping short of divorce (after all, the third verse says "Now we don't go there anymore")? Or is the Great Divide even between life and death, a vision of strangers entering our houses *à la* Beetlejuice? The poet sayeth not, but a mood has been created which even the more upbeat second verse about a child riding a carousel cannot dispel. The lyrics of *Silver and Gold* illustrate that Neil is still as in touch with his "darker side" (from "Looking for a Love," *Zuma*) as his inner child.

The next persona to make its appearance in Young's career is that of the Stoner, the rock and roll version of Spicoli (the Sean Penn character in *Fast Times at Ridgemont High*). Neil has been so convincing at this role that many folks believe he IS this cat, perpetually high. When P. J. O'Rourke wants a neoconservative laugh at the counterculture's expense, Neil provides a ready target.

As with all of Neil's masks, there is more than an element of truth here (consider some of the archival footage in *Year of the Horse*, for example, or the onscreen dope-smoking of Neil and current mate Carrie Snodgress in *Journey Through The Past*). Or Astrid Young's revelation that *Prairie Wind* was the first recording he made when he wasn't high (281)! But it is not the whole truth about Neil—anymore than any of these other masks. He uses it at certain times for certain purposes: to bond with his audience, to play a trickster or clown, to set an audience at ease so he can slip in more subversive ideas. And, as we shall see, so he can do a volte-face and renounce the Stoner. In other words, it's all showbiz; or, more to the point, it's all (modernist, Yeatsian) art.

The earliest appearance of the Stoner occurs in "After the Gold Rush" when he admits "I felt like getting high." (Don't you love how when Linda Rondstadt covers this song either on a solo outing or with Trio she changes the line to "I felt like I could cry"? I guess homegrown's not all right with her ... .) As with most of these songs, there's not much for the critic to do here except cluck or clap. Sounds like Neil wanted to get high. In live performance, this line always draws applause and cheers.

His 1972 tour with the Santa Monica Flyers—and subsequent release of this material on *Tonight's The Night* (1975)—offers the most extensive embrace of this persona, however. Stories abound regarding this tour, a sort of public wake mourning the heroin death of Crazy Horse guitarist Danny Whitten and roadie Bruce Berry. Neil guzzled tequila out of a wine glass on stage and treated the audience to stream-of-consciousness monologues about Nixon, Miami Beach and Bruce Berry (Downing 104-6). At the Roxy in Los Angeles, he even ordered a round of drinks for the audience (Petridis 23). Unlike some of Warren Zevon's antics in the seventies, however, this was theater. Neil was drinking heavily, but it was part of the show—not real alcoholism or drug addiction.

The dope and booze ended up all over the *Tonight's The Night* album: most obviously in the raggedness and off-key, off-rhythm quality of the playing, but also in the lyrics. "Borrowed Tune" uses a melody from the Rolling Stones' "Lady Jane" because Neil was "too wasted to write [his] own." "Roll Another Number" advocates doing just that, and the following track "Albuquerque" reiterates the lifestyle:

> Well they say that Santa Fe
> Is less than ninety miles away
> So I got time to roll a number
> And rent a car

Around this time, Neil also made his spectacularly wasted appearance in the film *The Last Waltz*. Editing has removed from general consumption the spectacle of Neil snorting coke on the way to the stage (and its falling out of his nose), but Neil wanted it retained to show the major theme of the film: rock and roll is a destructive lifestyle that will eventually do you in if you're not careful (Heatley 97-8). Stoner Neil in effect offered up his persona as a cautionary icon. As he would later sing in "Hippie Dream," "Take my advice / Don't listen to me."

The last full and unqualified embrace of the Stoner image is on the track "Homegrown" from *American Stars 'N Bars* (1977). Originally intended as a title song for a shelved project, this ditty celebrates the joys of growing your own marijuana: "plant that bell and let it ring." After this, Neil begins to fine-tune his attitudes toward alcohol and drugs. The Stoner still appears—for instance, the International Harvesters would play "Roll Another Number" in a country idiom—but his drug intake is confined to marijuana and this persona is chastised as well in a series of antidrug songs. Arguably, this process began with "The Needle and the Damage Done" to some extent, but Neil came to carry the critique much further in the latter seventies and eighties. A long-unreleased song from the seventies, "Hitchhiker," addressed these issues at epic length. Bootleg live recordings reveal that it has long been an insider fan favorite.

In 2010, Neil finally recorded it for the *Le Noise* project. Here is a typical verse from this straight-up chronological recounting of Neil's favorite drugs (and when he did them):

> You didn't see me in Toronto
> When I first tried out some hash
> Smoked through a pen and I'd do it again
> But I didn't have the cash
> I didn't have the cash

One can readily see why the confessional honesty of this song, a virtual drug diary, might have been deemed too candid for general consumption for many years. It is not only an example of the Stoner persona in eclipse, but a Mesoamerican lyric (he recycled one verse from it in "Like an Inca")—and indeed, one of many songs about his breakup with Carrie Snodgress ("we had a kid and we split apart"). Its 2010 release makes it technically the "newest" example of the Stoner persona, but I discuss it here because of its earlier composition date.

"Too Far Gone," written in the seventies but not released until *Freedom* (1989), takes an even more critical and renouncing stance towards the party life. This acoustic country-folk tune addresses a one-night stand bar meeting jeopardized by the intoxication of the protagonist:

> We had drugs and we had booze
> But we still had something to lose
> And by dawn I wanted
> To marry you ... .
>
> Was I too far gone
> Too far gone
> Too far gone
> For you.

Although the outcome is never revealed, there seems ample cause for doubting future success.

In the eighties, Neil renounced drugs and hippiedom on *Old Ways* (1985) and *Landing On Water* (1986). The title track of the former pledges a change in lifestyle and "Are There Any More Real Cowboys?" dismisses the fake ones who are "snorting cocaine when the honky-tonks all close." "Hippie Dream" from the latter is even more scathing, possibly an attack on Crosby and Stills' addiction at the time to crack cocaine. He singles out for repudiation a song they co-wrote together: "The wooden ships / Are just a hippie dream." Stephen Stills is also the likely target in "Cocaine Eyes," a song released only on the import EP *Eldorado* (1989).

Neil Young: Prisoner of Avant-Pop 157

"No More," also from *Freedom*, is an ultimate renunciation of harder drugs:

> You don't know which drug is right
> Can't decide which way you wanna go
> I feel the way you feel
> 'Cause not so long ago
> It had a hold on me
> I couldn't let it go
> It wouldn't set me free
> It wouldn't set me free
> No more, no more, no more.

The abnegation of the lyrics is reinforced by the fierce yet muted electric solo runs that close the song and by the sheer repetition of the vow to overindulge "no more."

These songs have proven to be the last lyrical hurrah of the Stoner figure, although Neil acknowledges that "psychedelic music fills the air" in the "Mansion on the Hill" from *Ragged Glory* (1990). Neil still performs old Stoner songs such as "After the Gold Rush" and "Roll Another Number," but he's not writing new ones anymore. In his sixties, it makes abundant sense to say "no more."

In marked contrast to the Stoner, Neil Young also wears the mask of the political activist, the writer of broadside ballads for the masses. Neil's further willingness to play benefit concerts for many causes reinforces the seeming authenticity of this persona. I do think Neil Young has a politics: it's very close to Frank Zappa's "practical conservatism," which is in turn close to libertarianism. Neil, like Frank, likes the idea of local governance and big government non-interference. Zappa was more liberal on foreign policy issues; as we shall see, Neil seemed to endorse in a qualified manner some of Reagan's overseas adventurism (against Libya, for example).

But as an artist, Neil likes trafficking in ambiguity—even in songs of social protest and commentary. Thus, I have found upon closer examination that Young's songs can work as a kind of political Rorschach test, enabling the listener to read in their own political values. This trend appears in the earliest political song by Neil put on vinyl: "Ohio" (1970) from Crosby, Stills, Nash and Young. (It's also telling how late this persona appears in Neil's work. Perhaps because of his Canadian origins, he left the political writing in Buffalo Springfield to Stephen Stills ["For What It's Worth," "Four Days Gone"].) The opening verse's statement of facts offers no hermeneutic difficulty, but consider the chorus:

> Gotta get down to it
> Soldiers are cutting us down

Should have been done long ago
What if you knew her and found her dead on the ground?
How can you run when you know?

We have a referent problem here, a recurrent grammatical trope in Neil's lyrics (cf. "She said you're strange / But don't change / And I let her" from "Mr. Soul": let her do what? Speak? Change?). What "should have been done long ago?" "Soldiers ... cutting us down" can't be the right answer, unless bitter irony is intended—which is after all possible. The National Guard's behavior is forcing the counterculture to mobilize finally. And grammatically, it is the closest potential referent for what "should have been done."

Nonetheless, most of the song's listeners would reject this bloodthirsty reading and posit what "should have been done long ago" is our realizing that we "gotta get down to it." (Although one should duly note how you can get this same meaning by way of an ironic reading of the line about the soldiers as shown above.) It turns out that Neil is using an obscure rhetorical figure known as "hyperbaton." Longinus describes it in his first century treatise on the sublime:

> Hyperbaton is an arrangement of words or thought which differs from the normal sequence ... It is a very real mark of urgent emotion. People who in real life feel anger, fear, or indignation, or are distracted by jealousy or some other emotion ... often put one thing forward and then rush off to another, irrationally inserting some remark, and then hark back again to their first point. (147)

His use of this trope gains further power from the likelihood that it was not a conscious choice.

Jessica Jenkot, one of the students in my Rock Generations class (and an English major) would remind us that "done" is also ambiguous here: it could mean either "acted upon" or even "completed." The anti-war movement (the revolution?), perhaps, should have been finished business by now?

And then we come to the very quintessence of the Neil Young inkblot test: what is the "it" we "gotta get down to?" Insert your own leftist agenda here! The song's politics with regard to a response are left completely wide open. Arguably, this is a virtue. The best political songs often leave room for ambiguity: what does "Blowin' in the Wind" really advocate doing, after all? Dylan's song becomes a flexible tool for sundry causes as a result, just as Neil could redo "Ohio" in 1989 as a response to Tiananmen Square (Heatley 166)—or "Blowin' in the Wind" itself for the Gulf War (*Weld*, 1991). By contrast, Stephen Stills' attempts to formulate counterculture politics during his "America's Children" rap on "49 Bye Byes" (*Four Way Street*, 1971) have not aged so gracefully.

Neil Young: Prisoner of Avant-Pop 159

And let's not forget that "Ohio" is also driving and intense rock and roll, that its amplified repetitions make it far more than its lyric content. It sounds like a battle cry, however unsure the marching orders. The same can be said of Neil's next major political song, "Southern Man" (*After The Gold Rush*, 1970). Based on my anecdotal sources, especially Alabama-born friend Johnny Langley, I can assure you this song has gotten Neil into a lot more trouble than "Ohio." Johnny tells me that Neil has received enough death threats to avoid the state of Alabama because of this song and its follow-up "Alabama." A glance at Pete Long's thorough listing of Young concerts in *Ghosts on the Road* confirms the last time he played in Alabama for over forty years was in April 1968 with the Buffalo Springfield—before penning "Southern Man" (Long 21). (In his memoir *Waging Heavy Peace* he recounts a 2010 concert in Mobile [377].) Neil eventually pinpointed some of the reason for this animosity in his liner notes on *Decade*:

> This song could have been written on a civil rights march after stopping off to watch "Gone with the Wind" at a local theatre. But I wasn't there so I don't know for sure. Actually I think I wrote it in the Fillmore East dressing room in 1970.

He admits not only that it's from an outsider's perspective ("I wasn't there"), but that the song is a mixture of civil rights era activism (reflected in lyrics such as "Now your crosses are burning fast") and Old South romanticism ("bullwhips cracking" and "Lily Belle"). The contempt which the Deep South tends to feel for this song has to do with, first off, its belatedness: this song was written well after the peak of the Civil Rights movement, so both its referents are in the historical past. Plainly put, it seems to be flogging a dead horse. And secondly, it's penned by a real outsider, a Canadian (worse than a damn Yankee!). The lyrics are a catalogue of button-pushing issues for the southern listener, touching such bases as reparations for slavery ("Southern man, when will you pay them back?") and miscegenation ("Lily Belle, your hair is golden brown / I seen your black man comin' round"). And the music is, of course, rock and roll: most assuredly a southern (Sun Studios, Memphis) and not a Canadian invention.

One can see how royally all this would piss off a southern listener, especially with the one-two punch of "Alabama" (to be discussed below). Lynyrd Skynyrd responded with "Sweet Home Alabama," of course, with its specific name-check of Neil Young. In typical Scorpio fashion, Neil responded not only by apologizing and becoming buddies with the band (and writing songs for them such as "Powderfinger" which they never got to cover because of the plane crash), but by actually performing "Sweet Home Alabama" himself in concert as an encore (Long 102). "Take my advice / don't listen to me."

But there's another turn of the screw, courtesy of another friend. American historian Jerry Hirsch contends with others in his field that the civil rights movement is when the Civil War actually ended, that Appomattox was a pyrrhic victory for the north given the failure of reconstruction. The goals for which the war eventually came to be fought were not realized until the 1960s. By this account, Neil's juxtaposition of antebellum and civil rights imagery is spot on and quite perceptive in an intuitive, outsider's, Canadian way. Needless to say, the arguable accuracy of the historiography in the song would further fuel resentments for the southern listener. But one suspects that Hirsch is right: if the song were merely flogging a dead horse, it would not have drawn such wrath!

"Alabama" (1972) rubs salt in the wound with its electric indictments. I recall Neil at the time commenting on the song's being about his disillusionment with the south for voting in Nixon (Nixon proves to be a recurrent obsession in his political writing, for easily comprehensible reasons). This target is clearer in the film version of the song in *Journey Through The Past*, where Nixon is added to the song in audiovisual montage. On the *Harvest* album, it is much harder to discern "What's going wrong?" in the state. Again, we have anachronistic imagery ("banjos playing through the broken glass"), here bordering on the surreal and fantastic. Some lines are just plain puzzling: "See the old folks tied in white ropes." Are these lynching victims or KKK members or both or either? Maybe that's the point ... . The final verse is a nadir of sorts, with its mixture of smugness (even neo-imperialism, as if we had a reverse perspective from "Cortez the Killer") and a complete misapprehension of how quickly and easily the south will embrace outsiders:

> Oh Alabama, can I see you and shake your hand?
> Make friends down in Alabama.
> I'm from a new land
> I come to you and see all this ruin
> What are you doing, Alabama?
> You got the rest of the union to help you along
> What's going wrong?

Ouch. Neil would seldom be this naive again on a political song, but the damage was done: he had made some enemies for life.

"Are You Ready For The Country?" (also from *Harvest*) is a much better indicator of where Young's political writing would go in future. It may not strike you at first listen as even being a political song; it seems to be more about a return to country values. This posture itself, of course, goes back to the Jeffersonian ideal of the gentleman farmer. (After the money started flowing in, Neil Young lost no time in becoming such an agrarian by buying a working ranch forty miles south of San Francisco—whence the inspiration for this song and, indeed, the new persona which it creates to be discussed below.) "Are You Ready For The Country?" also has a bizarre series of archetypal characters, a "preacher" and a "hangman." So what's political besides the agrarian gestures? The answer can be found in a throwaway line that is arguably the key to Neil's politics: "Lefting and then Righting, it's not a crime you know" (capitalizations are Young's from the lyric sheet). Neil takes political positions, but he's serving notice that they will be on a case by case basis, not because of a consistent commitment to leftist ideology. Neil Young has shown throughout his career that he can sympathize with the Right as well as the Left within the overall liberal (in a political science sense, i.e. non-fascist or socialist) consensus of a democratic polity.

A recent dramatic example would be on December 12, 2001, when Neil received a Spirit of Liberty lifetime achievement award from People for the American Way for "promoting freedom and justice in his adopted country" (infogate.com). He used this bully pulpit to defend Attorney General John Ashcroft's anti-terrorist measures that have curtailed some pre-September 11th civil liberties. Although conceding that such measures should not become permanent, Neil Young once again shocked the Left by refusing to adopt an expected stance. "Are You Ready For The Country?" is the moment when he gave fair warning that this would be his privilege—a move not unlike that of mentor Bob Dylan, who occasionally riles his fans by becoming born again or supporting Israel.

But if Young promised "Lefting and then Righting," his next political effort showed him (also typically) Righting and then Lefting. In 1972, he issued a rare single with Graham Nash in support of the antiwar presidential campaign of George McGovern. "War Song" was unavailable after its initial release until the 2009 arrival of *Neil Young Archives Volume I*, perhaps because Neil promised later on "This Note's For You" that he "won't sing for politicians." This song provides a typical exception to one of Neil's proclaimed rules (cf. no live rock and roll on television, no CSN & Y reunion till Crosby got off crack, etc.). "War Song" begins with imagery of Vietnam set to driving staccato guitar:

> In the morning, when you wake up
> You've got planes flying in the skies
> Dropping bombs meant to break up
> Other lies in your eyes.

Then it promises "There's a man / Who says he can / Put an end to war." McGovern is never named, but he is obviously implied.

Four years later, after an interval of the Stoner / "Tonight's the Night" persona, he would left, then right, again with a sympathetic song about Richard

Nixon, of all people ("Campaigner," 1976). The lyric portrays him as essentially a lonely, driven man; but "even Richard Nixon has got soul." The inspiration for this plaintive acoustic song was watching Nixon on television visit his wife Pat in the hospital (Downing 138). Somehow, the demon was humanized; this song was the result. I have always found in it a subtle implied parallel between the life of a politician and a travelling musician. Both are uprooted and alienated from the very popular base they wish to appeal to. It's probably not coincidental that "Campaigner" was written on the Stills-Young band's tour bus (liner notes, *Decade*). It's not so much a political song as a song about politics, perhaps. Nonetheless, any sympathy towards Nixon would carry implicit ideological weight in 1976 (after the Watergate scandal, Nixon's resignation and his pardoning by President Gerald Ford).

As the Reagan era began, Neil Young continued to fiddle on both sides of the bow, but generally shifted to the Right. *Hawks and Doves* (1980) and *Re.Ac.Tor* (1981; with Crazy Horse) show Neil taking simultaneously opposing positions on issues (a curse on / embrace of both your houses?). For instance, "Comin' Apart At Every Nail" (from *Hawks and Doves*) portrays America falling apart economically and militarily to the rhythm of Neil's country swing:

> It's awful hard to find a job
> On one side the government, the other the mob
>
> Hey, hey, ain't that right
> The workin' man's in for a hell of a fight ...
>
> Way up on the old DEW [Distant Early Warning] line
> Some of the boys were feelin' fine
> A big light flashed across the sky
> But somethin' else went slippin' by
> Meanwhile at the Pentagon
> The brass was wonderin' what went wrong
>
> Oh this country sure looks good to me
> But these fences are comin' apart at every nail

The song's form fits its function, since the verses are of uneven length (verse 1 has 4 lines, 2 has 6, 3 has 2). It too is "comin' apart at every nail."[4]

Yet the very next song on the album, its title track, crows:

> In history we painted pictures grim
> The devil knows we might feel that way again
> The big wind blows, so the tall grass bends
> But for you don't push too hard my friend
>
> Ready to go, willin' to stay and pay

> USA, USA
> So my sweet love can dance another free day
> USA, USA

This does not sound like a country coming apart at every nail, does it? How to reconcile these ambivalent readings of America's strength? Unfortunately, the easiest way might be to see the former as a Carter song, the latter as a Reagan lyric—especially since Neil held forth about voting for Reagan at some length in the 1980s. Needless to say, this juxtaposition puzzled many listeners expecting a less dialogical—in Mikhail Bakhtin's sense of being polyvocal—approach to the social lyric.

Another example of Neil's ambivalence would be his Janus-faced criticisms of both unions and management in the early eighties. "Union Man" on *Hawks and Doves* satirizes the musician's union in ways similar to Frank Zappa's "Rudy Wants To Buy Yez A Drink" (*Chunga's Revenge*). The comparatively rich rock musicians carry everybody else: "I pay my dues ahead of time / When the benefits come I'm last in line, yeah." The song replicates a meeting whose sole business ends up being the issuance of "Live music is better" bumper-stickers.

And yet "Southern Pacific," a far superior song on *Re.Ac.Tor*, poignantly portrays the sadness of forced retirement (for, in this case, a lifelong railroad worker). The train-like rhythms of the band and the unusually plaintive vocal reinforce the pathos of the lyrics:

> I rode the highball
> I fired the Daylight
> When I turned 65
> I couldn't see right.
>
> It was, "Mr. Jones,
> We've got to let you go.
> It's company policy.
> You've got a pension though." ...
>
> I put in my time.
> I put in my time.
> Now I'm left to roll
> Down the long decline.

As with "Campaigner," the power of the song derives from its wider applicability. It's about growing old in America, whatever your job. It's as much about Neil's feared obsolescence—or yours or mine—as it is about the most symbolically named "Mr. Jones" (Casey? Dylan's "Thin Man?"). In any event, this song questions the benevolence of management in counterpoint to Young's satire of the unions. And both union and management would probably like his jingoist gibe that "There's already too many Datsuns / In this town" (from "Motor City," *Re.Ac.Tor*).

As the eighties continued, Neil penned a few political songs on more international themes, perhaps indicating a greater confidence in his global stature and authority. "Berlin" (1982; only performed once in concert in Berlin, but on the eponymous video) offers a modest induction to these songs. Neil pleads to be taken "just the way [he is] after Berlin." The implication is that he has been changed and deepened by the experience of playing there:

> Cruising down the Corridor
> Seeing things I never seen before
> Where they lock you out
> Or lock you in ...
>
> Save me from the final days after Berlin.

Neil's vision is ultimately an apocalyptic one (as we shall see, another mask he wears occasionally if rarely): he can taste the escalating conflict between the eastern bloc and the west, and fears the "final days" are upon us. The video record shows that the young German audience was extremely moved by this song, with its expression of solidarity and sympathy. For a few minutes, Neil captured the absurdity of living in cold-war Berlin—living for the moment while feeling like you're sitting on a powder-keg.

Neil's richest political material of the eighties addressed the Middle East, however, particularly in the highly nuanced "Mideast Vacation" off *Life* (1987, with Crazy Horse). A much better song than the more well-known "Ohio," it merits close attention. In four short verses, it addresses the sadomasochistic relationship America has with the Middle East. We screw up their affairs by playing favorites, and they retaliate against us: a cycle that began with our assistance in the creation of the state of Israel (admittedly historically comprehensible; see Grose) resulting in the subsequent marginalization and exile of the Palestinian people and going right up to the new temporary friends and enemies we've made as a result of kicking the Taliban out of Afghanistan. Young begins the song by putting the blame for the situations about to be described squarely on certain tendencies of the American national psyche:

> I used to watch Highway Patrol
> Whittlin' with my knife
> But the thought never struck me
> I'd be black and white for life
> I was raised on law and order
> In a community of strife

Neil Young: Prisoner of Avant-Pop

>Became a restless boarder
>And I never took a wife

All this to the accompaniment of fierce electronic war-drums and a synthesizer sound resembling a jet taking off. The narrator is the archetypical rootless, single American loner who will take it upon himself to dispense frontier justice: James Fenimore Cooper's Leatherstocking, and ultimately John Wayne's character in *The Searchers*. But this guy can only see things in "black and white": there are good guys and bad guys, just like in *Highway Patrol* (and this dualistic thinking is partially a product of media brainwashing). Young suggests this mindset is a risky one to bring to a grey region like the Middle East.

So off our protagonist goes, seemingly now a surreal conflation of John Wayne and Ronald Reagan:

>I went lookin' for Khadafy
>Aboard Air Force One
>But I never did find him
>And the C.I.A. said "Son,
>You'll never be a hero
>Your flyin' days are done
>It's time for you to go home now
>Stop sniffin' that smokin' gun"

This verse points out the absurd inefficacy of American (or any) power when confronting the elusive individual enemy. Specifically, it addresses Reagan's airstrikes against Libya in order to attack Khadafy. The Libyan leader survived that attack—as did Idi Amin and (for that matter) Salman Rushdie. The prognosis is not good, of course, for reasons this song details: the limits of American air power and attacks mediated by technology. Still, we sniff the smoking gun and long for the justice of the mythic old west (*High Noon*).

Between this verse and the next, our antihero has made a concession to civilization and settled down with a family:

>I was travellin' with my family
>In the mideast late one night
>In the hotel all was quiet
>The kids were out like little lights
>Then the street was filled with jeeps
>There was an explosion to the right
>They chanted "Death to America"
>I was feelin' like a fight
>
>So I ran downstairs

> And out into the street
> Someone kicked me in the belly
> Someone else kissed my feet
> I was Rambo in the disco
> I was shootin' to the beat
> When they burned me in effigy
> My vacation was complete

These last verses capture the mix of anti-American and pro-American (or at least pro-tourist) stances one finds in the region—and how this ideological murk both brutalizes the American, turning him into simultaneously another icon of violence (Sylvester Stallone's Rambo), and a cultural masochist ("When they burned me in effigy / My vacation was complete"). On some level, the sensitive American visitor feels that she or he deserves the reprobation Muslim cultures often give us as a result of our complex relationships with the region. (If this sounds abstract, I am nonetheless speaking as a recent traveler to Morocco where I witnessed similar phenomena.) I have no evidence that Neil Young ever travelled to this part of the world, but the song captures well the ambivalent feelings of Americans who do. It also satirizes the anachronistic nature of our national myths, especially as they are gendered. John Wayne / Gary Cooper / Rambo confronts the feminized oriental ("Someone else kissed my feet"). Overall, a much harder (if surreal) look at American foreign affairs than "Hawks and Doves."

The next track on *Life*, "Long Walk Home," explores similar terrain on a more surface level. This song is explicitly about Reagan's authorizing the shelling of the Libyan coast by our battleships (it sounds like the synthesizer is sampling the big guns of the New Jersey going off):

> We balance the power
> From hour to hour
> Giant guns wail
> it's such a long walk home

The representation of American intervention "From Vietnam to old Beirut" is, to say the least, ambivalent:

> Why do we feel that double-edged blade
> Cutting through our hand?
> America, America
> Where have we gone?

In contrast to the more militant statements Young was making in interviews defending the Reagan-era arms buildup, this song portrays America, as does

"Mideast Vacation," as a kind of geopolitical lost soul (Heatley 139-140). We intervene, but cut ourselves with "that double-edged blade"—and only get in deeper with respect to some conflicts far older than our own history as a nation. Young believes that we have to live up to our obligations as a superpower ("We balance the power / From hour to hour"). Consider human rights issues, for example: how can we shirk such an ethical imperative? (Of course, we often do.) But such an obligation is a thankless duty. These songs show that, although Neil was stating many right-wing positions in his mid-eighties interviews, his songs tended to be politically ambivalent and dialectical—whereas slightly before, in the early eighties, they were seemingly contradictory from song to song.

At this same time, in conjunction with his work to create the annual Farm Aid benefits, Neil wrote a few populist anti-foreclosure ballads that hearkened in spirit back to Woody Guthrie's Dustbowl Ballads ("This Old House" and "Depression Blues"). "This Old House" is the more interesting of the two, since it was recorded by CSN & Y and seems, on some level, a sequel to Nash's hippie idyll (hippie dream?) commemorating his Laurel Canyon cohabitation with Joni Mitchell ("Our House" on *Déjà Vu*). In contrast to the Middle Eastern material, though, this was pretty safe stuff. Almost every American likes to think they are pro-farm and anti-bank, whatever the reality of our lived choices. It's a kind of national mythology. The problem was to get people to go beyond the sentiments and actually help the family farm. Over the course of later Farm Aid benefits, Neil would idealistically lament the fact that it was necessary to hold them every year. He hoped the farm crisis could be solved by a massive outpouring of generosity—one which never really came to the needed extent.

In 1989, after his long dalliance in the ditch of Geffen Records, Neil bounced back with a powerful political ballad that reads like a prophecy of September 11th:

> There's a warnin' sign on the road ahead
> There's a lot of people sayin'
> We'd be better off dead
> Don't feel like Satan
> But I am to them
> So I try to forget it, any way I can
>
> Keep on rockin' in the free world ("Rockin' in the Free World")

This polemical tune addresses many issues: the end of the Cold War, militant Islamic fundamentalism as the new foe, the pro-democracy movement in China and its brutal suppression in Tiananmen Square, homelessness and crack addiction in the United States, the "kinder, gentler, machine gun hand" of George Bush, Sr.'s Middle East policies, American overconsumption and environmental negligence ("Got Styrofoam boxes for the ozone layer"). Lots of problems, but we still have to "keep on rockin' in the free world." Things are bad here, but even worse elsewhere—and we have some semblance of democracy. "Rockin' in the Free World" is a typically ambivalent, if exceptionally passionate performance. The visual record shows that he performed it with the intensity of early Dylan finger-pointing, wearing a Chinese beret and combat pants while telegraphing the lyrics like a mad busker. The result was electrifying. It was a better State of the Union address than Bush Sr. was giving at the time!

Neil's political persona in the eighties focused on Middle Eastern policy and the farm crisis—with more than a nod to urban homelessness in songs such as "People on the Street" (*Landing On Water*), "Life in the City" (*This Note's For You*) and "Rockin' in the Free World." In fact, it might be fairer to link urban rootlessness and rural displacement and say his political mask addressed Middle Eastern exertions of force and varieties of American homelessness (urban and rural): strength abroad and weakness at home. In the nineties and the new millennium, he has retained his interest in the Middle East, but has expanded his agrarian polemics into something more closely approximating a Green politics of environmental preservation.

The Middle Eastern material came in at moments of actual wartime. On the "Smell The Horse" tour of 1991 with Crazy Horse, the eruption of the Gulf War led Neil to perform a dirge-like electric cover of Bob Dylan's "Blowin' in the Wind," replete with visual footage of the bombing of Baghdad and sound effects of air raid sirens and bombs going off. Much more recently during the war on terrorism in Afghanistan, "Let's Roll" commemorated passenger Todd Beamer's rally on Flight 93 on September 11th that led to the passengers overcoming the hijackers—which cost them their lives, but saved hundreds or even thousands more potential victims. This latter song is both familiar terrain for Neil ("Powderfinger" is also about existential resolve in the face of imminent death) and unusually different in its sound. Its gloomy marching bass figure and anguished mid-section sound more like Roger Waters, and his version of Pink Floyd, than typical Neil.[5] This song succeeds because, for starters, it avoids trying to do too much. It is tied to the point of view of a baffled persona, rather than any expert commentator, a common man like the heroes of Frank Capra's films:

> How this all got started
> I'll never understand
> I hope someone can fly this thing
> And get us back to land
>
> Time is running out
> Let's roll
> Time is running out

Let's roll

Whatever the complexities of the big picture (for example, the C. I. A.'s training of Osama Bin Laden to fight the Russians), Flight 93 is a story of good and evil—with good triumphing at a terrible cost. That's all in the song lyrically, instrumentally and vocally. As a result, it is one of Neil's most moving performances in a career replete with them.

The song's other strength is its concreteness. It looks at an immensely tragic day through the focused lens of one participant. Sir Paul McCartney's "Freedom" and Michael Jackson's "What More Can I Give," whatever their other virtues, lack this focus. There will certainly be more songs about this day, but Neil's is the first one likely to stick around.

On the *Weld* video with Crazy Horse (1991), the redoubtable slacker anthem "F*!#in' Up" became both a Gulf War and a Green statement by Neil's inclusion of footage of a bird covered with oil on the shores of the Persian Gulf at the song's conclusion. Throughout the nineties, he would make more explicit evocations of environmental concern—a lyric interest, after all, since the cryptic "After the Gold Rush" ("We got Mother Nature on the run").

"Mother Earth (Natural Anthem)" from *Ragged Glory* warns us over a plaintive, droning pump organ to "Respect Mother Earth and her healing ways / Or trade away our children's days." *Harvest Moon* (1992) featured two Green tracks. "War of Man" follows up on the Gulf War bird footage (which Neil alluded to on tour when he introduced the song) by describing human conflict from the perspective of bewildered animals:

> Out on the delta where the hoofbeats pound
> The daddy's runnin' on the frozen ground
> Can't smell the poison as it follows him
> Can't see the gas and machines, it's a war of man
>
> No one wins
> It's a war of man

Neil universalizes the situation by blurring geographic specifics; it doesn't seem to be about any war in particular—perhaps reinforcing the non-anthropocentric perspective of the song. The animals don't care about the politics in question. Curiously, Neil's take on war has crept into the cinema in such recent war films as *Three Kings* and *The Thin Red Line*, which both cut away from the human action to show animals responding to war.

"Natural Beauty," the other Green song from *Harvest Moon*, presents a series of tableaux unified by a recurrent trope of technology mediating nature (as such, it is compositionally similar to "Broken Arrow" and "Misfits"). The first verse has a baby's cry fading "[i]nto an anonymous wall of digital sound," paralleling the third verse's rodeo scene with "the moment of defeat / Played back over on the video screen." The lyrics trenchantly observe to what extent we encounter things indirectly these days, instead of directly living as our ancestors did. Add up the hours of staring at computer screens and television monitors. Young also has a specific axe to grind: his conviction that digital recording has taken out the intense high end of music that moves us most; the compact disk has ushered in "the dark ages of recorded sound" (in Downing 226-7). We're leading greyer, more mediated lives as a result.

His second verse considers a far bigger and more disastrous intersection between technology and nature, the devastation of the rainforests:

> Amazon
> You had so much and now so much is gone
> What are you gonna do
> With your life?
>
> What a lucky man
> To see the earth before it touched his hand
> What an angry fool
> To condemn
> One more night to go
> One more sleep upon your burning banks
> A greedy man never knows
> What he's done

The only problem with this well-intentioned representation—and it is a serious one—is that Neil stops with a contrast between "natural beauty" and the intervention of developers. Typically, but unfortunately missing, are the indigenous forest peoples. Their management of these resources deserves to be considered environmental science, not a mere practice of "ethno-science." One could go so far as to say "the Amazonian biosphere is an irreducibly human / non-human collective entity" (Haraway 310-314). This is an even more puzzling omission given Neil's indigenous mask—perhaps it confirms that his awareness of indigenous peoples is more mythic than intellectual (or even practical).

As with Neil's concerns about farm foreclosure, he has put his money and clout where his lyrics are on several occasions with regard to Green issues: performing at benefits for Walden Woods, speaking out about the environmental impact of corporate farming at Farm Aid, and other helpful gestures. I will reserve discussion of his post-millennial use of his political mask for a later section of this chapter, since it has arguably become his dominant persona in the first decade of the new century—largely thanks to the misadventures of George W. Bush and associates!

In any case, Neil's political persona is arguably a thankless mask: putting your opinions in progress on the line in a popular song renders a certain permanence to what may be a temporary perception. (Some of his songwriting in the early 80s bears this out.) At best, you may be only preaching to the choir; at worst, you may only be broadcasting your lack of expertise. Consider, for example, the close scrutiny Bob Dylan received for his unconditional support of Hurricane Carter. The temptation, and most pragmatic solution, seems to be hedging your bets through ambiguity. Even more famous artists than Neil Young have done this: consider John Lennon double-tracking "Don't you know that you can count me in / out" on the *White Album*'s version of "Revolution." Talk about having it both ways! So if Neil's sharpest political writing—"Ohio," "Mideast Vacation," "Rockin' in the Free World"—is vexed by ambivalence, he's in good company. The pop troubadour only has an easy time in moments of relatively complete clarity (like Flight 93), which history offers in short supply. The most one can typically hope for is a general encouragement of good people—which for Young is probably more effectively done by a good solo on "Old Black!" Give him credit for trying, and occasionally succeeding.

The last major persona to emerge in Neil Young's career is the gentleman farmer / country boy / agrarian. Neil has some legitimate credentials here, having spent some famous formative years in Omemee, Ontario, between living in Toronto and Winnipeg. But the persona emerged full-blown in his lyric writing in the early seventies after he acquired his ranch. As with the Stoner mask, this persona does not require much critical exegesis. These songs are among the most straightforward Neil ever wrote and performed. "Are You Ready For the Country?" (*Harvest*, 1972) starts the discourse with its embrace of country values (obliquely covered in "Lefting and then Righting" as noted). Other songs from this era allude to the ranch (like "Journey Through The Past"), but this is the only one to really traffic in a new image—a claim borne out both by Waylon Jennings' cover of the song and Neil's embrace of it when he went almost totally country in the mid-eighties with the International Harvesters. When he performed "Are You Ready For the Country?" on Austin City Limits in 1984, he changed the lyrics to flaunt his persona:

> Are you ready for the country?
> Are you ready for me?
> Are you ready for the country?
> Ain't I a sight to see?

This persona lay dormant between that song from *Harvest* and the early-mid eighties while Neil preferred the Stoner, Blakean innocent and politico masks. Then, in the midst of the Geffen "ditch," he went very country. Reasons he gave interviewers emphasized feeling old and worn out at the time and a suspicion that rock was strictly a young person's game. Country music, on the other hand, let you grow old:

> I see country music, I see people who take care of their own. You got seventy-five-year-old guys on the road. That's what I was put here to do, you know. So I wanna make sure I surround myself with people who are gonna take care of me. Because I'm in it for the long run. (in Downing 177)

In retrospect, this was a mid-life crisis. After acquiring a personal trainer and getting off any serious drugs, Neil would end up rocking even harder than he had in his youth. But for the years of 1984 and 1985, the country farmer reigned supreme in a whole series of International Harvesters songs: "Get Back to the Country," "Are There Any More Real Cowboys?," "Nothing Is Perfect," and "Farmer's Song," to name but a few (the last two unreleased officially as yet).[6] The persona even bled into other projects in the late eighties. He recorded "This Old House" with CSN & Y, and even did two shit-kicker romps with Crazy Horse: "Country Home" (*Ragged Glory*, 1990) and "Don't Spook The Horse" ("Mansion on the Hill" EP, 1990). Let me consider this last song as representative for the whole persona; I also favor this track because of its playfulness and its comparative rarity. Anyone who's read this far can deal with the sentiments of "Get Back to the Country" on their own!

Neil described this song to reviewers as a kind of "condensed books" version of *Ragged Glory*. It has all the features of that larger project: rough, loud and sloppy but energetic playing; politically incorrect lyrics; a refusal to take itself very seriously. (On the "Smell the Horse" tour, Neil would introduce songs by saying "Here's some more trash for ya.") An old-time sixties garage band ethos as a reminder to then-emergent grunge of where it came from, here with a country twist:

> If you want to go riding in the tall green grass,
> Try not to spook the horse.
>
> If you want to pet that old hound dog,
> Make sure he ain't rolled in shit.
>
> There's a pretty little girl, and she's living down there
> Down on her daddy's farm.
>
> If you're going to mess around with that chick,
> Be sure to close the barn door.
> Better not spook the horse.
> Make sure she ain't rolled in shit.

Neil Young: Prisoner of Avant-Pop

>There's a field of green and a big red barn
>Deep in the valley of hearts;
>If you want to go riding in the tall green grass,
>Try to not spook the horse [repeat this line].

The song ends, as does most of *Ragged Glory*, with some deliberately un-radio-friendly protracted feedback.

Cultural studies research has given us some ways to grasp the complex appeal of this song. As do most of Neil's country persona songs, it seems to be addressed simultaneously to an urban and a rural audience. City slickers will recognize every cliche in here—an iconography of the rural that goes back before Erskine Caldwell and Al Capp (to William Byrd's *History of the Dividing Line* in 1728?)—whereas a rural listener will appreciate the laconic good sense and practicality of the advice (and even forgive the misogynistic humor?). The scatology of the song reminds me of Laura Kipnis' scholarship on *Hustler* magazine. Using statistical information from Jeffrey Klein, she accounts for the popularity of the magazine across class lines, despite its blue-collar bias, as indicative of "a blue-collar urge" shared by American men (Kipnis 390-1). This bias is manifested by the relentless scatological humor of the Flynt publication.

I think her class analysis can be applied as well to Neil Young here. Despite Neil's atypical status as gentleman farmer, rural America is definitely poorer than urban America as a whole. But we have an agrarian urge as well as a blue-collar urge. The redneck is the rural version of the blue-collar. These mediated and mythic images are part of the cultural repertoire of all Americans. So this song can have a broad appeal to men across class lines (not that it got any airplay)—and to roaring girls as well, if not as much to female graduates of posh finishing schools. In other words, the class spectrum of Neil's fan base is arguably wider for men than women: a hypothesis worth testing. (I intuit this primarily as a result of having attended nine concerts featuring Neil Young in sundry configurations, and from the helpful audience footage in the *Weld* video.)

It would also be interesting to research what the country music world made of Neil Young and his farmer persona. Did they like him as much as he liked them? The answers would not be simple. Recall Young's alienation of the Deep South because of his political writing, but also remember that he played the Grand Ole Opry. Neil's friendships with Willie Nelson and Waylon Jennings are probably telling; he could have a market niche in at least the Outlaw variant of country. But Young is the ultimate outlaw in his willingness to slide in and out of this popular genre, so perhaps Bob Dylan is a closer analogue. Both artists have at least given something back to country, in the form of songs and participation in benefit concerts such as Farm Aid (which Neil helped organize). Like rock before it, country has become a diffuse enough body of work that it can accommodate almost anyone who wants to be there and touches some bases with its conventions. As Neil threatened David Geffen, he could have turned into George Jones. But given what we have seen about Young's malleability with regard to personae and genres, this was clearly an idle threat: how could Young have stood still artistically for that long?

So much for Neil's major masks: the Blakean childlike, wide-eyed innocent; the Native American; the surreal troubadour; the gothic gloom-bringer; the stoner; the political activist; the country farmer. There are other minor personae as well. A few times he has spoken from the subject position of another proletarian hero, the biker ("Motorcycle Mama" from *Comes A Time*, "Unknown Legend" from *Harvest Moon* and the unreleased "Live to Ride" from his 1993 tour with Booker T. and the MGs). Neil's street credentials include a serious fondness for Harley-Davidson bikes, complementing his antique car collection.[7]

A more interesting minor persona, a subset of the vatic troubadour, would be Neil as doomsayer penning apocalyptic jeremiads of the fall of western civilization—also a kind of flipside to the indigenous American persona nostalgic for the homeland he's never seen (indeed, with some canonical overlap). There aren't a great many of his songs in this vein, but they make an impression.

The earliest occurrence of this mask is on "L. A." from *Time Fades Away* (1973), which tenders a vision of the city ultimately swallowed up by "cracks in the earth" and the sea, the Big One (cf. his obsession with "rollers" in the *Human Highway* film). Only after its destruction will "[he] finally be heard by you, now, L. A. / City in the smog," a prophet validated.

A more elaborate, if mysterious, jeremiad occurs in "Goin' Back" on *Comes A Time* (1978). The lyrics invoke a vision worthy of Rousseau regarding a lost, nomadic Eden ("I feel like goin' back / Back where there's nowhere to stay"). This utopian picture of the chorus is contrasted with verses of destruction and alienation, all eerily undercut / complicated by the beauty of the folk melody and Nicolette Larson's backing vocals. The second verse has the protagonist recollect that

> When fire filled the sky
> I still remember that day
> These rocks I'm climbing now
> Have already left the ground
> Careening through space

Is this the eruption of a volcano or a nuclear explosion? It's hard to tell. The third verse provides similar ambiguities:

Neil Young: Prisoner of Avant-Pop   175

> I used to build these buildings
> I used to walk next to you
> Their shadows tore us apart
> And now we do what we do
> Driven to the mountains high
> Sunken in the cities gay
> Living in our sleep
> I feel like goin' back
> Back where there's nowhere to stay

The whole sense of the song is that urban civilization has had a catastrophic collapse, or at least a subset of it has fallen. The narrator records the destruction and his own escape, with an implied quest for a post-apocalyptic return to simpler living. The beauty of the production (subtle orchestration from the Gone With The Wind Orchestra, crisp miking of the acoustic guitar) glosses over the mysterious resonance of the lyric.

It is no coincidence that the bulk of these apocalyptic songs come around the time of the crises befalling the later Carter administration (the Iranian hostage situation, the Soviet incursion into Afghanistan) and the subsequent Reagan arms build-up and nuclear saber-rattling. We have already looked at "Comin' Apart At Every Nail's" vision of something slipping past the DEW line defenses on the arctic circle (from 1980's *Hawks and Doves*; cf. "the sky is falling" on "Misfits" [*Old Ways*, 1985]). "Shots" off *Re.Ac.Tor* (1981) offers a non-nuclear apocalypse of unrestrained urban violence ("I keep hearing shots"). The lyric is underscored by Crazy Horse's very raw, almost industrial sound—punctuated with the sounds of automatic weapons fire and a marching beat on Ralph Molina's drums. The aforementioned "Berlin" and "Like an Inca" from the *Trans* era recur to nuclear scenarios. As the latter song warns, "We're gonna lose this place / Just like we lost Atlantis."

After this burst of apocalyptic observation, Neil abandoned this minor mask with only one exception in the later career: "Trans Am" from *Sleeps With Angels* (1994, with Crazy Horse). As with "Goin' Back," the lyrics are murky. But they seem to imply a kind of *Road Warrior* post-apocalyptic scenario. The narrator hangs around the desert, fixing old cars (especially Trans Ams). Ominous and suggestive lines include a reference to a "nasty wind" (fallout?) and to a place "where once the angels stood and cried [where now] everything was new" (the destruction and renewal of Los Angeles?). There is room for disagreement here, but clearly Alexis Petridis is off base when he thinks it's a train song (he doesn't know what a Trans Am is, apparently) (109). I think we're in Mad Max country here, or the California glimpsed at the conclusion of indexSee, Carolyn!Golden Days@*Golden Days* Carolyn See's novel *Golden Days*.

These are the majority of Neil's sundry personae. I suggest that they are one reason why Young is an avant-popist. All such musicians traffic in them, but most are either very consistent (think Roy Orbison or Yoko Ono, for that matter) or very fluid and uncommitted to any narrator in particular (the Robert Browning dramatic monologue with invented speaker (think Elvis Costello or Frank Zappa). Even David Bowie, who most resembles Neil's project in his approach (especially on rare occasions where he recycles a persona, as in Major Tom's use in both "Space Oddity" and "Ashes to Ashes"), differs from Neil in that no one believes that Bowie IS any of his personae. (Although there were moments when the public thought he was Ziggy Stardust, Aladdin Sane or the Thin White Duke; but the marks soon wised up.) Young's genius, which I would ultimately link to the modernist approach to identity exemplified by the poetic career of William Butler Yeats, is to switch between masks that all have an authentic feel. Neil believes in his personae so much that we do as well. Their artificiality only becomes apparent when he does dramatic costume changes (as with the Shocking Pinks, for example).

Neil Young plays with his self-fragmented identity in an unusually overt way. This is manifest, of course, in Geffen's surrealistic attempt to sue Neil Young for not making Neil Young records. Or consider Neil's response to a fan in Canada requesting "Down by the River" at a Squires reunion: "We don't know that one. Some other guy did that one" (Einarson 15). When you feel the full seriousness of that drily ironic utterance, you will understand Neil's project a bit better. To see him in concert in a playful mood is to experience something akin to Yeats's poem "The Circus Animals' Desertion": a parade of personalities. Sometimes you get just one Neil (some of the earlier International Harvesters gigs); sometimes he is legion, Yeats, photographer Cindy Sherman, the most modernist / postmodernist (your call) of Canadian folkies gone south.

Journeys Through The Ditch

The third and final dimension of Young's avant-gardism is his willingness to go resolutely uncommercial as he has done at several points in his career, to destroy his fan base as a way to keep himself fresh and interested in his music—and to see "more interesting people" than you can as a protected pop superstar (*Decade* liner notes).

His first foray into the ditch occurred in 1972. Young was at the height of his popularity. He had consolidated his critical successes with Buffalo Springfield and Crazy Horse with the extreme popularity (and hype) of CSN & Y. Neil was both admired and consumed: *Harvest* was not only Neil's bestselling album ever, but the bestselling album of 1972. Neil would marvel at "the seemingly endless flow of money coming my way from you people out there" (*Decade* liner notes). He bought a ranch; he had a movie star partner (Carrie Snodgress); they had a son Zeke on September 8, 1972 (Downing 89). He was branching out into film direction for the first time with *Journey Through The Past*.

But there was trouble in paradise, as there would prove to be the next time Young would steer his career ditchward. Zeke was diagnosed as having mild cerebral palsy. On a much more somber level, Crazy Horse guitarist Danny Whitten died of a heroin overdose on November 18, six days after Neil's birthday (Long 55). Technically, Neil paid for the smack. (When Whitten proved unready for a forthcoming tour, Young sent him home with a plane ticket and the $50 he used for the overdose [Petridis 20]). Young "didn't feel very guilty, but [he] felt a little guilty"; he had a sense that the existential bill for the excesses of the sixties had come due (Downing 92). The decade that had been so astonishingly good to him was over, leaving a palpable taste of ashes.

Further pressure was created by a mammoth planned tour capitalizing on the popularity of *Harvest*. With Whitten's death hanging over the band, the tour was not well-timed. Neil nonetheless honored his commitment to the grueling four-month tour of mammoth venues, a heck of a way to get the first taste of one's gargantuan new level of personal fame as a singer-songwriter. It was not a pleasant experience for him. "Old Black" was out of commission because of a missing pickup, so Neil was not musically satisfied. He later told Cameron Crowe of his distress: "[Old Black] was never on the Time Fades Away tour. That's why I played like crap on that tour, too. Of all my memories of everything I've ever done, that's the worst tour I ever did. I hope that doesn't hurt anyone's feelings" (61).

But wait; there's more. On the tour, Young's roadies and band, sensing all the money changing hands, kept clamoring for raises. People that he considered friends began treating him in an overtly mercantile fashion. Passive aggressive manifestations of these issues would show up in the paradox of wonderful sound checks followed by sloppy shows (Downing 93). One can understand both the touring company's sense of inequity and Neil's feelings of being completely overwhelmed. Neil was just learning how to run his tours as a business—which someone like Zappa would candidly say is the only way to get it done. For Neil, the transition from friend to employer was traumatic.

Having said all this, I caught the January 5 concert in Milwaukee and saw none of the bad blood Neil has alluded to in interviews. My bootleg cassette of the show confirms that Neil was having a good time, joking with the audience and encouraging a sing-along on "Sugar Mountain." The seeming disparity is resolved by Pete Long's legwork: this was only the second date on the tour (after an opening gig in Madison, Wisconsin). The bloom was still very much on the rose. The only problem hinted at on the tape was the shoddiness of the sound. The Milwaukee Auditorium was never a good venue for live music, acoustic or amplified. As on my Zappa tape, echoes abound as the amplified sound ricochets around the cavernous venue. Neil could not have been pleased by the crudeness of the aural delivery.

But the bad vibes soon manifested. David Crosby and Graham Nash very selflessly tried to help out by joining in on later dates (the former had a dying mother; the latter just had a girlfriend murdered by her brother). This tour reached its nadir at the Oakland Coliseum on March 31. During "Southern Man," Neil saw a black cop beat up an enthusiastic white listener. The irony was overwhelming; he put down his guitar and walked off stage (Downing 93-4). There were two more dates, but Neil had lost any remaining verve for the proceedings. He had seen fame, greed, America, all at about their worst. The hippie dream of the sixties had thoroughly curdled (to mix a metaphor).

Another item in the mix about to inspire three brilliantly dark albums was the *Journey Through The Past* film. The soundtrack, released in November of 1972 before the film premiered (in April 1973), has been deemed by many critics to be "commercial suicide"—a complete dissipation of the career momentum that built up to *Harvest* (Heatley 77). Unlike the subsequent releases (*Time Fades Away, On The Beach, Tonight's The Night*), there have been no defenders of this audio souvenir of the movie. It has little to recommend it beyond the aforementioned new song "Soldier." The film itself is fairly interesting, although it got thoroughly mixed reviews.

Neil's approach as a filmmaker is intuitive, spontaneous, script-less: as he does with his songwriting, he tinkers and hopes for the best. The cinematic results were mostly watchable and entertaining; the visuals at times were beautiful and hallucinatory (grey riders on a beach). Young makes interesting films, because his vision is sufficiently skewed to not be cliched or dull. But as with Zappa's films, I think they are better geared to please the curious fan than to convert the cineaste. There is a lot of self-indulgence in Neil's method (recall the joint smoked onscreen in real time). One could argue that Bresson, Ozu,

Godard and Kiarostami all make demands as well—but the film scholars avoid discussing Neil in droves (a fate shared by Frank Zappa and Bob Dylan [*Renaldo and Clara*]). I would submit that Neil's films are still better than the majority of the films at your local cineplex. Take the ride for yourself and see. But Neil's economic imperative would remain musical (as would Joni Mitchell's). Movies would prove to be an expensive hobby for him, just as painting (albeit less costly) would be for Joni.

Given these various personal, existential and creative disappointments (to their varying degrees), Neil must have felt that 1973 was a serious pressure drop after the critical and commercial triumphs building up in previous years. What separates Neil from your average pop star at this point, and keeps him off *Behind the Music*, is that he was willing to explore this new state of affairs. He did not soldier on with more upbeat music—and he certainly would have had enough in the can to fill an album (then-unreleased but written and performed songs such as "Winterlong," "Wondering," "See the Sky About to Rain," "It Might Have Been," etc.). Instead he released a trilogy of harrowingly confessional albums that remain a kind of industry standard for how far you can peer into the abyss without teetering over the edge, stuff that makes *Jagged Little Pill* look pretty mannered. What Young was building on, of course, was the greatest confessional rock album ever recorded: John Lennon's 1970 *Plastic Ono Band*. To get from Lennon to Young, just add lots of Jose Cuervo Gold Tequila and record the band when they're drunk!

The first, somewhat transitional, recording released was *Time Fades Away* (September 1973). These were all live tracks, all but one from the ill-fated Stray Gators tour of 1973. There were three quiet songs on solo piano and harmonica akin to *Harvest* (and compositionally predating the release of that album): "Journey Through the Past," "Love in Mind," and "The Bridge." But the dominant tone of the album was established on its raw and ragged opening title track:

> Fourteen junkies pull into work
> One sells diamonds, for what they're worth
> Down on Pain Street disappointment lurks
> Son, don't be home too late
> Try to get back by eight
> Son, don't wait till the break of day
> Cause you know how time fades away.

Young had previously addressed heroin abuse ("The Needle and the Damage Done") and urban alienation ("The Loner," "Don't Let It Bring You Down"); but there was a sloppiness and jagged nakedness in the delivery here that was something new. And who would have thought that those nice Stray Gators players on *Harvest* could sound like this? The subsequent verses reminisced about Young's destitute year in Toronto as a folkie living in part off his dad (see Einarson 164-5) and fired an opening salvo regarding the increasingly troubled Nixon presidency, a subject that would come to obsess Young for several years ("all-day Presidents look out windows").

After a reassuring piano palate cleanser ("Journey Through the Past"), the new Neil returns with the ragged and funky rarity, "Yonder Stands the Sinner." This loosest song on a loose album features out-of-tune blues vamping, a raw Young vocal and obscurely retro lyrics ("You heard about the Great Pretender / I went to see him and he's not the same"). Neil even resorts to howling at a few points. The result is both a goofy novelty song and a sonic assault. Then side one ends with the apocalyptic "L. A." (see above) and another piano lyric ("Love in Mind').

The second side brings out the heavy artillery, sandwiching the third piano piece ("The Bridge") between two discordant and wrenching elongated electric workouts. "Don't Be Denied" is Neil Young's most straightforwardly autobiographical song. Its lyrics detail his parents' separation and divorce, his move to Winnipeg and subsequent harassment at school, his dreams of stardom with the Jades and the Squires, his move to Hollywood and crazy fame with the Buffalo Springfield, his ultimate disillusionment with fame ca. 1973:

> Well all that glitters isn't gold
> You know you've heard that story told
> I'm a pauper in a naked disguise
> A millionaire through businessmen's eyes
> Old friend of mine
> Don't be denied

The "old friend" can be variously construed to be Ken Koblun, Neil's bassist in the Squires left back in Canada, or Danny Whitten. In either case, the song provides a cautionary tale to seekers of fame on at least a par with Phil Ochs's "Chords of Fame."

"Last Dance," the album closer and the typical pre-encore set closer for many of the shows on the first part of the tour (including Milwaukee), moves the disillusionment from the singer-songwriter to the audience. The song is about waking up on "a Monday morning" and going to work—with lots of details about cold orange juice and hot coffee. Allegorically, of course, it recontextualizes the countercultural moment of the sixties as a "last dance": a brief romantic interlude before one has to return to the same daily capitalist grind as one's predecessors. It's a very seventies song declaring the sixties officially over ("It's time to go / Time to go to work!"). Crosby and Nash's closing "no, no, no" adds an extra poignancy to the wake. Time has faded away while we weren't paying attention.

Neil reinforces the message by the grim artwork on the album. The cover shows a typical stadium crowd for the 1973 tour: some happy faces, but some looking stoned and / or alienated. The color is a sickly grey-green combination from harsh house lighting and a room laden with marijuana smoke (trust me on this one!). A bouquet on a stand on the stage is tipped over and contains only one rose. The party is over, folks. On the back cover, there is a black and white photograph of a Hertz rental semi moving the band's equipment down an urban freeway. The art screams loud and clear that it's no fun anymore; it's just work. We're only going through the motions of something that was once real.

Neil Young was far from the first to make these statements, of course. Frank Zappa's *We're Only In It For The Money* and the Velvet Underground's *Banana* album (both recorded in 1967) rang the death knell for the sixties much earlier. I also think of Andy Warhol and Paul Morrissey's bleak films about the urban counterculture, such as *Trash* (1970). What makes *Time Fades Away* so significant is that it is apostasy. Zappa, Reed, Cale, Warhol, Morrissey were never especially linked with this hippie counterculture—which no doubt had a more tenuous hold on the east coast in any case.[8] Neil Young, by contrast, certainly was one of its icons. Dylan also abandoned it, but he did it very gently by going country and getting reclusive. If he trashed it, it was in relatively oblique and debatable ways. Neil, on the other hand, had bit the hand that fed him in a major and overt way—a move no other west coast artist had done, although others were to follow. Like Grace Slick, who would interject, after the line "They cannot tolerate our minds" (from "Crown of Creation"), "I can't either" (*Thirty Seconds Over Winterland*). But there was too much gold in them thar hills for most bands who had made their fortunes representing the counterculture to declare it defunct. Neil certainly differentiated himself from his peers. (On the 1974 tour of CSN & Y, David Crosby called Neil's recent output "dark shit numbers" [Petridis 127].)

The 1973 tour and *Time Fades Away* proved to be just an initial descent into the abyss. In fact, much more experimentation was to come in that calendar year! An unsuccessful attempt in the summer to make a CSN & Y album led Neil to head to Los Angeles and book studio time at Studio Instrument Rentals (SIR). The concern was owned by Ken Berry, brother of Bruce Berry. Bruce, as all Neil Young fans know, was a roadie for CSN & Y. He had also overdosed on heroin shortly before this time. The SIR sessions featured Neil, Billy Talbot and Ralph Molina (the survivors of Crazy Horse after Whitten's death), Nils Lofgren and Ben Keith (from previous studio work on *After The Gold Rush* and *Harvest* and, in Keith's case, touring with the Stray Gators). These sessions turned into a wake for Danny Whitten and Bruce Berry. The band guzzled tequila and rolled the tapes. The results were scary rough, out-of-tune, hoarse, jangled —a level of confessional honesty never surpassed in popular music. This survives on the 1975 released version of *Tonight's The Night*, but one should recall that this was not the original tape. Neil told it best to *Melody Maker*:

> The original version of "Tonight's The Night" was somewhat heavier than the one that hit the stands. The original one had only nine songs on it. They were the same takes, but the songs that were missing were "Lookout [sic] Joe" and "Borrowed Tune," a couple of songs that I added. They both fitted lyrically but they softened the blow of the album a little bit.
>
> What happened was the original had only nine songs but it had a lot of talking, a lot of mumbling and talking between the group and me, more disorganised and fucked-up sounding than the songs, but they were intros to the songs. Not counts, but little discussions, three-and-four-word conversations between songs, and it left it with a very spooky feeling. It was like you didn't know if these guys were still gonna be alive in the morning ... it was really too strong.
>
> I never even played it for the record company like that. We made our own decision not to do that. If they thought "Tonight's The Night" was too much the way it came out which they did, a lot of people—they're lucky they didn't hear the other one. (in Heatley 90-1)

Reprise's initial reluctance to release the album confuses the narrative of this trilogy a bit. Since *Tonight's The Night* was released after but recorded before *On The Beach*, the order in which Neil's listeners heard the recordings implied that Neil was getting darker and darker. In actual chronology, *On The Beach* marked him coming slightly out of the abyss recorded on the SIR tapes. But record companies care more about the bottom line than authenticity, which is why artists like Zappa and Young have problems with the business (cf. Zappa's problems with *Läther*).

To discuss these albums in order of release, then, I have to turn to *On The Beach*. But I must first duly note that the material from *Tonight's The Night* was showcased live first. Some was played on the 1973 Stray Gators tour, but left off *Time Fades Away* ("Borrowed Tune," "New Mama," "Lookout Joe"). Much more significantly, the SIR band, christened the Santa Monica Flyers, toured Canada, the United Kingdom and the U. S. in the fall of 1973. They showcased the new material from the unreleased *Tonight's The Night* sessions, but they did much more. This tour remains Neil's most edgy, bizarre, influential and misunderstood live outing ever.

According to many accounts, what you saw on stage would include (depending upon tour logistics) a potted palm tree (sometimes with a light bulb above it that could be switched on for "sun"), a wooden Indian, glitter-spangled boots dangling off the grand piano, and chrome hubcaps (Long 63-4). A scraggly, bearded and hirsute Neil, dressed in a sports coat, would drink tequila out of a wine glass and ramble drunkenly to the audience. One incessant tagline at all the shows was "Welcome to Miami Beach. Everything is cheaper than it looks" (*Speakin' Out* bootleg). The stream-of-consciousness raps would discuss, among other things, Richard Nixon, Watergate, Miami Beach culture and Bruce Berry ("You took Crosby's guitar and stuck it in your arm, man!") (Petridis 23). There were a few gestures towards drunken performance art: at the Roxy Theatre in Los Angeles, he offered to buy the audience a round of drinks and offered a boot off the piano to any woman who came on stage topless—an offer accepted by then-partner Carrie Snodgress (Long 63). (Was that rehearsed? We'll never know.)

Then there were the SIR songs, mixed with some older material. "Tonight's the Night," the Bruce Berry elegy, was especially featured. It would always be performed twice each night, and occasionally three times; its length clocked in as long as 35 minutes in a version performed in Chicago (Long 64). The shows were generous in length.

Needless to say, most of Neil's fan base was alienated and alarmed; for example, this was not a good concert to make the centerpiece of a romantic evening—unless the date was with Morticia Addams. But these shows had their admirers, too. Future punks especially enjoyed them and cited them as a seminal influence (Downing 106). Rock could take the piss out of itself!

Most of the Neil Young scholarship I have read stops here. They describe the shows and their baffling effect / crucial influence, but they never read them semiotically beyond Neil going through a rough patch and wanting to reinvent himself. Or mourning Whitten and Berry in a public Irish wake. These plausible readings leave out key elements, though: why Miami Beach? What does Bruce Berry have to do with that stage set?

I think I've solved Rosebud here, not that it's any great revelation. When I saw Neil in Milwaukee in 1973, he made extensive jokes about eventually playing Las Vegas and inviting us to come see him then and enjoy surf and turf. One of Neil's central concerns has been about the dialectic between "burn[ing] out" and "fad[ing] away" ("My My, Hey Hey"). The Santa Monica Flyers tour confronted those demons head on. It was about two romantic flameouts, yes (Whitten and Berry). But Neil also decided to act out as a kind of *mise-en-scène* the alternative case: a washed-up, drunken rocker gone sleazoid commercial with limited success. Instead of Las Vegas, we got a "Miami" lounge singer— perhaps because it had greater resonance with Nixon, given his associations with the place via Bebe Rebozo and the like?

The show was psychodrama exploring, as a kind of preventive inoculation, how Neil could end up in one of his worst case scenarios. And since he's in it for the long haul, Neil likes to anticipate the future of his career: the International Harvesters were also a form of imagining his future, albeit a far more benevolent one than that offered by the Miami Beach M.C. One last piece of evidence regarding the Miami Beach connection occurs on "Fontainebleu," a Stills-Young Band song from 1976. Regarding the Miami hotel in question (and the city itself by extension), Neil sings: "I guess the reason I'm so scared of it is / I stayed there once and I almost fit." That scary lounge guy was a part of himself, a road he could have ended up taking.

I strongly suspect those were Neil's intentions for the show, the first of a fair number which he arranged with a prominent theatrical dimension. The protopunk attendees drew other valuable lessons, no doubt: that rock music could be more honest by being more theatrically ersatz, that the bigger sham was not Vegas but the "sincere" hippie capitalism of sensitive singer-songwriters and progressive rock bands. Neil had sailed off to mostly uncharted territory at the time (except for work done by his odd doppelganger Iggy Pop). He had become a new kind of singer-songwriter, "one you never figured" ("Powderfinger").

On The Beach (1974) proved to be a more palatable incarnation of this new Neil for the record company: at least he appeared to be sober during the recording sessions. Unlike *Tonight's The Night*, it was released when delivered. A practical reason for this was that the same month it came out (July) saw the start of a highly profitable CSN & Y reunion tour. Reprise would benefit from having new Young product available, even this.

This recording found Neil in a better mood, but only marginally so. The title of the album surely evokes Nevil Shute's bestseller about nuclear apocalypse (and the Stanley Kramer film). The mood of the album is apocalyptic, but more concerning Nixon, Manson, and the oil crisis than the bomb. (Once again, though, British Young critics reveal their ignorance of American automobiles by labeling the Cadillac fin in the sand on the cover a "missile" [Heatley 84]. Then again, they are noticing something important about populuxe auto design!) The cover shows Neil in a *Tonight's The Night* sport jacket looking out on a beach. The weather is overcast. A remnant from the previous tour, a potted tree, graces the back cover. There is the aforementioned Cadillac fin stuck in the sand (a comment, no doubt, on the oil crisis), a Watergate-related headline on the newspaper in the sand ("SEN. BUCKLEY CALLS FOR NIXON TO RESIGN"), cheap beach furniture (the pattern of which is quirkily replicated on the inner sides of the album cover—a joke for the stoners?) and a few cans of Coors beer (downscaling from tequila). The mood set by the cover art is appropriately downbeat, but short of nihilistic.

The music inside is honestly previewed by these visuals. Neil has an interesting lineup of players: all of the Santa Monica Flyers except for Nils Lofgren, a few other Nashville players (Tim Drummond and Rusty Kershaw), and guest shots from Crosby, Nash and several members of The Band (Levon Helm and Rick Danko). For a one-shot ensemble that never got a name, they sound great—laid back, but not sloppy. You can take Rusty Kershaw's guarantee on the witty inner sleeve liner notes to the bank: "But what the Hell I give you my word there is good music in this album." Call me crazy, but ever since I heard it this has been my absolute favorite Neil Young album. (And I keep encountering "Rusties," Neil Young fans, who agree with me.) I think it's because Neil is so complex and dialectical—loud and soft, upbeat and gothic, polished and crazed. This is the one recording where he came closest to keeping those antipodal traits in perfect tension; hence, it's the one album that captures Neil's elusive and mercurial essence best. *On The Beach* is a critic's and fan's favorite: you have to listen to a lot of Neil to appreciate what I'm claiming here.

The crazy part of this assessment is that, like most of Neil's best, it's an uneven effort—more so than *Time Fades Away* or *Tonight's The Night*. There are arguably no throwaway tracks on either (although purists would probably chuck "Yonder Stands The Sinner" off the former). Whereas, depending upon your tastes, as many as four out of eight tracks here could seem comparatively nonessential ("Walk On," "For The Turnstiles," "Vampire Blues," "Motion Pictures"). The power of the album, and its uncanny balance of Neil's opposing aspects, lies mostly in the other four gems: "See The Sky About To Rain," "Revolution Blues," "On The Beach," and "Ambulance Blues." Perhaps the other tracks serve to cleanse the palate?

"Walk On," the album's opener, seems to have received undue appreciation as the one upbeat song on the record. Along with "For The Turnstiles," it was the sole representation of this album on the collection *Decade* (with zero tracks from *Time Fades Away* and two from *Tonight's The Night*—one version of the title track and "Tired Eyes"). On the *Decade* liner notes, Neil has claimed that "Walk On" was written in response to the record company's rejection of *Tonight's The Night*; critics have routinely reiterated this explanation.

Chronologically, however, this account makes no sense. Neil premiered the song in concert in August, 1973, before *Tonight's The Night* was even recorded—let alone rejected (Long 66). Neil is doing some creative memory work here. I'd submit the song is more likely addressing Neil's frustration with CSN & Y (he premiered the song after the failed attempt to make an album) and / or Lynyrd Skynyrd's release of "Sweet Home Alabama" with its anti-Young lyrics. (In an interview I can't relocate, Neil said, in effect, "They wrote a song and I wrote a song. Now we're even." If not "Walk On," what could that song have been he wrote in response?) In either case, "They do their thing and I do mine ... / Walk on." It's got a funky beat, and it was the only track to be released as a single from *On The Beach*, but I don't think it's a masterpiece.

The next track, "See The Sky About To Rain," is on a whole other level. Along with "Southern Pacific" (*Re.Ac.Tor*), "Red Sun," (*Silver And Gold*) and some of the instrumental music for *Dead Man*, it is one of Neil's best train songs. And he's written quite a few: Young loves the railroad, as his massive personal model railroading layout and co-ownership of Lionel Trains suggests. The secret centrality of this song for the Young canon can be found in his naming of his music publishing company, Silver Fiddle, after one of its lines. When the Byrds briefly reunited, they felt the need to cover this song as they had previously covered major Dylan.

Having said all that, it's hard to say why this song is so wonderful. It paints an efficient picture, one that any traveler through the west has seen, of a train moving across a great prairie under an overcast sky:

> See the sky about to rain
> Broken clouds and rain
> Locomotive pull the train
> Whistle blowing through my brain
> Signals curling on an open plain
> Rolling down the track again
> See the sky about to rain.

The "signals curling" line is unquestionable genius: getting a visual metaphor for the signals shifting in the prairie wind. (Neil is not as consistently wonderful a lyricist as Dylan or Joni Mitchell, which gives added power when he nails an image.) The gentle keyboard accompaniment perfectly sets the lyric, although I will confess I prefer the earlier bootleg (and now Archive) versions on piano to the Wurlitzer piano played on the album.

At least three other artists have noticed and captured the feel of such a moment and such a place as Neil has here: poet Jim Barnes in "Paiute Ponies" (*Season of Loss* 4), and filmmakers Satyajit Ray (the train scene in *Pather Panchali*) and Terence Malick (the train in the distance in *Badlands*).

As if all that weren't enough, there is the song's baffling lyric in the middle eight (which clearly meant something to Neil):

> I was down in Dixieland
> Played a silver fiddle
> Played it loud and then, hoo man,
> Broke it down the middle.

Autobiography? A comment on Neil's relationship with the South (extending "Walk On")? An allegory of Neil's need for musical self-overcoming, even to the point of perceived (self-)destruction? As Iris DeMent says, "Let the mystery be."

When discussing Neil's gothic mask, I addressed the next song ("Revolution Blues"). This dramatic monologue from the perspective of Charles Manson is the hardest rocking track on the album. Young and Crosby have a fine guitar duel in the instrumental break. As he would later with the Blue Notes, Neil got into a phase here of playing with standard blues changes and writing his own peculiar versions of the blues: along with the three songs on *On The Beach*, he performed other blues in concert at this time ("Love Art Blues," "Citizen Kane Junior Blues" [later renamed "Pushed It Over The End"]). The peculiarity of these songs resides in their occasional feel ("Revolution Blues" is too exuberant for a blue mood) and their consistent subject matter (Manson, the oil crisis, the fate of the sixties)—critical cavils to be repeated during the Blue Notes outing. These songs work, although you'll never confuse Neil with Buddy Guy or John Lee Hooker.

Side one ends with more pleasant, but less interesting stuff. "For The Turnstiles" sounds good with Neil's hot banjo picking, but is another Rorschach song inviting listener projection as to its meaning. Baseball players and seasick sailors cavort, but to what end? Neil returns to this one a lot in concert, so it means something to him! "Vampire Blues" has nice gothic imagery (bats outside your window pane) and a gurgling guitar solo emulating oil getting sucked from the ground. The lyric explicitly connects Dracula with Exxon and friends:

> I'm a vampire babe
> Sucking blood from the earth ...
> Sell you twenty barrels worth

But, as with "Motion Pictures," the playing is sooo lethargic (as if clinically depressed) that it's more interesting as a mood artifact than an actual piece of music. And maybe that's the point. Neil's playing is always expressive emotionally, but he's down here—and not afraid to show it to a sympathetic listener.

The title track opening the next side is an exploration of the alienation that can come along with fame: "I went to the radio interview / I was standing alone at the microphone ... I need a crowd of people / But I can't face them day to day" ("On the Beach"). Ben Keith's hand drums and the slow delivery of the song (also a blues, technically) fit the lyrics perfectly. This song sounds the way the cover art looks—blue and resigned.

"Motion Pictures" slows things down even further, almost too much. Again, this is a mood artifact. Its dedication to Carrie (Snodgress) and oblique references to the movie business mean it could go on what would turn out to be a substantial compilation of songs Neil wrote about this ultimately unsuccessful relationship (including "New Mama" [*Tonight's The Night*], "Already One" [*Comes A Time*] and "Separate Ways" [planned for the unreleased *Homegrown*, but only performed in concert]).

"Ambulance Blues" is the closing tour de force for the album. The sporadically cryptic lyrics feature Neil at his most Dylanesque. John Einarson has tracked down the Toronto references in the song quite helpfully in his book

Don't Be Denied (items such as "the Riverboat was rocking in the rain" being a reference to a folk club, "TO" being Toronto, Ontario, and the like). As with "Time Fades Away," there is autobiography here. But other subjects also make an appearance, such as the fate of the sixties ("All along the Navajo trail / Burnouts stub their toes on garbage pails") and Watergate:

> I never knew a man could tell so many lies
> He had a different story for every pair of eyes
> How's he supposed to remember who he's talking to?
> Well I know it isn't me, and I hope it isn't you.

Neil even confronts the critics who first deified him, then vilified him:

> And so you critics sit alone
> You're no better than me for what you've shown
> With your stomach pump and your hook-and-ladder dreams
> We could get together for some scenes

In other words, it's all showbiz. The rise and fall of the pop star is a "scene." The ritual interaction between artist and critic is a form of theater. (As Guy De Bord once said, "The spectacle of society is the society of the spectacle.") Lyrically, this song both beckons toward a thematic ("An ambulance can only go so fast / It's easy to get buried in the past") and doubts it ("I guess I'll call it sickness gone / It's hard to say the meaning of this song").

These remarks are only addressing the lyrics, however; the music is equally striking. Neil plays the rawest harmonica of his career on two instrumental breaks. The first time a friend heard the recording, he said that it was as if Neil was "chewing" the instrument—and taking big bites out of it at that! As with the rest of side two, the pace is that of a slow folk blues (except for "Revolution Blues," this is not a rocking album). The other instrumental touch of genius is Rusty Kershaw's slow, bluesy and passionate fiddling, which anticipates later and similar uses of the instrument by Bob Dylan (Scarlet Rivera on *Desire* and in the Rolling Thunder Revue) and John Mellencamp's band. *On The Beach* in general, and this song in particular, has a very special feel and flow. As with the two releases that bookend it, there is really nothing else in Neil's career—or pop music in general, for that matter—quite like it. And if some think that's just as well, never mind the bollocks!

A year later, Neil had completed another confessional album project entitled *Homegrown*. At a house party at his Zuma beach residence, he played the tape to relatively unimpressed listeners. Someone flipped it over, only to hear the still-unreleased *Tonight's The Night*—which drew raves (Downing 118). Neil decided, as an experiment, to finally release the latter almost two years after it had been recorded. This time Reprise agreed to do it. Neil Young critics have speculated that it may have been in exchange for a promise to do something more upbeat next time. This theory makes some sense, since a month after the album was released Neil began the sessions for *Zuma*—the beautiful Crazy Horse album (and first outing for replacement guitarist Frank Sampredo) that marked Neil's emergence from the abyss (Downing 118, Petridis 70-2).

Tonight's The Night never set any sales records when it came out initially, but it received critical adulation for its passion and honesty. As rock critic David Fricke once said, "in rock 'n' roll, attitude is at least seven-tenths of the law" (in Petridis 134). Along with some of the wilder experiments during the ditch excursion of the 1980s, *Tonight's The Night* showed just how much attitude Neil could muster. (One doesn't often associate drunkenness with courage, but that tequila fuelled some serious soul-searching.)

The album begins and ends with the title track, a straightforward elegy of Bruce Berry that in concert always threatens to become—and often does become—a public exorcism of the sixties' heroin demon. Neil never rushes the process; the following lyrics might be repeated twice, three times, or even more in live delivery. As long as it takes to do the job:

> Bruce Berry was a workin' man
> He used to load that Econoline van
> A sparkle was in his eyes
> But his life was in his hand
>
> Late at night when the people went home
> He used to pick up my guitar
> And sing a song in a shaky voice
> That was real as the day was long
>
> Tonight's the night
>
> Early in the morning at the break of day
> He used to sleep until the afternoon
> And if you never heard him sing
> I guess you won't too soon
>
> 'Cause people let me tell you
> It put a chill up and down my spine
> When I picked up the telephone
> And heard that he died out on the mainline
>
> Tonight's the night

(Typed from memory: every Neil Young fan knows this one by heart.)

The power of the song is mostly in the delivery; these lyrics are no threat to Sylvia Plath's reputation (although they are equally confessional). Neil's approach on this song, as with much of the album, is almost journalistic. He wants to show his audience as clearly as possible what hard drugs did to the "hippie dream" of the sixties. It's a very sad song about a very ugly situation.

Having set the scene, the rest of side one provides a series of ravaged and drunken / stoned musings, more mood pieces than invitations to analysis: "Speakin' Out," "World on a String," "Borrowed Tune." Neil's persona is depressed but surviving, and that's what the lurching accompaniment sounds like. "Come On Baby Let's Go Downtown" is an audio flashback to Crazy Horse in 1970, with a then-living Danny Whitten providing vocals for a burning Crazy Horse performance. The irony of the juxtaposition is not only how tight this sounds compared to the rest of the album, but that the song (co-written by Young and Whitten) is about scoring drugs:

> Sure enough they'll be selling stuff
> When the moon begins to rise
> Pretty bad when you're dealing with the man
> And the light shines in your eyes

The seeds of future destruction are already glimpsed. Then it's back to 1973 with side-closer "Mellow My Mind," the most-soused song on a drunken album: a plea for calm from a singer almost at the end of his tether and almost at the bottom of the tequila bottle.

The second side opens with two Stoner ballads with a ragged edge: "Roll Another Number" and the lovely "Albuquerque." As with "See The Sky About To Rain," Neil paints a vivid if sparse geographic picture in the latter song—arguably more through its loping rhythms than the actual lyrics. The former capture the laid-back, big sky enchantment of rural New Mexico; the latter are by now characteristic musings about fame and the need to escape from it. The narrator longs to find a roadside diner that serves "fried eggs and country ham / Somewhere where they don't care who I am." "New Mama" calms things down even more with the most upbeat moment on the album, a lyric celebrating Zeke's birth that goes back to the days of the 1973 Stray Gators tour—as does the subsequent "Lookout Joe," a song about veterans returning from Vietnam to find a different country.

This topical diffusion from the main event is halted by the harrowing "Tired Eyes," straight journalism about a failed cocaine deal resulting in "bulletholes in the [car] mirrors" and four shootings (and presumed deaths). Young ironically eulogizes and cajoles the love generation in its terminal fuck-up mode:

> He tried to do his best
> But he could not
> Please take my advice (please take my advice)
> Open up the tired eyes (open up the tired eyes)

All this delivered with a scary-wasted slurry vocal. After a career founded in high romantic idealism, Young shows here that he can be a consummate realist. "Tired Eyes" in its believable grimness makes Lou Reed's drug songs look like overblown poses (let those who doubt listen to *Berlin*). A reprise of "Tonight's the Night" finishes the wake and seals the coffin. "Classic rock" isn't supposed to sound like this; then or now, you didn't / won't hear this material on the radio. The Plastic Ono Band Lennon album had more commercial potential!

A month after *Tonight's The Night* was finally released, Neil went into the studio with a reformed Crazy Horse and began recording *Zuma* (Petridis 72). Its opening rocker "Don't Cry No Tears" reworked a composition of Neil's that dated back to the days of The Squires ("I Wonder," now on the Archives). Tellingly, Neil had to reach far back into his past to recover the joy he could find in his music. This self-therapy worked: light broke through the clouds on *Zuma*.

Neil had a second critical and commercial run that lasted through most of the latter 1970s. After the gorgeous power-chording of *Zuma*, Neil released an innocuous album with Stephen Stills that belied how good that band was live (*Long May You Run*, 1976). He recycled fragments from *Homegrown* on *American Stars 'N' Bars* (1977), giving his fans a first recording of the Crazy Horse showstopper "Like A Hurricane." Then came *Decade* (1977), a three-record retrospective with a mix of greatest hits and unreleased material that set an industry standard for what would eventually become the compact disk box set. *Comes A Time* (1978) revisited and improved upon the country-folk of *Harvest*: the writing was better and the accompaniment of the Gone With The Wind Orchestra was more lush.

Typically, Neil proceeded to do the unexpected. He had been hanging out with the spud boys from Akron, Devo, in connection with his second narrative film project (*Human Highway*). Unlike most of his peers, Neil liked punk and new wave versions of rock. So he released *Rust Never Sleeps* (1979) with Crazy Horse, a serious foray into the new sounds which got pretty punked out at times ("Sedan Delivery") and even praised Johnny Rotten of the Sex Pistols ("Hey Hey, My My"). He also toured with this material in 1978, using an elaborate stage show that mocked the size of the music industry by using Brobdingnagian props. He got a third film out of the tour (*Rust Never Sleeps*) and a live album (*Live Rust*). The *Village Voice* pronounced him the "artist of the decade." (And that was a tough decade!) Neil had ridden the changes from hippiedom to punk, never getting stale or fearing to innovate. Even the journeys into the ditch made increasing sense. Neil Young was a popular and critical success; he had fared better than anybody in the industry at this point—even Bob Dylan or the remnants of the Beatles.

Moreover, his personal life was going fine. He had finally met and married the love of his life, neighbor Pegi Morton. For a few months, it must have seemed like life couldn't have gotten any better.

But then a series of reversals occurred that would lead into a much longer and scarier trip into the ditch. One catalyst was the discovery that second son Ben (by Pegi) also had cerebral palsy—in a much more severe form than Zeke. Since this disease is not hereditary, and these children were from two different mothers, the odds of this happening are like that of getting struck by lightning twice. As Neil recounted later, he was devastated:

> It was too big a picture to comprehend ... I couldn't believe it ... It couldn't have happened twice. Somehow we made it out to the car. I remember looking at the sky, looking for a sign, wondering, "What the fuck is going on? Why are the kids in this situation? What the hell caused this? What did I do? There must be something wrong with me." (in Downing 150)

Neil had entered the realm of Job or King Lear suddenly. Fortunately, he eventually learned "that probably Zeke did not actually have CP—he likely had suffered a stroke in utero. The symptoms are very similar" (Young, *Waging* 207). (This medical information encouraged Neil and Pegi to try to have another child, the perfectly normal Amber.)

His music attempted to cope with this new state of affairs by initially if obliquely reflecting the situation (*Hawks and Doves*, *Re.Ac.Tor*, *Trans*). Then Neil shut down his confessional persona completely in the early eighties in favor of postmodern stylistic pastiche and masks that stayed on: the resurrected rockabilly leader of the Shocking Pinks (*Everybody's Rockin'*), country singer (*Old Ways*), new wave synthmeister (*Landing On Water*), grizzled bluesman Shaky Deal (*This Note's For You*). There was only a brief burst of the old Neil with Crazy Horse in 1986 (a tour and the album *Life*, which got passed over given all these other listening challenges). And even less successfully, a CSNY studio reunion that produced the underwhelming *American Dream* in 1988. In effect, Neil abandoned all except his hardcore fan base (i.e., people like me) from 1980 until 1989 (*Freedom*) a nine-year foray into the ditch that made the 1973-75 blip look like a dress rehearsal. Still, I kept listening and I want to show you why. He made some interesting music which has not yet had its day.[9]

Like *Time Fades Away*, *Hawks and Doves* (1980) was a transitional album. The major critical gripe was that it seemed a falling off of powers. As indicated above, Neil had serious family issues to deal with. *Hawks and Doves* also resembled *American Stars 'N' Bars* in being half leftovers (side one) and half a thrown-together session with a country-tinged band (side two). Some leftovers, like "Captain Kennedy," were from the unrealized *Chrome Dreams* recordings (which also contributed a great deal to *American Stars 'N' Bars*). As noted above, the lyrics for these were obscure but interesting. Some tracks used assigned dramatic parts for the vocals ("The Old Homestead," "Lost In Space," even the straightforward "Union Man" on the second side). Neil might have gotten the idea from Joni Mitchell, who did it first on "The Pirate of Penance" off her debut album—or from CSN, who employed the technique on "Wooden Ships."

Overall, this is one of Neil's quietest records. Songs like "Little Wing," "Lost In Space," and "Captain Kennedy" are almost delivered in a hush. It's all acoustic with close microphone placement. Side two gets only a little rowdier with a country swing band feel. With the country comes the previously noted turn to the Right: anti-Carter, pro-Reagan, pro-working man, anti-union. "Stayin' Power" and "Coastline" have a grim resolve to them that now seems to be confessional in nature: Neil serving notice that Pegi and he had the grit to accommodate the slings and arrows of outrageous fortune ("We don't back down from no trouble / We do get up in the mornin'" [from "Coastline"]).[10] Rufus Thibodeaux's gorgeous country fiddle injects a little sunshine into the proceedings.

A year later, the music got much grimmer with *Re.Ac.Tor*, his least accessible work ever with Crazy Horse. Neil has talked about how his son Ben was enrolled in a rigorous physical program (the Institute for the Achievement of Human Potential). For eighteen months, Ben was drilled physically and mentally to push him as far as he could hope for with his abilities (Downing 150-2). Neil had restricted free time. The Crazy Horse sessions reflected his predicament: the band produced loud, industrial, highly repetitive material that expressed Neil's frustrations with the world. "T-Bone" is the nadir of the album, nine minutes and fourteen seconds of Young repeating "Got mashed potatoes / Ain't got no T-Bone" over a thudding vamp. When I worked at a factory, sometimes the noise of the machines sounded almost musical: "T-Bone" is that process in reverse. *Re.Ac.Tor* carried to the extreme the Crazy Horse aesthetic that expressive honesty matters more than "chops" virtuosity. The Horse was never in a worse mood than during these recordings, and it shows. Neil Young's music has always been about communication—here he's communicating overwhelming pain, pain so intense it dulls his art. This is not the sort of tape record companies like to receive.

Having said all that, there are some great songs on the album: "Southern Pacific," another excellent train song, and the apocalyptic closer "Shots." Except for those two tracks, however, you have to be in a pretty brassed-off mood to play this recording. Its incredible sonic contrast with *Hawks and Doves* reveals how excessive Young's musical mood swings (always a feature of his career, of course) were getting.

In addition to musical and familial labors, Neil finished his second narrative feature film, *Human Highway*. It premiered on August 16, 1982 (Downing

157). Although critically ignored, *Human Highway* is a very interesting film and a much better movie than *Journey Through The Past*. Imagine John Cassavetes directing a Jerry Lewis picture about nuclear annihilation and you've got some of its special sauce. The film is highly improvised (with an interesting cast that includes Dennis Hopper, Dean Stockwell, Russ Tamblyn, Sally Kirkland and Devo). Young knew how to pick actors; David Lynch would find amazing things to do with some of them later in the decade. Neil himself plays nerdy Lionel Switch, an astonishing homage to the Jerry Lewis stock goofball that remains one of Young's most surprising turns. And the world ends in a big atomic fireball. For some perspective, watch *Human Highway* alongside Cassavetes films like *Opening Night* or *The Killing of a Chinese Bookie* (which resemble Young's film technically, but are noticeably better) and Bob Dylan's *Renaldo and Clara* (if you can get it; this film works like *Human Highway*, but is much more problematic). Neil Young is our best director from the rock world and its second-best actor (David Bowie is obviously superior).[11] That's not too shabby.

Although the film was edited in the early eighties, it was shot much earlier and hence resonates more with Young's *Rust Never Sleeps* work. By this time, Neil had left Reprise for the new Geffen label and had put together a new band: Nils Lofgren on rhythm guitar, Ben Keith on steel guitar and miscellaneous, Ralph Molina on drums (all three alumni from the *Tonight's The Night* sessions); but also Joe Lala on percussion (who had worked with Stephen Stills a lot in Manassas and in the Stills-Young Band) and Bruce Palmer on bass (from the Buffalo Springfield). They went to Hawaii and cut a session for *Island In The Sun*, a planned album of mellow, commercial material (*à la Harvest* and the sand-and-surf songs on *Long May You Run* [Petridis 31]). In what proved to be a pattern, David Geffen discouraged Neil from releasing it. Hearing the bootleg session for the unreleased "If You Got Love" and two of the three songs that ended up on *Trans* from these sessions ("Little Thing Called Love" and "Hold On To Your Love" but not the splendid "Like An Inca"), I can see why Geffen was unimpressed. Although pleasant enough, the lyric writing was pedestrian for Neil: three songs with the word "love" in the title about love must have looked like overkill.

Fortunately, Neil had a backup plan. He had been recording Kraftwerk-influenced songs about computers on synthesizers and vocoders—an electronic device that enables you to alter your voice in various desired directions. The technology was crude. Neil would never be able to realize wishes expressed in interview to sound like James Brown, for example (Crowe 99). But thanks to the machines, Neil did not sound like Neil Young anymore. He could and did put out six vocal recordings on *Trans* that concealed one of the most distinctive voices in popular music by replacing it with an electronic simulacrum. Obviously, this was a radical gesture that would alienate some older fans. Combined with three tracks from *Island In The Sun*, *Trans* was released in December 1982 (Petridis 87).[12] The first pressing was so slapdash that it had an erroneous listing for "If You Got Love," pulled at the last minute, and an errata sticker correcting the mistake.

Neil described the meaning of the album as being covertly confessional:

> [*Trans*] is about communication, about not getting through. And that's what my son is. You can't understand the words on *Trans*, and I can't understand my son's words ... . *Trans* was about all those robot-humanoid people working in this hospital and the one thing they were trying to do was teach this little baby to push a button ... . *Trans* is the beginning of a search for communication with a severely handicapped non-oral person. (in Downing 161-2)

Needless to say, only the few listeners who knew what Neil was going through could pick up on this explicit meaning; but most could feel the frustration behind the opaque presentation. *Trans* was not just a trendy homage to Kraftwerk designed to cash in on a subset of the New Wave audience (although it seemed that way to many); it was Neil's last serious attempt to relate honestly to his audience—without wearing an impenetrable mask—for seven years!

And yet these remarks are after the event. The 1982 *Musician* magazine interview with Cameron Crowe cited above seems much more joyous than the above quote. Neil was also breaking out of a conceptual cage and exploring new musical frontiers. You can hear that in the music as well.

Trans neatly divides into two types of songs—with one striking exception. There are the "human" love songs (directed to Pegi, from the *Island In The Sun* sessions: "Little Thing Called Love," "Hold On To Your Love") and the "computer" songs (directed to Ben, electronic: "Computer Age," "We R In Control," "Transformer Man," "Computer Cowboy," "Sample and Hold," "Mr. Soul"). The album closer, "Like An Inca," is a glorious exception. As discussed earlier, it is a non-electronic song warning of nuclear apocalypse and wearing Neil's Mesoamerican mask. Unlike *Hawks and Doves*, this suggests Neil's developing ambivalence about Reagan's military policies.

The human love songs are unexceptional, although in live performance "Little Thing Called Love" had a piano riff played by Nils Lofgren that would eventually turn into the melody for "Harvest Moon" (*Berlin* video). And "Hold On To Your Love" features harmonizing worthy of the Beach Boys on the chorus.

The computer songs are both quaint musically and prescient lyrically. The Kraftwerk / Gary Numan sound is completely of its era, but the lyrics anticipate further developments in some cases. "Computer Age" predicts the information superhighway:

> Precious metal lines

> Molded into highways
> Running through me
> So microscopically

That they are "running through" the narrator implies either that he is a computer or that he can directly "jack in" to the flow a la William Gibson's *Neuromancer*.

"We R In Control" is a more ominous vision reminiscent of *The Matrix*; these machines "control the TV sky" and "the FBI" in a vision of total cybermediation reminiscent of the more pessimistic musings of postmodern theorists such as Jean Baudrillard. The juxtaposition of these two songs suggests that for Neil this new frontier was both potentially utopian ("Computer Age") AND dystopian ("We R In Control"). As with so much of Neil's ideological positioning, he opts for an unresolved dialectic rather than a fixed position.

"Transformer Man" is the most melodically lovely of these songs. It is an ode to son Ben ("Your eyes are shining on a beam / Through the galaxy of love").[13] When he performed it unplugged a decade later, its virtues as a Neil Young song became even more apparent. Then side one closes with "Computer Cowboy (AKA Syscrusher)," ironically a dystopian prediction of the massive factory farms Neil would oppose in his work for Farm Aid:

> Well his cattle all have numbers
> And they all eat in a line
> When he turns the floodlights on each night
> Of course the herd looks perfect
> Computer cowboy

The plot is further complicated by the cowboy's alter ego as an urban hacker:

> Ride along computer cowboy
> To the city just in time
> To bring another system down
> And leave your alias behind
> Computer syscrusher

Presumably the last word is the alias. So what are we to make of this character? He's a kind of Clint Eastwood badass anti-hero. Perhaps Neil hadn't fully formulated his position on factory farms yet.

On side two, "Sample and Hold" provides a comic, if slightly misogynistic, highlight. This song joins Alice Cooper's "Woman Machine" (*Muscle of Love*) and Frank Zappa's "Ms. Pinky" (*Zoot Allures*) in its fantasy of an artificial substitute for biological womanhood—especially Cooper's, since Young's also involves robot / cyborg sex. Neil sneaks in a joke about PMS when describing the cyborg's specifications: "Mood Code—Rotary Adjustable." Laugh at your own risk; in fairness, the song is also thoroughly mocking its geeky narrator who would crave such a device. This ends up being the most rocking of the synthesizer/vocoder songs, and a good lead in to a vocoder version of "Mr. Soul" (the irony of a soulless song about soul scarce needs mentioning). Then "Like An Inca" brings on the nuclear apocalypse, and a longing to return to pre-contact Incan land in present-day Peru.

As the *Berlin* video shows, the Transband cooked in concert. Bruce Palmer delivered a definitive bass line for "Cinammon Girl;" Nils Lofgren jammed mightily; Neil and Nils hit upon the expedient of acting out the vocoder songs, so the audience could see the intended meaning (for not only were the vocals distorted, but they were sung to some audiences in Europe with marginal skills in English). The Berlin audience appreciated the special encore song written for them, but seemed to prefer the oldies. When Neil ventured out onto a runway to connect with them during "Sample and Hold," they seemed frightened! You can even see people backing away. Pete Long suspects that these shows led to Neil's very low turnouts—so bad as to result in cancellations—when he next returned to Europe in 1987 with Crazy Horse (Long 179). Neil had been too innovative, especially since these dates preceded the actual release of the *Trans* album. In all likelihood, Neil's vocoder material would have been a completely baffling and disorienting surprise. Unless the concertgoer liked Kraftwerk as well, it may not have worked. And some Kraftwerk fans probably thought Neil should stick to "Heart of Gold." In any case, commercial difficulties were on the horizon.

Neil's next project was a country album called *Old Ways*. Since Geffen declined to release it when it was first offered to them, we can only speculate how it might have differed from the 1985 version (Downing 172). Once again, Neil had a backup plan featuring his first completely invented alter ego (not counting Lionel Switch in the film *Human Highway*): the doomed leader of the Shocking Pinks, a retro rockabilly band. This album was released, with little fanfare, in August of 1983 (Petridis 88). As with *Trans*, a puzzling tour initially preceded the album. Video footage of a September concert in Dayton shows that audiences got three versions of Neil: a set of oldies, a vocoder / synthesizer Trans set and the Shocking Pinks. Not everyone was amused by Neil's deadpan pastiche of a fifties rocker.

I certainly got a chuckle, though, when I saw the bizarre cover of *Everybody's Rockin'* in the record store. The spectacle of Neil Young in pomaded hair, sideburns and a pink suit was alone worth the purchase price; that there was sound on the vinyl was a bonus. Neil's shortest release (also faithful to the fifties), it hardly gets a chance to wear out its welcome. Neil's musical personality is completely submerged, except for the fact that he can't help sounding like Neil even when he's imitating Elvis. Highlights include "Payola Blues" (a song both about Alan Freed and the Geffen records situation), "Wonderin'" (a Crazy Horse concert oldie reworked to sound really old) and the authentically double / single entendre neo-race rockers "Kinda Fonda Wanda" and "Jellyroll Man." He throws in a record four cover songs: "Betty Lou's Got A New Pair Of Shoes," "Rainin' In My Heart," "Bright Lights, Big City," and the Elvis classic "Mystery Train." Fun stuff, but guaranteed not to make a single new fan. I have yet to meet one individual who got into Neil Young on the basis of this recording. To David Geffen, it must have looked like over-the-top self-indulgence. To Neil, it was no doubt a diversion from various stresses—and a chance to quit being Neil Young.

As we have already noted, Neil was so successful at this curiously postmodern project that Geffen sued him when he resubmitted *Old Ways* for his next release. Neil Young was no longer making Neil Young records! Geffen could not have really expected to win this peculiar litigation, but Neil got the point. After the 1985 release of his purest country album, he mixed his experimentation with slight nods to the marketplace.

Nowadays, country music is a lot bigger because of people like Garth Brooks. In 1985, Neil putting out a country album meant that he would be appealing to a smaller consumer base than he would as a folk-rock popular artist—bad news for the record company that depended upon rock sales.

On the other hand, Neil did have a strategy. He no doubt noticed from his work in Nashville how many rock session players ended up there, especially as a result of the disco era (when their services were no longer needed as drum machines and the like replaced them).[14] Neil would have also grasped that aging baby boomers were the new audience for country, as they would cease to follow every twist and turn of the pop scene. Country, despite its penchant for murder ballads and drinking songs, has always been musical comfort food, particularly in its highly accessible musical dimensions. Despite Hank Williams being denied access to the Grand Ole Opry, one could debate whether "avant-garde country" is possible: the music of the people must be where the people are, not where they could be if they stretched their ears.

Neil being Neil, he in fact recorded to some extent this hybrid beast of avant-country. The proof is in the song "Misfits" off *Old Ways*. Admittedly, it sounds conventional (even Neil never figured out how to alter its musical conventions, except in so far as his country rock has always been doing that). But, as noted above in our discussion of his Dylanesque mask, the song's lyrics are exceedingly strange: a surreal and apocalyptic narrative triptych extending the work of Neil's psychedelic phase with the Buffalo Springfield (especially "Broken Arrow"). Country listeners who made it to the end of side one would have had something to scratch their heads about.

The rest of *Old Ways*, however, is fairly conventional country. As Neil sings on "Get Back to the Country," he's "back in the barn again." A big irony here is that Neil has been an influence on country music doing what he normally does (i.e., making country come closer to rock music). This is Neil doing a little post-Neil country ("Get Back to the Country"), but mostly all pre-Neil country. Some elements here work (the duets with Waylon and Willie, the haunting piano work of Hargus "Pig" Robbins, the equally striking backup vocals of Doana Cooper), some are debatable (the massive strings, which fit the musical function on a cover of "The Wayward Wind," but risk sonic overkill). As with *Everybody's Rockin'*, the lyrics take a back seat to the pastiche—with the obvious exception of "Misfits."

This sound enabled Neil to do a different kind of touring with his country band, the International Harvesters. For the first time, he got to play state fairs and country venues. The audiovisual evidence suggests that, like the Shocking Pinks, this band was better in live performance than in the studio (e.g., a 1984 Austin City Limits concert). Young complicated his allegiances by whipping out Old Black and playing a blistering "Down By The River." To say nothing of his sneaking off to the Catalyst Club in Santa Cruz for the odd gig with Crazy Horse (Long 143). Neil's premature retirement was beginning to end; he was not ready to go out to the country pasture yet.

After a rapid succession of style changes from one album to the next (synthesizer band, rockabilly, country), Neil next shook up the fan base with a modified synthesizer sound on the aptly named *Landing On Water* album (1986). He left off using the vocoder, but otherwise this session went for a mid-eighties pop sound (Neil Young does a-ha). We're really in the ditch now, but in the depths of pastiche—not the gritty authenticity of the 1970s excursion. *Landing On Water* is an underrated album with some fine songwriting on it ("Violent Side," "Hippie Dream, "Touch the Night"). [15] But the production values tie it to the moment of its creation. (The same is even truer of the bizarre videos of "People on the Street" and "Pressure" Neil produced for the MTV crowd!) Moreover, Neil was discovering the limits of his adaptability. His seventies audience was convinced by his sincere explorations of punk and new wave; the frenzied eighties genre-hopping seemed more contrived, even desperate. He didn't want to repeat himself, but his experiments were not succeeding.

An obvious plan was to revisit a band he had struck gold with in the past, to see if the magic could be rekindled: Crazy Horse. The resulting release, *Life* (1987), is arguably the best of the five Geffen contract recordings and a significant improvement over *Re.Ac.Tor*, his last outing with the Horse. Side one offers explicitly political songwriting ("Mideast Vacation" and "Long Walk Home" discussed above), a general state-of-the-planet rumination ("Around the World") and a fine return to the Mesoamerican mask ("Inca Queen"). The synthesizers from *Landing On Water* remain, however, updating but muting the force of the band.

Side two is rawer—and given this band, thus better! It begins with three straightforward rockers: "Too Lonely," "Prisoners of Rock and Roll" (an arch embrace of the band's garage status ["we don't want to be good"]), and "Cryin' Eyes" (a song originating with the Ducks experiment).[16] Neil hadn't sounded so authoritative, good-humored, and confident since *Live Rust*. The album closed with several slower love ballads ("When Your Lonely Heart Breaks" and "We Never Danced;" the latter was a reworking for rock band of a song Neil wrote for Alan Rudolph's film *Made In Heaven* [which also featured a Young acting cameo]). All in all, *Life* was a modest return to form, if not as confident as his work with the band in the previous decade.

But the commercial damage had already been done; only hardcore fans even bothered to listen to the album or attend the shows when Crazy Horse toured Europe around the time of the album's release. (American response to tours before and after Europe seemed better, at least on the visual evidence of the Westwood One broadcast from San Francisco's Cow Palace [November 21, 1986].)

After a low-profile Canadian reunion with the Squires in June of 1987, Neil was prepared to go even further back to his roots than with Crazy Horse. Even as he emerged from the ditch a decade earlier by reworking a Squires tune, Neil formed a ten-piece blues band, the Bluenotes, which would cover old Squires compositions such as "Ain't It The Truth." This proved to be the last musical pastiche project Neil would ever attempt. It was more of a popular and critical success than the Transband, the Shocking Pinks or the International Harvesters for several reasons.

For starters, Neil was off the Geffen label and back on Reprise. That had to feel good for all concerned, since Geffen and Neil had strained and unproductive relations, to say the least. In addition, this band sounded great. The horn players stretched out Neil's sound in a vital new way; they could play long and hard. In essence, this band delivered in concert what the Blues Brothers promised. An August 18, 1988 audience video from Toronto shows a generous and satisfactory delivery of Young roots music to an enraptured audience. And finally, sales benefited from a controversy connected with the "This Note's For You" video, directed by postmodern auteur Julien Temple. Temple's video, in keeping with the sentiments of the lyrics ("Ain't singin' for Pepsi / Ain't singin' for Coke"), parodied recent soft drink commercials done by Michael Jackson and Whitney Houston. MTV refused to air the video, fearing to offend its corporate sponsors. Neil razzed them and got lots of media exposure. Eventually, MTV not only relented but gave the video its award for best video of that year—an interesting maneuver to conserve their theoretical hipness!

"This Note's For You" was hardly the best song on the album. (Indeed, its line about not singing "for politicians" was revisionist history.) Actual highlights included "Ten Men Workin'" (a self-reflexive work song), "Coup De Ville" (a very moody and atmospheric piece that captures late-night melancholy with its gentle dynamics), "Twilight" (good horn textures and a rousing arrival of Chad Cromwell's drums at the end), "Sunny Inside" (excellent homage to the horn sound on Stax recordings), "Can't Believe Your Lyin'" (a big bass sound from Rick Rosas, who would later feature prominently on *Freedom*), "Hey Hey" (an homage to "Shake, Rattle and Roll" with more taunting of MTV in the lyrics) and "One Thing" (proof that Neil can play the blues). Admittedly, Neil's lyrical interests often did not dovetail with standard blues subject matter (as with his blues writing in the seventies). But the changes were there, and the band sounded fine. As the above list indicates, different songs showcased different players. This was a team effort.

The album only hints at the amount of material this band performed in concert. The Bluenotes are right up with the Ducks for underrepresentation. Not until the Young archives come out will the general listener be able to thrill to unreleased blues gems such as "Bad News" and "Big Room," to name but a few in the vaults (Long 203). "Sixty to Zero," later to become "Crime in the City" on *Freedom*, had many additional verses when performed with the Bluenotes. My Toronto bootleg video also shows that this band could play as scary and seemingly endless a version of "Tonight's the Night" as the Santa Monica Flyers, Crazy Horse or Neil's "friends and relations" entourage. The Bluenotes were a good thing, but Neil kept moving on.

Unlike the previous recordings of the eighties we have been discussing, CSN & Y's *American Dream* (November 1988) was for Young not so much a deliberate foray into the ditch—after all, he knew how to make "Neil Young records" and had enough in the vaults for an emergency bailout at any time—as an unsuccessful attempt to get back on the highway. I don't think Neil has the sole responsibility for that, to say the least. Too many chefs may have spoiled the broth. The biggest problems with the album are its overly slick 80s production values, which just aren't right for this band, and Stephen Stills's unfortunate adoption of the coke habit that David Crosby successfully kicked (Neil's precondition for making the album). As a result of the latter, the one Stills song that cooks is co-written with Neil ("Night Song")—although I'll confess to liking "Got It Made," because it reminds me of earlier and better Stills efforts. Neil doesn't give the band his best stuff here. Aside from "Night Song" (probably Neil's best piece here as well), he contributes "Feel Your Love" (a lovely soft rocker), "This Old House" (farm activism revising Nash's "Our House" from *Déjà Vu*), "Name of Love" (another state-of-the-world commentary that needs focus) and the title track (a dated indictment of Jim and Tammy Faye, partially redeemed by synthesized pan pipes, that overall pales in comparison to Zappa's more satiric takes on the subject). Because Neil was holding out, the best songs on the album are "Compass" (Crosby's honest confrontation with his addictions, using lovely alternate tuning), "Soldiers of Peace" (a Nash rabble-rouser), and "Nighttime for the Generals" (a Crosby political rocker with some fire in it).

American Dream was largely vilified when it came out, perhaps because it was not the parting of the Red Sea a *Déjà Vu* sequel was expected to be by the boomers. I even once saw it listed in a mall bookstore cutout tome about the Worst Albums of All Time—ranked number two (between Lou Reed's pure noise release *Metal Machine Music* and Elvis' spoken-word only *Having Fun With Elvis On Stage*). Funny, but mean. The album really isn't that wretched, especially if you've been following these guys over the years. In any case, they were discouraged from touring; they appeared only at a Bridge School benefit that December.

For Neil, the CSN & Y reunion was only a temporary setback. His career was back on track. With Rick Rosas on bass and Chad Cromwell on drums (both from the Bluenotes), Neil formed a power trio that ended up being the core of a new band: the Restless. Neil Young and the Restless—get it? They were the heaviest sound Neil ever obtained, between heavy metal and industrial (you can hear chains clanking on some of the recordings, such as "Don't Cry"). Neil released an import EP of just this band's work in early 1989 (*Eldorado*), then combined it with gentler acoustic material and a new political rocker ("Rockin' in the Free World") for the larger opus *Freedom* in the fall. Neil followed up this productivity with tours both deploying his new band and as a solo act throughout 1989. By working out physically beforehand, he burned down *Saturday Night Live* in an appearance there in September of that year (Long 215). Neil Young achieved critical and commercial successes he had not enjoyed since the late seventies; he was back on top of the world. And his confident return to working with Crazy Horse the next year, which resulted in *Ragged Glory*, clinched the deal. Neil was out of the longest ditch he had ever explored.

Why was this second journey an avant-garde gesture and not just a career mistake? I'll admit that it's a debatable point. Young himself has explained his eighties output in various ways, as we have seen: as a response to family and career pressures, as a desire to reinvent himself, as a desire to reach different audiences. When he collected some of the eighties work for a compilation CD (*Lucky Thirteen*—nice irony!), he subtitled it "Excursions Into Alien Territory." On VH1 *Legends*, he compared it to an artistic phase, a set of "pictures on the wall" he did a la Picasso's Blue Period.

To defend this work, I have to explode a few assumptions that may not even need exploding. First off, no artist is in complete control of their work. A work can run away from its creator's intentions and still be successful—or not. And that "success" is constantly negotiated by those who perceive it. So if Neil's eighties output was affected by outside influences, we have to deal with that—because complete control is never a possibility.

Secondly, all art has a commercial dimension. It costs money to make, for starters. A popular artist like Neil Young and someone like, say, Aaron Copland are on the same continuum of aesthetic producers in a marketplace. There are distinctions to be made, of course, but there is no commercial-free zone in a capitalist society. Ask any musician; they'll laugh in your face at the question. Frank Zappa was unusually direct on this subject.

In the 1980's, Neil Young saw a strangely fluid marketplace. Many musical styles proliferated, and nothing was sure-fire anymore. As Marx observed once, "Everything that is solid melts into thin air." The New York art scene had some bizarre success stories such as Julian Schnabel (who painted on black velvet) and Mark Kostabi (who created a factory where others did work in his name). The closest analogue to Neil Young's work, however, was Cindy Sherman: a photographer who played with the fluidity of identity in a series of images where she manipulated her identity through costume, makeup and *mise-en-scène*. One image was compelling; to see a series of them was terrifying and sublime, a revelation of the tenuousness of selfhood in an image-based society.

Neil's eighties output works in a parallel fashion. To experience its power, you have to listen to it all more or less back to back. The sublimity lies between the lines: the same person going from electronics to rockabilly to country to new wave pop to rock to blues. Where Neil in the seventies cut to a core, abject, confessional identity, in the eighties he gave us a terrifying shiny surface. By the time I bought *Landing On Water*, he had ME worried—and I was beginning to learn about postmodernism. Like the seventies work, this was an honest response to the era, a very different era.

As such, I think this stuff works in a way that Dylan's occasional variegations do only to a lesser extent (*Down In The Groove*, *Under The Red Sky* [unless the latter is supposed to be a children's album?]). Neil cares and is trying to communicate an aesthetic vision. This work alienated most of his fan base, as he may have suspected it would have. But it abides. I find it interesting that youth-oriented CD stores in Columbia, Missouri (a college town), keep it all in stock. As with all risk-taking art (even the popular variety), it may find its best audience in the future. If there is ever a cyborg hit parade, how could *Trans* stay off it?

Neil in the 1990s

I questioned for a decade and change how much sense it made to talk of Neil Young as a practitioner of avant-pop. This was not to imply that his work had fallen off significantly in quantity or quality. A better conclusion would be that the world has caught up with him, finally. Like Bob Dylan, Young is an icon—and it's very hard to be an avant-gardist under those conditions. Neil's multiple inductions into the Rock and Roll Hall of Fame (for Buffalo Springfield and as a solo artist) made the point in an obvious fashion. Neil IS classic rock, although I never hear them play anything later than "Rockin' in the Free World" on my local station in rural Missouri. He had returned to being Neil Young, and he didn't whoop it up like he used to; I had ceased to expect the ditch rides of the eighties or seventies anymore. Since he is Neil Young, though, no one should have ruled out a new foray into the ditch. But all signs suggested this was unlikely.

Nineties Neil and beyond oscillated between his two strengths: gentle country / folk rock *à la Harvest* and *Comes A Time* (*Harvest Moon, Unplugged, Looking Forward* [with CSN & Y], *Silver and Gold*) and passionate and raw electric work with Crazy Horse, Booker T. and the MGs, Pearl Jam or "friends and relations" (*Ragged Glory, Arc-Weld, Mirror Ball, Broken Arrow, Year of the Horse, Road Rock Volume One*). At his very best, he combined the two (*Sleeps With Angels* with Crazy Horse).

As noted at the beginning of this chapter, Neil's best claims to avant-pop in the nineties can be found in the *Arc* disk, *Sleeps With Angels*, and the soundtrack for *Dead Man*. The first and the third of these are primarily instrumental recordings showcasing Neil's guitar (*Arc* features some vocals; the soundtrack includes dialogue from the film). *Arc* (1991) is especially in your face: it's over thirty minutes of guitar feedback drawn from song conclusions on the Smell The Horse tour edited together into one suite. Thurston Moore of Sonic Youth (backing Crazy Horse on the tour) urged him to release it. Neil thought of it as a palate-cleanser for club use, something to fade in and out between other records: since it has no groove or beat, it is compatible with anything (Heatley 177).

The adventurous listener should sit through it all, however. It raises questions worthy of John Cage about noise vs. music (in this respect, it resembles Lou Reed's *Metal Machine Music*). Like Yoko's abject sonic blasts, it messes with the time-space continuum. Frank Zappa could have renamed it "A Small Eternity With Neil Young." *Arc* develops into an ABABA structure eventually, with A representing vocal repetitions from "Like a Hurricane" and B indicating vocal drones from "Love and Only Love." After this formal gesture, we get a clear ending from "F*#!in' Up" and a jazzy bass interlude from Billy Talbot (probably from "Welfare Mothers"). It then returns to the formal pattern with a B section (including one of the band [Billy?] yelling "No more pain!") and a concluding A section.

Arc is as close as Neil will probably ever get to writing a symphony. Take heed, Billy Joel: Neil was born to rock; he'll never be an opera star! It combines minimalism (repetition) and maximalism (a BIG loud sound). It works like speed; it is the sonic equivalent of the Gulf War that the band was touring in conjunction with; it is the ultimate encore for the two-disk *Weld* set it was initially packaged with. *Arc* is art, not commerce; David Geffen would not have been amused to receive it. But, as with the soundtrack of *Dead Man*, it was an unobtrusive side project. You could purchase *Weld* without *Arc*. Neither of these were big hyped Neil Young releases like *Tonight's The Night* or *Trans*. The avant-pop was still out there, but you had to look for it more actively.

The soundtrack for *Dead Man*, Jim Jarmusch's revisionist western (1996), is even better than *Arc* in some ways. The music is as loud, but it's more brooding, meditative and expressive. It opens with Neil's ultimate train music, mimicking the steam engine on his guitar by scratching the strings and deploying other unconventional effects. The rhythms eventually develop into electric picking reminiscent of the song "Eldorado" (off *Eldorado* and *Freedom*). Pump organ, sound effects and film dialogue complement the guitar soloing. It's an audio souvenir of the film, but it stands on its own as a mood-setter.

Sleeps With Angels (1994) is the closest Neil got in the nineties to an avant-pop release as a mainstream recording. As already noted, it's about repetition on many levels. The black label on the CD echoes the same color scheme on *Tonight's The Night*, even as the death of Kurt Cobain that inspired the title track conjures up the deaths of Danny Whitten and Bruce Berry. Melodies are repeated ("Western Hero," "Train of Love"); lyrics are repeated ("Blue Eden"—sandwiched between "Change Your Mind" and "Train of Love" on the disk—contain lyrics from both songs). Tack piano songs open and close the album ("My Heart," "A Dream That Can Last"). The longest jam on the album, "Change Your Mind," contains a lot of repetition in its somber development. The album seems to be completely about stasis, repetition, deja vu, the return of the blues. Crazy Horse hadn't sounded so haunted since they lost Danny Whitten and became the Santa Monica Flyers. Even as Neil recaptured *Harvest* on *Harvest Moon*, he had successfully held another musical wake for a man who had quoted him on his suicide note.

These three outings were the exception for a more contented and confident Neil. His career at the turn of the millennium seemed ditch-proof. And so it basically was, although Neil never has lost the capacity to alienate part of his fan base by lefting or righting or throwing some sonic curveball. If we can characterize his last decade of activity, it would be about making some avant-pop moves without heading into the ditch: the privilege of his iconic status. It all started with his response to United Flight 93's struggles on September 11, 2001.

From "Let's Roll" to "Let's Impeach The President": Neil Young's Conceptual Politics for the New Millennium

On the first "Topanga" volume of the Archives, there is a hidden "Easter egg" interview where Neil says, and I quote, "fuck the audience." His *cri de coeur* has to do with the sad fact that Neil has seldom had audiences who trust him to do his art—in contrast to, say, Bob Dylan. Dylan has surprised, defied and thwarted the expectations of his audience so many times that they have come to pretty much expect the unexpected. As Neil notes in this commentary clip, his audiences used to be ready for anything when he was a new face on the scene: he could do a concert of almost entirely new material and have an open-eared, receptive response. Now, after all these releases, he has an audience which contains members that have definite expectations regarding what they're going to hear. This is compounded by some fans' embrace of the Stoner persona as the real Neil: they show up drunk and / or high to the concert, yell random shit at him and throw him off his game. He's right: I've seen this behavior at a fair number of his gigs, especially in the more intimate settings when he tries to talk to the audience or play acoustically. On a bad day he has to wonder if anyone really listens to him closely anymore.

The 2002 release of *Are You Passionate?* confirms that this is not only a problem in live performance, but even with the reception of new recordings. It's like Neil's music has become background music to fire up the bong to. When this CD came out, some liked it and some didn't. But no one understood it (as far as I can tell from reading every review I could get my hands on). The buzz was all about Neil's 9/11 anthem "Let's Roll" (vs. "Ohio," the unreachable gold standard) or his choice to work mostly with Booker T. and the MGs. What no one seemed to notice was that this was Neil's first rigorously organized concept album (as such, a strong precursor to the *Greendale* projects). They weren't expecting such a move after decades of intuitively and pleasingly sequenced material. Neil gave a few clues on the cover art of the disc, but they were well-concealed.

Let's start with the back cover: twelve index cards laid out in rows (the eleven titles on the album and one, "Gateway Of Love," tantalizingly omitted). The sequence read vertically or horizontally yields a different order than the final version on the CD. So what? Well, this tells us that he was consciously thinking about the order of the songs: the final arrangement decided upon just might matter!

On the front cover, we get more information: the title, a rose, a fatigue jacket, and a mysterious photo of two lovers. (Neil and Pegi made up? Neil's parents? A soldier and his girlfriend? It doesn't matter.) This tells us that the album is about two things we get "passionate" about: love and war (and that they can be interconnected in strange ways, as we shall see). If we pay attention to the actual lyrics, we realize that the love portion of this release is Young's version of Dylan's *Blood On The Tracks*: his marriage was hitting a rough patch (worked out, apparently, for the time being). He tells us pretty explicitly what was going wrong and how he fixed it. This could be a purely fictional narrative persona, but I doubt it given the ready applicability of the lyric content. This material segues into the actual songs about conflict and war, followed by closure for both inter-related themes.

Let me give you the structure of the album if you listen to it straight through as intended. Indeed, that may be a partial reason why folks didn't catch the organization of the work. If it's not background music left playing, releases are cut up by shuffle play features or IPod selections. Anyway, here's how Neil laid it out:

- Songs of marital and family conflict: 1) "You're My Girl" 2) "Mr. Disappointment" 3) "Differently" 4) "Quit (Don't Say You Love Me)"

- Songs of war and political conflict: 5) "Let's Roll" 6) "Are You Passionate?" 7) "Goin' Home"

- Resolution of marital conflict: 8) "When I Hold You In My Arms" 9) "Be With You"

- Resolution of political anxiety (up to a point): 10) "Two Old Friends"

- Ultimate affirmation of his wife and marriage: 11) "She's A Healer"

I'll break it down in a little more detail. The CD's opener, "You're My Girl," starts out with only a slight hint of the trouble ahead. It's addressed presumably to his daughter Amber, and is a gentle lament about the costs of being a hands-off dad:

> Well I took you for a walk on the forest floor
> 'Cause I wanted to share some things
> But it sure looked like you'd been there before
> It was such a natural thing

My read on this opening is that Neil tried to give her the facts-of-life talk and / or dating advice, but she had beaten him to the punch by her actual experience. He's not too traumatized by this "natural" development, a mood reinforced by Booker T's upbeat Stax chooglÍng organ. But he is worried about her getting to leave the nest without his really spending enough quality time with her: "Please don't tell me that you're leavin' me quite yet."

The next song deepens the critique by acknowledging the narrator needs to take the "blame ... [f]or livin' [his] life in a shell." He hasn't been accessible to his loved ones, causing a "change" in their attitude towards him and his encounter with his doppelganger "Mr. Disappointment." Once again, he's let folks down. "Differently" offers more fence-mending, the wish that he'd behaved better. Amber's maturation is revisited in a more somber way in his address to his wife:

> Yeah I know you tried and tried
> But your signal I just missed
> When you said my little girl would soon be gone
> Yes I didn't hear you then
> And it might be too late now
> That's another thing I'd do
> Differently

These sentiments go all the way back to a Neil country cover: "The saddest words / are these four words ... / it might have been."

"Quit" brings this thematic aspect of the collection to a crisis with its dramatic opening: "Don't say you love me / That's what she said." The protagonist's neglect and substitution of hollow words for actual behavior is called out, resulting in much eating of crow: "I know I treated you bad ... / And I'm the one / The one who did you wrong." He knows that this could be the last straw, prompting a rearguard promise: "I'm never quittin' you / Even if you quit me." As Paul Williams reminds us in his brilliant writing about Bob Dylan, performance is far more important than the mere lyrics of a song. On the page, these words may well strike one as trite. But with Booker T. and the lads providing backup, it's a whole other story. Neil's choice of sidemen gives him a new persona, in effect: the soul man screw-up who wants to make it right through song, a character who runs like a rich vein through the Stax catalogue. ("Mr. Disappointment" no doubt alludes to Otis Redding's "Mr. Pitiful.") It provides a kind of intertextual musical assurance to the person we could call the "Pegi figure:" these things have happened before and can be dealt with.

Then we get the big curveball: ominous drones, cell phone sounds and the call to arms of "Let's Roll." Most listeners are tempted to dismiss this collection as a pleasingly sequenced grab bag of songs like most Neil releases at this point. But I'd submit this is a brilliant segue to the second "passionate" theme of the album. After all, 9/11 happened—just like Neil's marital squabbles—as a result of NEGLECT, this time on a global geopolitical level. You can pick your own area of coverage here, from our abandonment of the Afghan people after the Soviets left which led to the hegemony of the Taliban (the subject of *Charley Wilson's War*) to the Bush administration's disinterest in intelligence reports about Bin Laden. How much did Neil look into all this? It's hard to tell, but he's smarter than most people give him credit for. In any case, his instincts are spot on here: there is an odd parallel to be made. Some internet commentators point out that the references to "Satan" and "evil" are an overripe return to Young's early Reagan-era jingoism, but (once again) they're not paying sufficient attention: like "Powderfinger," this is a dramatic monologue—and the point of view is that of Todd Beamer just before he storms the hijackers. How do you think the situation looked to him that day?

I suspect the title track comes far closer to Neil's actual, highly nuanced and ambivalent take on the situation. Its politics are strange, to say the least. His haunting blues guitar expresses the sorrows of the world for a situation running completely out of control: "Are you scared of it? / Do you wish that it would stop?" In between these questions and his refrain about a "turnin'" world (cf. "Two Old Friends" below), he offers two distinctive and peculiar scenarios. The first is easily the more bizarre of them, delivered with a gentle lyricism resembling Neil's Blakean child persona:

> Once I was a soldier
> I was fighting in the sky
> And the gunfire kept comin' back on me
> So I dove into the darkness
> And I let my missiles fly
> And they might be the ones
> That kept you free

Militarily, of course, this is painted with broad and somewhat inaccurate strokes. He seems to be depicting a Stealth fighter ("I dove into the darkness") eluding anti-aircraft shells (although surface-to-air missiles would be as equally in play as "gunfire") and launching cruise missiles and the like. "You" in the last quoted line is to me ambiguous: probably American civilians, but possibly Afghanis or Iraqis—if you give the line a very optimistic reading that our interventions might lead to a sustainable democracy in those regions. The odd vocal tone of the delivery might reflect Neil's belief that young soldiers are somewhat idealistic, even innocent, in contrast to the experiences they are about to encounter. And maybe the optimism here comes from the fact that this is their narrative point of view (it is, after all, in the first person).

The second scenario is about a "prisoner" on "public display" who lets onlookers "see [their] soul on that day." An American prisoner? A Taliban? An Iraqi? We're not told. The end result of all this ambiguity is a sense that Neil is stoically expressing military conflict as a condition of life, a result of political passion. But that's where he stops: you can pretty much create your own ideological adventure based on what you want the song to be about. He's simultaneously "lefting and then righting." Unlike the view from Todd Beamer's head, Neil's multiple personae here don't yield up a firm point of view beyond general sympathy for all concerned.

The next war song, "Goin' Home," throws a further spanner in the works. The only song featuring Crazy Horse, this track finds Neil back wearing his Native American mask. The lyrics are pretty surreal/mystical, beginning with a vision of the "wind" from Little Big Horn and Custer's last stand blowing though present-day "buildings" and "streets," thereby making the protagonist feel like they—I choose a neutral plural because of some gender ambiguities we shall see below—are "goin' home" (to that homeland they've never seen?). The second verse could be about either broken treaties or bad business negotiations (with your former record company?):

> Droppin' in on you my friend
> It's just like old times
> Said the fool who signed the paper
> To assorted slimes
>
> It's hard to get blood from a stone
> But I'll give it a try
> To provide your accommodations
> And leave you satisfied
>
> You'd think it was easy
> To give your life away
> And not have to live up to
> The promises you made

Once again, we have the rhetorical figure of hyperbaton in the last two lines; in their intense emotion there is a switch from referring to the victim (the "fool") to the promise-breaking "assorted slimes." So the conjunction "and" is somewhat misleading. But then again, who's studying the lyrics while Ralph Molina's intense war drums are beating?

The final verse has a female protagonist in the third person (vs. a gender-neutral first-person narrator whom we might easily link with Neil). She returns to the battlefield of the opening stanza, and wackiness ensues:

> [She m]ade a turn on a wooden bridge
> Into the battleground
> With a thousand warriors on the ridge
> She tried to turn her radio down
>
> Battle drums were pounding
> All around her car
> She saw her clothes were changing
> Into sky and stars

This final metamorphosis and fusion with the past and the natural world is reminiscent of Native American beliefs regarding the Ghost Dance: that with the right ritual it is possible to reconnect with the ancestors. Musically, Crazy Horse gives it all they've got here until the abrupt conclusion. Clearly the music is meant to be a kind of accompaniment to the final transformation (an optimistic hope these days that this song would ever get played on the radio!).

Now recall the context: three songs about war and conflict. If the title track replaces the clear point of view of "Let's Roll" with more universal ambiguity, this Native American mystical turn further generalizes the theme into coverage of conflict in general. As such, despite appearances, *Are You Passionate?* is more about politics than political per se (as opposed to follow-up releases such as *Greendale, Living With War* and *Fork In The Road*—unquestionably Young's most overt sustained ideological statements in his entire career). As such, it's a kind of transitional release from the somewhat safer product of the 1990s.

Then we get the closure and resolution of the themes addressed in these first seven songs. The marital difficulties prove easier to fix. "When I Hold You In My Arms" is a soulful affirmation of his love providing stability in ominous, even apocalyptic times ("We'll be blowing up the planet just like an old neighborhood"). "Be With You" is far more sanguine and hopeful:

> Girl it shouldn't be too hard
> To live with you
> It's really not complicated
> Until I get the blues

He can do this, and Booker T.'s big funky sound seals the deal.

The closure to the themes of military and political conflict is more tenuous and less satisfactory, as we might expect. In "Two Old Friends," Neil gives us a fable of a preacher meeting God at "the Golden Gate." Given the preacher's question, it is more probably atop the Golden Gate bridge than the entrance to heaven: "I'm dreamin' of a time when love and music is everywhere / Can you see that time comin'?" Not surprisingly, God answers "No my son. That time is gone." Notice is served that the sixties are over, never to return (still news in some quarters, maybe even to Neil a bit). The song is a kind of theodicy, an attempt to account for "so much hate" in the world. The preacher can only ask for God to help him to keep evil out of his "old black heart"—a rueful descriptor worthy of later Yeats or the poetry of Stephen Crane. As in the title track, the only constant we can be assured of is "the way things change." At least they had this little talk, in a locale described by the preacher as "a world where we're from another place." I see that allusion as not just a comment about the transcendental, but an oblique acknowledgment from Neil Young that those who lived through the sixties experienced something magical that remains if only as a memory. It was indeed "another place."

"She's A Healer" gives us the big resolution the preceding track could not: a thorough affirmation of the woman in his life. It was an unusual musical palate for Neil at the time (and at most times): extended and jazzy—with funky organ from Booker T., trumpet (Tom Bray), bongos (Steve Potts) and great blues piano from Neil. The song has a spacious, wide-open prairie sound (a geographical location referred to in the third verse). I think of it as an anti-matter universe version of angst-ridden early explorations such as "Down By The River" and "Cowgirl In The Sand:" a celebration, not a lament or a murder ballad.

This fine album pretty much vanished without a trace critically, perhaps because he was touring with CSN & Y at the time rather than behind this with just the studio band (although Booker T. and Duck Dunn were providing backup keyboards and bass for the tour). When I saw the February 15, 2002, "Tour of America" date in St. Louis, Neil showcased "Let's Roll," "Two Old Friends," and "Goin' Home." The first two worked every bit as well as on the CD; the last rocked out, but did not match what the Horse could do with it. All the while an even more ambitious project was percolating: a tour, film and CD (and eventually even a graphic novel) about an imaginary California coastal town named Greendale.

In the intriguing booklet which accompanies the CD, he recreates a kind of primal scene he had with his novelist and journalist father, Scott Young:

> ... i went up in the attic to see my daddy, who's a writer: he's written many books. he had an old underwood typewriter. i walked up there and it took a lot of nerve to go up there, because you weren't supposed to go up there because he was writing, so i walked over and i looked up at him and i said, "what're you doing, daddy?" and he said, "well, I'm writing," and i looked up at him and said, "what're you writing?" he said "I don't know." he said, "i just come up here every day and start writing, sometimes i don't write anything, sometimes i write all day. i don't know what i'm writing." i said "well" to myself, "there must be something to learn there." my 3-year-old brain was churning on overtime. [punctuation and capitalization are Neil's]

He offers this anecdotal memory as a kind of insight into how he just produced the Greendale project. He imagined a place and some characters and would make up stories and write songs about them on the way to the studio:

> i realized the same characters were in the second song as were in the first song. it was a big surprise. we were all keeping track of it. it was like watching a soap or something. every day I'd come in with a new song. usually i wrote it on the way over there. i'd stop my car and write a little bit. then when it stopped coming, i'd

> move my car about 500 yards and stop again. there was a whole
> bunch more material there. [Neil's punctuation and capitalization]

Even by Neil's standards, this was a gift from the muse. It flowed torrentially, except for a few days of writer's block after he killed off his favorite character (CD notes). And in all the concert performances, he told lengthy additional stories about the characters—never the same as far as anyone could tell. It was as if Neil Young walked into a fully realized world the way William Faulkner inhabited Yoknapatawpha County or Thomas Hardy knew Wessex. Reviewers would duly note that he was only following in the footsteps of his novelist father (whom he was especially aware of as his dad's health declined with dementia). But I also find it significant that he would take this unprecedented approach after the neglect his far more personal previous release received. Not only is this much more impersonal; it can't be neglected! Because it's a narrative, you have to pay attention to the whole thing. You snooze and you lose. Neil telegraphed this aspect of the project by not including the lyrics on the CD (as opposed to notes about the songs) and by using a stripped-down version of Crazy Horse: just Neil, bassist Billy Talbot and drummer Ralph Molina (no Frank Sampedro on the studio version vs. the tours). This arrangement makes it easier to hear the lyrics.

I had the good fortune to see the Greendale show on August 9, 2003 (Starlight Theatre, Kansas City) before the CD came out. The audience was completely in the palm of his hand. He sweetened the deal with the elaborate stage show: a cabin on stage left with smoke coming from the chimney, a jail, costumes, slides and film. But for the first 90 minutes (before an encore set of crowd-pleasers), you had to go where he wanted you to go. Given his disdain for being a human jukebox, a very empowering arrangement he clearly relished.

Although this was experienced as the shock of the new (no small feat for a popular artist with this long a career), it wasn't as much so as one might think upon further reflection. Given Neil's fondness for masks and personae expounded at great lengths above, of course, the Greendale project was just an extension of the masks into full-blown fictional characters (and yes, there is still a lot of their creator in each of them). Still, genre considerations with all this proved interesting. Obviously, this was an old-fashioned concept album ... maybe even a (gasp) rock opera. But no one uses those terms these days if they can help it. Critics (and Neil) were more comfortable deeming it a musical novel. Sun Green's final dream in the booklet of "a high school play" is germane, since what she envisions matches exactly the "Be The Rain" staging of the tour, which had that cheesy amateur theatrical feel (cf. the Miami beach set for the Santa Monica Flyers but more populated with actors). Since the devil is a major character in the drama, I'm tempted to call it a modern morality play in the grand medieval tradition (however unintentionally).

Paradoxically, the externalized nature of the presentation enables Neil to make several lyrical jokes at his own expense. In the opener "Falling From Above," Grandpa comments on Neil's ridiculously prolific career: "Is there anything he knows that he ain't said?" Cousin Jed in the jail later tells Sun Green that he's written a song "longer than all the others combined / and it doesn't mean a thing." These lyrics occur in "Grandpa's Interview," a long song (and one of the longest on the recording). Later in that song, Grandpa again breaks the fourth wall, lamenting (as he dies):

> That guy just keeps singing
> Can't someone shut him up?
> For the life of me I don't know
> Where he comes up with that stuff

As you might gather, this is very loose and fun material (albeit with some serious issues worked in). The Greendale project works best if you roll with it and don't sweat the slapdash nature of its narrative. The songs are performed in all formats (CD, concert, film) in the order in which they were written, which violated plausible chronology and clarity on more than one occasion: the media would certainly hassle the Green family before Officer Carmichael's memorial service, for example. And is Lenore the cop's wife or his mistress? She has her name on an envelope with money in it which the widow's friends hide from her, but their specific motives are somewhat unclear beyond sparing her pain (what's the potential reason for the anguish?) And the widow is never named in the song as Lenore. Perhaps these lacunae were meant to give the listener interpretive options. But if you leaned too hard on this soap bubble of a tale, it popped.

Until the film came out, that is—to some extent. In the movie we find that the songs are "chapters" which are not given in linear order—a modernist move readily found in writers like Faulkner or Louise Erdrich. And yes, we also found out that the widow and Lenore are played by separate actors. Carmichael was having an affair, thus clarifying Neil's cryptic remark at a Dublin acoustic concert (included as a DVD in the first edition of Greendale) that the officer had "a bunch of secrets."

"Falling From Above" is a kind of overture, introducing many of the characters in the Green family. Grandpa posits the first of several sage bits of advice:

> a little love and affection
> in everything you do
> will make the world a better place
> with or without you

Then we get the shuffle blues of "Double E" with more pastoral effects: the grandmother is mentally "livin' in the Summer of Love." Yes, it has been that long since 1967. We're back in the lyric territory of "Two Old Friends"—with a dash of Thomas Pynchon's novel *Vineland*. Conflict doesn't really emerge in the plot until the third track, which introduces not only the devil, but Grandpa's brother Captain John Green, who won't set foot on land because of his concerns about the moral rectitude of Greendale. He seems to be another older ex-hippie, since he quotes John Lennon's "Come Together" in his soliloquy in "Devil's Sidewalk." (On the Dublin DVD, Neil gives the ages of both the Captain and Grandpa as around 75.)

"Leave The Driving" relates the first dire turn of the plot: Cousin Jed Green's killing of Officer Carmichael during a routine traffic stop (because Jed's car was full of marijuana and cocaine): a "tragic blunder." The song's lyric focus curiously expands to discussing terrorists using the internet to plot future attacks and critiquing the Patriot Act (which Neil initially endorsed, as we have seen). He seems to want to simultaneously sympathize with the police, question the surveillance of ordinary citizens, and warn about terrorism. He thus covers all the possible bases at the expense of a clear agenda beyond trying to balance these conflicting considerations. The final stated "moral" of the song is a more pointed if broad denunciation of the powers that be: "some people have taken pure bullshit / and turned it into gold." Insert your agenda here.

"Carmichael" ironically borrows from the Beatles' guitar riff on "Ticket to Ride" to convey the memorial service for the slain cop and that mysterious envelope with money for Lenore. Neil explains his intentions in the accompanying booklet: "some people think that police are evil and hippies are good, but it may not be true. [T]here's a gray area." The next song focuses on Earl Green, Vietnam veteran and painter ("there's a lot of those," Neil correctly notes). "Bandit" is the only acoustic song on the CD, featuring a lovely, yearning vocal and a rough quotation from Dylan's "Like a Rolling Stone"—Young name-checking his perceived peers (Lennon and Dylan). In concert this proved to be a show-stopper.

With "Grandpa's Interview" we get the next catastrophic development: Grandpa's heart attack and death resultant from an encounter with a television interviewer. Grandpa holds forth again:

> It ain't an honor to be on TV
> And it ain't a duty either
> The only good thing about TV
> Is shows like "Leave It To Beaver"

The lyrics eulogize him as a "hero ... fighting for the freedom of silence, / trying to be anonymous." The media are a consistent target in this song cycle and presentation, from Sun Green's book report on *How To Use the Media* to the Clear Channel billboard in the stage show and Grandpa's demise.

As noted, this is where Neil was momentarily blocked as songwriter. He had killed off his favorite character. But thinking about Grandma (and granddaughter Sun) led him to switch things up again with "Bringing Down Dinner," the only track on which he plays keyboards (his trademark pump organ). The slow march of the opening drums is highly reminiscent of the old Buffalo Springfield chestnut "Broken Arrow" to these ears, which adds additional resonance to the song.

Then the torch gets passed to Sun Green, who assumes center stage (figuratively and literally) for the last two cuts. "Sun Green" showcases her civil disobedience: she welds herself to an eagle at "Powerco." The political target here is the collusion between the Bush White House and the utility companies to cause rolling blackouts which could be blamed on the democratic governor of California, who was replaced by Arnold Schwarzenegger in a special election. As the DVD included in the second edition of *Greendale* shows, Neil had a lot of fun with these last two songs playing with a megaphone and getting feedback on it from a vocal microphone. The vocal distortions of his trademark voice are oddly reminiscent of the vocoder experiments on *Trans*—only grittier and dirtier. Like Sun Green says, "Hey Mister Clean! You're dirty now too!" And the psychedelic processing of the phrase "golden moment" (when talking about the media coverage of Sun Green's action) is a throwback to the Buffalo Springfield days.

We get a rapid burst of additional plot developments in "Sun Green." The FBI kill Sun's cat (because it scratched one of them) and plant marijuana in her room (a charge which doesn't stick). Sun meets Earth Brown at John Lee's bar, a troubled young man who gets a potion—put in his glacier water by the devil—that causes continual anxiety and thirst. Sun impulsively decides to go to Alaska with Earth Brown to "be a goddess in the planet wars" like Julia Butterfly Hill (who is referred to in the song). The film shows the devil riding on the back of the camper with them to Alaska.

My interpretation of these odd juxtapositions is that Neil wants to avoid an unrealistically upbeat ending to the tale. Both literally as a character and allegorically as a planet, Earth is in big trouble. The devil wants to get Alaska under his sway as well. Neil wrote all this in 2003, well before Sarah Palin arrived on the national scene to underscore his concerns.

The closing anthem "Be The Rain" offers a musical last stand in defense of America's last wilderness. In Sun's dream vision of the high school play and at the conclusion of some of the concerts, her cheerleading cohorts come on stage in camouflage and war paint waving "a flag with a black monkey wrench on it" (CD booklet): a clear reference to Edward Abbey's novel *The Monkey Wrench Gang*, the Earth First! movement and eco-terrorism. (Actually, costuming and makeup at the finale were a constant; this particular flag was not.) Like Abbey himself and post-Abbey eco-writer Mark Spitzer (in *Bottom Feeder* and *Age of the Demon Tools*), Neil is walking a fine line: showing characters embracing extreme environmental activism without explicitly and directly advocating such behavior himself. Think of it as a kind of suggestion! Then a suitably grungy guitar solo takes us out of *Greendale*, Neil's most political and wittiest and conceptually dense production: a big surprise on all levels from a guy who a decade ago was beginning to look reasonably predictable as an artist.

Neil's film version of *Greendale* is quite interesting as well, firm proof that Neil keeps getting better as a director. (Unlike his previous efforts, including guilty pleasure *Human Highway*, *Greendale* actually gets airplay on cable channels like Sundance.) The film was shot on Super-8; the soundtrack was the album and appropriate sound effects (waves, cars going by). As a result, there was no actual script. The actors lip-synched the dialogue from the songs: the only voices you hear in the entire film are from the musicians (Neil, Crazy Horse, the Mountainettes back-up vocalists). No actor per se makes a sound in the film. To get their performance right, Neil urged them not to think of delivering their lines "as singing; think of it as talking" (DVD bonus features).

The songs appear in the same order as on the CD, but they are given the following chapter numbers to add the modernist twist alluded to above. Respectively, the chapters are III, II, VI, I, IV, V, VII, VIII, IX and XII. Upon closer inspection, this does not solve the chronological problems of the CD and in fact creates new ones. If "Leave The Driving" is chapter I, resulting in the incarceration of Jed, how can he be relaxing on the porch with Grandpa in "Falling From Above" (chapter III)? Grandpa's harassment by the media (VII) comes six chapters after Carmichael's shooting and three chapters after Carmichael's memorial service—a highly unlikely progression. Most intriguingly, there are two missing chapters between "Sun Green" and "Be The Rain." Is Neil just messing with us, or is he weak on his Roman numerals? Does it matter? And art gallery owner Lenore is an evocatively mysterious character. Not only is she Carmichael's mistress (and she attends the memorial service), but via Sun Green she slips Jed a note in prison which makes him smile. Since Jed killed her lover, what would be so positive in that letter? It's like Bobby Gentry's "Ode to Billie Joe." And Lenore's taste in art is hilariously off-kilter, preferring a representational painting of the devil holding a sign marked "Alaska" to Earl's psychedelic abstracts.

The charm of the film, as is the case for all of Neil's films, is his laid-back approach to *mise-en-scène*, acting and plot logic. He wants to give the audience a good time, sugarcoating his strong messages. We get wacky effects like the devil getting a shock (with animated skeleton effects) when he touches a church door; he also breathes colored smoke when he cleans Earl's glasses to send the latter's art career in a new direction. Lenore and Edith Green "sing" the falsetto parts on "Bandit." The "helicopter" buzzing the Green house is a cheap improvised prop (the production crew said such effects were "MacGyvered" into existence (DVD bonus features). As a result, the feel of *Greendale* is somewhere between a home movie made by a gifted child and a midnight movie or drive-in classic: kind of like Zappa's films but warmer and nicer. Neil would look back on his two-year dalliance with the Greendale material as a "gift" right up with his personal best work. As he says in the making-of featurette, "I like to keep the door open and let the wind blow." The wind of inspiration blew hard and strange over this material—and one can only hope we haven't seen the last of Sarah White, the spunky Sun Green lead. It can't be easy to turn in a good performance with palpable star quality when you're only lip-synching!

After Neil's two-year long exploration of Greendale in 2002 and 2003, he embarked on another extended project: the *Prairie Wind* CD and DVD, culminating in Jonathan Demme's concert film masterpiece *Heart of Gold*. In the context of this section, its continuity is more formal than thematic. Neil's new standard operating procedure after *Greendale* has been to at least release a Bernard Shakey DVD with every new CD offering (if for no other reason than his preference for the audio quality on the DVD format). If possible, however, he also tries to produce a theatrical release for art-house distribution as well: true for *Greendale*, *Prairie Wind* and *Living With War* (*CSNY/Déjà Vu*)—but not *Chrome Dreams II* or *Fork In The Road*. Maybe because he's too busy trying to develop a roomy fuel-efficient car?

Another formal resemblance to *Greendale* (and *Are You Passionate?*, for that matter) is that *Prairie Wind* is clearly a concept album as well. The best proof for this is that the concert film follows the exact order on the CD release. Director Jonathan Demme opted to exclude the mood-breaking Elvis tribute, "He Was The King," which appears as an extra on the DVD. But you can tell by an audio edit in the film—the only sonic discontinuity of house noise that one hears—that this too was played live between "This Old Guitar" and "When God Made Me."

Thematically, *Prairie Wind* is a divagation from the more political material which preceded and followed it. By no means a breather, as we shall see below, it is in fact a culminating act of his career: his ultimate Nashville statement (just as *CSNY/Déjà Vu* might be his ultimate CSN & Y gesture).

The opening lyrics of "It's A Dream" imply such a momentary renunciation of political events: "I try to ignore what the paper says / And I try not to read all the news." The only political song on the album is "No Wonder," which alludes to a "fallen soldier" from some war and to September 11th:

> That song from 9/11
> Keeps ringin' in my head

I'll always remember somethin' Chris Rock said
"Don't send no more candles
Whatever you do ... ."

This last reference recalls not only the many memorial vigils after the attacks, but also Neil Young's candle-filled set at a memorial benefit concert when he performed an exquisite cover of John Lennon's "Imagine" (changing the lyrics to "imagine no possessions / I wonder if I can"). That was then; this is now.

Neil also addresses in this one song the environmental and governmental issues that came to pervade Greendale:

Back when I was young
The birds blocked out the sun
Before the great migration south

We only got a few
They last the winter through
Mother cooked them good and served them up

Somewhere a senator
Sits in a leather chair
Behind a big wooden desk

The caribou he killed
Mean nothin' to him
He took his money
Just like all the rest

The references to his childhood here not only evoke the theme of memory that unifies this CD, but provide a marked contrast to the thoughtless hunting of the public official. The last stanza quoted has obvious connections with some of the megaphone statements on "Be The Rain" ("Let the caribou stay!"; "They're all bought and paid for anyway!"). But that's it for the politics of *Prairie Wind*: as we shall see, he had bigger existential fish to fry which put even the absurdities of George W. Bush's presidency on momentary hold.

After the *Prairie Wind / Heart of Gold* Nashville country rock roots project, Neil put forth the most ambitious—and, I would argue, successful—political statements of his career. Six months after the concert at the Ryman Auditorium and the subsequent assistance he provided Jonathan Demme in mixing the film, Neil reconvened bassist Rick Rosas and drummer Chad Cromwell (who had worked on the previous project). From March 29 to April 2 of 2006, they recorded nine new songs about the second Iraq war, the environment, the Bush presidency and the state of the nation and the world at large: *Greendale* minus the narrative sweetening. Tommy Bray (from the *Are You Passionate?*

sessions) eventually showed up to add some martial trumpet. On April 5 and 6, Neil added to the mix a 100 voice choir at Capitol Records studios in Los Angeles. By April 28, Neil was ready to give away the entire release of *Living With War* online free as a total song cycle (so you couldn't cherry pick just the most controversial stuff). The official CD came out a little later and climbed to #15 on the U.S. charts (it went to 7 in Canada, 14 in the U.K. and 24 in Ireland) (DVD with *Living With War: "In The Beginning"*). In the next five months, Neil rehearsed and toured behind the new songs with Crosby, Stills and Nash. By 2008, the *Living With War* material had yielded 3 CDs (the original, *In The Beginning* and the film "soundtrack" to *CSNY/Déjà Vu*), a lively and active website, a concert tour and Neil's finest work as a videographer and film director. I also strongly suspect, although I can't prove it, that these efforts helped turn the tide towards the Democratic party in the 2006 and 2008 elections. Not bad for a rocker in his sixties!

Perhaps we should begin by noting how Neil Young works these days. As we saw with *Greendale*, he likes to wait for the muse to arrive and then he writes approximately a song a day. Up until the last decade or so of his career, he would occasionally move song fragments around until they were in some satisfactory recordable form. Once the studio arrangements existed, he tended to keep the lyrics stable in performance (excepting adjustments for the decade referred to and the like). He does not keep fiddling with his lyrics in performance like Bob Dylan. But initially there used to be some fluidity and mutation of lyric and song.

Since *Greendale* at least (and probably earlier: *Silver And Gold*?), that has not been the case. Nowadays Neil comes in with a song, tweaks it a bit and records it. The result stands. Because he's been writing songs for a long time, the results are usually between very good and exceptional. (I will suggest that there is a slight falling off of powers in *Fork In The Road*, though he quickly bounced back.) But that songwriting methodology which he uses will help to account for some of the lyrical oddities we shall find in what is essentially an amplified version of broadsheet folk song composition and performance. He cites Phil Ochs and Bob Dylan as inspirations for his work here in the liner notes, appropriately enough. But John Lennon and Yoko Ono's *Some Time In New York City* is an even closer analogue—and a comparison that can only redound to Neil's credit!

So what we have here are some simple electronic folk protest songs written in the heat of the moment that are then interpreted and complicated by video and cinematic presentations. Each song on *Living With War* exists in as many as five forms: 1) the completed mix on the eponymous CD / website; 2) the rawer mix lacking the choir and Bush sound bytes, etc., on *Living With War: "In The Beginning"*; 3) the videos for the songs directed by Neil available on DVD either with #2 or #5 texts; 4) the CSN & Y version of the song on the *CSNY/Déjà Vu* "soundtrack" CD (in quotations because there are almost no complete performances in the film itself); and 5) the *CSNY/Déjà Vu* film / DVD. Presentations 1, 2, and 4 simply offer varying degrees of complexity in the arrangements—and different kinds of complexity (a choir harmonizing vs. Crosby, Stills, Nash and Young). The videos (3) thematically enhance the songs with images and are thus the fullest embodiment of what Neil Young wanted to convey with the lyric content. The film (5) is Neil trafficking in the aesthetics of reception, showing how this material was received by actual audiences. (The postings on his website served a similar function.) In short, he used the full resources of the contemporary mediascape to voice some pointed opinions while sincerely wanting to facilitate a dialogue with anyone who wished to engage him in agreement or disagreement.

No wonder the tour was the "Freedom of Speech" tour: it was a celebration of the implications and tolerances of our first amendment rights, rights which were indeed compromised by the Patriot Act that Neil, ironically as we have seen, initially endorsed. Neil changed his mind in public about government surveillance with *Greendale* first, of course. But this broadband call to conscience worked on a whole other level. In fact, as the film of the tour shows, the response to the show was a kind of litmus test as to how well Americans understood and appreciated their first amendment rights: a test we did not pass with flying colors.

Because of the complexity of these various versions of the songs, I prefer to discuss briefly each song in all relevant forms (as opposed to running through all the separate showcases for the whole song cycle), following the track order on the first three ways in which they were presented. Such a way of proceeding ought to allow us to see hidden connections, convergences and developments among the various formats (ultimately anchored, for me, in the bold video statements).

"After The Garden" opens the *Living With War* song cycle. It both revisits the environmental concerns of *Greendale* and reminds us that the environment is an even bigger issue than the concerns addressed in the material to follow:

> Won't need no shadow man
> Runnin' the government
> Won't need no stinkin' war ...
>
> After the garden is gone

The anthemic guitar work on "Old Black" reinforces the message with a clarion call worthy of the finest protest folk rock. This may not seem to be a very subtle song; but, like most of these tracks, there are lyrical curve balls to be discovered by the discriminating listener. The reference to the environment as a "garden" and the odd drug reference to 1960s acid varieties in the second verse ("won't need no purple haze / won't need no sunshine") reveal that this is a direct address to the Woodstock nation and younger wannabe members of same. After all, Joni Mitchell's anthem to Yasgur's Farm—covered by CSN & Y—told that generation that "we've got to get back to the garden." Here's the update. In the movie, Graham Nash makes a similar point when he acknowledges that the band is in part preaching to the boomer choir: "I'd like the choir to get off their ass and do something" (*CSNY/Déjà Vu*).

Neil's ambitious video for the song raises its message to a whole other level. I won't break it down for you second by second, but what the video does is nothing less than offer a several minute condensation of Vice President and should-have-been-President Al Gore's book and film *An Inconvenient Truth*. Neil obviously did this with Gore's cooperation, since clips from the film and book abound. Using charts, CNN style ticker tape text and documentary footage of ice formations collapsing, the video recapitulates all the major talking points of Gore's work. Since I already knew his stance from exploring the original sources, there was nothing new here for me. But I am incredibly impressed with how Neil managed to boil all this down so that a media-savvy generation impatient with the long form could extract Gore's informed polemic by just watching this video (and maybe hitting the freeze frame a few times).

The following title track addresses the way that the Iraq War (now, in 2013, it's more the war in Afghanistan) permeates our lives subtly "everyday." The musical highlight of the song is a reworking of the "Star Spangled Banner" in the bridge, a haunting and pointed reminder that Neil Young considers this talking back to power a profoundly patriotic act—and that his beef is not ever with the actual armed forces serving our problematic leaders (texts 4 and 5 are dedicated to them). On the other hand, the reference to "how the west was won" reminds us that our expansionist interventions go back to the call of Manifest Destiny: a gentle if pointed history lesson. The video accompanying "Living With War" is again brilliant with its deployment of rapid-fire footage of the missing man formation in a memorial fly over, Iraq war imagery, views of Mecca, Stealth fighters and the juxtaposition of returning Iraq veterans with historical films of the celebrations for returning soldiers at the end of World War II. It shows us the obsessive and passionate immersion in the military effort which the lyrics address—and Neil's hopes for closure and peace ("[t]ry to remember peace," his version of John Lennon's "Give Peace A Chance").

I think time will confirm my strong sense that "The Restless Consumer" is the conceptual highlight of the release. Its lyrics are darkly witty and far-ranging: from our oil dependence through the Iraq war to the Bush presidency, globalized consumer culture, mass starvation and our refusal at the time of the song's release to conduct serious diplomacy with parties we don't agree with ("Hate don't negotiate with Good"). All this delivered with blistering guitar, bass and drum attack. As drummer Chad Cromwell observed in the rehearsal sessions on the DVD documentary, "it's a lot of information." I am reminded of the modernist aesthetics of poets such as Ezra Pound, T. S. Eliot and Charles Olsen. As with these avant-garde poets, the meaning of the lyrics has to be derived by thinking about the rapid-fire juxtapositions here. Neil chooses not to connect the dots for the listener as opposed to just bombarding us with diverse concerns that only a little reflection will reveal are deeply interconnected: we fight wars for oil to support our overindulgent lifestyles—instead of feeding the world—and "elect" liars to do our dirty work for us, etc. etc.

Again, the video vastly enhances the presentation with a blitzkrieg of images. In fact, Neil quotes from most of the other *Living With War* videos in just this one by split-second cutting, making this one visual text a condensation of the whole project's argument just as "After The Garden" summarized Al Gore. He achieves other stellar effects as well. A shot of post-Katrina New Orleans over the lyric line "You're not even tryin'" reminds us that neglect of the poor is abundant in our domestic policies as well. The central image of the video is a private jet dancing in the clouds with a stripe painted on the front of its fuselage which curiously resembles a smile: a potent symbol for the "restless consumer." And it ends with a pointed montage of yuppies sipping red wine and eating pasta edited against Iraq war footage. In its filmic form I am reminded that Neil's technique hearkens back not only to Pound and Eliot, but also to Soviet filmmaker Sergei Eisenstein at his most advanced: the intellectual montage of *October*. We're not talking about direct influence here; although it is possible, there are endless ways to be indirectly influenced by a giant like Eisenstein. But I am asserting Neil's arrival as a mature and sophisticated filmmaker. "The Restless Consumer" is not a glorified home movie!

By contrast with this hyperkinetic assault, "Shock And Awe" is almost (key qualifier) musical comfort food. And indeed, in standard folk procedure, the melody is largely recycled from "My My Hey Hey (Out Of The Blue And Into The Black)." Behind this familiar hard-rocking melody, Neil addresses the superbia of the "Mission Accomplished" photo shoot and the ban on presenting the return of flag-draped coffins in the news media (a recurrent beef of Neil's redressed by his videos, concert tour presentation and tour documentary). The final verse ("We had a chance to change our mind") addresses the 2004 election, a point rendered more clearly in the video with its images of John Kerry. Clearly Bush's reelection (if we grant him Ohio) was a kind of tipping point for Neil ending his silence. The video ends poignantly with an Iraqi wall hanging of a woven souvenir rug depicting the World Trade Center, followed by archival time-lapse footage of same prior to its destruction. We suffered; the world had to suffer too—even if we didn't go after the actual perpetrators ... .

"Families," the next cut, continues the imagery of homecoming (perhaps in a flag-draped coffin) which permeated the three previous songs. The lyrics are consistently ambiguous as to whether this is the return / existential situation of a live or deceased veteran: at times implying both possibilities; at other times favoring one reading over the other. The request in the first verse implies that this is not a living soldier: "When you try to bring our spirit home / Won't you celebrate our lives." The entity is pointedly referred to as a "spirit," as opposed to a living body. On the other hand, the second verse could refer to any veteran: "When you write your songs about us / Won't you try to do us justice." The third verse, like the first, favors being read as the voice of the dead with its imagery of going back to the light familiar from accounts of near-death experiences: "I see a light ahead. There's a chill wind blowin' in my head." When the next verse opines "There's a universe between us now," it could be addressing either the gap between life and death or between Iraq and America. But the last verse's closing affirmation implies a living soldier returning: "I just got my ticket today / I can't wait to see you again in the / USA." After all, dead soldiers can't obtain tickets—unless, of course, this is figurative language (which it certainly could be).

The video of "Families" enriches the song's ambiguities even further by providing the information that, for Iraqis, the family is the most important cohesive social unit (followed by tribe and nation). So the song is even in part about the Iraqi side as well. The video's concluding footage of a military funeral reinforces the suspicion that the returning vet is a casualty of war.

The final interpretive wrinkle is provided in the *CSNY/Déjà Vu* film by Iraq veteran Bo Alexander, who felt the song was a personal communication from Neil to him. Bo's father was killed in Vietnam, so he felt with total conviction that the song was about "not coming home." As part of the tour's modus operandi, Neil had the "totally unbelievable" experience (Neil's words) of meeting Bo at one of the shows. What is implicit here is that Neil is not trying to police our response to this deceptively simple lyric. Especially if you're a veteran, you can steer its meaning any way that works for you. As such, "Families" is a throwback to Neil's earlier and more wide-open political utterances—and to Bob Dylan's "Blowin' in the Wind," the ultimate one-size-fits-all activist song.

Speaking of Dylan, the sixties icon haunts the succeeding "Flags Of Freedom" both in the lyrics (where he is named) and in the melody (which is borrowed from "Chimes Of Freedom"). In the spirit of Bob, Neil also throws in a hefty harmonica solo. Lyrically, this song is an exceptionally powerful choice to follow "Families"—since it is about the troops leaving to go off to war. One might expect Neil to present these two images in chronological order: departure, then homecoming. By reversing the presentation he gets a much more complex effect (plus, don't forget, he's recording the songs in the order that he wrote them; he received the sequence in this order). We know how it will all end when we see the "younger son ... going off to war." In the DVD documentary, Neil says that playing the song reduced him to tears and snot, giving his wife Pegi some cause for concern regarding his health; the 100 voice choir seems similarly moved. In the video, documentary footage of departure parades is accompanied by a ticker tape listing all the wars the United States has fought in, including campaigns against Native Americans and the Cold War. There are far more conflicts than you might have thought. The running header also duly notes that the second Iraq war was our first "pre-emptive strike," a new level of imperialist engagement.

It's taken Neil six songs to set up the situation for his most controversial—and misunderstood—political statement ever: "Let's Impeach The President." His account of the genesis of the song is both revealing and hilarious. In the rehearsal documentary on the DVD, he tells the band "I didn't want to write this." But on the morning of April 1 (!), 2006, Neil Young found a rat chewed in half (presumably by one of his cats) in his "favorite bathroom" and took it as a "sign" that it was okay to write the song. He jokingly told the band "You guys are free to go ... . This is a volunteer mission." He later told a Hollywood reporter that the piece was essentially a list of reasons for impeaching Dubya: "it's a long song" (*Living With War: "In The Beginning"* DVD).

Well, actually it isn't that long—although it might seem to last forever for fans of Fox "News." As many of us know, it cites numerous misbehaviors of the Bush administration that will keep historians scratching their collective heads for centuries: starting the war in Iraq based on deliberately misleading intelligence, getting our nation up to its ears in debt to China to pay for it, violating the essential rights to privacy guaranteed in the Bill of Rights with the Patriot Act, neglecting the citizens of New Orleans after hurricane Katrina, appointing incompetents and "criminals" to positions of power, and dividing the country ideologically and manipulating religion "to get elected." But look at the last verse of the song:

> Thank God he's cracking down on steroids
> Since he sold his old baseball team
> There's lots of people looking at big trouble
> But of course our President is clean
>
> Thank God

Friends, "Ohio" it's not—not with this ending. I am forced to conclude that this tub-thumping barn-burner of a song, after its passionate presentation, takes a comic turn. It's as if Neil knows that the system would never let George W. Bush get impeached, despite the earnest efforts of a few committed people (in contrast to Bill Clinton, who was impeached for committing fellatio with an intern!). So this song becomes a wish-fulfillment fantasy (a sing-along in concert: follow the [literally provided] bouncing ball!). The lyric ultimately tips its hat by self-deconstructing in its conclusion. Instead of building up a stronger and stronger case, it ends with a mild gibe about Bush's hypocritical regulation of major league sports. This is a *cri de couer* to be sure—but not the angry, hateful and revolutionary tract it was demonized as in some of the media.

On the DVD bonus features, we discover that a reviewer from the *San Francisco Chronicle* aptly described the media collage in the center of the song as "messy but effective." Yes indeed. In the final version of the song, Neil juxtaposes contradictory sound bytes featuring the President reversing his positions on weapons of mass destruction in Iraq, the Saddam Hussein connection to Al Qaeda, the need to go to war and the like to a chorus of "Flip ... Flop." This last of course refers to the 2004 smear campaign conducted against John Kerry, citing his record as contradictory. On the video, this gets rubbed in by showing footage of delegates at the Republican national convention waving flip-flop footwear. In fact, the entire video is the political equivalent of shooting fish in a barrel: the Bush presidency gives the videographer so much to work with, beginning with Bush's photo op in front of St. Louis cathedral after Katrina.

Nonetheless, any time a Canadian resident of the United States who is not a citizen pens a song about impeaching an American president—no matter how droll the song is—some people are going to be offended. The *CSNY/Déjà Vu* film almost lovingly documents that moment. It occurs in Atlanta, Georgia, when the Freedom of Speech tour hits a red state. Atlanta's radio stations were the first to boycott the Dixie Chicks after they dissed Bush in concert; we have already seen how Neil has riled up the South with "Southern Man" and "Alabama." When Crosby, Stills, Nash and Young performed "Let's Impeach The President," a third of the audience booed and many walked out. The cameras recorded the colorful parting verbal shots of the frustrated concertgoers: "Neil Young can stick it up his ass ... . The worst concert I ever went to ... . He can suck my dick, that son of a bitch ... . You don't come to the South and do this [because half of the Iraq war casualties were from this region]." Heavens to Betsy! And of course a few flipped the bird to the camera. The band ended up abandoning their tour bus and flying out of Atlanta on a chartered jet because of "growing security concerns."

I suppose Neil derived a perverse glee from the anger of these people. Since his intent for the show was not to leave the audience with "fuzzy, warm feelings" but simply to make them "feel," mission accomplished (*CSNY/Déjà Vu*). And it was gratifying for the band to be more than just a nostalgia act; as in the Vietnam era, they were again contributing to a national dialogue. But, on the other hand, it is hard not to regard these naysayers as anything but cretins. What rock were they living under to not know what material Crosby, Stills, Nash and Young were going to present? The briefest of media or internet inquiries would have revealed what Neil and the boys were up to. Even "Freedom of Speech" on the concert ticket provides a slight clue. Or maybe—here's the rub—they knew and showed up just to see how bad it all was in order to get pissed off: an increasingly popular American pastime. Is that a more charitable reading of the situation? Arguably all parties concerned were a bit disingenuous.

My final take on the tune is that "Let's Impeach The President" was a sincere if quirky hand grenade thrown by Neil into the mediascape. It stirred the pot, but that was about it—as opposed to the next track, "Lookin' For A Leader," which was the first popular song to mention Barack Obama as a suitable candidate for President! The documentary DVD reinforces Neil's status as presidential prophet. When the band asks him who Obama is, Neil says "a lot of people know about him ... . His time may be sooner than he thinks." He also says that the song "has continuity" with the previous one: out with the old, in with the new. The choir happily gives a "sexy" accompaniment to the song, thereby selling its positivity. And the video gives another history lesson, showcasing all the presidents of the United States.

A few additional aspects of the video are worth noting. It uses portraits until motion picture footage exists. Each president is described with a tag line. Tellingly, Andrew Johnson is cited as the first president to be impeached—a reminder that this is a possible course of action. For a change, Neil makes nice with Nixon by only describing his diplomatic triumphs; less surprisingly, Reagan is also complimented for his "peace through strength" policy (a reminder that Neil supported him initially). A brief shot of Al Gore precedes the image of George W. Bush to remind us who really won the 2000 election, which is why the lyrics urge that "We got to have a clean win / To regain confidence." Then the video ends with a question mark: who's next? Now we know—and Neil was one of the first to recognize it: "And maybe it's ... a black man after all."

The next cut, "Roger And Out," lets Neil remind us that after all he's really part of the Vietnam generation. In the *CSNY/Déjà Vu* film, he even makes explicit parallels between that band and Vietnam vets: "There's a bond ... . We're still here against all odds." The song is a memorial to a fallen Vietnam veteran (the war is never explicitly named, but the references tellingly refer to their driving along "that ol' hippie highway"):

> Wonderin' how it really was for you
> And how it happened in the end
> But I guess I'll never know the truth
> If you were really all alone

In the studio session, Young opted for an electric guitar despite the elegiac feel and slow pace of the song because "it's an electric record." He also coached the choir to hold back and "come in gently" since they were conjuring up a ghost: "don't scare him away." The video appropriately juxtaposes road footage (from the hippie highway) with stock Vietnam battle imagery (those omnipresent Huey helicopters). We are reminded that this too has been a conceptually unified statement: from the environment through the Iraq debacle to the people responsible for it, our hope for the future and a reminder that, yes, as David Crosby put it in "Déjà Vu," "we have all been here before."

The song cycle effectively could have ended here—and did in its first incarnation captured on *Living With War: "In The Beginning."* But Neil added some insurance for the main release, the choir doing a gospel-inflected reading of "America The Beautiful." Since "When God Made Me" off *Prairie Wind*, Neil seems to have discovered the beauties of gospel music. (Maybe because of Bob Dylan's gift to him of the Dust-to-Digital box set *Goodbye, Babylon?*) In any case, this serves as a reminder to the naysayers that Neil does indeed love his adopted country where his wife and kids were born. It's okay to love America and yet raise an eyebrow about George W. Bush, despite the relentless counter-suggestions from big right wing media.

Not only was *Living With War* an astonishing populist statement about the state of the planet; Neil's videos directed for it showed a new maturity as a filmmaker. This impression was verified by *CSNY/Déjà Vu*. Neil's tour documentary was his first in-theaters project that looked like the work of a professional film director instead of an enlightened and quirky amateur. It stands on its own and surpasses the Dixie Chicks documentary *Shut Up and Sing*. At last Neil had arrived to excel in a second medium (something Zappa never lived to accomplish). And the tour which the film documents was itself a carefully contrived aesthetic experience.

What the ostensible soundtrack CD to the film accomplishes, even more than the film, is a convincing demonstration that this band at its best has always been a political band. In addition to the great harmonic boost the other three members give to Neil's new material, these songs as done by Crosby, Stills, Nash and Young fit comfortably alongside older and still relevant material. The CD sequencing of "Roger And Out"—> "Find The Cost Of Freedom"—> "Teach Your Children" is especially moving: a succinct statement of the price of war and the need to transcend reaching for it as a solution. The band can still joke around with its audience as well. Neil begins "After The Garden" by observing "Nice weather we're having, folks;" Graham Nash precedes "Wooden Ships" with an admonition not to "eat the brown acid"—an in-joke for the Woodstock generation.

Given the availability of the music elsewhere, the documentary *CSNY/Déjà Vu* wisely sidelines it in favor of the larger story of the tour in all its aspects. Embedded tour reporter Michael Cerre seeks out connections with Iraq and Vietnam veterans in the areas the tour passes through. He also interviews detractors and naysayers, who get their shot at freedom of speech as well. The opening credits of the film establish it as an historical record of a moment in our nation's history of interest to later times. As such, the documentary contains polemical material, but genuinely attempts to be fair and balanced.

Most remarkably, we learn of dissension even within the band. David Crosby acknowledges that the group is a "benevolent dictatorship" run by Neil. Stephen Stills goes even further, ridiculing the yellow ribbon wrapped around the giant microphone onstage as a "political cartoon" turning them into "Tony Orlando and Dawn" (of "Tie a Yellow Ribbon 'Round the Old Oak Tree" fame). He says he's of "two minds" about the tour and believes that his stumping for local political races is more important than the concerts (and in fact, seven out of ten of the Democratic candidates Stills worked for won their races—a good track record).

Graham Nash seems closest to Neil in spirit regarding the tour (which may be why on the poster Stills and Crosby are on one side of the image, while Young and Nash are together on the facing side). Nash notices how on this tour (as opposed to the one in 2002) audiences will sing "no more war" at the end of "Military Madness." He perceives "a tipping point:" "this hammer is going to fall." And so these aging rockers (average age 62) kicked out the jams one more time.

The band even resurrected "Ohio" (not on the soundtrack, by the way). Neil explained that he felt it was no longer "trading on somebody's misfortunes" now, but "history ... what folk music does." Neil's ambivalence about profiteering off suffering is also why he gave away "Let's Roll" and *Living With War* to radio stations and the internet: any money he received for those broadsides was strictly on a voluntary basis. The film also clarifies why an incident like the Kent State campus shooting commemorated by the song is unlikely to recur: we now have no draft and an all-volunteer army. The middle class are no longer forced to join the service, so our campuses are much quieter—while the poor get exploited. It's not personal for as many college students.

I will simply send you to the film for all the meaningful encounters the tour has with the military, noting only the sad story of Karen Meredith, the mother of a son killed in Iraq who was denied a photograph of her son's returning flag-draped coffin for reasons of "privacy"—an obvious dodge since she was family. She watches with tears in her eyes as the band performs "Find The Cost Of Freedom" to a backdrop of turning faces showing all the soldiers who died in Iraq. The full presentation of the song is included as the saddest of bonus features on the DVD: a kinetic updating of Maya Lin's Vietnam Memorial that deserves to be widely seen. The number of faces stops at 2645, but we know they keep coming ... .

After this sustained political activity, Neil in characteristic fashion moved on to other projects. He released *Chrome Dreams II* in 2007, a collection of miscellaneous songs he had lying around (some going as far back as "Ordinary People," an unreleased composition from the Blue Notes band era). Good stuff in the tradition of *American Stars 'N' Bars* (or for that matter the never-released original *Chrome Dreams*), but not a concept album like his previous efforts in the new millennium. Neil also embarked on a long tour showcasing this new material and older songs he was revisiting in his assemblage of the Archives.

His most recent foray into political commentary ended up being the title track on *Fork In The Road* (2009), his first CD release in the post-Bush era. It's a very quirky recording, even by Neil's standards. There are a lot of what can only be described as green car songs. As we know, the car song has been a venerable staple of rock music since its inception: "Little Deuce Coupe," "Pink Cadillac" and myriads more. Car enthusiast Young has contributed his fair share to the genre: "Long May You Run" and "Trans Am," to name a few. *Fork In The Road* has no less than seven out of ten. In addition to the driving references in the title track, we have "When Worlds Collide," "Fuel Line," "Johnny Magic," "Get Behind The Wheel," "Off The Road," and "Hit The Road." All of these six songs are celebrating his Lincvolt project, a Lincoln Continental whose engine has been redesigned to get 100 miles per gallon on the highway. This car is Neil's ultimate automotive dream, a big car with the highest standard possible of fuel efficiency. So this new collection showcases the vehicle with a series of driving (ouch) electric rock songs pumped out on Old Black. Another song even explicitly backs off from the possibilities of political songwriting (vs. building a green car, for example: "just singing a song won't change the world" (from "Just Singing A Song").

That leaves two songs making political statements beyond the tacit environmental aspects of the car songs. "Cough Up The Bucks" addresses the economic bailout of the banking industry in a somewhat simplistic and repetitive fashion (cf. *Re.Ac.Tor*'s "T-Bone"). The title track, however, is a return to political form engaging the bail-out, the effect of internet downloads on Neil's career, the economic downturn and the continuing conflict in Iraq and Afghanistan:

> Forgot this year, to salute the troops.
> They're all still there in a fucking war.
> It's no good. Whose idea was that?

All this is delivered with a driving boogie beat from standby players Chad Cromwell and Rick Rosas. Neil directed an amusing, extremely low-tech video for this piece, shot on a digital camera, which features him eating an apple while lip synching and playing a solo on air guitar. The implications of the key lyric are mysterious: "There's a fork in the road ahead. / I don't know which way I'm gonna turn." Is he talking about lefting and then righting politically? Giving up touring for just assembling his massive Archives? Or just a real turn coming up for him to negotiate in his Lincvolt? We had to wait and see.

"We Left Our Tracks In The Sound:" Neil Young's First Last Statement

When I planned to write about the 2004-5 *Prairie Wind / Heart of Gold* project, I thought you'd get the few paragraphs above concerning its status as an aberration from his far more political work in the new millennium. But then I did something always very dangerous for a rock writer: I actually listened closely to what he was putting out. Before reading further, I suggest, dear reader, that you do the same. Specifically, if you haven't yet, watch Jonathan Demme's *Heart of Gold* DVD on a good home theater system—the best you can find without too much trouble. Take the ride. Trust me—it's worth seeing even if you don't consider yourself a Neil Young fan, maybe even if you're one of the many who can't stand his "whiny" voice. Then we can talk about how two years of effort culminated in this work of absolute musical and cinematic alchemy.

The clear impetus for this material was another rocky patch in his personal life: the decline and death of his father and a very scary medical discovery of a brain aneurysm in his head. As Samuel Johnson once said, "Depend upon it, Sir, when a man knows he is to be hanged in a fortnight, it concentrates his mind wonderfully" (Boswell 748). After a two-year break from songwriting, these songs came in a flood of creativity. His wife Pegi observed that he saw "his life flashing before his eyes" (*Heart of Gold*). As such, *Prairie Wind* is a kind of last statement to the world. Neil Young had no way of knowing that the experimental operation to remove the aneurysm—putting tiny biodegradable springs in his circulatory system to free the clot—would be successful. Fortunately it was; but he by necessity already looked into the abyss and used it for a powerful muse.

As with *Greendale*, he wrote the songs in an intense burst of creativity: according to Ben Keith on the bonus features of *Heart of Gold*, ten songs in ten days (one per day). They were recorded as they were written. The result is that you see him in the act of discovering his subject matter. The first two tracks are comparatively diffuse thematically. "The Painter" is a portrait of the artist rendered obliquely across gender and artistic medium: she is a visual artist, not a (masculine) musician. More genderfuck from Neil? Another element of complexity is the song's switching between third and first person. Is the song just about the painter and her point of view, or does it cross-cut between her and an observer? Arguably the latter, since the first-person remarks sound very close to Neil's perspective:

> I keep my friends [not "have" as in the lyric booklet]
> Eternally

> We left our tracks in the sound
> Some of them
> Are with me now
> Some of them can't be found

These comments reflect Neil's loyalty to his inner circle (repeatedly stressed in the film's interviews) and the larger themes of memory and loss. But it's as if Neil can't quite go there completely yet, so he uses the female artist's struggles ("But in the end / She fell down / Before she got up again") as a distancing device for discussing his own angst and existential dread. In some ways, this song is reminiscent of "Bandit"—Earl Green's dark-night-of-the-soul soliloquy on *Greendale*.

"No Wonder" is even more murky with its scattergun political commentary noted above. This track provides another link with *Greendale*, reinforced even more by being the only song with any electric guitar on it (a few power chords from Old Black). Constant references to clocks ticking and bells ringing in the chorus evoke mutability and the transitory nature of life, but we stay on a fairly general level here. These observations of a turning world are in keeping with a number of lyrics on *Are You Passionate?*, but we're still not quite where this song cycle wants to go.

Until the third song, that is: "Fallin' Off The Face Of The Earth." The lyrics here resolve into crystal clarity and accessibility: this is a response to the medical news and an attempt to manage the resultant fears. On the CD, it seems like it's directly addressed to wife Pegi, thanking her and apologizing (again) "for all the troubled times." In the concert film, it's absolutely clear that this is also addressed to Neil's listening audience—one of the songs in the film that director Jonathan Demme describes as a Neil "valentine to the whole human race" (bonus features). He certainly leaves his emotional tracks in the sound on this one!

In case we had any doubts, "Far From Home" brings in some funky Memphis Horns and a semi-borrowed melody from the Rolling Stones ("No Expectations") to punctuate a mix of childhood reminiscences and burial instructions ("Bury me out on the prairie"). Neil makes a curious slip in the memory portion that invites some psychological speculation. He remembers his father singing "Bury Me On The Lone Prairie," which turns into Neil's own wishes as noted. The song alluded to, however, is called "Bury Me Not On The Lone Prairie:" it's about a cowboy's fears of ending up isolated from everyone in death.[17] Neil's 180 degree re-imagining of its sentiments speaks volumes about his sensibility and fondness for his Canadian roots in this time of crisis. He remembers what he needs to remember. And just like John Keats's famous mistaken allusion to Cortez (how ironic in a Neil Young context) as the discoverer of the Pacific Ocean (when he meant Balboa) in "On First Looking into Chapman's Homer," the slip stands—and works!

The following piece, "It's A Dream," is nothing less than an instant classic, a blazing Neil Young masterpiece that takes the train memories and childhood nostalgia of such previous songs of note as "Helpless," "See The Sky About To Rain" and "Red Sun"—then ramps them up into an unforgettable celebration which then turns into a lament for the impermanence of all good things. It's all about the performance. This song is tailor-made for Neil's voice and vocal range: I can't imagine any other artist successfully covering it. Art like this reduces the critic to pointing and putting on the CD. It is ineffably fine.

The title track that comes after is no slouch, either. It's also about a fragile memory, "tryin' to remember what [his] daddy said," a tale of Native American visions glimpsed on the Canadian prairie. The Memphis Horns here become the symbolic force of the wind, overpowering the mix at times (but ever so slightly) when they enter the music. The "prairie wind blowin' through [his] head"—extensively reiterated by the backup vocalists—connotes not only the literal force of nature, but symbolically both the healing of the aneurysm and his father's dementia. When Neil alludes to his dad talking about "a place on the prairie where evil and goodness play," we have a clear sense of the abraxas experience of both the memory and the current state of his personal affairs. And, yes, Neil's powerful muse as well. Recall how he likes "to keep the door open and let the wind blow." That wind is a strong prairie wind as well.

After these four epiphanies of increasing power, beginning with "Fallin' Off The Face Of The Earth," Neil has to downshift a little to keep the listener from being overwhelmed by the intensity of these offerings. "Here For You," a song he labels an "empty-nester song" in the concert film, revisits Amber's going off to Kenyon college and leaving the ranch (cf. "You're My Girl"). It's a universal enough situation to transcend the personal. In the *Heart of Gold* introduction, he wryly observes "I used to write these kind of songs about girls my own age." He follows it with a glance at Pegi, then a quick save: "I still got a few of them left in me."

Then we head back to the depths with "This Old Guitar," an ode to his Martin acoustic guitar which once belonged to Hank Williams. Musically, it borrows a little from the "Harvest Moon" riff—not a bad thing. He acknowledges the guitar is not his "to keep": musical instruments outlive their players. Neil salutes the guitar for never "search[ing] for gold": it's never been used for slick, commercial purposes. Perhaps most cryptically, "When [he] get[s] drunk and seein' double / It jumps behind the wheel and steers." I read this as a reference to the guitar's sound carrying him through musically when he wasn't in an optimal state to perform (as opposed to any actual automotive skills displayed by the instrument). This claim has obvious applicability to its previous owner as well. The backing vocals from Emmylou Harris take this to country music heaven so that Hank can enjoy it!

After this tribute to Hank Williams, a celebration of Elvis seems a logical enough segue. "He Was The King" is the closest this collection gets to a throwaway, an evaluation reinforced by Jonathan Demme's leaving it out of the concert film. Funky (those horns again), seemingly improvised (studio chatter on the CD) and kind-spirited (this is Elvis the iconic figure, not the complex human being), this breaks the mood one last time before the straight-up gospel sound of the concluding number, "When God Made Me."

This last is Neil's only foray into a gospel sound so far, an appropriate gesture for a recording so interested in American musical roots. The Fisk University Jubilee Choir provides the highly appropriate accompaniment. If the sound is traditional, the lyrics are not. They explore the likely diverse tolerance of the Creator in contrast to His / Her acolytes through a series of musical questions:

> Did He create just me in his image
> Or every living thing? ...
>
> Did He think there was only one way
> To be close to Him? ...
>
> Did He give us the gift of love
> To say who we could choose?

This last question offers Neil's first strike against homophobia since the soundtrack to *Philadelphia*. And after this non-restrictive vision, a long piano fade to silence a la "A Day In The Life" (a Beatles song Young has taken to covering in concert recently).

The film *Heart of Gold* adds even more power to these new songs by giving them a concert film setting at the historic Ryman Auditorium in Nashville. The Ryman was a church originally (as is hinted at by its gorgeous stained glass windows); then it was used for many years by the Grand Ole Opry. On the DVD interviews, Neil praises it as "a church of American music" that "any musician could call home," "a spiritual place to play." His purpose in performing there was to "pay respects to the old muse." There is an air of mutability in this choice as well, since developers were building a "super-scraper" (Neil's term) right next to it which would permanently obscure the church windows. So this concert film was intended to capture one last glimpse of the building's full history and glory.

Much of the film's power can be attributed to Ellen Kuras, the Director of Photography, who came up with separate and appropriate color schemes for each musical number. For example, "The Painter" gets swathed in the yellow color of a prairie wheat field; "Far From Home" has a warm reddish-orange-yellow of a family hearth (reinforced by the backdrop painting); "The Needle And The Damage Done" is shot in a single long shot with a white spotlight on

Neil dwarfed by the bluish-black darkness around him. These choices make the film work on our emotions in subliminal ways. As Neil attests in the interviews here, the film works on a deeper level for the viewer than an ordinary concert film. It's about the songs, "not hero worship" (the agenda of most concert films). Jonathan Demme describes it as a film of "a dream concert," an ideal concert as Neil would dream it.

Neil pulled this miracle off by getting the best musicians and technical crew money could buy, by rehearsing the band until their parts were second nature, by keeping all filming at a distance with long lenses so that audience and musicians didn't have to notice the cameras. (The one onstage Steadicam used in a tracking shot showed up at every rehearsal so it wouldn't distract anyone.) As is Neil's wont, he chose the night of a full moon (8/18/2005) for the magical event. His final pep talk before they walked out said it all: "Let the Muse have us. Send it out. Take a shot." Did they ever!

After the complete performance of the *Prairie Wind* material, Neil and company did an encore set highlighting Neil's previous Nashville work on *Harvest*, *Comes A Time* and *Harvest Moon*. The *Harvest* material seems prophetically apt, proof that Neil was always an old soul. When he sings "and I'm getting old" on "Heart Of Gold," a certain resonance is added. Similarly, his claim that "I'm a lot like you were" on "Old Man" is now bankable.

The memory theme recurs and persists with his tributes to the deceased, both human and animal, "The Needle And The Damage Done" and "Old King" (this last thoroughly enlivened by Emmylou Harris' exuberant contributions). He brings out a stellar line of guitars in a row (including wife Pegi and backup singer Diana DeWitt) for "Comes A Time" and his cover of Ian and Sylvia's "Four Strong Winds" (here DeWitt plays autoharp). The conclusion of the concert is utterly and literally sublime, a musical apotheosis: "One Of These Days" from *Harvest Moon*. On its first studio appearance, it was not a standout track. But now it's the big global valentine Jonathan Demme (and the viewer) perceive. The lyrics name-check Neil's power spots (L.A., Nashville, New York and Canada), his many friends and collaborators ("some are weak, / some are strong") and his own regrets ("I know I let some good things go"). But it's the delivery that makes this so transcendent. He uses all the resources of the band, including the Memphis Horns and the Fisk Choir. Moreover, he telegraphs every word. You realize from this performance that this song is not about writing a letter to all your old friends; it's about the sad realization that such a letter will never be written. The song planning to write the letter is as close as he can (and we can) ever come to such an ultimate closure.

Neil could take it no farther. After the concert ends, the credits roll to Neil Young solo on the empty Ryman stage playing "The Old Laughing Lady"—another early song which has shocking applicability to this particular existential moment. Its opening line "Don't call pretty Peggy / She can't hear you no more" is downright eerie, given his eventual marriage to Pegi. Neil's look into the abyss had brought his artistry up to a new level. Like Yeats and Dylan, he has a strong muse in his maturity—one as unafraid of taking chances as it was 45 years ago (and counting).

The Archives: Neil's Ultimate Avant-Pop Gesture

Finally, we must briefly touch upon the significance of Neil Young's 2009 release of the first volume of his Archives project. In some ways, it's his most radical production. Not for the music itself in volume 1, which covers the Squires through *Harvest*; indeed the *Journey Through The Past* film reissue which closes the set is both the most avant-garde material on it and a harbinger of the glorious things to come in subsequent volumes (which we have been discussing at length).

What is astonishing here is the presentation, which provides "Unparalleled Access to Neil's History" (*Archives* trailer on the bonus disc). To see this, you have to investigate the DVD or Blu-Ray versions of the box: the CD version really doesn't even give you a clue as to the proceedings. Mind you, you can simply play the former formats as CDs in your player with the picture off. But again, this approach would be missing the point.

For the DVD / Blu-Ray discs are set up as a file cabinet, song by song, which enable one to access 1) song lyrics, 2) manuscript drafts of the song, 3) period photos from the relevant time frame, 3) press clippings about the song or sets in which it was performed, 4) odd memorabilia such as record sleeves from other countries, promotional materials and the like, 5) audio clips from interviews or promo spots explaining / featuring the song, and 6) video performance footage of the song if it exists (or filmed interviews). The songs themselves in these enhanced formats sound even better than vinyl (as we know, Neil has never cared for the CD format—although he is willing to compromise about HDCD technology). It is instructive to contrast the sound on these DVDs with the much-ballyhooed recent Beatles reissues: one can only imagine what the results might have been if the latter had been released in Neil's chosen format.

And each song has a whimsical minimalist film to go along with its audio track: a tape recorder with the reels where Neil's eyes are on the cover of his first solo album (for "I've Been Waiting For You"), a turntable in the sand for "Cowgirl in the Sand," a Buffalo nickel weighing down a phonograph tone arm on a Buffalo Springfield song ("Out of My Mind"). The recurrent thread here is an emphasis on the original technological means of reproduction for the audio source material: Neil letting his inner gearhead out with strange resultant lashings of Walter Benjamin's interest in technology and archives.

Besides all this, there are many hidden "Easter eggs": hidden tracks, family photo galleries, videotape of him commenting on the archival materials, performance clips on a biographical timeline bonus feature and random oddities (film footage of Neil touring a record plant manufacturing the cover for *Harvest* or confiscating a bootleg album from a record shop). In preparation for these words, I spent over a month mining the set's resources. The online community proved to be an invaluable source of information regarding the many obscure treasures to be found.

Aside from the discs, there is also a leather-bound booklet reproducing lyric scribblings, photographs and press clippings, a poster (of the file cabinet!) and a stash box containing a bonus concert disc, a code to download the songs and a little notepad copied from the original at the Whisky A Go-Go.

At this point it would be fair to ask: so what? Why does this matter? What makes this more than just an ultimate pop collectible? I think the answer has to do with Neil's complex attitudes toward fame and his fans.

On the one hand, from his earliest lyrics for the Buffalo Springfield, Neil has had a kind of existential dread about being in the media spotlight. Neil prefaces a granted request for "Out of My Mind" at Ann Arbor's Canterbury House (on the bonus disc) by observing that he "wrote it before anything happened" as a "premonition." Two years later the band listened to it again: "it blew our minds and we broke up." He never liked being in a place where "all [he] hear[s] are screams / from outside the limousines." By the end of the box set, he can talk in interview about his recently purchased ranch as "a chance to live a normal life" because people "freak" when they meet Neil in public: "They know about you, and you don't know about them" (video log for "Words," disc 8).

But on the other hand, Neil has always embraced honest contact with ordinary people (also a recurrent lyrical obsession from songs like "Albuquerque" through "Ordinary People"[!]). You can hear his evident rapport and intimacy with his audience on the three acoustic sets in this first volume of the Archives (at Toronto's Riverboat and Massey Hall and at the Canterbury House). I know two people who have interacted with Neil personally: a colleague who talked to him when he was just hanging out at a bar in Ohio after a concert and a friend who took care of his son Zeke for him during the Ducks era. I know people (including myself) who have met other famous musicians; but the Neil interactions sound more extended and, well, more authentic. Every serious Neil Young fan feels that (s)he knows Neil in some fashion: we dream about interacting with him, repeatedly. (I also have these dreams about the Rolling Stones, but nobody else on a recurrent basis. Zappa and Yoko once or twice; never Bob Dylan or the Beatles.)

The Archives provide a kind of synthesis for these two dialectical positions by creating a kind of virtual intimacy between the performer and his public. We can't really hang out at Broken Arrow ranch, but the Archive provides a simulacrum of that kind of proximity which satisfies us but does not intrude on Neil's privacy. And Neil is careful to explain why this is the way it has to be in the interview materials on the box, as noted. He's both being generous and drawing lines. Having read father Scott Young and half-sister Astrid Young's memoirs, I am tempted to conclude this is a family trait. Despite Neil's protected spaces, he seems more like a normal human being than a stereotypical rock star. We would do the same things he had to do to protect himself if we were in his shoes—i.e., if we were intuitive musical geniuses!

And perhaps that's Neil's greatest sleight-of-hand: he downplays his exceptional gifts enough so that we can relate to him. But it's magic, not a con. And these Archives, in a gesture worthy of Penn and Teller, give us unprecedented insight into how he worked the magic, note by note and chord by chord. But it's still magic for a' that—magic which he has been working for 45 years with his odd mix of intuition and perfectionism, big heart and steady head. As an avant-pop musician, Neil Young is beginning to approach the longevity of Frank Sinatra, the founder of the Reprise label he has mostly recorded on. Neil turned the jackpot boomer zeitgeist strike of *Harvest* into a seemingly endless sonic cornucopia. The Archives consolidate these riches in a cyber-savvy way all serious twenty-first century musicians should emulate; they provide a workable blueprint which can only become more viable as the costs of the technology decrease.

P.S.: Forever Young!

The discussion of the Archives project would have provided nice closure to this chapter, except for one inconvenient truth: Neil keeps working and surprising us. In the banner years of 2010 and 2011, Neil reinvented himself with a new sound that enabled him to play solo electric guitar and tour small venues doing just that. More astonishingly, after more than four decades, he reunited and toured with the surviving members of the Buffalo Springfield (original bassist Bruce Palmer died in 2004; drummer Dewey Martin in 2009). That left guitarists Richard Furay, Stephen Stills and himself, backed by Rick Rosas on bass and Joe Vitale on drums. (Richard Furay's return was the big surprise, given his commitment to his religious ministry the past few decades.)

The new sound largely came courtesy of producer and technician extraordinaire Daniel Lanois—whose quirky Canadian mispronunciation of his last name gave the project its title: *Le Noise*. Lanois has worked magic (alone and with Brian Eno) for the likes of U2, Emmylou Harris and Bob Dylan; it was probably only a matter of time before he got to work with Neil Young. He brought to the table a specially designed amplified acoustic guitar capable of all sorts of electronic processing effects. Lanois also found a way to alter and manipulate electronic guitar sounds to give Neil such a full sound that the entire album is just his vocals and these complex guitars recorded by Mark Howard and produced by Lanois. As you can see on Youtube, Neil eventually learned how to deliver this same rich noise in concert (check out his version of "Hitchhiker" at the 2010 Farm Aid in Milwaukee). The closest analogy to this approach, albeit much simpler, would be Robert Fripp's Frippertronics technology on his solo guitar releases.

The album's sequencing reverts back to Neil's approach on *Are You Passionate?*: a move from more personal material to larger social concerns. The first of two songs unquestionably about and for wife Pegi, "Walk With Me" is distinguished by a looping on the fade which makes the music itself sound like it's walking. "Sign of Love," also on the louder end of Neil's dynamics, elicits a "That was pretty good" from him at the end of the very live and non-overdubbed recording. "Someone's Going to Rescue You" has a bigger if vaguer circle of concern: who is this song about? Stephen Stills? Neil Young? Anyone in trouble?

After this better-than-adequate opening, we get the first of three bonafide instant classics on the recording: "Love and War." In interviews we find this was actually the first new song Neil wrote for the album to fit the modified acoustic guitar. My neighbor compared it to Schubert—that's just how romantic and moving it is. The guitar sound is reminiscent of classical Spanish work, an approach Neil occasionally explores ("Eldorado" on *Freedom*). The lyrics are nothing less than an assessment of Neil's career-long thematic obsessions:

> When I sing about love and war
> I don't really know what I'm saying
> I've been in love and I've seen a lot of war,
> Seen a lot of people praying
> They pray to Allah and they pray to the Lord,
> But mostly they pray about love and war ... .

He acknowledges (again) the pain of war ("Daddy won't ever come home"), but he saves his most scathing critiques for himself. He acknowledges that both his political and romantic songs can "hit a bad chord" and that "[t]he saddest thing in the whole wide world is to break the heart of your lover. I made a mistake and I did it again and we struggled to recover." Politically, he admits "I said a lot of things I can't take back but I don't really know if I want to."

It's all here in review: his marital lapses, his Reagan support, his attacks on Dubya. A flawed human being baring his soul and looking back on his long, imperfect record—with the tacit interrogation: listener, are you any better? Have you done any better? Combined with the haunting melody line, it's a wise and brilliant song which is light years from the bravado and confidence of some of his early work ("Southern Man," "Alabama")—to say nothing of contemporary rap lyrics.

Form fits function with the next track, "It's an Angry World" which raucously points out the obvious —"[s]ome wish some would go to hell's inferno for screwing with their life in Freedom Land" (gee, who could that be?)—but dares to hope "everything will go as planned." The fading vocal loop contrasting "hate me" with "lo ... " (I don't hear the complete enunciation of "love") is a nice touch.

Then we have the next two masterworks on the release back to back: "Hitchhiker" (an older song discussed above and his ultimate Stoner statement) and "Peaceful Valley Boulevard." The latter is Neil's best environmental fable, far more focused than "After the Gold Rush" or even "War of Man" or "Mother Earth." This cautionary tale on the modified acoustic guitar begins with the aforementioned "peaceful valley ... before the railroad came from Kansas City and the bullets hit the bison from the train." Next we have a Native American (or Mormon?) massacre of a wagon train in the spirit of a song like "Powderfinger" and a rush "for gold and then for oil." The punch line comes in the present when an "electro-cruiser" pulls off the "Peaceful Valley Boulevard" exit and sees the town's slogan on a billboard: "People Make the Difference." (Doubly ironic for me, since Kirksville, Missouri, my base of operation, chose a slight variant of this highly unoriginal phrase for its town slogan.) It's the old environmental joke: places are named for the natural features which they've displaced / destroyed. The song could have stopped there; but, Neil being Neil, he wanted to work in the polar bears too! Still, it's some kind of pinnacle for this branch of Young's lyric output.

Le Noise ends with "Rumblin'," a vaguely apocalyptic blast on buzz saw electric guitar about earthquakes ("I feel the rumblin' in her ground") and climate change ("I can feel the weather changing"). The whole of this disk is certainly more than the sum of its parts, although three of the eight songs are utterly remarkable in their own right. The big news is that Neil at the age of 65 can put out a sound unlike any other he's had in his previous career (the instrumentals on the *Dead Man* soundtrack come closest, but are again much simpler). Neil Young, needless to say, loves to keep us guessing!

In March of 2011, I got from the Neil Young website tour dates for his solo performances of this material ... and a handful of Buffalo Springfield dates! Needless to say, I was gobsmacked at the prospect of seeing this literally legendary band live. The closest (i.e., non-west-coast) performance was at the Bonnaroo festival near Manchester, Tennessee. So I managed to cross two items off my bucket list because of this information: attend a music festival for more than one day and hear the Buffalo Springfield.

My "Bonnaroo Letter" in the appendix covers my experiences pretty adequately and gives the reader a sense of what the Springfield show was like (right down to the set list). Interpretively for this chapter, a few words are in order concerning what Neil's up to with his latest provocations. Part of my read is that, like Kurt Vonnegut's Billy Pilgrim, Neil Young has become "unstuck in time." A perception confirmed by what I found in my mailbox today: a new release of a 1985 show with his International Harvesters called *A Treasure*. Working on the Archive has no doubt led Neil to revisit his entire vast career. A corollary of this journey through the past is a desire to fill in some gaps in the record. The biggest of such lacunae, as the beginning of this chapter indicates, is the almost complete lack of live recordings of the Buffalo Springfield—who were nonetheless touted as an amazing live band by all who heard them.

We know that Neil had been thinking of this for a while. After all, in 1987 he even reunited the far less significant Squires! There were rumors of annual Buffalo Springfield jam reunions up at his ranch and the release of wistful songs like "Buffalo Springfield Again"—and a Buffalo Springfield box set. Even the resurrected "Hitchhiker" on *Le Noise* has a lot to say about the Buffalo Springfield era of his career. So all considered, the signs were propitious for the reunion.

What did I learn by actually hearing them? On the down side, the guitar evidence was inconclusive. After forty years, these guys couldn't blaze like they must have in the day. Don't get me wrong: they're fantastic musicians and it was a superb concert. But Neil had to sort of rev them up with the vocal harmonies on the first two numbers to get them to the right tempo. They couldn't possibly have played with the adrenaline rush they must have originally exhibited. Neil says all over the Archives that the Springfield's guitar solos far surpassed those of CSN & Y regarding sheer risk and energy as opposed to showy calculation. The Bonnaroo concert did not prove that claim.

What was evident was the importance of Richard Furay as a balancing force between Stills and Young. Vocally, this band was every bit as lovely to hear as the more successful CSN & Y: a different kind of vocal blend, but equally potent. In that sense they totally lived up to the hype—and even surpassed it.

One wonders what Neil has planned next for this band. There are already rumors afloat that they will undertake a more extensive tour next summer. A live album seems inevitable and just; a studio album of new material risky, less likely, but possible. One senses that Neil Young has stopped making collaborative music with many of his former bands: it's been a long time since new studio work from CSN & Y. So time will tell if this was a nostalgic one-off—albeit, as noted in the appendix, one delivered with a lot of panache and postmodern simulational irony (working up to the "hit single")—or the start of a more extensive rekindling of the old flame.

And as noted, Neil released *A Treasure* at the same time that he was touring with the Buffalo Springfield. This CD documents the live tour of his country band, the International Harvesters, in the mid-1980s. Like its predecessor in the performance archives, *Dreamin' Man Live '92*, the release is compiled from various tour dates (although a review inside might mislead one into thinking it was a September 1985 Miami show). The title comes from Ben Keith's appreciative remark about the compilation. And indeed this is gorgeous country music, confirming my remark above that this band was much better in concert than in the studio.

"Amber Jean," Neil Young's ode to his healthy daughter (after two sons with disabilities by two separate mothers), opens the set up on a heartfelt note about love "still that hasn't been lost / there for you, my Amber Jean." "Are You Ready For The Country?" gets a much more countrified reading than on *Harvest*, enhanced by Rufus Thibodeaux's down-home fiddling. (Curiously, he gives the lyrics an update by making the "preacher" a "pusher" in the second verse.) His cover version of "It Might Have Been" is also pushed closer to its cry-in-your-beer jukebox weeper status with this stellar cast of Nashville studio players.

"Let Your Fingers Do The Walking" offers a more comic take on heartbreak with its droll lyrics: "I used to be happy when you gave good phone ... . / I'm listed under broken hearts looking for a good time." The Buffalo Springfield's "Flying On The Ground Is Wrong" is greatly enhanced by Ben Keith's work on pedal steel. This eclectic set continues with "Motor City" from *Re.Ac.Tor*, Neil's love / hate valentine to Detroit carmakers with its economic xenophobia that hasn't necessarily aged too well ("there's already too many Toyotas in this town"). And "Soul of a Woman," a song more associated with the Blue Notes later. In this one, the political incorrectness comes from Neil's most heteronormative lyrics ever: "soul of a woman / soul of a man / perfect combination ever since the world began"—a long way from "Philadelphia!"

Redemption for this more conservative iteration of Neil comes with "Southern Pacific," also initially from *Re.Ac.Tor* with Crazy Horse. I had marveled at the Harvesters' reading of it on a bootleg, but the version here alone justifies seeking out this recording (the one track to download?). Everything about this performance gives me chills: the fiddle doing the diesel horn, the cymbals serving as air brakes, the high hats for the station bells, the rest of the band choogling along. And as observed above, its poignant commentary on the eventual obsolescence of all workers: "Now I'm left to roll / Down the long decline." Still the Southern Pacific rolls on "on your silver rails / through the moonlight." Along with "See The Sky About To Rain" and "Red Sun," this is Neil's greatest train song—one more than worthy of being placed alongside classics such as Steve Goodman's "City of New Orleans."

The set winds down with the hitherto unreleased "Nothing Is Perfect," Neil's acknowledgment of the mixed bag of life, and the visionary "Grey Riders." The imagery of this last recalls the iconic fantasy sequence in his film *Journey Through The Past*. With its big electric guitar crunch and Ben Keith's keyboard stylings on the Stringman, this closer ends up being the most raucous number on an overall laid-back album. No doubt, the sequencing was intentional—and a reminder that Neil Young never settles down anywhere musically for too long, thereby giving the lie to the Miami reviewer in the booklet who confidently predicted in 1985 that, "as his new theme song, Back to the Country [sic] attests, [Neil Young] has rediscovered his musical roots and he's settling there." Wasn't it pretty to think so?

With some reluctance, I must mention for the diehard fan a bootleg release entitled *Live On Air: The Lost Tapes Volume 2*. It contains six tracks originally broadcast over the radio. The signal cuts out for a second here and there; some of the recordings end abruptly. And there is no provenance with regard to year, band or venue (although Neil name checks Rio de Janeiro in "Like a Hurricane"). The problem is that the playing is fantastic. So after you buy every legitimate release of his, you might want to investigate a great extended version of "Cortez the Killer" (without the fake Rastafarianisms of *Live Rust*), the noise art and feedback sculptures of "Like a Hurricane" and a "Rockin' in the Free World" that morphs into the Star-Spangled Banner. Neil delivers a tuneful, well-acted dramatic monologue—and a great solo—on "Powderfinger." And the apocalyptic version of "Down by the River" included here proves that Neil is only getting better at playing these songs with age.

I have far less reserve about noting the fall 2011 release of a double CD and a triple DVD package celebrating the twenty-fifth anniversary of the Bridge School Concerts—and the innovative progressive school for the differently abled that the Young family helped found and support to an immeasurable extent. The contents of the two media platforms slightly overlap but are distinct, so check them both out for a good cause if you can afford it. Neil Young is not center-stage in either format. On the CD his acoustic "Love and Only Love" with Crazy Horse is an interesting alternate approach to the song. (The Bridge School Concert's policy is to play strictly acoustic.) He also joins his occasional band mates Crosby, Stills and Nash for an extended take on "Déjà Vu," replete with a fine harmonica solo from Neil and some trademark vocal and guitar weaving. And Neil assists REM on acoustic guitar for "Country Feedback" (which also features an intense and passionate vocal from Michael Stipe).

The first disk of the CD abounds with other acoustic non-Neil treats from his posse and allies: an emotionally intense and dramatic "Born in the USA" from Bruce Springsteen, the Fleet Foxes channeling CSNY's superb harmonies with an Appalachian twist ("Blue Ridge Mountains"), Sonic Youth burning down the house ("Rain on Tin"), Willie Nelson's always-consolatory nylon guitar strings ("The Great Divide") and Nils Lofgren's homage to the late Bill Graham ("Cry Just a Little").

Highlights from the second disk include a Spanish-inflected acoustic guitar performance by Metallica of their anti-war anthem "Disposable Heroes" ("I was born for dying"). Thom Yorke of Radiohead does a straight-up cover of "After the Gold Rush." Odd man out Tony Bennett swings the house with "Maybe

This Time," featuring a false ending and an extended piano and vocal coda. And the Who give us an acoustic but equally long and exuberant "Won't Get Fooled Again" with a piano standing in for the original synthesizer. All the rest is pretty good too: how can you not like Jonathan Richman working up the audience with "I Was Dancing in the Lesbian Bar"?

The DVDs take us on a deeper journey which carries forward the lessons of virtual intimacy Neil Young learned in preparing the Archives. One disk is non-music documentaries: *The Bridge School Story, Backstage at the Bridge School Benefit Concert,* and *Bridge School Network Interviews* with the performers—all further signs of the maturation of Shakey Pictures. The first documentary, worthy of broadcast on PBS, tells the amazing story of how the Bridge School developed from humble beginnings in the mid-eighties to care for Ben Young and folks like him. (Ben is now in his thirties and a certified organic egg farmer!) Now it is a state-of-the-art facility with a global outreach that helps differently abled kids to transition into the public school system by means of technologies that compensate for verbal limitations Their graduates have gone on to college study at places like Berkeley. As one of the staff says, it's all about helping the students "find their voice."

The backstage documentary is the least compelling of the three, being a tribute to the massive undertaking involved in putting on these annual shows at the Shoreline Amphitheatre in Mountain View, California. They even have a "tea wrangler" to keep things steeping. But the Bridge School Network backstage interviews are quite fascinating. The students interview the artists using "augmentative and alternative means of communication" (AAC)—except for Ben Young, who directly talks to his subject, Eddie Vedder of Pearl Jam. They ask some unusual questions and get candid answers. Most germane to this chapter would be an inquiry to Neil as to how he balances being a celebrity with "family life." He answers that it's easy: "one is real, one isn't."

The concert DVDs are less ground-breaking, although they add the nice touch of having the Bridge School students introduce each clip using AAC. There are a few more heavy-hitters on the DVDs (Billy Idol, David Bowie, Bob Dylan, Simon and Garfunkel, James Taylor), but they're serving up exactly the well-delivered sonic comfort food you might expect in the grand tradition of benefit concerts since the Concert for Bangla Desh ("Rebel Yell," "Heroes," "Girl From the North Country," "America" and "Fire and Rain" respectively). Admittedly, Billy Idol rocks the entire house—and even the camera crews—with his energetic antics not to be tamed by lower amplification. By song's end, everyone's pumping their fists that can! And "Heroes" has a whole different feel as an acoustic performance. But these are lovely versions designed to give the audience exactly what it wants.

Patti Smith's palpable interaction with the kids behind the stage is wonderful, as is getting the visuals for REM and Neil (nice beard) in collaboration. Neil also sings backup vocals on Brian Wilson's (and Chuck Berry's) "Surfin' USA" (along with Pegi Young, Roger Daltrey of the Who, Eddie Vedder of Pearl Jam, Sheryl Crow, etc.). Neil's solo performance, a much more passionate reading of "Crime in the City" than on the bootlegs, features Neil pounding on his guitar for percussion effects when he plays his harmonica. Son Ben gives his dad a charming introductory set-up: "Here's a guy I never get tired of hearing."

Non-Neil surprise highlights include the Fleet Foxes again (the mojo of the shimmering harmonies and the dulcimer wizardry comes through even better on DVD). Fleet Foxes are from Seattle; but they sound like they're from the Blue Ridge Mountains they're singing about, not the land of grunge. Obviously, a musical sea change is afoot up there. Tom Waits is suitably seedy on "16 Shells from a Thirty-Ought Six," which has a nice slow-burn fade. Elton John and Leon Russell trade honky-tonk piano on "A Dream Come True" backed up by an entire tent show band (shades of Joe Cocker's Mad Dogs and Englishman tour). And on the visuals for the Who, we have rare footage of the late John Entwistle playing an acoustic (but not upright) bass and getting some nice effects by sliding his hand down the strings. All this for a very, very good cause ... .

In 2011, Neil also made some contributions to his wife Pegi's third album *Bracing for Impact* (with her band the Survivors). (Is the title riffing on Neil's less successful *Landing on Water?*) Neil played electric sitar on one song from her debut CD and left her alone for the second release. My guess is that she's established enough in her own right as a musician that he concluded he would not be perceived as propping her career up by contributing more to this effort. Not that there's anything avant-pop here. He plays subdued electric guitar backup on "Lie" and "Song for a Baby Girl" (and a solo on the former) as well as train-sound harmonica on her cover of Tarheel Slim's "Number 9 Train." Neil even contributes a song, "Doghouse," a lighthearted tale of marital transgression that sounds like it emerged from the *Fork in the Road* sessions (down and low vocals like the title song in question).

In fact, Neil is far from being the best or only reason to investigate Pegi's smoky-voiced lyrical tour through the lives of various down and out individuals—her band is aptly named Pegi Young and the Survivors. She joins the many fine artists who've covered original Crazy Horse guitarist Danny Whitten's haunted and haunting "I Don't Want to Talk About It." Neil's guitar technician Larry Cragg contributes some nice dobro on "Daddy Married Satan" and "Song for a Baby Girl" features one of the last performances by the late Ben Keith on pedal steel.

A more important Neil Young release of late is *Americana* (2012), his first studio album with Crazy Horse since 1996. But the importance of this is not only a re-visitation of the Horse, but a far more important act of historical preservation. The two biggest missing pieces of Neil's musical career—that is to say, not caught on tape—were the live Buffalo Springfield (remedied in the summer of 2011 by the reunion of surviving members) and the folk-rock freak-outs the Squires did in Fort William in 1965 witnessed by Stephen Stills when he was in the Company folk ensemble touring up there. Neil himself reminisces about it best:

> Stephen and the Company did "High-Flyin' Bird." "Clementine" [by the Squires] was influenced by seein' the Thorns—they did "Oh Susannah." The Thorns came through playin' in nightclubs that we were playing in afternoons. They were the original folk-rock band, okay? Tim Rose and two other guys—no drums, but they had bass, two guitars, I think it was. They did some really nice stuff and sang really well. One of my favorites was "Oh Susannah"—they did this arrangement that was bizarre. It was in a minor key, which completely changed everything—and it was rock and roll. So that idea spawned arrangements of all these other songs for me. I did minor versions of them all. We got into it. That was a certain Squires stage that never got recorded. Wish there were tapes of those shows. We used to do all this stuff, a whole kinda music—folk-rock. We took famous old folk songs like "Clementine," "She'll Be Comin' Round the Mountain," "Tom Dooley," and we did them all in minor keys based on the Tim Rose arrangement of "Oh Susannah." (in McDonough 112-3; italics removed)

Jump forward forty-seven years and this is to a tee the *Americana* project, with Crazy Horse filling in for the Squires (both loose and soulful garage affairs). Every single song Neil mentions in this interview appears on the new release—and more as well, of course. But they're all covers of folk songs, except for a wacky version of the doo-wop hit "Get a Job" (originally done by the Silhouettes). In the liner notes, Neil claims that this number "is included in *Americana* because it is a genuine folk song with all of the true characteristics." But he does not elaborate what any of those "characteristics" are! Disingenuous? Definitely. A joke? Probably. But who cares? Like the rest of the CD, it's serious fun. (Did the Squires cover it in this fabled Fort William era? Did the Shocking Pinks?)

The other indication of the fun factor here is the inclusion of studio patter after the takes. After their version of the Thorns' arrangement of "Oh Susannah," Neil observes "it sounds funky … . It gets into a good groove." More tellingly, after "Clementine" he laments "I fucked up." But nonetheless that's the take he uses! Sonic perfection is not the goal here as opposed to spirited, rough readings of the material, warts and all.

Maybe it's the unusual approach, but this album restores some of the uncanny aspects of the folk material. I had never noticed before the contradictory lyrics of the third verse of "Oh Susannah":

> It rained all night the day I left
> The weather it was dry
> The sun so hot, I froze to death
> Susannah, don't you cry

Whaaa? And is the second verse of "Travel On" about post-traumatic stress disorder: "Papa writes to Johnny, But Johnny can't come home / 'Cause he's been in the war too long?"

Heard in this context, "Clementine" sounds like a tamer germ for "Down by the River": a drowning, but not a murder. "Tom Dula" (aka "Tom Dooley") IS a murder ballad. There's some good sequencing here: "Clementine" to "Tom Dula" to "Gallows Pole." This last features the most passionate vocal delivery on the project from Neil. Check out the way he deploys terrified melisma on the word "hangin'" only when the narrator who's awaiting death by same sings it (as opposed to other characters he's speaking for)—it's a wonderful touch. "High Flyin' Bird" offers sizzling blues, great soloing and a nod to Stephen Stills's roots. Stephen himself shows up on back-up vocals (also with Pegi and a choir) on the next track, Woody Guthrie's "This Land Is Your Land." Neil includes all of the subversive socialist lyrics usually not sung when the tune is covered—and is careful to remind the listener in the liner notes that "the lyrics sung in the *Americana* version were in the original manuscript of the song." It turns out "Let's Impeach The President" has a pedigree as well.

The album winds down with an acoustic "Wayfarin' Stranger." Its lyrics of reunion after death with one's parents no doubt hold special resonance for Neil (and anyone, like me, in a similar existential situation). The raucous closer, "God Save the Queen" (the original, not the Sex Pistols anthem) is a suitable valentine for Queen Elizabeth II in the year of her diamond jubilee. Its medley of those lyrics with "My Country 'Tis of Thee" keeps the proceedings fair and balanced.

In October of 2012, Neil Young published a memoir, *Waging Heavy Peace: A Hippie Dream.* It's something he said he'd never do, but a broken toe that grounded him from touring changed his mind—as well as temporary songwriter's block resultant from going completely pot and alcohol free. You can read the book for yourself. It's very straightforward if chronologically nonlinear. As reviewers have noted, it reads like a series of entertaining blog postings.

As Neil wrote in "Wrecking Ball," his "life's an open book / you read it on the radio." If you listen carefully to the music, you know about this guy. Thus I had to make only two factual corrections to this chapter after reading the 500 page book (both cited above). There are no deep revelations therein, as even he jokingly acknowledges when he lets us in on the secret that Linda Rondstadt was once "addicted to peanut butter ... . Isn't that exactly the kind of interesting information you expect from a book like this?" (414). Along with anecdotes about the music, the artists who played it and the staff who helped get it out there, we learn much about Neil's two big technological interests: the abovementioned Lincvolt large-size hybrid car he wants Detroit to produce —and Pono. Pono, which means "righteous and good" in Hawaiian, is a new music delivery platform which Neil helped develop that offers unprecedented audio reproduction—like you're there in the studio (428). It sounds vastly better than vinyl, let alone the CDs or MP3 files which Neil Young heartily despises. If Neil can ever bring these projects to fruition, they may become his most important historical legacy. But neither has been picked up as of this writing, so he's in a limbo between being Mark Twain with his financially disastrous investment in the Paige typesetter and Thomas Alva Edison.

This month also saw the release on DVD and Blu-ray of the third film in Jonathan Demme's documentary trilogy on Neil, *Journeys*. (For some reason, as of this writing, the second film documenting his 2009 tour, *Trunk Show*, remains unreleased.) Both of these two films contrast strongly with the first film in what turned out to be a trilogy, *Heart of Gold* (discussed above). While that was a concert especially staged for a film, the other two works document actual tours and are not as elaborately staged. Several aspects distinguish *Journeys* from *Trunk Show*. First of all, it is only at one venue: Toronto's Massey Hall (a return to the scene of his famous concert released on the Archives). Secondly, Neil is playing strictly solo. And finally, the concert is intercut with road movie footage of Neil's return to Omemee, his North Ontario hometown. From there he drives to the venue in a 1956 Crown Victoria, telling stories on the way.

In the interview with 92Y on the bonus features Neil elaborates on the importance of Massey Hall as a location. Like Constitution Hall in Washington, D.C., it has a thrust stage, not a proscenium stage: it's "like a giant speaker .... You're playing in the hall" as opposed to "playing into the hall." The player immediately hears how the sound is going out rather than hearing an echo off the back walls. Neil prefers this effect, while conceding many musicians do not (like symphony orchestras).

This sound is used to advantage with the Dolby surround. Although Neil is playing alone, he's using a bevy of electronic toys from the *Le Noise* sessions to make a single guitar sound like a full band. Between the electronics and the Dolby, the result is an auditory experience unlike any other. When he's playing electric guitar, it actually sounds like you're inside the guitar hearing the sound move around.

The visual compensation for just having one guy on stage is also more than adequately compensated for by Demme's Director of Photography, Declan Quinn, who isn't afraid to take a few risks. Most notably, he placed a small digital camera very close to Neil for especially dramatic songs such as "Down By the River" and "Hitchhiker." How close? You can only see his mouth delivering the words. On the latter song, he's so close that he's spitting on the lens which creates a low-grade psychedelic effect (as Demme jokes in interview). Lighting is also used for dramatic effect: on "Hitchhiker" green spots for the marijuana verse, red for the cocaine verses. The only additional *mise-en-scène* besides Neil and the instruments is a giant cigar store Indian who gets an occasional close-up. One last innovative idea is the use of actual archival footage of the Kent State shooting on "Ohio"—as well as superimposing the names and faces of the four victims (with permission of the families). These choices deliver the historical gravitas of the song to younger generations.

The concert itself, as you may gather, is all good. He does fourteen songs, including an encore and an audio-only version of "Helpless" over beautiful closing credits of rural Ontario. Six are from *Le Noise*, the other eight are largely from his earlier career ("Ohio," "Down By the River," "After the Gold Rush" [on pump organ], "I Believe in You," "Helpless"). "My My Hey Hey" is an expected exception.

And there are two new songs, the last he wrote before his year-long post-sobriety songwriter's block: "Leia" and "You Never Call." The former is a piano ballad of Blakean innocence about a friend's infant daughter. It's interesting that Neil can still go here as he approaches seventy: "We're going back to grandpa's house / And rocking on his knee." The song ends with some ephemeral piano noodling meant to replicate Leia at the keyboard. It's a little gem of a song. "You Never Call" is a tribute to his late friend and collaborator Larry Johnson, who helped Neil edit his films (among many other services). Actual footage Larry shot is shown during the very personal elegy.

Other musical highlights include that uncanny and dramatic re-invention of "Down By the River" (like "Hitchhiker," played on Old Black) and definitive live renderings of "Love and War" and "Hitchhiker." The passion and energy that come through on all these one can hardly imagine ever being surpassed; it's great that the cameras were rolling.

The documentary trip down memory lane interspersed between the concert footage, as well as the conversational bonus features, is another example of the virtual intimacy Neil Young is comfortable establishing with his fan base first made prominent by the Archives project (as noted above)—but previewed by between-song patter in early concerts and gestures like smoking a joint in real time onscreen in the *Journey Through the Past* film. As in the case of the memoir, Neil seems to be exactly whom we might expect him to be. He looks right into the camera, casually dressed, and tells us goofy little stories about his childhood entrepreneurship (pulling a wagon full of fish he caught, raising chickens and protecting them from foxes by sleeping near them in a pup tent). The only time things get heavy is when Neil comments on loss and change triggered by all the places from his childhood no longer there: "It's all gone. It's in my head. That's why you don't have to worry when you lose friends.

'Cause they're still in your head and still in your heart." Appropriate thoughts for a year in which he lost longtime collaborators Larry Johnson and Ben Keith.

Like they say on the infomercials: but wait! There's more! Not only did October, 2012, see a book and a new documentary concert from Neil. There was also *Psychedelic Pill*, a triumphant return to songwriting and his first double studio CD with Crazy Horse—more remarkable acts of closure. The double CD opens with "Driftin' Back," an epic workout for Neil in his activist persona, 2012 style. Clocking in at over 27 minutes, it's the longest studio effort of the Horse. It begins with an acoustic section recorded separately in Hawaii that laments that the listener cannot hear much of what Neil's recorded, a worry that recurs once the song kicks into full electric strangulation mode " "Don't want my MP3 ... . You only get 5% / You used to get it all now." Young connects this with the difference between an actual painting and computer wallpaper in a manner evocative of Walter Benjamin's classic essay "The Work of Art in the Age of Mechanical Reproduction," where the latter comments upon the loss of "aura" when a work is copied: "I used to dig Picasso / Then the big tech giant came along / And turned him into wallpaper." These are the most pointed lyrics in what is overall a loping, stream of consciousness set of associations reminiscent of an amplified "Last Trip to Tulsa." He sings about how he got his mantra from the Maharishi, his likely paganism and how he wants "a hip hop haircut" (???). The stretched-out feel of the song makes it a western *rāga*, perfect traveling music. It's incantatory, a sober re-grounding of his muse with Crazy Horse—and the best they've sounded since *Zuma*.

The title track which follows is, ironically, a return to the stoner persona without actually being high. He gets a trippy effect by flanging the entire song. You can get a nice technical definition of "flanging" on Wikipedia. Suffice it to say, it's a distortion effect caused by a slight tape delay doubled onto the original signal. The Beatles used it subtly if extensively on *Revolver*; Jimi Hendrix used it a fair bit on all his studio albums. Its most pronounced use was on "Itchycoo Park," a single by the Small Faces readily hearable on Youtube. Neil himself slightly deployed it in "Sun Green" on *Greendale*. Here he goes the next step by flanging the entire song, something I'm not aware that any other artist has done. With the "Cinnamon Girl" variant melody, this could be a bid for a single. But everyone besides me who's heard it that I've talked to thinks the flanging is too much of a good thing, which is probably why the non-flanged version is a bonus track on the CD.

The lyrics reinforce the stoned-out feel:

> The way she dances makes my heart stand still
> When she's spinning in the sky
> Every move is like a psychedelic pill
> From a doctor I can't find

Neil and the lads get off a great musical joke here, too. They repeat "I can't find" several times to the exact melody of "I can't hide" from the chorus of the Beatles' "I Want to Hold Your Hand." The joke is that Bob Dylan thought the lads were singing "I get high," so he brought some marijuana to their New York hotel. Crazy Horse carries the play to the next level.

As Neil points out in his memoir, he constructs his albums in a carefully sequenced way. And so it certainly is here. The track which follows this faux stoner rocker is "Ramada Inn," another long song about a battle with the bottle which seems to be an actual bidding of adieu to the party animal persona. It's none of our business how precisely autobiographical the lyrics are, but this track is easily the saddest, most moving and most powerful cut on the album—regardless of whether it's about Neil and Pegi or some folks like them. Given his revelation in *Waging Heavy Peace* that he needed to give up alcohol as well to facilitate giving up pot, one can draw one's own conclusions (9-10).

After that heaviness, the band lightens it up for a few shorter numbers. "Born in Ontario," the last song on the first disk, is a revival of the country shit-kicker persona—replete with pump organ—that would not have been out of place on the *Harvest* album. Its opening line holds out another olive branch to the folks he offended in his youth: "You might see me in Alabam'." But he's from the place "[w]here the black fly bites and the green grass grows." "Twisted Road," the second disk's opener sets to music his anecdote in the memoir about the first time he heard Bob Dylan's "Like a Rolling Stone" on the radio (as well as his fondness for the Grateful Dead and the joy he got playing a venue where he once heard Roy Orbison). And "She's Always Dancing" is another energetic tribute to Pegi.

"For the Love of Man" is the most uncharacteristic cut on the album, a quiet number with stringman synthesizer about social injustice, albeit on a very abstract level:

> For the love of man
> Who could understand what goes on
> What is right and what is wrong
> Why the angels cry, and the heavens sigh
> When a child is born to live
> But not like you or I

By his own admission, Neil has more questions than answers about life.

The CD proper ends with another monster jam to bookend "Driftin' Back." "Walk Like a Giant" confronts some of Neil's biggest concerns: it looks back to previous failures and hopes for future successes (no doubt Pono and Lincvolt). First the bad news:

> Me and some of my friends

We were going to change the world ... .

But the weather changed
And the white got stained
And it fell apart
And it breaks my heart
Go think about how close we came

The second section is a murky allegory about a train heading into "Spiritual" that jumps the tracks; the third chunk worries about "the big fire comin' / Comin' to burn down all my ideas." This lyric could refer to the actual fire that burned up the first Lincvolt prototype or to Neil's anxiety about potentially encroaching Alzheimer's which led him to go straight. On the spectacular video of the song, mushroom clouds are shown, suggesting that his perennial concern about nuclear weapons might be in play here as well. (For the record, the videos for both this and "Driftin' Back" are amazing. Both have lots of psychedelic animation hearkening back to vintage-era light shows; the former also has footage of Big Foot walking [Neil's primitive double!] and a train wreck.)

In any case, Neil wants to get back to former glory: "I used to walk like a giant in the land / Now I feel like a leaf floating in a stream / I want to walk like a giant." The lyrics are reinforced by full-tilt Crazy Horse. Neil even whistles on the chorus and the band provides doo-wop harmonies that reach back to Danny and the Memories, the band they were before they became the Rockets and subsequently Crazy Horse. The song ends with an extended coda with the whole band replicating the walking giant's footsteps as he walks away, then with hopeful connotations returns—followed by a last blast of vocal harmonizing (Crazy Horse does the Beach Boys). All three of these texts (book, film, CD) show a man at a significant crossroads: a fork in the road indeed.

So these are the projects Neil Young's been working on—and the loose ends he's been carefully tying up (cf. Frank Zappa finishing the *Uncle Meat* film and putting out the 12 CD live box set). What's next for Neil? Perhaps another book which he wants to call *Cars and Dogs* (*Waging* 140), a finished director's cut of his film *Human Highway* (he wants to re-edit it for better comic pacing). And yes, the Lincvolt car—and a documentary film about it—and the Pono audio platform, plus three or four more volumes of the Archives. Quite an ambitious agenda! And hopefully even more ... . Long may he run.

Works Cited

Barnes, Jim. *A Season of Loss.* West Lafayette, IN: Purdue University Press, 1985.
Boswell, James. *The Life of Samuel Johnson.* 1793. New York: Everyman's Library, 1992.
Buffalo Springfield. *Buffalo Springfield Box Set.* Rhino R2 74324. 2001.
Crowe, Cameron. "Neil Young: Still Expecting To Fly." *Musician.* November 1982, pp. 54-62, 96-9.
Downing, David. *A Dreamer of Pictures: Neil Young: The Man and His Music.* New York: Da Capo, 1995.
Einarson, John. *Don't Be Denied: Neil Young: The Canadian Years.* Kingston, Ontario: The Quarry Press, 1992.
Gibson, William. *Neuromancer.* New York: Ace Books, 1984.
Grose, Peter. *Israel in the Mind of America.* New York: Schocken Books, 1984.
Haraway, Donna. "The Promises of Monsters: A Regenerative Politics for Inappropriate/d Others." In *Cultural Studies.* Ed. Lawrence Grossberg et al. New York: Routledge, 1992. pp. 295-337.
Heatley, Michael. *Neil Young: His Life and Music.* London: Hamlyn, 1994.
<infogate.com> "Neil Young Defends Anti-Terrorist Crackdown." December 12, 2001.
Kipnis, Laura. "(Male) Desire and (Female) Disgust: Reading Hustler ." In *Cultural Studies.* Ed. Lawrence Grossberg et al. New York: Routledge, 1992, pp. 373- 91.
Lifton, Robert Jay and Richard Falk. *Indefensible Weapons: The Political and Psychological Case Against Nuclearism.* New York: Basic Books, 1982.
Long, Pete. *Ghosts on the Road: Neil Young in Concert.* London: The Old Homestead Press, 1996.
Longinus, "On Sublimity." Trans. D. A. Russell. In *The Norton Anthology of Theory and Criticism.* General editor Vincent B. Leitch. New York: W.W. Norton & Company, 2001.
McDonough, Jimmy. *Shakey: Neil Young's Biography.* New York: Random House, 2002.
Petridis, Alexis. *Neil Young.* New York: Thunder's Mouth Press, 2000.
Young, Astrid. *Being Young.* Toronto: Insomniac Press, 2007.
Young, Neil. *Decade.* Reprise 3RS 2257. 1977. Liner notes by Neil Young.
——. *Waging Heavy Peace: A Hippie Dream.* New York: Blue Rider Press, 2012.

Again, I am not listing a discography here, readily available through 1999 in Petridis. See Long for bootleg and video releases. Post-1999, indeed all, official Young recordings can be found on Neil's website (<www.neilyoung.com>).

Appendix: The Bonnaroo Letter

To whom it may concern:

I had originally intended to write a letter to my friend Shawn, who is in a place that is pretty much the exact opposite of Bonnaroo. But then I thought: why not make this text available to any interested party? It's a lot easier to hand them this missive than to try to sum up the Bonnaroo experience in a few words.

My two traveling companions left Kirksville early on the morning of Wednesday, June 8, 2011 to pick up an RV in Springfield, Missouri—which we proceeded to hump across southern Missouri and western Tennessee. By midnight, we had gained our fourth member, the wife of one of us three guys. We stayed at a campground and drove into the Bonnaroo site the next day around noon.

Thursday was largely considered a day for settling in, so when we went onto the actual site it was to see only small indie bands. We began the long process of discovering our perquisites as VIP guests (e.g., the ability to bypass long lines of people). The initial impression of the site was that it was packed with people and extremely dusty (some of our party was reminded of Calcutta, India). The dust would build throughout the weekend to Dust Bowl proportions, prompting many wise festival-goers to wear bandanas over their mouths.

The first band we heard was Uncle Skeleton, an eleven-person ensemble that could rock out on *Remain in Light* Talking Heads covers. After some Thai food (pad thai) and libations, we heard three bands back to back in That Tent (as the venue was called): Futurebirds (a country-tinged group out of Athens, Georgia), Freelance Whales (an eclectic New York collective that had the same devil-may-care attitude of the Velvet Underground, if more in the way of electronic keyboards) and School of Seven Bells (abetted by a powerful Irish female vocalist). All were very good, if not sublime. Then we headed over to the opening VIP buffet reception (yum). Bored by a mediocre comedian, we went back to the RV for bevvies and much-needed rest, wafted off to sleep as we would be by the late-night acts (Bonnaroo only sleeps about 4 AM - noon—less if you go to the headphones-only rave tents).

The next day I discovered the wonders of coed showering and pressure-cooked bath-rooming before enjoying a smoked salmon egg burrito and venturing over to Centeroo for the action. I underestimated the power of my VIP pass and thought I couldn't get into the Comedy Theatre to hear Cheech Marin and several young acts (by the account of my fellow attendees, I didn't miss much). Plan B was to hear the New Orleans Allstars at the Sonic Stage featuring Jamie McClean, Kirk Joseph and Ivan Neville (of those Nevilles). They kicked it out on some excellent covers such as "Papa Was a Rolling Stone" (Temptations), "Let's Go Crazy" (Prince), "Big Chief" (Professor Longhair) and

Appendix: The Bonnaroo Letter

"Superstitious" (Stevie Wonder)—all with a N'Awlins flair. The sousaphone certainly helped in that regard.

The behavior at this set reminded me of one of several aspects of etiquette by the youngsters at Bonnaroo I found slightly problematic. The open smoking of marijuana was ubiquitous by the attendees (despite threatening official rhetoric about zero tolerance); but, unlike their sixties counterparts, they didn't share with strangers. So I got a lot of second-hand and ONLY second-hand smoke over those four days.

Then it was time to head to Which Stage (the second largest on the grounds) for the first act whose name I recognized—and had even seen before: Bela Fleck and the Flecktones. Original member Howard Levy rejoined Bela on banjo, Victor Wooten on bass and Futureman on homemade instruments for a typically indescribable instrumental set of bluegrass-jazz-rāga fusion. Bela has certainly reinvented the banjo with results always pleasant if never really edgy or challenging (as jazz can certainly be). But he was very enjoyable.

After his set, we headed back to the RV and met our neighbors: two women and a man in a three-way marriage arrangement. The gals are an on-line item known as the Doublemint Twins after the gum. They sported a lot of lime-green (clothes, pasties, lipstick, peace signs) and were ideal neighbors. Grilling was in process—which I could only sample as I had to run off to see Wanda Jackson, who proved to offer one of the three sublime musical experiences of Bonnaroo for me.

A contemporary of Elvis, this Queen of Rockabilly got her career revived by Jack White's production of her comeback effort, *The Party's Not Over*. The years melted off this seventy-plus-year-old gal as she stormed through a series of scorchers like "Riot in Cellblock #9" (her opener), the single-entendre "Rock Your Baby," "Fujiyama Mama" (where she tastefully promises to leave her lover in the condition of Hiroshima and Nagasaki) and "Shakin' All Over." Her sequined red top was indeed shakin'! She even threw in a little yodeling despite the dust that turned her bottled water into mud ("I always was a gal with more guts than talent"). Overall, her voice alternates between a croon and a compelling buzzsaw growl. She paid homage to Elvis with a few songs (e.g., "Heartbreak Hotel"). And she gave us a gospel moment with "I Saw the Light," telling us that she was born again in 1971. Given those rockabilly years, undoubtedly a good thing. Fantastic lady, amazing show. Here I benefitted from some great Bonnaroo staff who let me sit in an unoccupied seat for the mobility-impaired. Along with the dope stinginess, a second downside of the youngsters was their wanting to stand for EVERYTHING; it was very hard to get a good view in any of the tents without doing the same. This proved to be the one exception.

After Wanda, I wandered over to This Tent to hear . They sounded good— both powerful and ethereal—but I was too far away to even see them, given the crowds. So I wandered over to the What Stage (aka the main stage) for the back-to-back thrills of My Morning Jacket and that year's Grammy winner Arcade Fire. My Morning Jacket were great but not sublime IMHO. The Louisville-based band can do almost anything, sounding by turns like Pete Townshend, Bob Dylan, the Band, or Dino Valenti's Quicksilver Messenger Service. But unlike Wanda Jackson or Arcade Fire, they don't have a sonic thumbprint. You can't recognize an MMJ song on the radio if you don't know it's by them. Very postmodern, but maybe a problem for their career in the long term. If you're that eclectic, you had better be the Beatles.

Arcade Fire on the other hand transcended the hype and exceeded expectations—thereby giving me the second sublime thrill and making me an instant fan. Since I was previously unfamiliar with this Canadian bunch (although one of the leaders grew up in Houston), I can't give a very detailed blow-by-blow of the proceedings. Suffice it to say they had a superb light show (including fake movie trailers before they came on—Pink Floyd with a sense of humor) and a driving rhythm enhanced by two violinists and fantastic keyboards. The lyrics were modern William Blake meditations on childhood (especially in the suburbs) counterpointed with songs about Haiti and unadulterated weirdness ("I know a place where spaceships never land"). Damn good stuff. Those of our crew who went were so pumped up we stayed up till four, drinking and overhearing rapper Lil' Wayne exhort us repeatedly to "raise [our] motherfucking hands." I drifted off to sleep to the ambient *rāga* of the Shpongletron Experience.

Saturday, June 11, was the Big Day that inspired my journey: a chance to see the last date of the brief Buffalo Springfield reunion tour! But first we ventured over to the Which Stage to catch , a bluegrass-tinged southern band that scored a hit with "Wagon Wheel." We even caught a little of sanctified shouters who preceded them. After the Crow, occupied the stage for ninety minutes. Occupied, but did not hold.

For those of you counting, here are my third and fourth (final) objections to today's nouveau-pseudo-faux hippies. They largely suffer from attention deficit disorder which leads them to, first of all, talk and text through the musical acts rather than LISTEN. It's multi-tasking: they can simultaneously chat and piss me off. No wonder they say that they "see" bands; they don't hear them. (Only in-your-face highly amplified acts like MMJ, Arcade Fire and rappers can get their undivided attention. A mellow gal like Allison Krauss doesn't stand a chance.) One of the non-stop chatterers (who did not appreciate my calling them on it) even knew the lyrics: every now and then she'd burst into song. The second facet of their AAD is that they lose interest in an act quickly, compelling them to move on to some new stimulation. All it takes is one song with a slower tempo to incite a mass exodus. Since Krauss has a lot of those, it was a free for all so bollixed up that I can't say I really enjoyed it. She deserves more than to be aural wallpaper for these people.

After this semi-debacle and more delicious Thai food (drunken noodles!), we went over to That Tent for Loretta Lynn. She was fabulous, if a bit frailer than Wanda Jackson (she sang one song twice). She avoided her Jack White work in favor of her earlier classics. But since those include "Fist City," "The Pill," and "Coal Miner's Daughter," who could complain? Not me! The departed she chose to honor was Patsy Cline with an extended medley with the likes of "Crazy" and "Walkin' After Midnight."

Then it was time for my main event. We got great seats in the VIP bleachers at the Which stage for the Springfield, top row, above the goofballs. At 9:30, Richard Furay, Stephen Stills and Neil Young hit the stage together (with drummer Joe Vitale and bassist Rick Rosas replacing Dewey Martin and Bruce Palmer respectively) for one of the first times in forty years. Here's the set list, which I will follow by a few general observations:

1. "On the Way Home" (written by Neil, sung by Richie as on the album *Last Time Around*)

2. "Rock and Roll Woman" (Stephen Stills)

3. "Burned" (Neil Young)

4. "A Child's Claim to Fame" (Richard Furay)

5. "Do I Have to Come Right Out and Say It" (written by Neil, sung by Richie as on their first album)

6. "Go and Say Goodbye" (Stills)

7. "I Am A Child" (Young)

8. "Hot Dusty Roads" (Stills)

9. "Kind Woman" (Furay)

10. "Mr. Soul" (Young)

11. "Nowadays Clancy Can't Even Sing" (written by Young, sung by Furay as on the first album)

12. "Bluebird" (Stills)

13. "Sad Memory" (Furay); Neil switching from guitar to piano on this

14. "Broken Arrow" (Young); Stephen on piano for this

15. "For What It's Worth" (Stills)

16. "Rockin' in the Free World" (Young)

An amazing set list that would leave any fan of the Buffalo Springfield vastly satisfied. They played almost everything one might want to hear, including a number like "Broken Arrow" which I doubt was ever attempted live previously by the original band.

Some random notes:

- A very brief lightning storm ensued beginning on "Burned." Neil made it rain again (cf. the *Road Rock* video). We had to vacate the bleachers from song 5 until song 11—the only rain that fell on Bonnaroo!

- The youth thought the band wasn't loud enough (see previous kvetches: throughout the openers they kept chanting "Turn it up!" At one point I yelled back: "Listen!"). Only the final number met their sonic approval.

- Neil was especially charming and ironic throughout—and an obvious fan of the festival. He made sure to showcase equally his band mates, although he was willing to be the jovial emcee. After a few of the openers, he announced "we're from the past." He made sure we knew that the band was leading up to their hit single (15) ("and we do have a hit single!") after playing the B-side earlier (5). He avouched that they were "happy to be here" (i.e., both at Bonnaroo and alive) and marveled that this was the "biggest gig this band's ever done."

- Stephen Stills looked better than I'd seen him in ages, for artificial (hair dye) and natural (weight loss) reasons. He wore glasses for a professorial look. The jam on "Bluebird" paid homage to the epic closers of the band's original live shows, culminating in an electric guitar call-and-response led by Neil on the riff that precedes the banjo studio coda (not delivered live—a pity since Bela Fleck was around and interested).

- The other great little jam was the jazz coda at the end of "Broken Arrow," which was more extended than the studio version.

- Neil gave a rap introducing the final song, positing it as a "new cover" and an alternate history example of where the band might have gone before admitting he was just putting us on and doing the song to round out the set. In effect, the song—albeit fabulously—broke the magic spell the Springfield reunion cast upon the true believers, reminding us that it was in fact 2011 and not 1968 (as it was for 75 minutes). But after all, both "For What It's Worth" and "Rockin' in the Free World" are political anthems. There is continuity as well as change!

After this, we headed off to the RV to the soothing strains of Eminem on the main stage. As much as I wanted to see him, we were satiated—and you really can't go to everything you want to hear at a music festival of this scope.

The final day of Bonnaroo proper began for me with the great Mavis Staples on the main stage at 1:15 PM. As she pointed out, her show was as close as Bonnaroo was going to get to a church service. She did a wonderful melange of spirituals old and new, including a song Jeff Tweedy of Wilco wrote for her and a cover of the Band's "The Weight" backed up by Patty Griffin. Her surprising encore was the Buffalo Springfield's "For What It's Worth," thereby extending the enchantment of the previous night.

I proceeded over to That Tent for back-to-back Bruce Hornsby and Gregg Allman. I only heard the former, since we were sitting on a blanket throughout the mellow keyboard-driven set. What we saw were white frat boy asses lamely shaking to the music (see complaints above). Same for Gregg Allman, except that I stood up for his "Whipping Post" closer. (The other exquisite Allman Brothers oldies he did were "No Way Out" and "Sweet Melissa.") The newer stuff was highly listenable if not lyrically challenging (e.g., "Going Back to Daytona" [as in Beach, his hometown]).

After a designer beer, I headed over to the general vicinity of This Tent, where the Odessa-based post-rock noise art band Explosions in the Sky alternated between ambient gentleness and King Crimson levels of decibel blowout. Because of the massive crowd, I could only hear not see them. From my picnic table listening post, I could also hear the band Beirut from another tent and, more obnoxiously, broadcast coverage of what turned out to be the NBA final game. My odd personal sound mix was very Brian Eno—or should I say very Shpongletron?

I also saw briefly the dark side of Bonnaroo when a couple of faux-hippies cornered a terrified squirrel who had wandered onto the grounds. What did they think they were doing by ratcheting up a wild animal with sharp teeth? Fortunately, Explosions in the Sky went into very loud mode, pushing the animal into running rapidly through the circle of entrapment, off into the woods, sadder but wiser. Saved by the music! It was time to go back to the RV and home.

At the RV, the Doublemint Twins and friends lit up a hot air balloon powered by charcoal. In a final irony, they offered me my first marijuana of the entire festival as we were about to leave. In a further irony, it was California medical marijuana which one of them had a prescription for. So for the second time in 24 hours, it was 1968!

Our return journey was uneventful mostly. We stopped at Denny's (whose shrimp and grits are no match for the fare you get in the Carolinas). We caught two hours shuteye in a truck stop and hit heavy rain and hail by the Lake of the Ozarks. After sleeping for 14 hours in the past 24 and unpacking, I thought I'd better strike while the iron was hot and write this, my Bonnaroo, down. There's nothing like it. Let me give Lewis Black the last word (from the 6/11/11 in-house newspaper, the *Bonnaroo Beacon*): "Bonnaroo is always amazing. It's never not been amazing. Even if you had this many people standing around, not listening to anything but themselves, it would be amazing."

—Tuesday 6/14/11, 5:45 PM

Notes

[1] Tellingly, his 1978 "Rust Never Sleeps" tour, with its innocence-turned-into-experience theme, began with Neil performing "Sugar Mountain" and "I Am A Child."

[2] On the 1978 tour, Neil's set design also included lowering Frank Sampedro's Stringman keyboard onto the stage in a large Thunderbird for "Like a Hurricane." His third film, *Human Highway*, is full of Native American references and visuals as well. Wooden Indians abound in the film (especially in its dream sequence); Young's character (Lionel) serenades one in one sequence. Lionel also reads a newspaper headline that says "Oil-Rich Indians In Space." In the dream sequence, Young breaks out the old Comanche jacket for one scene.

[3] "We R In Control" from *Trans* (1982) first uses this image, though, so Gibson may not be relevant. (*Neuromancer* was published in 1984.) Still, Neil could have encountered that lovely opening line in the interval between *Trans* and *Broken Arrow*: "The sky above the port was the color of television, tuned to a dead channel" (Gibson 3).

[4] To avoid confusion, let me point out that the last two lines of the block quotation are not the third verse, but the chorus. The third verse follows and is a repeat of half of the first verse.

[5] I feel totally validated about this observation after reading, much later after writing this originally, that Neil's half-sister Astrid Young also "thought it was Roger Waters" when she first heard the song on her car radio (253).

[6] "Farmer's Song" is really a political song as well. It not only celebrates / mourns the farmer as the last of a dying breed, it talks about "fighting for a change / We're looking for a country that don't need Farm Aid." In 1993, it was especially performed as a provocation to the non-participation of the new Clinton administration. "Where's the change?" Neil lamented. Incidentally, "Farmer's Song," retitled "Last of a Dying Breed (The Farm Aid Song)," is now available on the Farm Aid benefit CD.

[7] And how can I forget his performance as "Westy," the owner of a motorcycle shop, in Steven Kovacs' film *'68* (1987)? This film, like Alan Rudolph's

Love At Large, is worth tracking down for proof that Neil is a fine character actor. (He works harder for other directors than himself!) Young's thespian skills offer collaboratory evidence that he can deliver convincing personae from the stage as well. And the subplot of the Hungarian family's gay son in '68 adds to the roster of Neil's queer projects ... .

[8] Frank Zappa was mistakenly linked with the counterculture, of course, despite his careful attempts to differentiate between the Los Angeles "freak" and the San Francisco "hippie"—a distinction which began to blur in any case when the drugs moved in. Zappa's anti-drug stance should have separated him from the ranks, but no one believed him. They mistakenly assumed he had to be ripped to produce such far-out music, unaware of its complexity—which required sobriety.

[9] I think the real ditch excursion was 1980-88. This sequence has been blurred because of some tendency to consider the five Geffen recordings as a sequence, a decision partially reinforced by the 1993 compilation *Lucky Thirteen*. (However, note even there the inclusion of Bluenotes material—a band that ended up back on Reprise.) This is not to deny that Neil's dealings with Geffen records were exceptionally dysfunctional; only that he had other demons as well that influenced recordings—both prior to and after the Geffen contract—which were released on Reprise.

[10] By this time, Pegi was also diagnosed with a brain illness. She had only a fifty-percent chance of survival. Fortunately, the Youngs lucked out that time (Downing 151). This also factored into the mood of *Hawks and Doves*.

[11] Having said this, I guiltily concede that David Byrne might be the best director from the rock world on the basis of *True Stories* (1986). But that's beginning to look like a one-shot deal. And, in any case, Frank Zappa is not far behind—especially on the evidence of *200 Motels*. Yoko Ono is a special case, both because she directs experimental films and because she was a filmmaker before she was a rock musician (hence, another kind of filmmaker than Young, Zappa, Byrne).

[12] In addition to the *Trans* band, the rest of Crazy Horse (Talbot and Sampedro) graced a few tracks.

[13] And in fact one of Ben's nicknames is "Benny the Beam" (Astrid Young 46).

[14] I am grateful to artist and country music fan Steve Shepard for this observation.

[15] Astrid says that Neil considers this "his least favorite record—he's said that a million times" (42).

[16] Alert and astute readers may have wondered why I did not discuss the 1977 summer in Santa Cruz with the Ducks in the seventies "ditch" narrative, although I alluded to it in the beginning of the chapter. For three reasons: 1) Neil was already "back" as a result of *Zuma* and the Stills-Young Band. The Ducks was too underground an experiment to jeopardize his international rep-

utation. 2) The music this band made was conventional if wonderful bar-band rock and roll. The avant-gardism was thus more in the concept than the actual musical execution of the material. 3) Although I have heard this material, courtesy of friend Jane Donovan who lived with Neil's entourage that summer, most of my readers will not have. When Neil releases his promised archival materials, fuller and fairer discussion of the Ducks will be appropriate.

[17]Then again, Neil could be remembering his father's performance of another song, "Carry Me Back to the Lone Prairie," which does have a request in the chorus for a similar prairie burial. "Bury Me Not On The Lone Prairie" might in fact be a rejoinder to this song. I first became aware of this other tune while watching the 1935 Busby Berkeley musical *Stars Over Broadway*, where it is featured.

Joni Mitchell's Musical Hejira

Joni Mitchell's life experiences have certain parallels, perceived by her, with Neil Young. Both Scorpios (Neil on November 12, 1945; Joni on November 7, 1943) grew up in western Canada (Neil in Winnipeg; Joni in Saskatoon, Saskatchewan). Joni noted the effect this had on their music: "I think that there is a lot of Prairie in my music and in Neil Young's music as well. I think both of us have a striding quality to our music which is like long steps across flat land" (in Luftig 70). Moreover, they both contracted polio in the summer of 1952 "both in the back, in the precious spine, and in the right leg. That's a great will-forger, you know." Joni suspected that Neil's medical difficulties led to "a lot of peer group disadvantage at an early age. Maybe that gives him a tailwind" (in Luftig 131). Joni's remarks would apply to herself equally well, of course. She would add on to this list of similarities a dry sense of humor as a result of listening to the BBC (Luftig 130). Given their respect for each other, it's in fact surprising how little they've collaborated on each other's work: Joni has yet to show up on a Neil Young album, and Neil's sole appearance on a Joni Mitchell record is his turn on harmonica for "Furry Sings The Blues" (*Hejira*). They contribute together on a few collective gigs, of course, such as *The Last Waltz* concert and Farm Aid.

With some modifications, then, I believe Joni Mitchell's stretching of the boundaries of pop music can be considered in a parallel manner with the gestures of Neil Young. Like Neil, she has some intrinsic experimental features in her musical art (Joni's phenomenology). They are all completely divergent from Neil's, naturally. For Joni, the unusual aspects of her music include its emergence from her interest in painting; her remarkable alternate guitar tunings, which began as a compensation for the polio, but took on much greater aesthetic interest; and her resistance to the established genres of popular music. In this latter regard, she has gone so far as to claim that her music really needs a genre all its own (Luftig xviii).

Also as with Neil, the issue of persona is important. But unlike Neil, Joni does not offer a proliferation of masks. She is either confessional and autobiographical, or she crafts a persona for a specific song (as with the dramatic monologues of Robert Browning). In this respect, she more closely resembles Yoko Ono than Young, who (as we have seen) plays with various personae across songs. Joni's avant-pop claim to fame in this regard is *Blue* (1971). If John Lennon's *Plastic Ono Band* and Neil Young's *Tonight's The Night* are the most confessional rock albums ever recorded, *Blue* is certainly the most confessional folk-rock album ever put to vinyl. This album offers a rare example of an uncompromising aesthetic statement that became a commercial success.

And finally, Joni had some wonderfully productive forays into the ditch. After her successful fusion with light, pop, west coast jazz—personified by Tom Scott and the L. A. Express—on *Court and Spark* and *Miles of Aisles* (both 1974), she proceeded to much more thoroughly investigate Afro-centric rhythms and approaches in a series of albums which culminated in her collaboration with Charles Mingus. As with Neil's turn to country, Joni's embrace of jazz marginalized her from her more narrow-eared pop and folk fans. The jazzier Joni became, the fewer records she sold. And, of course, the jazz press also were reluctant to embrace her: she wasn't "pure" enough; she hadn't paid her dues enough; she wasn't really making jazz (back to that genre issue again). Even Joni would agree with that last charge: on the liner notes for *Mingus*, she described herself as "dog paddling around in the currents of black classical music." But for her it was all about the music, not the section of the record store you could store it under.

After a modest comeback effort which combined earlier approaches with her jazz interests (*Wild Things Run Fast* [1982]), she headed for the ditch again with *Dog Eat Dog*, a 1985 collaboration with synthmeister Thomas Dolby. This album combined scathing satire of the Reagan era with sampling technology and massive electronic effects. Neil may have gotten as far as what Kraftwerk were accomplishing in *Trans* (1982), but Joni was pushing the envelope a lot further—both emulating and anticipating trends in hip-hop and techno, yet making an album that still sounds sui generis.

These features justify including Joni Mitchell in my partial roster of practitioners of avant-pop. Needless to say, this focus excludes other worthy dimensions of her career: many other fine albums released besides the ones discussed; Joni's career as a producer (she has unobtrusively produced nearly all her recordings); Joni's paintings and photography, which have begun to draw interest from the art world. Even the music we are not discussing is interesting and complex. For example, the Berklee College of Music in Boston used the bridge arrangement from "Car on the Hill" (*Court and Spark* [1974]) as the basis for a final exam question in music theory classes (Luftig 190). This chapter will only discuss a few exceptional stretches in a career never characterized by complacency.

Joni's Special Sauce

Cultural studies scholars Simon Frith and Howard Horne, in their book *Art Into Pop*, have demonstrated the significance of the art school (especially in Great Britain) for fostering future pop musicians—a stunning roster that includes members of the Beatles, the Who, the Rolling Stones, the Sex Pistols and the Clash—as well as other key figures such as Eric Clapton, Syd Barrett, Jeff Beck, Jimmy Page, Ray Davies, Cat Stevens, Brian Ferry and Brian Eno (to name but a few). In America, art school students who have gone into pop music include such folks as Patti Smith and bands like Devo and Talking Heads

(Frith and Horne 73, 115, 116, 125, 126). Yoko Ono's art background scarcely needs mentioning. And on another level, musicians like Frank Zappa and David Bowie learned various arts and worked commercially in graphics (Zappa, for example, designed greeting cards) without ever having actually attended an art school (Frith and Horne 115; Zappa, *Real Frank Zappa Book* 40).

Frith and Horne's book does a good job of explaining why this should be so. On the one hand, art students often became frustrated with the forced career dualism between fine art and commercial art training (a not-so-subtle replication of the British class system)—which tempted many to simply walk away. On the other hand, the techniques learned tempted them to come up with a way to combine commercialism and fine arts aesthetics: pop art! (Even avant-pop art!) Why honor that dodgy dualism? Blend the aesthetics from either side of the divide. After all, they were given preliminary training in both dimensions. And this was easier for many to do in music—although a visual artist such as Peter Blake (who did the cover for *Sergeant Pepper*) showed that a way could be found in the visual arts as well.

Yoko Ono and Frank Zappa's subversive approach to the fine arts demonstrates that their art training was not lost on them. Yet Yoko was far more weighted in her education towards the fine arts, and Zappa was informally trained on the job more in the commercial arts. Of the seven figures we are considering here, Joni Mitchell's background most resembles the classic journey of the art school student into pop music that Frith and Horne finger as the foundation for such massive musical developments as the British invasion, punk and new wave.

Joni's journey from the visual arts into music began in public grade school. As she has often related, a free-spirited teacher assured her that "If you can paint with a brush, you can paint with words." Mr. Kratzman encouraged her as a budding poet, steering her away from cliches and advising her to "Write about what you know, it's more interesting" (Luftig 12).

These words of advice came back to Joni when she became frustrated during her first year at the Alberta College of Art in 1963: "the first year was like a time to decide whether you wanted to be a commercial artist or fine artist. They were going to decide what your fate would be" (Luftig 15). Like many of her peers across the pond, she resented having to make such a choice—and turned to music, deciding to use that career to free her to be both a fine artist and a commercial artist (her album covers) without having any pressure on that vocation. As she later told a curator, "Music is my sorrow, painting is my joy" (Hebert 23).

But painting is at the core of her identity; Joni describes herself as "a painter who writes music," even though the public might see things the other way around (Luftig 203). Indeed, Joni's music and lyrics are influenced by her love of the visual arts in very important ways. For starters, to get back to Mr.

Kratzman, Joni as a songwriter is unusually visual. Think of how technicolor her lyrics are compared to most tunesmiths:

> Woke up, it was a Chelsea morning, and the
>   first thing that I saw
> Was the sun through yellow curtains, and a
>   rainbow on the wall
> Blue, red, green and gold to welcome you,
>   crimson crystal beads to beckon
>
> Oh, won't you stay
> We'll put on the day
> There's a sun show every second ("Chelsea Morning," *Clouds*)

Joni's fondness for colored glass effects also turns up in the "fiery gems" of Graham Nash's song "Our House" (*Deja Vu*). The point is that you can see this imagery quite clearly. And a quick run through Mitchell's lyrics reveals an abundance of color imagery, all quite significant and resonant: blue, turbulent indigo, kelly green ("Little Green," *Blue*).

In addition to color imagery, Joni has a painterly eye in her lyrics generally. They abound in precisely rendered visual detail. Consider four of my favorite lines from the song "Hejira":

> White flags of winter chimneys
> Waving truce against the moon
> In the mirrors of a modern bank
> From the windows of a hotel room

She is more of a romantic than an imagist; Ezra Pound would dun her for indulging in the pathetic fallacy here (the "truce" is her agenda, not the smoke's). But that's mere hairsplitting: this is a marvelously vivid scene. Her use of mirrors and windows is especially astonishing, beckoning the listener to think about the play of light on surface—a written equivalent of effects produced by painters such as Velasquez and Parmigianino. Painting with words indeed!

But beyond pictorial effects in Joni's lyrics, her approach to sound itself is deeply shaped by her training in and love of the visual arts. As she has repeatedly conceded, this was making a virtue out of necessity:

> ... I not only couldn't read [music], but I didn't know—and don't to this day—what key I'm playing in, or the names of my chords. I don't know the numbers, letters, or the staff. I approach it very paintingly, metaphorically: so I rely on someone I'm playing with, or the players themselves, to sketch out the chart of the changes ...

> I see music very graphically in my head—in my own graph, not in the existing systematized graph—and I, in a way, analyze it or interpret it, or evaluate it in terms of a visual abstraction inside my mind's eye.
>
> I see music as fluid architecture. For me, the chords are colors that you stir into mutant shades, as in painting. (Luftig 93-4, 155)

Whence the importance of Joni's work as her own producer: she makes sound recordings as opposed to merely writing songs. Textures and timbres are important to her because of their synaesthetic parallels to visual effects in painting. For example, she describes the open-tuned bass strings that she plays against in many of her songs as resembling "a wash" in the visual arts:

> In painting, if I start a canvas now, to get rid of the vertigo of the blank page, I cover the whole thing in olive green, then start working the color into it. So every color is permeated with that green. It doesn't really green the colors out, but it antiques them, burnishes them. The drones kind of burnish the chord in the same way. That color remains as a wash. Those other colors drop in, but always against that wash. (Luftig 223-4)

You can hear this technique in many of Joni Mitchell's recordings. Musicologist Jeffrey Pepper Rodgers cites "Chelsea Morning" as an early example: an open E tuning which juxtaposes a bass "wash" with a riff played on the top two strings (in Luftig 223). But it is impossible to ignore the effect by the time she works with bass players like Jaco Pastorius. Every song on *Hejira* has a pronounced "wash" / drone in the lower registers which the sparse melody plays off.

Both musically and lyrically, Mitchell's songs incorporate synaesthetic effects; more so than most popular music, they are literally paintings in sound—and should be contemplated visually as well as aurally. Such a project links Joni with some interesting company, ranging from the French symbolist poets through the painter Kandinsky to such fellow musicians as Scriabin and Sun Ra (who actually played a color organ at one point to provide instant visual equivalences for his music). All these individuals, among many others, sought to break down the barriers between sensory perceptions and give us color we could hear, sound we could see.

Joni's alternate tunings, already hinted at, are another unusual feature of her music—also resultant from necessity. Because her left hand has limited movement as a result of the bout with polio, Joni experimented with many alternate tunings of the guitar which would enable her to evoke the sounds she wanted without having to move her hand too much (Luftig 23). She cites as parallels and influences black blues players and Hawaiian slack guitar—and indeed some of the open tunings of Keith Richards and Neil Young (Luftig 203, 220). Joni has described composing some of her songs by going into nature and tuning the guitar to "the pitch of birdsongs" nearby (for "The Magdalene Laundries" [Luftig 221]). To date, she has deployed a remarkable number of alternate tunings for her songs: 51 separate tunings. Only three of her songs ended up in standard tuning (Luftig 222, 220, 229). Since her own technical knowledge is limited, she used to rely on multiple guitars onstage. The Joni Mitchell homepage, sundry other websites and music books share these tunings with the general public. Recently she has been using a Roland VG-8 Virtual Guitar which can program all of these alternate tunings into a single guitar—a great convenience (Luftig 228).

So what does this alternately tuned guitar music sound like? The answer to this question touches upon the issue of Joni's resistance to easy genre labeling. Here is her own description of the sound:

> It's closer to Debussy and classical composition, and it has its own harmonic movement which doesn't belong to any camp ... . It's not jazz, like people like to think. It has in common with jazz that the harmony is very wide, but there are laws to jazz chordal movement, and this is outside those laws for the most part. (Luftig 221).

You can hear these effects on any Joni Mitchell composition except for the three in standard tuning ("Tin Angel," "Urge for Going," "Harlem in Havana"), but again *Hejira* proves to be a rich resource. "Black Crow," for example, has a nonce tuning of B flat / B flat / D flat / F / A flat / B flat with the fifth and sixth strings an octave apart. The result is "a thousand miles from standard tuning" (in Luftig 223).

A final avant-pop aspect of Mitchell's music as a whole is its resistance to easy genre categorization. Like Sun Ra, Joni Mitchell has never been happy with the labels used to describe her music. Not even her initial arrival as a "folksinger": "I looked like a folksinger, even though the moment I began to write, my music was not folk music ... . It was something else, maybe closer to German *lieder*, or it had elements of romantic classicism to it" (Luftig 28). She covered folk songs before making records, but never wrote any by the standard dictionary definition of simple melodies paired with archetypal motifs. And as noted above, her music of the seventies and beyond is not really jazz either. It has family resemblances to all these categories—folk, classical, jazz (and of course rock and pop)—but it is none of these entirely. So her placement in a music store is a matter of convenience that conceals as much as it reveals.

Joni's genre troubles suggest gender issues as well. The music industry is an undeniably patriarchal institution, one that has never hesitated to oppress women like Mitchell any way it could. Early demeaning ads described her music as "90% virgin" (since Judy Collins' cover of "Both Sides Now" sold ten times as well as Joni's records [Luftig 35]).

Rolling Stone magazine dubbed her "Old Lady of the Year" in 1972 and provided a dubious flow chart of her affairs with other pop musicians (Luftig xvi). Consider the blatant double standard in play here: what male rock star received such critical sexual scrutiny? The music industry's most serious form of oppression, however, is keeping Joni's music off the airwaves, as she duly notes in interviews:

> ... being shunned from the airwaves in favor of tits-and-ass bubble gum kind of junk food is a tragedy. And there is no other arena for me to make music in. So I feel constantly in a position of injustice. There's a civil liberties thing here. Is it my chronological age? That should never be held against an artist. We're all going to grow middle-aged. We need middle-aged songs. (Luftig 200- 1)

Her early songs strike her as "ingenue roles" unsuitable for her present identity. While Neil Young, Bob Dylan and others can continue to perform even their earliest material (men can be forever young), Joni senses that she—and her music—have evolved beyond its origins (Luftig 204). But only the earliest music might manifest on a "classic rock" station: the cruel irony of that format is that it only plays what baby boomers heard when they were teenagers. Recent music by any artist who flourished in the sixties will be neglected. As a result, the main Mitchell music heard is the CSN&Y cover of "Woodstock" on classic rock and performances of "Big Yellow Taxi" and "The Circle Game" on children's shows. All of the recent lifetime achievement awards and adulations she has been receiving have not changed this sorry state of affairs which impoverishes everybody. What kind of fucked-up world makes it easier to hear Britney Spears than *Hejira*?

No wonder that Joni refuses to play by the rules. She resists genre the way Woman escapes previous patriarchal categorizations (as described by French feminists such as Helene Cixous and Luce Irigiray). Joni Mitchell makes Joni Mitchell music, just as Sun Ra made Sun Ra music (or Mingus made Mingus music). Free your ears, and your mind will follow.

Blue

It is a banal truism to suggest that music communicates emotions, but a more focused inquiry to speculate when it began to reveal personal and autobiographical circumstances regarding the performer. No doubt many folk songs by anonymous composers addressed direct situations. But only with the emergence of mass media and the culture industry have we been able to confirm these communications with any semblance of exactitude. Joni has joked about this new state of affairs with her audience: "that's one of the tests for schizophrenia, isn't it? 'Do you hear people speaking to you from the media?'" (Luftig 183).

Before popular songwriting became overtly and consistently confessional, the personal communication would come under the veil of a persona. The listening public might feel they were getting to know Edith Piaf, Frank Sinatra or even Elvis Presley because they favored certain types of lyrics and performance styles. These artists sold themselves as tender-hearted victims of love who still regretted nothing, late-night boozehounds, swaggering sexual conquerors or delicate delinquents (to cite only a few masks). Here the persona is created by the selection of other writers' songs to cover in order to present a consistent yet complex character. (A stellar example of this would be *Frank Sinatra Sings for Only the Lonely*.) By contrast to these great interpreters, the balladeers on teenage death songs (like "Tell Laura I Love Her") seem to be only going through the motions.

The confessional turn probably began with Bob Dylan. "Positively Fourth Street" had such conviction in its delivery that listeners suspected they were hearing about a real situation in Dylan's life, although they would have to wait for biographers to track down specifics. Dylan's candor in turn derived from literary developments of the 1950s and early sixties which included confessional poetry (Robert Lowell, Sylvia Plath) and, especially, the raw honesty of the Beats (Jack Kerouac, Allen Ginsberg, William Burroughs). Dylan simply adopted this approach to the pop song. But not consistently: other than "Positively Fourth Street," such clear communiques from Dylan come only sporadically (*Blood on the Tracks, Time Out of Mind*). Other pop singers adapted Dylan's approach, though, and the confessional singer-songwriter was born: James Taylor, Laura Nyro, Yoko Ono (as we have seen) and a host of others. In rock (as we have also seen), the rawest confessional material came from John Lennon (*Plastic Ono Band*) and Neil Young (*Tonight's The Night*).

Joni Mitchell's *Blue* is a special case even in this illustrious company. She has been very forthcoming about the origins of the album. Her first three albums (*Joni Mitchell* [1968], *Clouds* [1969], and *Ladies of the Canyon* [1970] led her from obscurity to a dizzyingly large following. She wrote "Woodstock," after all: an anthem for an entire generation. Other songs such as "Both Sides Now" (with its old soul worldliness) and "Big Yellow Taxi" (a timeless ecological campfire sing-along) didn't hurt either. Joni had the alarming and disillusioning experience of seeing her popularity exceed her audience's accurate appreciation of her. One might think that's an enviable problem to have; but as Neil Young also discovered on the 1973 tour that led to *Time Fades Away*, the results can be devastating to a confessional songwriter. And along with her anthems, Joni had been penning a few tentative confessional songs about relationships she was in: "I Had a King" (about ex-husband Chuck Mitchell), "The Dawntreader," and "Cactus Tree" (about David Crosby and his boat), "Willy" (about Graham Nash)—to name a few where the content has been readily divulged. By 1970, Joni's identity—and heart—was on the line in concert (and she has always been a somewhat nervous performer). Her audience more often than not was an uncomprehending beast, using the music for an excuse to get wasted on whatever was available. That's the reality of a rock concert today, let alone then. The recently released documentary of the Isle of Wight festival shows Joni reduced to tears by acid casualties storming the stage (she missed Woodstock, ironically). The paradox of her situation was not lost on her:

> I thought, "You don't even know who I am. You want to worship me?" That's why I became a confessional poet. I thought, "You better know who you're applauding up here." It was a compulsion to be honest with my audience. (Crowe 49)

> I used to go in the dressing room after a show and just ... cry. People were just discovering you, so you received this radiant enthusiasm, and you'd think, "What are they applauding for, that was horrible what I just did out there." There was emotional deception, there was technical failure. I couldn't get into this song and they didn't know the difference. There's a danger of becoming contemptuous of your audience at that point. (Garbarini 47)

> I don't like receiving things that don't mean anything ... . I couldn't get work in these little piddling clubs, and then I couldn't believe that suddenly overnight all these people loved me for the same songs. These same people sat in clubs where I was the opening act and talked through my show. Now suddenly they were rapt? I wanted to see where they were at. I wanted to show them where I was at. (Luftig 40)

The ultimate product of her disillusionment with her audience was the "terrible opportunity" to "discover to the tips of [her] toes that [she was an] asshole[]" (Crowe 50). In other words, her critical attitude towards her audience did not spare herself, either. It was all going wrong: everyone was misbehaving.

These perceptions coincided with the dissolution of the counterculture's more idealistic phase. Like Neil Young, she noticed that the hippies were turning to much harder drugs:

> Well there're so many sinking now
> You've got to keep thinking

Joni Mitchell's Musical Hejira 275

> You can make it through these waves
> Acid, booze, and ass
> Needles, guns, and grass
> Lots of laughs, lots of laughs
> Well everybody's saying
> That hell's the hippest way to go
> Well I don't think so
> But I'm gonna take a look around it though ("Blue")

All of these forces led to the production of her 1971 album *Blue*. She has repeatedly spoken of its unique position in her career:

> ... there's hardly a dishonest note in the vocals. At that period of my life, I had no personal defenses. I felt like a cellophane wrapper on a pack of cigarettes. I had absolutely no secrets from the world and I couldn't pretend in my life to be strong. Or to be happy. But the advantage of it in the music was that there were no defenses there either. (Crowe 52)

> ... I'll never be that pure again. (Garbarini 49)

> I guess you could say I broke down, but I continued to work. In the process of breaking down there are powers that come in, clairvoyancy and ... everything becomes transparent. It's kind of an overwhelming situation, where more information is coming in, more truth than a person can handle.

> So it was in the middle of all this that I wrote the *Blue* album. It is a very pure album; it's as pure as Charlie Parker. There aren't many things in music that pure. Charlie Parker played pure opera of his soul—especially the times that he was extremely sick. He had no defenses. And when you have no defenses the music becomes saintly and it can communicate. As one group of girls in a bar that accosted me put it, "Before Prozac, there was you," and especially that album. Somehow it had more power than an aspirin for the sufferer ... . (Luftig 182)

Now that some time is passed, it has become easier to see the thematic foci of the album: her complex relationship with James Taylor (who had heroin problems at this time), her ambivalences about her ex-husband, and—most obscurely—her angst about Kelly Anderson, the child out of wedlock she put up for adoption. None of these were happy themes. When the album was first released, few of us caught the referents (how could we have known these details?). But the sheer naked power of the album let the listener supply their own emotional contexts. As Joni says, it was a communication.

The album begins with a few songs about the Taylor relationship. "All I Want" offers classic Petrarchan observations about romance ("I hate you some / I love you some"), while "My Old Man" has some more original poetic conceits. When her man is gone, "The bed's too big, / The frying pan's too wide." As always, there is a good music/text relationship with Joni: listen to the way she conveys her "lonesome blues" as she sings the words. The musical accompaniment is sparse and unobtrusive; it never gets in the way of the lyrics and the singing.

"Little Green" is the first masterpiece on the record, although it may not have seemed that way upon its initial release. It is an anomaly, a 1967 composition amongst all the other songs written in 1971. This song explicitly if obliquely addresses the birth of the daughter Joni put up for adoption. "Little Green" is code for Kelly Anderson, a child named for a shade of green. She was "Born with the moon in Cancer" (February 19, 1965). Joni named her green so "the winters cannot fade her" and "for the children who have made her" (Joni and a Calgary artist named Brad MacMath).

The second verse talks of MacMath's leaving Joni to go to California, circumstances that factored into putting Kelly up for adoption. She sends Brad a letter telling him "'Her eyes are blue'"; then Kelly is "lost" to the mother. The chorus offers the child advice that there will be much joy in her life, but "sometimes there'll be sorrow."

The third verse describes Joni as a "Child with a child pretending / Weary of lies [she is] sending home" (Joni did not inform her parents of the pregnancy initially). The birth papers are signed "in the family name" (Joni was born Roberta Joan Anderson; this is Kelly's last name). The narrator is "sad and sorry," but "not ashamed." She wishes Kelly to "have a happy ending" before the chorus of advice repeats (Luftig 190-191).

This bare bones summary of the song does not convey its devastating emotional power, which I confess I have limited technical resources to comment on. Clearly, the minor keys combined with the passionate yet restrained vocal delivery and the cryptic yet suggestive lyrics create these effects. But I will note that my Rock Generation students responded emotionally to the song on hearing it before we even began analyzing it. Following "My Old Man," it leads the listener from the "lonesome blues" of an absent lover to a far more cutting sense of loss, Joni's primal scene of absence: her difficult and haunted decision to give up a child. There is no song like this around that I am aware of. It is a unique vision of loss that moves even the uncomprehending listener.[1]

After the abyss of loss in "Little Green," Joni lightens things up again with "Carey," one of the two most upbeat songs on a very downbeat album. "Carey" is a thinly disguised tribute to Cary Raditz, a free spirit from North Carolinia who ran a taverna on Crete that Joni visited in the early spring of 1970. Their encounter led to her cohabiting his cave for a month and change, getting to explore her wilder side (Weller 299). Its quasi-calypso rhythms assure its subject that "Oh you're a mean old daddy, but I like you fine." I have already quoted from "Blue," the closing song on side one which moves from the intensely personal to more general social commentary on the fate of the sixties, with its narrator willing to "take a look around" the new drugged-out, interpersonal "hell." The final four lines of the song unexpectedly recur to Kelly and "Little Green." Kelly Anderson's eyes are blue, after all; so blue is both her and the condition of the blues. Joni directly addresses her:

> Blue, here is a shell for you
> Inside you'll hear a sigh
> A foggy lullaby
> There is your song from me.

A poignant use of the mass media to sing "a foggy lullaby" to a lost child. But the matter-of-factness of the delivery and the restraint of the lyrics keep this from cloying sentimentality. It's Charlie Parker, not Bobby Goldsboro ("Honey"). We leave the singer in a double mood of qualified romantic fulfillment and haunted desolation and regret about the past—and it's only the end of side one!

Side two of the vinyl record opens with "California," the other upbeat song which begins with bad news read on a park bench in Paris ("They won't give peace a chance / That was just a dream some of us had"). This reference to the Paris peace talks for Vietnam continues the larger social vision of "Blue" on the previous side. But the narrator shakes off the blues of the old world with the promise of "coming home" to California to "even kiss a Sunset pig" (see Luftig 146 for Joni's peculiar intimacies with police officers). She tells her rock and roll band (CSN & Y!) to make her "feel good" because she's their "biggest fan" and she's "strung out on another man" (James Taylor; note the oblique heroin reference).

The album proceeds to its more downbeat conclusion with "This Flight Tonight," a song of regret about leaving a lover before difficulties are resolved. Clever sound effects duplicate listening to music on headphones during the flight. The next song, "River," plumbs far more profound depths of regret for making the narrator's lover weep during the Christmas holidays: "Now I've gone and lost the best baby / That I ever had." Joni's simple piano accompaniment plays off a minor key rendition of the riff from "Jingle Bells," while her lyrics offer extravagant symbols of regret:

> Oh I wish I had a river
> I could skate away on
> Oh I wish I had a river so long
> I would teach my feet to fly

The evocation of holiday melancholy and romantic loss makes this one of the most universal songs on the album. If the previous songs have been glimpses into Joni's problems, with this song she shows us that her woes are our sadnesses as well. Who can't relate to this song?

"A Case of You" also explores universal passions, although it is also more explicitly confessional (she draws a map of Canada in a bar with her lover's face sketched on it twice). The song's imagery is intense, comparing her love to a case of wine, with implicit eucharistic imagery:

> But you are in my blood
> You're my holy wine
> You taste so bitter and so sweet
> Oh, I could drink a case of you, darling
> And I would still be on my feet
> I would still be on my feet.

If her lover is communion wine, he is also sacred smack "in [her] blood" — another acknowledgment of James Taylor's presence in these songs. Sheila Weller suggests that this song is also partially about her relationship with Leonard Cohen (which makes sense, given the references to the map of Canada), an affair also alluded to in "Rainy Night House" off *Ladies of the Canyon* and several other compositions (241).

The album ends with an encounter with her ex-husband in "Detroit in '68" ("The Last Time I Saw Richard"): "he told me all romantics meet the same fate / cynical and drunk and boring someone in some dark cafe." The ex-husband criticizes the narrator for thinking she's "immune" to the ravages of romance; she duns him for his drunken self-pity ("When you gonna get yourself back on your feet?"). The final verse offers a Joycean epiphany of emotional devastation tempered with hope for an unforeseen future:

> Richard got married to a figure skater,
> And he bought her a dishwasher and a coffee percolator
> And he drinks at home most nights with the T.V. on
> And all the house lights left up bright.
> I'm gonna blow this damn candle out,
> I don't want Nobody coming over to my table.
> I got nothing to talk to anybody about
> All good dreamers pass this way some day
> Hidin' behind bottles in dark cafes
> Dark cafes
> Only a dark cocoon before I get my gorgeous wings
> And fly away
> Only a phase, these dark cafe days.

When Joni sings of her "gorgeous wings," the vocal momentarily soars and leaves the melancholy that otherwise permeates the song (see Lloyd Whitesell for Joni's consistent use of bird and flight imagery in Luftig 237-250). But the dominant closing note is one of the narrator's acute perception of all the absurd irony of life's dashed hopes and dreams. Her "dark cafe days" take her from being a mislabeled folksinger to an iconic resident of the same regions inhabited by Rilke, Piaf and Parker (Dorothy or Charlie, take your pick).

Blue is a masterpiece (mistresspiece?) of concentrated beauty and pain, as bone-true as Sylvia Plath's *Ariel*. Its lyrics are poems in their own right, augmented by the carefully conceived musical settings. A quantum leap beyond Mitchell's first three very fine albums, it showed what a transcendent artist she could be. *Blue* would never—and could never—be repeated, but Joni would make more kinds of great music. Even, I believe, a greater recording than *Blue*.

Joni's Journeys Through The Ditch

The Hissing of Summer Lawns

"I was completely out of whack with the public taste throughout the late '70s and '80s. People aren't always going through changes at the same time as me, and sometimes I get so far ahead I look like I'm behind."—Joni Mitchell, 1994 (in Luftig xv).

After *Blue*, Joni Mitchell had an option which Sylvia Plath did not have, alas: to go into semi-retirement and take a sabbatical from all the forces and pressures that were wearing her down. She bought land in Canada, laid back and eventually got around to a more playful, less confessional type of songwriting which led to songs such as "You Turn Me On I'm A Radio." Not that there weren't confessional moments on her next album, *For The Roses* (1972); but they were mixed in with other kinds of material and not as relentlessly probing as the earlier release. Also of significance was her choice to collaborate with California jazzman Tom Scott on some of the tracks. His reed and woodwind work began Mitchell's ever-deepening embrace of jazz. "Cold Blue Steel and Sweet Fire," a very urban song about heroin addiction, especially foreshadows sounds to come.

A year later, Joni would achieve her greatest commercial and critical success to date with *Court and Spark*, a radio-friendly confection of pop and light jazz. She had a fuller sound, eschewing folk arrangements for Tom Scott and the L. A. Express. Singles were released and charted ("Raised on Robbery," "Help Me"). The inside cover showed Joni in a glamour shot, her folk tresses shorn and coiffed. She seemed to be saying, like the French feminists across the pond, that it's okay to wear lipstick and celebrate your sexuality. One doesn't have to be a waif to have integrity. The music was also getting increasingly complex, as the charts for songs like "Car on a Hill" and "Down to You" demonstrate. (On the latter, Joni and Tom Scott were writing full-blown orchestral arrangements.)

The success of *Court and Spark* was amplified and consolidated by a highly successful tour with the L. A. Express that led to Joni's first live album, *Miles of Aisles* (also 1974). The banter and joking with her audience on the album shows an unprecedentedly relaxed Joni, happy to be sharing the spotlight with others. These were the perfect concerts to bring a date to; Joni had become the soundtrack for romance in mid-seventies America.

Once again, Joni must have felt her fame exceeded the comprehension of her work by her audience. She decided to do something different with her next album, *The Hissing of Summer Lawns* (1975):

> *The Hissing of Summer Lawns* is a suburban album. About the time that album came around I thought, "I'm not going to be your sin eater any longer." So I began to write social description as opposed to personal confession. I met with a tremendous amount of resentment. People thought suddenly that I was secure in my success, that I was being a snot and attacking them. The basic theme of the album, which everybody thought was so abstract, was just any summer day in the neighborhood when people turn their sprinklers on all up and down the block. It's just that hiss of suburbia. (in Crowe 51)

She reinforced the theme by an inside cover shot of her in her swimming pool. This was also misread as indulgent narcissism and a betrayal of her social conscience (you can see how her fans were hanging on her every gesture); all she intended was a reinforcement of the suburban setting.

The Hissing of Summer Lawns thus contained a new approach to her lyric writing (social observation rather than personal confessions). It also served as a transition from the friendly pop music of the previous albums to the more rigorous experimentation of the three albums that lay ahead. Its opening song, "In France They Kiss On Main Street," could sit comfortably with the songs from *Court and Spark*. It is a celebration of young love adorned by the backup vocals of past lovers (Crosby, Nash and Taylor) and the drums of current boyfriend John Guerin.

"The Jungle Line," the very next track, pushes the casual listener off the dock into something far more sonically adventurous. She accompanies frenzied lyrics celebrating the dual pulses of lust and modernity with a moog synthesizer and sampled warrior drums of Burundi, a world music gesture well before David Byrne, Paul Simon, and Peter Gabriel:

> In a low-cut blouse she brings the beer
> Rousseau paints a jungle flower behind her ear
> Those cannibals—of shuck and jive
> They'll eat a working girl like her alive
> With his hard-edged eye and his steady hand
> He paints the cellar full of ferns and orchid vines
> And he hangs a moon above a five-piece band
> He hangs it up above the jungle line

Joni's cover drawing juxtaposes an urban and suburban landscape with bas-relief Africans handling a snake. This juxtaposition "rhymes" the hissing of sprinkler systems on suburban lawns with the snake-handling of the African jungle line. As with the actual lyrics of this song, Mitchell implies that the frenzy of capitalist modernity and lust are congruent: a rhythmic pulse which sublimates sex into commodity fetishism, or can desublimate the latter into the former. This two-way traffic epitomizes the many dualisms of this rich album. Even as "The Jungle Line" contains dialectical tensions, it serves in such a contrast with the soft-pop opening song: the drummers of Burundi speak of a different kind of sensuality than Crosby, Nash and Taylor!

"Edith and the Kingpin" offers another contrast, an encounter between a corporate bigwig and a woman of lesser means he encounters: the master/slave dialectic, seventies style. Unlike "In France They Kiss On Main Street," this is a song of romantic experience, not innocence. The musical accompaniment is lovely and seductive, reinforcing the two main characters' mutual seduction in their negotiation which swaps beauty for material goods:

> Edith and the Kingpin
> Each with charm to sway
> Are staring eye to eye
> They dare not look away
> You know they dare not look away

The potential Olympian distance of the song's tone is undercut by the music: there is sympathy here as well as judgment. Both protagonists are playing the hand they were dealt.

The next song, "Don't Interrupt The Sorrow," seems like a confessional moment on a non-confessional album. But that might only be because of the first person narration and the conviction of its tale of a wine-drenched war between the sexes:

> He says "We walked on the moon
> You be polite."...
> He says "Bring that bottle kindly

> And I'll pad your purse—
> I've got a head full of quandary
> And a mighty, mighty, thirst ... ."
>
> It takes a heart like Mary's these days
> When your man gets weak.

In any case, it's a closely observed moment of post-feminist gender tension; its offer of money for service echoes the financial transactions of "Edith and the Kingpin."

Side one concludes with one of Joni's most overlooked songs, "Shades of Scarlet [think Scarlett!] Conquering." This lyric resituates the gendered master/slave dialectic of the previous two songs historically in the cult of southern womanhood:

> Out in the wind in crinolines
> Chasing the ghosts of Gable and Flynn
> Through stand-in boys and extra players
> Magnolias hopeful in her auburn hair
> She went to a school of southern charm
> She likes to have things her way
> Any man in the world holding out his arm
> Would soon be made to pay

Once again, the lush orchestration of the music takes the edge off the acute social observation. This woman is using her power as best she can under straitened circumstances. Mitchell admires her (anticipating her love of the southern United States on *Hejira*). When she says "A woman must have everything," how can Joni deny her? The last three songs have all portrayed woman as a commodity, an object of beauty for patriarchal consumption; Scarlet's modest strategy is to get full value for the exchange.

This is an album of profound realism: relationships here are about mercantile exchange, not love. So much for the sixties, or Joni Mitchell as a good accent for a date. Any couple that listened to these lyrics would lose the romantic mood they might have thought they were setting. No wonder this album drew critical and commercial wrath: no one wanted to hear this then except for ardent feminists. And all this was accomplished on one nearly perfect first side of the record.

The second side does not let up, either. Its opening title track describes the suburban splendor achieved by the kind of wheeling and dealing portrayed in the previous three songs:

> He bought her a diamond for her throat

Joni Mitchell's Musical Hejira 283

> He put her in a ranch house on a hill
> She could see the valley bar-b-ques
> From her window sill
> See the blue pools in the squinting sun
> And hear the hissing of summer lawns

The woman is described as a "diamond dog" with her bejeweled necklace/collar (a curious reference to David Bowie's apocalyptic 1974 release of the same name?). She's a kept woman / wife, the absolute antithesis of the life which Joni Mitchell created for herself. And yet, there is sympathy. Once again the album stops short of condemnation, content to observe how lives are pushed into certain channels, how character is fate is character. The characters that populate this album seem a long way from the golden stardust of the Woodstock generation, but they live in Joni's neighborhood.

As with "The Jungle Line" on side one, the second track on side two provides a significant contrast. Even as the warrior drums demystified the romantic negotiations and celebrations of the other more melodic songs, "The Boho Dance" leaves suburbia only to show that the same dynamics are operative in downtown Bohemia. Mitchell has acknowledged that the song's inspiration came from reading in Tom Wolfe's *The Painted Word* about this dance, the gestures the artist makes when she or he crosses class lines (think Jackson Pollock pissing in Peggy Guggenheim's fireplace to preserve his authenticity).[2] The key line in the interchange between the Bohemian foil and a character much like Joni is her perception that "the virtue of your style [is] inscribed in your contempt for mine" (curiously, the last five quoted words are in the song but not on the lyric sheet). Much the way Swiss linguist Ferdinand de Saussure described language, the semiotics of cultural placement is a system constructed on differences: the Bohemian is the not-popular-artist. Avant-garde or popular, downtown or suburban: you can't be both. Musically and conceptually, this album relentlessly challenges those dualisms. As a result, it pays the price of the reduced commercial sales of the avant-pop artifact. But as Lawrence Fishburne said in his tribute to Joni Mitchell on a tribute special, she "didn't let the market dictate her aesthetic choices" (*An All-Star Tribute To Joni Mitchell*).

The final three songs on the album provide a triple closure to the proceedings. The medley "Harry's House—Centerpiece" shows the nearly inevitable divorce settlement that follows the sterile negotiation and habitation of suburban courtship and marriage:

> Shining hair and shining skin
> Shining as she reeled him in
> To tell him like she did today
> What he could do with Harry's house
> And Harry's take home pay.

Her cover of Mandel and Hendricks' song "Centerpiece" reinforces the theme of commodification resonant throughout the album. In this covered lyric, the narrator's "pretty baby" is the centerpiece of his home; in "Harry's House," the centerpiece has left the building.

Further closure is provided by "Sweet Bird," a meditation on the fleetingness of youth (the title alludes to Tennessee Williams' play *Sweet Bird of Youth*; cf. her later interest in Williams evinced by "Night of the Iguana" off *Shine*). From the aegis of eternity, these romantic moves look pretty silly:

> You must be laughing
> Behind our eyes
> Calendars of our lives
> Circled with compromise
> Sweet bird of time and change
> You must be laughing[3]

Joni's final gestures here move the album from its realism to her more characteristic romanticism: this is her update of Keats' "Ode to a Nightingale." We are bound in time, but we can have glimmers of transcending it; we have left the linearity of the album's plotline.

The final track, "Shadows and Light" ties everything up in a celebration of dialectics, Saussurean semiotic construction of meaning by contrasts, Emersonian compensation, yin and yang: "Every picture has its shadows / And it has some source of light." There are devils, gods and men of cruelty and delight. Everything is affirmed, ultimately; it all comes out in the wash. There is a cosmic perspective as well as a time-bound one. Like Thomas Pynchon before her, Joni can "keep cool, but care."

My comments have tried to exfoliate what Joni herself claimed in her liner notes about this album: "This record was a total work conceived graphically, lyrically and accidentally—as a whole ... . The whole unfolded like a mystery. It is not my intention to unravel that mystery for anyone." Fools go where angels dare to tread. I have tried to show you how this recording hangs together as a song sequence to at least one listener, the journey it takes me on. Conceptually, this album is even richer than *Blue*. It has a real sense of architecture to it; it is thoroughly conceived and well-built. My advice is to take the ride yourself and see what you discover. Time will be this album's friend; the contemporary listener won't have the preconceptions that led to such complete incomprehension of the project upon its initial release.

Hejira

Although the reception of *The Hissing of Summer Lawns* must have been a great disappointment and bafflement to Joni, she soldiered on to produce

Hejira, the greatest album of her illustrious career—indicative of a confidence that she was on the right musical path, whatever others told her. The genesis of the album was a car trip from the west coast to the east and back again:

> I had an idea; I wanted to travel. I was sitting out at the beach at Neil's [Young; his house at Zuma beach (before it burned down) which also inspired *Zuma*] place and I was thinking, "I want to travel, I don't know where and I don't know who with." Two friends of mine came to the door and said, "We're driving across country." I said, "I've been waiting for you. I'm gone." So we drove across country, then we parted ways. It was my car, so I drove back alone. The *Hejira* album was written mostly while I was traveling in the car. That's why there were no piano songs, if you remember.
>
> *Hejira* was an obscure word, but it said exactly what I wanted. Running away, honorably. It dealt with the leaving of a relationship [with John Guerin], but without the sense of failure that accompanied the failure of my previous relationships. I felt that it was not necessarily anybody's fault. It was a new attitude. (Crowe 52)

She has recommended that the album be listened to while driving across America for maximal impact: "Given the right setting, all of my albums have a certain power. I wouldn't recommend them for certain moods, I'd say, 'Take this pill and stay away from that one!'" (Luftig 174).

The lyrics of *Hejira* exemplify a new, unprecedented approach to writing in Mitchell's career. Because of the focus this album has, they offer a conceptual unity. Generically, they are a mix of confessionalism, romantic lyricism, travel writing and even journalism. They are tied to place and event; they read like a set of wonderful diary entries set to poetry.

Musically, the album is also unique. She double recorded her guitar sound —not precisely, but like silk-screening where the lines do not exactly coincide. (Since this album, Roland built a Jazz Chorus amp that replicates this technologically [Luftig 245].) The guitar melodies are sparse, favoring in fact the rhythmic dimensions of the songs. When coupled with John Guerin on drums and incomparable jazz bassist Jaco Pastorius, this is driving music in every sense of the word. It cooks; it's in motion. I have never heard an album that conveys a feel of relentless car travel as well as *Hejira*; musically, it's almost programmatic. It creates a simple but constant sound picture as a backdrop for the lyric observations. Since its occasion is car travel across America, it's a kind of feminine, musical counterpart to the masculinist writing of Jack Kerouac in *On The Road*. *Hejira* ultimately deserves that kind of iconic status. What could be more 20th century American than crossing the country by car? It's as close as you can get to an embrace of this problematic and multi-textured vastness.

And thanks to Ike and his allies in congress, we've got the roads! As Whitman has noted, if you have a great subject you can produce great art. Her very approach to this album promised success, but what she delivered can exceed your wildest expectations if you pay attention.

"Coyote" gets things off to a rollicking start with its tale of a casual tryst with a free spirit who is arguably playwright and actor Sam Shepard. They first met on Dylan's Rolling Thunder Revue in 1975, where he inspired this song as "she wrote pieces of it during the bus rides" (Weller 420-1). Its opening line, "No regrets Coyote" sets the tone for the entire album: running away without blame. The details are closely and wittily observed. Although love is a "passion play," Joni can revel in its paradoxes, even its obscenities: "He picks up my scent on his fingers / While he's watching the waitresses' legs." Joni possesses a confidence here not always evident in her earlier work, reinforced by the always cooking instrumentation.

On a more symbolic level, Coyote is the Native American archetypal trickster; his showing up in the first song on the album lets us know we're in for a wild and unpredictable ride.

"Amelia," the next track, shows us how deep the journey will also be. One of Mitchell's very best songs, it is a lyric address to the spirit of Amelia Earhart, the mysteriously downed aviatrix also commemorated in song by Ian Matthews and Plainsong (*In Search of Amelia Earhart*) and the Cocteau Twins ("Amelia"). Its opening guitar line shows how haunting a simple melody can be. Then we get a striking visual, indicative of Joni's skill as a painter:

> I was driving across the burning desert
> When I spotted six jet planes
> Leaving six white vapor trails across the bleak terrain
> It was the hexagram of the heavens
> It was the strings of my guitar
> Amelia, it was just a false alarm

The linkage of the vapor trails with her guitar resembles the romantic fusion with nature typical of Keats's great odes, here given a technological twist. The "false alarm" probably refers to her failing relationship, which she confides to Earhart. Joni's self-examination becomes more and more candid. She notes how her life has become "a travelogue / Of picture-post-card-charms"; her rootlessness makes her hard to get along with:

> Maybe I've never really loved
> I guess that is the truth
> I've spent my whole life at icy altitudes
> And looking down on everything
> I crashed into his arms

Joni Mitchell's Musical Hejira

Amelia, it was just a false alarm

The song ends with her pulling into the "Cactus Tree Motel" (a sly reference to "Cactus Tree" off her first album, whose protagonist has a "heart ... full and hollow / Like a cactus tree / While she's so busy being free"). We leave her dreaming of "747s / Over geometric farms," obsessed with flight despite its risks (apparent in her references to Amelia Earhart): you can leave and never come back.

The next song, "Furry Sings The Blues," broadens the journey to social commentary. Joni has given a thorough description of the germinating circumstances for the song:

> ... [W]hen we got to Memphis ... I hit on this cop, and he agreed we should trade a badge for a record. Then he said we should go see old Beale Street, which used to be the heart of blues music in the town. Well, it was an amazing vision, like a Western ghost town three blocks long. Shards of wreckage all around, cranes with wrecking balls still standing there. [It has since been rebuilt as a Disney theme park for white tourists.] Two pawn shops were functioning, and there was a modern theater with a double bill of black machine-gun movies—next to a statue of W. C. Handy, a trumpet player of the jazz era. We came down the street, and, if I'm not embellishing, a tumbleweed drifted across in front of the car—it seems to me it did.
>
> Standing in front of one of the pawn shops was a guy in a purplish-blue shirt, bright blue blazer with brass buttons on it, bald, smokin' a stogie. He looks at me and says, "You Joni Mitchell?" I think, "Culturally this is impossible. This guy should not know my name." However, I had heard that Furry Lewis lived in Memphis, so I mentioned it to the pawnbroker. He says, "Oh sure, he's a friend of mine. Meet me here tonight and we'll go over and see him. Bring a bottle of Jack Daniels and a carton of Pall Mall cigarettes."
>
> Furry was in his eighties or nineties and senile at this point. Lived in a little shanty in the ghetto there. It was quite a nice visit until I said to him—meaning to be close to him, meaning "We have this in common"—"I play in open tunings too." Now I dunno, people must have ridiculed him about it or something, because he leaned upon the bed and said ... "Ah kin play in Spanish tonnin'." Real defensive. Somehow or other I insulted him. From then on it was downhill. He just said, "I don't like her," as I wrote in the song. (Luftig 146-7)

This encounter turned into a very sad song about how America cannibalizes its past and turns it into a simulacrum, a glitzy tourist attraction: "history falls / To parking lots and shopping malls." Yeah, she knows that parking lots are historical too (*pace* to Perry Meisel, the reviewer in the *Village Voice* who objected to this line [Luftig 81-2]). But the buildings had a different value, which was not honored when they were demolished. The back story here, of course, is white entrepreneurs exploiting the black cultural past for profit. The song is prophetic not only of what happened to Beale Street, but of even greater Memphis tourist atrocities like the Civil Rights Museum built at the Hotel Lorraine (where Martin Luther King was assassinated) by the same folks who brought you Graceland (no longer the tackiest spot in Memphis).

Joni is, as always, careful to implicate herself in the proceedings. She too is ripping off black culture by her visit: "Why should I expect that old guy to give it to me true ... / While our limo is shining on his shanty street." She admits to the statue of W. C. Handy that she's "rich and ... fay" and "not familiar with what you played." Just another tourist, ultimately. Joni underlines her outsider status by having Neil Young, of all people, play backing harmonica on the track. Both music and text reinforce that these are white folks looking in on and even ventriloquizing a fading black culture. Joni knows and shows this, but lacks the power to stop the process—and even admits her complicity in this development. She makes her living off musical influences ultimately of African-American origin. At least she's honest enough to admit it in this uncompromisingly critical and self-critical song.

The next song, "A Strange Boy," is a kind of palate-cleanser set between the more intense offerings that precede and follow it—a return to the romantic whimsy of "Coyote." This time, Joni describes an encounter with a man-child in New England ("Even the war and the navy / Couldn't bring him to maturity"). She explored similar terrain in "Rainy Night House" (*Ladies of the Canyon*). "A Strange Boy" is far more playful, however, with its depiction of Mitchell playing piano in the boarding house where he lives, "fire in the stiff-blue-haired-house-rules." The antique dolls in the cellar staring at her lend a suitable touch of New England gothic.

Side one closes with the title track, another major wedding of music and text and a grand statement of the album's themes. The sinuous guitar opening and bass accompaniment draws us onto the endless road:

> I'm travelling in some vehicle
> I'm sitting in some cafe
> A defector from the petty wars
> That shell-shock love away
> There's comfort in melancholy
> When there's no need to explain

> It's just as natural as the weather
> In this moody sky today
> In our possessive coupling
> So much could not be expressed
> So now I am returning to myself
> These things that you and I suppressed
> I see something of myself in everyone
> Just at this moment of the world
> As snow gathers like bolts of lace
> Waltzing on a ballroom girl.

That's quite an opening verse! It sets the scene and the season (dead of winter), shows both the breakup and a romantic hope fusing the narrator with "everyone." The lace imagery both echoes the snow and anticipates the long flashbacks in the next cut (Joni and Sharon attending weddings and marveling at the bridal attire).

The second verse offers general ruminations on love and life. Joni's observation that "the slightest touch of a stranger / Can set up trembling in my bones" eventually made its way onto one of her canvasses. "Hyde Park" (1996) depicts this electric moment of contact (Hebert 31). I have also always liked the wonderful use of metonymy in these lines:

> We all come and go unknown
> Each so deep and superficial
> Between the forceps and the stone

This last reflection leads to the third verse's trip to the "granite markers" of a cemetery. This final full verse also employs the closely rendered visual of "White flags of winter chimneys" discussed above. "Hejira" has a nice balance between abstract thought and closely rendered image, all underpinned by a powerful musical drive. It holds all its forces in a delicate balance, and we are enraptured.

Joni admits in interview that "Song for Sharon," the first cut on the second side, was written under the influence of cocaine (Luftig 144). It is the longest and wordiest song on the album, and has an associative logic to its construction—all perhaps reflecting the drug's effects. For all that, it's a fine song. It moves from a wedding gown glimpsed in a New York storefront window to Native American construction workers building Manhattan to a visit to a fortuneteller to more reflections on love to an acquaintance's suicide to Joni's guilt about not embracing a cause to childhood memories to skaters ... and finally to Sharon of the title, who has a husband, a family and a farm in contrast to Joni Mitchell. At any given point, the transitions are logical, thematically.

For example, her reflection that "love's a repetitious danger" leads to the account of the suicide; the suicide's being "so far from satisfaction" segues into the need for taking up a cause.

Musical leitmotifs in the song provide a dry humor as well. Joni uses a Native American background chanting riff both for the account of the construction workers and for her discussion of causes ("put some time into Ecology"). The music free associates as well as the lyrics. The whole package comes together as well as a long song from Dylan such as "Highlands" (*Time Out of Mind*). There is freedom here, but also control.

I have already mentioned the unusual tuning of "Black Crow," which follows. Unquestionably the most rocking track on *Hejira*, the song is almost a pure driving sonic force emulating the energetic crow of its title (another trickster by the way, celebrated by Native Americans and Ted Hughes, among others).

"Blue Motel Room" slows things down with its slow and (appropriately) bluesy vamp. The song is set in Savannah, Georgia, during a rainstorm. The narrator, in a reflective mood, wonders whether her estranged partner will "still love [her] / When [she gets] back to L. A. town." The highlight of the song is a comparison of the two lovers to the superpowers, an extravagance worthy of the metaphysical poets:

> You and me we're like America and Russia
> We're always keeping score
> We're always balancing the power
> And that can get to be a cold cold war
> We're going to have to hold ourselves a peace talk
> In some neutral cafe
> You lay down your sneaking around the town, honey
> And I'll lay down the highway

John Donne, yes; but, more current for the time, with also the wit of a good blues lyric.

Hejira concludes with "Refuge of the Roads," another summative statement like the title track. It arguably begins with a rare portrait of Neil Young:

> I met a friend of spirit
> He drank and womanized [Neil was between marriages]
> And I sat before his sanity
> I was holding back from crying
> He saw my complications
> And he mirrored me back simplified
> And we laughed how our perfection
> Would always be denied [an allusion to "Don't Be Denied"?]

"Heart and humor and humility,"
He said "Will lighten up your heavy load."
I left him then for the refuge of the road.[4]

At this same time, Joni also drew a wonderful felt marker portrait of Neil (see Hebert 36). The song echoes her interview accounts of leaving Zuma Beach (and Neil) to travel with her friends. The following verses are part diary, part travel writing; we get both "Winn Dixie coldcuts" and the "clouds of Michelangelo / Muscular with gods and sungold." "[A] photograph of the earth / Taken coming back from the moon" seen on a gas station wall recalls the use of NASA for gender warfare in "Don't Interrupt The Sorrow" (*The Hissing of Summer Lawns*). Same old, same old. Jaco Pastorius' bass exertions, as lovely as a lullaby, take us, Joni Mitchell and the album home. Although mostly neglected at the time, *Hejira* has aged like a fine Bordeaux. In recent concert specials (*An Evening With Joni Mitchell: Painting With Words and Music*), it's the album she performs the most material from. Well she might: it has some of her very best writing on it and it is her most unified album conceptually and sonically. The band and production perfectly suit the material. The whole package provides a detailed postcard of the mid-seventies reflected through a sensitive register. *Hejira* is both of its time and out of it (like all successful romantic gestures).

Don Juan's Reckless Daughter

Don Juan's Reckless Daughter (1977), her next album and her only double studio album, made for even more challenging listening. It marked a quantum leap in Joni's embrace of jazzlike textures, serving as a kind of sketchbook of sonic explorations and ideas. Much looser and more diversified than *Hejira*, it was critically drubbed upon release and still remains the least accessible Mitchell offering, even for fans. All of which goes to show how well pop music conditions us. The willingness to both diversify and extend an idea to elaborate lengths raises few eyebrows in the jazz world: think of John Coltrane's hour-long version of "My Favorite Things" on *Live in Japan*, which opens with a half-hour bass solo, or Sun Ra's moog synthesizer forays in the late sixties and early seventies. Jazz artists could play with sound as they wished; but Joni Mitchell was still in the pop ghetto. If *The Hissing of Summer Lawns* and *Hejira* didn't kick her out yet, this album certainly helped. The *Court and Spark* devotees just didn't get it; but listeners such as Prince, Miles Davis and Charles Mingus did. They knew the blackface and cross-dressing on the cover photo went into the grooves as well: inside this white girl a black man was trying to get out!

Joni herself has implied there were difficulties with the project (when asked by Cameron Crowe about her response to the album's reception):

If I experience any frustration, it's the frustration of being misunderstood. But that's what stardom is—a glamorous misunderstanding. All the way along, I know that some of these projects are eccentric. I know that there are parts that are experimental, and some of them are half-baked. I certainly have been pushing the limits and—even for myself—not all of my experiments are completely successful. But they lay the groundwork for further developments. Sooner or later, some of these experiments will come to fruition. So I have to lay out a certain amount of my growing pains in public. I like the idea that annually there is a place where I can distribute the art that I have collected for a year. That's the only thing that I feel I want to protect, really. And that means having a certain amount of commercial success. (Crowe 51)

Don Juan's Reckless Daughter, then, was a kind of annual exhibition of her musical art—transitional, a sign of growing pains, experimental, eccentric, even "half-baked." It builds the bridge between *Hejira* and what would become *Mingus*.

Insofar as the album has a structure, it moves from confessional writing (sides one and two) to portraits of others (side three) and back to confessional (side four). Musically, it sandwiches in two sides of sonic experimentation (sides two and three) between two sides of more familiar Mitchell sounds (one and four). But this is a loose hanging in the music gallery, in contrast to the highly planned groupings and transitions of the previous two albums. *Don Juan's Reckless Daughter* just flows along in your ear, if you relax and let it.

Side one opens with a brief instrumental overture before taking us down to "Cotton Avenue," a celebration of African-American nightlife that anticipates the last verse of "Goodbye Pork Pie Hat" (*Mingus*). Instrumentation is simple but satisfying: Mitchell on guitar, John Guerin on drums, Jaco Pastorius on bass. Rhythm is thoroughly foregrounded with this setup.

The next track, "Talk To Me" is even sparser—just Mitchell and Pastorius. Joni uses *sprechstimme* with Jaco, matching the music to the speech rhythms of the lyrics (all this before Frank Zappa used the technique). The short side (a little over thirteen minutes total) closes with a studio version of "Jericho" (one of two new songs on the live *Miles of Aisles*). This version adapts to the jazzier context of the rest of the album, augmenting the trio of "Cotton Avenue" with Don Alias on bongos and the incomparable Wayne Shorter (of Miles Davis, Weather Report, and solo fame) on soprano sax. The result is that Joni's songwriting from the L. A. Express days receives a far more stately and less pop-oriented reading. In the decades ahead, Mitchell would continue to use Shorter as an accent to uplift and enrich her less experimental (by contrast) projects (e. g., *Wild Things Run Fast* and all recent releases).

The genesis for "Paprika Plains" (side two's sole track, a composition for piano, bass, drums, saxophone and orchestra) was a discussion Mitchell had with Bob Dylan:

> The next time we [Dylan and Mitchell] had a brief conversation was when Paul McCartney had a party on the *Queen Mary*, and everybody left the table and Bobby and I were sitting there. After a long silence he said, "If you were gonna paint this room, what would you paint?" I said, "Well, let me think, I'd paint the mirrored ball spinning, I'd paint the women in the washroom, the band ... ." Later all the stuff that came back to me as part of a dream that became the song "Paprika Plains." (Crowe 51)

She has said elsewhere that Native Americans were also a big part of the later dream, as is evident from the lyrics of the song (Garbarini 52).

> When I was three feet tall
> And wide eyed open to it all
> With their tassled teams they came
> To McGee's General Store
> All in their beaded leathers
> I would tie on colored feathers
> And I'd beat the drum like war ...
> I would beat the drum like war ... .
> But when the church got through
> They traded their beads for bottles
> Smashed on Railway Avenue
> And they cut off their braids
> And lost some link with nature ... .

The surreal plot of the song moves from the ladies' room on the *Queen Mary* to a flashback to Joni's childhood in Saskatchewan, especially an encounter with Native Americans. This leads to another vision of "Paprika plains / and a turquoise river snaking" (more likely a New Mexican landscape than a Canadian one at this point, linked by free association with the Native Americans). At this point an orchestra kicks in. It's not in tune with the piano, as that part of the recording has a different time and source. The result is surreal and jarring, like Charles Ives' experimentations with dissonance in his symphonic writing. A long orchestral tone poem follows, lavish and romantic. The lyrics continue to describe the landscape, nuclear testing, and much else besides. But they are not sung: they exist only as programmatic notes for the instrumental music, in a manner favored by late nineteenth-century composers such as Edward MacDowell. Only at the song's very end does Joni sing again, returning lyrically to the ladies' washroom on the *Queen Mary* for closure. Musically, the song ends with a blast of jazz from Shorter, Pastorius and Guerin.

You can readily see what a challenge this sixteen-minute piece would be for the casual Joni Mitchell fan. Dylan's extended writing never attempted anything so outrageous: a fusion of stream-of-consciousness narrative with nineteenth-century orchestral program music and Ivesian dissonances. The results are both quaintly retro and daunting. "Paprika Plains" is a creation of the studio; one cannot easily imagine it being performed live with the piano and the orchestra battling each other in different tunings. Eccentric, experimental ... half-baked? You be the judge; this piece will really stretch your ears and is not user-friendly, even by avant-pop standards. I think it would sound great if the listener were running a high fever! That seems to be the kind of effect it's trying to duplicate (actually a dream state, but only in a fever can you be awake and dreaming at the same time). Given "Dreamland" on the next side, the dream state seems to be a recurring thread in the album's concerns.

Side three begins with "Otis and Marlena," a portrait of a couple visiting Florida comparable to some of the character sketches on *The Hissing of Summer Lawns*—and Neil Young's song "Fontainebleu" off *Long May You Run*. Otis and Marlena are paranoid and xenophobic ("They've come for fun and sun / While Muslims stick up Washington"—a reference to the oil crisis, probably, since this is pre-hostage crisis). As always, Joni closely observes details of dress and manners ("All those Pagliacci summer frocks / Otis is fiddling with the TV dial"). The boob tube seems to induce a trance for them, as the lyrics reiterate "Dream on." The song segues into "The Tenth World," a long percussion instrumental with a great groove featuring players like Jaco Pastorius, Don Alias and even Airto (on the surdo bass drum). If side two featured mostly melody without rhythm (until the end of "Paprika Plains"), side three is mostly rhythm without melody. Side two is Joni's European influences and interests; side three is African, Latin, Caribbean—her racial cross-dressing, since the drum is an instrument traditionally reserved for men in these cultures! The side ends with "Dreamland," a chant that describes an initially Caribbean setting ("Walter Raleigh and Chris Columbus / Come marching out of the waves"). In effect, Otis and Marlena, while staring at the television, have made a dream flight from Miami to the islands. Or perhaps we have segued truly to other characters and other places, a description of a real Caribbean trip. The song ends on an ambiguous note:

> African sand on the trade winds
> And the sun on the Amazon
> They push the recline buttons down
> With dreamland coming on

Are they "On a plane flying back to winter" (previous verse) hitting the recline buttons on the plane, or just watching TV and kicking back in their La-Z-Boys? Could go either way; in any event, the listener makes the journey vicariously by listening to the drums. As with side two, we are in Dreamland.

The album concludes with three slightly more typical songs on side four, which also returns to a more confessional mode. The title track sounds like an outtake from *Hejira*, which it could very well be. It was initially written in 1976, the same year as the songs on that album. Furthermore, its guitar strumming closely resembles the same riff as on the previous album's title track. One can readily see why it's on this album, however: its lyrical engagement with the mysticism of Carlos Castenada (the eagle and the snake) make it belong here with other surreal material rather than with the more down-to-earth lyrics of *Hejira*. Joni declares that she is "Don Juan's reckless daughter," a reference to the Yaqui sorcerer of the Castenada tomes as well as to the famous lover. Love and magic: that's what Joni and this album are all about!

The side closes with two songs about love. "Off Night Backstreet" seems to be about the breakup with John Guerin, a tale of being put on the margins by his "sneaking around the town" ("Blue Hotel Room," *Hejira*). It complements the more positive "Jericho" on side one with its tale of loss; tellingly, Guerin drums on both tracks. Her ex-lovers usually remain friends and musical collaborators.

The final song, "The Silky Veils of Ardor," is a solo effort on guitar. Its lyric warning hearkens back to the conventions of Appalachian folk ballads such as the Carter family's "Wildwood Flower":

> Come all you fair and tender school girls
> take warning now—when you court young men
> They are like the stars
> On a summers [sic] morning
> They sparkle up the night
> Then they're gone again
> Daybreak—gone again

The narrator compares herself to Noah's dove looking for land in her quest for "the one I love" (an echo of Billy Holiday's "I Cover the Waterfront"?). The ornithological imagery and references to flight recall earlier Mitchell songs like "Song to a Seagull," "Sweet Bird," "Amelia" and "Black Crow." Like Icarus descending, however, she has to come down at song's end:

> But I have no wings
> And the water is so wide
> We'll have to row a little harder
> It's just in dreams we fly
> In my dreams we fly!

The concluding motif of flying in your dreams hearkens back to the dream flights in "Paprika Plains," "Otis and Marlena / The Tenth World / Dreamland" and the actual writings of Castaneda. This last reference underlines the album's concept as a surreal musical journey, a dreaming counterpart to the journey of *Hejira*. I hope Joyceans will pardon my sacrilege: if *Hejira* is Joni Mitchell's widescreen version of *Ulysses* (we traverse a whole country instead of just Dublin), then *Don Juan's Reckless Daughter* is her version of *Finnegans Wake*. And like that latter tome, this album is highly experimental, very ambitious and much misunderstood.

Mingus

After *Don Juan's Reckless Daughter*, where could Joni go next? She seemed to be leaving her pop career to travel even further into the ditch than Neil Young ever ventured; she was exploring musics and textures and song lengths guaranteed to deny her radio play and public exposure as the looser FM formats of the late sixties slowly constricted to the conditions of the present day (where only jazz, classical and college stations allow you to play songs longer than you could fit on a single). Clearly, she was becoming jazzier by the minute; when a dying Charles Mingus asked her to collaborate with him, it must have struck her as pure kismet. Mingus liked her music, her thirst for growth and her audacity. Initially, he wanted to work with her on a musical adaptation of T. S. Eliot's *Four Quartets* (Luftig 145). When she demurred, he offered his last melodies for her to write lyrics to.

Joni struggled for quite some time to get the sound right for the Mingus album. She was seeking a real conversation with her players, not just jazz chops that would overwhelm the material with pure virtuosity. She ended up just playing guitar (no piano) with a band that included Jaco Pastorius on bass, Wayne Shorter on soprano sax, Herbie Hancock on electric piano, Peter Erskine on drums, Don Alias on congas and Emil Richards on percussion. The sound is stately and restrained, not flashy. The music is not really jazz, but it's certainly not pop either. It is a true blend of Charles Mingus and Joni Mitchell, so much so that some fans of either were bound to be disappointed. You are best positioned to appreciate it if you like both musicians.

Mingus opens, after a snippet of recorded dialogue, with "God Must Be A Boogie Man," one of two songs on the album entirely written by Joni Mitchell. The spirit of Mingus pervades the song, however. It is derived from the opening chapter of Mingus' autobiography, *Beneath the Underdog*, in which he discusses his perception of his three personalities as he reveals himself to his analyst:

> "In other words, I am three. One man stands forever in the middle, unconcerned, unmoved, watching, waiting to be allowed to express

Joni Mitchell's Musical Hejira

> what he sees to the other two. The second man is like a frightened animal that attacks for fear of being attacked. Then there's an over-loving gentle person who lets people into the uttermost sacred temple of his being and he'll take insults and be trusting and sign contracts without reading them and get talked down to working cheap or for nothing, and when he realizes what's being done to him he feels like killing and destroying everything around him including himself for being so stupid. But he can't—he goes back inside himself."
>
> "Which one is real?"
>
> "They're all real." (3; see also 217 for further discussion of this self-division)

Mingus also asks the analyst if he believes in God "[a]s a boogie man," the source for the song's title (5). Joni's lyric picks up on all these themes about "Mingus one, two or three" and the "cock-eyed" divine plan of God, the boogie man. Behind the song's lyrics, of course, is a sense of Charles Mingus' impending mortality, as he slowly died from Lou Gehrig's disease. God must be a boogie man, indeed.

What is most puzzling about the song, perhaps, is that Joni stopped reading the book after chapter one, the first seven pages. We have already seen that this is typically how she reads, stopping when she gets a revelation she can turn into a song. In addition to that procedure, I think her reticence confirms her status as his last Mingus chick. The autobiography is a long account of his hiding things from his women: he led many lives as a musician, a pimp and the like. Joni in effect, like so many other women, would rather not lift up the rock. And finally, her stopping at chapter one confirms her independence in the project—as does the fact that she wrote the music for this song. She's collaborating with Mingus, but this is still a Joni Mitchell album. The song's intermittent rhythms show a new complexity resultant from grappling with his music. Clearly Mingus taught her something; this track pays tribute to the result. Lyrically, it's only a snapshot of the man. You can read the whole book (highly recommended) if you want to learn more.

The next musical track (dialogue snippets are between most of the songs), "A Chair in the Sky," is the most moving Mingus composition on the record. It's no surprise that the Charles Mingus Big Band—a ghost band that plays at the Fez in New York on Thursday nights—features this piece in performance. The song stands on its own as a haunting instrumental. But Joni has added poignant lyrics that capture the song's sense of regret for missed opportunities at the conclusion of a life:

> There's things I wish I'd done

> Some friends I'm gonna miss
> Beautiful lovers
> I never got the chance to kiss ...
> Daydreamin' drugs the pain of living
> Processions of missing
> Lovers and friends
> Fade in and fade out again
> In daydreams of rebirth
> I see myself in style
> Raking in what I'm worth
> Next time
> I'll be bigger!
> I'll be better than ever!
> I'll be resurrected royal!
> I'll be rich as standard oil!
> But now—Manhattan holds me
> To a chair in the sky
> With a bird in my ears
> And boats in my eyes
> Going by.

These lyrics allude to Mingus' Eastern belief in reincarnation, his wheelchair-bound status from the disease, his regrets and desires. The "bird in [his] ears" could be a Charlie Parker recording. The music/text relationship is what really makes the song sublime. Joni's understated approach to the accompaniment reaps the richest benefits here: the music sets the lyrics like a jewel, and vice versa. Neither overwhelms the other. The song is a middle-aged song (at least), but it deserves a wider hearing.

Side one ends with a seemingly utterly incongruous Mitchell composition (her second one of two on the album), "The Wolf That Lives in Lindsey." Its tale of a serial killer haunting the Hollywood hills does not have any obvious resonances with the Mingus material on the album; it is a very bleak moment on a fairly downbeat album. Why is it here? Perhaps because of its very negativity, as if Joni had to go outside of the songs Mingus wrote for her to get an even more somber text to express her emotions about the collaboration. The track also demonstrates what she learned from Mingus musically: its throbbing bass and guitar interplay pays homage to the rich literature Mingus produced for the bass, his instrument of choice.

Then there are the wolves. In the Garbarini interview for *Musician* magazine, Joni spins a long tale of serendipity involving her quest to get a recording of wolf calls to accompany the song. Not only did she succeed through a chance, drunken meeting in a hotel; the wolf tape she obtained was already in key with the recording (48-9). This must have all seemed portentous. Compare the wolf call coincidence with her liner notes for the *Mingus* album:

> Charles Mingus, a musical mystic, died in Mexico, January 5, 1979, at the age of 56. He was cremated the next day. That same day 56 sperm whales beached themselves on the Mexican coastline and were removed by fire. These are the coincidences that thrill my imagination.

The serendipity of the wolf call tape must have been equally thrilling for her; no doubt the song's inclusion pays homage to Mingus the mystic as well as the bass player. For all that, "The Wolf That Lives in Lindsey" is an odd fit with the rest of the album—although a compelling track in its own right. Mitchell may have acknowledged as much herself when she put it on the wittily titled *Misses* compilation (1996) as one of her songs that got away.

Side two begins with "Sweet Sucker Dance," a love song that comes the closest lyrically to favored Mitchell themes. Love is a ritual dance of fools: the Mingus melody is suitably jaunty, and Jaco Pastorius gets in some good licks at the conclusion.

The last two songs on the album, "The Dry Cleaner From Des Moines" and "Goodbye Pork Pie Hat," are the songs Joni featured most frequently in live performance, even long after the album's release. "The Dry Cleaner From Des Moines" approaches the loping-yet-capable-of-turning-on-a-dime rhythms and melodies of scat. I can imagine Ella Fitzgerald doing a marvellous job with this tale of a lucky tourist in Las Vegas. But Joni's rendition is just fine; in fact, it's arguably her best jazz vocal on this album or anywhere—as close as she gets to the real tradition. Jaco's frenzied bass charts are a treat as well.

The closing cut, "Goodbye Pork Pie Hat" pays musical and lyrical homage to Lester Young. The song also addresses the problems Young (and Mingus) faced with racist club hiring practices and interracial dating. The song (and the album) ends on another note of serendipity: Joni describes journalistically an encounter she and conga player Don Alias had in New York with African-American kids tap dancing in front of what turns out to be the "Pork Pie Hat Bar," named after Lester Young (Crowe 48). As a result, the song ends up being about how great jazz artists eventually enter history and become an oblique part of the landscape—a consoling final gesture for Charles Mingus. After mortality comes immortality for some.

Mingus proves to be a reverential tribute album (some said almost too reverential with the snippets of dialogue) and the closest Joni Mitchell ever got to jazz. As you can infer, I prefer (in order) *Hejira*, *Blue* and *The Hissing of Summer Lawns*. But this is a fine album that deserved more attention than it received. Charles Mingus is an avant-pop artist in his own right: although labeled a jazz musician, his work comes closer to Charles Ives than Count Basie in many respects. It is playful, risk-taking, at times devilishly witty and complex. A whole Mingus canon awaits you, but a good place to start might be with "Fables For Faubus" (a circuslike and sardonic musical response to Orville Faubus, the segregationist governor of Arkansas when Mingus penned the composition). The songs on Joni's album are his last efforts. They are not always his best. "A Chair in the Sky" is up with his most powerful writing, though, and "The Dry Cleaner From Des Moines" and "Goodbye Pork Pie Hat" are not far behind. Hearing the Charles Mingus Big Band in concert will be enough to hook anyone interested enough in music to be reading these words. As with Ives, Ellington, Sun Ra and Joni Mitchell herself, there's a substantial and varied musical corpus out there to be explored and appreciated.

After *Mingus*, Joni toured behind her seventies work (with some earlier songs thrown in as well). She put together her best band yet (and possibly ever) with Jaco on bass, Don Alias on drums, a young Pat Metheny on guitar, Lyle Mays on keyboards, Michael Brecker on saxophone and the Persuasions on backing vocals. She played electric guitar. The resulting tour, double live album and video got her some critical and commercial attention. (Both album and video were called *Shadows and Light* [1980]; the latter was directed by Joni.) The live renditions of material from *The Hissing of Summer Lawns*, *Hejira* and *Mingus* were riveting (*Don Juan's Reckless Daughter* was downplayed, represented only by "Dreamland"). Joni seemed to be back in the public eye in a more modest capacity.

She consolidated these gains in 1982 by switching to David Geffen's new Geffen label and releasing *Wild Things Run Fast*, unquestionably Joni's happiest album. She was basking in her new relationship with and eventual marriage to bassist Larry Klein. Musically, she combined her early quasi-folk, lieder-style songwriting with all the jazz inflections she had been learning in the previous decade. (Wayne Shorter was a crucial presence here.) As with Brecker earlier, she also turned to Zappa alumni (Vinnie Colaiuta on drums). Guest vocalists represented both the old (James Taylor) and the new (Lionel Richie). The result was a pleasing negotiation between sixties Joni and seventies Joni. Its opening medley of a new song, "Chinese Cafe," and a cover of "Unchained Melody" was a possible single. But you can't be twenty on Sugar Mountain; Joni was exiled from the radio by and large.

Dog Eat Dog

Then things began to turn sour, beckoning Joni into one last foray through the avant-pop ditch. She explained to an interviewer:

> The '80s were very difficult for me, physically and emotionally.

> A lot of financial betrayal, a lot of health problems. My housekeeper sued in a version of the new palimony; simultaneously I was butchered by a dentist ... . [T]he '80s for me were like being a prisoner of war, what with the physical and mental pain and general climate of mistrust ... .
>
> ... I was one of 12 artists in the state [California] who had 85 percent of our income taxed in a kind of experimental levy. Maybe the greed of that decade was supposed to descend on me more heavily, or more irrationally, than on other people. But I did feel like Alice with the Red Queen; I felt I was in a world where irrational law was coming at me from all directions. (Luftig 162-3)

In addition to her personal travails, Mitchell was deeply concerned about the Reagan presidency— more so than fellow Canadian Neil Young:

> I'm talking about everything from the insane arms race to the current attempts to censor lyrics by various extreme rightwingers. Basically, I feel that a lot of strides were made in this country during the '60s—equal rights, feminism, freedom of speech, etc.—but under Reagan's new conservatism, much of that's being eroded and undone. (Luftig 136)

Feeling "a sense of responsibility to speak up now or forever hold [her] peace" in those "dangerous times," Joni decided to produce and write *Dog Eat Dog* (1985). This would be her most political album ever, in-your-face jeremiads instead of the subtler commentaries from earlier works. "There's a lot of blood on those tracks," she would remark (Luftig 135). Musically, she also went for a brand new sound by co-producing with synthesizer wizard Thomas Dolby. Mitchell explored sampling technology and a bevy of new electronic keyboards such as the Fairlight CMI. The resultant sound on the album is unlike any heard before or since, strictly speaking, but it has affinities with both rap and techno. It exudes both anger and technocool. Comparisons with Neil Young's *Trans* (1982) are illuminating. Neil seems in the kiddie pool, while Joni seems to have jumped off the high-dive. Lest we be too invidious, however, one should note that this technology came a long way in three years!

The opening track, "Good Friends," shows little of what's to come. Like the album's closing track "Lucky Girl," it's a throwback to *Wild Things Run Fast*—a reminder that even in the treacherous times delineated on the rest of the album there are repositories of sanity to be found in friendship and love, respectively for the two songs. Michael McDonald's smooth backing vocals reinforce the fragile serenity adumbrated here.

In the next cut, "Fiction," Joni tips her hat towards the album's main concerns. Its driving electronic rhythms and samples point us towards the postmodern abyss of the simulacrum discussed by such eighties theorists as Jean Baudrillard—and eventually popularized by films such as *Wag the Dog*: how can you tell what's real in an age of media saturation and boundless image manipulation? Like Neil, Joni isn't afraid to be "Lefting and then Righting": despite her clear stance against the arms race in interviews, the lyrics have the more nuanced ambiguity of the "Fiction of the pro and the no nukers." It's hard to infer fully what she's getting at with this line. Is she simply recreating the confusion of the average citizen, or is she finger-pointing at some distortions of fact in the anti-nuke movement? For example, Carl Sagan's "nuclear winter" writing was rushed into a Sunday supplement (*Parade* magazine) before it received scientific validation through regular review. Would Joni have known that from cocktail conversation, or is she just playing a hunch?

In any case, it's not all simulation—or is it? The track ends with the "Fiction of the monuments reduced to zero" and a recording of a nuclear blast. All this posturing could lead to nuclear holocaust, on one level; more profoundly, nuclear holocaust is more media hype. The song ends with a fake, simulated apocalypse—not a real one. It's a counter-fiction, but it's not "Truth" either. Unlike the tracks to follow, "Fiction" has an unresolved ambiguity to it reminiscent of Neil Young's political writing. As Neil once penned, "Take my advice / Don't listen to me" ("Hippie Dream"). Joni is confronting a paradox in this song: her album is adding to the media saturation. Can you trust *Dog Eat Dog*? Is it truth or fiction? Before she delivers her jeremiads, she is careful to include some self-criticism and to acknowledge the problematic status of her own participation in the media flow. And if you don't want to enter this conceptual abyss, hey, you can just dance to the cut's rocking synth beats!

The next jeremiad concerns "The Three Great Stimulants" of "the exhausted ones." No, not sex, drugs and rock and roll as one might expect: "[a]rtifice, brutality and innocence." Joni explains: "Innocence has always been a stimulant ... especially when a culture is entering a decadent period. You get kiddie porn, the cult of the youth, an obsession with youth, in fact, and stuff like face-lifts—yech!" (in Luftig 136). Artifice refers to the obsession with surface characteristic of the postmodern eighties moment, starting top down with an actor-president and ending up with the paradoxes of the previous song. Brutality was evident in everything from our aggressive foreign affairs to the abandonment of the domestic war on poverty, a new litigiousness ("it's so easy now, anyone can sue"), and a new self-righteousness ("They're gonna slam free choice behind us"). It all adds up to global disaster:

> Last night I dreamed I saw the planet flicker
> Great forests fell like buffalo

> Everything got sicker
> And to the bitter end
> Big business bickered

As of this writing, one can still think these thoughts: forests are still falling and the planet is getting sicker (physically and mentally). Joni, appropriately, doesn't offer grand solutions (although she invokes her personal values). She just wants us to wake up from our collective complacency and think about these issues. The music on "The Three Great Stimulants" is electronically driven, but not as hyperkinetic as the preceding and following tracks; the subject of the song is too downbeat to merit such an arrangement. As its closing lyric sighs, "Oh, these troubled times."

"Tax Free" is Joni's densely produced blast at the televangelists, joining Neil Young ("American Dream") and Frank Zappa ("The Meek Shall Inherit Nothing," "Jesus Thinks You're A Jerk" and oh so many others). Like Frank, Joni questions what gets done by these schmucks using their tax-exempt status. (As Zappa used to say, "tax the churches!") Actor Rod Steiger plays a preacher on the track, mouthing a credible pastiche of actual tele-sermons (cf. Zappa's similar gambit on "A Few Moments With Brother A. West" off *The Best Band You Never Heard In Your Life*; it must have felt like old home week to Mitchell's ex-Zappa drummer Colaiuta). Joni's not afraid to state her allegiances here loud and clear:

> Lord, there's danger in this land
> You get witch-hunts and wars
> When church and state hold hands
> Fuck it!
> Tonight I'm going dancing
> With the drag queens and punks
> Big beat deliver me from this sanctimonious skunk
> We're no flaming angels
> And he's not heaven sent
> How can he speak for the Prince of Peace
> When he's hawk-right-militant
> And he's immaculately tax free

While Joni was getting gouged by the state of California, as noted above. Little has changed here, alas, only the faces as scandal toppled some.

The side ends with a bagatelle called "Smokin' (Empty, Try Another)" in which our heroine confronts her nicotine addiction and plays a cigarette machine in its percussive aspects. After the last three songs, Joni needed to light up, no doubt.

The second side keeps up the pressure with the title track about a "culture in decline" desperate for sensation and run by "Snake bite evangelists and racketeers / And big wig financiers":

> People looking, seeing nothing
> Dog eat dog
> People listening, hearing nothing
> Dog eat dog
> People lusting, loving nothing
> Dog eat dog

Joni obviously wasn't buying the "morning in America" rap from Ronald Reagan; from Los Angeles, it looked to her more like the later ages of the Roman Empire.

"Shiny Toys" sustains the critique with its mockery of consumerism and materialism—again, especially as viewed from southern California. Zappa did this (uncharacteristically?) with a more Horatian touch in "Valley Girl"; Joni is up to a more Juvenalian satire. Guess who got the hit single out of the deal? Uncharacteristically again, Zappa—which tells you something about how Americans like their satire. (In fact, most took Frank's record at face value and didn't realize Moon Unit was trafficking in satire at all! And that tells you even more ... .) With Thomas Dolby's wizardry on the track, "Shiny Toys" sounds like pop eating itself: an eighties production mocking eighties productions!

The album's most brilliant move is to follow all this with "Ethiopia," a somber reminder on acoustic piano from Joni about how the rest of the world lives: "Hot winds and hunger cries—Ethiopia / Flies in your baby's eyes—Ethiopia." Her haunting vocal cements the music/text relationship. She uses a strategy similar to Robert Bly's juxtaposition of Vietnam and suburbia in "The Teeth Mother Naked at Last" with her imagery of "Famine phantoms at the garden gates." The two worlds, as always, are really one. Joni has a characteristically keen eye for detail: she notes how a celebrity visiting the famine-torn country refers to a baby as "It" to the child's mother. Curiously, this song is published by "The Tenth World" (ASCAP) publishing company instead of her usual "Crazy Crow" (BMI), perhaps indicating an intended charitable use for the royalties.

Dog Eat Dog can't get any more downbeat than this, so Joni lightens up on the last two tracks. The arrival of Wayne Shorter on soprano and tenor saxophones (on the last two cuts, respectively) brings a utopian musical presence to a very dystopian album. "Impossible Dreamer" seems to be about Joni's reaction to the murder of John Lennon. She recalls an unnamed dreamer and quotes Lennon lyrics obliquely ("Imagine") and directly ("Give Peace A Chance," which she also cited on "California" [*Blue*]). Perhaps Lennon's vision is as close as this album gets to offering solutions: remember his ideals, and try to figure out how to implement them.

"Lucky Girl," the closing track, offers symmetry and closure with its rapture about her redemptive love for Larry Klein:

> I never loved a man I trusted
> As far as I could pitch my shoe
> 'til I loved you.

Even in the harsh Darwinian world of this album, some good things abide. If more turbulent indigo than blue at this point, Joni seemed nested for the moment.

Although an early sixties folk audience would be baffled by its production techniques, they would applaud *Dog Eat Dog*'s passionate finger-pointing reminiscent of early Dylan. Joni stepped up to the plate here while Bob was trying to decide if he was a Christian or not. But an eighties audience? Forgeddaboudit, as Joni recalls:

> With *Dog Eat Dog* , the press went to sleep en masse: Ronnie Reagan could do no wrong. It took a few years for the press to wake up. This Japanese interviewer said to me, "Joni, you used to be a poet and now you're a journalist." And I said. "That's because America is a land of ostriches and somebody's gotta be Paul Revere." People didn't like the politics on that album. *Time* magazine called it an adolescent work, yet it contained two of their subsequent cover stories. (in Luftig 171)

Even more strikingly, the politics of the album still sounds fresh today. We have additional problems whose impending arrival was only hinted at by this record, but her basic critique of contemporary American culture remains valid—as does Frank Zappa's, for that matter. Living in Los Angeles puts you in the belly of the beast—the Galeria vs. Walmart—but southern California has no monopoly on artifice, brutality, innocence, materialism, consumerism, sanctimonious religiosity and a subtle contempt for the full implications of ostensible democracy. The transition from Jimmy Carter to Ronald Reagan made these trends instantly more observable, and made Joni a "journalist" for one uncharacteristic and unpopular album. For all that, it's still a beautiful piece of work musically and ideologically. It awaits your interest.

The Persistence of Joni

For all intents and purposes, *Dog Eat Dog* was Joni Mitchell's last foray into the ditch from a position of cultural power. This is not to say she has stopped making excellent music: just that she is no longer putting her career (such as we shall see it is) at risk to make highly experimental statements.

To give a brief overview of the more recent material, she followed up *Dog Eat Dog* with *Chalk Mark in a Rain Storm* (1988). This recording continued some of the criticism and techniques of *Dog Eat Dog* (e.g., "Lakota" [a lament about Native Americans reminiscent of "Ethiopia" in its feel and sound], "The Beat of Black Wings" [a Vietnam veteran narrative] and "The Reoccurring Dream" [a collage of sound-bytes from television ads]). But she tempered the critique with more accessible material such as a cover of "Cool Water" (with Willie Nelson) and even a comic song about romantic rivalry ("Dancin' Clown" with Billy Idol and Tom Petty). The high-profile guest artists and the varied moods made this a less harsh album—not that the radio stations noticed.

Joni began the 1990s with a guest vocal on Roger Waters' mammoth restaging of *The Wall* at the former Berlin Wall ("Goodbye Blue Sky," accompanied by Irish flautist James Galway). Her next solo project, *Night Ride Home* (1991) was greeted critically with the same relief as Neil's *Freedom*: back to love songs and/or reflective autobiography on piano and acoustic guitar (mostly). This was the first stereotypical Joni Mitchell album since *Wild Things Run Fast, Court and Spark* or even *For The Roses* (depending upon how strict a constructionist the listener was).

Turbulent Indigo (1994) caught Joni in a somewhat fiercer mood reflecting upon her romantic (but not professional) breakup with Larry Klein ("Last Chance Lost"), the AIDS epidemic ("Sex Kills"), the O. J. Simpson case ("Not to Blame") and even the Book of Job ("The Sire of Sorrow [Job's Sad Song]"). The production used reliable players (Wayne Shorter, Seal [whom she also did a guest vocal for on his second album]) and her trademark mature jazz-folk hybrid sound.

The CD contains one incredible mistresspiece, "The Magdalene Laundries" (about a Catholic charity for fallen women). *Turbulent Indigo*'s version is superb; her version with the Chieftains on their *Tears of Stone* (1998; anthologized on *The Wide World Over* [2002]) is sublime, essential Joni Mitchell ranking with the best stuff I have been describing here—proof that she can still part the heavens on occasion!

Turbulent Indigo won two Grammy awards, including Album of the Year (resembling similar late-career kudos bestowed on Bonnie Raitt, Santana and Steely Dan). In 1996, Mitchell released two compilations, *Hits* and *Misses*. They work as samplers/introductions to the larger body of work, but cannot suggest the architectural unity of her best recordings. In 1997, she was inducted into the Rock and Roll Hall of Fame. The awards and tributes just kept on coming; I shan't list them all here. More importantly, she was reunited with the daughter she had put up for adoption—a miracle of existential fulfillment.

In 1998, she released *Taming The Tiger*. This CD addressed the mother and child reunion ("Stay in Touch"), offered some social commentary in the title track, and had more romantic autobiography—and, again, a trademark sound with excellent work from Wayne Shorter and some younger players. *Both Sides Now* (2000) offered a big-band suite of romantic covers (including her own "Both Sides Now" and "A Case of You") that traces the course of a love affair (oddly reminiscent, in fact, of the use of cover songs to tell a love narrative in the later film *Moulin Rouge*). Her smoky vocals and soulful delivery are perfect for the material: she's much closer to Peggy Lee and Julie London than Linda Ronstadt and Carly Simon (who preceded her on big-band projects—proof that it pays to wait for some things).

In 2002, she followed up *Both Sides Now* with *Travelogue*, another big-band outing exclusively reworking her original songs. As such, it is not avant-pop by any means—although it has its charms. The band accompanying the orchestra is stellar: it includes Herbie Hancock on piano, Billy Preston on B-3 organ and Wayne Shorter on soprano sax. The sequencing is inspired as well, taking the listener on a true musical "travelogue" (referring to a line from "Amelia"). For example, the mutability theme which shapes "Hejira" of time passing segues into a series of songs about memories, beginning in late childhood and moving forward chronologically ("Chinese Cafe / Unchained Melody," "Cherokee Louise," "The Dawntreader," "The Last Time I Saw Richard"). Some songs are enhanced by this treatment: the post 9/11 martial drumbeats work well for "Otis and Marlena" and "Slouching Towards Bethlehem"; the elaborate developments of "Refuge of the Roads" and "Hejira" seem justified (the former featuring a harp rendering of the melody line).

Most recently, Joni has released her first CD of (mostly) new compositions in almost a decade (*Shine*, 2007). As in the case of *Turbulent Indigo*, there is one great keeper here: "Night of the Iguana" (a return to Tennessee Williams for inspiration; cf. "Sweet Bird"). This straightforward retelling of the play / film juxtaposes Joni's rare raucous electric guitar (a whole new development!) with suitable tropical beats and textures. It's the one moment where she seems to let the music completely take her away. The rest of the album is, lyrically, a series of jeremiads a la *Dog Eat Dog*—but with smooth jazz settings rather than more harsh electronica. Maybe this cognitive dissonance IS the point, an attempt to sugarcoat the pill of environmental concern. But I suspect a) she's preaching to the boomer choir (who still haven't fixed things), b) she has never really improved on her ahead-of-the-curve "Big Yellow Taxi" (reworked here, in fact) and c) like Neil says on *Fork In The Road*, "just singing a song won't change the world." Maybe a download of "Night of the Iguana" is the way to go here. But then again, the actual music is up to her usual compositional standards. Maybe just listen to it and don't dwell on the lyrics?

Not that 2007 was a bad year for Joni Mitchell musically. Herbie Hancock's jazz homage to Joni, *River: The Joni Letters*, won a Grammy for Album of the Year in 2008—only the second time in the 50 years of the awards that a jazz instrumentalist's recording received such recognition. This confection combined an unbeatable list of players (Wayne Shorter again, Dave Holland on bass, Zappa alumnus Vinnie Colaiuta on drums), some very inspired guest vocalists (Tina Turner on "Edith and the Kingpin") and a choice selection of some of Joni's best compositions. She herself did a cameo vocal on "Tea Leaf Prophecy"; ex-lover Leonard Cohen showed up to treat "The Jungle Line" as a *recitatif*.

The musical trifecta for this Year of Joni Mitchell came from her previous label Nonesuch (she is now on Hear Music, a label owned by Starbuck's coffee). They released *A Tribute to Joni Mitchell* (also 2007, natch). This Whitman's sampler offers a wide variety of collectible covers: Sufjan Steven's quirky and overblown "Free Man in Paris," Annie Lennox's psychedelic and Indian-inflected "Ladies of the Canyon," Emmylou Harris' transcendent "Magdalene Laundries" (a photo finish with Joni and the Chieftains' reading), Elvis Costello's deliberative treatment of "Edith and the Kingpin" as *lieder* and k. d. lang's "Help Me" (like buttah—trust me).

This trio of releases gets to the heart of the paradoxes of Joni Mitchell's musical career in the twenty-first century (as opposed to her burgeoning career as a painter). Her muse of late—and really since *Dog Eat Dog* a quarter of a century ago—has been fitful and sporadic, only occasionally turning up a gold nugget in the pan. But the sheer power and complexity of the work I have been considering in this chapter keeps getting rediscovered and reinterpreted (with Grammy-winning results): proof positive that Joni was way ahead of her time back then. The rediscovery of the compositions on *The Hissing of Summer Lawns* is especially gratifying to followers of this arc. Finally the world seems to be catching up!

Joni Mitchell still has a contract with a major label (if you don't have a problem with the Starbuck's connection), but (like most of her sixties peers) she is no longer a best-selling artist with her own releases (Luftig 153). She acknowledges that many of her fans were fair-weather listeners who only used her as the soundtrack to "their youth and their best years," but that she also attracts "a loyal body of people" who follow everything she does as they might read the latest book by a favorite author (Luftig 164, 199). I confess to being one of the latter. Joni deserves as much, as that Chieftains version of "The Magdalene Laundries," *Both Sides Now* and "Night of the Iguana" would indicate. I find it sad that a television salute in the 1990s, *An All-Star Tribute To Joni Mitchell*, didn't cover any of her songs later than "The Dry Cleaner From Des Moines"—as if she hadn't written anything of note since then! With a "tribute" like that, who needs critics?

Joni is both famous and unknown. One Saturday in 2002, I had the serendipitous happenstance—while grazing the questionable DMX cable music service—

of hearing two Joni Mitchell songs back to back: "Big Yellow Taxi" on the children's channel and "Both Sides Now" on soft rock. Neither were sung by her, of course. The former was done by those anonymous and underpaid purveyors of cover songs for kids; the latter was (of course) covered by Judy Collins. A strange and somewhat cruel fate for a living artist—to be trapped in what she calls "ingenue roles." Aging women musicians have the same problem as aging actresses, it appears. (Unless, of course, you're Yoko Ono and were never perceived as an ingenue.) Her loyal fans will have to support her until the rest of you catch up. I hope I have planted a suspicion in your mind that there's a body of work worth investigating out there: Joni has never been just for kids, hippies or soft-rockers. As she once described herself, she is a "woman of heart and mind"—in equally abundant proportions. I hope you're ready for that.

Works Cited

An All-Star Tribute To Joni Mitchell. Musical director Larry Klein. Turner Broadcasting, 2000.
Crowe, Cameron. "Joni Mitchell: The Rolling Stone Interview." *Rolling Stone*, No. 296 (July 26, 1979), pp. 46-53.
Frith, Simon and Howard Horne. *Art Into Pop.* New York: Methuen, 1987.
Gabarini, Vic. "Joni Mitchell." *Musician.* January1983, pp. 42-52.
Hebert, Gilles, ed. *Voices: The Work of Joni Mitchell.* Saskatoon: The Mendel Art Gallery, 2000.
Luftig, Stacey, ed. *The Joni Mitchell Companion: Four Decades of Commentary.* New York: Schirmer Books, 2000.
Mingus, Charles, edited by Nel King. *Beneath the Underdog: His World as Composed by Mingus.* 1971; rpt. New York: Vintage, 1991.
Mitchell, Joni. *The Hissing of Summer Lawns.* Asylum Records 7E-1051. 1975. Liner notes by Joni Mitchell.
——. *Mingus.* Asylum Records. 53-505. 1979. Liner notes by Joni Mitchell.
Weller, Sheila. *Girls Like Us: Carole King, Joni Mitchell, Carly Simon—and the Journey of a Generation.* New York: Atria Books, 2008.
Zappa, Frank. *The Real Frank Zappa Book.* With Peter Occhiogrosso. New York: Poseidon Press, 1989.

Discography is available in Luftig, updated on the Joni Mitchell homepage and numerous websites. Luftig's book is the only major book-length critical anthology on Mitchell; there are no major single-author studies of her as yet. (Joni is also rumored to be writing an autobiography.) This state of affairs demonstrates another way in which Joni's work has been neglected.

Notes

[1] The astonishing postscript, of course, is that Joni was reunited in 1997 with her daughter, a fashion model in Toronto now named Kilauren Gibb (Luftig 191). Their amazing reunion prompted another remarkable song from Joni, "Stay in Touch" (from *Taming The Tiger*, 1998).

[2] Joni admits in interview how she only dips sporadically into books until she gets an inspiration for a song. She compares the reading process for her to casting the I Ching: "the answers come to you through your inquiry" (in Luftig 19-20). This serendipitous approach to research is best exemplified by "God Must Be A Boogie Man" (*Mingus*), a song which she composed after reading just the first chapter of *Beneath the Underdog* (Mingus' autobiography).

[3] In addition to the Keats reference below in the body of the text, I think this is also William Butler Yeats's bird in the Byzantium poems ("Sailing to Byzantium," "Byzantium") who transcends time and mortality. Joni set his poem "The Second Coming" to music ("Slouching Towards Bethlehem," *Night Ride Home*), so she would be familiar with his work.

[4] Sheila Weller claims that these lines refer to then-lover John Guerin, drummer for Tom Scott's L. A. Express. But she acknowledges that Joni's trip started from Neil's beach house (415, 422). Given Neil's comparative earthiness, I think either attribution works.

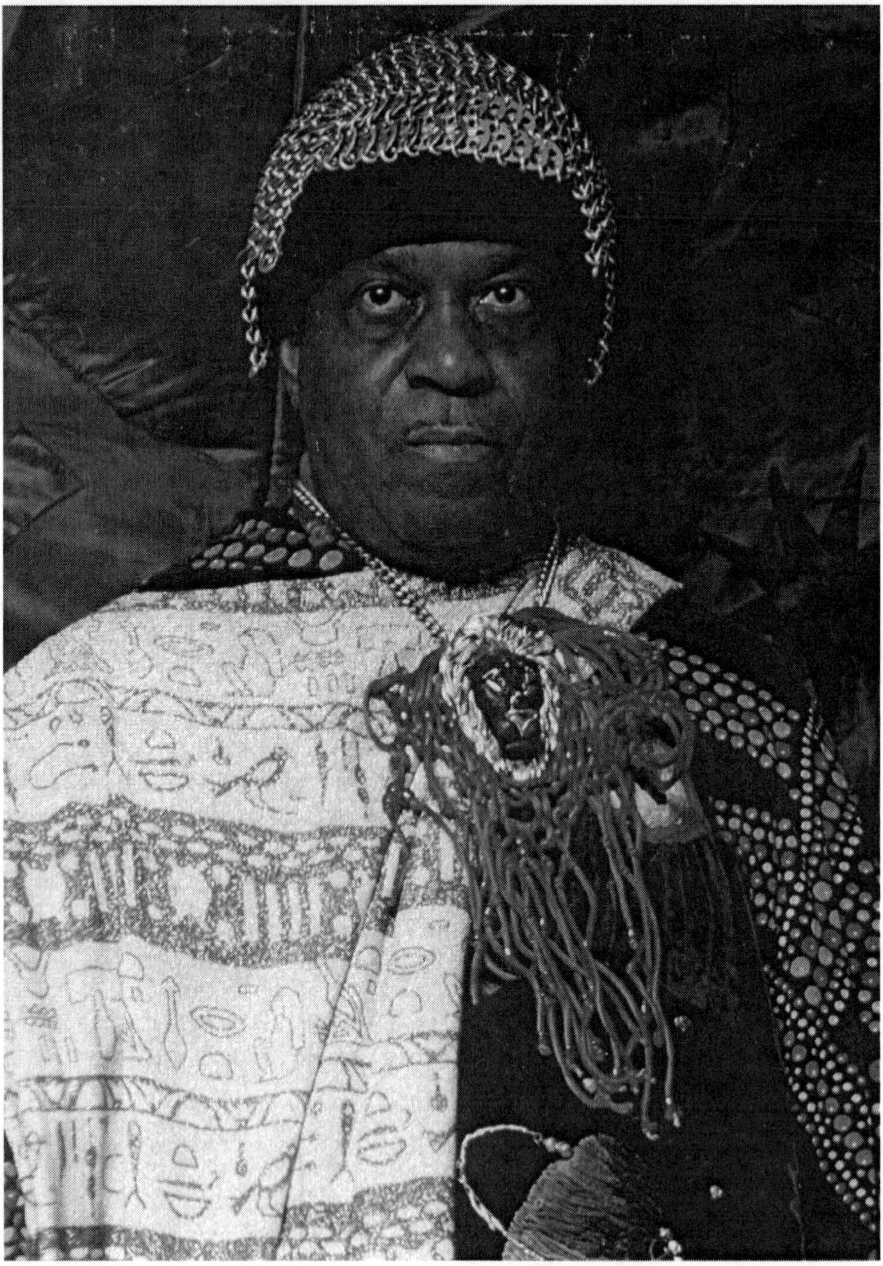

We Travel Ra's Spaceways

Cosmo Sun Connection to the Alter-Destiny

The first and only time I ever heard Sun Ra's music on the radio (unless I played it on my own campus radio shows) was in late May or early June of 1993. The place was Washington, D. C.; the station was the then-incredibly-hip Radio Pacifica. My delight turned to sorrow when I heard a second Ra tune played in a row. "He's passed on," I immediately and correctly concluded. When I saw Sun Ra and his Arkestra a few years earlier at the Artist's Glam Slam nightclub in Minneapolis, Ra was wheelchair-bound and frail. I knew he was feeling poorly. It took his departure from Earth to get him some brief radio exposure.

Because of his sub-underground status, every Ra fan has a story about how they first came to discover his work, a veritable secret musical history of the omniverse (which is bigger than the universe, in case you're wondering). Until the end of his career, the only way his home label El Saturn got distributed was by mail order, hand delivery to specialty record stores or off the bandstand at concerts (Szwed 170). Like many mid-western Ra fans, I got my first exposure to the Man from Saturn in a cut-out record bin where I acquired *The Solar-Myth Approach, Volume 2* on the French Actuel label for a buck or two in the early seventies. What made a nice caucasoid high-schooler like me buy an album with a black guy on the cover wearing a Mexican hat and some freaky orange glasses with only tiny slits to see through? On the back he and his band were clad in capes and bizarre jerry-rigged helmets and *dashikis*; nowhere was there any listing of the musical contents of the recording. The abundance of reeds suggested that they could be playing jazz, although the record might have been in the rock bin. I didn't normally check the jazz section back then; Ra was my first jazz purchase! So how did curiosity catch this particular cat?

I grew up listening to some pretty god-awful music. My older parents were big fans of Lawrence Welk, a fourth remove from decent jazz (Ellington to Goodman to Glenn Miller to Welk's fusion of big band with mitteleuropic ethnic effects like the polka). They also liked Bob Kames's Hawaiian-inflected organ records. My brother snuck off to hear Ahmad Jamal and George Shearing in Chicago, but his record club purchases stuck to Ferrante and Teicher, Martin Denny (I unapologetically grooved and groove to *Quiet Village*), the soundtrack to *West Side Story* and an early album by Peter, Paul and Mary (admittedly big improvements on the parental selections). My sister was hippest with Elvis (on 45s only, alas—the problem with being in the Columbia record club vs. RCA). I forget which sibling had *Trini Lopez Live at the Purple Onion*, but both liked it. The only Negroes allowed in our white-bread house (ironically in an African-American ghetto in the making) were the Platters and Nat King Cole. You get the picture.

Needless to say, the British couldn't have invaded too soon. Even there I got off on the wrong foot. I was taking a bath when the Beatles first played Ed Sullivan, so I had no way of knowing my neighbor and playmate Duane Kirchner was completely full of shit when he told me that the Dave Clark Five were destined to contribute more to western civilization. The good news is that I learned after I heard my first Beatles record TO TRUST MY OWN EARS, the secret to music appreciation when all is said and done. The bad news is that Duane's love of the DC5 proved to be the harbinger of a series of existential wrong turns for him. I lost track when he dropped out of my high school.

Once I got the Beatles issue straightened out, I took the journey of many fellow boomers and watched them evolve from a rocking teen combo to avant-popists in their own right with the increasing experimentation that began with *Rubber Soul*. Soon I was also investigating the new psychedelia: the Moody Blues, King Crimson, Pink Floyd and so many others. An even more crucial development for my musical ear was my appreciation of Stanley Kubrick's 1968 movie *2001: A Space Odyssey*, which led me to purchase the soundtrack recording. Luckily, and thanks to tolerant music teachers, I had an unbiased ear. I didn't know the cardinal rule of musical socialization in western culture: that consonance sounds good and pretty and dissonance sounds evil and ugly. To me, this has always made as much logical sense as a color preference: green is beautiful and purple is ugly. Consonance and dissonance were just different musical effects, but either could be wonderful depending upon their use. So I intuitively loved the three compositions by Hungarian composer Gyorgy Ligeti on the 2001 soundtrack. This was real "space music," conveying the feel of contact with the alien. Unquestionably, it was the most adventurous record in my house—and the one that best prepared me to appreciate Sun Ra.

The final piece of the puzzle was a series of references to Sun Ra (even a cover story) in *Rolling Stone*. At the time, I was assisting a peer who was in the business of providing light shows for Milwaukee bands. I was intrigued to learn that Ra was doing light shows and space spectacles long before the acid rock bands emerged on the scene. *Rolling Stone* gave him credit for being an innovator in this regard, as well as being the earliest user of exotic electronic keyboards. In fact, Ra's earliest recording "Deep Purple" (between1948 and 1953, depending on your sources) uses a Solovox (an odd proto-synthesizer electronic keyboard [Corbett 164, Szwed 427]). Thirdly, Ra and his band wore exotic costumes in Chicago in the 1950s, long before Arthur Brown and Doctor John kicked psychedelic fashions up a notch with their regal robes. Sun Ra, according to *Rolling Stone* was a secret progenitor of the new counterculture. Even as Pat Boone homogenized Little Richard a decade earlier, white entrepreneurs had seen the Ra spectacle in Chicago and New York (especially at Slug's tavern every Monday night) and adapted it for new scenes like the UFO club in London.

This information led me to buy the Ra cutout album when I saw it; I needed to *hear* this guy, and buying the record seemed like the only way that could happen. But it was my fondness for Ligeti that kept my ears open when I put it on the turntable. The first track on *The Solar-Myth Approach, Volume 2* is "The Utter Nots," an uncompromising example of Ra's space music. It sounds like a round of free solos, but Ra explained that he had to compose those levels of chaos (mere improvisation couldn't guarantee results that wild!). The reed instruments are burning the zoo down, then drums and piano come in, Marshall Allen on alto saxophone with frenzied percussion backing, Ronnie Boykins on bowed bass. To bring things to a climax, Ra uses the "space key" or "space chord": "a collectively improvised tone cluster at high volume" (Szwed 214). (In concert, he could use this as an all-purpose transitional device for the program.) It sounded like nothing I had ever heard before, but I liked its fierce energy and curious mixture of freedom and control. This band knew what it was doing; there was a structure to the sonic extravagance. On first listens, I couldn't tell for sure if this was programmatic science fiction music portraying a world of chaos and negation best not spoken of ("The Utter Nots," after all, is a pun) or just some funky African-Americans baiting the bourgeoisie with signifying sounds—a logical extension of James Brown on the TAMI show. After all, I could hear even then the abundant humor in Ra's music. John Gilmore's falsetto squeaks on tenor sax and Pat Patrick's honking on the baritone create risible as well as profound effects (lessons not lost on emergent Chicago musicians like the Art Ensemble of Chicago). The Arkestra gives you consistent virtuosity with a signifying swerve. As we shall see, these guys aren't for real: they're for myth!

The second track, "Outer Spaceways, Inc." was my favorite at the time. Clocking in at a mere 1:05, it is a good example of Ra's "space chants." These are eminently hummable and singable ditties that the Arkestra began to record and include in their live shows as early as 1960 ("Interplanetary Music" and "We Travel the Spaceways"), quasi-pop songs with hooks. They have a way of sticking in your mind.

My attraction to the song was no coincidence. Sun Ra was first and foremost a teacher. Like Ralph Waldo Emerson, that other great American romantic pedagogue, Ra realized that you had to meet your audience on many levels and give them many things (advanced and elementary instruction); moreover, that it pays to restate complex teachings in simpler, varied forms. A typical Emerson address contained aphorisms and proverbs, poetry, straight exposition and philosophical explanation—often reiterating similar points about self-reliance or the Oversoul or fate in these various idioms. Similarly, a Ra concert or recording can include poetry, sermonizing, space chants, traditional jazz, "outside" (but not free) playing, dance, lightshows, film, and theater to reinforce his message in sundry media. (Don't worry; we'll address what that message might be below. As he wrote in a later song, "I'll wait for you.") He can attract most people on some level. Biographer and Ra scholar John Szwed explains:

> With Sun Ra, it was up to you to make sense of what he said, to find in it what you could use. You had to engage your spirit to understand him, but it was your spirit which was always in control, not Sun Ra. It was that attitude that audiences who responded to Sun Ra's music took to the performances. You accepted what you liked and ignored the too-far-out, the obscure or embarrassing parts. And he in turn ignored the Philistines in his audience. Or transvalued their comments. A teenager once said to him, "This is sixth-grade jazz!" "Yeah," he answered, "because the average American has a sixth-grade education, so thank you, I'm reaching them."
>
> "Sun Ra didn't say you had to believe what he says; you should just check it out for yourself," said Danny Thompson [baritone sax player and flautist for the Arkestra]. (385)

Ra, after all, was trained as a teacher at Alabama A & M in 1936, and would eventually give public lectures and teach a course at Berkeley. He knew how to communicate knowledge to people. As Ra said elsewhere, "A natural musician should 'move' all the people—whether they love him or not. It's like the rain, or the sun which shines in many different ways" (Carles).

On that second track, I got his message loud and clear:

> If you find Earth boring
> Just the same old same thing
> Come outside
> Come to Outer Spaceways, Inc.

How could I resist? He was offering to get me off the planet to explore the cosmos.

We Travel Ra's Spaceways 317

The next track, "Scene 1, Take 1," was a Moog synthesizer solo (possibly his very best ever) that veered from ethereal shimmering to gutbucket abrasiveness. But was it jazz? On the one hand, in name only because it was on a record best filed under jazz. On the other hand, as Thelonious Monk once said in defense of Ra as a jazz artist, "it swings" (Szwed 219-20).

The second side had more unusual sounds: "Pyramids," a spacemaster keyboard solo with drums in the background; "Interpretation," a brooding chamber piece for strange stringed instruments and a "space dimension mellophone" [a mellophone fitted with a mouthpiece for another instrument, perhaps a bassoon]; "Ancient Ethiopia," a big Cadillac arrangement of an older Ra composition highlighting drums and baritone saxophone; and finally "Strange Worlds," another alien soundscape with trumpet flares, James Jacson playing the ancient Egyptian infinity drum with his curved candy cane mallets, and the great vocals of June Tyson evoking "strange worlds" with her space ethnicities and distortions. A final blast of the space key and the needle went off the record. Amazing stuff! I had heard Sun Ra's "angels and demons at play," an intriguing mix of consonance (the angels) and dissonance (the demons). My ears stayed open.

After that, I was always on the alert for Sun Ra cutouts. The first few I acquired after *The Solar-Myth Approach, Volume 2* were pretty conservative for Ra. *Sun Song* and *Sound of Joy* were Delmark reissues of 1956 recordings that were much more "inside" than what I had previously heard (although avant-garde jazzer Anthony Braxton recommends "Brainville" off the former as one of two essential Ra compositions for study [in Corbett 217]). When I went to graduate school in North Carolina, I made happier discoveries on Franklin street in Chapel Hill at Schoolkids Records: a cut-out double album *Live at Montreux* (1976) which contained a vital mix of adventurous soloing, quintessential Ra compositions such as "Lights on a Satellite" and "El is the Sound of Joy," and a sublime cover of "Take the A Train" (Billy Strayhorn's signature composition for Duke Ellington). At Schoolkids, I also acquired my first really homemade El Saturn release, *Sound Mirror* (1978); it had minimal information on a piece of paper taped to the front of the otherwise blank record jacket. Eventually I would come to acquire a lot more of these from mail order (Rounder Records in Boston), Schoolkids and at live gigs.

For I became a hopeless Ra admirer in the late seventies when I first saw him in concert at D. C. Space (aptly named) in Washington, D. C.. If you have open eyes and ears, once you see the Arkestra you're hooked! When Sun Ra came out in his purple robes and stared into my eyes, I had no doubt of his sincerity or his genius. He projected a gentle seriousness, tempered by a hint of whimsy. In a word, his presence was regal even in that dingy punk club.

The show, of course, was fantastic—a veritable anthology of the black arts from Africa through Harlem to the space age. Saxophone players climbed up on our tables to blow us personal solos; dancers and players marched and chanted through the space of the nightclub. This version of the Arkestra was smaller than some of the more elaborate presentations which included fire-eaters and tumblers. But it was more spectacle than I had ever seen before or since in concert (except for the other four times I saw the Arkestra). Sun Ra knew how to mix it up with an audience and give them a tailor-made concert.

The music was wonderful as well, naturally. By then Ra had patented a mix of group improvisation, his own compositions, a standard or two and some closing space chants. During these the band would march offstage, wend through the audience, go backstage and return for the encore singing, playing and clapping all the while. I have since seen Moroccan bands in Marrakech execute these maneuvers, but such an approach is a rarity in these United States.

After seeing the cosmo-drama, the rest is history. I am grateful to a late friend, Greg Bovee, for taping four sets over two days at a Milwaukee jazz club in the early 1980s, and for helping me to obtain some of the rarer Saturn offerings. I don't have all of Sun Ra's recordings. (Does anyone? I doubt it.) But I have enough to share with you some highlights and give you something to look for in used record stores, at yard sales, or online.

But Is It Jazz?

One logical place to start considering the music of Sun Ra is to address the serious issue of its genre. Like Joni Mitchell, Ra was somewhat resistant to easy labeling and aware that he was doing something ultimately outside the categorical boxes listeners rely upon to process the shock of the new. (Think of how people hasten to read titles and accompanying text in art museums.) A closer examination of this music will frustrate any attempt to box it in.

The Arkestra emerged in the mid-fifties during the mass popularity of be-bop jazz and were naturally associated with that movement, especially by white jazz critics. Be-bop (later bop) was characterized by a freer relationship towards the melody and harmony of the source material than earlier eras of jazz attempted. The improviser could just cut to the chords of the song and play them forwards, backwards or sideways—a sonic breakthrough comparable to cubism in the visual arts. When coupled with driving rhythms ultimately derived from West African techniques, this was a frenetic music well-suited to the post-atomic age of anxiety. Too far out for some listeners, it attracted progressive audiences across ethnic lines and made careers (if not wealth) for players such as Charlie Parker, Dizzy Gillespie and Thelonious Monk. There is no doubting that individual members of the Arkestra thoroughly understood this music and could deploy its approaches: John Gilmore's work on tenor sax immediately comes to mind.

But, as critic Art Lange reminds us, be-bop "held no charms for Ra," whose roots and initial allegiances as an older man who arrived on Earth in 1914 were in the Swing Era (liner notes for *We Travel the Spaceways*). As is often documented, Sun Ra served an apprenticeship with the Fletcher Henderson orchestra after he moved from Birmingham to Chicago. Fletcher Henderson (1897-1952), one of the founders of swing, was based at the Club DeLisa, a south side juke joint and casino. In the late 1940s, Sun Ra (then technically Herman Poole Blount) took over as pianist and eventually co-arranger for the Club DeLisa's house bands, first Henderson and then later Red Saunders (Szwed 53-7). He received a fine training for a future band leader; the point of this narrative, however, is that Ra initially learned Swing Era, big band compositional approaches. Specifically, he acquired a taste for discipline—a touchstone throughout his career. Be-bop would have represented the opposite values for him: wildness, self-indulgence and indiscipline. Although the Arkestra produced far more adventurous music than the bop players throughout its career, there were always contexts and codes—even scores—constraining the expressive elements of the band.

There are plenty of be-bop moments in the Arkestra's long performance history, acknowledging its presence as a possible jazz idiom. For example, the trading of solos rapidly between players on a cover of Gershwin's "But Not For Me" is standard bop practice (on *Standards* [2001, but recorded 1962-3]). And John Gilmore's earlier solo work often resembles be-bop in technique (e.g., "Urnack" off *Angels and Demons at Play* [recorded in 1956, issued in 1965 (Szwed 177)]). But Sun Ra was expanding the Swing Era into the space age, first and foremost; be-bop was only a sideshow for him.

Generically, the same is even more evident in the case of the free jazz movement that began with Ornette Coleman and eventually flourished in the sixties and early seventies. Again, Sun Ra and his Arkestra seemed to embody its approach, and even anticipate it. Free jazz employed techniques like simultaneous soloing and an emphasis on conversationally improvised communication between players of a highly spontaneous and unrepeatable nature. It sounded like Ra was doing this from as early as the appropriately named track "The Beginning" from *The Futuristic Sounds of Sun Ra* (1961). And by 1965, he was clearly recording pieces with a strong family resemblance to free jazz, like "The Magic City" (off the eponymous recording)—which John Gilmore admitted was "unreproducible, a tapestry of sound" (Szwed 214).

Nonetheless, Ra always took care to dissociate himself from the movement. In a 1975 interview he joked:

> A lot of musicians have been trying to come to Philadelphia and stay with me ... . I say, "Stay where you are if you're one of the freedom boys, because I'm dealing with discipline." All men can get

into the freedom thing, but I'm on the discipline plane. I tell my Arkestra that all humanity is in some kind of restricted limitation, but they're in the Ra jail, and it's the best jail in the world. (in Blumenthal)

More technically, he pointed out that "I can write you something so chaotic you would say you know it's not written. But the reason it's chaotic is because it's written to be. It's further out than anything they would be doing if they were just improvising" (liner notes, *When Angels Speak of Love* [2000]).

A simple test case you can make is to play side by side one of Ra's "freer" compositions with any straight-up example of free jazz. The trick nowadays can be getting ahold of a recording of the latter; much fell out of print. I conducted this experiment by juxtaposing "The Magic City" by Ra with Alan Silva's Celestrial Communication Orchestra's recording of "Seasons," a six-sided improvisation with some minimal scoring. This latter is an especially interesting case: not only was Alan Silva in the Arkestra, but he made this recording in Paris only a month after playing with Ra in West Berlin (his recording is from December 1970). Although "Seasons" is not without merit or interest (its main theme recalls the Mexican horror film "Braniac" music used by Zappa on *Bongo Fury*), it is palpably not as compositionally complex as the Ra composition—despite having six times the length! There is a great deal of noodling and self-indulgent blowing with no seeming direction. Sun Ra, by contrast, is always conducting and taking the listener along on a cognitive and emotional ride. The Arkestra has freedom, but it is always constrained by discipline—wild solo moments in a larger structure. This is more easily heard than described, and it may be a difference of degree rather than kind. Nonetheless, it is a serious misnomer to lump even Ra's most adventurous work in with free jazz.

But why quibble about be-bop and free jazz when Ra occasionally denied he was even really playing jazz? In the liner notes he wrote for *Jazz in Silhouette* (1958), he described his music as "THE SOUND OF SILHOUETTES IMAGES AND FORECASTS OF TOMORROW DISGUISED AS JAZZ" (block capitals are Ra's). In other words, jazz music itself was just a generic mask he wore for his actual purposes, something to file his music under for convenience.

Finally, although "some may recall him as one of the great avant-gardists of the second half of the twentieth century," Ra did not like that label either (Szwed 382). John Szwed points out on this same page of his biography how Ra's music was too positive and inclusive to resemble the pessimism and nihilism of much of the avant-garde. But Ra says it best again: "[my music is] more than avant-garde, because the 'avant-garde' refers to, I suppose, advanced earth music, but this is not earth music. It has nothing to do with it. Music that's from a celestial plane, it's not a part of this planet" (Corbett 311).

For Sun Ra himself, this was space music when all was said and done—

not jazz or avant-garde earth music (Szwed 141). He was trying to depict his mental (the safest position, I know) travels through the cosmos by means of sound. His co-partner in Saturn Research, Alton Abraham, gives some ultimate insight into how serious this all was for the inner circle when he talks of secret codes that produce the music belonging only to the Ra "frat," and when he assures interviewer Corbett that he, Alton Abraham, "can write the music, the space music" (225, 227). Alton Abraham attributes the change in John Coltrane's style after 1956 to Arkestra member Pat Patrick slipping him some of the codes (Corbett 225). If this all smacks of Pythagoreanism, Gnosticism and hermeticism, so be it. Ra ran not only one of the best jails in the world, but one of the most interesting ones. Let's investigate this space music disguised as jazz and the man who transcribed it, after laying one last generic issue to rest.

But Is It Avant-Pop?

By this point, you might be questioning why Sun Ra is in this book. If Yoko Ono and Frank Zappa tended towards the avant-garde end of avant-pop, and Neil Young and Joni Mitchell towards the pop end, Ra seems off the charts altogether—literally. I have already mentioned how Radio Pacifica gave him rare airplay only after he died; none of his records ever graced the Billboard charts. Ken Burns neglected to mention him even once in his mammoth *Jazz* documentary (which did take time to name-check musicians influenced by Ra such as the Art Ensemble of Chicago). We have already seen Ra's problematizing of his avant-garde status; what on earth makes him a pop musician?

I will submit, as I will later for Sigmund Snopek III, that it is a matter of intention rather than necessarily achievement. If Ra never charted, it wasn't for his lack of trying. Unlike avant-garde musicians such as Anthony Braxton or John Cage, Ra and his Arkestra repeatedly reached out to the masses—albeit unsuccessfully by industry standards. I have already suggested, for starters, that Ra was a consummate showman. The Arkestra always gave its public top value on their entertainment dollar. No wonder promoter and activist John Sinclair described his double bill of Sun Ra and the Arkestra opening for James Brown at the 1974 Ann Arbor Blues and Jazz Festival (in exile in Windsor, Ontario) as the "Dream Show of All Time" (liner notes, *It Is Forbidden*, capitals Sinclair's). The aforementioned space chants sung in the show especially gestured towards the most accessible kinds of popular music.

Aside from Ra's popular outreach as a performer, which won him fans at rock festivals as well as jazz gatherings, he took part in many commercial projects without any elitist condescension. In fact, Sun Ra's first recorded work (under the name of Herman "Sonny" Blount) was playing barrelhouse piano for the lewd blues shouter Wynonie Harris. (One of another connections between Ra and James Brown is that Brown initially went for a vocal delivery like that of Harris [Smith 56]). The four songs, singles on Nashville's Bullet label that required Ra to travel from his Chicago home base in 1946, were double-entendre blues and boogie (the word itself a double entendre!). Sun Ra would seldom revert to this style of playing with his own band, but it is telling if not surprising that he could readily work in such an idiom thoroughly associated with "race" records. Ra's most energetic playing is on "Dig This Boogie." The other tracks are of more interest perhaps for Harris' lyrics, which are not like anything else in the Ra catalogue of originals or covers. "Lightnin' Struck the Poorhouse" seems to be about white lightning moonshine bankrupting the singer who hasn't "got a dime" after the meteorological event. "Drinkin' By Myself" (because he's "feelin' low down and lonesome") contains a blues trope that becomes almost ubiquitous after Fats Domino: "You never miss your water / Till your well runs dry."

In addition, Ra released many 45 rpm singles throughout his career—enough to more than fill a double CD compilation on the Evidence label. Ra began working with doo-wop groups like The Nu Sounds and The Cosmic Rays in Chicago during the mid-fifties.[1] A casual listen to the CD will tell you these are pure pop songs, only hinting at Ra's metaphysical interests:

> If you live in fables
> Then you'll know what I mean
> For that is a world
> Where things aren't what they seem ("Dreaming," The Cosmic Rays
>   [1956])

Sun Ra released many other such pop projects on his Saturn label, including holiday songs that he co-wrote with Alton Abraham ("Happy New Year To You!" and "It's Christmas Time" with The Qualities [1956]; Ra also played harmonium on the tracks [liner notes, *The Singles*]). Or how about his piano work on the Saturn single "Teenager's Letter of Promises" (Juanita Rogers and Lynn Hollings with Mr. V's Five Joys [1958 or 1959])? Is that pop enough for you? I don't think there's anything like that lurking in the John Cage catalogue.

Other more commercial single releases include several with a character named Yochanan, a vocal wild man cut from the same cloth as Screaming Jay Hawkins. In addition to gutbucket race records like "Muck Muck" and "Hot Skillet Mama" (both 1957), Yochanan had his own extraterrestrial rap down claiming to be "The Sun Man" on several tunes (1959 or 1960). The Arkestra and Sun Ra accompanied him on all these ventures (liner notes, *The Singles*).

Sun Ra and the Arkestra themselves released at least two potential chart-toppers. "I'm Gonna Unmask The Batman" was a novelty release hampered undoubtedly by its infelicitous 1974 issuance between the Batman television series and the character's pop culture revival courtesy of Frank Miller's *Dark Knight* graphic novel and Tim Burton's films. Its flipside, "The Perfect Man," was pure synthesizer pop music in the same ballpark as other seventies products like Emerson, Lake & Palmer.

In 1965, Ra played piano and harpsichord for jazz vibist Walt Dickerson on an unusual outing entitled *Impressions of a Patch of Blue*. This was a series of jazz extensions of the Jerry Goldsmith instrumental music for the Sidney Poitier film of the same name. Although the interplay was lovely (Ra would work intermittently with Dickerson over the years), the project was doomed because of the marginal interest the public had in the original film score. Who cares about a jazz interpretation of pop melodies that aren't popular? Francis Davis admits in his witty liner notes on the reissue that the album "was aiming for the sort of casual record buyer who thinks he likes jazz but prefers hearing songs with which he is already at least vaguely familiar." This target audience was never reached, but a great album of chamber jazz was produced.

The Arkestra's own album releases delve less frequently into gestures towards the mass market, but there are stellar exceptions. Most oddly, there is the much better timed (but nonetheless not terribly successful) 1966 *Batman and Robin* record marketed for children. On this gig, the Arkestra played with members of the Blues Project rock band (including Al Kooper joining Ra on organ). This amalgam was called for little apparent reason other than its catchiness "The Sensational Guitars of Dan and Dale." Although Danny Kalb was one of the guitarists there was no Dale. The music is pretty much what you'd expect: cheesy sixties instrumental music. There are some good musical jokes, however. Ra sneaks in a Tchaikovsky quote on his organ during "Penguin's Umbrella"; "Batmobile Wheels" recycles the melody from the pop hit "A Groovy Kind of Love" (itself based on a Clementi *sonatina*). There's also some respectable playing from Gilmore's gutbucket tenor on "The Bat Cave" and the whole ensemble grooves at length on "Batman and Robin Over the Rooftops."

Then there was Sun Ra's disco phase in the late seventies! Like Frank Zappa and James Brown (and even Yoko Ono if you consider "Walking on Thin Ice" as a club track, which it was), Sun Ra saw musical opportunities in the disco craze. He made his band members listen to examples of the genre. When they told him it was "hokey shit," he responded that "[t]his hokey shit is somebody's hopes and dreams ... . Don't be so hip!" (Szwed 352). Ra made a series of records that attempted to please these listeners, beginning with the drum machine and keyboard groove of "Constellation" (1978, issued on both *Other Voices, Other Blues* and *Media Dream*). Pre-programmed keyboard sound loops and drum machines accompanied Ra's organ work and various horn and reed players on a series of late seventies recordings: "Disco 3000," "Dance of the Cosmo-Aliens" (both off *Disco 3000* [1978], the former was also issued as the edited single "Disco 2100") and "UFO" (off *On Jupiter* [1979]).

There is no evidence to suggest the disco community embraced these rather eccentric efforts, too complex to be really danceable. John Szwed honestly and charitably labels them "revisionist disco" (350). As some of the titles indicate, one could also think of them as a kind of science-fiction projection of what disco might sound like had it continued to be musically dominant—a quaint sonic equivalent to the Futurama exhibit at the 1939 New York World's Fair, an alternate tomorrow.

I am puzzled as to why Szwed refers to *Lanquidity* (1978) as also revisionist disco, however. Now that Evidence has reissued this rare recording, one can see it was a serious bid for a larger audience. But its popular genre is not so much disco as smooth or mellow jazz of a sort produced at the time by the likes of Eddie Harris, Grover Washington, Jr., and Stanley Turrentine. Certainly Sun Ra's most accessible album, it has a late-night urban feel reflecting the circumstances of its recording: an all-night session in New York at a professional studio (Buchler, liner notes). Only the surreal whisper-chants of "There Are Other Worlds (They Have Not Told You Of)" break the trance induction of the rest of the album ("They want to speak to you"). The lineup of the Arkestra was very full and strong for this session: John Gilmore on tenor, Marshall Allen on oboe and alto, James Jacson on bassoon, relative newcomer Michael Ray on trumpet, several hot guitarists—to name only a few players and instruments. As a result, *Lanquidity* manages to be both of its time and genre and fresh (unlike most seventies smooth jazz, which sounds like a soundtrack for a coke binge!). The players made all the difference here; they're making a pop record, but they hint of other worlds. Musical ones as well as physical ones ... .

In the early eighties, the sixty-eight year old Ra recorded a timely "protest rap" (Szwed 353) with "Nuclear War" (on the eponymous release and *A Fireside Chat with Lucifer*). Released in 1982, the same year as Grandmaster Flash's "The Message" and well before Public Enemy, "Nuclear War" skewers the militaristic pretensions of winnable nuclear war originally espoused by the Reagan administration:

> It's a motherfucker
> Don't you know
> If they push that button
> Your ass got to go

From my admittedly biased perspective, I think this is Ra and the Arkestra's wittiest moment among many. He was caught in a catch-22: to really tell it like it was, he had to transcend FCC regulations. It should have been a monster hit, and was indeed covered by some rock musicians (Brian Ritchie of the Violent Femmes, who also has a Sigmund Snopek connection, and Yo La Tengo [in four separate readings; see below]).

Sun Ra's last massive pop gesture began when the Arkestra was asked to contribute a song to *Stay Awake*, a 1988 tribute to the film music of Walt Disney. The band performed "Pink Elephants on Parade" from *Dumbo* with zany brio. Perhaps responding to Disney's discipline and technological innovation, as well as the ubiquity of this music in our culture, Ra embraced him as a genius on a par with Fletcher Henderson and Duke Ellington. Renaming the Arkestra (a band with many thematic sub-names over the years) as the Disney Odyssey Arkestra, he toured in 1989 with a largely Disney program to "show the cosmic forces that there have been some people who came this way who were very nice ... . [I]t's a shield of beauty" (Szwed 361-2). I've always wondered whether he noticed or cared about Disney's racist moments (the crows in *Dumbo* come to mind), or whether he simply transcended such issues from his extraterrestrial perspective. In any event, the Arkestra took back Disney songs like "Zip-A-Dee-Doo-Dah" (from the essentially suppressed *Song of the South*) more dramatically than U2 did "Helter Skelter" on *Rattle and Hum*. It's a rare treat to hear these Arkestra covers on *Second Star to the Right (Salute to Walt Disney)* (1989). John Szwed beat me to the punch in observing that "The Forest of No Return" (from *Babes in Toyland*) sounds like it already was a Ra composition (362)! This live compilation could also work as a children's record.

Even after Ra's passing, the ghost band Arkestra continued to perform Disney material. In the late nineties, I saw the band cover the Mickey Mouse Club Theme, replete with a dancer dressed like Minnie Mouse and audience participation, as well as "Zip-A-Dee-Doo-Dah." It was real, it was natural: everything was satisfactual!

Throughout its career, Sun Ra's Arkestra made gestures of popular outreach not only to children and trend-following young adults, but also to older generations. Consider how many standards the Arkestra played through the years, always reverentially in intention even if the execution might have been unusual: "I Could Have Danced All Night" (*Sound Sun Pleasure!!*, 1958), "Autumn in New York" (*What's New?*, 1962), "Nature Boy" (*Some Blues But Not the Kind That's Blue*, 1977), "Smile" (*Celestial Love*, 1982) or "Days of Wine and Roses" (*Live at Praxis '84 Volume III*), to name but a few. In addition to show tunes and pop ballads, the Arkestra also repeatedly covered the standards of the jazz canon (Ellington and Strayhorn, Fletcher Henderson, Thelonious Monk). Any demographic which braved the concerts would have found something tailored for its tastes.

A final popular dimension of Sun Ra worth noting is his 1974 film *Space Is the Place*. Although it remained sub-underground in distribution until its 1993 release on video (from Rhapsody Films), it was a fine contribution to the popular blaxploitation genre. The film is only 63 minutes in length because Ra vetoed the sex scenes that were otherwise typical for this popular genre (Szwed 332). What remains is a mythic tale of Sun Ra playing for "the end of the world" with a mysterious adversary called "The Overseer." Ra flies a spaceship that runs on music and has various encounters with the residents of seventies Oakland. Its most memorable line is his threat to teenaged girls who don't want to go to outer space with him that he might just "chain [them] up, take [them] with [him]" like their ancestors. Like Neil Young's *Human Highway*, there is a suitably apocalyptic ending to this funky rewrite of *The Seventh Seal*. *Space Is the Place* was certainly populist in intent, if not popular in box office take: Sun Ra's imaginative bid for a black space program.

Where Is Sun Ra Coming From, Besides Saturn?

John Szwed begins his biography of Sun Ra with a 1954 quote from Louis Armstrong: "Our music is a Secret Order" (vii). Along with the previously mentioned remarks of Alton Abraham, this comment reminds us that there has always been a hermetic element to the jazz tradition—one which Ken Burns was certainly not given access to as an outsider when he made his documentary, which accounts for its superficial coverage. I'm not claiming I have much contact with it either, being an extreme amateur as a musician. But I know folks who do! On the most mysterious level, jazz has its "codes," which Abraham claimed he, Ra and some Arkestra veterans possessed. Perhaps these are no more than the space-age versions of Frank Zappa's remark that accomplished musicians know how to manipulate the emotions of their listeners. Or an extreme version of the obvious ways jazz technique is passed on: tutoring worthy disciples, humiliating rivals in all-night "cutting contests," wood-shedding in private after being exposed to new ideas (sometimes for years).

Sun Ra repeatedly admitted that his earthly hometown of Birmingham, Alabama, exposed him to all the music he would ever need to hear in the form of largely undocumented African-American touring big bands such as the Carolina Cotton Pickers:

> I never missed a band, whether a known or unknown unit. I loved music beyond the state of liking it. Some of the bands I heard never got popular and never made hit records, but they were truly natural black beauty. I want to thank them, and I will give honor to all the sincere musicians who ever were or ever will be. It's wonderful to even think about such people. The music they played was a natural happiness of love, so rare I cannot explain it. It was fresh and courageous, daring, sincere, unfettered. It was unmanufactured avant-garde, and still is, because there was no place for it in the world; so the world neglected something of value and did not understand. And all along I could not understand why the world

> did not understand.
>
> What happened is that, in the Deep South, the black people were very oppressed and were made to feel like they weren't anything, so the only thing they had was big bands. Unity showed that the black man could join together and dress nicely, do something nice, and that was all they had ... . So it was important for us to hear big bands. (Szwed 16-7)

Anyone who listens to the Arkestra will hear this tradition preserved, if transformed—which is what any jazz player inevitably does to the tradition. But Ra concedes the origins of his music are but a memory, for reasons as diverse as racism, economics and technological limitation. The earliest roots on record available to the genealogically inclined would be the swing records of Fletcher Henderson, which young Herman Blount had listened to for years before he moved to Chicago and actually played with Henderson's band (Szwed 11).

What does one hear on these records that became Ra's? A tough question, because most of Henderson's contributions to the idiom can be found elsewhere. Big band swing is an over-determined text: who can say for sure who contributed what? (A problem that extends, of course, to all music.) What matters most is not whether Fletcher Henderson did something first, but that Sun Ra heard it very early on.

Fletcher Henderson is credited in the jazz histories with the incorporation of the innovations of Louis Armstrong into the larger jazz ensemble, a development that turned jazz into swing (Schuller 1-2). What Louis Armstrong did was to develop a playful relationship to melody and rhythm: you could bend the notes of the song, or sustain them, or omit them altogether. (Listen to "Potato Head Blues," for example.) Sun Ra has commented on the importance of this approach:

> You should play it wrong—a little ahead of the beat. That's the way the older jazz musicians played it. They played it a little ahead, then later, Chicago musicians decided to play a bit behind the beat and that's not easy to do. It's a little ahead or behind. Then there's music that's right on the beat. Well, white people can do that. If it's on the beat they got you, and say, "That's my stuff!" If you get ahead of the beat or behind the beat they be talking about you and say it ain't even music, 'cause they can't play it. If you can play on the beat you can forget it, you won't have a job. So stay ahead of the beat, something you can't count. (Szwed 99-100)

Fletcher Henderson got his band to do this, emulating what he heard from Louis Armstrong himself when he was in the Henderson orchestra. At first only a few soloists, like Coleman Hawkins on tenor sax, could pull it off. But by the thirties, Henderson's entire band could swing.

Other innovations accomplished by Fletcher Henderson included composing for the orchestra sectionally (like classical musicians had been doing, but unlike earlier jazz practice). The reeds would be doing one thing, the trumpets another, the percussion section would be laying down a different rhythm than the rest (Schuller 2). Often this would be refined into a call-and-response effect, with one section answering another like the African-American congregation responding to the exhortations of the preacher. (Check out Henderson compositions such as "The Stampede," "Copenhagen" or "King Porter Stomp" [this last covered by the Arkestra] to hear this in practice.) The Arkestra's careful mixture of composed material and solo improvisation is an elaboration of the Henderson approach heard as early as "Copenhagen" (recorded in 1924). The insanely tight and fast reed section work on a Ra composition such as "The Shadow World" seems to be pushing the innovative approach of Henderson to a kind of sublime *reductio ad absurdum.*

Other elements that arguably passed from Henderson's practice to Ra's were the former's love of lush "Cadillac" arrangements (e.g., "Wrappin' It Up") and even occasional tendencies towards exotic and / or orientalist scene-painting ("The Gouge of Armour Avenue," "Shanghai Shuffle"). You can hear exfoliations of Henderson's Cadillac approach on Ra compositions such as "Saturn" or "Lights on a Satellite." As for Ra's scene-painting, it extends from the local (Birmingham ["The Magic City"], Chicago ["El is a Sound of Joy"], New York ["Manhattan Cocktail"]) through the terrestrial exotic ("Overtones of China," "Ancient Ethiopia") to the vast universe itself ("Friendly Galaxy," "Strange Worlds"). Duke Ellington also had these elements in his work, of course; but Henderson was doing it first. Sun Ra's writing seems to be an extension of both into the space age.

Along with the great African-American swing tradition, Sun Ra also seemed to be aware of a fifties trend in Euro-American music: the high-fidelity lounge exotica of composers and performers such as Les Baxter and Martin Denny (Szwed 151). After its initial popularity in the 1950s, this was a neglected music until *Re/Search* magazine put out its *Incredibly Strange Music* issues and CDs in the early nineties. Exotica, and the lounge genre it was a subset of, were buried by rock and roll before the fairly recent lounge revival. Its initial popularity was a result of a concatenation of circumstances: American exposure to Oceanic culture as a result of the second World War's Pacific theater, which culminated in the statehood of Hawaii; the boom in audio-electronic innovations, which led to a craze for high-fidelity and stereo experimentation; the conspicuous consumption of the Eisenhower populuxe era, which caused a boom in cocktail, space-age and / or tiki paraphernalia. After all, this last juxtaposition became the caucasoid version of Sun Ra's juxtaposition of outer space and ancient Egypt (co-opted by the *Stargate* film and its televisual spinoffs). If you find the right bar on Cocoa Beach, Florida, you can see simultaneously a fake Easter Island head and the launch pad for the space shuttle! I've done it. Future primitive was in, and still leaves its traces on the space coast.[2]

Sun Ra certainly picked up on many elements of this music, and it helps give the Arkestra its uncanny ambience: it's the added ingredient outside the main tradition of the jazz big band, although the exotica of Henderson and Ellington are a plausible influence upon Les Baxter and Martin Denny. Les Baxter is an especially crucial link here. Like Ra, he was interested from the beginning in electronic instruments. Baxter pioneered the theremin synthesizer on *Music Out of the Moon* (1947), a year before Ra may have recorded "Deep Purple" (with Stuff Smith) playing his Solovox.

Some Arkestra selections pay deep homage to this music. Consider, for example, the hypnotic drumming and processionals of "Watusa" (or "Watusi," depending upon the recording: they are slightly different pieces sometimes but other times it's just an interchangeable name) or "Africa"—both off *Lady with the Golden Stockings* (recorded 1959, issued 1966, reissued 1967 as *The Nubians of Plutonia* [Szwed 171, 429]). Sun Ra could have almost made it as a lounge act, in fact; his only problem was that his music was often too intense to be truly ambient background for bachelor pads. In Brian Eno's famous formulation of the criterion for ambient music, Ra's music was not "as ignorable as it is listenable" (liner notes, *Music for Airports*). The Arkestra has a way of waking you up, unlike Denny or most of Baxter (whose emotional sonic experiment, *The Passions* (1954), is a telling exception: check out "Terror," for example).

Big band swing and hi-fi exotica, when combined and extended with post-bop innovations in playing technique, offer a plausible lineage for the sounds of Sun Ra and his Arkestra. But that's only half the story, of course: the Arkestra is a marching (literally) encyclopedia of black performance and spectacle. The roots for these elements go as far back as Herman Blount's exposure to precision marching at age ten as a member of the American Woodmen Junior Division, a Euro-American philanthropy for African-Americans comparable to the Boy Scouts (Szwed 9-10). The travelling big bands undoubtedly also showed performance tricks and techniques to an admiring youngster. All these elements entered into the mix of the Arkestra's development. By the time they held down Slug's tavern Monday nights in mid-sixties New York, all the elements of the Arkestra show were in place. As Szwed says:

> They were reasserting black performance values which were completely alien to white experience, conventions drawn from the church, the black cabaret, bar life, and the community picnic; they were reclaiming the aesthetics of those Amiri Baraka called the Blues People: honking and shrieking saxophones, bar walking, guitar play-

ing behind the head, eccentric dancers, capes and exotic costumes, weeping and pleading on bended knees, ecstatic states of speech and dance—the flash of the show, the elements which James Brown and Jimi Hendrix were startling whites with elsewhere: "They didn't know how to take us," [James] Jacson said. "As a bunch of drunks? Some slightly crazy people? A bunch of addicts? But whatever we were, they knew we were not broken men." (227-8)

Such were the main ingredients in the cosmo-drama's sound and look. But there were conceptual elements in it as well.

Was Sun Ra From Saturn?

As John Szwed ruefully acknowledges, much of the white critical discourse around Sun Ra inevitably genuflects at this tedious honky shrine: was Sun Ra a "genius," a "charlatan" or a "madman" (xvii)? Look at all the liner notes written by white critics for his various albums and CDs. However much they may admire Ra and his music, they feel compelled to bring this question up—even if only to dismiss it. They protest too much. Like those first concertgoers at Slug's, they still don't know how to take Ra, really.

I'd like to sidestep this minimally interesting question and address the far more compelling consideration of Ra's beliefs. James Jacson hits the nail on the head in the above quote when he asserts "they knew we were not broken men." Sun Ra's insistence that "[he] never felt like [he] was part of this planet" was an empowering one for him: as June Tyson would sing in the Arkestra, Ra became "the living myth" (Szwed 6).

I have an odd perspective on all this, because as a middle-schooler I briefly claimed I was from another planet! I parlayed somatic tricks such as the hereditary ability to make the pupils of my eyes vibrate, and some rhetorical skills, to maintain this ruse—frankly, as a gambit to get attractive lasses intrigued with me. Such a stratagem was compensation for my blue-collar origins and uncouth appearance. As we shall see, James Brown likewise compensated for his own hardscrabble origins by turning himself into a living myth; Elvis did the same. My own foray into self-mythology was briefer, because my circumstances were better than these other folks'. But for James Brown, Elvis Presley and especially Sun Ra, the persona was sustained seamlessly in public for much longer. Though Brown and Presley occasionally slipped, no one ever saw Ra drop the mask in a moment of fatigue—or at least no one ever reported seeing such a thing. He was the Man from Saturn 24/7. What do you call a persona that you adopt around the clock? An identity, I would think. Sun Ra was the only version of Herman Blount we were ever going to get to know. Only the squares were bothered by that; the rest of us got with the program and acknowledged the living myth. It was the only game in town—or more accurately, in the omniverse!

Although I shall return to Ra's sense of alienation (literally being an alien!) from his arrival in Birmingham, Alabama, a clear watershed moment in Ra's self-formulation was his narration of alien abduction in the late nineteen thirties. This foundational account is worth quoting at length:

> ...[T]hese space men contacted me. They wanted me to go to outer space with them. They were looking for somebody who had that type of mind. They said it was quite dangerous because you had to have perfect discipline ... . I'd have to go up with no parts of my body touching outside of the beam, because if I did, going through different time zones, I wouldn't be able to get that far back. So that's what I did. And it's like, well, it looked like a giant spotlight shining down on me, and I call it transmolecularization, my whole body was changed into something else. I could see through myself. And I went up. Now, I call that an energy transformation because I wasn't in human form. I thought I was there, but I could see through myself.
>
> Then I landed on a planet that I identified as Saturn. First thing I saw was something like a rail, a long rail of railroad track coming out of the sky, and landed over there in a vacant lot ... . Then I found myself in a huge stadium, and I was sitting in the last row, in the dark. I knew I was alone. They were down there, on the stage, something like a big boxing ring. So then they called my name, and I didn't move. They called my name again, and I still didn't answer. Then all at once they teleported me, and I was down there on that stage with them. They wanted to talk with me. They had one little antenna on each ear. A little antenna over each eye. They talked to me. They told me to stop [teachers' training] because there was going to be great trouble in schools. There was going to be trouble in every part of life. That's why they wanted to talk to me about it. "Don't have anything to do with it. Don't continue." They would teach me some things that when it looked like the world was going into complete chaos, when there was no hope for nothing, then I could speak, but not until then. I would speak, and the world would listen. That's what they told me.
>
> Next thing, I found myself back on planet Earth in a room with them, and it was the back room of an apartment, and there was a courtyard. They was all with me. At the time, I wasn't wearing robes. I had on one of theirs, they put on me. They said, "Go out

there and speak to them." And I looked out through the curtain and people were milling around in the courtyard. And I said, "No, they look like they're angry. I'm not going out there." So they pushed me through the curtain, and I found myself on a balcony, people milling around in the courtyard. They said, "They aren't angry, they're bewildered."

All of a sudden, the people were turning around, looking up to me on the balcony. (I was living in Chicago at that time.) I saw that I was laying down on a park bench, a stone park bench, in some park, near a river. There was a bridge. I knew it was New York City. I had done very well in Chicago and I thought that was one thing that could not happen. I looked and saw the sky was purple and dark red, and through that I could see the spaceships, thousands of them. And I sat up to look, then I heard a voice [say] "You can order us to land. Are conditions right for landing?" I think I said yes. They started to land, and there were people running to come to the landing, and they shot something like bullets. But they weren't bullets. They were something that when they hit the ground they were like chewing gum. It stuck people to the ground.

I came out of that. But [later] when I got to New York City, I was up near Columbia University. I saw the bench, I saw the bridge, so those things have been indelibly printed on my brain. I couldn't get them out if I tried. (in Szwed 29-30)

Both true believers in aliens and UFOs such as Whitley Streiber—as well as more skeptical analysts of UFO lore—have noted how UFO narratives like Ra's take on the coloration of the historical era in which they are experienced and recounted. From the Biblical claims of fiery wheels spinning in the air through the lore on goblins and fairies to the modern "grey" aliens in flying saucers, the variations of the tales produce a subject / object problem in accounting for the discrepancies. For example, John Keel posits thusly:

That unidentified flying objects have been present since the dawn of man is an undeniable fact. They are not only described repeatedly in the Bible, but were also the subject of cave paintings made thousands of years before the Bible was written. And a strange procession of weird entities and frightening creatures have been with us just as long. When you review the ancient references you are obliged to conclude that the presence of these objects and beings *is a normal condition for this planet*. These things, these other intelligences ... either reside here but somehow remain concealed from us, or they do not exist at all and are actually special aberrations of the human mind— ... hallucinations, psychological constructs, momentary materializations of energy from that dimension beyond the reach of our senses and even beyond the reaches of our scientific instruments. They are not from outer space. There is no need for them to be. They have always been here. (15, italics Keel's)

This speculation might strike the casual reader as wilder than Ra's claims, but Keel gives himself several empiricist escape clauses courtesy of abnormal psychology. I appreciate, however, that Keel makes room for these encounters betokening some kind of reality—if not necessarily the one claimed by the informant. For Ra's account is a creakily anachronistic one: its tales of interplanetary monorails and chewing gum weapons align it solidly with science fiction writers such as A. E. Van Vogt and Cordwainer Smith, as well as fifties alien contactees like George Adamski. It has E. H. Gombrich's "invisible style" of its historical moment. So do Gilgamesh and the Book of Ezekiel. This is not to debunk, but to acknowledge the subject / object blurring in these mysterious accounts. The archetypal tale must pass though its particular teller. As for its ontological status, we could pick up Julian Jaynes' *The Origin of Consciousness in the Breakdown of the Bicameral Mind* and say that it's a mental phenomenon that we are hardwired for; or we could believe that other entities are surreptitiously co-inhabiting our world. John Keel's most subversive insinuation is that it really doesn't matter which option we pick: either way something odd is going on. Sun Ra clearly leaned towards the latter explanation, but we needn't if we don't want to—and we can still respect his account.

As Szwed notes, this narrative also resembles "a conversion experience and a call to preach in the Afro-Baptist tradition" (31). From this epiphany, it all proceeded: Ra's cosmo-doctrines, the music, the costumes, the drama. Sun Ra was a teacher first and foremost. It never got as much in the way of his art as it did for poet Ezra Pound, but these two men shared a certain obsessive dedication to their respective projects—as well as associational habits of mind divergent enough from conventional modes of thinking to inspire accusations of insanity from the skeptical. I cannot hope to convey to the general reader the full scope of Ra's beliefs and doctrines (which shifted over time in any case), but I can at least reference some of his most recurrent observations and assumptions.

Most of Ra's beliefs have pedigrees in world religious and philosophical thought; they result from his voluminous reading with Alton Abraham in Chicago. For example, consider his central doctrine on birth and death:

...[I]t is important to liberate oneself from the obligation to be born, because this experience doesn't help us at all. It is important for the planet that its inhabitants do not believe in being born, because whoever is born has to die. (Szwed 6)

For Sun Ra, life and being were opposed values to the cycle of birth and death, where death always and inevitably triumphs (as he joked in "The Possibility of Altered Destiny" lecture, "Die" is the one commandment of the creator we haven't been able to break yet!). Ra believed that you could transcend this mortal cycle through attaining access to a more spiritual plane through discipline and, yes, music. He would ask audience members to "give up [their] death" for him and travel the spaceways. Otherwise, the unenlightened are trapped on and in a world of death.

This belief obviously resembles many doctrines in world religion, ranging from all forms of Platonism and Gnosticism to Hindu and Buddhist doctrines of reincarnation and satori. The importance of music for the task recalls the doctrines of Pythagoras; the emphasis on discipline for transcendence reminds one of the teachings of Gurdjieff and Ouspensky. Ra had read all of these people, in fact, as Szwed's biography and Ra in interview demonstrate. His teachings were a syncretistic synthesis of what he liked about each set of beliefs—a mix-and-match approach to philosophy and religion reminiscent of his predecessor Emerson.

Sun Ra's dismissal of Christianity was no doubt abetted by his exposure to and interest in the German philosopher Nietzsche (Corbett 221). Ra was most hung up on the significance of the crucifixion:

> ... [W]hatever they're doing ends up in the graveyard. Even the Son of God ended up in the graveyard. Now, how could they teach a limited philosophy or a limited position like that...?
>
> ... He came and went right to the cross and said, "This is what God wants you to do: follow me." Ever since then they've been dying. If the Son of God died, well, God didn't save His own son; how can anybody think He's gonna save anybody else? His Son had to buy death; so will everybody else. He just came and showed them the way ... the way not to go. (Szwed 303)

Using his semantic equations, Ra would proceed to link the cross with the letter "X," the cruciform, the Roman numeral for ten. "Ten" reversed is "net," which he linked with Christ's injunction to his disciples to be "fishers of men" (Matthew 4:19; Szwed 303). Ergo, for Ra the cross was a net to snare men into the path of death.

The manner in which Ra argues involves etymological investigation and punning. He believed that God hid the truth after the fall of the Tower of Babel by using "phonetics" to hide true meanings in the great codes of world language and the Bible (in Meltzer 247). The undoing of post-Babel chaos and confusion occurs by means of a playful attention to counter-meanings revealed by etymology, wordplay and palindromic reversal. As the "X / ten / net" progression shows, Ra had no problem hopping from one language to another to follow a lead.

Ra's project has resonances with the linguistic experimentations and procedures of such luminaries as James Joyce, Jacques Derrida and John Cage. Like these gentlemen's efforts, his demonstrations of the fluidity of thought and language are both highly playful and imposing. For one thing, Ra was the master linguistic sorcerer: he would not be amused when band members he was instructing attempted these procedures themselves (Szwed 98). His thought processes were highly spontaneous and improvisatory in the spirit of jazz. But he assumed only a true leader of men could deploy his subversive approach—whence the importance of his foundational vision / calling. Such a stance seems highly plausible for an intelligent and creative autodidact. Behind all the wit and bluster, there must have been some lingering insecurities masked by the rigorous disciplining of his musicians.

And indeed, as Ra's take on Christianity shows, there is ample cause for doubt. Ra's obsession with the crucifixion leads him to neglect the resurrection part of the Gospel narrative! Ironically, his own *contemptus mundi* neoplatonic stance seems very harmonious with Christian doctrine. But his concentration on the sacrifice of the Son by the Father—itself plausibly defended as heralding an end to the sacrificial order by Rene Girard in *Things Hidden Since the Beginning of Time*—blinds Sun Ra to other aspects of Christian doctrine he might find more congenial to his own formulations.

My purpose here is to explicate Ra's beliefs rather than to defend or attack them, but this seems as good a moment as any to say *caveat emptor*. There are lots of interesting nuggets of insight scattered in Ra's works, but also all the deficiencies and cul-de-sacs of the street intellectual. Danny Thompson's advice to "just check it out for yourself" is again germane. Sooner or later everyone except Ra disagrees with Ra; if you don't, you're just not paying attention!

With this warning given, let's return to more of Sun Ra's especially recurrent claims. He also believed that Earth was inhabited by disguised angels and demons that interact among us. Again, this is a doctrine with a rich pedigree. The teachings of Emmanuel Swedenborg come to mind immediately. Swedenborg also believed in this concealed celestial conflict; Ra seems to have additionally absorbed the Swedish mystic's doctrine that "it's after the end of the world" (from the album of the same name). Both Ra and the Church of the New Jerusalem believe the last judgment has already occurred: we're just living out a kind of cosmic endgame! I raise this more obscure second point only as proof that Ra was very familiar with Swedenborgian doctrine and unafraid of incorporating it into his own doctrinal mosaic.

Ra's interest in the hidden angels and demons manifested in album titles (*Angels and Demons at Play*), song titles ("A Call for All Demons," "Demon's

Lullaby") and the lyrics of space chants ("I know that I'm a member of the angel race / My home is over there in outer space" ["Angel Race," *Live from Soundscape* and elsewhere]). In a 1984 article in *Semiotexte*, Ra unpacked this belief at greatest length:

> You have to realize this planet is not only inhabited by humans, it's inhabited by aliens too. They got the books say they fell from heaven with Satan. So, in mixed up among humans you have angels. The danger spot is the United States. You have more angels in the country than anywhere else. You see, it was planned.
>
> I'll tell you something fantastic. It's unbelievable. They say that truth is stranger than fiction. Never in this history of the world has there been a case where you take a whole people and bring 'em into the country in the Commerce Department. Never before has that happened. It happened here. They bringing 'em in through the Commerce Department. It was possible for aliens and angels and devils and demons to come in this country. They didn't need no passport. So then they'd come in as displaced people. Perfect setup. So they come right on into the United States. They could come here and act like poor people, they could come here and act like slaves because they didn't keep up with what was happening. They just brought some people in ... and said Oh you, they is nothing, they beastly. They brought 'em in here and doin' that, they allowed anything to come here. (in Meltzer 246-7)

Perhaps it is easier to grapple with this narrative as parable or myth rather than literal truth revealed by Ra. After all, his suggestion that angels, demons and aliens would have been caught by immigration if they hadn't gone through the Commerce Department seems unlikely at best. More likely, this tale is about the African-American paradox. Sun Ra early on realized that the skin game of being black in America was one he couldn't win, so he changed the rules and repatriated himself as a Saturnian.[3] The narrative above attempts to help other African-Americans by dialectically juxtaposing a myth of self-empowerment (they could be actually aliens, demons or angels) with the existentially crushing historical reality of slavery. It offers a redemptive counter-history for the standard accounts of the African diaspora.

Ra dwelt on the diaspora only obliquely and always subversively. For instance, he told an African well-wisher who welcomed him "home" upon his January 1977 arrival in Nigeria that "Your people sold mine. This is no longer my home!" (Szwed 342). He preferred to emphasize the pre-diasporic glories of ancient Egypt and Africa and the future promise of the space age. What happened between in the present and recent past was an unpleasant time of travail.

He explained his ambivalence about black folks, which he typically dissociated himself from, to poet Henry Dumas through the use of his linguistic "equations." "Negro" also referred to "Necro," the word for death, and "NeCROW," a black bird. From there Ra could leap to another black bird, Edgar Allen Poe's raven. "Quoth the Raven 'Nevermore.'" And "Raven" backwards is "naver," which sounds like "never" (*The Ark and the Ankh*). In Ra's cosmology, contemporary black people are semantically rhymed with death, birds of ill-omen and ill-repute, and the spirit of negation itself.

He had other critiques of this ethnicity as well. Ra called them "block people" because they hindered his career (Szwed 366). In the film *Space Is the Place*, he hires an African-American street wino at his "Outer Space Employment Agency" to do "nothing" and be paid "nothing" since his qualifications are "nothing." Ra explained in interview about the film's message that he wanted to work with "black folks because they're priceless. They have no price. They're worthless. They ain't worth nothing. Priceless. Give them to me. That's in the film" (Szwed 332). As noted above, Ra threatens in the film to drag them in chains into outer space, if necessary. Ra is not a gentle redeemer of this race which he dissociated himself from. He once told Alton Abraham: "I hate black people ... . I don't know about white people. I don't know any. But I know I hate black people" (Corbett 176).

In fuller context, however, these disparaging racist and even misanthropic remarks are only one side of a two-sided dialectical coin. Black people are worthless AND aliens, angels, demons in disguise; powerless and empowered; slaves AND pharaohs. Ra himself is from Saturn AND at times an African-American ("Your people sold *mine*," italics added). Every African-American intellectual has had to confront this double heritage / inheritance / identity of pride and shame: W.E.B. Du Bois, James Baldwin, Richard Wright, Paule Marshall, Toni Morrison, Malcolm X and, yes, James Brown. Ra's mythic rewrites of self, history, and ethnicity show how he negotiated these treacherous existential shoals, how he "got over." Who are we to gainsay his myths if we haven't had his experiences growing up in early twentieth-century Birmingham, Alabama?

Fortunately for Ra, he was not alone. He had a musical family and body of disciples: the Arkestra. Sun Ra has explicated some of the connotations of the name he gave his "outer space orchestra":

> "A covenant of Arkestra": it's like a selective service of God. Picking out some people. Arkestra has a "ra" at the beginning and the end ... . Ra can be written as "Ar" or "Ra," and on both ends of the word it is an equation: the first and the last are equal ... . That's phonetic balance ... . Besides, ... that's the way black people say

"orchestra." (Szwed 94)

John Szwed adds a few other references besides the obvious one to the Ark of the Covenant. The Egyptian sun god Ra had a solar boat or ark. "Kest" in the middle of the name evokes "kist" as in "Sunkist"—kissed by the sun. In Sanskrit, "kist" means "sun's gleam" (94). I would additionally add the very obvious reference to Noah's ark: the Arkestra is on a mission to transport black people (and eventually all followers) safely to outer space before planetary destruction occurs. (This scenario is played out literally in the film *Space Is the Place*.) I also find Ra's reference to the selective service interesting, since he was a conscientious objector during World War II. Rather than play by the white man's rules, Ra devised an alternate draft for worthy musicians. This parallelism in effect resembles similar trends such as black freemasonry. I won't be the first to observe that the Arkestra in performance looked like extraterrestrial Shriners!

By now one can readily see that there was a great degree of esoteric doctrine and pedagogy behind the music and the visual cosmo-drama of this band in performance. Not surprisingly, Ra's mysterious presence spawned miraculous tales, some repeated enough with variations to suggest urban legends. There are many stories of the Arkestra's playing ostensibly causing electrical failures; Ra would even take such outages as indications that they "got it right" (Szwed 125). Most auspiciously, the lights in the Great Pyramid went out when Ra approached the King's Chamber on a tour (Szwed 293). Several accounts describe audience members claiming that the Arkestra was playing "God's music" or "the forbidden sacred music" of India. In these anecdotes, Ra always responds "That's what I hear" (Szwed 180, 221). Finally, Ed Michel (one of the band's producers) recounts the Ra contingent's ability to call him before he could dial a number to call them. He'd just pick up the phone, on numerous occasions, and they'd already be there (liner notes, *The Great Lost Sun Ra Albums*). All of this certainly adds to the legendary status of the band and its leader. Then there's the music, readily available from Amazon and other sellers, or on Youtube and Google.

Some Omniversal Listening Suggestions

For several reasons, I am not going to proceed as I did in the Zappa chapter with a ranking of Ra's recordings. The most practical one is that only a handful of people—and I am not one of them—have them all. The Saturn releases were too obscure and backdoor an operation for gaps not to appear in the most ardent Ra collector's holdings. As it is, I will be referring here to many releases which you will only be able to obtain at the most serendipitous of yard / estate

We Travel Ra's Spaceways 339

sales, off e-bay or at a vintage vinyl store (in the latter two cases, at exorbitant prices). The good news is that much first-rate Sun Ra is available easily, and more is being made available as we speak—largely due initially to the Evidence label in Pennsylvania, which contracted to undertake massive reissues of the original Saturn recordings. Other labels have since come on board with both old and previously unissued Ra music: John Corbett's Unheard Music series, Leo records, Art Yard and Transparency.

A second reason for less thoroughness is the reduced status of the recorded artifact for Sun Ra. There are reasons for this tied in with African-American and jazz aesthetic preferences. Like James Brown, Ra eschewed Euro-American linearity and progression in favor of repetition and circularity (Rose 120). Arkestra trumpeter Lucious Randolph describes this proclivity on the level of the individual composition:

> Sonny gave his drummers long solos ... and sometimes asked them to play the same thing over and over until you could hear something else in it. You'd ask him, "How long is this going to go on?" and Sonny would answer, "I'm trying to tell you something else ... like, if you keep eating peach pie every day, [sooner or later] it's going to taste like something else." (Szwed 144)

Ra's career was cyclic on the macroscopic level as well. The classic Ra show (as it certainly developed by the mid-seventies) had a circular structure as well: an invocation of Ra by the band and June Tyson, ecstatic soloing by the Arkestra to scare off the musically timid, a space sermon from Ra like "I, Pharaoh" or "Discipline 27-II" (optional—if Sun Ra was in a good mood), a blend of jazz classics (from Fletcher Henderson, Todd Dameron, Duke Ellington and even Thelonious Monk and Miles Davis) and classic Ra compositions ("Lights on a Satellite," "Fate in a Pleasant Mood"), closing space chants and a prolonged exit involving the band circling through the audience, offstage and onstage again (usually to the tune of "We Travel the Spaceways" or "Space Is the Place"). In other words, the shows began and ended with the space material framing a more conventional jazz concert. And then on to the next gig. This is not to deny that Ra introduced variations into this outline, but to suggest that there was a basic structure. You can hear it quite clearly on the 1976 recording *Live at Montreux* or 1983's *Love in Outer Space: Live in Utrecht*—or any of the more documentary-like recordings of live performances.

Larger cycles in the career included his occasional emphases upon synthesizers, organ or solo piano. At certain times he would get into a groove relying upon one of these instruments especially for awhile, give it up more or less, and then return to it. This can be heard when you listen to the recordings chronologically. And Ra's biggest cyclic act was to record shortly before his death a tribute to Stuff Smith, the violinist he played with on his earliest recording "Deep Purple." On this later session, he even re-recorded it. Sun Ra had come full circle.

This sense of a long project unfolding, combined with every musician's tendency to privilege live performance, meant that Ra had less fetishistic regard for the recording process or its results. Saturn recordings are markedly casual: one hears tape recorders being turned on, phones ringing in the background, abrupt starts and stops. The idea of producing a concept album that would take the listener on a narrative journey was alien to Ra; the records were audio souvenirs of live musical events. One finds a similar attitude in James Brown's recorded work. James thought more on the level of the individual studio track than the album, which is why only his live albums (like some of Ra's) have a feeling of development at all (circular though they might be, live shows at least have to end!). Neither Ra nor Brown gave us a *Sergeant Pepper*—or wanted to.[4] It would take a later African-American artist like Prince to want to attempt such a development (especially on *The Rainbow Children*).

All by way of saying that Sun Ra's recordings merit discussion more for the quality of the songs on them than the albums as conceptual wholes. The best releases contain a critical mass of superb material, but overall Ra beckons the collector to shuffle the material onto customized mix tapes.

As with Frank Zappa, all of Ra's music is extraordinary. The gap between his "best" stuff and his least interesting material is small, so one personally negotiates to what extent Sun Ra is a musical seasoning in a record / CD collection or a source of fetishistic pursuit. I don't think one can own just a single Sun Ra recording (Evidence's greatest hits single CD is ultimately a genial in-joke directed at real Arkestra aficionados). Since you can't own them all, let me point to what I think are some landmark recorded musical moments, arranged chronologically to show the band's development.

The Chicago Years (1948 - 1960)

Sound Sun Pleasure!! (1958, reissued by Evidence in 1991) is a good place to start any Ra listening voyage. It contains his earliest "Sun Ra" recordings as bonus tracks. I have already referred several times to "Deep Purple" with Stuff Smith; the vocal ballad "Dreams Come True" is also remarkable because of the gentle surrealism of its lyrics delivered by Clyde Williams (with a classic Billy Eckstine voicing). Off the original album, "Enlightenment " stands out as Ra's earliest standard. Destined to be performed throughout his long career, this jaunty tune (co-written with trumpeter Hobart Dotson) appears in its early instrumental guise. The lack of words in this early rendition is more than compensated for by the wild generic shifts in the presentation of the melody: now it's a cha-cha, now it's a march. Other highlights include "Back in Your Own Backyard," an ironically terrestrial sentiment for Ra, and a samba version of Lerner & Lowe's "I Could Have Danced All Night" that provides a showcase for the Arkestra's innovative use of flute textures (probably from Marshall Allen, but not credited as such). For Sun Ra, this is a very accessible and mainstream recording; but already the novice listener will detect a different approach to music than she has ever heard before.

Our next stop would be the *Sun Ra Visits Planet Earth / Interstellar Low Ways* twofer on Evidence (from 1957-1960 sessions). "Interplanetary Music" especially hits the main vein with Ronnie Boykins managing to make his bowed bass sound like a trumpet. The vocals for this song are beyond belief: doom-laden yet archly signifying space-age camp that you dare not laugh at. The Arkestra would do this for over three decades, but the tone is struck early here. "Interstellar Low Ways" is a lush mood piece for flute and soft percussion which also became a Ra standard.

In 1960, the last year the Arkestra was based in Chicago, several notable recording sessions were produced. *Fate in a Pleasant Mood* contains several Ra compositions destined to be revisited often over the years. The title track hits upon the major philosophical theme of changing your destiny (presumably to the alter-destiny) by finding fate in a pleasant mood. The various catchy riffs in the song could be extended in live rendition as long as desired; its conclusion often resulted in an Arkestral promenade around the performance space.

"Lights on a Satellite" from the same session shows the lush influence of Duke Ellington; its main flute melody mimics the spinning lights on the orbiting object. This composition is outer space program music perfectly in line with the zeitgeist of sputnik and Telstar. (I can recall going out at night in a much less polluted Milwaukee and being able to see these objects in the heavens—and wanting to see them as a great novelty!) Ronnie Boykins again delivers impressive arco bass. The piece's main theme resembles the alien melody enough in *Close Encounters of the Third Kind* (1977) to lead Ra admirers to suspect homage (or plagiarism) from Steven Spielberg / John Williams, but I fear it's just a happy coincidence. How sad, though, that the makers of science fiction films never realized what a goldmine these Ra compositions could have been as instant scores. I predict some day this oversight will be spectacularly rectified.

In typically mercurial fashion, Ra also recorded some jazz standards on the same day as his futuristic compositions, later released as *Holiday for Soul Dance*. The whole CD is wonderfully accessible, but a live recording of "Early Autumn" (from a slightly later gig that year) is nothing short of sublime because of Ricky Murray's dramatic vocals and John Gilmore's haunting tenor saxophone solo. Amidst the adventurous sonic exploration, Ra never forgets to remind you that he can be a better jazz traditionalist than those who never leave that idiom.

The New York Years (1961-1968)

Although Sun Ra and the Arkestra returned to New York City periodically for the rest of their respective lives to play live and make recordings, these eight years mark the extent of their actual residence in the Big Apple. They were appropriately based in the East Village, Alphabet City, at 48 East Third Street (Szwed 194). Paralleling the biography to the music, one could similarly note that although Ra made post-avant-garde gestures at least until the mid-1980s, the New York years marked the height of the band's experimentation. They equaled the musical events of those years, but they never surpassed them. Disciplined by a regular Monday night slot at Slug's tavern in the same area where they lived, the band developed a truly fierce energy which fortunately shows up even on the recordings. When drummer Tommy "Bugs" Hunter returned from Sweden and heard the Arkestra in 1965, he marveled that "It was like a fire storm coming off the bandstand" (Szwed 212).

You can hear this new attitude from the first recording made on the east coast, *The Futuristic Sounds of Sun Ra* (1961; Newark, New Jersey; on the Savoy label). The key moment of paradigm shift is on a track aptly entitled "The Beginning." (Like James Brown, who knew he was inventing a new genre when he called his first funk single "Papa's Got a Brand New Bag," Ra must have sensed the importance of the occasion.) "The Beginning" is an extended percussion experiment with fabulous guest congas contributed by Leah Ananda from Kashmir. It inaugurates a spatial approach to the music, a use of the band to create sonic landscapes rather than merely to play a melody and then offer solo variations on it (which, of course, Ra and the Arkestra always continued to do as well). There IS no melody discernible on this track, only rhythms and textures—a jazz equivalent of what Edgard Varese was doing in the 1920s as an avant-garde classicist. "The Beginning" offers a paradigm shift, and is the most important part of an overall wonderful session that features other fine tracks (including more vocals from Ricky Murray on "China Gate," the theme from the Sam Fuller film).

The following year brought several landmark recordings. *Art Forms of Dimensions Tomorrow* featured another experiment in sonic space, "The Outer Heavens." This composition has no drums, only a rhythmic piano accompanying reeds and trumpet. The music evokes floating bodies weightless in deep space, very reminiscent of Varese's turning crystalline sound structures. You can see this music if you let it take you where it wants to. Marshall Allen goes wild on alto sax; Ra's piano work demonstrates an energy that has led many jazz enthusiasts to compare him to Cecil Taylor (when he's in this mode of playing).

Secrets of the Sun (recorded in 1962, released in 1965) also finds Sun Ra and His Solar Arkestra (the name then) transitioning between the tight arrangements that characterized the Chicago years and the more open form explorations of the New York period. "Friendly Galaxy" and "Solar Differentials" are extraterrestrial versions of Les Baxter exotica (the latter highlighting "space bird sounds," Art Jenkins' "space voice" and reverb drenches from Tommy Hunter's tape recorder tricks). "Space Aura" is a piece originally from the Chicago days, but it is executed at "a psychotropically slow tempo" (as Ra scholar John Corbett accurately says in the liner notes to the CD reissue.

An early version of "Love in Outer Space" features John Gilmore wailing on bass clarinet for a change—and lots of "space drums." This piece would become a Ra standard whose gorgeous melody would be performed over the entire career; in later incarnations, it provided a showcase for extended Afrocentric drumming.

"Reflects Motion" offers a great showcase for Gilmore's more typical tenor saxophone and fine drum interplay between Tommy Hunter and C. Scoby Stroman. "Solar Symbols" ends the original album with a pure percussion workout.

The CD adds a long bonus track "Flight to Mars," which was intended for the entire B side of an unreleased El Saturn long-player. It begins with a blast-off crescendo and Gilmore enthusing "all the way into space" before a tape edit transitions into stretched-out swinging and extended soloing from Marshall Allen on flute, Scoby Stroman on heavy drumming, Calvin Newborn on scintillating and subtle electric guitar and Ronnie Boykins bowing away on the upright bass. After seventeen minutes and thirty-five seconds of this solid groove, the tape abruptly ends. In length at least, this track presages wilder journeys to come.

The breakthrough recording of this year, however, is *When Sun Comes Out*. This is the first release where the experiments dominate the proceedings. "Circe" begins with big gongs played by Ra leading into Yma Sumac vocal stylings from Theda Barbara. (Ra's interest in Les Baxter is quite evident here.) "The Nile" provides more thick atmosphere with lots of percussion and Marshall Allen on flute. "Brazilian Sun" gives us Latin piano and percussion.

Then we leave our tour of the ancient world and head out into outer space! This journey is appropriately inaugurated with "We Travel the Spaceways," the space chant destined to close many an Arkestra concert. This is the definitive version, fully developed instrumentally and, as they say with a new meaning when applied to the Ra project, "far out." The soloing sure sounds free, even if it's scripted. "Calling Planet Earth" keeps up the pressure with echo-laden drums and Pat Patrick playing the baritone sax as if it's an alien message communicated to earthlings. The band plays slightly more conventionally on the next two tracks ("Dancing Shadows" and "The Rainmaker"), but the reed solos keep threatening to collapse the structures. "The Rainmaker" concludes with an early example of the space key / chord, a burst of noise worthy of the most discordant gestures of Charles Ives. The title track really cuts loose with outside horn work, piano played as a rhythm instrument with the drums, a squiggly Danny Davis alto solo and Walter Miller's trumpet on top of the proceedings. "Dimensions in Time" concludes this landmark session with John Gilmore playing a rare (and sporadically honking!) bass clarinet with the percussion section. The trajectory of the Arkestra's future experimentation was already cast as early as these 1962 recordings. What followed would extend their innovative discoveries.

Such is literally the case with "Next Stop Mars" off *When Angels Speak of Love* (1963). This track is the earliest in a series of sound sculptures long enough to fill the side of a long-playing album. It begins as a space chant, then proceeds to serious sonic experimentation: Cecil-Taylor-style piano from Ra, intense saxophone soloing by Allen (alto), Gilmore (tenor) and Pat Patrick (baritone).The solos are interspersed with wild echo effects produced by "Bugs" Hunter. He had discovered that he could achieve these results by recording with earphones on and running a cable from an output jack back into the input for the recorder. Without the headphones, only feedback would result; with the headphones on he could obtain massive reverb and control its speed by adjusting the volume on the tape recorder (Szwed 187). These effects made the music sound like it was being beamed into your stereo from a distant galaxy. "Next Stop Mars" was pre-psychedelic psychedelia.

In 1964, John Gilmore had a brief falling out with Sun Ra and the Arkestra. Immersed in the New York jazz scene, he thought he heard a lot of musicians stealing his ideas and making a lot more money when they played them in various venues. So he took a break from the group and toured Europe with Art Blakey's Jazz Messengers. It turned out that he had too big of an ego for Blakey to deal with, so he returned to the Arkestra in 1965 and stayed with the band for the rest of his life except for a few brief side projects (Szwed, *Space* 204-5, 213). This state of affairs led to Pharaoh Sanders, a much better known tenor saxophonist than Gilmore, joining the Arkestra. (Any Ra fan will tell you Gilmore is as good as or better than Sanders, but Pharaoh has more name recognition because of his distinguished solo career.)

The results of this realignment can be heard on *Sun Ra Featuring Pharaoh Sanders and Black Harold* (a flautist), an ESP Disk recording of a New Year's Eve 1964 concert at New York's Judson Hall (long unavailable on vinyl, but reissued in 2009 with 45 minutes of additional material). This is fabulous music, although one can tell that despite the brilliance of Pharaoh Sanders, Gilmore was a better fit for this band. Black Harold (Harold Murray) is arguably the more intriguing new sonic seasoning. On "The Now Tomorrow," his interplay with Sun Ra (playing piano and celeste at the same time)—later joined by Ronnie Boykins and Alan Silva (both on bass)—is remarkably nuanced and sensitive to the other musicians. When you add Art Jenkins' "space voice" to all of this. you have an improvised composition that is both wonderful and strange.[5] Jenkins also contributes spooky vocalese to "Discipline 9" (really a version of "We Travel The Spaceways"). "The Voice of Pan" offers more ethereal flute from Black Harold. When he intones into his flute some vocal stylings in the spirit of Rahsaan Roland Kirk (why should Jenkins have all the fun?), you can hear nervous laughter from the audience. This stuff sounds pretty unusual today; in late 1964, it was almost indescribable, as A. B. Spellman (the reviewer of the concert for *The Nation*) conceded: "how to render a sympathetic appraisal for what was one of the most exciting [concerts in the] series without making this group seem either utterly insane or sickeningly corny? ... well, you had to be there" (Szwed 206).

The Magic City (1965) continued Ra's experimentations, especially in its 27 minute title cut. This was collective improvisation, organized by hand signals to cue the individual Arkestra members to play certain prearranged sequences or effects (a method very similar to Frank Zappa's method of conducting). The result is musical freedom with a hidden structure. "The Magic City" was never performed in concert later: as John Gilmore said, it was "unreproducible, a tapestry of sound" (Szwed 214). Its title paid homage to the nickname of Birmingham, Alabama (Ra's terrestrial point of entry). But it also suggested an exotic realm of urban enchantment, closer to what you hear in the music. This piece sounds more like Samuel R. Delany's cities (in novels such as *Dhalgren*) than its ostensible referent. Still there is no doubt that Birmingham seen through the eyes of a youngster could be magical, especially if that child were Sun Ra.

The composition begins with the use of clavioline, a gentle electronic keyboard Ra favored at the time. A section of flutes come in imitating bird song. Gradually there is interplay among a baritone sax, arco bass and the clavioline; then more birdsong. John Gilmore and Danny Davis give reed solos of augmenting chaos, eventually joined by a whole saxophone ensemble simultaneously soloing. At around 24 minutes in, the sound thins to clavioline, piano and bass. At around 26:50, there is a final blast of the space key and a fade. You've been on an interesting journey and glimpsed a landscape, if not necessarily one in Dixie!

The Magic City recording also features "The Shadow World," a sporadic concert favorite with a torturously fast melody line for a bevy of saxes (its signature riff). The piece refers to Ra's quasi-Swedenborgian belief that other dimensions coexisted with ours. The spiritually attuned individual could catch glimpses of these other realms as shadows in our world. Ra also revealed that it's musically a serial composition deploying a twelve tone row (Szwed, liner notes for *The Magic City*). Ra's adaptation of Schoenberg's methods illustrates how far the band was moving from the sound of a jazz ensemble. Once in a guest lecture on modernism and postmodernism, I played an excerpt from the similarly adventurous "Atlantis" (see below). A room full of bright students took a very long time to guess its genre. They ventured jazz as an option after essaying classical and rock—only prior to country and western. To their ears, and that of many other listeners, Ra's music sounded like the farthest thing imaginable from jazz—especially as it is pumped out on digital music services. Like other composers such as Anthony Braxton, Sun Ra was beginning to create sound textures in a region somewhere between big-band jazz and twentieth-century avant-garde European classical. (For some of Ra's releases, you'd want to add a third musical lineage of sixties psychedelia achieved, like Zappa's, without the use of any chemicals.) *The Magic City*, and a few other releases of the years 1965-1968, offer clear aural evidence for this claim.

The Heliocentric Worlds of Sun Ra (Volumes 1 and 2) from 1965, for example, are avant-garde chamber jazz: a smaller version of the Arkestra playing meditative and complex compositions as close to Anton Webern as they are to Duke Ellington. The suitably named "Cosmic Chaos" off the second volume offers an early example of the reed battle royals that would constitute a significant portion of the Arkestra's music in performance and recorded legacy. Although Ra aficionados have their favorite examples of this routine, the sonic contours from one to the next are fairly consistent. The battle royals essentially consist of the reed section delivering highly athletic performances on their saxophones, soloing both serially and (sometimes) simultaneously. As good tone scientists, they use the saxophone in ways never imagined or intended by its developer: pushing the reed into making sounds at frequencies guaranteed to bother dogs, or using sustained circular breathing to keep the sound going. This rather free jazz in effect explored all the sounds one could get out of the sax. Its sonic vocabulary was not only extended but seemingly exhausted. I haven't heard any new ways to play it since the innovations of this decade.[6]

In May of 1966, Bernard Stollman arranged for the Arkestra to tour colleges in New York state with other avant-garde acts on his record label. Stollman was the owner of ESP Disk which Ra was now also recording for (the *Heliocentric Worlds* series) in addition to his own El Saturn releases. (ESP, by the way, refers to the invented Esperanto language—another Stollman interest—not extrasensory perception. Ra would have loved this linguistic serendipity, of course.) Forty minutes of one of the concerts at St. Lawrence University in Potsdam came out on ESP vinyl in 1969 as *Nothing Is* (Szwed, 237). In 2010, ninety additional minutes of the Potsdam shows came out on CD as *College Tour Volume I: The Complete Nothing Is ...* . (This numbering suggests more is to come!)

One of the highlights of the original release was "Exotic Forest," a loping percussion exploration augmented by Marshall Allen's North-African inflected oboe accompaniment. The result is an aural equivalent of Henri Rousseau's painting *The Dream* (which Ra had no doubt admired at New York's Museum

We Travel Ra's Spaceways 347

of Modern Art). On this expanded version, there are many additional delights including a long, subdued take on "The Satellites Are Spinning" and two highly obscure piano-driven nonce pieces ("Nothing Is" [which was NOT on the original *Nothing Is*] and "Is Is Eternal"). The college audience is attentive and supportive: 1966 was truly a year poised to embrace any new cultural idea. On the cusp of the incrementally radical years that ended the decade, it seemed that ANYTHING was possible. You could walk from your dorm room into a concert hall and see black people from outer space wearing exotic costumes and blaring "Interplanetary Chaos" (an aptly titled improvisation on the expanded release).

The recent reissue of the hitherto rare *Strange Strings* set confirms that 1965-67 of the New York years showcased the most extreme experiments of an always-adventurous band (no date on the reissue, but the liner notes are dated 2006). I agree with Ra Scholar Hal Rammel that this 1966 recording should be linked with *The Magic City* (1965) and *Atlantis* (1967) as a trilogy of "master works" of epic proportions (liner notes, *Strange Strings*). The recording begins with "Worlds Approaching," an uncanny and atonal alien processional march, chock full of reverb and distortion. Ra even plays on a metal sculpture in homage to creators of sound sculpture such as Bernard and Francois Baschet, who were displaying their work at the Museum of Modern Art at the time. It is instructive to compare this piece with Zappa's processionals for the Grand Wazoo bands (including "Regyptian Strut"). Zappa sounds like muzak compared to this sublime feast reminiscent of more ominous and mysterious alien encounters like those in *2001* and *The Fifth Element*.

The aliens arrive in the remaining tracks. "Strings Strange" and "Strange Strange" are the result of Sun Ra's going to music stores and import shops in the city and buying up all manner of exotic stringed instruments—none of which his band knew how to play! They built a few more homemade ones as well, including sheet metal constructions that could produce thunderous noise. He called this "a study in ignorance." He was interested in the effect of highly trained musicians being put on a level playing field, all disadvantaged, with unfamiliar instruments. He was also thinking about how stringed instruments can emotionally affect listeners "in a special way" (Szwed, *Space* 237-8). He wanted to see if this communication could occur under these odd laboratory conditions with the aid of his aptly named "tone scientists" (often his preferred name for the musicians of the Arkestra).

The results? Hal Rammel tries to deliver program notes in the CD booklet, but I think there are some things language just can't accomplish. But I'll try: the truest statement is that this is like nothing you've ever heard before (or will hear since). It sounds like classical music from an alien civilization. Or, to be more banal, it evokes Sun Ra moving into the territory of Harry Partch— the maverick composer who built his own instruments (as here, mostly strings and percussion) and invented his own 32 note microtonal scale (because, yeah, exotic microtones abound). You know you're out there sonically when Arthur Jenkins' space vocals (lip-vibrating and "gargling" into various tubes and cylinders) are a reassuringly familiar strangeness (Rammel). At least we've heard this kind of oddity before in Ra's canon ... .

The surprise here is that this is not chaos. Ra is conducting them: structures and patterns emerge. These are improvised compositions, not mere noodling. Along with Ra's conducting, kudos should go to Clifford Jarvis on percussion and Ronnie Boykins on bass for laying down a focal groove for everything else to dance around. The results are sublime in the sense the Romantics intended, exactly the kind of sonic adventure I promised in the title of this book.

The reissue clinches the deal by an even more bizarre bonus track from the same sessions, "Door Squeak." This features Ra playing a squeaky door in the studio! He revels in its mix of gritty lows and high piercing tones, playing it like a "Mini-Moog" synthesizer (Rammel). Over the course of this ten-minute exploration, percussion and "strange strings" are eventually added to the piece. At this point in his musical development, Ra clearly felt almost anything was possible sonically. From a completely different background, he had come to embrace convictions similar to those of John Cage. (The difference, as oft noted, is that John became more minimalist as Ra became more maximalist.)

Then there's *Atlantis* (1967), the high-water mark (ouch) of the Arkestra's experimentalism. The major title work extends the discoveries of "Next Stop Mars" and "The Magic City" by fusing musical intensity with genuine program music. Apocalyptic program music, in fact, as Michael Shore asserts in the CD liner notes. You can hear the destruction of Atlantis conveyed through music. Given Ra's apocalyptic proclivities in interview, we are invited to read the fate of Atlantis as an allegory of what's in store for at least America, and most likely Planet Earth. As Ra told a French interviewer in 1984, we have to "turn or burn" (*Mystery, Mr. Ra*)

"Atlantis" begins, after a brief drum burst, with electronic keyboard beeps that various listeners have construed as either alarms or sonar pings probing the depths of the ocean in search of the lost city before flashing back to its destruction (the James Cameron reading of the composition). In either case, we transition into a highly theatrical keyboard meltdown on organ that certainly suggests massive sonic flooding. Eleven minutes into the piece Ra's Farfisa organ solo abruptly ends; at 11:30, a brooding French horn comes in. The keyboard returns soloing in a quieter fashion as if to offer a requiem for the initial catastrophe. At 13:30, the keyboard builds up again, giving us the aftershocks. At 15:30 a trombone comes in, followed by other horns playing a doom-laden theme. After 16:10, the horn section sounds exhausted by the crisis. (Ra discographer Robert Campbell has described this sound as the Arkestra doing Guy Lombardo [Shore, liner notes for *Atlantis*].) After 17:30, the keyboard returns for more electronic blasts, followed by percussion. The postmodern coup de grace happens at 21:25 when the Arkestra sings "Sun Ra, and his band, from outer space, have entertained you here": the apocalypse and/as show biz schtick. As the track fades, we hear the opening riff for a concluding "We Travel the Spaceways." This astonishing piece was recorded live at the Olatunji Center of African Culture, an utterly remarkable nonce event (Szwed 432).

The Transparency label has recently issued a double CD of the band live in early 1968 at New York's Electric Circus nightclub and at the Newport Jazz Festival in 1969 (after the move to Philadelphia). The sound quality is substandard, bootleg level (from audience tapes). But if you can overlook that deficiency, there is some interesting music on these discs. Newport reveals a version of "Shadow World" played at warp speed—the fastest reading of this lightning-paced piece that I've ever heard. The New York set has a 25 minute "untitled improvisation" with lots of electronic keyboard washes, and a reading of "Space Aura" that allows Gilmore to burn the zoo down with some wild soloing (to the amusement of the audience). As such. a fitting end to the highly formative New York years of the Arkestra.

The Philadelphia Years and the Arkestra on World Tour (1968-1992)

Studio Work (1968-1970)

In the fall of 1968, Sun Ra and the Arkestra moved into a row house in Philadelphia owned by Marshall Allen's father. Their East Village digs were drawing noise complaints from the neighbors, and the landlord was in the process of selling the property (Szwed 266). But who could have imagined that the house at 5626 Morton Street in the Germantown section of Philly would become the Arkestra's home for a quarter of a century (and beyond)? The band still played and recorded in New York on a regular basis—to say nothing of grueling global touring that took them all over the United States and to Mexico, Canada, Western and Eastern Europe, Russia, Egypt, Sub-Saharan Africa and Japan. But there was always a home base to come to, no matter how raggedy and dilapidated it might be at any given moment. For throughout this quarter century, there were never flush times. Although the perks for any given performance date could be flattering, the Arkestra's financial status was always in peril. Like Fletcher Henderson and Duke Ellington before him, Sun Ra learned how to keep a big band on the road—a miracle of economic and existential levitation.

These first years after the move were the time when Ra recorded *The Solar-Myth Approach (Volumes 1 and 2)*. I have already discussed the second volume, the first Ra recording I ever purchased in the opening section of this chapter. Volume 1 contains "Seen III, Took 4." Along with "Scene 1, Take 1" off Volume 2 and the *My Brother the Wind* sessions (all 1969-1970), these are Ra's earliest recordings with Moog synthesizers. Like Edgard Varese before him, Ra was obsessed with the possibilities of the new electronic instruments duplicating potentially any sound. The synthesizer, however crudely, offered the promise of musical creation *ex nihilo*: if you could imagine it, you could program it and play it. These first recordings are humble efforts compared to what Ra could accomplish as the synthesizer itself expanded its capacities. (For instance, listen to the rich textures Ra could even get in live performance on a later recording such as *A Night in East Berlin* [1986].)

But Ra's synthesizer work has always been compelling. He used the synthesizer from the first as a sonic sketchpad to delineate his intergalactic visions. It was a bold accent in his concerts. He never tried to tame it like other jazz musicians such as Herbie Hancock and George Duke did. Although he could make it "swing," he never treated it as just another jazz keyboard to vamp on. Ra dared to outrage his audience with sublime celestial fire and thunder to a far greater extent than even psychedelic space-rock groups dared. (Nothing in Pink Floyd's or Hawkwind's catalogue matches the intensity of some of Ra's efforts.) If he risked leaving the jazz idiom altogether (although he was retaining its improvisatory aspect), so be it. Jazz was never more than a means to an end for Ra in any case.

My Brother the Wind, Volume 2 also features a few haunting Ra ballads. "Somebody Else's World" showcases June Tyson doing a modest version of Yma Sumac vocalese. Its lyrics are resolutely neoplatonic / Gnostic:

> "Somebody else's idea of somebody else's world / Is not my idea of things as they are."

"Walking on the Moon" is a tribute to the Apollo 11 moon landing and a warning to black folks to get with the space age:

> "If you wake up now / It won't be too soon."

One of Ra's baritone saxophonists contributes a sultry solo. (Danny Thompson? Or Pat Patrick? Information regarding personnel, let alone who's soloing, is typically sparse.)

Night of the Purple Moon (1970) is one of the best instrumental studio albums from the beginning of this era of the Arkestra, showcasing a return to a more concise approach to composition and a funkier aspect that would linger through the 1970s. Sun Ra was willing to engage the same issues as James Brown and

Parliament / Funkadelic, albeit in his own distinctive manner. This outing also showcases a much smaller quartet version of the band: Sun Ra on keyboards (especially his new favorite, the gritty Roksichord [sic: the manufacturer called it a Rocksichord]); John Gilmore mostly on drums for a change; Danny Davis alternating among sax, clarinet, flute and more percussion; and Stafford James on electric bass. On the first side of the album (tracks 4-6 on the CD), Ra solos on two Mini-Moogs simultaneously with very sinuous and funky results.

The title track is light instrumental funk with a shimmering Roksichord keyboard leading the way. "A Bird's Eye View of Man's World" follows, emulating sudden aviary motions and offering wonderful bass work from Stafford James. "21st Century Romance" has a giant and insistent bass beat in the back and marvellous soloing by Danny Davis on alto. Then comes "Dance of the Living Image" with its way out bongo exotica and more Roksichord. The album concludes with a version of "Love in Outer Space" reinvigorated by alternate timbres: roksichord, Danny Davis' alto, jaunty percussion from John Gilmore and Danny Davis (doing double duty).

First European and African Tours (1970-1971)

The onset of the Arkestra's extensive touring in the early seventies led to the production of many live recordings. Some of these were issued contemporaneously; other sets, like the material in the vaults of activist / music promoter John Sinclair, have just shown up in the last few years as his personal affairs have begun to settle down. *Nuits de la Fondation Maeght, Volume 1* is the better half of a double release commemorating two August 1970 concerts in St.-Paul-de-Vence, France. This concert gives you a fine reading of Ra's classic "Enlightenment" and the lovely melody of "The Star Gazers." "The Shadow World" receives an intense workout with wild and sustained hocketing from the reed section and massive solos from everyone until blasts from the Moog and the space chord offer closure. "The Cosmic Explorer" is a long nonce Moog solo, augmented by percussion and Ra doing some doubling up on organ. He does indeed sound like he's exploring the cosmos in this engaging event.

Two later fall concerts in Germany from the same year have been collected on the double CD *Black Myth / Out in Space*. The latter disk is of special interest. The Arkestra typically began their concerts with group improvisation before settling into completely composed material. At 37 exuberant minutes, the opening title track from the Berlin show demonstrates how long they could keep this up without boring the sympathetic listener. It remains the longest and most thorough illustration of this facet of the Arkestra. This major piece opens with a chamber jazz segment; then African percussion and bass; a space chant assuring us that "Out in space is no disgrace"; a long series of uncompromising solos, including Ra turning his thunderous organ on and off for effect and playing a big Moog solo; and a final concluding space chord. Ra has talked about the effect his music can have on animals (liner notes, *Hours After*): this piece completely excites one of my cats! The rest of the set sustains this energy.

Of perhaps more historical / archival interest only (in other words, if you're becoming a diehard Ra fan) would be the November 9, 1970 UK debut of the Arkestra at Queen Elizabeth Hall in London (now available as a two-disc release from Transparency). The sound quality is that of an in-audience bootleg with lots of tape hiss. Its charms are largely ideological: the pounding percussion session of this massive touring ensemble talking back to the Empire! There is a lovely vocal rendition of "Planet Earth" in the second set, a full-tilt synthesizer buzz-out on "Myth vs. Reality"—and even a moment when the string section is getting sounds very akin to those heard on Gyorgy Ligeti's "Atmospheres." Even through the weak audio one can detect the utterly uncompromising nature of 1970's Sun Ra, perhaps the peak of the ensemble's favoring experimental improvisation rather than recognizable melodies (as with *Out in Space*, a minority element in the proceedings). And there is no doubt in the listener's ear that the Brits are more shocked than the French and the Germans by these extreme sonic assaults: applause begins to occur rather late into the first set (but one can hear the gradual learning curve towards the shock of the new).

The following year also proved to be a banner year for global touring, taking the Arkestra to such far-flung spots as Finland and Egypt. As in the case of Frank Zappa, Helsinki proved to be a highly accepting and inspirational venue. In 2009, Transparency issued a two CD and DVD coverage of Ra's performance there in October of 1971. Although these live versions tend to go on at some length (because there is a theatrical and dance element which the musicians are accompanying), this is a highly rewarding listen because of the sheer size and exuberance of the band. (And the recording quality is quite good.) "Love in Outer Space" gets a magisterial, highly percussive reading; "Watusi" provides polyrhythms galore when this large ensemble starts tub-thumping. The second disc features an extended, untitled flute interlude, some very soulful vocals on "Space Is the Place," bass minimalism on "Angels and Demons at Play" and a very funky "Second Stop is Jupiter" with wild shrieks from one of the female vocalists (I hope it's Wisteria el Moondew, then a member of the group!). They end this second set with some transcendentalist praise directed "To Nature's God" ("lightning, sunshine, wind, the leaves on the trees ... . Give some credit where credit is due") and an urgent invocation to "Prepare for the Journey to Outer Space" ("This world ain't gonna be here long ... . Time to go"). Fun stuff, and even a good set for initiating the novice listener: I got four people interested in Sun Ra's music by playing this material.

The accompanying DVD has a brief interview with Sun Ra where he mainly discusses the need for laws to provide alien visitors with some rights and protection, a reciprocal necessity in the space age (we'll need them when we visit

We Travel Ra's Spaceways 353

other inhabited worlds). And while we're at it, how about some laws for angels too? Since Sun Ra believed he was an extraterrestrial and an angel, this might be special pleading. Fortunately, the Finnish interviewer takes it all in stride.

In 2010, Art Yard and Kindred Spirits jointly released *The Paris Tapes*, a concert at Le Theatre du Chatelet performed six weeks after the Helsinki show. Also extremely well-recorded, this set opens with a fine synthesizer workout, including ray-gun blasts of a highly percussive nature. "Discipline 27" really swings out and evolves into some trademark saxophone dueling among the usual suspects (Pat Patrick, Danny Davis, Marshall Allen, John Gilmore, Danny Thompson). A very sinuous rendering of "Somebody Else's Idea" (aka "Somebody Else's World") becomes a repetitive mantra with exotica lounge vocalese. As Knoel Scott says in the liner notes, "Watusi" showcases an "African Drum Choir," featuring James Jacson's Ancient Egyptian Infinity Lightning Wood Drum (carved from a tree struck by lightning in defiance of Native American taboos). The audience screams with delight at the intense results.

As with the Helsinki concert, "Space Is the Place" gets a very energetic reading (albeit quite different, more in the spirit of gospel shouting): "Your thought is free / And your life is worthwhile." "Angels and Demons at Play" (i.e., flutes and drums) also gets a different treatment than Helsinki. This concert concludes with a jaunty, rare unnumbered "Discipline" that evolves into an organ solo and a cacophonous horn and reed blowout followed by a synth solo with enough square wave action to break up a listener's kidney stone! Suitably big sounds from one of Ra's largest touring Arkestras ever (27 members including dancers and a light show coordinator).

The Arkestra finished up the year in Egypt, which resulted in three albums worth of live material from sundry concerts and television appearances. I think the best of these is *Horizon*, taken from a December 17 concert at the Ballon Theatre in Cairo (and sponsored by the Egyptian Ministry of Culture!). Noteworthy moments include the obscure "Discipline #2," a flute workout for Marshall Allen, Danny Thompson, and Danny Davis. The title track is another Ra synthesizer extravaganza. And "We'll Wait for You" (later known as "I'll Wait for You") is delivered as a poem, not a song by June Tyson (she includes the "like the lash of a whip" simile from the poem that would get deleted from the song lyrics; see below).

Stateside Live Appearances, Studio Work, and a Jaunt to Paris (1972-1975)

The recently released *Life Is Splendid* documents more thoroughly the Arkestra's 1972 performance at the Ann Arbor Blues and Jazz Festival (previously only briefly excerpted on a compilation album). This concert, the beginning of a three-year tradition for Ra, gave the band its best and biggest American reception to date. They more than rose to the occasion with wild "space ethnic" vocals, a fierce demonstration of African-inflected drumming on "Watusi," and the by-now trademark cosmo-spectacle.

A much rawer sounding but more thorough documentation of the summer 1972 Arkestra is available on Transparency's six CD box set *Live at Slug's Saloon*. Ra returned that summer sporadically to his former main venue during the New York residency. These tapes capture a June and an August show with slightly different personnel. The August show is by far the better of the two, although the June show captures a very gritty and grimy synthesizer solo (no one played the instrument like Sun Ra did—ever) and an organ solo that erupts into Vesuvian maximalism. (And for what it's worth, the long instrumental prelude of that show woke up a bat sleeping in my basement: Ra's effect on animals is always worth noting.)

The August date has an extended anti-apocalyptic gibe on "At First There Was Nothing": "Is that all you got to do? / Sitting around waiting for the end of the world? ... / You got to find something else to do." In any case, every Ra aficionado knows what the band later reveals: "It's after the end of the world. / Don't you know that yet?" The percussion workout on "Watusi" turns into a Haitian ra-ra procession replete with whistles. The new "Discipline 27-II" gets a lush, slightly different reading than the studio recording from around the same time (see below). But best of all, the August 19, 1972 version of "The Shadow World" gets into some really alien hybrid instrumentals cum vocalese, the true "space ethnic voices" promised on many a liner note.

These recordings confirm Los Angeles-based Transparency founder Michael Sheppard's claim that his label's partial specialty with regard to Ra is "the really psychedelic stuff from about 68 into 72, maybe even 73 or 74, where it's almost like they've stopped playing jazz entirely" (Gershon 111). In other words, Ra's avant-pop at its most avant—as much space liturgy as concert!

Around this same time the band made the studio recording *Space Is the Place* in Chicago. On first listen, I thought the title track was too repetitive; repeated listenings have opened up a lot of interesting elements in the piece: a fine horn chart, gentle Moog bleeps, gibbering ape noises in the back channels (it was originally released in quadraphonic four-speaker sound), a twisted overall funk effect that definitely shows Ra reaching out to a younger audience. In the original quad, or even in simulated surround sound, it offers a genuine soundscape. Ra was never interested in making concept albums, as noted. (After all, why make a conceptual album when your whole *oeuvre* is just one big concept / body of doctrine?) Nonetheless, his brief series of quad releases at least demonstrated that Sun Ra was beginning to take the vinyl record as a medium in its own right—one he could use in special ways to get his message across.

The other side of the recording provided a uniquely conscientious sampling of the Arkestra's variety: the classic inside jazz of "Images" with traditional piano and a lyrical tenor solo from Gilmore; "Discipline 33" 's Egyptian-sounding processional riff and space organ solo; "Sea of Sound" 's chaotic reed soloing; and finally, a reworking of the "Rocket Number Nine" space chant. Because of this range, *Space Is the Place* (not to be confused with the film soundtrack of the same name) might be a better place to start listening to Ra than any ostensible greatest hits collection.

During the same Chicago session date, the Arkestra also made the much more obscure Saturn release *Discipline 27-II*, a far more challenging affair but arguably an even more major work. "Pan Afro" demonstrates how close Gilmore could get to the feel of John Coltrane's tenor when he wanted to. "Neptune" is both a mellow sax jam and one of June Tyson's best space chants: "Have you heard the news from Neptune, Neptune, Neptune, Neptune?" The title track is Ra's major piece in the discipline series of compositions and his fullest musical sermon statement regarding his beliefs:

> For you, I gave everything I never had.
> They call this life?
> They really think this is life?
> This is not life.
> We know what life is.
> Life is splendid.

For the entire side of a record, we get these call-and-response doctrines repeated by Ra, June Tyson and the other ethnic space vocalists. The absurdity of terrestrial existence leads Ra to proclaim that "The world ended 3,000 years ago" and that we are "on the other side of time": "Where's your sense of humor? / Let's all have a good laugh." At which point the Arkestra cracks up, both vocally and with laughter replicated on the saxophones in emulation of the "laughing blues" novelty tradition. A remarkable record badly in need of release on CD, and a thorough canvass of Ra's beliefs.

Around this time, because of the growing word-of-mouth reputation of the live shows and some critical recognition in jazz circles, Sun Ra was able to work with major labels as well as El Saturn. These mainstream flirtations happened throughout the later career in cycles, always ending in eventual abandonment by the major label in question. Despite his cult following, Ra has never been a way to wealth for the corporate music industry—not even by the more relaxed criteria for jazz music. *Space Is the Place*, for example, was released on Blue Thumb records (a pop label that took a few chances: e.g., Captain Beefheart's *Strictly Personal*).[7] But both artists only had one record on the label.

The big score of the early seventies, however, was an ambitious contract with ABC-Impulse. This was the most distinguished label for sixties jazz in

America, after all, with an impeccable roster of artists that included John Coltrane, Pharaoh Sanders, Archie Shepp, Albert Ayler, and McCoy Tyner (to name only a few). To be released on this label was in effect critical canonization as well as an economic proposition. ABC planned to reissue a massive 21 of the original Saturn records (an arrangement now actually realized by the smaller Evidence label) and contracted for four new releases (Szwed 333; Ed Michel, liner notes for *The Great Lost Sun Ra Albums*). This sweet deal soon went sour when the numbers came in.

Which brings us to the next Ra highlight, *The Great Lost Sun Ra Albums*. These were *Cymbals* and *Crystal Spheres*, two Impulse albums recorded in 1973 but never released until 2000. They are both superb instrumental albums. The highlight of *Cymbals* is "Thoughts Under a Dark Blue Light," a seventeen-minute "monumental soul blues" (Robert Campbell, liner notes). Replete with funky sax charts and generous helpings of Gilmore, Ra and Boykins, this track is an ultimate example of Ra's many engagements over the years with the blues form. (Highlights of Sun Ra's collected blues-based recordings would easily stretch to about 5 CDs.)

Crystal Spheres has a few equally ambitious moments. "The Embassy of the Living God" has a great deal of diverse soloing and reed ensemble work; "Sunrise in the Western Sky" contains THE major solo statement of tenor John Gilmore. This latter track is the only opportunity Ra ever gave him on record (or, as far as I know, in concert) to stretch out and blow as long as the major Coltrane solos. Needless to say, he could do it! His sax has a fabulously metallic sound, in part because of Ed Michel's professional production. Because of the depth of Ra's career-long collaboration with Gilmore and Marshall Allen, "Sunrise in the Western Sky" is an important document.

I would also like to mention a 1973 live recording, *Sun Ra live in Paris at the "Gibus"*—a club that attempted to emulate the vibe of the Arkestra's New York home base, Slug's, but was deemed "much too nice" for that comparison by the band (Szwed, *Space* 228). It's worth checking out for one standout track. "Salutations from the Universe" is a fifteen minute Moog and Space Master organ Ra solo that truly explores the absolute limits of the sounds these instruments can make. This music will clean out your ears, scare your pets and threaten your speakers. The rest is a good selection of what the large live ensemble was doing then (Ra originals, a Fletcher Henderson standard, etc.). The liner notes in the Italian reissue are hilariously (?) racist, dropping the n-bomb repeatedly ("Sun Ra was a n——") because of a mistranslation from the French *negre*. Someone needs to fix that.

Thanks to the 2009 reissue by Art Yard, one can also hear the 1974 El Saturn recording *The Antique Blacks* (off a live Philadelphia radio show on August 17 and unavailable for many years). This is an unusual set for several reasons. First off, it showcases a mellower and smaller Arkestra. The opening track,

"Song No. 1" is mostly straight-ahead jazz, with a round of solos, spiced up by some alto wildness from Marshall Allen. The title is curious: is this Ra's first composition he considered a "song?" (Not that there are any lyrics.) This more relaxed sound anticipates later seventies releases such as *Lanquidity* and *Sleeping Beauty*.

Secondly, this outing features a lot of Ra's poetry, constituting a virtual tutorial for humans. The abundance of spoken word material (albeit mostly accompanied by the band) may reflect the absence of vocalist June Tyson—who in previous years held up the lion's share of the vocals. It may also reflect Ra's perceptions of the opportunities provided by a live radio broadcast to get his cosmic message out: an opportunity not to be squandered! And finally, this was the historical moment of Watergate and Nixon's resignation. Sun Ra could sense the confusion of the moment and use it to his advantage as a kind of messianic cosmic messenger. A few examples will serve as illustration (and bear in mind none of these pieces I'm quoting entered the standard Arkestra repertoire; they are relatively rare examples of Ra being totally in the historical moment, albeit in his own peculiar manner):

> They do not know how loud the silence can be ... .
> [They're on] the right road, the wrong direction ... .
> The arrow points to pointlessness ... .
> The people and the leaders walk hand in hand [on the right road, wrong direction;
> they need to go to "space"] ("There is Change in the Air")

> The antique blacks belong to me ... .
> I plan to present them to the greater universe ... .
> I plan to place them in Lucifer's care [because Whitey fears Lucifer; *The Exorcist* is still in the mix!] ("The Antique Blacks")

> You would like to go into outer space, into our territory ... .
> We're all around you ... .
> We've been here a long time watching you ... .
> We are not your enemy
> You refuse to be our friends ... .
> Take the big gamble ... .
> I am the magic lie greater than your truth ... .
> You can't even take care of the fishes in the sea ... . [part of a larger environmental rap]
> I will not let you go there [into space] until you learn how to treat me ... ,
> [and yet, on the other hand]
> Why don't you visit me?
> You have nothing else to do.

And always remember:
If you are not my friends, I am not your enemy. ("You Thought You Could Build A World Without Us")

We have an intriguing set of shifting personae within these texts, a mixture of threatening and welcoming that perhaps ultimately derives from Michael Rennie's alien Klaatu in *The Day the Earth Stood Still*. As Ra repeatedly opined in text after text, humans are an immature species. The Man from Saturn can help them if they "treat" him right (which begins for any musician with money and perqs, of course!). In this context, "Song No. 1" is another carrot for the listener to balance the stick of Ra's semi-jeremiads. If not the first Ra you should hear, *The Antique Blacks* captures a very interesting and brief seized moment in a long, diverse career. And bottom line: the music's great. Gilmore is playing his most lyrical tenor saxophone and Sun Ra has utterly mastered the newer electronic keyboards with truly unearthly results.

Also of some transitional interest is the 2009 Leo release *Live in Cleveland* (January 30, 1975). The concert opens with a rare space chant called "Astro Nation": "We hereby declare ourselves to be of another order of being: / an Astro Nation of the United Worlds of Outer Space." Dale Williams funks the melody up with some fine electric bass. We also get an early version of the "I, Pharaoh" declamation (see below); in fact, one gets sonic whiplash by the transition from "I, Pharaoh" with its conjuration of ancient Egypt through an eight-minute synthesizer solo to an extended and lush reading of Duke Ellington's "Sophisticated Lady." This last homage—a classic big band arrangement especially highlighting the bass, Ra's piano and John Gilmore's tenor sax—serves as a harbinger of Ra's desire to integrate the Arkestra with jazz history as a whole in concert on a consistent basis (a tendency which began with the Fletcher Henderson covers at Slug's in the sixties but did not become standard Arkestra practice until the mid-seventies). Sun Ra wanted the Arkestra to do it all, pretty much—and they delivered! As does Ra himself, although his vocal delivery of the song ("smoking, drinking / never thinking of tomorrow") falls well shy of crooner status.

In 1974 and 1975, El Saturn records issued two of the rarest Arkestra recordings, the "*Sub Underground Series*." These only became generally available in 2012, courtesy of England's Art Yard label. The 1974 album opened with "Cosmo Earth Fantasy," an extended free performance that actually dates back to the *Strange Strings* sessions in the late sixties. This piece is all about the lovely and unusual timbres; it is utterly unclassifiable, at the very limits of jazz (and not recognizable as such to most ears). There is no discernible melody line. The only jazz element is its improvisatory nature. After the opening strings, Sun Ra weighs in on Hohner Clavinet, eventually duetting with Marshall Allen on oboe. Ronnie Boykins plays some fuzzed-out bass, followed by wild and intense xylophone work from an unknown player which is eventually accompanied by Danny Davis on flute. This exploration hangs together as an esoteric listening experience—sub underground, indeed. There is a build-up to a sonic climax of xylophone, clavinet, bass, flutes and percussion. But one suspects, in a parallel to the structure of live Arkestra performances, Ra chose this sidelong excursion as a way to scare off the casual listener. Sun Ra demanded unconditional acceptance from his listeners. They could have preferences and judgments, but he needed the right to play anything he was interested in. And he loved to stretch our ears: that's what "Cosmo Earth Fantasy" does, like the other *Strange Strings* work.

The second side of the original album rewarded the listener with three more accessible treats. First off, there were two numbers from a 1974 concert at Temple University. "Love is for Always" offers lyrical interplay between Ra on piano and John Gilmore on tenor sax. "The Song of Drums," with its African language singing against a drum line, could pass for African world music—but is in fact a Sun Ra composition. This paradox is also true for "The World of Africa," a 1968 rehearsal tape featuring June Tyson singing African vocals. Ra scholar Paul Griffiths lays this all out in the 2012 liner notes. When the album was first issued, the average fan assumed incorrectly it all came from 1974.

The 1975 Sub Underground release was even more peculiar, offering no track titles on the record. Side one of it was relatively tame stuff from 1962, two covers of jazz standards and two originals from other members of the Arkestra (a quite rare arrangement) that sounded like jazz standards. We have here an early rendition of "What's New" with great solos from Al Evans on flugelhorn and Calvin Newborn on electric guitar. Ra's approach to the song is typically unconventional, an upbeat reading lacking any of the lachrymose regret that most crooners bring to this material. "Wanderlust" and "Jukin' " follow (written respectively by Newborn and Evans). That side closes with a lovely and simple jazz quartet performance of "Autumn in New York" (Ra, Gilmore, Boykins on bass and Thomas Hunter on drums). Here is Ra at his most lyrical and accessible. Even my cats loved zoning out to this—always a sign of audio quality.

The second side is the joker in this particular deck, a space chant and declamation, eventually given the title "We Roam the Cosmos," from 1975. The fire and fury of this space sermon—as always, telling us to get off our mortal butts and "try something else than planet Earth"—anticipates some of the drama of the declarations made during the Detroit Jazz Center residency considered below. The combined series offered two sides of intense and uncompromising Ra bookending two other sides of the Arkestra in a mellower mood. The 2012 compact disk gives you all of it.

A weird side note: El Saturn kept reshuffling the material from the second release: one El Saturn release replaced "We Roam the Cosmos" with "The Invisible Shield"; another retitled it "What's New?" (it was originally just marked "Sub Underground Series") and substituted a Ra original ("State Street") and more standards for "We Roam the Cosmos." Odd behavior even for El Saturn.

Back in Europe (1976)

I have always been fond of *Live at Montreux* (1976); as with *Space Is the Place* (1972), this is a well-rounded introduction to the Arkestra's variety. It includes a reverential yet subversive cover of Billy Strayhorn's "Take the A Train." Thus, except for the absence of Ra's keyboards, *Live at Montreux* sounds like what you would hear if you could catch the touring Arkestra today.

The French studio recording *Cosmos* (on the Cobra label, also from 1976) offers several delights, including the lilting space chant "Moonship Journey." "Journey among the Stars" presents chamber jazz, with much flute exploration augmented by R. Anthony Bunn's electric bass and Ahmed Abdullah's trumpet. And "Jazz from an Unknown Planet" combines a fine Cadillac chart with a stirring round of solos from Abdullah, Ra and Gilmore.

The much harder to obtain *Unity* (the Italian Horo label, 1976) has a rare recording of "Halloween in Harlem," perhaps Ra's finest processional, featuring lots of electronic wizardry on the space organ and spooky horn charts. This song highlighted the Arkestra's Halloween shows, and was often accompanied with costumed dancers jumping into the audience. The album's title perhaps refers to his telescoping of past, present and future in the song selections (which are heavy on covers from Henderson and his peers).

The Late Seventies: Outburst of Productivity

The late seventies offered a proliferation of superb Ra releases. 1977 saw a live concert which eventually was issued as *A Quiet Place in the Universe*. This recording is another way to obtain "I, Pharaoh." Along with "Discipline 27-II," this is a major Ra sermon in which he reveals that he formerly "dwelt in Egypt land" in a "kingdom ... splendid without compare." He lost his kingdom, preserving only "the secret of immortality." Even as he urged his audience to travel the spaceways with him, Ra now asks us to become his servants: "Why don't you be my people now? ... Behold me—Pharaoh!" An interesting offer from the living myth which many accepted (and many more did not).

In that same year, Ra also issued two more recordings of solo piano (*Solo Piano Volume I* and *St. Louis Blues*; the first were two volumes on Saturn entitled *Monorails and Satellites*). As a player, Sun Ra splits the difference between the grand old stride stylings of Earl Hines and/or Jelly Roll Morton and the avant-garde sound clusters of Cecil Taylor, often in the same piece. The results are distinctive and memorable. *St. Louis Blues* extends the instrument experimentally in "Sky and Sun" (favoring the very upper end of the keyboard) and "I Am We Are I" (slamming and plucking the strings in the piano á la American classical composer [and John Cage mentor] Henry Cowell's "Banshee").

Somewhere over the Rainbow (Saturn, 1977) adds the Arkestra, but continues Ra's infatuation with the piano. In the title track, he takes you over the rainbow by creating a rumbling thunderstorm on the lower registers in juxtaposition with a gorgeous reading of the melody. Another version of "Take the A Train" has a lyrical piano introduction. "Make Another Mistake" chants more Ra philosophy:

> You made a mistake
> You did something wrong
> Make another mistake
> And do something right.

Words to live by which prompted one member of the Bloomington, Indiana, concert audience to yell "bellissimo" at song's end.

Some Blues but Not the Kind That's Blue (Saturn, 1977), except for the title track, consisted of cover versions of sundry jazz and popular standards. The introductions to all these pieces are unusual (especially so for the title track, which appears to be an edit from a completely different session). They offer oblique little Ra piano solos in their own right until he showcases the main melody. "My Favorite Things" is the expected nod to John Coltrane, with Gilmore producing some appropriate sheets of sound on the tenor.

The Morrison / Lawrence / Gross composition "Tenderly" opens with a quotation from Sun Ra's own piece "Interstellar Low Ways." It turns out the two pieces are very similar melodically in their opening phrasing.

The CD reissue on the Unheard Music series (2007) adds two earlier readings of "I'll Get By" with a different lineup. More interestingly, it adds an unreleased (and untitled) Ra original from the 1977 session. This piece offers some intense tenor soloing from John Gilmore which is even more rambunctious than that provided on "My Favorite Things."

The same year and label's *The Soul Vibrations of Man* is distinguished by an "Untitled Improvisation" with the wildest reed soloing in the recorded canon (in order, Pat Patrick or Danny Thompson, baritone; Marshall Allen, alto; John Gilmore, tenor). As noted above, there is plenty of this material available since it was a component of almost every Arkestra concert since the mid-sixties. But this is the most extreme example. I also recommend the Rhapsody Films video documentaries *Sun Ra: A Joyful Noise* and *Mystery, Mr. Ra* for video footage of what this activity looked like in performance. It was not only music, but also dance and theater!

This incredibly active and diverse year of 1977, lastly, also includes a live solo piano recital in Venice, available on Leo Records in CD format. It provides a great complement to the studio solo work and shows how readily Sun Ra all by himself with a piano could captivate a diverse audience. Offering a program which mixes improvisations, originals and covers of standards, Ra gradually heats up his reverential audience. "Love in Outer Space" soars as a lilting piano vehicle; his cover of "Take the A Train" ends in some piano-bashing that sounds like the train approaching the concert hall. His work on "St. Louis Blues" reminds us that Ra can deliver straight ragtime with the best of traditionalists. By the time he delivers a jaunty and lyrical reading of Jason / Burton / King's "Penthouse Serenade," Ra has the audience in the palm of his hand—giving him the confidence and authority to treat us to a rare solo vocal on a lovely version of "Angel Race." And he introduces the experimental improvisation which follows by telling the audience, "I want to invite you to attend the party in 1980 on Jupiter." Great stuff worth hunting for ... .

I have previously discussed the quasi-pop work of *Disco 3000* and *Lanquidity* (both from 1978), but I would add that the recent release on CD of the complete *Disco 3000* concert in Milan, Italy (January 23 1978) during Ra's extended Italian sojourn is well worth a listen. In addition to all the Crumar Mainman drum machine soloing by Ra, this quartet—Ra, Gilmore, Luqman Ali on drums and new member Michael Ray on trumpet and vocals (and a vocal assist from June Tyson)—burned long and hard. "Third Planet" features intense hard-bop interplay between Gilmore and Ali. The track called "Spontaneous Simplicity" (which may really be "Dance of the Cosmo Aliens"; title labeling here is flawed) offers squiggly synthesizers juxtaposed with Ray's soaring funk trumpet. They introduce a live version of "When There Is No Sun," a lovely new song (off the Italian studio release *New Steps* on the Horo label). Gilmore, Ray and Ali harmonize on the typically vatic lyrics: "The sky is a sea of darkness / When there is no sun to light the way." After an explosive free jazz climax of simultaneous soloing at top volume, Ra calms everybody down with a completely straight piano rendering of "Over the Rainbow."

In 2009, an obscure Ra reissue label called "Atomic Records" released *New Steps*, one of two studio recordings done by this quartet for the Italian Horo label in early January 1978 prior to the Italian tour with its live recordings. The studio version of "When There Is No Sun"—the only vocal on the album—offers even more exquisite vocal harmonizing from Gilmore, Ali and Ray. The session also features a great run-through of the jazz standard "My Favorite Things" and some quirky Ra compositions, doubly rare in this quartet format, such as "Moon People" (Michael Ray creating goofy horn effects to simulate extraterrestrial chatter accompanied by Ra playing his Crumar Mainman like a cello), "Sun Steps" (a lyrical meditation on piano that builds to a Michael Ray solo and a wildly dissonant ending), "Friend and Friendship" (with good call and response between the piano and the horn and reed combo), "Rome at Twilight" (a sonic picture of the city's bustle that hearkens back to early Ra compositions like "Chicago USA") and "The Horo" (an extended workout for the entire quartet with much sensitive musical conversation).

Media Dreams (1978) also features the quartet. The title track (almost) "Media Dreams" takes the listener on an interesting ride. Ra was fascinated at this point with the new keyboard synthesizers. He tinkers with quasi-minimalist "chords and obligatti," while Michael Ray soars around him (Szwed 349-50). The very rare recording *The Sound Mirror* from the same time has another major Ra sermon in its title track, as well as some mellow, "inside" Gilmore work ("Jazzisticology") and mostly solo sound sculpture for electronic keyboard ("Of Other Tomorrows Never Known").

By chronology of the original recording date, we next come to one of several Ra cosmic singularities, courtesy of the Transparency label: a 10 CD box set documenting three 1978 dates (with overall fine audio quality) of the Arkestra at Toronto's Horseshoe Tavern (with a bonus disk showcasing a 1968 Ra interview on Radio Pacifica). On the one hand, as Art Yard consultant Michael Anderson says disparagingly of the Transparency label, "Those are bootlegs ... . I don't know where those tapes came from." On the other hand, as Ra critic Pete Gershon notes, "even Ra's own releases of the Arkestra's music were often low budget affairs that were rather imprecise with respect to such details...[;] those aspects of the Transparency program might well have appealed to the intergalactic trickster" (Gershon 112). By all accounts, Transparency founder Michael Sheppard is in good standing with the surviving members of the Arkestra (which must mean among other things that he's helping them financially with his windfall).

I give this context because part of me says that if a slightly curious listener just obtained this one box set, they would pretty much have a thorough representation of what the mature Arkestra did as I described it at the beginning of my "Omniversal Listening Suggestions." From this one recording you could decide whether you wanted to delve deeper into Ra or whether you had heard "quite enough," as they say. To me as a Ra enthusiast, the most interesting show is the first one on March 13, 1978 (discs 1-3). This shows a Canadian audience responding to the band with more enthusiasm than I ever heard a European or American audience ever muster. At the final outer space altar call, for example, when Ra informs them "Get your tickets here please. Do you want one way or round trip?," they yell out "One way," "Take me with you," "Space is the place" while banging on beer mugs for percussion accompaniment and even chanting "day-o." (I said that they were enthusiastic, not sober.) Ra responds to their accolades by letting his hair down as much as I've ever heard Ra do in concert, going all the way back to *Spaceship Lullaby* days by interpolating "Stranger in Paradise" in "Discipline 27-II"—and even "As Time Goes By"! It's a sonic love feast unparalleled in the Ra discography.

All three shows feature interesting and radically different improvisations from the band before Sun Ra appears on stage. The March date showcases Michael Ray's trumpet in dialogue with the percussion section at some length; the September 27 preamble starts out with Egyptian snake charmer sounds evolving into trumpet, and a meditative exploration in the spirit of fusion-era Miles Davis without sounding derivative of it in any way; the November 4 show begins with electric guitar, drum and vibraphone interaction before an echo-laden trumpet enters at approximately 11:00, followed by reeds a minute later, bass and (at around 18:00) a trombone solo. Three completely different sets of textures and moods from almost the same personnel ... . Once Ra arrives, the three concerts are more similar but still satisfyingly varied. All three showcase a variety of jazz standards covered with great care and respect (e.g., Fletcher Henderson, Duke Ellington and the like), Ra sermons and compositions, and a wide variety of space chants.

There are a lot of little surprises and treats here as noted; the only major unprecedented weirdness is on disc 5 when one of the Arkestra declares himself to be the "Birdman" during "Love in Outer Space" (is it wild man Michael Ray?) and gives the audience a mix of instructions ("sing with the birds ... they are way out") and critiques of earthly mores ("all through history truthful men are shot"). The bonus disc reiterates many of Ra's ambiguities and mysteries to the interviewer. Ra admits his music is "slightly evil in a sense" (because it's beyond good and evil) and that he's a "world teacher," "a double order of being," conducting a "knower's ark" trying to remedy the sad fact that "black people in America have been deprived of beauty." There is abundant beauty—and strangeness—on these ten disks. As noted, for some this may be enough Sun Ra to satisfy them (or even an overdose?).

Ra ended the decade with a few more gems. *On The Other Side of the Sun* (1979), the New York program music of "Manhattan Cocktail" captured well the discord and complexity of the island and provided another instance when Ra's writing seemed curiously similar to that of Charles Ives (who also captured urban sounds in compositions such as "Over the Pavements" and "Ann Street").

The title track of *On Jupiter* (1979) is a lush seventies mellow jazz reading of a then-new Ra space chant destined to become a solid part of the later Arkestra repertoire ("On Jupiter, the skies are always blue"). June Tyson's lilting vocal is accompanied by suitable loping percussion and some very mellow piano from the man from Saturn.

"UFO" is the real ear-opener: Sun Ra doing straight-up disco! This is a serious commercial bid—far more so than the odd keyboards on *Disco 3000*. This is New York disco 1979: "UFO, UFO / Take me where I want to go." Lots of electric guitars, that signature beat white people can dance to ... it's all here. As with Neil Young's Shocking Pinks or Frank Zappa's doo-wop (or his disco for that matter), when you're a far-out avant-popist, the most radical move you can make is to go far in. There isn't a single second of free jazz or atonality on this track. It's as if Sun Ra noticed what George Clinton and P-funk were doing with his concepts with their Mothership Connection—not to mention Earth, Wind and Fire— and decided to school them by giving them back their own approach raised to a whole other level of teen appeal. This reading seems to be reinforced by the signifying nature of some of the lyrics intoned by Ra: "You can fool some of the people some of the time, / You can't fool all of the people all of the time."

"Seductive Fantasy" is the third and final track comprising *On Jupiter*. Here Ra works in his more typical proclivities. The composition begins by living up to its title with heavy wah-wah guitar and a fine piano accompaniment that evolves into a sinuous and rapid solo (all at once, a neat sonic trick which reminds us that Sun Ra has few musical limitations). A few raucous bursts from the horns and reeds break our trance and remind us that this is the Arkestra after all. Cello and violin interplay further unplug the fantasy until the piano returns to try to restore the mood, abetted by percussion and James Jacson on bassoon. Finally, a blast of the space key / chord and one last highly discordant piano note cluster ends this interesting and complex piece. What we hear here is a complex negotiation with a new audience, a willingness to meet them more than halfway as long as Sun Ra can reserve the right to take them out of the musical shallows into the cosmic depths (cf. Zappa's negotiations with the disco crowd on *Sheik Yerbouti*).

And then on *Sleeping Beauty* (also 1979) we find the mellowest Ra ever recorded, from his lush seasonal chant "Springtime Again" through "Door of the Cosmos" ("Love and life interested me so / That I dared to knock at the door of the cosmos") to the fractured fairy tale of the title track. Ra traffics in his own version of Zappa's conceptual continuity in the lyrics here. The juxtaposition of the tale of Sleeping Beauty with his desire "to speak of Black Beauty to you" at first glance seems to make little sense beyond ethnic inclusiveness (cf. Black Jesus or Black Barbie). And then, one recalls the 1968 Pacifica observation cited above where Sun Ra observes that "black people in America have been deprived of beauty." Eleven years later, Ra tries to rectify this state of affairs explicitly. Abetted by Damon Choice's vibraphone stylings and exotica-influenced background vocalizing, Ra directly addresses Black Womanhood: "I know you don't want to hear it ... . Without Prince Charming, there's nothing, Black Beauty ... . Nothing will ever happen." Ra insinuates that he is the Prince Charming in question that can wake Black Beauty by showing this Eternal Black Feminine her own beauty through his music. Such a claim and persona coming from this celibate, queer extraterrestrial transcends even his other outrageous masques as Satan or as Pharaoh. And yet his curiously gentle approach promises to seal the deal—and might have worked if a critical mass of African-American women had been listening! If you want Sun Ra in a very pleasant mood, this has been conveniently reissued on CD in the Unheard Music series.

Finally, *God Is More than Love Can Ever Be* (1979) presents Ra's music in a trio format (piano / drum / bass), which frees him up more for improvisation than on the solo piano recordings.

The 1980s

The first recording of the new decade worth mentioning for non-completist interested parties is a Transparency release called *Live in Rome* from March 28. The fine audio quality and abrupt breaks between songs eliminating applause (cf. Grateful Dead live releases) suggest that this double CD may have been originally intended for the Italian Horo label as a live album. Highlights include a flashy Michael Ray trumpet solo in the beginning of the concert that features his playing the impossible by holding a trumpet note for minutes with circular breath technique—and a comic closing gesture for the solo. We are also treated to a more piano-driven version of "Lights on a Satellite." As with the Swiss concert from a month previous issued as *Sunrise in Different Dimensions* (on Hat Hut / Art), there are a lot of older jazz standards covered; but in this show, Ra slips in his new "Springtime Again" amidst them (as a future standard?). There is even a rare new chant worth quoting in its wacky entirety, tentatively titled "Hit That Jive Jack":

> Hit that jive Jack
> Put it in your pocket till I get back
> I'm going to outer space as fast as I can
> I ain't got time to shake your hand

As Doctor John would say, mos' scosious!

Ra also released his first classical cover, a jazzy rendition of Rachmaninoff's "Prelude in C# Minor" (on the solo piano Saturn release *Aurora Borealis*). On *Dance of Innocent Passion* (also Saturn, 1980), Ra favored a theatrical organ sound on the title track (accompanied by light jazz guitar, drums and trumpet), "Cosmo Energy" (with arco bass and synthesizer), and "Omnisonicism" (with an appropriately wide range of timbres such as conga, saxophone, synthesizer and vibes). This latter adventurous set was recorded live at the Squat Theater in New York.

At the end of the year, the Arkestra recorded some even more challenging material excerpted from their 6-day, 11-performance residency at the Detroit Jazz Center. Two El Saturn releases emerged from this outing—and now there is a mammoth 28 CD Transparency release (2007). To consider the El Saturn excerpts first, *Beyond the Purple Star Zone* is worth checking out primarily for the deep space electronica of "Immortal Being." Also of some interest is the electric guitar soloing on "Romance on a Satellite" and the sweeping organ tone clusters on "Planetary Search" that suggest Sun Ra had been listening avidly to the Gyorgy Ligeti compositions in *2001: A Space Odyssey*, a decade earlier.

Oblique Parallax contained uncompromising Detroit moments as well such as "Vista Omniverse" for gritty, distorted organ and synthesizer, "Celestial Realms" for organ and Michael Ray's trumpet and "Journey Stars Beyond" for synthesizer (after a full-band free jazz introduction). After some of the cosmic hi-jinx on this last piece, an audience member (or an Arkestra member adding to the drama?) can be heard to marvel "What was that?" The Arkestra may have been aging and slightly mellowing, but they could still freak out their listeners if the stars were in proper alignment!

And then there's the 28 CD Transparency release of *The Complete Detroit Jazz Center Residency* by Sun Ra and the Omniverse Jet Set Arkestra (so named because he was into the newly discovered omniverse vs. the universe then [the former is even bigger!] and because the Jazz Center flew the band into Detroit?). Everything I said about the Horseshoe Tavern box set goes quintuple here: this is all the Sun Ra you might ever need—especially if you supplement it with downloads of "The Magic City," "Atlantis" and "Nuclear War." But it doesn't work that way, does it? A casual listener testing the waters with regard to an unfamiliar musical act doesn't begin with this much of a sonic investment! So, in actuality, this is an acquisition for hard-core devotees of the band. Since an exploration of this material as a result transcends the mere "Omniversal Listening Suggestions" promised early in this chapter, I have relegated my listening notes (with an ear towards absolute highlights) to an appendix.

As was the case with all the artists we have considered previously (and as will be the case for Sigmund Snopek if not James Brown), the Reagan presidency drew an aesthetic response from the man from Saturn. Sun Ra wrote the most political lyrics of his career in the early eighties in response to the nuclear buildup and the Strategic Defense Initiative. On the aptly titled *Ra to the Rescue*, he warned his audience on the otherwise lilting ballad "They Plan to Leave" of what was potentially in store:

> They plan to leave this world one day
> In sundry rocket ships to sail away
>
> They plan to go to somewhere there
> In splendid ships of models rare
>
> They plan to leave this world forever
> To lead the kingdom of Never-never

> They plan to find another place in the sky
> Without saying farewell, without saying goodbye
>
> They plan to put the White House on the moon, soon
> And the Kremlin on a satellite, soon

If the lyrics have an Oliver Stone paranoid tang, consider it a sign of those times. The High Frontier think tanks were probably not far off from Ra's accusations in their more speculative moments.

I have already mentioned Ra's best pop song, "Nuclear War." It is readily available on the reissued CD of the same name, but you will get more great music if you can find the two original Saturn Gemini releases: *A Fireside Chat with Lucifer* and *Celestial Love* (both 1982). On the former album (but not the *Nuclear War* CD) are "Makeup," a funky organ workout with lyrical Gilmore accompaniment, and "A Fireside Chat with Lucifer" itself. This latter piece takes up the entire second side of the album, deploying space organ, trumpet, theater organ, gentle electronics, piano, synthesizer and flute. What makes it unusual is its restrained, brooding and meditative quality—far from sixties and seventies extended rave-ups such as "Atlantis" or "Out in Space." The feel is closest to *Pangea*, the last music Miles Davis was recording in the seventies prior to a long sabbatical. Sun Ra seemed determined to explore at least once every jazz idiom that was ever attempted: here is his version of later fusion Miles.

On the original *Celestial Love* lp, one can find another version of "Interstellar Low Ways" (re-titled "Interstellarism" and re-orchestrated more for reeds and trumpet than flute) and a luscious cover of Duke Ellington's "Sophisticated Lady" (featuring Michael Ray on trumpet). The rest of the major material is on the much more easily accessible *Nuclear War*: "Retrospect," the appropriately dolorous ballad that follows both the title track on the CD and its appearance on *A Fireside Chat with Lucifer* (a rare example of Ra doing thematic sequencing!); "Blue Intensity," another funky organ vamp; and stellar covers of standards "Sometimes I'm Happy" and Charlie Chaplin's "Smile." This last has been re-done by everyone from Nat King Cole to Michael Jackson. Sun Ra, June Tyson (on vocals) and John Gilmore offer the definitive reading here, even against this level of competition. Only on the CD version of these sessions do you also get "Drop Me Off in Harlem," another Ellington cover that switches from organ to full Arkestra.

In 1983, the following year, Sun Ra returned to Egypt and collaborated with drummer Salah Ragab, paying Ragab the rare compliment of recording two of his compositions with the Arkestra as well as letting him play on the recordings. "Egypt Strut" is a processional march (Ragab directed military bands). Eloe Omoe plays marvelous bass clarinet here, and the tune has a fine hook of an Egyptian cast. Also on the compilation *The Sun Ra Arkestra Meets Salah Ragab in Egypt* is "Dawn," with a melody based on an Islamic hymn suitable for that time of day. Ra delivers the melody on a Hohner Melodica; the Arkestra churns up a mean percussion line; Gilmore delivers another splendid tenor solo. (The Egyptian jazz from Ragab's band fills out the record nicely; the CD version has additional jazz from Ragab in a "free" vein as well as another Arkestra track, an epic live version of "Watusa" [aka "Watusi"].)

Stars That Shine Darkly (Volumes 1 and 2) contain two sides (one on each lp) of the 1983 Montreux festival concert by the Sun Ra All Stars. Besides Ra, Gilmore and Allen, this band featured jazz masters Archie Shepp and Don Cherry (who was later destined to make several more recordings with the Arkestra) as well as members of the Art Ensemble of Chicago, Lester Bowie and Don Moye (Szwed 356). It was a veritable supergroup of avant-garde players, and the results do not disappoint. The title of their collective improvisation (also "Stars That Shine Darkly") refers to black holes: like the astrophysical phenomenon, this band also combines blackness with great power and force. Archie Shepp's saxophone solos deliver gorgeous full tones; Richard Davis supplies memorable bass; John Gilmore offers another workout; Ra contributes a thunderous piano solo; Lester Bowie adds some characteristic comic effects on trumpet. This nonce band sounds like they've been conversing all their lives. (Or at least keeping tabs on each other's efforts!)[8]

The second side of the first volume is devoted to "Hiroshima," another composition evincing Sun Ra's nuclear concerns. The atomic bombing of Hiroshima, like the Holocaust or the events of September 11th, is a challenging subject for program music. Arguably, it can't be done. But then again, Ra was always interested in the impossible. The meager body of music about Hiroshima falls into two general categories: soft requiem pieces (such as Hikari Oe's subtle yet moving "Hiroshima Requiem") or attempts to convey the horror of the devastation through sound (Krystof Penderecki's "Threnody for the Victims of Hiroshima"). This piece by Ra is solidly in the latter tradition ("Retrospect" on *Nuclear War* might be an example of the former approach). "Hiroshima" is a giant theatrical organ solo accompanied by drums and percussion. The music combines ominous low notes with Japanese-inflected melodies. Its feel is gothic, intense and pained. Although Penderecki's composition remains the best ever written on this somber theme, Ra's work manages to convey his sincerity and concern. How amazing that it took Ronald Reagan to overtly politicize Ra's music, a body of work which largely avoided terrestrial politics throughout the sixties.[9]

By this time, given the Arkestra's arduous touring schedule, live recordings came to dominate the recorded canon. To make this generalization concrete (using Robert Campbell's discography in Szwed), between the 1983 studio session in Egypt with Salah Ragab and Ra's earthly demise, the Arkestra issued four times as many live recordings as studio releases. Once again I would state that all of this is good, but a few of the live recordings deserve special mention. A case in point would be *Love in Outer Space*, a December 1983 concert from Utrecht. Although there are no rarities on it, this disk offers a classic eighties Arkestra set with the band in fine mettle: its virtue is its well-delivered typicality of this nevertheless atypical music. This version of "Fate in a Pleasant Mood" has a definitively lyrical piano introduction and fabulous hand drumming at its conclusion. The Utrecht audience were also treated to a stately cover of " 'Round Midnight" (with memorable solos from Gilmore and Ra) and a well-drummed version of the title track with superior piano accompaniment.

The 1984 *Live at Praxis* concerts from Athens, Greece reveal the Arkestra in a longer performance format (3 albums). The interesting material here includes a version of "Nuclear War" with alternate lyrics ("First comes the heat / And then comes the BLAST!"), Marshall Allen soloing on the *kora* (an ancient African string instrument made from a gourd and used by *griots*), a rare cover of "Mack the Knife" replete with vocal tribute to Louis Armstrong, another rare cover of "Satin Doll" and an early version of the Egyptian-inflected processional march "Carefree." The Arkestra always rose to the occasion when they visited locations associated with antiquity; NASA missed a good bet by not inviting them to play the Kennedy Space Center! (After all, outer space was always the matching bookend for the ancient world in Ra's cosmology.)

A Night in East Berlin (1986) features a lovely piano reading of "Interstellar Low Ways" and a wild battle royal on "The Shadow World" that whips even subdued East Berliners into a Dionysian frenzy. The CD version contains an amazing bonus track ("My Brothers the Wind and Sun #9" from the otherwise impossibly hard-to-obtain last Saturn vinyl release *Hidden Fire 2*). This extended piece of improvisatory chamber jazz from space most closely resembles "Stars That Shine Darkly"—although it is much more exotic. Since it was recorded live at New York's Knitting Factory, the Arkestra picked up a few extra alumni who prefer not to tour. Most notably, Art Jenkins returns for extraterrestrial scat with his space ethnic voice filtered through various horns. Combined with lots of violin and synthesizer textures, this music may be as close as Ra ever came to making really alien jazz with equal emphasis on both terms. I pity the poor fool who showed up for this gig on any hallucinogen; the Arkestra was playing the Bellevue waltz that night! Would that the rest of this music be released; it's truly one of the Arkestra's last post-avant-garde hurrahs.

I have already alluded to Ra's late-career fascination with the music of Walt Disney. The 1988 anthology *Stay Awake* has only one track from the Arkestra, "Pink Elephants on Parade." But that cut is so fabulously carnivalesque that it's worth obtaining for that reason alone—and there are other delights to be had as well on the disc, ranging from Yma Sumac to Ringo Starr with Herb Alpert. If you want much more of the same, *Second Star to the Right (Salute to Walt Disney)* is indispensible, even though it's a CD derived from an audience tape.

This 1989 concert from at the Jazzatelier in Ulrichsberg, Austria, displays the band in high surrealist mode as they romp through a series of Disney film tunes. "The Forest of No Return" proves a perfect marriage between the mouse and Ra—the only Disney lyric with the earthbound claustrophobia and paranoia Ra felt about this planet ("You can scream, you can shout / But you can't get out"). "Zip-A-Dee-Doo-Dah" transforms the song's original minstrelsy into a vague menace behind the grins, more than hinted at by Marshall Allen's squiggly alto solo. The highlight of the session is the title track, surely one of Disney's most haunting songs, here rendered reverentially by Ra through piano and vocal. "Heigh Ho! Heigh Ho!" and "Whistle While You Work" seem to be caught between being paeans to discipline and quasi-Marxist critiques of the exploitation of the workers. This tension, I think, results from the gap between what Ra intended the songs to convey and the subtexts delivered by the Arkestra's performance of them. (Easier to hear than explain.) From either perspective, the point is that these last two covers will last longer than you want to hear them. And be it discipline or exploitation, from either perspective that is precisely the point. After listening to this music, you will never think of Disney the same way again.

Final Recordings, or, Sun Ra Leaves Earth

All of Ra's later studio releases have something to recommend about them (for example, *Blue Delight* [1988] has an exquisite version of "Days of Wine and Roses"). But the best of these is *Mayan Temples* (1990), his last studio recording with the Arkestra. Ra reworks older material such as "El Is a Sound of Joy" and "Theme of the Stargazers" into updated, extended and more lush versions. One key difference in these readings is his addition of rich synthesizer textures to the original piano melodies. And "Sunset on the Nile" is the last great Ra composition, a mood-setter with sumptuous polyrhythms that transcends even such idylls as "Springtime Again." This final track ends Ra's studio career with his band on a grand note of sublime closure.

The late live recordings kept coming, though. There are moving rarities such as June Tyson's violin solo, as fragile as a spider's web, on "Discipline 27" (*Stardust From Tomorrow*, 1989 concert). There is even exuberance, as Michael Ray plays the jester to get us to give up a smile. But there is also the sadness of encroaching mortality, most evident in the way "We Travel the Spaceways" comes to sound like a dirge on these late recordings. It had been a long road, and the travelers were weary.

Despite the exuberance of an opening romp through "Frisco Fog" and a fun "Blue Delight" (with Michael Ray quoting from Gershwin's "Rhapsody in Blue" for a few bars), the dominant note of the *Live in London 1990* concert is struck by a somber cover of Lalo Schifrin's "Down Here on the Ground." Ra's vocal laments his earthbound, mortal status: "Down here on the ground / Is not a place for living." He finds himself "wanting something better ... wanting something more"—to emulate the birds "flying so free ... . If you hear this sound / Down here in the ground / It's only me trying to fly." Sun Ra delivers this vocal with a haunting stoicism that the concluding space chants' promises of interplanetary travel cannot mollify.

And further ironies abound when the first post-stroke live recording (*Friendly Galaxy* from Montreuil, France, in 1991) ends with the band announcing that t-shirts are for sale after the concert. Like Gustav Mahler before him (who scored his fatal heart arythmia into his ninth symphony), Ra knew how to put his own dying into his music both thematically and sonically. These concerts are important documents, but definitely not preferred entry points into Ra's music. The aftertaste of soul fatigue is too much to offer the novice listener; it can be appreciated and respected only after some exposure to Sun Ra and the Arkestra at their peaks.

Sun Ra ended his career in a strange double register. On the one hand, *Destination Unknown* (1992) is a joyous last live recording from the Moonwalker Club in Aarburg, Switzerland. The melancholy of later live works such as *Stardust from Tomorrow* and *Friendly Galaxy* is missing as the band cooks through a pleasing mix of standards and Ra compositions and chants. If one didn't know better, that is. For by this time singer, dancer and violinist June Tyson was unable to tour, fighting the breast cancer that would end her life that November; Gilmore was also absent, declining from emphysema (Szwed 376). This band sounds reinvigorated because the elder statesman in it is the healthy Marshall Allen (the now-marginalized Ra recovering from his strokes). Trumpeter Michael Ray is really directing this show, a trial run for his own post-Arkestra ensemble (Michael Ray and the Cosmic Krewe). He even gently tweaks the master during a now-joyous "We Travel the Spaceways," asking him if he's fastened his seatbelt and assuring the audience "Ra's all hooked up"—a somewhat grim joke given Ra's wheelchair-bound status. At the set's conclusion, he exhorts the small audience to "Give it up for Sun Ra." It's a fun time, but it's more Michael Ray's joy than Ra's at this point.

On the other hand, Ra's last studio recording, *A Tribute to Stuff Smith* (1992), offers more satisfying if melancholy closure. This is really violinist and former Arkestra member Billy Bang's record. Bang leads a quartet including Ra on keyboards, Thelonious Monk and Arkestra alumnus John Ore on bass and Cecil Taylor alumnus Andrew Cyrille on drums. Ra had turned his disability to advantage by offering wild melodic leaps of faith in his perforce simplified solos. As Steve Holtje says in the liner notes about Ra's solo on "Only Time Will Tell": "Almost any pianist could play it—but only Ra would think of it." The eight-song set covers standards associated with violinist Stuff Smith, including a haunting version of "Lover Man." But the epiphany is "Deep Purple," a song

Ra played with Stuff Smith on Ra's very first recording. If one has any doubts of Ra's sense of his imminent departure from Planet Earth, consider the significance of his re-recording the first song he ever taped on this, the last session he ever played on in his life. If you're enthralled by now with Ra's previous work, you'll want to take this sentimental journey with him.

Let me emphasize that this has been an extremely truncated overview—believe it or not!—of some of the highlights of Ra's music (in my humble opinion). I have discussed less than half of his recorded output, and would not dissuade the committed or even interested party from any of it. Sun Ra had too much integrity to put out half-baked playing, even if the technical standards of many of these sonic documents are palpably lower than industry standards. Which begs the question: would you prefer the well-recorded treacle of Wynton Marsalis or Kenny G., or the sometimes rough-cut diamonds (stardust from tomorrow) of the Arkestra? We know where Ken Burns stands. But as Ra would ask, what's your story?

Posthumous Discoveries and Tributes

Discoveries

As I have been indicating in this march through the catalogue, a great deal of material has been released since Sun Ra's departure from Earth in 1993. In addition to John Sinclair's release of tapes from the Ann Arbor Blues and Jazz Festival, no less than five labels have emerged that are heavily invested in making Ra's music available to the listening public: Leo Records, Evidence Records, John Corbett's Unheard Music series, Transparency and Art Yard. Transparency and Corbett have also been releasing DVDs of films featuring Sun Ra and / or Arkestra performances. The result is that a search on Amazon, for example, will turn up nearly 400 Sun Ra recordings and a double-digit amount of video material. This readily makes him the most prolific musician I am considering in this book.

In fact, so much is out there that it's easier to say what's not available. As alluded to above, the complete *Hidden Fire* recordings (as opposed to the teaser excerpt on *A Night in East Berlin*) are the only major Ra music a fan might want to hear that is not readily available (as of fall 2013). Everything else is well-documented. I have discussed some album reissues and new concerts made available above in the chronological order of their original performance. Let me devote a little time here to some numbered series of releases—Transparency's 6 live DVDs, the "Audio Series," and their later "Lost Reels" audio series—as well as to a consideration of some of the more important tribute recordings, including the Arkestra's continuation after Sun Ra as a "ghost band" under the direction of Marshall Allen.

Transparency's DVD series is a motley assortment of performance footage ranging from professional editing with multiple cameras to a single camera held by an audience member. The tradeoff is a chance for new fans to see Ra in performance at the expense of optimal visuals. The first volume of these releases, *Sun Ra Arkestra Live at the Palomino* (November 5, 1988; North Hollywood) offers a case in point.

On the one hand, the footage is somewhat low-fi: an audience member who knew how to work a zoom on his (I presume the gender) video camera. Nonetheless, the concert has some real surprises. Because of that early November date, we get a super-rare performance of "Halloween in Harlem" in all of its splendor: monster movie chord changes, Frankenstein lurches from the dancers, spooky cackles and calls of "trick or treat." As the title of the piece indicates, Ra uses this composition to super-size the racially exotic. Since the 1920s, white bohemians have wanted to check out Harlem. Here's Halloween in Harlem, the Other raised to the nth power: the African-American as the monstrous in this problematic culture. (And maybe a sly concession that Ra knows he's in costume?) Michael Jackson was making similar connections in "Thriller," but Ra gets the slam dunk here!

This performance also has plenty of footage of Michael Ray playing the (wise) fool, flirting bodaciously (and archly) with the women in the group on a cover of "Easy to Love" ("It gets no better than this")—and playing a mean trumpet. Despite its technical deficiencies, this DVD will get the casual reviewer interested in What The Heck Is This Guy Up To: the primal scene of a Ra encounter.

The second volume is another mixed bag. There are two sets from a 1986 show in East Berlin which are professionally shot in black and white (with faded picture quality). The visuals allow us to see the big band choreography (no dancers or women on this outing). And there are some musical highlights: a shimmering and ethereal synthesizer solo on "Prelude to a Kiss," a stately and deliberative reading of "Interstellar Low Ways," a bopping Gilmore solo on "Velvet." The show-stopper, however, is the "Shadow World" encore. The band shakes up the polite audience by tearing up the stage: throwing chairs around, twirling on the floor while playing their instruments, even going up to cameramen and making insane grimaces into the lens. The audience goes wild, of course, at this serious extraterrestrial invasion of the eastern bloc—a somewhat wilder affair than, say, a Billy Joel concert in Moscow!

Also on this DVD is a filmed segment of one of the Sun Ra All Stars shows from 1983 (for symmetry from West Berlin). This footage is of very high quality: color, multiple cameras on stage, professionally shot. I have discussed the music from these shows above; what the visuals add is a sense of Ra's bizarre leadership of this avant-garde ensemble. He'll do some hand conducting with little symbolic gestures that the band obligingly responds to in some mysterious fashion. Then he'll sort of prowl around the stage, hovering near individual players to listen to what they're trying to do. After that, he'll head back to his keyboards and throw a musical idea out. In contrast to the absolute power Ra wielded over his Arkestra, this looks more like herding cats. (And Lester Bowie, Don Cherry, Archie Shepp, Famoudou Don Moye and Philly Joe Jones are some mighty hep cats indeed!)

The third DVD has three separate concerts. The first is off Italian television, excerpting a solo piano concert by Sun Ra from Venice in 1978. There is some documentary footage of him walking along the canals and telling the interviewer that one's "ears have to be in tune with the cosmos" to appreciate his music. The actual concert footage shows Sun Ra in subdued costume (black and white colors and a beret) playing three original compositions for piano. His general approach, as always with his own solo piano pieces, is to alternate between thunderous dynamics and dramatic blurry fast runs (Conlon Nancarrow compositions played live instead of punched into a piano roll) and heartbreakingly gentle lyric explorations: the paradoxes of the omniverse.

The second concert is the visual record of the July 9, 1976 Arkestra concert at the Montreux Jazz Festival (released as the double album discussed above). As one will see, the visuals were half the show. He had a bevy of talented and energetic dancers in leotard, with outer-space accent, accompanying the space tunes (vs. the standards, which highlight the big band). Close-up camera work allows one to observe the hyperkineticism of Marshall Allen in alto sax skronk mode (a much better view than one ever got at an actual live show). Sun Ra flails on the electronic keyboards—at one point he's playing them behind his back. And what you SEE in the piano intro to "Take the A Train" is a man possessed by the spirit of music in Dionysian abandon. (You can only hear a little of that on the audio recording.)

The third show is from an outdoor public plaza in Lugano, Italy from 1990. Despite the late date, the Arkestra is as energetic as they were in the earlier glory days. Sun Ra hand-conducts them in a similar manner to Frank Zappa before "Discipline 27-II" cuts in. We see the band marching around on stage (on "I'll Wait for You"), more close-up Allen skronk (on the deconstructed "Prelude to a Kiss") and another crazy sax duel on "The Shadow World" (as in the second volume, but here in color). Younger electric bass and electric guitar players give the music a slight jazz-rock accent. The footage ends with a rare live recording of the late composition "Sunset on the Nile" (from *Mayan Temples* in 1990, his elegy to all things Egyptian—and life itself). In addition to the beauty of the tune, we get an electronic keyboard solo and some appropriately thematic dancers.

The fourth DVD volume is a 1987 performance at the Pacifica Radio Cap City Jazz Festival in Washington, D.C. (the same FM station whose playing of back-to-back Sun Ra in 1993 told me that he must have died). The source of this material is a semi-professional audience tape (one camera, but good zooms and close-ups). I will only consider here the unusual aspects of what is a good, but fairly typical Arkestra outing (insofar as one can ever apply the word "typical" to this group). The highlights all come well into the concert. First off, we have a highly satisfying visualization of "Love in Outer Space" with a choreographed swaying horn section. The dancers somersault, tumble and give pelvic thrusts. John Gilmore works the drums instead of his saxophone. June Tyson not only dances, but provides the only occasionally heard vocal for the song: "sunrise in outer space / love for every face."

Then Sun Ra steps up to the microphone for a relevant thematic cover of "I Dream Too Much: "I only dream to touch your heart ... . / My dreams have shown / Perhaps I dream too much alone." A big percussion break (including moving drummers for a carnival atmosphere) segues into "I'll Wait for You" and a generous sampling of space chants (I count ten distinct ones). The showstopper here is the final one, "Greetings from the Twenty-first Century which Ra hand-tailors for the Washington audience to their obvious delight:

> There's no need to cry. I'm with you now ... . I'm here now, I'm watching nations. They must do right. I am an agent of the living God. I'm watching every world including the USA. If they worship God, they must not kill. Because every person is a child of God.

As he declaims, the band exits but returns for an encore of "Spaceship Earth," a reminder to the audience that they need to pay their union dues for the "Fellowship of the Brothers of the Universe" and a final blast of the space key.

This DVD also has bonus footage of the Rufus Harley Quintet at the same festival apparently on the theory that Sun Ra fans will like this guy too. Harley plays more conventional jazz, but he packs a serious joker in his deck: he plays jazz bagpipe (in a kilt, no less)! You have to hear and see his bagpipe versions of John Coltrane's "A Love Supreme," "Greensleeves," "Stormy Weather" and "Amazing Grace" to believe them—not to mention his jazzy versions of various Scottish bagpipe melodies.

Volume Five has two New York area concerts from 1989: most of a set from the Lone Star Roadhouse in the Big Apple itself and a generous chunk of a performance at the African Street Festival in Brooklyn. The two dates must be fairly close together: the band personnel are the same (including a guy who does call-and-response bird noises with the audience during the warm-up) and both shows have a rare, zany cover of "Let's Go Fly a Kite" from *Mary Poppins*. The Lone Star gig is very heavy on the Walt Disney, in fact: we also get "Wishing Well" and "Zip-A-Dee-Doo-Dah" (this latter always a mind-bending performance of ironic minstrelsy). There also seems to be an exotic instrumental arrangement of "When You Wish Upon a Star" that only flirts with the melody.

The Brooklyn concert begins by having a giant puppet with a man inside (in the Caribbean these are called "Mocko Jumbies") lead Sun Ra onstage while embracing him—a theatrical gesture Ra imitates later by hugging and moving with a young female dancer in the Arkestra. He varies the opening space chants to tell the audience "this world is not your home" (either). Michael Ray contributes an arch vocal on "East of the Sun." Besides another soaring rendition of "Let's Go Fly a Kite," the other rarity here is a vocal performance of "Africa" (highly appropriate given the occasion). Unfortunately, the tape runs out before the piece ends.

The last DVD in the series (to date) is certainly the latest video footage of the Arkestra with Sun Ra I've ever seen (although I personally saw a show from a later date). It's two complete sets from Oakland, California on November 2, 1991. The sound is mono; the camera work is semi-professional (smooth zooms, good close-ups [you have to love James Jacson working that infinity drum]). The position is from stage right. The advantage of this set-up is an unusually intimate glimpse of the band; you can actually hear titles being called out on occasion. The downside is that Sun Ra's keyboards are on stage left, so all you see of him is an occasional head sticking above the instruments. But his health is already in decline. He's in a wheelchair (as when I last saw him) and he does not interact with the audience at all aside from playing and singing a few muted vocals in chorus.

The other Arkestra members pick up the slack and give the audience the sonic spectacle they came for (with special kudos to baritone saxophonist Pat Patrick, John Gilmore, Michael Ray and Marshall Allen). There is a dancer as well. On the one hand, this is an unusually conventional concert for this group: they take turns soloing like a regular jazz ensemble, stretching out each number in a way Ra would not consistently do in his prime. But the good news is that this show spotlights many wonderful pieces in the playbook that would only sporadically be played in concert ("Interstellar Low Ways," "Planet Earth," "El is the Sound of Joy"). "Opus in Springtime" is a mellow rarity from *Mayan Temples* (1990) with several bracing tenor solos from John Gilmore.

Perhaps the most telling moment in the concert is at the end of the second set. The concert closer is not a medley of space chants (there are none in the show; at the end of the first set "We Travel the Spaceways" is performed as a song not a chant) or a rousing "Space Is the Place" (not done at all in the show). Instead we get "They Plan to Leave." In its original context of the Reagan era, it was a jeremiad about world leaders planning to leave Earth to be safe from seemingly imminent nuclear war. As performed here, it's a haunting and melancholy song of departure. "They" are the Arkestra, and especially Sun Ra. As the song continues, the band leaves the stage, one by one; Sun

Ra is escorted off; only Marshall Allen and another member abide to get the audience to give it up for Ra—and sell some merchandise. No admirer of this music will be unmoved, As T. S. Eliot says in "The Hollow Men," "This is the way the world ends / Not with a bang but a whimper."

To turn to their audio offerings, the first Sun Ra set of CD releases for the Transparency label, before individual projects and the "Lost Reels" series, were several concerts simply labeled the "Audio Series." Volume One, a somewhat inauspicious start, was recorded at Myron's Ballroom in Los Angeles (4/2/81—just a few months after the Detroit residency). It's not that it's a bad Arkestra performance; in fact, it's a rather generous one at over three hours. The audience is enthusiastic; the band is delivering on all booster rockets. The problem is that it is for the most part a very standard Arkestra show in its offerings as opposed to the idiosyncrasies that merit a live recording. Nothing unusual happens until the second disk, which features a rather carnivalesque reading of "Enlightenment." The band turns the lyric "strange mathematics, rhythmic equations" into a background chant for the other lyrics and a few Ra declamations. Not too unusual, but noteworthy when everything else so far was by the book (albeit Sun Ra's book).

The third disk gives us Sun Ra's creation myth in a brief sermon: "At first there was nothing ... . Nothing turned itself inside out and became something." (As good as any I've heard or read.) We also get a solid reading of "Lights on a Satellite" with shimmering piano and a gorgeous, restrained John Gilmore tenor solo. "Springtime Again" is equally lilting, courtesy of June Tyson's vocals and Gilmore (again)—the right song for a gig in early April. And finally, Ra's prophecies over the concluding "Discipline 27- II" optimistically predict "Someday soon there'll be shuttles to the moon." At least in *2001: A Space Odyssey* ... .

The Audio Series Volume Two release—a live date from December 14, 1985, at Club Lingerie in Hollywood—is far more indispensable for both the completist and the curious investigator of the spaceways. I suspect this show was inspired by the decadent location (even the name of the venue speaks volumes). In any case, we get a concert that Nathaniel West would have enjoyed. You won't even mind that it's an audience member's tape (the loud clapping close to the microphone gives it away now and then); the audio quality is quite adequate.

June Tyson does a variation on the "Mystery" invocation of Sun Ra: he is "the king of the kingdom of Mystery." Ra also deviates from the standard script by saying he has "names of splendor" and "names of shame," choosing to focus on the latter: "I am Sin!" Ra proceeds to explore his somewhat cheesy dark side (and ours):

> When they close the door

And the lights are low
What do they do?
They s-i-i-i-i-i-nnnn! [with Ra's version of melisma!]

He brings "pleasure without measure" to "five million people" (a kind of Doctor Evil low-balling number!). Amidst this hilarious rap the band interrupts for a funky low-down-and-dirty jam. Can you be funky and funny at the same time? If you're the Arkestra, you can.

The "sin" rap is a tacit criticism of the Hollywood audience, however good-humored, which is continued in the "Discipline 27-II" sermon: "If I told you I was from outer space, you wouldn't believe a word I said. Would you? Why should you? ... You lost your way; you should have nothing to say ... . You can't go to Saturn. You can't go any place ... . Shame." After this chastisement of sorts, he kisses and makes up with a fine cover of "Prelude to a Kiss" replete with jazz guitar grace notes and witty alto skronk from Marshall Allen.

The typical mix of standards and Sun Ra compositions follow, but even here there's a nice curve ball: a rare cover of "Mack the Knife" which features a band member doing a cod impression of the Louis Armstrong vocal (that wacky Michael Ray?) and an extended tenor solo of the highest lyricism from John Gilmore. After Ra takes over the vocals, he even lets Gilmore end the song by himself with an extended and witty solo (it ends with the "shave and a haircut, two bits" riff).

The highlights of the second disk include a bravura Ra solo piano composition which segues into and interweaves with "Over the Rainbow": he enjoys alternating between the two texts. Obviously, it's an appropriate cover for film land. Even the concluding space chants / ring shouts have a little something extra in the mix in the form of an additional and rare chant: "No news is good news on Planet Earth." Announcer Brendan Mullen describes Sun Ra at show's end as "the Emperor of the Omniverse" in tribute to his regal performance.

Transparency also issued a nonce project on CD, *Untitled Recordings*, which doesn't fit into any of their other categories of the Audio Series, specific residencies or tours, or the Lost Reel series. Although it may not be for all casual listeners, it is curious enough to be worth mentioning—especially if one wants a look behind the scenes. The release has three separate components. The first is an audience tape from a 1985 Brooklyn concert with a quintet featuring Sun Ra, John Gilmore, Art Ensemble of Chicago percussionist Don Moye and New York Black Arts Movement jazz fixtures Andrew Cyrille on drums and Milford Graves on bass. The highlight here is "Opus in Springtime," which gets pretty free between Gilmore's tenor skronk and Sun Ra's frantic organ work.

The real rarity is the second text, a tape of a Sun Ra rehearsal at the band's Philadelphia house from circa late 1978. As with some of the recently released Frank Zappa rehearsal tapes, you get to hear the training process: Sun Ra doing a vocal scat of the desired performance, calling out the chord changes and indicating where performers should take solos. All this may be too technical for some, but it will certainly interest those with any musical background and dispel any notions that the Arkestra were playing it fast and loose on stage. Sun Ra was a diligent taskmaster. The best thing here—everything else involves rehearsing standards—is a Ra composition called by him "Tone Poem #9." This exquisite piece was scored for the reeds and horns (John Gilmore and Michael Ray eventually take solos). Given the melody and the date involved, I suspect the piece evolved into "Springtime Again" off *Sleeping Beauty*.

The other treat from the rehearsal tape is the weird dialogue among the band members as the session winds down. Sun Ra in a matter of fact way talks about encountering people who have risen from the grave (they smell like "mildew") and a musician who said that he "died in Casablanca." Another member of the Arkestra (Gilmore?) brings up the guy they saw at a concert with actual green skin. Oddly enough, this is exactly what one might think this band would be talking about! Such uncanny interests were all part of the esoteric package of Arkestra membership and communal living.

The final part of the CD is an at-home jam session from 1973 showcasing bass, synthesizer, reeds and trumpet. Good stuff, but not as revelatory as the rehearsal.

Transparency's final series, *The Lost Reel Collection Volume One: The Creator of the Universe* offers some real rarities. The first disk is from a June 1971 concert at the Warehouse in San Francisco. After a "Discipline" piece of unknown number, there are twenty minutes of Sun Ra declaiming to the audience. Unlike most such events, this is not over the band's vamping. Rather we have his pronouncements unaccompanied, with the band responding to them in rather free ways. The result is highly theatrical, in the spirit of the *Black Mass* collaboration with Amiri Baraka.

Since the CD booklet has a complete transcription of the text, I won't dwell on the (somewhat familiar) details. The main note is a Nietzschean transvaluation of values. Ra claims that hell propaganda is designed to scare folks (especially black ones) from outer space. The "bottomless pit" really refers to the depths of space: hell "is an ancient name for the sun" (he's no doubt thinking of "helios" here). Sun Ra actually admits he is "black and part of the black race"—a position he typically denied and thus a tribute to the orbital pull of the Black Power movement even on the man from Saturn. His assurance that "[t]here's nothing that can stop black people from having their own government" secures Ra's place in the tradition of liberatory black nationalism alongside other such luminaries as Marcus Garvey and Malcolm X. Finally, Sun Ra explains the decline of black folks from their Egyptian pyramid-building heyday along Gnostic lines: they have "neglected ... the creator of the universe" in favor of a lesser deity, "the white man."

This epic exegesis is followed by a trumpet and percussion interlude, more percussion and a blasting Moog synthesizer solo that thoroughly investigates the instrument and takes the audience into outer space. Some comfort is provided for the bewildered by a soothing delivery of "The Satellites Are Spinning" which underscores by background chanting that the Arkestra's ultimate goal here is to "abolish sorrow."

The second disk is even more esoteric: it's a tape of Sun Ra's third class in a course he taught at UC Berkeley in the spring of 1971 (a month before the concert on disk one). Known as "Sun Ra 171" or "The Black Man in the Cosmos," this course accommodated both students taking it for credit and local folks who wanted to sit in. John Szwed's biography goes into detail on its depth and rigor (Sun Ra after all had some training as a teacher). But an actual audio document from it is revelatory. Ra had both a message and a method: his message, as one might expect was a threefold project of 1) reminding African Americans of their glorious past; 2) confronting them with their hideously debased present; and 3) helping them toward a glorious future which involved not just Black Power and empowerment (economic and political), but ultimately moving into outer space.

His method was cultural deprogramming and reprogramming: both a matter of directing his audience to esoteric readings and his cross-lingual deconstruction of etymologies—for he believed, as did William Burroughs and many others (any linguist?), that language is the primary means of control and concealment for the powers that be. Hence, for example, "human" suggests both "hue-man" (the color factor) and "hew-man" (mortality, our inevitable date with the Grim Reaper). Or consider the connection between "sins" and "sense" and "cents." Ra believed that one had to confront and acknowledge one's own evil as well as good to be honest about the human condition and to survive in and profit from life—once again, more than a whiff of Nietzsche who mistrusted Christianity as a slave religion. For him, the message of the Book of Job is to "drop your righteousness and you'll get everything you want."

As the audience's appreciative laughter suggests, Sun Ra was an entertaining lecturer. He would allow for a question and answer period to interact with his students. And for the record, here he claims he is "not a human being"— a month before the concert where he says he is "part of the black race." So clearly there was some waffling going on, as well as the strong siren call of the Black Power movement at Berkeley and the Black Panther party. Sun Ra not only taught here; he was transformed by what he experienced as well (if only momentarily).

Intergalactic Research, the second "Lost Reel," combines two shows: a summer 1971 performance at Berkeley's Native Son club (around the time of the material documented in the first of this series) and an unknown location from 1972. The Native Son gig is on the cusp of the European tour that featured concerts like the Helsinki date: that band at that level of proficiency. The sound is very experimental, to say the least, with plenty of wailing skronk from both Allen's alto and whoever was on baritone sax. The themes from the lectures recur in the space chants. On "Why Go to the Moon?," the band adds "try Sun Ra" and "be your natural self." There's also some nice loopy synthesizer work from the maestro and a delicate interchange between the *kora* and the bass.

The second concert recording begins with another fine Moog solo, over which June Tyson eventually sings "Outer Space (Is a Pleasant Place)." A synth cascade of sound eventually leads to the band in free jazz mode both blowing simultaneously and taking solos—with further full band interjections (the sound of a crowded zoo burning down!). Ra's piano lead into the title track calms things down. "Intergalactic Research" also features a fine tenor showcase for John Gilmore. Given its repetitiousness, one suspects that this rare piece is probably in the "Discipline" series (which favors repetition)—and a very good example of same at that.

Volume three, *The Shadows Took Shape*, has two disks worth of an early 1970's concert labeled only "Spacemaster Concert." This excellently pristine recording is aptly named, for it begins with the full band blowing free jazz which morphs via a percussion break into a long solo on the electronic keyboards. After a while the Arkestra adds lyric-less chanting with an Egyptian melodic inflection: think of the soundtrack music for a film like *Land of the Pharaohs*. Sun Ra responds with muted synth overlays.

This improvisation is followed by a jaunty "Stardust from Tomorrow" and an extended reading of "Exotic Forest." This piece is the auditory equivalent of a Henri Rousseau painting or the sound of a giant progress through a jungle by a slow-moving army with elephants out of the *Mahābhārata*! Its plodding, steady beat is utterly hypnotic; a splendid trumpet solo adds some flair before the big percussion climax and the soft piano denouement.

The second disk begins with extended full-band fury lead-footing it on the space key; a little electric guitar at the end extends a hand to the rock audience before tranquility is restored with piano and bells. The space chants urge us to "[p]repare for the journey to other worlds ... . You better get ready for outer space," A previously unheard Ra poem recited by June Tyson to electronic keyboard accompaniment gives this release its title before we get another rhythmically driven number, "Friendly Galaxy." This last has an otherworldly synthesizer solo (an unusual setting) before a percussion break and a close on the "Watusi" theme.

Volume four, *Dance of the Living Image*, is another rehearsal tape from San Francisco, December 1974. Arkestra members have praised the rehearsals as often having better music than the concerts, and Sun Ra was known to have released some rehearsal sessions on the El Saturn label. So, as this music demonstrates, such material is worth putting out there. There are numerous treats on the first disk: a cocktail-lounge version of the theme from "Discipline 27-II" (listed as "unidentified title" for track 2), an oddly dissonant cover of "Sometimes I'm Happy" and a funky original with a big baritone sound and a spacious trumpet solo. But the highlight is unquestionably another original, an exotic yet tuneful processional that sounds like a fusion of Miles Davis' work in the *Sketches of Spain* era with his later electronic space funk (replete with guitar), one style evolving into another. A real gem of a rarity, in short.

The first half of the second disk involves Sun Ra showing the band a 1924 Charles L. Bates tune, "Hard Hearted Hannah." They first learn a Latin beat instrumental arrangement; then he teaches them the over-the-top lyrics, which crack the band up initially before they perfect the necessary deadpan delivery: "I saw Hard Hearted Hanna pour some water on a drowning man ... . Hard Hearted Hannah just love to see men suffer / Life is tough, but with Hard Hearted Hannah it's tougher."

The proceedings get even sillier with a Ra (very) original, an ode to flatulence which the compilers have called "Passin' Gas": "When you eat, don't eat too fast / Or you'll make music with your ass." This clear proof of Ra's deeply terrestrial humor was probably too outre even for the Arkestra to deliver in live performance. (The farting backup vocals are also quite special.) And then, turning on a dime, a straight and lovely run-through of Duke Ellington's "Sophisticated Lady" (except for some work on the ending and the vocals after the initial pass). In rehearsal as well as in concert, Sun Ra likes variety and the shock value of abrupt transitions. The tape ends with a version of the "Watusi" riff arranged just for the horns, reeds and flutes.

The Universe Sent Me, Lost Reel Collection Volume Five, presents excerpts from two concerts in the early 1970s. The first, a 1972 outdoor performance at the South Street Seaport Museum in New York City, is chiefly distinguished by an early, lush instrumental-only rendering of "Discipline 27-II." The subdued conclusion is probably as quiet as the Arkestra ever got, especially in the early 1970s—and indeed previously in the set there's lots of more characteristic free-blowing full-band space key and solo skronk.

The second show is from Paris a year and several months later. The microphone placement is near the reeds and horns, so they come through with exceptional clarity. But the vocals are muddy, which is not initially a problem since the declamations over "Discipline 27-II" (again) are also available in clearer form on the Club Lingerie tapes (Audio Series Volume Two; see above). It's worth straining to hear the rap over the improvisation in the latter part of the show, however. It's a rare recording of a legendary rant John Szwed refers to in his Ra biography (258): "Anyone can give up their life. Why don't you give up your death? ... I require you to give up your life and to give up your death." I guess that's the only way to enter the impossible world of Sun Ra's mythocracy: to go beyond life AND death. He's clearly holding his own with

Philip K. Dick (check out his recently published *Exegesis*!) and / or the Gnostics here ... .

The sixth (and last as of this writing) Lost Reel is *The Road to Destiny*, an October 18, 1973 date at the Gibus in Paris (not the same music as on the other Gibus CD discussed above). Arkestra drummer "Bugs" Hunter made the recording. As he turns the tape on, he pronounces "Arkestra" with a short "e": "Erkestra." (Irkestra?!) A puzzling moment probably attributable to a regional accent. Highlights of the actual concert include an "Astro Black" that ends with "space ethnic voices": the women singing at the top of their vocal register without actually screaming (it sounds more like a very high-pitched rasp). We also get a very mellow reading of "Discipline 27" with a shimmering vibes effect on the electronic keyboards. "Discipline 27-II" features a very long cosmo-drama dialogue between Sun Ra and June Tyson (which also has a "give up your death" moment—not surprising given the proximity in date to the Paris show on Volume Five). The Arkestra throws in a repeated quotation of the main motif from John Coltrane's "A Love Supreme" on top of the "Discipline" theme. A final treat is the inclusion of the spiritual "Swing Low, Sweet Chariot" among the space chants. The vocal approach is whimsically retro: think of how the slaves would sing in a 1930s Hollywood film about the antebellum south. If Al Jolson did this, it would be racist; coming from the Arkestra, it's a loaded deconstruction of black "identity."

To turn from Transparency's abundant offerings, the most recent Sun Ra rarities release (2013) is from England's Fantastic Voyage oldies label. *A Space Odyssey: From Birmingham to the Big Apple—The Quest Begins*. According to its compiler and annotator Kris Needs, this ambitious three CD package is a "tribute and beginner's guide" to Ra. It certainly is the former; but I think it would prove the latter for only a select and unusual demographic. The first disk, "Pre-Flight," assembles a generous amount of Sun Ra's pre-and / or-non Arkestra activities. The tracks include the ultra-rare: Clarence Williams and His Orchestra performing in 1933 "Chocolate Avenue," a composition then-teenage Ra mailed him—as such, the earliest recording of a Ra piece. (It's mainstream thirties Big Band writing with little indication of what's to come.) There's also a memorably catchy novelty record Ra arranged for bandleader Red Saunders (for the "race records" Okeh label) called "Hambone" after the technique African Americans developed for using the body as a percussion instrument. There's lots of other good stuff as well, about forty per cent of which is available on other compact disks from Evidence and Unheard Music. But this is a convenient if highly specialized compendium far more likely to interest diehard fans.

The other two disks, "Lift-Off" and "Future Shock" document the early days of the Arkestra in Chicago up to the cusp of their New York sojourn. Everything here is available elsewhere, but to my ears the sound is more pristine than on the Evidence reissues. As such, it's a pleasant enough selection of early releases showcasing his instrumental avant-garde jazz exotica in a way that helps you appreciate the rapid growth curve of the band in this era. Another interesting move here is to sequence eight compositions that appeared in diverse places as "A Suite of Philosophical Sounds," a longer work comprised of these shorter pieces which Sun Ra referred to in his notes. The anthology appropriately culminates with "The Beginning," a turning point on *The Futuristic Sounds of Sun Ra* discussed above.

One senses that Needs—who writes highly detailed and helpful liner notes—may be planning to continue this chronological project, which could make Fantastic Voyage a sixth label deeply invested in Sun Ra's work. The historical approach, which I have also tried to use here to some extent, is helpful given that Ra offers, as Kris Needs notes, "one of the world's most impossibly-convoluted [sic] discographies" (e.g. recordings released many years after they were made by Impulse records and the El Saturn label itself). This series if continued might truly be a good "beginner's guide" from which one could branch off into many interesting tangents based upon listening taste.

Tributes

And, as in the case of the death of Frank Zappa, a number of tribute CDs covering and / or honoring Ra appeared and continue to appear. The most important of these was *A Song for the Sun* (1999, El Ra Records), the first Arkestra release after the demise of their leader. The band uses the opportunity to unveil several previously unheard Ra compositions. The most beguiling of these is "They're Peepin'," a ditty of extraterrestrial voyeurism co-written with Allen: "They're peepin' in / They're doing it again." Space ethnic vocalist Art Jenkins adds his characteristic zaniness, and the band levitates (as it also does on "Cosmic Hop," an Allen composition that shows how closely he paid attention to Ra's lessons). "Blue Set" is another Ra blues piece that's nice to hear, but no great revelation. The rest of the CD mixes standards ("The Way You Look Tonight," a pointed and poignant "There Will Never Be Another You") with tributes to Ra ("Song for the Sun," "Watch the Sunshine," "Spread Your Wings") and new compositions in the style of Ra ("Galactic Voyage"). Respectfully, the Arkestra leaves the keyboard spot vacant to remind the listener who's absent as well as who abides.

Music for the 21st Century (2003, El Ra Records) is a live date from the Uncool Festival in Poschiavo, Switzerland. This recording shows how Marshall Allen learned to solve the two biggest problems of a post-Ra Arkestra: the lack of a keyboardist and the diminished uncanniness resultant from the lack of Ra's philosophical declamations to the audience. He compensates for the lack of electronic keyboards by extensive use of the EVI (Electronic Valve Instrument), a new windblown device that gives off the same timbres and loopy effects as a good synthesizer. And for the weirdness, he gives a lot of leash to the space vocalist Art Jenkins (now going by Arnold, it turns out). The result is not identical to Sun Ra's concerts, but something very much in the spirit of same (audio and visual methadone for the Ra junkie). Not for nothing is Sun Ra listed as "executive producer" on this release.

Marshall Allen's composition "Light and Darkness" has a nice hocketing introduction before it resolves into a theme. "Super Nova" offers us the triumphal return of Michael Ray on trumpet; Arnold Jenkins' space vocals grace "Voices from Outer Space." As John Szwed suggests in the liner notes, Allen's compositions hang together as a kind of suite in the spirit of Duke Ellington—which is why these somewhat elderly (in part) musicians play them straight through without a pause. "Blues Intergalactic" has a fine opening clarinet solo from Allen, and "Blue Sun" has lyrics worthy of Ra delivered by Jenkins: Today I saw a blue sun in the southwest corner of the sky ... I've never seen such beauty in a blue sun."

"In-B-Tween" has a nice vamp reminiscent of Ra's processionals over which Marshall Allen can deliver some free jazz skronk on his alto sax. On "Mr. Mystery," Arnold Jenkins assures us that "Sun Ra left in a flying saucer": the beginning of the posthumous (and postmodern) Sun Ra mystery religion! After this, the first pause in the concert. A deep cut Ra cover follows ("Reflex Motion," not heard on any recording since 1962's *Secrets of the Sun*). "When You Wish Upon a Star" gives us an appropriate slice of Walt Disney to evoke the later incarnations and interests of the Arkestra when Ra was still on-planet. It's a jagged, edgy—and yet oddly moving—reading. As performed, the songs and its lyric have real resonance: "If your heart is in your dream / No request is too extreme." The concert appropriately ends with "We Travel the Spaceways," now a battle-scarred anthem for the band's strange celestial road. Allen's EVI's boops and blurps rev up the spaceship one more time to end the space memorial service as the extraterrestrial second line joyously comes back from the cemetery (which may contain an empty tomb).

The most recent release of the post-Ra Arkestra is a live date from the Paradox Music Club in Tilburg, the Netherlands, on June 20, 2008 (the last night of a five-day residency, released in 2009 on In and Out Records from Freiburg, Germany; I mention all this to indicate how the Arkestra is still all about finding supporters for temporary alliances rather than being regarded as the global cultural treasure they are and given a sinecure). This beautifully recorded set— my, how technology has advanced—is nicely balanced between four Sun Ra compositions (actually five, since there's a medley), four Marshall Allen pieces and a Fletcher Henderson cover. Arnold Jenkins and Michael Ray are not in attendance; but for the first time in fifteen years, the band has a keyboardist: Farid Barron on piano and organ. A wise decision, I think, since so many of

Ra's works were designed to emphasize his keyboards.

The opener, Allen's "Space Walk," is a warm-up piece very similar to the improvisations that Sun Ra's band would play before he came out, a chance for the group to collectively stretch out. An instrumental "Discipline 27-II" follows (here called "27-B"; whatever) in medley with "I'll Wait for You." The former is instrumental only (no declamations, of course); the latter has group vocals and even some side excursions into other space chants ("This World Is Not My Home," "Angel Race"). Then we get more Ra originals: the deep cuts of the very early (1956) "Dreams Come True" (with a Knoel Scott vocal and a fine trumpet solo from Charles Davis) and "Velvet" (a driving instrumental from *Jazz in Silhouette* [1958] that ended up on the set list of some dates on the 1966 campus tour of the northeast).

"You'll Find Me" (Allen's instrumental rejoinder to Sun Ra's "I'll Wait for You"?) is a lovely, lyrical tune with an ear-catching piano solo from Barron. Appropriately, he does not try to sound like Sun Ra—nor could he, being more polished and less fiery. Allen's "Millennium" uses the full resources of the Arkestra in a big Cadillac arrangement to celebrate the new era and invite the audience to "come ride with us on cosmic dust." His "Take Off," given the title, is appropriately far out EVI-led electronica: the band at its spaciest. Then, just like Sun Ra used to do, Marshall Allen turns the band on a dime for a faithful reading of Ra mentor Fletcher Henderson's "Hocus Pocus." The recording ends with the hitherto-unreleased Sun Ra original "Space Idol," a boppy tune with an initial exploratory piano solo. No doubt there's much more of this quality in the vaults and notebooks of this astonishingly prolific musician.

But how much will we get to hear? *Points on a Space Age*, a 2009 documentary about the Marshall Allen Arkestra, directed by Ephraim Asili, is somewhat pessimistic. There really isn't anyone as qualified as Marshall Allen to carry on, and he's in his late eighties. Members see the current state of the band as the end of the line, even though there are young players joining it: it's a question of leadership.

This film (available on DVD) is a fine tribute to Sun Ra in its own right. It skillfully intercuts JFK speeches and NASA footage with archival films of Ra in Egypt and the contemporary band to establish the historical context for Ra's space-age agenda and mission. We hear from the Arkestra about diverse proclivities of their late leader: his wanting to vary the band with different personalities and skill levels to create a microcosm of the omniverse; his visiting electronic keyboard factories to show them what he wanted to hear from the instruments; his desire to appeal to all the senses in his shows (hence the strong visual element); and his interest in "moving orchestration" resulting in the performers moving through space as they played (cf. similar sonic interests on the part of Charles Ives and Edgard Varese). One band member describes what they play as "African American classical music." The most striking concert footage in the documentary shows us a dancer in a kind of trapeze cage lifted off the stage and executing an aerial ballet to "Love in Outer Space" while a psychedelic abstract film plays in the background.

In addition, Arkestra members have spun off into other solo projects. Most notably, trumpeter Michael Ray and the Cosmic Krewe showcase Ra material in their concerts and recordings. Ray and keyboardist Adam Klipple execute an especially delicate reading of the lesser-known "Island in Space" (now available in its original Ra version as "Island in the Sun" on *Janus*). Marshall Allen also led a quartet for several recordings with reedist Mark Whitecage, bassist Dominic Duval and drummer / Arkestra member Luqman Ali. As with John Gilmore's side outings, it's interesting to hear Allen playing in another context. Ra's spirit nevertheless presides understandably over some of their choice of standards ("When You Wish upon a Star," "Fly Me to the Moon"). The sensitive production values make these CIMP (Creative Improvised Music Projects) releases well worth a listen.

Of the tribute albums by non-Arkestra personnel, *Wavelength Infinity* is the best (and even features a few cameos from Arkestra members). The players here don't really try to sound like Ra's band; they use the music to do their own (often unusual) thing. Steve Adams and Ben Goldberg's duet workout for reeds on "Transition" is spellbinding, as is The Residents' adaptation of "Space Is the Place." The Splatter Trio do much justice to bassist Ronnie Boykins' composition "Tiny Pyramids." Then there's "Miss Muragtroid" (Alicia J. Rose) accompanying her recitation of Ra's poem "Nature's Law" on accordion. The Residents, Miss Murgatroid and Eugene Chadbourne with Zappa alum / drummer Jimmy Carl Black (on another version of "Space Is the Place") all separately manage the enviable feat of playing cover versions of Ra stranger than the originals by the master. We also get an appropriately electronic version of "Disco 3000" from Elliot Sharp. But the absolute highlight of the double CD is a "Tri-School Artestra" of elementary school players performing "Planet Earth." The joyous simplicity and genuine wildness of the kids captures an element in Ra perfectly that the more adult and sophisticated Arkestra could only approximate. When they whisper "the spirit of Sun Ra" at the end, you can believe that Ra truly lives!

I am less enamored of *Spaceways Incorporated: Thirteen Cosmic Standards by Sun Ra and Funkadelic*. This tribute from reedist Ken Vandermark, bassist Nat McBride and drummer Hamid Drake has some fine original jamming on "El is a Sound of Joy" and "We Travel the Spaceways." It even has the blessing of the great Ra scholar John Corbett, who co-produced. (In fact, it illustrates the argument of his opening essay in *Extended Play* by gesturing toward a genealogy that links Ra with Funkadelic.) So what's my gripe? Only this: Ra was a teacher, first and foremost. And this set provides a misleading lesson to the novice jazz fan most likely to pick this up as an introduction to the material it covers. The Ra songs are quieter jazz numbers; the Funkadelic covers are loud, kicking funk. Why such a neat division of labor? There are plenty of loud funk jams in the Arkestra's late-seventies repertoire (and scads of loud Ra generally). Why make Ra the high-art chamber alternative to Funkadelic? It's a neat structure, but I fear it's also facile. I'd prefer the cosmic slop of the truth—which would establish the linkages even better.

I am much fonder of alt-rock band Yo La Tengo's one-off, 2002's *Nuclear War, Or How I Learned to Stop Worrying and Love the Bomb*. This CD offers four versions of Sun Ra's soulful Reagan-era agit-prop classic. The first version is a highly percussive but quite faithful reading of the original version's call-and-response vocals. The only change made is an addition of "neutron bombs" to the chanted arsenal (which I don't hear on the Arkestra versions). The second take adds didgeridoo and a spirited children's chorus (getting to cuss up a storm on the lyrics, including an opportunity to drop the "M" bomb). You can hear one kid softly chuckling at song's end.

Version three is a longer, jazzier take with piano and horns added to (again, as in take one) heavy percussion. The saxophonist throws out some free-jazz skronk in the spirit of the Arkestra; the trumpeter lights off some Michael Ray inspired flares. The jazz players sing and chant as well; one muses about the oddity of "walking around without an ass." And finally we get a techno remix of the second reading by Mike Ladd: four diverse ways of looking at the song for a tribute that's both respectful and irreverent—respectful to the irreverence of the material! Would Sun Ra want it any other way?

No doubt there will be more to come of Ra's music as reissues proceed, audience tapes surface and his music enters further into the repertoire of classic jazz. All likely developments, *pacé* Ken Burns. Meanwhile, there is plenty to listen to if you find earth boring.

Why Sun Ra Matters

The *Washington Post* obituary for Sun Ra, I recall, described him as "the missing link between Duke Ellington and Public Enemy." Although a glib soundbyte, it captures a certain truth about Ra. He was not only a collapser of all periods of music, though, from the ancient world to the space age; he was also a synchronic absorber of whatever was most interesting as a sonic possibility. Perhaps little that he did per se was truly unique: on that score, his greatest contribution might have been the addition of electronic keyboards to the Big Band ensemble. But the fusion of musical influences gave him an utterly remarkable sound that helped kick start post-bop jazz into all sorts of experimentation. (Some, like free jazz, partially arose from a misreading of the Ra project. Even mistaken apprehensions of the Arkestra proved fertile.) Who else combined dissonance, microtones, the bottom end of the orchestra so loved by Edgard Varese, electronics, playing chords on top of each other (the "space key"), the relentless polyrhythms of Africa, enough repetition to satisfy Phillip Glass or John Cage—plus costumes, dance, theater, spectacle? That was the live show; the recordings anticipated punk production with their avoidance of glitz and willingness to experiment with unusual techniques of recording. Before *White Light / White Heat*, there was *Art Forms of Dimensions Tomorrow*. And all delivered with precision and discipline. First and foremost as a musician and showman, Sun Ra carved out a special niche in American popular culture.

But as we have seen, Ra was also a poet and a philosopher. Although I have concentrated understandably upon his music and ideas, his poetic output also figures into his importance—even though it is as destined to be marginalized by literary anthologies as his jazz is from some flat-browed approaches to the tradition. It would strike many as not poetry at all because of its high level of abstraction. Like Ra's music, it is not necessarily trying to fit in with the conventions of its form.

But I would submit that Ra is not writing in a vacuum. His verse combines the aphorisms and parables of an eccentric American poet like Stephen Crane with the repetition and wordplay of a Gertrude Stein. Here is "The Foolish Foe," Sun Ra at his closest approach to Stephen Crane:

> There were some things I never tried to do
> And most of them were things I wanted to do
> ... There were opposing forces
> Why should they oppose me?
> Why? Why?
> Now and then I thought, there is
> No such enemy as I think they are.
> But then, it is beyond thought ... it is beyond thought
> I feel
> These opposing forces whose power is their weakness
> The power they grant to their servants / subjects
> They exist, Indeed they do.
> I feel and always have felt
> It is, it always was true
> Since this plane of existent I came to be, to know
> They are are/were here!
> I never resisted them,
> They think I did
> It was only pretense desires I projected to them
> Were my non-resistance weapon/shield of defense
> I do not desire what they thought I desire

> Neither now nor ever then
> Non-resistance became my resistance
> My resistance is non-resistance. Do they challenge?
> I resist the challenge
> Foolish foe!
> I have already won the victory
> How? You will never know.
> I have forgotten the how I did
> I only know I know only
> I only know ... .
> It was never your game,
> It is always mine
> I resist the challenge
> Foolish Foe
> I always win the victory
> You did not know the secret code
> If I win, I win and if I lose I win!
> You did not know
>
> You do not know! (Szwed 326-7)

Although longer and slightly more abstract than a typical Crane poem (and containing more Steinian grammatical perplexities and repetitions), "The Foolish Foe" can still bring to mind a Crane poem such as the following:

> Why do you strive for greatness, fool?
> Go pluck a bough and wear it.
> It is as sufficing.
>
> My Lord, there are certain barbarians
> Who tilt their noses
> As if the stars were flowers,
> And thy servant is lost among their shoe-buckles.
> Fain would I have mine eyes even with their eyes.
>
> Fool, go pluck a bough and wear it. (#52, Katz 56)

The archaic language is the main clue here that the above is by Stephen Crane and not Sun Ra. While there is little evidence to suggest Ra was necessarily exposed to Crane (or Stein, for that matter), these iconoclasts innovate in their verse in resonant ways.

A good example of Ra in a more Steinian voice can be found in his poem "Nature's Laws" ("Nature's Law" is the title given on the Miss Murgatroid version):

> According to nature's laws and laws
> I be as I am and what I am not even
> Because and yet not even because
> Because, for, and, that is ... . why ... .
> Because, should and why. If then
> Then and so
> Perhaps
> May
> If I do, I will
> And if I don't I won't
> Either way I do and don't perspectively
> Why, when, how, what, which
> Yes, no, neither. (Abraham 84)

Any random sample of Gertrude Stein's writing will show parallel interests in repetition as a way to restore to words their uncanniness. I open *The Heath Anthology of American Literature, Volume 2,* to the following excerpt from Stein's *Geographical History of America*:

> *Page III*
>
> Human nature has nothing to do with it.
> Human nature.
> Has nothing to do with it.
>
> *Page IV*
>
> Emptying and filling an ocean has nothing to do with it because if
>   it is full it is an ocean and if it is empty it is not an ocean.
> Filling and emptying an ocean has nothing to do with it.
>
> *Page IV*
>
> Nothing to do with master-pieces.
>
> *Page V*
>
> Nothing to do with war. (1261-2)

Und so weiter. You get the general resemblance, I trust!

Sun Ra used his poetic writing to illustrate his cosmology and to aid in deprogramming his audience from its mistakenly earthbound and death-oriented ways. It was a teaching tool, in short, as was his music. The published poetry often overlaps with the song lyrics, as in the case of "In Some Far Place" (which became the lyrics for the song / space chant "I'll Wait for You"):

> In some far place

> Many light years in space
> I'll wait for you.
> Where human feet have never trod ... .
> Where human eyes have never seen,
> I'll build a world of abstract dreams
> And wait for you.
>
> In tomorrow's realm
> We'll take the helm
> Of a new ship ... .
> Like the lash of a whip
> We'll be suddenly on the way
> And lightning-journey
> To yet another other friendly shore. (Abraham 31)

The whip simile is an unusually poetic touch for Ra, and recalls his threats to chain up black people and drag them into outer space (in the film *Space Is The Place*). Ra saw himself as a revisionist slave master. Whereas the white slavers disciplined their charges to dehumanizing ends, Ra's disciplinary regime will ultimately liberate his followers from the deathly ways of earth. Through music, drama and words he offered this charismatic promise.

Sun Ra was also of some interest and importance as an amateur street-corner philosopher and sage. Consider his unusual philosophical position, as helpfully unpacked by John Szwed in the biography. Ra's beliefs were an unusual, but not unprecedented, fusion of Nietzschean iconoclasm and platonic idealism. On the one hand, Ra attacked the same targets as Nietzsche: Christianity and democracy. The way of the cross and an overemphasis upon freedom were gross misapprehensions to him. Like Nietzsche, Ra was a transvaluer of such fundamental western assumptions. He preferred Egyptian discipline and leadership (as he perceived it) to Christianity's slave religion which turned the other cheek; he preferred enlightened autocracy (or his preferred term, mythocracy) to the illusory freedom of democracy that gave the incompetent the same access to power as the enlightened pharaoh leader.

But he also preserved some absolute values from his skeptical transvaluations, however inexplicitly he evoked them: "beauty, discipline, space, the Creator, infinity" (Szwed 383-4). There were absolute values in the universe that offered connections to an ideal world of beauty as in the writings of Plato and Pythagoras. His reconciliation of these two positions was simply that these values were not the values of earth. Ra hop-scotched over Christianity, St. Paul and the enlightenment itself to offer a fusion of ancient Greece and Egypt with a pisgah view of the cosmos.

Curiously enough, this reconciliation of Plato and Nietzsche was done before, by the German philosopher Max Scheler in his 1914 treatise *Der Formalis-*

mus in der Ethik und die Materiale Wertethik (roughly translatable as "Formalism in Ethics and the Material Ethics of Values"). This work has never been translated into English, so it is unlikely Ra was ever exposed to it. But Scheler's project, which came to be known as "ethical platonism," was independently charting the same northwest passage between Plato and Nietzsche that so interested Sun Ra. A final curiosity here is that Pope John Paul II's theological scholarship prior to his papacy concentrated upon Scheler, ethical platonism and the issues it raised. No doubt Ra would have been mightily amused by these ironies![10]

Besides Sun Ra's importance as a musician, showman, poet and philosopher, he deserves some credit for having "kept the sixties going a long time," as John Sinclair has observed (in Szwed 354). Ra's musical commune of musicians, charismatic playfulness, and obliging fusion of experimentation and joy were the very best of what the sixties had to offer culturally and existentially. For most of us, this experience was a brief epiphany before things went sour. But Ra kept the soap bubble up in the air for three decades: for this alone he deserves much credit.

Nonetheless, Sun Ra genially saw himself as a failure, albeit a "successful" one:

> I did never want to be successful. I want to be the only thing I could be without anyone stopping me in America—that is, to be a failure. So I feel pretty good about it, I'm a total failure ... . So now as I've been successful as a failure, I can be successful. (Szwed 366)

There is much to be said about his observations. He is addressing the ultimate separation of art and commerce in America—a serious problem for all of the musicians I have been discussing at least at some point in their careers. (Yoko Ono and Neil Young have been the luckiest in this regard.) If you choose the path of art, you will in all likelihood be an economic failure. Ra's remarks are a typical transvaluation of these considerations. If the sentence of Earth is one of death, America's is one of failure for the artist who refuses to compromise. That might be Earth's sentence as well, for what country really supports its artists? Where is arcadia? When was the golden age?

These comments also underline Ra's connection with the sixties; as we all know, that too was a "successful failure." It accomplished some goals regarding civil rights and ending the war in Vietnam, but it fell far short of its expectations.

In the packaging for *Blue Delight* (1988), Sun Ra included a valedictory poem for his audience:

> We are approaching the twin roads of the future,
> One day planet earth must choose to change;

And you must choose
There is no other way.
Don't forget the alter hints I give to you ...
One day, you must choose to change
Be sure your intuition's voice is not defied
Or perhaps neglectfully denied.
No other voice will speak to you
No other voice knows what to say. ("You Must Choose")

Ra's confidences to the reader / listener ally him with that most intimate of nineteenth-century American poets, Walt Whitman. In 1855, Whitman ended "Song of Myself" with this assurance:

Failing to fetch me at first keep encouraged,
Missing me one place search another,
I stop somewhere waiting for you. (89)

Whereas Whitman advised us to look for him under our boot-soles, Ra's promise of future rendezvous is celestial and intergalactic: in some far place, many light-years in space, he waits for us.

So much for Sun Ra's universal message and significance. I want to conclude by briefly addressing his specific importance for African American culture. For like many artifacts of same culture, Sun Ra's work was double-coded: it had a universal message and a specifically targeted meaning for black audiences. I am not saying anything new here. Graham Lock in his liner notes to *Live in London 1990* (with the help of Victor Schonfield, John Szwed and Julian Vein) makes the same point. I would only add a critical concept by way of a prelude from Henry Louis Gates, Jr. In his seminal work *The Signifying Monkey*, Gates notes how African American texts are unusually intertextual: they bounce off each other in two distinct ways which he calls "unmotivated" and "motivated" signifying. Unmotivated signifying is done in homage to a preceding text (he uses the example of Alice Walker's recycling of tropes from Zora Neale Hurston). Motivated signifying offers a critique of the earlier text: it is a parody, not a homage or a pastiche (Gates 346).

Although Lock does not use this terminology, he astutely discovered that Sun Ra was deep into motivated signifying on several counts. For starters, his use of Egypt as a cultural touchstone turns on its head the standard identification in the spirituals of African Americans with the Israelites (e.g., "Go Down Moses"). Along Nietzschean lines, Ra perceived that such a linkage was disempowering: why be slaves when you are descended from pharaohs? The sorrow songs' vehicle of escape was a "sweet chariot coming for to carry [them] home" (and indeed, as we have seen, the Arkestra would even include this in the space chants sometimes). But Ra's vehicles of preference were moonships, rockets, flying saucers. And his goal was not heaven, but outer space: "pluto too"—and beyond (Lock).

All this Graham Lock correctly observes. I'd add a few more examples of motivated signifying upon spirituals and the black church. Where this body puts its ultimate faith in the suffering Jesus, Sun Ra countered with himself as a "living myth" who even had aspects of Lucifer in him. Sun Ra was very interested in the Creator, but he had a profound distrust of the Son (vs. the SUN!) as a bad example of suffering and passive endurance of the world's woes. Lucifer's rebellion was a more useful role model. (In this respect, Ra is solidly in the earlier, more European Romantic tradition alongside William Blake, Lord Byron, Walt Whitman and many others).

And lastly, Sun Ra trumped the alienation expressed in many spirituals ("sometimes I feel like a motherless child") with a far more profound distancing claim: "this *world* is not my home" (italics mine). The problem was not being black; it was being human, terrestrial. The solution was to transcend the human and discover one's inner alien—and join other beings in the omniverse.

Considered in this light, Sun Ra offered a major alternative to his people through his lyrics, music, and writings. He offered a space-age version of black power that can be profitably compared with the labors of a Marcus Garvey or a Malcolm X. Like the former, he by his own admission was "a total failure" (Szwed 366 again). His program never caught on as a mass movement; it was embraced only by a few fans and band members—and they're / we're not getting any younger! It is gratifying to note that some younger listeners are discovering this enticing singularity in our cultural cosmos (and I hope this chapter piques some further interest in Sun Ra for the reader). In this regard as well, he waits as an alternative for anyone who "find[s] Earth boring." Or worse ... .

Works Cited

Abraham, Adam, ed. *Sun Ra Collected Works Volume I: Immeasurable Equation*. Chandler, Arizona: Phaelos, 2005.

Blumenthal, Bob. Liner notes for *Sun Ra & his Arkestra Live at Montreux*. Inner City 1039. 1976.

Campbell, Robert L. Liner notes for *The Great Lost Sun Ra Albums*. Evidence 22217-2. 2000.

——. Liner notes for *The Singles*. Evidence 22164-2. 1996.

Carles, Philippe. Liner notes for *Unity*. Horo HDP 19-20. 1978.

Cassenti, Frank, director. *Mystery, Mr. Ra: Sun Ra and his Arkestra*. Rhapsody Films, distributor. 1984.

Corbett, John. *Extended Play: Sounding Off from John Cage to Dr. Funkenstein*. Durham, NC: Duke University Press, 1994.

Works Cited

Gates, Henry Louis, Jr. "Introduction to *The Signifying Monkey*." In *African American Literary Theory: A Reader*. Ed. Winston Napier. New York: NYU Press, 2000. Pages 339-347.

Gershon, Pete."Twenty First Century Music: Reissues, Memorabilia & the Ongoing Activities of the Sun Ra Arkestra Under the Direction of Alto Saxaphonist Marshall Allen." In *Sun Ra: Interviews and Essays*. Ed. John Sinclair. London: Headpress, 2010.

Katz, Joseph, ed. *The Complete Poems of Stephen Crane*. Ithaca, NY: Cornell University Press, 1972.

Keel, John. *Visitors from Space: The Astonishing, True Story of the Mothman Prophecies*. St. Albans, Great Britain: Panther, 1976.

Lange, Art. Liner notes for *We Travel the Spaceways / Bad and Beautiful*. Evidence 22038-2. 1992.

Lauter, Paul, general editor. *The Heath Anthology of American Literature: Volume Two*. Third edition. Boston: Houghton Mifflin, 1998.

Lock, Graham. Liner notes for *Live in London 1990*. Blast First BFFP60 CD. 1996.

Meltzer, David, ed. *Writing Jazz*. San Francisco: Mercury House, 1999.

Michel, Ed. Liner notes for *The Great Lost Sun Ra Albums*. Evidence 22217-2. 2000.

Ra, Sun. *The Ark and the Ankh: Sun Ra / Henry Dumas in Conversation 1966, Slug's Saloon NYC*. IKEF02. 2001.

——. *The Immeasurable Equation*. Xerox of collected edition compiled by Hartmut Geerken, courtesy of BenWa.

——. Liner notes for *When Angels Speak of Love*. Evidence 22216-2. 2000.

——. "You Must Choose." In liner notes for *Blue Delight*. A&M 5260. 1989.

Rammel, Hal. Liner notes for *Strange Strings*. 1966. Unheard Music Series ALP263CD. Ca. 2006.

Rose, Cynthia. *Living in America: The Soul Saga of James Brown*. London: Serpent's Tail, 1990.

Schuller, Gunther and Martin Williams. Booklet essay for *Big Band Jazz: From the Beginnings to the Fifties*. Washington, DC: Smithsonian, 1983.

Shore, Michael. Liner notes for *Atlantis*. Evidence 22067-2. 1993.

Smith, R.J. *The One: The Life and Music of James Brown*. New York: Gotham Books, 2012.

Szwed, John F. Liner notes for *The Magic City*. Evidence 22069-2. 1993.

——. *Space Is The Place: The Lives and Times of Sun Ra*. With a discography by Robert L. Campbell. New York: Pantheon, 1997.

Whitman, Walt. *Leaves of Grass: Comprehensive Reader's Edition*. Eds. Harold W. Blodgett and Sculley Bradley. New York: W. W. Norton & Company, 1968.

Discography is available in Robert L. Campbell's *The Earthly Recordings of Sun Ra* (Cadence Jazz Books, 1994) or in Szwed. John Szwed's scholarly biography is the only book-length study of Sun Ra readily available—a handy compendium of information. So, as in the case of Joni Mitchell, I have had to rely on one book more than scholarly conventions deem advisable. At this point in time, the four major Sun Ra scholars are Robert L. Campbell, John Corbett, Hartmut Geerken and John F. Szwed. They have all been crucial informants for my undertaking.

Appendix: Musical Highlights from The Complete Detroit Jazz Center Residency

Disc 1: A very generous serving of jazz standards. John Gilmore takes a superb tenor solo on "'Round Midnight" (the Thelonious Monk composition). "Cocktails for Two" gets a highly mutated rendition. The Ra original "Love in Outer Space" has a funky organ solo and whistles in the style of a Haitian ra-ra procession. (Perhaps a sonic pun. Ra likes to work his adopted name in whenever he can!) James Jacson's Ancient Egyptian Infinity Drum also gets a long workout on this number's very serious drum break—even longer ones are to follow in this box set!—before the piece's huge, dramatic finish.

Disc 2: The end of the first set on Friday December 26, 1980, showcases a brief and wacky a cappella reading of "Interplanetary Music." The second set has some noteworthy "untitled improv[isations]." Track 9 has a fine John Gilmore tenor solo with some serious skronk (what Arkestra fans refer to when the reed player goes up into pitches only dogs can hear interspersed with low honking—challenging listening at first which was designed to drive off the uncommitted). The next track has some simultaneous soloing in the spirit of the free jazz movement (despite Ra's dislike for it, and even for freedom for that matter!). His last "Unidentified Title," oddly enough, has a kind of Bach feel to it with its sinuous variations on a musical theme. From Szwed's biography, however, it is apparent that Sun Ra was well-versed in the classical canon courtesy of at least Lula Hopkins Randall, a professor from Alabama A & M for Negroes [sic] (*Space* 27).

Disc 3: We open with "Spontaneous Simplicity," a wonderful and understated Ra composition. "Images," which follows, contributes a soaring Michael Ray trumpet solo. The rare "Stompy Jones" is very funky and gut-bucket.

Disc 4: The first Saturday set opens with impressive Marshall Allen skronk. A brief flute interlude is followed by Tony Bethel on trombone, more skronk from Gilmore, a Michael Ray and Walter Miller trumpet duet, and more skronk from Allen: the Arkestra following its director's urgings to play the impossible to provide cosmic tones for mental therapy. Then Ra himself steps in with an intermittently mellow organ solo. Another "Unidentified Title" offers lashings of musical exotica with its percussion effects. And finally with regard to highlights, Sun Ra uses his organ to imitate a subway train arriving and leaving on the bookends of their cover of "Take the A Train."

Disc 5: This is the first disc in the set to show you some virtually unheard, ultra-weird facets of Ra (yes, beyond the high standards already available). It begins with "Slippery Horn," well-played if innocuous kitsch designed perhaps to lull the listener into a false state of relaxation. "Solitude," with its dramatic and showy organ, hints at the turbulence to come. Ra's "Right Road, Wrong Direction" rap from *The Antique Blacks* (see above) evolves into a full-blown, angry diatribe against Planet Earth, "a cursed and doomed planet." It gets even wilder with the "Bad Truth" declamation. Ra screams and shouts: "The truth about the nations of Planet Earth is a BAD truth ... . The history of the people of Planet Earth is a BAD truth." Then Ra turns into a drill sergeant and gets the band and audience marching in a manner reminiscent of his childhood membership in the Boy Scouts knockoff American Woodmen Junior Division (see Szwed 9):

> Shoulder to shoulder
> Man to man
> March as men should
> March as men should

Ra's militancy gets augmented by the band playing a marching beat to this. He exhorts the audience to "fight against the common enemy of all humanity, namely DEEEAAATHHH!": "Don't be a slave / Lay down in the grave / Bow down in the dust." These proceedings are very theatrical. It's almost like hearing a play (cf. his collaboration with Amiri Baraka).

Lastly, he reminds his audience that "When you travel through outer space, you use the password, the word of victory: Ra, Ra, Ra Ra Ra!" The band turns into his cheerleaders. Even for Ra, this is as weird as it gets. His switch to "Over the Rainbow" on piano chills things out and cools them down. But for a few minutes the listener can hear how ambitious (and, yes, strange) Ra's agenda is: to unite humanity and get them to leave Earth, the planet of death and false freedom (freedom to die), for his discipline and the immortality of outer space travel and living mythology.

Disc 6: Another deluxe version of "Love in Outer Space" occurs, with "alien" groans and guffaws during James Jacson's Infinity Drum solo.

The second Saturday set also finds Ra in an extremely didactic mood, willing to share with an enraptured audience his unusual and complex beliefs. Over the musical strains of "Discipline 27-II," a frequent setting for such ruminations, he reveals that "the sun is a computer that cannot lie ... the big eye ... God's private eye in the sky ... a cosmic spy." The sun sees all, knows all and tells God what's really going on in the solar system, especially on Earth. Ra once again draws a line in the sand between himself and the audience—until they sign up for his space program:

> Everything is my brother except man and woman ... on Planet Earth ... . Am I 666? What kind of mystery am I? ... You're the alien. You have no birth certificates; you have death certificates. So I pronounce you dead until you can prove to me you're alive. Is it right for people to bow to Death? That's your master. The Unknown sent me to break all the laws of nature. I am authorized to do wrong. The universe sent me to be wicked and evil ... . You talk about rights for women ... . Do you have rights for angels? No! ... How do you dare go into outer space? You're just babies in the universe.

There are obvious evocations of all kinds of Gnostic and neoplatonic thought here, all of which Ra voraciously read. The creator of Earth is an inferior deity (the Gnostic demiurge), and what is threatening that creation is paradoxically a higher good—so Satan and Cain can be heroes in this context. Sun Ra always wanted to be, as such, both good and evil to accomplish what he saw as his other-worldly task.

Keeping with the martial theme of the previous set, the "Astro Nation" chant (discussed above in the context of *Live in Cleveland*) gets a tattoo drumbeat accompaniment for the marching Arkestra and audience.

Disc 7: "Lights on a Satellite" features an extended Gilmore solo with Marshall Allen and Danny Ray Thompson on flute backup.

Disc 8: The last part of the second Saturday set has a great and stoic version of the new space chant "Strange Celestial Road": "We're traveling a strange celestial road / to endless ever." The road-weariness of the Arkestra really comes through. As it should, for these two shows (on discs 4-8) pushed the band about as far as it could go!

Disc 9: After the *sturm und drang* of the night before, the Sunday matinee begins on a suitably restrained note with Marshall Allen plucking the *kora* (a traditional African stringed instrument). This use of an ancient musical platform is reminiscent of the slogan of Chicago's AACM movement (the Associated Artists of Creative Music): "ancient to the future." These musicians, including Muhal Richard Abrams and members of the Art Ensemble of Chicago heard Ra and were influenced by him (Szwed 176). Some would even play with him in Europe as members of the 1983 Sun Ra All Stars.

John Gilmore mellows the crowd even more with a be-bop cover of "Jingle Bells" in honor of the season. "Hymn to the Sun" is a gentle composition for flutes that seamlessly leads into the invocation and arrival of the man himself, "the living myth." As Ra often did, he tells the audience "You can call me Mister Mystery." This time he lives up to his name by introducing brand new material the compilers of this box set cannot identify even to this day. Track 3 contains a wild baritone sax solo from Danny Ray Thompson with lots of choogling and backing from trumpet and French horn. This piece is followed by a very angular composition for bassoon, flute, trumpet and French horn with no percussion until the very end of the piece—real outer space music! Track 4 is an odd, very deliberative original for organ. The band's eventual entrance into the piece and subsequent repetitive playing of the main motif lead me to believe this is an unknown number of the "Discipline" series of Ra compositions.

Disc 10: Here we have a rare live "Sleeping Beauty" with Ra singing in a relaxed mood backed by on-point vocal harmonies—which also grace the following "Fate in a Pleasant Mood." Ra assures us "The time is fast approaching when fate will be in a pleasant mood." This mood arrives with the Ra classic "El is a Sound of Joy," which has a jumping middle section and Michael Ray cutting loose in addition to the basic presentation. "South America" is a Latin-influenced number with a massive percussion line. Ra and the band continue the positivity with the wistful vocals:

> South America, such a nice place ... .
> I plan to visit there one day.
> And if it's as nice as they say it is,
> Perhaps I'll be tempted to stay ... .
> I know I'm going to stay.
> Ole!

The geographical tour continues with "Africa," which we are assured is a "romantic land of treasure ... . There's never skies so blue as in Africa." The percussionists drive the beat hard and stretch it out, eventuating in another Infinity Drum solo. These works showcase not only Ra's more earthbound side (and after the day before, certainly more Earth-friendly approach!) as well as his interest in lounge music and exotica. (Les Baxter could have readily covered this material.) The matinee ends with space chants about Ra's very favorite place, Saturn, his home planet: "Saturn rings, rings around Saturn ... . Who put those rings around Saturn? ... I am Sun Ra, Lord of the Saturn Rings." (Eat your heart out, Sauron!)

Disc 11: The evening show on Sunday finds Ra returning to a tutorial mood, revisiting his more esoteric doctrines (again to the tune of "Discipline 27-II"): "Time was crucified 2,000 years ago ... . You are living on the other side of time ... . Confusion and chaos" knock on every door ... . "I have come to make you confess to me 'I know I don't know.'" What he means by this is certainly up for grabs, but I am reminded of science fiction author Philip K. Dick's theory, based on some of his mystical visions, that we are really still living in the first century of the Christian era and the devil is deceiving us to delay the Second Coming. Sun Ra could have encountered these theories in his voracious reading of speculative fiction and would have found them congenial to his basically Gnostic outlook (matter is evil and must be transcended through knowledge, spirit and discipline).

Ra's Sunday anti-sermon also reprises his interest in his demonic side (cf. the night before): "I am the mystery of iniquity ... . I am Sin ... . I bring you pleasure without measure ... the sin that does not bring death ... . In ancient days they knew me ... . It is written ... in the last days Ra will visit the western lands." Compared to this, the Rolling Stones' "Sympathy for the Devil" looks fairly elementary. Here Ra claims to be a conflation of the devil (broadly considered) and the Egyptian god of the sun he takes the name of.

Then we get another blast of solar paranoia: "You've got to mind what you're talking about ... . You've got to give account in judgment ... . The witness against you is the Big Eye in the Sky." John Gilmore gives us the benediction with a hearty dose of tenor skronk, burning the message in our brains with his high-pitched squeals.

Disc 12: Sun Ra calms things down with some jazz standards. As promised in the rare editorial note in the Transparency box set, there is a "[b]eautiful Gilmore solo at [the] end" of "Body and Soul." Marshall Allen also gives a fine closing solo for Coleman Hawkins' "Queer Notions" (a standard the Fletcher Henderson orchestra played when Ra was a member). We are also treated to a rollicking "Discipline 99," highlighted by some fine bass playing from Richard Williams.

Detroit Jazz Center Residency 403

Disc 14: The Monday set opens with a nice reading of the "Pleiades" composition for flute and bells. Michael Ray executes some tough circular breathing during an improvisation, which is followed by Gilmore displaying some "sheets of sound" on his saxophone in the idiom of John Coltrane—whom his playing is always in dialogue with but never imitating—as well as some characteristic skronk moves.

Disc 15: The concert continues with an exquisite reading of "Lights on a Satellite" with great solo contributions from both Ra on organ and Gilmore. Ra also shines on "Love in Outer Space," which is also enhanced by the usual great drumming—but in this rendition also by some funky horn riffs for further punctuation. In the initial section of this long performance, there is a more equal distribution of labor among the entire Arkestra than is typical for this song (which is usually an excuse for most of the band to take a bathroom break by all accounts!). Eventually we do get the drummers carrying the burden, the Infinity Drum solo, and a theatrical bit with alien groaning while a band member asks "What planet is this?" (The answer he receives: "Planet Earth.") Then the music gets even quieter as the band plays with "little instruments" (to use the stock phrase from Art Ensemble of Chicago albums—the group which pioneered these ultra-pianissimo effects for the new jazz in the late sixties). A soaring full-band Cadillac arrangement of the main theme brings this epic version of the piece to a climax. The follow-up "We'll Be Together Again" also swings with just organ and drums, building up to a dramatic solo conclusion on the former instrument.

Disc 16: After all this fine playing, Sun Ra felt that some discourse was in order. He announces that "the spaceship Earth is scheduled to be leaving soon ... to find another place in the sun" because it is "at present living in the shadow of death"—as opposed to "the shadow of other planets" which are "converging" on Earth. Ra laments that he "could've enjoyed [him]self on this planet if the people had been alive." But they're not, so it's time to go! A series of typical space chants follow. The band encores with another martial march version of "Astro Nation," a sparkling Gilmore solo on "King Porter Stomp," and a stately version of "Fate in a Pleasant Mood." On this last, the organ performs the vocal line to good effect and solos a little; the a cappella vocals, briefly accompanied by a little sax, get softer and softer to end the show.

Disc 17: The Tuesday show opens with some good skronk from Gilmore in the improvisation that leads into "Discipline 27." Marshall Allen also gives us some skronk showmanship on his alto saxophone to set the mood for Ra's apocalyptic warning: "Impressions misinterpreted can destroy a planet."

Whimsy is mixed in with the warnings this time: "People walk around in a daze ... . The daze makes them crazy ... . They're crazy as a daisy." Then we get some standards, including a very upbeat and up-tempo "What's New?" (pretty consistently the way Ra likes to cover it in contrast with the more wistful and dolorous reading given the piece by the likes of, for example, Linda Ronstadt).

Disc 18: Amidst the standards, Ra sneaks in his classic composition "Lights on a Satellite"—lovely and subdued with lots of Gilmore soloing. Another editorial note for "Love in Outer Space": "40 minutes!" Yep. This is the most epic reading of the piece available, full of the Arkestra's complete bag of tricks: hocketing and staccato playing by the reeds and horns, percussive banging on metal sheets to give an industrial sound, the "What planet is this?" skit, little instruments, a long Infinity Drum solo. The "Enlightenment" vocal invitation to "be of our space world" is reinforced by an extra-raucous opening of "The Shadow World" from both the reeds and horns and Ra on exuberant organ and synthesizer.

Disc 19: "The Shadow World" continues with some serious Marshall Allen skronk at very high pitches, preceding the already available "Journey to Stars Beyond" discussed above. After that sublime strangeness, "Over the Rainbow" settles things down (as it did on disk five after the "Shoulder to Shoulder" → "Ra Ra Ra" sequence). It's Ra's way of acknowledging that we're not in Kansas (or Detroit) anymore! "Space Is the Place" has gut-bucket tenor and baritone sax soloing that at one point even quotes from "Tequila"! The chants offer a slight lyrical variant on "Moonship Journey": *"Prepare yourself for the* moonship journey" (my italics).

Disc 20: These last nine discs capture the excitement of the three culminating concerts on New Year's Eve of 1980. The eight o'clock set begins with a long improvisation with the African *kora*, percussion, and the horns intermittently probing like sonar signals (cf. "Atlantis"). A beautiful untitled flute composition follows, very much in the spirit of Ra's "Pleiades" pieces. The music gets gradually edgier and more akin to free jazz, culminating in an overlay of "Auld Lang Syne" over the mounting cacophony of the simultaneous soloing. June Tyson's "Astro Black" vocal is accompanied by nice trumpet flourishes from Michael Ray. A rare performance of "Tapestry from an Asteroid" ensues: a Tyson showcase about the "space joy" you receive when you get "vibrations from an asteroid" (then "the spaceways are not so far"). And finally the standard processional "Along Came Ra." We are reminded that there was a time, pre-Ra, "when the world was in darkness / and darkness was ignorance." Thanks to Ra, now darkness is "Astro Black," not ignorance. After over half an hour of gorgeous music, Sun Ra steps on stage.

He begins by conducting "Discipline 27" with lots of dramatic interludes from various instruments between statements of the main theme, thereby showcasing the band. Michael Ray contributes much wildness and more sonic sonar probing; seasonal sleigh bells and other percussion frolic (including what the Art Ensemble of Chicago call "little instruments"); more horns crescendo. Then we get a mellow change of pace with a rare reading of "Island in the Sun," an organ-and-percussion-based idyll augmented with horns and flute that provides a smooth transition to the standards to follow.

Disc 21: The Gershwin brothers' "A Foggy Day" begins with that heavy Ra ballpark organ before easing into a jaunty full-band chart with deft solos. A sultry "How Am I to Know?" follows with fine solos from alto sax Marshall Allen and (again) trumpeter Michael Ray. Ra sneaks in a few of his own compositions bidding for the jazz canon, including a swinging "Images" with a lyrical tenor solo from John Gilmore that evolves into an organ duet with Ra. "There Will Never Be Another You" showcases more tenor splendor from Gilmore, followed by the meditative Ra / Ray dialogue "Celestial Realms" already discussed in its El Saturn appearance on *Oblique Parallax* above. A fine reading of the ubiquitous "Enlightenment" sets us up for the intense sermonizing about to follow.

Disc 22: From this extended residency, we can observe something pertinent about Sun Ra as a teacher—and indeed he always regarded pedagogy as a major aspect of his mission on Earth. I only saw him twice at one-night stands (D.C. Space in Washington, Glam Slam in Minneapolis). Both times he downplayed the sermonizing in favor of standards, original compositions and space chants. Ra had to have a special relationship with an audience—the weekly gigs at Slug's in New York, his annual appearance at the Ann Arbor Jazz and Blues Festival for a while, or a residency like this—to carry the lessons further. As we saw already on disc five, he felt unusually comfortable conveying his belief system to this audience. (One suspects, for starters, there were a number of repeaters who would attend multiple shows.) In any case, here on New Year's Eve he really lets it rip.

After a lovely (and rare) vocal duet with June Tyson on "Somebody Else's World," he unveils his quasi-Gnostic opinion that this world was NOT his idea; in fact, it's "a damnable conception": "in my most evilest moments, I wouldn't make a world like this" (throughout, all this is accompanied by hypnotic drumming akin to a voodoo ceremony). He practically screams at the audience in his passionate declamation that "this planet is a disgrace to the devil and a shame to God. This planet is out of order." Only "the unknown ... magic myths of the impossible" can save his auditors from the pain of this existence. He puts a specific historical spin on his jeremiad by reminding us "somebody might push the button" (a reference to the re-heating of the Cold War in 1980 and a dry run for his later "Nuclear War") and asserting that "the truth about the President on Planet Earth is a bad truth" (a nod to the arrival of Ronald Reagan).

After the nuclear fire and brimstone, he makes his cryptic altar (alter?) call: "The impossible is your only hope ... . Join my mythocracy." When I give talks about Sun Ra, audiences always wonder what this would entail—as well they might. It's clearly reminiscent of what existentialist philosopher Soren Kierkegaard called "the leap of faith." As was the case with his leap to faith in a mysterious God, the leap to Ra's mythocracy is "impossible" and absurd. You have to believe ridiculous stuff ultimately (e.g., that Sun Ra is from Saturn). But I believe he was serious about this, not a pure con man. As with the Masons, there were / are degrees of initiation ranging from actually joining the Arkestra to being a casual fan who likes the music without getting into all the weird stuff. As with any other belief system, levels of commitment and engagement will vary. And Sun Ra completely understood this. But like Sly Stone, he wanted to take us higher in a great black tradition that goes back to tribal priests through Marcus Garvey to not just Sun Ra, but the shamanistic grooves of James Brown.

June Tyson adds to the consummate strangeness at this point by doing vocalese that sounds like a moog synthesizer. A few more imprecations hurled at Planet Earth ensue: "What has Planet Earth done for you? Even the first man and woman ended up bad." Then the band breaks out in a fierce improvisation redolent with skronking reeds and repeated crescendos—an unleashing of all the pent-up emotion Ra's sermon has inspired and a translation of its message into musical sound. Finally, some calm resumes as the Arkestra pulls back to just acoustic bass, percussion and drums and trumpet. Sun Ra and June Tyson share vocals again on "They'll Come Back," which in turn inspires Ra to reveal a few more truths from the magic myth world: "Prepare to meet them ... . Other worlds wish to speak to you through the universal language: music. I know they exist because they sent me to you."

Brilliantly, Sun Ra re-conceptualizes the leap of faith as a gamble (in terms reminiscent of the chess game battle with the devil in the film *Space Is the Place*): "I took a big gamble on you. Take the big gamble on me. Take the big gamble on the dark horse ... . It's a fixed race. If I win, I win. If I lose, I win. I'm the dark horse." Perhaps he's getting at his own sense of cosmic connection beyond the beleaguered fate of 1980's Earth. He's part of the universe, not just tied to Earth. We need him; he doesn't necessarily need us.

End of the set, except for him interrupting the emcee with his special offer to the audience: "You are cordially invited to visit Planet Saturn any time you choose. Any time you want to visit Planet Saturn, get your passport from me."

Disc 23: After the usual improvisational warm-up, the eleven o'clock set begins in earnest with a closely harmonized a cappella "When There Is No Sun." Sun Ra continues his heavily theatrical performance from the last set with a zany query to the audience: "Are you spotless? I am the sun. I have spots. Sun spots. Just because I have spots, does that make me sin? Well then, I'm sin. I'm still the sun." One can only speculate where Ra learned of this imagery, so redolent of my Catholic religious training regarding sin as stains on the soul.

After this setup, "Discipline 27- II" kicks in, where Ra reveals more over the vamp: "I am the Tempter. I've come to tempt you to leave Planet Earth, This is a cursed place ... . I'm the troubleshooter of the universe. I never visit a planet until there is no hope. I do not belong to any particular one planet. I use planets for stepping stones." This commodious composition takes the concert right up to the New Year and a swinging (and straight-up) "Auld Lang Syne"—Sun Ra channeling Guy Lombardo just because he can! (Admittedly, a brief interpolation of "Pop Goes the Weasel" mutates the moment a bit.)

Then the Arkestra morph into a full-blown, blast-from-the-past old time dancehall big band with a deluxe poker face cover of "Big John's Special" replete with lovely tenor soloing from John Gilmore. Ra's own composition "El Is the Sound of Joy" gets a similar reverential pastiche. After the electronic explorations of "Beyond the Purple Star Zone" (available elsewhere as noted), the band plays the lesser-known piece called "The World of Africa": an epic tsunami of polyrhythmic percussion so hypnotically trance-inducing that it makes up for what it lacks in complex melody through its therapeutic value. (Not for nothing did Sun Ra title one of his releases *Cosmic Tones for Mental Therapy*.) After that frenzied workout, the standard "Rose Room" gets us back in a mellow lounge mood with Gilmore and Ray kicking it very old school in their gentle solos.

Disc 24: This CD opens with an ultra-rare vocal version of "Halloween in Harlem." For some reason, this composition has become one of my all-time favorite pieces by Sun Ra. Perhaps it's because of its loping melodic complexity which reminds us that Ra was right up there as a composer with the two American guys named Charles (Ives and Mingus). Or maybe it's the thematic riffing on white fears—for the bulk of Ra's listening audience was always ofay. (He was and is too strange for many African Americans.) What could be more super-spooky than to spend Halloween in Harlem? Never mind that this was performed on a completely different holiday: he is Mr. Mystery. The deep voice of bassist Richard Williams ups the uncanniness of it all.

The band takes us even farther out, off-planet, on a "Journey to Saturn" with Ra's usual offering of one-way or round-trip tickets. His exhortations to leave Earth end up in a recitation of "Never Never Land" from *Peter Pan*, an early indication of his interest in Walt Disney.

This disc also showcases an extremely rare bop vocal version of "Medicine for a Nightmare," the nightmare in question being—you guessed it—life on Earth: "You need this medicine bad!" Following this, Marshall Allen provides some strong alto medicine with a skronking solo of alien animal cries so high-pitched that it actually cleans out my sinuses when I listen to it. That's real medicine! A very dramatic reading of "Rocket Number Nine" led by John Gilmore follows while Ra informs us that "the Space Age is here to stay" over the "Zoom! Zoom! Up in the air!" backdrop. He explains that "the music of the Space Age" is "not mind music, it's music of the unknown ... . Even if you don't understand, you still got to face the music." An appropriate setting for the a cappella soulful vocal harmonizing on "Face the Music" which follows.

Disc 25: The music to be faced turns out to be W.C. Handy's "St. Louis Blues," a song Ra has also recorded on solo piano. Here it gets the royal treatment with majestic solos from Gilmore and Ray, a fine walking bass line from Richard Williams and a Ra vocal. I can see why he'd connect with the song; it's about departure, even if it's only about leaving the Gateway to the West and not Earth: "If I feel tomorrow like I do today / I'm going to pack my trunk and make my getaway."

The more terrestrial groundedness continues for the next three songs, beginning with an organ-heavy "Watusi" with rare Ra scat vocalizing before the standard "What planet is this?" theatrics and an Infinity Drum solo from James Jacson. June Tyson sings of the "Lion of the Heavens," the sun. Then we get another of my all-time favorites, "Planet Earth," with vocal harmonizing from Tyson, Ra and Gilmore before the band marches around the venue: "This song an anthem is of Planet Three, Planet Earth." Ensuing space chants remind us that Earth is only "the third heaven." We can "try Pluto too," or anywhere our imagination takes us: "If we come from nowhere here, why can't we go somewhere there?"

Disc 26: The last three o'clock in the morning set cuts right to the chase with a straight-ahead rendition of the standard "On Green Dolphin Street" featuring a solid contribution from John Gilmore's tenor sax. After this, Michael Ray performs a be-bop trumpet improvisation interacting with the drum line and the reed section. June Tyson takes us back to the cosmos with her sung assurance that "outer space is such a pleasant place." Then Sun Ra gives a far more succinct declamation: "if you're not a myth, whose reality are you? If you're not a reality, whose myth are you?" A puzzling dualism for the uninitiated (or even the partially initiated). He's a poet, not a philosopher.

Disc 27: An untitled group improvisation—heavy on saxes, drums and trumpet—woke up the sleepers. The wildness continued with "Vista Omniverse" for organ and synthesizer, which inspires one auditor (band or audience member?) to interject "right on, man, right on" and "mmmm." Then we get audio whiplash from a bevy of big-band standards, an appropriate move given the lateness of the hour. Sun Ra has done enough preaching for the night. Highlights include a "Tea for Two" which segues from a shimmering organ solo to full band solos in turn. A rollicking "King Porter Stomp" offers more sonic time travel to the heyday of the big bands. Ra sneaks in a few of his own compositions: the lovely "Interstellar Low Ways" with organ and trumpet showcases, and a martial-beat rendition of "The Satellites Are Spinning." The ultimate standard "Stompin' at the Savoy" keeps up the nostalgic groove, followed by a baritone sax and percussion driven processional: the Ra original "Mayan Temples." Marshall Allen also works in some nice filigree on flute here.

Disc 28: This last recording from the residency opens with an unidentified title, possibly a rare number of his "Discipline" series. Like the others, it is fairly repetitious—but in a good way. The track has a nice feel of carnival parade to it. Coleman Hawkins' be-bop classic "Queer Notions" succeeds, then a soulful organ workout on "Willow Weep for Me." As per his practice, Ra inserts another older original (the bopping "Space Loneliness") amongst the standards—and indeed Thelonious Monk's "'Round Midnight" comes next, distinguished by good solos from Ra on organ and the reed section, culminating in sheets of sound off Marshall Allen's alto to close the piece. A suitably *echt* "Limehouse Blues" gives us the frenzied feel of a Tex Avery cartoon before the Arkestra slows down for a stately "Discipline 99." The concert closes with standard fare: "Space Is the Place" (with a noisy synthesizer burst) and some space chants. Like many others, Ra gets his math slightly wrong when he reminds the audience it's "only nineteen years" until the twenty-first century ("The year

2000 is knocking at your door"). In any case, the Omniverse Jet Set Arkestra was, and is, ready, willing and able to hug that future.

Notes

[1] In addition to the singles collection on the Evidence label, there are three other CD compilations of Ra's non-Arkestra doo wop and vocal group arrangements. The most efficient collection for the curious is John Corbett's *Spaceship Lullaby* on his Unheard Music label. You get some interesting original compositions such as "Chicago USA," his sonic tribute to the Windy City reminiscent of some of Charles Ives's urban sound paintings, as well as the sublime corn of some inspired covers. The Nu Sounds version of "Stranger in Paradise" really takes off when the lyrics approach pianist / arranger Sun Ra's interests: "somewhere in space / I hang suspended." (Cf. "Just One of Those Things" with its"trip to the moon on gossamer wings.") "Holiday for Strings" is given a manic treatment with resultant amusement for the listener—surpassed only by the toy romance of "The Wooden Soldier and the China Doll." Clearly Ra's tastes are thoroughly eclectic: he can hear something of interest in schmaltz even Lawrence Welk might have taken a pass on.

This compilation features, in addition to the Nu Sounds and the Cosmic Rays, the thoroughly unwashed Lintels, a street corner doo wop group not afraid to croon, "you my only love."

[2] See Dan Noel's fascinating book *Approaching Earth* for a Jungian interpretation of why our culture, including Ra, would be so compelled to link the space-age with antiquity. Stanley Kubrick's *2001: A Space Odyssey* is as obvious an illustration of this habit of mind as the oeuvre of Sun Ra.

[3] Sun Ra was also an angel and a devil as well as an alien. He explained his lifelong celibacy by citing Matthew 22:30 ("They neither marry nor are given in marriage but are like angels that shine forth like the sun" [in Szwed 347]). Ra's biographers have speculated more pragmatically that it had something to do with his nearly lifelong untreated hernia (cf. Henry James's "obscure wound"). Ra's death is linked to its operative repair without anyone's consent when he was being treated for pneumonia in Alabama (Corbett 174).

As for his status as demon, consider that Ra made the doo-wop groups he worked with in Chicago call him "Lucifer": "That was the only name he would have us call him. Even after a year when he changed to Sun Ra we still called him Lucifer" (Szwed 91). As late as 1982 he kept that name; he issued an album called *A Fireside Chat with Lucifer*. Alien, angel, devil: Ra wanted to hog all corners of the Greimasian semiotic square except human!

[4] To continue this discussion, after Ra and Brown I'd rank Neil Young in descending rank as a "circular," non-conceptual artist overall. (There are big ex-

ceptions as noted in some of the more recent work which has carefully thought-out conceptual order: *Are You Passionate?*, *Greendale* and *Prairie Wind*.) He works out satisfactory song orders which can resonate from track to track, but that's as far as it goes. Yoko Ono, on the other hand, dabbled sometimes in the concept album with her sense that some of her recordings worked like plays (e.g., *Double Fantasy*) while others were looser collections (*Approximately Infinite Universe*). Zappa overtly produced narrative concept albums (*We're Only In It For The Money*, *Joe's Garage*, *Thing-Fish*) and worked towards the project / object as a whole, however miscellaneous the release (e.g., *Them Or Us*). And lastly, both Joni Mitchell and Sigmund Snopek were quite fond of linear development on their recordings and very interested in the recorded release as an aesthetic (and even narrative) construct in its own right. Sigmund Snopek has written symphonies, operas and rock operas, but he's also put together wacky party albums like *Beer*; whereas Joni Mitchell has consistently paid attention to architectural considerations and narrative flow on her recordings. I think, as with Brown and Ra, we have a photo finish here.

Here is how my remarks look diagrammatically on a continuum:

tending toward circular, repetitious structures				tending toward linear, "progressive," Aristotelian narratives
James Brown Sun Ra	Neil Young	Yoko Ono	Frank Zappa	Joni Mitchell Sigmund Snopek

[5] Art Jenkins had been in the Arkestra since 1962's *Secrets of the Sun*. He wanted to join the band as a vocalist, but was told by Ra that the band needed a singer who could deliver the impossible: "The possible has been tried and failed; now I want to try the impossible." After many unsuccessful attempts at fitting in using various effects, Jenkins finally succeeded when he sang into a ram's horn backwards and manipulated the little opening with his hand. Ra laughed, "Now that's impossible!"—and Jenkins joined the Arkestra (Szwed, *Space* 192-3). "Solar Differentials" off *Secrets of the Sun* is the first example of this material; the Judson Hall concert shows that Jenkins was getting ever more adept at this technique!

[6] A strange personage known as "The Good Doctor" delivered to the ESP label a third lost volume of these 1965 sessions, resulting in the 2005 release of *Heliocentric Worlds Volume 3: The Lost Tapes*. If you like this era and approach (avant-garde chamber jazz instrumentals), you'll want to listen to this as well if only for one long seventeen-minute track: "Intercosmosis." Like "Cosmic Chaos" on volume two, it features an epic battle royal in its mid-section between Pat Patrick (baritone sax), John Gilmore (tenor) and Marshall Allen (alto). The first third of the piece is a Patrick solo; the last third is a more meditative and subdued interplay between Ra on piano and Ronnie Boykins on arco bass. As in much of the work from this era, the Arkestra is doing some sound-

painting on a very large canvas. If "Intercosmosis" were a painting, it would be a Jackson Pollock or a Mark Rothko—guaranteed to take any open-eared listener on an epic space journey!

[7] In fact, avant-popist Beefheart's relationship with major labels provides a good parallel with Ra's misadventures. Both innovators were equally hot potatoes in the culture industry.

[8] More recently, the Transparency label has released *The Sun Ra All Stars*, four pre-Montreux European dates for this amazing ensemble on five discs. The first two discs cover an October 27, 1983 show in Milan. The opening improvisation features careful dialogue and exploration before exploding into a climax of free-jazz soloing. The next piece has fine piano-reeds-drums and percussion interplay before the trumpets kick in; Archie Shepp's tenor solo is a standout. The closing percussive interaction segues into a driving, simple yet dramatic bass figure from Richard Davis that eventually draws the ensemble in for some serious cooking. After all this improvisation, Don Cherry adds a lush vocal to Sun Ra's equally opulent piano and Davis' walking bass lines on the "sun" standard "East of the Sun"—which leads to even more retro ragtime piano work on "King Porter Stomp."

The second disk reminds us why this band was called the Sun Ra All Stars. Their repertoire consisted of group improvisations, jazz standards and Sun Ra compositions. Although the other members of the group had written a lot of music in their own right, this was Ra's show: he was the master of ceremonies. So we get a lovely reading of "What's New?" with more lovely bass work (bowing, soloing, interacting with the percussion section) and a mutated "Cocktails for Two" (because of Marshall Allen's alto skronk). Then two Ra originals conclude the show. "Spontaneous Simplicity" gets enhanced by a trumpet solo from Lester Bowie and Archie Shepp's full-bodied tenor sax. And finally, a highly polyrhythmic "Space Is the Place": after all, this band had three master drummers / percussionists (Famoudou Don Moye, Philly Joe Jones and Clifford Jarvis) and an astonishing bassist. Small wonder the former keep soloing after the piece ends.

The next day they opened their performance at the Zurich Jazz Festival with an improvisation that began with martial drumming and arco bass, followed by a soaring soprano sax solo from Archie Shepp and attentive percussion dialogue leading up to a Philly Joe Jones drum solo. Then Sun Ra played a piano solo, lyrical and pounding by turns, with trumpet grace notes in the background from Don Cherry. This eventually evolved into a barrelhouse blues with witty flourishes from trumpeter Lester Bowie. The highlight of the set from the standpoint of a Sun Ra follower would be their reverential and skillful reading of his standout composition "Lights on a Satellite." I would argue that this band performed the piece best of the many available recorded versions—a result of a jazz super-group instead of the always motley character of the Arkestra which mixed the old pros with rougher younger players in training. Not a false note here.

Then the show closes with some standards: again "What's New?" (its extended piano introduction eventually augmented by bass and drums and solid reed work) and "Cocktails for Two" (another "drunken" playful version courtesy of the reeds). The set concludes with "Poinciana," a piece they must have enjoyed playing since they also did long versions of it at the next two dates. As they should have. Not only does the tune have a lovely melody (which is why so many crooners [e.g., Frank Sinatra] have covered it), but the solo work showcases the diversity of the group—from the lyrical approaches of Shepp and Cherry to the subversions of Bowie. Richard Davis contributes an exquisite and multifaceted bass solo before the percussion section lands the spaceship with their subtle rhythmic conversations.

The Berlin concert (like the Paris show on the fifth disc) suffers from some inferior audio quality (more pronounced tape hiss). But in both cases, it's worth getting past that (and some receiver technologies can compensate for it). The Berlin show is also on DVD and discussed as such later. It opens with "Stars That Shine Darkly," a mostly free jazz romp with emerging climactic be-bop reed and trumpet work. The loose jam that follows is highlighted by Lester Bowie interpolating the New Orleans classic "Big Chief" (by E. Gaines). Bowie also throws a little "Rockin' Robin" at the end of the Ra composition "Somewhere Else." Then we get "Early Morning Blues" from Ra, with "laughing" reed and horn effects and a wacky Don Cherry vocal: "It's early in the morning / and I ain't got nothing but the blues / SUN RA."

Another fine reading of "Poinciana" ensues, featuring great tenor variations on the theme from John Gilmore. At the end of the interpretation, we transition from synthesizer to drum soloing and a quiet percussion break segueing into an unusual "Shadow World": after the head, we get synthesizer, piano, trumpet and walking bass, gong and didgeridoo (the Australian aboriginal drone tube, courtesy of Don Moye), trumpet and reed—all before extensive power drumming ("at the edge of magic," percussionist and Grateful Dead member Mickey Hart would say). Philly Joe Jones, Clifford Jarvis and Don Moye engage in a three-way cutting contest which includes some serious cymbal play. The following jam that ends the tape moves the Battle Royal over to the reed section which gets its skronky wailing on. The Germans loved every second of it as perennial supporters of Sun Ra and all his works.

The Paris concert (which concludes the collection, but not the tour) is the one where they really push the envelope—a combination of playing together for three previous shows, then having two days off? One thing this ensemble did share with the Arkestra's approach was an inclination to play the adventurous improvisatory stuff (in part) as a lead-in to the standards (including Ra's own older compositions). By Sun Ra's own admission with respect to the

Arkestra, this was a prophylactic gesture designed to clear the house of any closed-eared individuals who wouldn't give the band their absolute commitment. So it is here with the didgeridoo leading the way. The second improvisation has a bowed bass introduction, Archie Shepp running some bop scales, Ra's reeds wailing, a percussion interlude, some sensitive dialogue between bassist Davis and trumpeter Lester Bowie and even more intense reed wailing from Marshall Allen on alto sax to wrap it up. Then it's on to the standards ...

Sun Ra takes us once again "Over the Rainbow" on piano (with occasional thunderous cascades of sound) abetted by Don Cherry's trumpet and Archie Shepp's sax. The first big surprise is a completely against-the-grain (but equally brilliant) reading of Ra's "Lights on a Satellite." Where the Zurich version was an utter realization of the score's intentions (what the Arkestra tried to do fully delivered), this reading is relentlessly against the grain: a sonic deconstruction that moves the margins of the piece to the center. For starters, it's done to a calypso beat and the melody gets drowned out by bursts of responsive sound. Much of the time only one player is holding down the melody line—and even then, messing with that in some way (the bassist fiddling with the duration of the notes and the tempo). The mocking interrupters remind me, oddly enough, of the responding instruments in Charles Ives's "The Unanswered Question."

A loose and upbeat "What's New?" follows. One is reminded that this can be a sad and wistful evocation of lost love (the way Linda Ronstadt / Frank Sinatra and Nelson Riddle's orchestra deliver it, for example). But not here: it's either just a musical text or all is forgiven in the unsung lyrics (how ya doing, ex-love?). We get alternating energetic solos from Bowie, Davis, Shepp and Jones. The performance of "Poinciana" is also against the grain of the Zurich and Berlin readings. After the piano statement of the theme, Sun Ra solos on organ; Don Cherry gives us full-throttle trumpet; Lester Bowie slides in a quotation from "Tropical Heat Wave"; little instruments give us a Spanish flair; the didgeridoo shows up one more time. Then Ra restates the theme on a wild synthesizer setting (think Keith Emerson's approach to the conclusion of "Lucky Man"!). Another standard transformed, even from this band's previous takes on it.

The Sun Ra All Stars conclude by rewarding the persistent conservative listeners for hearing all this avant-garde stretching with a straight-up version of "'Round Midnight." John Gilmore's closing tenor solo brings us back to Earth after an amazing ride. As you might be gathering, this is some astonishing music.

[9] The obvious exception being *A Black Mass*, the Arkestra's collaboration with Amiri Baraka.

[10] I am grateful to my German colleague Rod Taylor for these helpful insights.

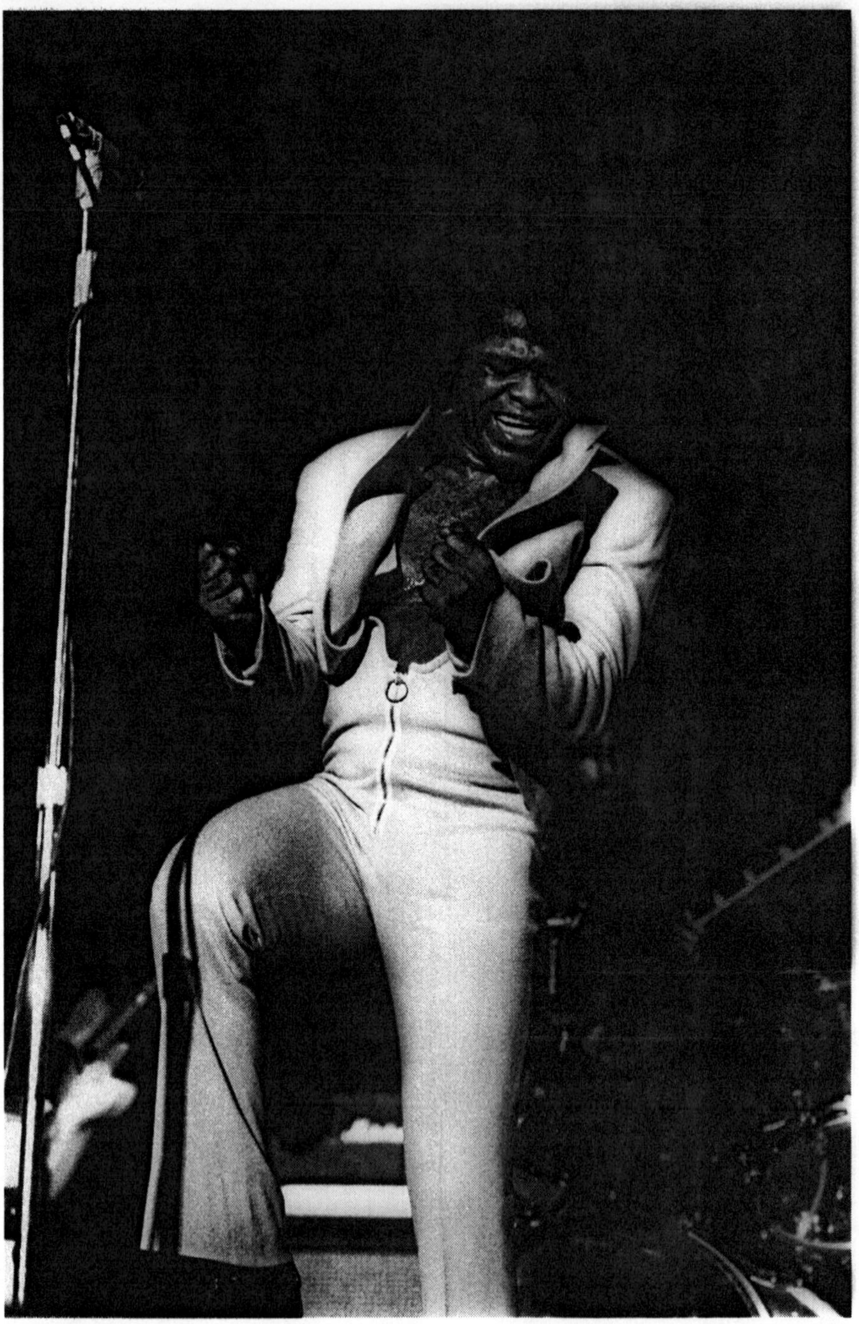

James Brown: Funky Surrealism, Surrealist Funk

"The pure products of America go crazy."—William Carlos Williams

"If you leave me, I'll go crazy. 'Cause I love you, I love you, I love you too much."—James Brown

James Brown is probably the oddest figure included in this thoroughly nonexhaustive representation of avant-gardists within pop music. On the one hand, Brown suffers the fate of successful innovators whose contributions to the discourse become so prevalent that the originating gesture becomes nearly invisible to the general public—an especially possible fate for an African-American in a country which still conducts much of its cultural business with certain ethnic biases. To a much lesser extent, this appropriation has also happened to Neil Young, Joni Mitchell and even Yoko Ono. (Sun Ra and Frank Zappa remain largely quarantined and unduplicated.) But James Brown is a whole other case. Not only was he as important as the Beatles at several points in his career, he was arguably more influential than they were to other musicians and diverse musics.

Put succinctly, James Brown catalyzed two major musical developments in popular culture: soul and rap / hip-hop. And he was the originator of a third, funk. As Bruce Tucker (the editor of Brown's autobiography) suggests, this makes him at least "the most *influential* [at the time of writing] living American musician" if not the greatest one (Brown xiii). Brown's sideman Fred Wesley tried to explain it in another way:

> Music was changing and he was changing it. James Brown changed everybody's ideas about music. Everybody. It's like saying "shit" and "damn"on TV. Once somebody says it and the censor lets it slide, okay, it's gonna be everybody. Redd Foxx gets away with it, so there's Richard Pryor—and then you get Eddie Murphy.

> Once you get away with something, you've set a precedent. And back there in the '60s, James set a *hell* of a precedent. All music that we hear today is influenced by James Brown. I stand on that—everybody today who calls himself a creator of music has been influenced by James. (Rose 37)

At least anyone you're going to hear on American pop radio (aside from the country stations) or on MTV. James Brown, as we shall see, originated a musical revolution when he brought Afrocentric polyrhythms to a dominant place in pop, overturning its prior European bias towards melody and harmony. Not only was this the foundational procedure of funk; it is the sine qua non for rap and indeed all contemporary urban stylings. But, like Fred Wesley says, James Brown set the precedent.

On the other hand, though, James Brown is also the consummate outsider (in the sense of an Outsider artist such as Howard Finster, James Harold Jennings or Henry Darger). Brown was never given entry into the mainstream culture in his formative years, so he was freed up to be the kind of innovator that he ended up being. For starters, like many Outsider artists, he was virtually uneducated. He had "less than a seventh-grade education" before he was incarcerated in the Georgia penal system in 1949 for minor theft connected with the need to meet dress-code requirements to attend school (Brown 110, 28). Brown duly notes the paradox of this:

> Mine was a kangaroo court. I knew that. What I have always felt was unjust in this country is that they didn't allow us to get an education, and yet when we went to court they treated us like we were impresarios who knew what was going on. We can't be wrong on both ends. *If you don't allow a man to get an education, don't put him in jail for being dumb. That's what they did in Augusta—they sent me to prison for being dumb.* (Brown 33; his italics)

His love of gospel music "got [him] through" and eventually released from prison in 1951 at age eighteen (Brown 42, 48). James Brown had served several years of an eight-to-sixteen year sentence.

His lack of education further haunted him through his endless dealings with the IRS that began in the late sixties. He ultimately wasn't able to control the crazy money that was coming into his hands. Brown owned radio stations and restaurants, but he didn't know how to manage the proceeds or obtain honest accountants. When he appealed directly to the government for help, he didn't receive it. So despite his cooling influence on the tense racial situation—and even endorsements of Hubert Humphrey and Richard Nixon (in 1968 and 1972, respectively)—Brown was harassed by the IRS nonstop for 35 years (Brown 200-1). When he released "Don't Be a Drop-Out" on *Raw Soul* in 1967, he was ruefully if indirectly acknowledging his disadvantaged upbringing and its consequences.

Brown's outsider status is also evident in his cavalier treatment by his record labels. Except for a few years in the 1980s with the Scotti Brothers, James was treated as a pure commodity by his other labels, with King and Polydor being especially problematic. Syd Nathan of King never seemed to fully appreciate what he had in Brown, fighting every career move of his along the way. After "Please Please Please" was a hit in 1956, Nathan just wanted him to keep imitating that song over and over. Brown relates how he was pressured to record "I Won't Plead No More" as an answer song (cf. Hank Ballard and the Midnighters' endless reworkings of "Work With Me Annie"):

> "I Won't Plead No More" was supposed to be the answer to "Please Please Please." Mr. Nathan kept saying, "Give us another 'Please Please Please'." That's typical of a white record company; they want you to keep cutting something just like your first hit. I gave them that, but I didn't want to. They did not want to change. (Brown 87)

Nathan also thought that *Live at the Apollo* was a bad idea, re-releasing live versions of studio hits. He was so disgusted by the proto-funk "Papa's Got a Brand New Bag" recording that he threw the acetate of Brown's first international best-seller on the floor (Brown 130, 159-60). Although Syd Nathan had the sense to sign Brown, he clearly had no idea of what to do with him and continually resisted Brown's incredible aesthetic intuitions.

The Polydor label, his label in the late sixties and beyond, was even worse. Brown has lamented that while the IRS "hurt [his] business," Polydor "destroy[ed him]" (Brown 238). Polydor was a German-run company that wanted to sell product in America. Brown notes that they never comprehended the American market, or how to "promote or distribute" their releases (239). Even worse,

> They weren't flexible about creativity, either. They expected you to go into the studio on such and such a day at such and such an hour and finish up at a certain time. Like a factory. At King we went into the studio and put together arrangements and worked at all hours until we had it *right*. Polydor back then didn't work that way. They had no respect for the artist, no personal feeling for the artist, no concern for what he had in mind. They would say this is what's going to happen: blah, blah, blah. And what the artist felt meant nothing.
>
> I'd mix a song until I thought—until I *knew*—it was right, but they would want their machines to say whether it was right or not. It

> had to register certain numbers on the machines. It didn't matter whether the track was alive and moved; all that mattered was the numbers. I had a warmth in my sound I was trying to preserve, and I wanted the track to be an instrumental before it was a vocal. I wanted it to have the right feel before I put any words to it. It's like having a good bedspread but wondering if the mattress is comfortable. They wanted a pretty bedspread. I wanted to make the mattress comfortable. (Brown 239)

Which translated into slicker production values (in keeping with the disco era) at the expense of the gritty soul / funk warmth Brown got on his releases for the King and Smash labels (the former despite Syd Nathan's misprisions). Although James capitulated to disco, he regarded it as a simplified subset of his richer sound (Brown 242-3). Eventually, the entire record industry began losing money in the late seventies because of the effects of all this bad decision-making (and economic recession, one should add). Only in the 1980s with the Scotti Brothers and CBS did Brown receive some real respect as a recording artist—and that all ended in 1988 when a high-speed chase (and the PCP abuse that inspired it) led to another prison sentence.

It is astonishing that an artist of James Brown's influence and stature should have had a decade of fighting tooth and nail to get his sound out (the sixties), followed by a decade of being unable to get his music released the way he wanted it (the seventies). By contrast, Frank Zappa and Neil Young's hassles with their record labels over the years seem benign. In the last chapter, I indicated how Ra and Brown both had less obsessive interest in the recorded artifact as opposed to the live concert—thus having less ambition to produce the "concept album" song sequences so popular at the time. We can now ruefully see that Brown had no choice in the matter: he was fighting to get individual tracks out the way he heard them in his head. Neither King nor Polydor had the sophistication to let out his leash more, as Berry Gordy did for Marvin Gaye to facilitate *What's Going On*. James Brown was strictly a revenue maker for his label. No wonder Brown identified with Elvis; James had the same aesthetic constrictions without even a Colonel Parker to blame!

As a result, there is no organized archival access to James Brown's recordings. It's catch as catch can as they have been allowed to fall out of print. Sporadic re-releases and overlapping anthologies appear, but Brown's catalogue has received little of the systematic care accorded the other six artists discussed in this book. Yoko Ono, Frank Zappa, Sun Ra and Sigmund Snopek III all have CD labels reissuing and maintaining their work; Neil Young and Joni Mitchell can keep all of their major output in print. James Brown credits Polydor for some good work on their reissues of his work (Brown 263). (These would eventually include the 4-CD *Star Time* box set, the closest thing we have

James Brown: Funky Surrealism, Surrealist Funk 421

to a James Brown retrospective, some reissues with bonus tracks, and anthologies of his singles.) But in contrast with the other six musicians discussed here, Brown seems neglected. No one has put this confused house fully in order as of 2013, and that's a shame for the music.

The oddity of Brown's handling becomes apparent when one looks at and listens to the original vinyl releases. For starters, there is the gratuitous habit of adding taped applause onto studio tracks to make them appear to be "live" concert recordings. A few examples of this practice would be the entire album of *Showtime* (Smash, 1964), "Tell Me That You Love Me" (off *Raw Soul*, King, 1967) and even parts of the mostly live *Sex Machine* (the title track, "Brother Rapp," a medley and "Lowdown Popcorn"; King, 1970). (All discography information is from Cliff White's fabulous work in the James Brown autobiography.) The results are mostly contrived, unconvincing and ultimately puzzling—unlike, say, Neil Young's playful fake live opening on Buffalo Springfield's "Broken Arrow." It seems to show contempt both for the artist's work and his audience.

As many critics have suggested, the semiotics of James Brown's album covers alone would be a book-length study of the representation of racial otherness in America. You might find flagrant flaunting of the sales volume of songs contained on the record: *Papa's Got a Brand New Bag* (King, 1965) boasts "2 MILLION SELLER." Or there might be cheesy paintings of James (*Raw Soul*) and / or the bums of female admirers (*Take a Look at Those Cakes*; Polydor, 1979). On the back covers, most King albums simply display other Brown product. On none of these albums (until the Scotti Brothers or the Polydor CD reissues) will you find any indication of who's playing on the recording beyond a passing allusion to a player or arranger in the liner notes. (Whence the helpfulness of Brown naming musicians on the actual tracks: "Maceo! Maceo!")

I want to focus on one typically loaded album cover: *I Can't Stand Myself When You Touch Me* (King, 1968). James Brown is neatly dressed on the cover, smiling and looking out at the viewer, sporting a goatee (his belated appeal to beatniks also demonstrated by the bongos on "Bring It Up" from the same era). There are three models to his left and our right (ironically, they get album credits on the back!). The one nearest to James is a white woman in a rust-colored pantsuit. She is actually the most erotically charged, given the era. Her jet-black hairdo makes her look like a sexy younger incarnation of then-first-lady Lady Bird Johnson (or Bobbie Gentry, for that matter). Her erotic attraction to James, amplified by her proximity, is dialectically muted by her more modest attire and the fact that she alone of the three is trying to look James in the eye (she can't because he's looking at us). The middle model is another Caucasian with long hair and a miniskirt. Although forbidden fruit, she is much more available for James and is clearly staring at his crotch! (Get out a straight-edge and follow the line of sight if you are skeptical.) Young Lady

Bird blocks the middle model's access to JB a bit: by being slightly in back of the other two women, the Caucasian in the miniskirt may be the farthest from James in three-dimensional space. On a strict left to right two-dimensional sweep, the middle mini-skirted model is closer than the third woman, the only black woman of the three, also mini-skirted and ogling James's family jewels. Did I mention that there's a cheesy wooden love seat behind James?

The not-so-subliminal messages this display conveys strike at the very heart of Brown's paradoxical status as insider / outsider. On the one hand, the cover suggests black women now have to share James Brown with the majority white culture (on the two-dimensional plane, whitey even has more ready access to him). As the middle model suggests, some white listeners fantasize about him more profoundly than others—and may even want to slip him some booty. James is politely pleased by these offerings of interest and affection.

But there is menace as well, beginning with the goatee that says Brown might play by Bohemian rules. The title track, "I Can't Stand Myself (When You Touch Me)" begs the question: why can't you stand yourself? Because these women might make you come, thereby soiling your lovely suit? Because you might just have to fuck them then, even if they have subsequent regrets—and then you won't be able to deal with the post-rape guilt? The love seat behind James is the fuse poised to light the powderkeg. Even the color scheme has a subliminal message: blue walls (read the blues, a metonym for blackness) and a white floor on the bottom of the cover: if things get busy, James Brown will be on top.

I admit the above paragraphs are the kind of thing that give critics a bad name, but don't shoot the messenger. Take a good look at this cover and see for yourself. The Outsider dimension of Brown's status is as amply conveyed by the thrown-together graphics of the album cover as it is by the funk surrealism in the actual recorded grooves. Extending to the ultimate degree the trash fetish appeal of the young Elvis, James Brown shows us he is simultaneously in the mainstream and utterly unable to be assimilated all at once: the paradox that has been fuelling these extended opening observations on my part. RJ Smith's recent biography of James Brown, *The One*, offers even more surprising evidence for the subversive power of this album cover. Henry Glover, Syd Nathan's assistant at King Records, claimed that this cover precipitated Nathan's final demise from heart attack and pneumonia. Glover explains Nathan's objections: "' How on earth am I going to sell this to redneck distributors in the South? I don't know what I'm going to do about him, Henry' ... . [T]hat was the thing that made him really sick" (184).

James Brown is quite conscious of, and articulate about, the semiotic confusion—even crisis—that his public career has created: an amplification of the double consciousness possessed by every African-American and discussed since at least the writings of W. E. B. DuBois. *The Godfather of Soul*, James Brown's autobiography, confronts these issues from the very first page, his preface:

> I was marked a lot of different ways. With names, for example. I was marked with a lot of different names. And each one has a story behind it.
>
> As a kid growing up in a whorehouse, I was known as Little Junior. After I broke my leg a couple of times playing football, I was nicknamed Crip. In prison I was called Music Box.
>
> The name of my first group, the Famous Flames, caused Little Richard to say, "Y'all were the onliest people who ever made yourselves famous before you were famous."
>
> As a performer, I had names like Mr. Dynamite, The "Please Please Please" Man, The Hardest Working Man in Show Business, Soul Brother Number One, The Sex Machine, His Bad Self, The Godfather of Soul, and The Minister of the New New Super Heavy Funk ... .
>
> But of all the names I've been marked with, James Brown is probably the most mysterious. In school the kids and the teachers always called me by it like it was one word: Jamesbrown. Just like that. But originally my name wasn't supposed to be James Brown at all. It should have been something else. (v)

This last remark alludes to both the fact that his original name was planned to be Joe Brown, Jr. (the James on the birth certificate was spontaneously placed in front of the Joe) and that his father's last name was originally Gardner (Brown 1). Along with the fact that he nearly died in childbirth, these unusual circumstances give him some of the resonances of Joseph Campbell's *Hero with a Thousand Faces*. James Brown had the miraculous birth of the hero—as did Elvis, with his twin brother dying at birth.

James Brown also seemingly shared with Elvis a complex ethnicity. In his lifetime he claimed he had a lot of Asian and Native American (Cherokee) blood in him. Brown compared his Asian roots with the dark-skinned residents of Surinam (Brown 2). Coming to awareness of this background made Brown feel that he could connect with any human type while ultimately belonging to none exclusively. This paradoxical universality / marginalization led him to identify and sympathize with other liminal groups such as the Jewish people. Bruce Tucker observed that Brown "will insist that any white person he likes has 'got some Jewish in them,' even if they deny it" (Brown xxii).

This last remark suggests that Brown's ethnic claims require some fact-checking: "[h]is daughter, Deanna Brown-Thomas, joked that every time he went to a country and felt the love, he perceived a genetic connection." RJ Smith's recent genealogical detective work limits Brown's ethnic background pretty much to African-American and Native American (on his mother's side) (8-9). The latter bloodline, of course, could suggest Asian elements given the ancient crossing of the Bering Sea by indigenous peoples.

Brown's early childhood involved being alone a lot, playing in rural South Carolina. It affected him "in a big way," as he relates: "It gave me my own mind" (Brown 5). Behind the flickerings of persona and imposed identity, Brown acknowledges an unshakable and inaccessible core to his being, a James Brown only he knows and can commune with:

> Where I grew up there was no way out, no avenue of escape, so you had to make a way. Mine was to create JAMES BROWN. God made me but with the guidance of a Ben Bart, I created the myth. I've tried to fulfill it. But I've always tried to remember that there's JAMES BROWN the myth and James Brown the man. The people own JAMES BROWN. That belongs to them. The minute I say "I'm JAMES BROWN" and believe it, then it will be the end of James Brown.
>
> I'm James Brown. (Brown 267; block capitals are Brown's)

The public persona / myth which he eventually developed, evidenced by the sundry Homeric epithets his announcers would rattle off about him (listed above), link him up with not only classic American self-reinventors such as F. Scott Fitzgerald's James Gatz (who becomes Jay Gatsby), but other mercurial pop music figures like John Lennon (who was Dr. Winston O'Boogie in the seventies) and Neil Young (aka Bernard Shakey and a host of other pseudonyms). The narcissistic wound of a pained and neglected core identity gets transcended by a proliferation of masks.

At one point, James Brown even let his manager pull a publicity stunt by spreading a rumor that Brown wanted to go to Europe for a sex change operation to marry one of his band (Brown 161, 167). Ironically, this was the first discourse about James Brown I ever heard! Courtesy of Duane Kirchner, secret hero of these pages, who gave me a wide-eyed rendition of the rumor on our inner-city playground. Brown's play of identity seemed boundless. By careful hair care and costuming, he had supplanted the adolescent prisoner who was "the one that no one came to see" during Sunday visiting hours (Rose 34). He now "look[ed] like somebody you would PAY to see" (Brown xi; block capitals mine). James Brown had learned the ropes about living in America. He offered us the music, but he lured us with the spectacle.

Soul Power: James Brown's Contributions to Soul Music

A lot of sundry ingredients went into the musical gumbo that became James Brown's patented soul music. As a child, he lived at his aunt's bordello in Augusta, Georgia (after his parents split up and couldn't properly care for him). Music is part of even the humblest of red light houses, so he came to learn from the patrons and associates how to play drums, piano, and guitar (in that order [Brown 17]). He heard a great variety of music as well: gospel, pop tunes, rhythm and blues, big band jazz. At church, he was mightily impressed by a revival preacher who "was just screaming and yelling and stomping his foot and then he dropped to his knees" (Brown 18). All Brown would have to add to this drama to make it his own would be getting covered with the soon-to-be-shrugged-off cape, a routine he borrowed from the wrestler Gorgeous George (Brown 106). Unlike other transplanters of gospel into the blues, James wasn't afraid to be a "sanctified" shouter. His rawest vocal performances—such as "Lost Someone" live at the Apollo or "I Got a Bag of My Own"—create abject ecstasy that is equal parts sanctified church music, field holler and animal cry: the human at the edge of radical Otherness.[1] Little Richard opened this door with his inspired rave-ups in the early fifties, but James Brown kicked the door off its hinges. Often imitated, James has never been surpassed as a soul vocalist.

I am speaking of James in his powerful screaming and shouting soul mode; when he sings ballads, he emulates the "cry singers" of rhythm and blues (like Wynonie Harris and Roy Brown) who beg and plead with the listener as well. This is the root of early performances such as the 1956 hit "Please Please Please" and "Try Me" (Rose 27). Brown's considerable expressive talents as a singer were honed by the no-bullshit attitude of the black audience, especially at punishing venues like the Apollo Theater in Harlem, where he first performed on April 24, 1959 (Brown 99). Here would be found no tolerance of anything less than musical excellence: this was a stage you could readily get booed off. Early concert footage of James Brown and the Famous Flames is rare. But the *T. A. M. I. Show* footage suffices to illustrate the evidence. Here you see James Brown set performance standards for a lineup of Caucasian groups that they have no possibility of emulating. See for yourself on Youtube. Before the Who and Jethro Tull spanked the Rolling Stones at the long-suppressed *Rock and Roll Circus*, James Brown effortlessly cut Mick Jagger at this earlier 1964 venue. (Back in the days, there was always somebody outplaying "the world's greatest rock and roll band." Time was on their side, though, because of their longevity as a unit.)

James Brown expresses skepticism about the "soul" genre labelling reminiscent of his suspicions about his various imposed personal namings:

> See, musicians don't think about categories and things like that. They don't say, I think I'll invent bebop today or think up rock 'n' roll tomorrow. They just hear different sounds and follow them wherever they lead. Let somebody else give it a name. Like they named the stuff we'd been doing rhythm and blues. It would take the world a long time to catch up to what we were fixing to do, but when they did, they gave it a name, too: soul. (Brown 119)

The musical developments came gradually enough; but at some point the sound was different enough to merit its own genre description.

I agree with James Brown that the earliest recording you can hear this new sound on is "I'll Go Crazy" (recorded in November of 1959; released in January of 1960). He says that the band was doing this type of performance significantly earlier: this is merely its first recorded documentation. Brown helpfully describes his soul as not just a fusion of gospel and R & B, but a fusion of gospel, R & B and jazz (Brown 120). This last is a key ingredient.

What you hear in classic rhythm and blues is the group in question—say, Hank Ballard and the Midnighters doing "Annie Had a Baby"—moving through standard blues changes with regard to chording and measures, tightly bound to the syncopated beat. Whence the label rhythm and blues: delta blues, being played on acoustic guitar and harmonica, was less tied to the rhythm. Rhythm and blues expression consisted of close vocal harmonizing, tight instrumentation, racy lyrics or occasionally bending the typically tight structures—this last the lesson of Louis Armstrong.

James Brown's love of jazz led him to seek out this very method of putting his own signature on rhythm and blues. His earliest recordings, "Please Please Please," "Why Do You Do Me?" and "Try Me" (1956-58) show a far greater interpretive freedom than can be heard on the R & B of Hank Ballard, Fats Domino or even jet-propelled Little Richard. These Brown songs are still R & B, but the delivery is a more playful jazz-influenced timing. James Brown is trying to bust out of the cage imposed by the rhythm and the changes.

An easy indication of a true soul recording is its elasticity. You can imagine the artist doing any part of it faster or slower, depending upon the feeling of the moment or the groove the band is generating. The interpretation has a temporal flexibility classic R & B lacks. Even if you play with the tempo in R & B, you do so throughout the song; with soul music, you can speed it up and slow it down in the same tune.[2] Brown's earliest soul masterpieces ("I'll Go Crazy," "Lost Someone") have precisely this freedom. By the time of "Lost Someone," James Brown is no longer even doing standard blues changes: there is an openness to the structure of this song that enabled him to perform it as a romantic mini-epic in concert. This freedom comes from jazz, of course, but also from sanctified gospel.

The other key distinction between rhythm and blues as opposed to soul has to do with the amount of melisma, or melodic ornamentation. Once again this is a matter of degree, not absolute differentiation. But you will find overall far more melisma in a soul performance than in R & B, which is content to deliver the melody with less embellishment. Listen to any Hank Ballard number, then put on Brown's "Lost Someone" or Otis Redding's "Try a Little Tenderness." You should be able to hear the greater freedom with the melody.

James Brown was not the only musician making these discoveries at the time: you can hear similar and independent developments in artists such as Wilson Pickett, Otis Redding and Aretha Franklin, to name but a few. Seems like everyone was using gospel and jazz to loosen up the strictures of R & B. (White musicians like the Rolling Stones and the Beatles were happy just to catch up with R & B! Blue eyed soul was a much rarer commodity: the Righteous Brothers and eventually Van Morrison, Joe Cocker and Janis Joplin.) But James Brown released the Rosetta stone of soul music in January of 1963, arguably the greatest live popular recording ever made: *Live at the Apollo*. After that, he was unquestionably Soul Brother Number One.

The liner notes for the CD reissue remind us that the recording was made at the height of the Cuban Missile Crisis: "Nuclear war was a real possibility" (Weinger). That must have been in the mix, because the show has the intensity of pre-apocalyptic ecstasy. Band member Bobby Bennett recalled, "It was like compiling a gift from God ... . It was perfection" (Weinger). James Brown was equally awestruck by the concert:

> As soon as I was into "I'll Go Crazy" I knew it was one of those good times. That's a hard feeling to describe—being on stage, performing and knowing that you've really got it that night. It feels like God is blessing you, and you give more and more. The audience was with me, screaming and hollering on all the songs, and I thought, "Man, this is really going to do it." (Brown 135)

God (or the muse, if you prefer) descending. I wasn't there that night (!) and can only hear the impressive recorded results, but I have seen actually unfolding some stuff like that must have been: Sarah Hughes's gold-medal performance in figure-skating at the 2002 Winter Olympics (even over the television it was electrifying); Crosby, Stills, Nash and Young's final encore of "Eight Miles High" at their February 15, 2002 concert in St. Louis. (Two sublime moments in one year ain't too shabby.)

You can hear the ripples of the event in the live recording. The intense audience response matches Beatlemania scream for scream a year and two months before the British Invasion. And this is a funkier audience, too: way down in the mix, some elderly woman is yelling "Sing it motherfucker, sing it." "Lost

Someone" turns into an epic psychodrama. James Brown draws out call-and-response like a backwoods preacher: "when I say that little part that might touch your heart, I want you to scream ... . I believe somebody here lost someone ... . It's getting a little cold outside [this last a reference to the arctic weather outside that night] ... . I feel like I want to scream." And just when it's all hanging out over the emotional edge, he drops immediately into a dramatic rendition of "Please Please Please" without missing a beat. The whole album sounds like a climax, in both the sexual and dramatic senses. This moment is the climax of the climax! You can hear it all much better on the CD; the vinyl version had the amazing insensitivity of breaking "Lost Someone" up into two parts, forcing the listener to stop the momentum and flip the record over to continue. It's as if Syd Nathan thought there was just too much soul on the record, and tried to insert some cadmium rods into the reactor.

When disk jockeys received the album, especially those on black-oriented stations, they made the unprecedented decision to play it in its entirety—an accolade accorded James Brown well before similar honors were bestowed on FM progressive rock (Brown 139). These radio guys intuited that this performance was a seamless event (broken only by the oddly programmed end of side one). Although it wasn't as dead danceable as Brown's later funk phase (except for "Night Train," the show's closer), there were plenty of opportunities on the record for slow dancing and grinding with special people. And no matter how hard his auditors worked it, how sweaty they got, we had to know it was a pale shadow of what Butane James was putting out. This was his self-acknowledged gift to the fans, a ritual immolation of clothing and processed hair: "The artist has to reach, you know? You come to see my show, you get the atmosphere and the feelin'. And I don't care how well-dressed I am, when I come off, I am drenched in sweat. You know that I was workin' for you" (Rose 74). By the time of *Live at the Apollo,* James Brown was the hardest working man in show business.

As we shall see, he worked so hard that he invented on his own a whole new bag a few years later. Whereas soul music was a parallel development by several R & B players, funk can be laid to rest solely at James Brown's door. But I hasten to add that he never abandoned his earlier idioms. Throughout Brown's recorded and live career, he would return to R & B and soul music. Like one of the promotional buttons declared, he was "The Man Who Never Left" (*Solid Gold* gatefold).

Take the somewhat controversial "It's a Man's Man's Man's World" (1966), a distillation of the main argument of Camille Paglia's *Sexual Personae* masterwork into a 2:46 soul statement: "This is a man's world / But it wouldn't be nothing, nothing / Without a woman or a girl." As with most Christian denominations, homosexuality isn't an option here. Get past the lyrics, and you can hear the fascinating psychodrama in play throughout the vocal: an oscillation between *braggadocio* and vulnerability that perfectly fits the sentiments of the lyric. It's a great song that only James Brown has ever been able to get away with.

And there would be a lot more where that came from, although the sound would get slicker in the seventies when Polydor started dictating terms (e.g., "I'm Broken Hearted" off *Reality* [1975] or "Kiss in 77" off *Bodyheat* [1976]). But, by then, James Brown was up against Al Green and Barry White! His soul music became a sideline to the funk—and, less fortunately for Brown, to the disco.

Papa's Brand New Bag

As with James Brown's transition from R & B to soul, his move from soul to funk was a gradual one. By his own accounts readily confirmed by your own ears, the beginning of the move occurred in "Out of Sight" (1964). What comes to the foreground on this song is a sense of the rhythm dominating the melody. Brown was fully aware of this development:

> You can hear the band and me start to move in a whole other direction rhythmically. The horns, the guitar, the vocals, everything was starting to be used to establish all kinds of rhythms at once. On that record you can hear my voice alternate with the horns to create various rhythmic accents. I was trying to get every aspect of the production to contribute to the rhythmic patterns. What most people don't realize is that I had been doing the multiple rhythm patterns for years on stage, but Mr. Neely and I had agreed to make the rhythms on the records a lot simpler. (Brown 149)

In other words, the world was not initially deemed ready for the funk initially.

What James Brown is describing here is, of course, polyrhythm: the maintenance of diverse tempos by the separate instruments to create a complex and highly danceable stew of beats. It is an old procedure which leads us back to both African drumming and Native American drum circles. Brown has this dual ancestry (and then some), but a more ready source of exposure would be the musical proclivities present in New Orleans—especially the Congo drumming in the square by St. Louis cathedral. Crescent City musicians learned much from nineteenth-century drummers fresh off the boats from Africa. Their rhythmic innovations came to be known as the "New Orleans beat," an emphasis upon the first downbeat of every bar—"the One"—as opposed to the 2nd and 4th beat emphasis of most western popular music. Funky drummer Clyde Stubblefield, who joined the band in 1965, epitomized this approach (Rose 47; Brown 218).

But Brown accomplished the rhythmic revolution before Stubblefield joined the band with "Papa's Got a Brand New Bag" (1965), his musical declaration of independence that reduced everything to propulsive polyrhythmic jazz licks (Brown 158). With this remarkable track funk arrives full-blown; it just needed a name! Which is not to deny that Stubblefield helped Brown carry it further. As Dave Marsh seriously jokes, "one day in 1967, James Brown grew weary altogether of the tyranny of chord changes and so he banished them and thus begot 'Cold Sweat' "(in Brown 278). Clyde Stubblefield was drumming on that track. By 1967, the funk revolution was accomplished. Polyrhythm *uber alles*—over chords, over melody, over harmony.

Marsh again: "if you don't think it amounted to much, try turning on the radio" (in Brown 278). In other words, pop music over the years has come to be dominated by a dummied-down and simplified version of James Brown's revolutionary paradigm shift. We will discuss rap music later; but what of the plethora of rhythm-driven pop tunes for teens by girl and boy groups / soloists? A quick eavesdrop into the playlists of non-oldies stations and / or MTV tells the tale. Almost everything you hear is post-Brown, but it's not as complicated or funky. Most of today's current pop megastars (Janet Jackson, Britney Spears, Beyonce) don't even have to play instruments: the rhythm tracks cover for them. This is all an etiolated version of Brown's project, hence he should not be blamed for its vagaries. But his influence must surely be acknowledged. After "Papa's Got a Brand New Bag" and "Cold Sweat," the deluge!

The move to funk by Brown also influenced jazz, and was ultimately responsible for fusion. In his autobiography, Miles Davis talks of changing his sound in 1967 because of James: "I was already moving toward a guitar sound in my music because I was beginning to listen to a lot of James Brown, and I liked the way he used the guitar in his music" (288). Miles decided he would rather reach black youngsters than the predominantly white listeners of jazz: this resulted ultimately in albums like *On the Corner* (1972), his self-proclaimed combination of his own style "with a little bit of Sly and James Brown and the Last Poets" (Davis 320, 322). James Brown always acknowledged his jazz influences; with funk, he was doing the influencing on jazz's greatest players. (You can also hear the sonic shadow of Brown on jazz recordings such as Joe Henderson's *Multiple* or Donald Byrd's *Ethiopian Knights*, to name but a few examples.)

In addition to the funk influences, there were a whole series of purveyors of this new music, straight up no chaser, after Brown. Parliament / Funkadelic are an obvious example since they took on members of Brown's band such as Bootsy Collins, Maceo Parker and Fred Wesley. (Bootsy later carried the funk on his own with the Rubber Band.) Earth, Wind and Fire, like Parliament / Funkadelic, seemed to borrow from both James Brown (the funk) and Sun Ra (Egyptian and extraterrestrial references). Miles Davis himself described Prince as "from the school of James Brown" (Davis 384). In 2002, my university had an operational funk outfit called Hazard to Ya Booty. The funk goes on. The torch Brown lit in 1965 still burns brightly years later both directly as funk and indirectly through jazz fusion, rap and contemporary urban and / or pop. As Salt 'N' Peppa might sing, "What a man, what a man, what a mighty mighty good man."

If musicians like Parliament / Funkadelic or Prince could eventually approach James's funk (and some would argue equal or transcend him), it was certainly many years after 1965 before anyone could touch him. (Kind of like America's five-year monopoly on atomic weapons.) As Cynthia Rose observes, "Papa's Got a Brand New Bag" "sounded like the initiation of a programme" (41). And it was: until pressures from Polydor to go disco diluted the sound, James Brown and the JBs churned out a decade's worth of fabulous funk. I hesitate to do more than describe a few personal highlights because it's almost all good. You're on extremely safe ground purchasing any reissues of this material or acquiring any original recordings from *Papa's Got a Brand New Bag* (1965) through *Hell* (1974). The first cheesy results of Polydor's pressures on James Brown manifest on *Reality* (1975) with its moronically repetitive soundbytes between songs. Although there are good things on all his albums, the rest of the non-reissue Polydor catalogue after 1974 is spotty—with the stellar exception of the double 1980 live album recorded in Tokyo, *Hot on the One*. Stick to reissues on Polydor after that, and look for eighties Scotti Brothers recordings such as *Gravity* (1986) and *I'm Real* (1988)—or his 12-inch *Unity* EP with Afrika Bambaataa on Tommy Boy Records (1983). That's enough funk to keep any party going a long, long time.

On the historical tip, we already know that "Out of Sight," "Papa's Got a Brand New Bag" and "Cold Sweat" are essential exhibits (respectively protofunk, funk and big funk). I'd also include "I Got You (I Feel Good)" (later 1965, after "Papa's Got a Brand New Bag"). This single was Brown's Pauline moment when he spread the gospel to whitey. Sure, this song is rhythmic and obviously funky, but it's so stripped down that even white folks can sing it and dance to it. In Kirksville, we have a bar with a karaoke night. There's lots of John Conlee, Garth Brooks and Dixie Chicks on the song menu, but only one James Brown number to choose from. You guessed it. This is meant by way of praise, actually—it's a universal communication with its cool reed breaks and its unabashed minimalism. John Lennon once compared the blues to a chair, simple and functional. "I Got You (I Feel Good)" works the same way. If you play it, they will dance.

Even a year later, James would risk far greater complexities with his earliest funk sermon, "Money Won't Change You." Like the best of his stream-of-consciousness preaching, this seems more directed at himself than the black bourgeoisie emerging. It's a cautionary tale set to cooking sax work: "Money won't change you / But time will take you OUT." Amiri Baraka recommended playing it in a bank to transform the space: not a bad idea. It takes you to "[a] place where Black People live" (Baraka 191).

"Let Yourself Go" (1967) in live performance would send Brown off into the stratosphere. On *Live at the Garden*, a rare King release now on CD, check out how "Let Yourself Go" leads into the intense nonce workout "Hip Bag '67."[3] Or even more remarkably, listen to the second side of the double album *Live at the Apollo, Volume II* (also reissued on CD). It is arguably the funkiest side of music James Brown ever recorded, and it has burned down the house at every party I've attended where it has been slapped on. In this live sequence, "Let Yourself Go" segues into "There Was a Time," "I Feel All Right" and "Cold Sweat." The damn thing never lets up. Although the original Apollo recording is overall superior, the best sides of *Volume II* beat the original. Side 2 showcases the new funk, and side 4 ranks as one of Brown's most soulful achievements with epic readings of "It's a Man's Man's Man's World" and "Lost Someone."

I must also duly note "I Got the Feelin'" (1968), the single which initiated Brown's trademark utterance of "Baby, baby, baby / Baby, baby, baby."

In 1970, James Brown trashed his newfound respectability which resulted from endorsing Hubert Humphrey and cooling down potential ghetto flare-ups. Not only was "Get Up, I Feel like Being a Sex Machine" serious funk, it was the raunchiest single-entendre race record since the heyday of Hank Ballard and the Midnighters or the Five Royales. Brown has claimed he "never gave a dirty show," but the seventies material had an intriguingly blue tinge that makes one suspect he was only referring to the letter of the law here (Brown 166). You tell me: what does a "sex machine" do? What does it manufacture? Or as Brown would say in live performance, "When we say 'get up,' what do we mean?" Not that anyone was complaining very much: even Richard Nixon hung out with him a bit in those days. (Maybe Neil was right singing that Nixon had soul!) But before Prince / The Artist, there was Brother James stirring it up.

The *Sex Machine* double album (also 1970) had other outstanding funk tracks besides the title jam: "Give It Up or Turnit a Loose" featured Johnny Griggs on congas while James urged the band to go "in the jungle, brothers"; "Mother Popcorn" had James demanding "You got to have a mother for me" at this height of one of his starch surrealist phases (to be discussed below).

A year later, "Hot Pants" kept up Brown's new lowdown heat. This was his paean to the most leg-revealing fashion to come out of the stylistic revolutions of the time: "Hot pants make you sure of yourself ... . The girl over there with the mini-dress / I ain't got time to dig that mess." James assured his female admirers that hot pants "let me see where you're coming from." The objectification of womanhood was so over the top that it was hard for anyone except Andrea Dworkin to take this stuff seriously. Camille Paglia, I'd bet, would gloss this material as proof of Brown's profound fear of the devouring Great Mother, a homeopathic incantation to hold the feminine at bay. And I would be inclined to agree: Brown doth protest too much on these highly danceable tracks. Since "It's a Man's Man's Man's World," the world would "mean nothing without a woman or a girl" for James Brown. Behind the hyper-macho posing lurks a realization that masculine Apollonianism is a mere afterthought. The cosmos of James Brown pivots around Woman.[4] (Once again, the rumors he allowed to spread about a planned sex change on his part seem germane.) Hence songs like "Hot Pants"—to say nothing of later fare such as "Take a Look at Those Cakes" (1979)—smack of male hysteria, which is not an oxymoron when you hear the grooves. The churning instrumental polyrhythms in this light seem another aspect of the charm, the counter-spell of ritual drumming that is exclusively a male privilege in traditional African cultures.

Revolution of the Mind, James Brown's third volume from the Apollo (1971) continues the tradition of funk excellence. James still has hot pants on his mind: during a soulful rendition of "Bewildered," he cautions the ladies, "Don't let anybody tell you how to wear your pants." But the band is incredible, turning the whole concert into one continuous flow of funk. Guitarist Hearlon "Sharp Cheese" Martin plays on "Make It Funky," by JB's admission, "funky guitar ... funky as it want to be ... cornbread licks with a little hoecake on the side." Fred Wesley's trombone conjures up "crowder peas" and "lima beans" for the Godfather of Soul.

Rather than just endlessly reiterate how funky seventies and early eighties James Brown is at his best, let me just list a few more funk classics from that era. These are all readily available for an ultimate party mix tape. They all have their individual virtues as well as a great deal in common musically. James Brown had a seeming patent on the funk until others caught on. These tracks all had the New New Super Heavy Funk: "Get on the Good Foot" (1972); "Sexy, Sexy, Sexy" and "People Get Up and Drive Your Funky Soul" (from *Slaughter's Big Rip-Off* soundtrack, 1973);[5] "Stone to the Bone" (from *The Payback*, 1974); "I Can't Stand It '76'" and "Papa Don't Take No Mess" (from *Hell*, 1974); "Hot (I Need to Be Loved, Loved, Loved)" (1976; main guitar line plagiarized by John Lennon and David Bowie on "Fame"!); "Get Up Offa That Thang" (1976); "It's Too Funky in Here" (from *The Original Disco Man*, 1979); "Rapp Payback (Where Iz Moses)" (from *Soul Syndrome*, 1980); and "Popcorn 80's" and "Super Bull / Super Bad" (from *Nonstop!*, 1981). There is far more available than this, of course—to say nothing of live versions of such material—but this list provides a respectable sampling of James Brown's greatest funk workouts from his later career. James Brown invented and perfected the funk; the proof is in the music.

Brother Rapp

James Brown certainly contributed to rap music as well as soul and (obviously) funk. I think those who claim "King Heroin" (a rhymed allegory of addiction Brown released in 1972) to be "the first rap record" are greatly mistaken (Brown xvi). By Brown's own estimate, it's not even his first rap recording! He bestows that honor upon "Choo-Choo (Locomotion)" (1963), a train song describing the towns passed through (Brown 227). Brown also considers tracks like "Say It Loud, I'm Black and I'm Proud" (1968), "America Is My Home" (1968) and "Get Up, Get Into It and Get Involved" (1970) to be in the rap genre as well (Brown 200, 227). "Brother Rapp" (1970) even uses the term in the title and in its lyrics, albeit with a nonstandard spelling. And funk tracks such as "Hot Pants" (1971) certainly have strong rap elements.

I think it's safer to say Brown is a contributor and an inspiration to this discourse rather than an originator. Clarence Major's *Juba to Jive: A Dictionary of African-American Slang* traces the word back to Sierra Leone, where it means to "tease" or "taunt." Since 1870, it's meant "to talk or converse"; by the late 1940's, it had all the modern implications of a "rhyming monologue" (Major 376-7). James Brown would have been aware of all these culturally specific aspects of the term when he used it.

The practice of rapping goes back to the African signifying monkey, ultimately—the first rapper playing the dozens on the big bad lion. It is an Afrocentric, pre-diasporic practice. Rapping came to the new world via the slave ships, of course. Although white folks were initially not privy to the practice, it came to be known somewhat through the verbal activities of folks like Cab Calloway and (especially) Cassius Clay / Muhammad Ali ("float like a butterfly, sting like a bee"). Zora Neal Hurston includes text you'd call rap in *Mules and Men* (1935).

James Brown certainly did not invent rapping; but did he release the first rap record? I don't think so. The records he cites don't really sound like rap technically. There's too much live playing of sundry instruments, and the vocals aren't sufficiently at hyper-speed. (Compare them with the Sugarhill Gang's 1979 "Rapper's Delight," which might well be the first modern rap record.) But Brown is a precursor to the genre, as are—to an even greater extent—the Last Poets and Gil Scott-Heron. James Brown did two major things for rap music. First, by creating the funk, he made possible rap. Rap is an even more rhythm-based genre: at its sparsest, it's just beats and rhyming—funk taken down to the minimum. So James Brown was at least rap's John the Baptist; he smoothed the way and made rap viable. Our ears were prepared. Secondly, as rapper Melle Mel once said, "Everybody samples James Brown. You can't make a rap record without sampling some James Brown" (Rose 151).

Hyperbole with a grain of truth: Brown was abundantly sampled in rap recording. ("Funky Drummer" alone was appropriated to an extraordinary extent.) So one can see why contemporary rappers cite Brown with affection.

James Brown returned the favor by contributing to the new form of expression himself a bit. In 1980, by his own description, he "mixed rap and funk together" on "Rapp Payback (Where Iz Moses)" (Brown 257). Two years later, he collaborated with rapper Afrika Bambaataa on the six-part antinuclear, pro-peace 12 inch Unity rap for Tommy Boy records. Later in the eighties and early nineties, he became a huge supporter of M. C. Hammer (then the only rapper who paid James for sampling him, a much appreciated gesture). Brown would appear in Hammer's video "Too Legit to Quit" and even do an HBO special with him.

Although James told Rick Dees once on *Into the Night* that he had lost "four fortunes," Brown's economic woes would seem small potatoes compared to Hammer's spectacular flameout. The sinister side of rap music was that it guaranteed built-in ephemerality for most of its practitioners, an African-American version of the boy/girl singers/groups (not to neglect Vanilla Ice or Eminem!). It remains to be seen whether any rap act can sustain a career as long as the artists we have been discussing. What will rap nostalgia look like? James Brown touched bases with the music—after all, it was the latest phase of black expression, and he's "the man who never left." But he understood his strongest musical suits were to be found elsewhere.

Starch Surrealism: Let a Man Come In and Do the Popcorn

Among other Brown scholars, Cynthia Rose has noted the surrealist element in Brown's style—an extension of the pop madman persona developed in the fifties by Little Richard, Screaming Jay Hawkins, Jerry Lee Lewis, even Elvis Presley.[6] She cites especially the revolutionary impact of Brown's cameo in the movie *Ski Party* (43-4). Out of nowhere he manifests with the Famous Flames, stretch pants and Cuban heels under his parka, to burn the ski lodge down with "I Got You (I Feel Good)" (suitable fare for white teenagers). Over the years, his five minutes are now the only reason anyone ever watches this teen exploitation flick. It became Brown's point of entry into the white youth market, all he really needed to connect. Once we saw him do the James Brown, young America was hooked.

In Brown's able hands, the dance craze became something more artistically interesting. His dance projects were closer to Pablo Picasso phases like the "blue period" than mere dance offerings like Chubby Checker's twist. There were two major dances Brown promoted throughout his career: the Mashed Potatoes and the Popcorn. Because of Syd Nathan's lack of support for the project, Brown had to release "(Do the) Mashed Potatoes, Parts 1 and 2" under the alias of Nat Kendrick and the Swans on the Florida Dade label. After it became a national hit, the deluge: "Mashed Potatoes, USA" (1965), "Mashed Potatoes '66," even a return to "Mashed Potatoes" ("Mashed Potatoes one more time!") on *Soul Syndrome* (1980)—to say nothing of endless references and name-checking of the dance in concerts well into the eighties (for example, on "Papa's Got a Brand New Bag" off *Live in New York* [1981]).

The Popcorn was created well after Brown's transition to funk, and you can hear it in the grooves. I am still trying to track down any eyewitnesses who can testify as to how you DANCE the Popcorn. Maybe that's ultimately beside the point. On the cover of *James Brown Directs and Dances with the James Brown Band The Popcorn* (King, 1969), he seems to be doing a kind of Spanish toreador gesture—a fascinating glimpse into a possible Popcorn move. The dance dominated his late sixties and early seventies output. *Sex Machine* (1970) had two versions of the Popcorn: the organ instrumental "Lowdown Popcorn" (also available in a "Hot Buttered Version" on *Soul Pride*, an instrumental anthology) and the funk in extremis "Mother Popcorn (You Got to Have a Mother for Me)."[7] The latter features fine solo work from Maceo Parker on tenor saxophone.

But the greatest example of the Popcorn phase is the utterly surreal 1969 single "Let a Man Come In and Do the Popcorn," most readily obtainable on the 1996 *Foundations of Funk* anthology. The lyrics catalogue Brown's obsessions, which are predictably different from Salvador Dali's:

> Way over yonder can you
> Dig that mess
> Sister standin' out there
> In a brand-new minidress
> Look
> Hey! over there
> Do you see that boy
> Playin' that horn?
> And get back—that soul brother
> Look at him doin' that
> Popcorn!

The scene has been set. In the second half of the song, after the band takes some solos, Brown raps a bit before uttering screams and howls on a par with "I Got a Bag of My Own"—the gold standard in these matters. It's an amazing track, with an earthy undertow equal to "Sex Machine."

As with the mashed potatoes, Brown would continue to reference the popcorn in his later career. Most notably, he re-recorded "Popcorn '80s" with new

James Brown: Funky Surrealism, Surrealist Funk 437

and exotic world percussion effects for his 1981 *Nonstop!* album. Other starchy food products such as cornbread and grits would show up in song titles and associational lyrics as well—as did other soul food treats such as collard greens and hambones. Art historian Robert Farris Thompson explains how central food imagery was for James:

> I only interviewed James Brown once ... and it was hard to keep track of him, hard to pin him down. But when we moved onto food, suddenly he warmed up. He started talking about the BONE, the ham bone, and the way it cultures the greens. Pretty soon, I realised that the food and the sound were going in and out of each other's focus. That to him, they were things both at one and separate. Both distinct and united. (in Rose 88)

Perhaps because for James the music and the dance and the food were all spiritual and physical nourishment. Given his impoverished upbringing, he understood deprivation; with success, he came to know its opposite. Brown wanted to nurture his audience with the gift of his spectacular show: the culinary allusions underline the proposition that he saw this as a kind of communal dining, perhaps even Eucharistic in nature. James Brown, his band and his audience literally *fed off* each other. And it was soul food in the truest sense.[8]

In James Brown's surreal libidinal economy, breasts and genitals are largely displaced by a far greater interest in the more basic (in a strictly Freudian sense) drives of orality and anality. Dare we say a reflection of unresolved issues from his troubled and mostly parentless childhood? If there is a lot of food in Brown's lyrics, there is also a lot of ass. In 1975, he encouraged everybody to do the hustle "dead on the double bump"—double ass cheek contact. Three years later, he introduced a new dance, "The Spank" (on *Jam 1980s*).

The culmination of all this imagery was "Take a Look at Those Cakes" (1979), a track which combined oral and anal interests by referring to the butt cheeks as cakes. From a first glimpse of the eponymous album's sleazy cover painting showing Brown leering at two gals thrusting their "cakes" at the viewer, one suspected that we were heading for deep psychic waters. The cut itself is undoubtedly James' most overwrought performance. He is nakedly honest about his desires, but it's all so over-the-top that little gets communicated (in a viral sense) to the listener—as is not the case with, say, "Sex Machine." The music is a recycled riff from "Call Me Superbad." We are invited into the Godfather's magic theater:

> Take yourself to the disco ... .
> When you see it,
> You're bound to put on brakes
> For goodness sakes,

Take a look at those cakes ... .

She can be tall and slim,
Brown and fat
But if she's got cakes,
I'll have some of that!
You like cakes?

Eventually, he invites the band members to earn their cakes by soloing; he even asks "Ray Charles, Stevie Wonder, did you see those cakes?" Augmented further by his gob-smacking "my, my, my," dubious taste and unrestrained vulgarity lurk behind the popping bass riffs. The great paradox here is that these very qualities make this one of Brown's most surreal raps. For the surrealist aesthetic has always involved getting in touch with one's most suppressed psychic interests at the risk of transgression. (If you doubt this claim, leave Salvador Dali behind and look at the paintings of Paul Delvaux and Clovis Trouille.) On the liner notes for *Take a Look at Those Cakes*, James says this is his "greatest [album] since THE PAYBACK." In terms of the psychoanalytic exploration it allows him to do, this is arguably the case—although he modestly demurs on the same liner notes that he only wants "to keep [us] boogieing."

Not all of James Brown's stream-of-consciousness sermons concern food or ass, of course. The 1972 "Like It Is, Like It Was (The Blues)"—unreleased until 1990 on *Messing With The Blues*—delves into autobiography and Brown's sense that he can't "sing the blues like [he] used to" because of his lack of the appropriate "environment" (White, liner notes). "Mind Power" from *The Payback* (1974) is unquestionably Brown's strangest rap. It covers a range of topics: ESP, "vibes," astrology, theft, mind over hunger ("If you don't work, you can't eat / So you got to have mind power to deal with starvation"), and the "JBE" ("James Brown Experience"). His intent is to offer comfort to his impoverished constituency via the power of positive thinking. Perhaps too New Age a statement to have gotten over fully, "Mind Power" remains an excellent example of the flights of fancy Brown could attain while the tape was rolling—not only funk surrealism, but the audio equivalent of Jackson Pollock's action paintings. For James Brown, the funky journey matters at least as much as the arrival at the musical bridge. "Take me to the bridge," he eventually says; but there's never a rush once he achieves the funk.

He's Real

In Bruce Tucker's introduction to Brown's autobiography, he makes an important observation of how Brown's status as a public icon of Otherness pro-

James Brown: Funky Surrealism, Surrealist Funk 439

duces problematic results, especially when the Godfather was arrested and imprisoned in 1988:

> In line with my argument about the burdens of otherness, ... I would point out that beneath the smugness in the reporting of James' plight, there was often a note of comedy, a nudge in the ribs about the wild man who drove six miles on his wheel rims before the police could catch him. Or later, the sly dog who was caught with, haw haw, $40,000 in his cell. For me, the nudges in the ribs have been more than metaphorical. Perfectly well-meaning people, a risible gleam in the eye, talk to me about his troubles in tones usually reserved for the appreciation of Road Runner cartoons; though having twenty-three bullets pumped into your vehicle by enraged southern cops is no joke. (Brown xxv; italics are Tucker's)

At least Brown was spared the televisual accompaniment of the chase later provided for O.J. Simpson in his white Bronco.

In 2002, I saw James Brown alluded to twice on television when I was drafting this chapter. On the Christmas episode of *The Osbournes*, Ozzy receives a dancing and head-bobbing James Brown doll that sings (yes) "I Got You (I Feel Good)" when you activate it. Ozzy reacts as if it's his favorite present. More recently, a claymation James Brown appeared with a claymation Danny De Vito in a Lipton's iced tea ad. It sounds like Brown is supplying the voice. All of these references confirm Tucker's suspicion that the Godfather of Soul had been assimilated as the Road Runner of Soul. And this is a process that has been happening for quite some time in both the black and white communities. In the early seventies, militants in the former group coined the slogan "James Brown—Nixon's Clown" after Brown endorsed Tricky Dick (Brown 232).[9]

Small wonder that James Brown entitled his last major studio effort *I'm Real* (1988). A man like James shouldn't have to point that out, but he clearly felt he did. I recall a telling moment in *Shakey*, the Neil Young biography by Jimmy McDonough. After five years of obsessing on Young, McDonough had a revelation:

> Neil had no more idea why he'd written "Nowadays Clancy Can't Even Sing" than I did ... .
>
> As banal as this is going to sound, it was actually beginning to poke through my thick skull that Young wasn't his music or his persona—he was a human being. (McDonough 706)

Bruce Tucker in turn described the authentic James Brown (to friends who asked for the inside scoop) as "the most complicated human being [he had] ever known" (Brown xiii). People, they're real.

There is so much to be said on behalf of James Brown's amazing contributions to world music, his simple inventions that changed the shape of sound. Until Polydor tried to make him The Original Disco Man in the late seventies, Brown mostly marched to his own beat—and he had some funky drummers! Who else would do straight covers of "Mona Lisa," "I Want to be Around," and "Nature Boy" during the summer of *Sergeant Pepper* (on *Cold Sweat*, a July 1967 King lp)?[10] And let's not forget that James Brown was the only one of these figures discussed here to play for the troops in Vietnam, cancelling $100,000 worth of bookings to do so (Brown 192).

Without even fully knowing what he was doing, James Brown brought Africa to America on a meaningful and egalitarian basis. Musicologist Miller Chernoff has noted that "James Brown's lyrics ... are 'thick with proverbs' comparable to the most philosophical [Ghanaian] highlife songs ... . Many of my [African] friends were eager for my help in translating James Brown's slang, which they interpreted with no end of enjoyment and wonder" (in Rose 123). By a diasporic miracle, James Brown carried over and carried on African beats and folkways. Like his dancing, he made it all seem like an effortless miracle. But we know he's really The Hardest Working Man in Show Business.

And he does get the blues sometimes from all the mess he's had to take. Check out the haunting ballad "How Do You Stop" from *Gravity* (1986)—a tale of infinite loss, obsession and failure. Joni Mitchell's cover of it on *Turbulent Indigo* (1994) is one of the best and sincerest tributes Brown has ever received from another artist, one outsider nodding to another.

Brown scholar Cliff White's liner notes for the British compilation *Solid Gold* summarize James Brown's Revolution of the Mind best:

> When [James Brown] started it was an era of black solo stars and vocal groups fronting anonymous bands. Now most of the creative work is done by self supporting groups of singer musicians—an evolution often attributed to Sly's Family Stone but deeper rooted in Brown's complex relationship with his bands and the independence of his self contained revue, on the road ever since the late fifties.
>
> When he started a lot of the bite of black music was disguised in the euphemism and double-entendre of the blues. Now the writers who have something to say can tell it like it is. In 21 years, fundamental changes. [This was written in 1977.] And while Brown is only one man in an army of agitators he's had his hand for all of those years on the pulse, the extreme example of the whole revolution. (punctuation as found)

Lest we ever forget who started so many cultural developments: the avant-pop artist who made himself the mainstream by sheer talent, genius and the will to power. Ain't it funky now.

Works Cited

Baraka, Amiri. *The LeRoi Jones / Amiri Baraka Reader*. Ed. by William Harris. New York: Thunder's Mouth Press, 2000.

Brown, James. *James Brown: The Godfather of Soul*. With Bruce Tucker, Dave Marsh and Cliff White (who did the excellent discography attached). New York: Thunder's Mouth Press, 1997.

———. Liner notes for *Take a Look at Those Cakes*. Polydor PD1-6181. 1978.

Davis, Miles. *Miles: The Autobiography*. With Quincy Troupe. New York: Touchstone, 1990.

Major, Clarence. *Juba to Jive: A Dictionary of African-American Slang*. New York: Viking, 1994.

McDonough, Jimmy. *Shakey: Neil Young's Biography*. New York: Random House, 2002.

Rose, Cynthia. *Living in America: The Soul Saga of James Brown*. London: Serpent's Tail, 1990.

Smith, RJ. *The One: The Life and Music of James Brown*. New York: Gotham Books, 2012.

Weinger, Harry. Liner notes for *James Brown Live at the Apollo*, 1962. Polydor 843 479-2.1990.

White, Cliff. Liner notes for *Messing With The Blues*. Polydor 847 258-2. 1990.

———. Liner notes for *Solid Gold*. Polydor 2679 044. 1977.

Notes

[1] See my remarks on Julia Kristeva's concept of abjection in the Yoko Ono chapter.

[2] No wonder twenties intellectuals called Louis Armstrong a "Master of Modernism." The same revolution was happening in poetry with free verse being preferred to standard meters. Robert Frost compared it to playing tennis without a net; T. S. Eliot fired back that that was much harder! So it goes with the music here in question. Standard meter : free verse :: R & B : soul.

[3] This is a suitable occasion to praise the 2009 Polydor reissue of *Live at the Garden* (which was actually recorded at the Latin Casino in Cherry Hill, New Jersey in January of 1967—more playing fast and loose with the truth for a greater hype factor by King Records). On the first disk, the CD repeats the original album with its added fake applause on the studio recording of "Let Yourself Go" and its truncated reduction of "Papa's Got a Brand New Bag" into the admittedly funky, mostly instrumental "Hip Bag '67." The remainder of

the release tries to provide a far more authentic audio souvenir of the show by culling together the best performances from four taped evening shows.

So the rest of the first disk showcases a series of organ instrumentals played by James as a show opener (and less fortuitously, a chitlin circuit comedy bit executed by several band members). But the second disk is a revelation—far superior to the original album. James Brown rips up the standard "Come Rain or Come Shine" in a full-tilt soul rendition which anticipates his enthusiastic readings of standards on *Soul on Top* (1969) and other earlier sporadic covers. He works in his own lyrical agenda: "if we're out of money, we can ride the night train home ... try me." Then we get the full live version of "Papa's Got a Brand New Bag" with funky drummer Clyde Stubblefield utterly transcending the accompaniment on the single. "Prisoner of Love" showcases Bobby Byrd and Bobby Bennett, the last remainder of the Famous Flames, on backup harmonies far more dead-on than on the original release. Again, this version is significantly more stretched-out and intense: "I want you to try me ... . You, you, you, you, you, you made me a prisoner of love."

The string accompaniment here also comes in handy on another relentless extension, this time of "It's a Man's Man's Man's World." We get slightly bluer nightclub lyrics: "Don't worry about the motion on the ocean / Just be there when I get a notion." All this with dramatic pauses, the clink of glasses and an interpolation of "When a Man Love a Woman."

The release ends with the rehearsal sessions for and recording of "Let Yourself Go" in the empty casino. Ronald Selico adds some tight bongos to bring out a new vibe for the funk. Ironically, an abbreviated version of the final take was reinserted into the original live album with fake applause. It still was good, but this longer read is better and of course a lot more honest. All in all, proof positive that James Brown was too much of an innovator for his record labels to understand him, let alone trust him.

[4] Alas, here we must also acknowledge Brown's well-documented abusive tendencies towards his wives. Such behavior also springs from fear, in fact: abusive men are not confident or secure in their relationships with women. Spousal maltreatment is a desperate act. Before judging James Brown too readily or harshly, consider his own upbringing as described in his autobiography. One can readily see him as part of a cycle of abuse he both received and perpetuated.

[5] A superior, uncut version of this non-stop groove jam can be found on the 1988 Polydor compilation of unreleased material from the vaults aptly entitled *Motherlode.* Fred Wesley really works his trombone and Jimmy "Chank" Nolen keeps his guitar churning for over nine minutes. Other highlights from this anthology of rarities include "Since You've Been Gone," a duet with Famous Flame Bobby Byrd that features the unbeatable combination of "Bootsy" Collins on bass and Clyde Stubblefield on drums. On the 2003 CD reissue, there's a

bonus track of a longer "Bodyheat" from 1976 which proves *Reality* (1975) wasn't the absolute end of the line for studio quality on Polydor for James Brown. What makes this extended take shine especially bright are the funk contributions of Mike Lawler on clavinet and "Sweet" Charles Sherrell on the bass. Was there ever an artist who had so many masters of the funk in his band over the years, especially in the 1960s and 1970s? Undoubtedly James ran a funk academy, but he had an incredible ear for potential talent he could help develop.

[6]RJ Smith more recently also links James Brown to surrealism, especially citing his short-lived 1976 television show in Atlanta, *Future Shock*, which showcased a younger generation of dancers even wilder than Brown himself. Smith describes a five minute performance on the show of a dancer named "Bojangles" as "surrealism's finest hour ... as unfathomable as any five minutes of *Un Chien Andalou* or a film by David Lynch" (358-9).

[7]RJ Smith helpfully informs us that "[p]opcorn itself was another euphemism for booty." Not too surprising a revelation ... . And "a 'mother' was his honorific for a big butt" (220). Ergo "Mother Popcorn" is as good as it gets.

[8]The last example of this food obsession occurs on "Good and Natural" off of what as far as I can tell is James Brown's last studio album, *The Next Step* (2002) before his death in December 2006. I qualify because his studio releases after the 1980s are somewhat jerry-rigged affairs. This item on Fome Records had the instrumental tracks laid down in Charlotte, North Carolina; James Brown added the vocals in Augusta, Georgia—not the way Brown ever got his best results in the studio as opposed to interacting with the musicians. It's a slick, overproduced high-tech attempt to simulate the funk and it doesn't really work: only his vocals contain vestiges of the funk. RJ Smith in the latest biography doesn't even bother mentioning this production.

But, having said that, "Good and Natural" is a kind of ultimate statement about James Brown and food. He compares himself to "mashed potatoes and collard greens ... pork chops on the side ... corn bread and black-eyed peas ... a four-course meal ... . That's the way the Lord made me." Dietitians might question how much of this fare is truly "good and natural," but his soulful Eucharistic communion with his fans is at its most nakedly perceptible here.

The other track of note on this late effort is "Killing is Out, School's In," his post-Columbine revisiting of "Don't be a Dropout," and even "Say It Loud" (this new song also has a children's chorus): "get the gun out of your pants." A last gesture towards topicality ... . But the rest of the CD is pretty sad, literally (some lyrics full of regret and loss). Then-wife Tomi Rae even gets a solo vocal—unheard of on a classic Brown album—on "It's Time." Although her voice was good enough to imitate Janis Joplin in a Las Vegas "legends" review, she's no Pegi Young (and this ain't no *Double Fantasy*) (Smith 362). The lyrics co-written by the couple are mind-numbingly repetitive along the lines of Dylan's "All the Tired Horses" or the Beatles' "Why Don't We Do It In the Road?" She provides another cringe-worthy moment on their duet "Baby, You Got What It Takes" when she reverses decades of Brown musical injunctions by requesting "don't you hit me"—which is hard not to read outside of the context of his spousal abuse. This CD is probably PCP rock (I wasn't there) and thus only for the completist or people who like to watch *1,000 Ways to Die* on the Spike Network. This is what content footnotes are for!

[9] To this list of kitsch I'd have to add my James Brown "Celebriduck" bath toy (which James Brown Enterprises did authorize in his lifetime). It's an authentic likeness except for the orange beak! I have an Elvis Presley "Celebriduck" as well, one more thing the two legends have in common.

[10] In this regard, James Brown's biggest stretches were his several jazz-oriented albums which he recorded to show the listening public that jazz was the third ingredient in his gumbo (along with gospel and rhythm and blues). The most noteworthy of these was *Soul on Top* (1969)—with jazz lying beneath, get it? Recorded in Hollywood with west coast session players (including Ernie Watts, who played with Zappa on *The Grand Wazoo*) under the conduction of Oliver Nelson, this is a whole other kind of jazz fusion.

"That's My Desire" opens the proceedings with a solid tenor solo from Maceo Parker, the only band member from Brown's funk outfit allowed to participate on this session. Hank Williams' "Your Cheatin' Heart" gets an astonishing makeover as a boogaloo. (As Brown's appearance on the Grand Ole Opry indicates, he always wanted to get country music into his project as well—his furthest stretch.) He connects well with the lyric of "What Kind of Fool Am I?" Leslie Bricusse and Anthony Newley's tale of well-earned loneliness. (Unlike his take on "September Song," which completely misses the Kurt Weill and Maxwell Anderson *weltschmerz*. One added word destroys his "September Song": "These precious days I'll spend with you—OVERNIGHT!" It's like adding "in bed" to a fortune cookie sentence. Like he says in the same song, "I'm a mess / People, can you guess?")

James Brown's own compositions get fantastic new arrangements here. "It's a Man's, Man's, Man's World" has a nice piano vamp from Frank Vincent. "Papa's Got a Brand New Bag" gets a jazzy, driving, shrieking send-up with a big horn section as solid as any other reading of this breakthrough statement. Nelson's big band arrangement of "There Was a Time" works as well.

One final gem worth noting is his cover of production manager Bud Hobgood's "The Man in the Glass," which could have been a single. Brown can again relate well to the lyric: "You pass the most difficult test / If the man in the glass is your friend." I wonder if Michael Jackson heard this before he came up with "The Man in the Mirror"?

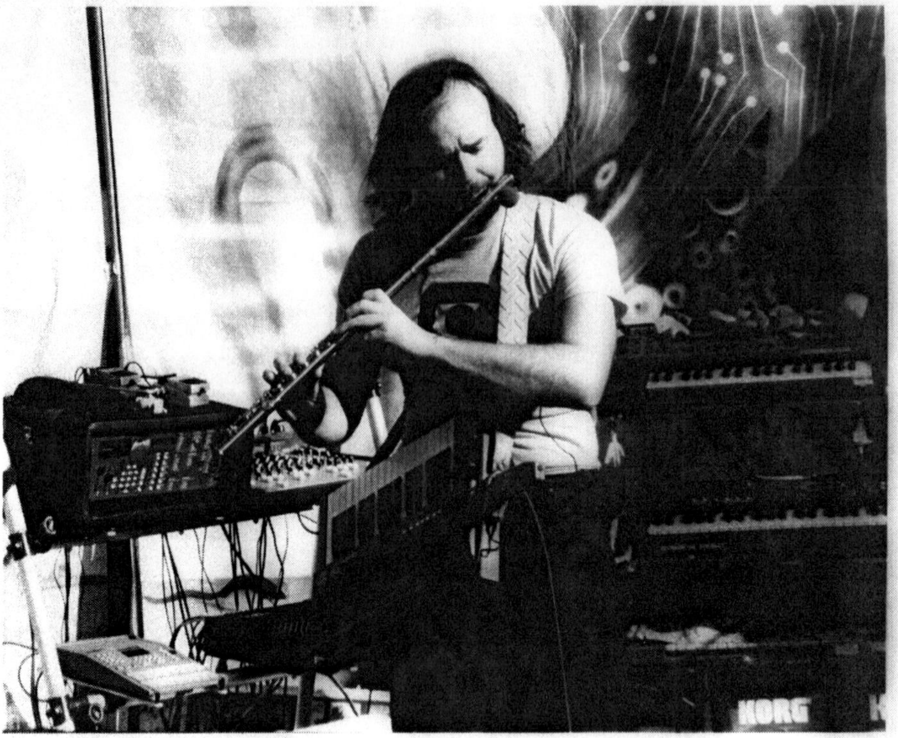
KORG

Who's Afraid of Sigmund Snopek III?

"Sometimes I don't know why I stay here."—"Sing for Me," Sigmund Snopek III

Location Is Everything

Where have all the good times gone, as Ray Davies once asked? Although these first six careers were fraught with chills and spills, one can look back and say that once upon a time the culture industry sort of *worked* in its own greedy way—an allegation that would be hard to defend today. These artists could assert in varying degrees their autonomous aesthetics while more-or-less sustaining a living and a career.

Now the fix is on. Nirvana and grunge were the last time oppositional youth culture seized the corporate reins with any clout. The pop music industry is now divided into three basic camps. First we have the disposable corporate swill targeted for maximal and ephemeral impact, acts that will make some money but will have a modest shelf life. The key indicator for this category is the inability to play instruments: Britney Spears, Back Street Boys, Destiny's Child, endless rap acts (James Brown could play instrumental music, after all, unlike most of his rap successors). No wonder Madonna started strumming guitar on *Music*: she didn't want to be lumped in with these folks. (And no wonder the King of Pop thought that he was the victim of a racist conspiracy!) Acts like Bob Dylan or Neil Young cost money over time, whereas the world will outgrow Britney. Bet on it! She's not about to write the next *Pet Sounds*.

A second category would be the big acts that hearken back to what now seems a relative golden age. They'll be around because they have been around and have a loyal fan base: Neil, Bob, the Rolling Stones, Lou Reed, what's left of The Who, Sir Paul, David Bowie. They've got the boomer bucks flowing in, and can fill stadiums at big ticket prices as they ride the demographic into that generation's retirement. Younger bands have crossed over into this cash cow as well: Tom Petty, Prince, REM, U2 ... maybe even Moby, Beck, Arcade Fire and/or Jack White! Boomers don't listen to much new music, but occasionally they hear something that they can recognize to be in the tradition.

Finally, there's the underground scene that has quality new avant-pop acts that receive little or no exposure in the mass media (busy catering to the first and second categories): bands like Goldfrapp, Trailer Bride or the affiliates of the Elephant Six group (Olivia Tremor Control, Of Montreal, Neutral Milk Hotel, The Apples in Stereo, Elf Power). As the internet websites and online reviews show, these groups inspire a devoted following. (And I've only named a few among thousands of possible examples.) But, unless they have as much luck as the youngest category two acts (Moby et al.), they are destined for obscurity and relatively modest sales figures. Category one listeners don't have the ready access to this new avant-pop that any kid with a transistor radio had in the sixties. The internet moderates these claims, of course, although one can certainly debate its fiscal benefits for the acts in question.

For another economic complication applying to musical categories one and three is the ready availability of music downloading off the net. Whereas wealthy boomers don't bother to steal their favorites by and large, the younger listening base really doesn't have to pay for its music if it doesn't want to. As a result of massive home-taping and CD / MP3 burning, the profitability of new music has never been lower, especially for the long term. The industry is overall targeted for the quick score, except for the aging giants of the past. Rock is running onto the same corporate shoals that jazz hit a while back when its newer music couldn't break unless it was slick. Three categories, three economic tiers and one bad situation for encouraging the music and the artists who make it. The bigger the access, the more watered-down the product: it wasn't always this way.

But perhaps the truth is even worse. There may have never really been a true golden age of avant-pop, only a few lucky souls who slipped through the system. Which brings us to the curious case of Sigmund Snopek III, an avant-pop artist of the first order that few have heard of. I will let his case stand in for the many folks who labored in the same vineyard as the more successful artists I have discussed. Snopek has had almost as long a career as these other artists. His first recording was released in 1969 (on Page Records) and he's still writing, playing and recording. So why haven't you heard of him?

Like James Brown, Sigmund Snopek III is "The Man Who Never Left." Unlike James Brown, however, the place he never left was Milwaukee, Wisconsin (my hometown, which is why I received abundant exposure to Snopek). Which is not to say Sigmund hasn't toured extensively over the years—both with his own bands and as a keyboardist for the better-known Violent Femmes—but that he has never relocated his base of operations outside of Wisconsin. This means that despite a forty-plus year career, he has an odd cult following. Few Wisconsinites even acknowledge him (even in his hometown of Waukesha), although he has a solid, if small fan base there. They respect him in France and Germany, as those two countries are responsible for keeping his first three solo masterworks in print (cf. Germany's assistance to the unjustly overlooked San Francisco group It's A Beautiful Day). And based on Amazon's reader reviews, they listen to Snopek in Silicon Valley. I have made a few converts in Missouri; after all, to hear him is to like him. There's some value for everybody in his complex and beguiling compositions.

I have to talk about Snopek not only because of regional allegiances, but because Snopek is actually the best illustration possible of the paradox this book has been discussing. What could be more avant-pop than starting your career writing rock operas and song cycles fit to be included amongst the works of Zappa, Pink Floyd and King Crimson (and better than the Moody Blues or Yes) and releasing thirty years later *Beer*, a CD of polkas and drinking songs (Irish and otherwise)? But wait, there's more: all the while composing symphonies, operas and other classical forms on the side. So much for NPR's cultural watchfulness. But that's why I'm here, I guess.

My bibliography will alert you to the relative ease with which you can acquire the recordings I will be discussing. The good news is that you can get the majority of them, and more are being reissued as we speak. Snopek may get the last word yet. His work roughly breaks into five categories of musical output:

1. progressive rock concept albums and rock operas: *Virginia Woolf* (1972), *Trinity Seas Seize Sees* (1974-1999 [!]), and *Nobody to Dream* (1975-1997 [!]);

2. more commercial pop fluctuating between prog rock and new wave: *Thinking Out Loud* (1978), *First Band on the Moon* (1980), and *Voodoo Dishes* (1982);

3. stand-alone collections of sundry compositions: *Roy Rogers Meets Albert Einstein* (1982), *Miasma Fragments: New Music for Pipe Organ* (2001), and *Jade* (2003);

4. pop music specifically addressing Wisconsin folkways and his residency in that state: *WisconsInsane* (1986), *Elephant* (1989), *Beer* (1998), and *Baseball* (2006); and

5. holiday music broadly considered: *Christmas* (2001), *Ornaments* (2010) and *The Easter Bunny's Christmas* (2011).[1]

(I am less concerned about Snopek's guest appearances with other bands on over one hundred different albums, although his playing trumpet and hunting horn on a cover of Sun Ra's "Nuclear War" for Violent Femme Brian Ritchie's *The Blend* seems auspiciously fortuitous!)

Sigmund Snopek III got his start in 1968 with a progressive rock band called Bloomsbury People. Their somewhat pretentious title no doubt reflected a sense that they represented an elite, oppositional culture in contrast to what passed then for the Milwaukee music scene (a lot of "pychedelic" jam bands, many of whom covered Iron Butterfly's "In-A-Gadda-Da-Vida"). By alluding to the London modernist vortex of Virginia and Leonard Woolf, Clive Bell and the like, the Bloomsbury People were proclaiming their difference from the hoi polloi—eminently audible in their progressive rock compositional complexities. Few got the reference, of course, and their only release on MGM was long out of print until it was reissued as a CD for Snopek's Couth Youth Productions in 2004. *Bloomsbury People* is very much a young man's album full of intense emotional states and lots of *sturm und drang*. Snopek's lyrics address archetypal symbols like water as a source of both death and rebirth with less sophistication than he will wield them on *Virginia Woolf* two years later. Musically, the standout track is arguably "Have You Seen Them Cry," which begins and ends with a quotation from "Greensleeves" and has a lovely interlude in the middle right up there with a Frisco act such as It's A Beautiful Day. "Birdsong" has an accomplished jazzy break in its middle. "Demian" features a fine piano introduction. And "So It Seems" has a nice organ / drums / percussion break—compelling prog rock insertions that suggest things to come.

But overall, the album is very much part of its time not only regarding Snopek's adolescence but the arrival of the counterculture in Milwaukee full-blown in 1970. "Witch Helen" evinces the fascination and dread for wiccan gals that Stevie Nicks would build a career on—and that Frank Zappa would parody thoroughly in "Camarillo Brillo." "Lake of Sand" has vocals delivered through a megaphone for a retro feel (a popular gimmick for about fifteen minutes). More amusingly on the same track, drummer Ding Lorenz drops a stick and curses. "State of Confusion," the only non-Snopek composition on the recording, ends in guitar wankery. "The Resurrection" quotes the famous chorus from Handel's *Messiah*.

"Suite Classical #11" foreshadows Snopek's interest in longer compositions and even has a rare Wisconsin allusion to one of Lake Michigan's more distinctive fishes: "[a] tall lean smelt felt." (Apparently this was a typo for "smell," but Sigmund Snopek says he likes "smelt" better! [Big Interview]) Another eccentric lyric from same: "Foolish faun / seriously basking." A nod to Debussy? "Gingerbread Man" and "Madeline" are relatively rocking. The album closer, "Saga of the Red Sea," returns to the obsessive water imagery and rounds things off with a peppy bolero. All in all, apprentice work with only a glimmer of the great stuff to come. On the plus side, you can hear the band's—and especially Sigmund Snopek's—chops.

The record drew enough attention to help Bloomsbury People achieve some critical acclaim and a few decent gigs. Most notably, they played with the likes of Jimi Hendrix, Traffic, Ten Years After and Mott the Hoople at the Atlanta Pop Festival. National exposure and popularity seemed inevitable. But then MGM's national distributors went bankrupt. And as in the case of the Buffalo Springfield, the more money they made the less they saw (Borden 147). Their youthful idealism was exploited by the industry (after all, some members of the band were still in their teens).

The final irony was that Milwaukee promoters billed them as outsiders:

> "Direct from Frisco," said one ad. In others, they were billed as a Chicago group. "We got into business through the back door," explained Snopek. "We had to. This is a back door state. There aren't any front doors out of this place." (Borden 147)

By 1971, the Bloomsbury People were defunct. Sigmund Snopek III decided to record the music he had written for their next album anyway, assisted by some former members of the rocking teen combo. The result was his first progressive rock masterpiece, *Virginia Woolf* (1972). My original vinyl version features a hand-lettered back cover which throws down the gauntlet: "This album is dedicated to those who say Milwaukee has no talent ... ." (Its 1994 German CD reissue with bonus tracks is re-titled *Who's Afraid of Virginia Woolf?*.)

What's so beguiling about Snopek's music is that it has its own individual sound, as unmistakable a sonic fingerprint as any of the other six artists I have been discussing. Perhaps the closest family resemblance is to Frank Zappa. Snopek shares with Zappa a wicked sense of humor (evident in the musical jokes as well as the lyrics) and a love of complex time signatures and rich musical textures. But he doesn't rock out as hard as Frank (he's a keyboardist after all, and few guitarists can match Zappa). Furthermore, he's much prettier sounding—reflecting his interests in nineteenth-century romantic music. The only sixties group that sounded lovelier than Snopek when he was in this idiom was the aforementioned It's A Beautiful Day; he could easily surpass the Moody Blues because he could outwrite them.

Progressive Snopek

It's an uncanny experience the first time one listens to *Virginia Woolf* (going by the original title throughout here). On the one hand, it is very much marked by its time: the early seventies, which is when the late sixties fully arrived in Milwaukee! Except for the title track, the lyrics are typical products of the psychedelic era: hippy-dippy surrealism, paeans to freedom (remember freedom?), juxtapositions of urban alienation ("Ciudad / hiding everyone / in their tiny / private space", from "Ciudad"), and pastoral faery women cavorting on the seashore ("Elizabeth," what remains of an unreleased album entitled *Nine Women* [Big Interview]). These lyrics are all in keeping with the issues of the time as expressed in prog rock. Think Pete Sinfield's early writings for King Crimson ("21st Century Schizoid Man," yet "Moonchild"), Marc Bolan and Tyrannosaurus Rex in their Tolkien phase, even David Crosby's "Guinevere."

But also there's something universal and familiar about the recording. Perhaps because of Snopek's clear love of romantic classicism as manifest in the melodies, one experiences a kind of *déjà vu* hearing the music. It's not borrowed directly from any particular source I can detect, but it sounds oddly familiar—an archetypal sixties band frozen in suspended animation, a bottle of that great vintage at last uncorked by the Germans in the nineties.

Then, on even closer listening, you realize that Snopek had a truly unique niche in progressive rock in this music, a kind of *via media*. His lovely and lush compositions have far more twists and turns than the simplicities of bands such as the Moody Blues, Pearls Before Swine and It's A Beautiful Day—although the vocals of James Gorton match the splendor of these more well-known outfits. Yet, on the obverse, Snopek's prog rock compositions avoid the time-signature-obsessed wankery of chief offenders like Rush, Yes, early Genesis and Emerson Lake and Palmer (and even King Crimson, whom I like for other reasons). Don't get me wrong: the music of Sigmund Snopek III is every bit as complicated as these others, even more so overall. But it has a restraint they often lack, a willingness to avoid rocking out into testosterone-laced guitar frenzy. And finally, Snopek allows for jazz and improvisation without descending into psychedelic jam band noodling. He balances romantic beauty, compositional rigor and improvisation in a delicate three-way equilibrium: Frank Zappa with a sunnier disposition! When you consider all these factors, you can see why no one really sounds like the band you hear on this first record—even though its family resemblances to other works of the era were legion.

Virginia Woolf

Virginia Woolf opens with a musical prologue that offers an instrumental version of the title track's main melody, a leitmotif for the album if you will (which will be reprised vocally in the epilogue). This music is a programmatic evocation of the moment when the writer Virginia Woolf walks into the water with her pockets full of stones, a suicide given much publicity in the novel and film *The Hours* (2002). This unifying interest in Woolf's death makes the album part company with the happy consciousness of prog rock bands the group otherwise resembles—and may well be an in-joke about the demise of Bloomsbury People. The original liner notes clarify Snopek's interest in Virginia Woolf: "Virginia Woolf came to me one early morning, told me of her suicide and her hate for the war ... . In her song the Nazi *war drums* tell of her death as she sinks into the sea ... ." Snopek's remark takes artistic license with the facts for greater dramatic effect (Woolf drowned in a river). And, he notes, it rhymed better (Big Interview). We learn that the origin of the song cycle is Snopek's dream vision encounter with the writer where she tells him that World War II was a factor in her suicide. This pointed comment invites us to consider the Snopek album as a statement against the Vietnam War and the Nixon administration. Woolf's suffering is a distant mirror on Snopek's current situation in 1972. Other moments in the album will also suggest this.

After the leitmotif of "Prologue," we proceed to the two-part song (of five originally) of urban alienation entitled "Ciudad" (Spanish for "city"). It bears a slight resemblance, as intimated above, to King Crimson material like "Pictures of a City" (off *In the Wake of Poseidon*). The low vocal rumblings in part one also evoke Frank Zappa's vocalese on *Freak Out* (especially "The Return of the Son of Monster Magnet"). The mix of influences keeps "Ciudad" fresh, but it is only a prelude in turn for the real masterwork of the album, "Orange / Blue."

It is not surprising that "Orange / Blue" was written both for rock players and for a full symphony orchestra. (The Milwaukee Symphony has performed it.) "Orange / Blue" has an inventive richness, variety and beauty more typical of the classical world than rock music (excepting, of course, the likes of Brian Wilson, Zappa and psychedelic-era Beatles). By contrast, most prog rock sounds pretty flat-footed and leaden.

The opening "Orange" section is simply a lovely melody, sixties wine from the same harvest that gave us the Moody Blues and It's A Beautiful Day. At 3:02 on track 3 of the German CD, the tour de force of "Blue" begins with a burst of electronic *musique concrete*. At 3:21, a harpsichord comes in with the main melody, soon augmented by the dreamy vocal and lyrics (3:31). Michael Lorenz bursts in with dramatic drum underpinnings at 3:44, and we rock out for a few minutes with the song. At 4:30, driving violin is added. Then everything quiets down to romantic piano and strings (5:12), soon turning into a straight jazz interlude (beginning at 5:17). At 6:28, a blast of electronic rock guitar shifts the mood again. The harpsichord reenters with choral voices (6:49), followed by a xylophone (7:11). This sounds disjointed but the effervescent melody keeps the composition unified despite the constant shifts in tempo, dynamics and tone color.

At 7:47, Snopek starts playing inside the piano, stroking the strings in a manner reminiscent of the experimentation of Henry Cowell, John Cage's teacher (check out Cowell's piece "The Banshee," for example). Then the xylophone reenters with more keyboards in a burst (8:21). At 8:52, another jazzy passage begins, emphasizing saxophone and drums. This riffing continues until 10:30 in the piece, when the band switches to a kind of classical march played at rock tempo (both genre fuck and yet exemplary of some quintessential prog rock moves). The harpsichord returns to the main theme at 11:44; then, from 12:05-13:14 (the piece's conclusion), the music dissipates into sundry dissonances for a final freakout.

These notes can only guide you through the major musical events of the piece as a rough listening map; they cannot convey its overall beauty and power. "Orange / Blue" is quintessential avant-pop, a neglected gem far superior to most of what ends up on prog rock box sets.

A few shorter pieces follow. "Elizabeth" closed side one of the vinyl release with its vision of faery love, showcased by a lovely melody, some ethereal and echoey drumming and the wonderful voice of James Gorton. Side two opens with "Soothsayer's Dove," a hippy-dippy pop ballad with operatic backing vocals. Given its classic position on the album (the first song on the second side is a frequently relied on location for a potential single), one suspects that Snopek hoped this might have been radio-friendly. Although this was a reasonable hypothesis—after all, Syd Barrett's version of Pink Floyd fired off some pretty wild 45s in the U.K.—there were no takers in Milwaukee. Sigmund Snopek's strengths have never been as a commercial composer. There's something almost tongue-in-cheek about his bids for mass acceptance (cf. Joni Mitchell's ironic hit "You Turn Me On (I'm a Radio)" from *For the Roses*). The main result of "Soothsayer's Dove" was that I played the first side of the album ten times as frequently.

Which was unfortunate, because the title track which followed is almost as fine a piece of music as "Orange / Blue." Like the latter, "Virginia Woolf" has an intricate if ultimately unified structure. On the German CD, it begins with a string quartet stating the theme at 2:37 on track 5 (they break up the tracks in an odd fashion not matching the actual vinyl cuts). The lyrics convey his dream vision of Woolf previously discussed. At 4:20, the main motif repeats as a chorus. The CD then switches to track 6 (although it's the same piece!) and Milwaukee jazz guitar great George Prichett comes in for a jazz interlude with Richie Cole on alto saxophone. Given the Milwaukee origins of the players, the feel is appropriately that of a Weimar cabaret.

At 2:13, the Nazi war drums discussed in the original liner notes arrive (along with many other drums). Programmatically, this works: it's as if we're in the mind of Snopek's version of Virginia Woolf hearing her mentally replay Germany's transition from the decadent freedoms of the Weimar Republic to its repressive Nazi fascism. Again, this is arguably a distant mirror for Snopek comparable to the counterculture's being violently suppressed by the Nixon administration at Kent State and the like. If this puts Snopek in a parallel position to Woolf on the verge of suicide, so be it. Snopek's first five solo albums all are rather death-obsessed, as we shall see—even obsessed with suicide on more than one occasion. For whatever reason, Sigmund Snopek is quite capable of contemplating the abyss: a trait more endearing to some of his listeners than others.

Of course, in the early seventies, no one felt they needed to apologize for a drum solo! It was the veritable heyday of the form (following in the footsteps of "In-A-Gadda-Da-Vida" [Iron Butterfly], "Toad" [Cream] and "Moby Dick" [Led Zeppelin]; I heard a live version of this last extend 45 minutes at a Zeppelin concert in Milwaukee!). The Nazi programmatic references help justify the fact that this piece features two drum solos, albeit ones of economical length.

After the first drum burst, electronic textures intrude (3:15, track 6) including an electronically distorted voice chanting "woman ... tired of war ... tired of life ... put herself to death." At 4:00, the second drum solo begins. Drummer Michael Lorenz showcases his chops by incrementally and precisely increasing the tempo. The result is an unusually mathematically accurate and technically astute variation on what would otherwise be seventies rock indulgence. Given the expressive and programmatic content of the piece, it seems justifiable. At 6:00, we have more electronics from the synthesizers, followed by a reintroduction of the jazz guitar (6:28). Then a second major theme is introduced instrumentally and vocally: "here it comes near my door" (7:30). The piece closes with a whispered chant: "Virginia walked into the sea / because she wanted nothing to be / Virginia is nothing and so are we" (8:20-8:59). The last four words reemphasize Snopek's own abyss-gazing. Like Hamlet, young Sigmund has his doubts about what it all adds up to.

A few brief tracks conclude the album. "Song of a Nation" is a strange sing-along ditty. Snopek has quite a few of these in his catalogue, part of his populist aspect maintaining a tension with his avant-garde proclivities. The piece bears a family resemblance both to Sun Ra's space chants and more well-known works such as "Hey Jude" or Donovan's "Atlantis." Its simple and repetitive chant seems addressed to the Woodstock Nation (whence its title), a nation gone underground. Or rather aboveground, as Snopek whimsically re-envisions it: "we're all hiding in the trees / you know that's the place to be." The point of the piece seems to be a further connection between Woolf's despair and current (1972) anxieties about war and politics. Finally, an "Epilogue" reprises the "Virginia Woolf" main theme vocally one more time for closure.

Virginia Woolf was an impressive solo debut recording for Sigmund Snopek, even though its reach somewhat exceeded its grasp. Like *Sergeant Pepper* (and that's respectable company to keep!), it's more of a song cycle than a concept album. "Prelude," "Virginia Woolf," "Song of a Nation" and "Epilogue" seem fairly related thematically—and given Snopek's relocation of Woolf's death to the sea, a case could even be made for including "Elizabeth" on this roster.

But much of the album seems unrelated to this overriding theme, including the musical highlight "Orange / Blue." By contrast, Snopek's next two progressive projects would have far greater unity, even on the level of narrative continuity in the lyrics.

The German reissue of *Virginia Woolf* also has two bonus tracks: "Lifencave Book Two," an extended sample of Snopek's classical side (keyboard and electronic settings of sundry poems from 1973), and an updated 1987 instrumental reworking of "Orange / Blue." (This is also available on vinyl as a double album from Gear Fab Records, which also carries the CD.) This new version offers an interesting variation on the original with its big rock guitar sound from Ramy Espinoza, its use of a sampling keyboard for choral vocals and its lush romantic piano work. Like Pete Townshend, Sigmund Snopek likes to revisit and polish his progressive projects.

Trinity Seas Seize Sees

His next opus, *Trinity Seas Seize Sees*, offers an exceptional illustration of this tendency: it was written in a single month during the spring of 1973 (the lyrics were composed in one day); it was partially recorded in 1973 and released in 1974; the rest was recorded between 1996 and 1999; the complete opera was finally released in 1999 (Snopek, *Trinity* liner notes). That's a saga comparable to Pete Townshend's complexly fated *Lifehouse* rock opera.

Sigmund Snopek got the idea for the science fiction progressive rock opera from reading about bands like Hawkwind and Aamon Duul who were associated with the new genre of "space rock." *Wunderkind* that Sigmund was, he decided to emulate them without actually hearing them since he "was already an avid science fiction reader" (Snopek, *Trinity*). Given the quality of his work compared to the groups he read about, this proved to be a wise decision.

The plot of the opera has some resonances with Sun Ra's actual biographical claims. The narrator and main character "is a nameless extraterrestrial who has lived on Earth so long that he has come to think of himself as human" (Snopek, *Trinity*). He gets kidnapped by other extraterrestrials at a wedding in Waukesha, Wisconsin. They abduct him and return him to his home world of Seize. He finds out that he is a "Bubble Freak," an easygoing guy who carries his own environment with him—thus making him capable of instant space travel. Seize is a utopian world, albeit one designed by outside forces: the Controllers Ockar Thrinking, Blacmar Crinking and Osmidachoo (who apparently like designing perfect worlds for sundry species).

Enter the Bubble Man, a Bubble Freak who has visited other worlds and encourages the Bubble Freaks to leave Seize with his traveler's tales. The Bubble Freaks make a mass exodus, exchanging unknown adventure for "the shackles of the Controllers' benevolence" (Snopek, *Trinity*). Unfortunately, they wreak havoc wherever they go. They visit two other worlds, Seas (an aquatic planet) and Sees (a planet populated by 1,000 "all seeing and all knowing" eyes led by the Hypnotic Eye) (Snopek, *Trinity*). The Bubble Freaks grab the water from Seas and the eyes from Sees, planning further galactic explorations. The Hypnotic Eye observes that the Controllers are massing forces to capture the Bubble Freaks lest they cause further environmental damage.

Warfare ensues. Both sides are devastated beyond measure. Time and space itself is rent, and the survivors tumble through a dimensional warp glimpsing many other worlds. Our narrator ends up in the Hall of Godcar, a repository for "all the religions and belief systems in the universe" (Snopek, *Trinity*). There he meets the Goddess (who speaks to him in Lithuanian). She returns the narrator back to Earth where he resumes his human form, sadder and wiser. The opera ends as it began, back on terra firma.

There are a lot of interesting thematic concerns in the plot. The trope of being really an alien in human form abounds not only in Sun Ra's self-mythologizing, but in the work of science fiction writers such as A. E. Van Vogt ("Asylum" comes to mind immediately) and even contemporary UFO mythology (they are among us!). In general, science fiction writer Philip K. Dick made a career out of postulating that things are not what they seem, a general form of epistemological alienation: being an alien without knowing it would be a specific illustration of his general approach.

The plot of the opera also engages in adolescent fantasies. The Bubble Freaks are flower children disobeying their parents (the Controllers). Historically, the Bubble Freaks are the hippie counterculture. As happened historically, their rebellion leads to environmental damage (think of what a field looks like after a rock festival) and violent confrontations with their opponents (the Chicago convention of 1968 and Kent State). Biblically, the plot has some resonances with the Israelites' exodus from Egypt into the Promised Land (where others had to be dispossessed). Archetypically, the opera moves from alienation through discovery of one's real identity to a synthesis of the two realities—a mature compromise and acknowledgment of the limits of freedom. Given rock's ultimately adolescent appeal, this last sentence also sounds like the Ur-plot of all three of Pete Townshend's rock operas for the Who (*Tommy, Lifehouse, Quadrophenia*)!

What about the music? It's different in some respects from *Virginia Woolf*, both because it's more consistently programmatic (illustrating a narrative) and because it is overall briefer in length with regard to each individual piece. Act I ("Discovery") begins with the melodramatic "Spirit Song" forecasting the upcoming interstellar violence and warfare with a critique of the behavior of Earthmen: "you've got to kill one another now / if not in body in spirit somehow." David Phillips provides a dramatic bass accompaniment. "Escape" deploys a beguiling motif with its "open sky" phrase and VCS3 synthesizer vamp. "Trinity Invitation" is Snopek on piano at his most lush and romantic, followed by the driving power pop of "Return of the Spirit."

"Waukesha Windows" (track 7 on the first CD) is the musical highlight of the entire space opera for me for several reasons. For starters, the lyrics are wonderfully precisely rendered yet surreal. This is the moment when the protagonist gets abducted by aliens and taken back to his home world:

> I saw Waukesha windows they were
> Moving down from the skies
> I reached for them I could not see
> I had no eyes

(All lyrics are by Sigmund Snopek unless otherwise noted.)

You can visualize the windows rushing past (cf. the trip in *2001*, or—even more accurately—the way car headlights can make a reflected light image of a window whip across a room at night). But they're "moving down from the skies," something you might see in the nocturnal phenomenon just mentioned but not from a UFO leaving Earth (unless this is a poetic vision of the takeoff of the craft?). In any case, the next two lines clarify that this is a purely mental image ("I could not see / I had no eyes"). In some mysterious fashion alluded to elsewhere in the song, "[his] soul was stolen put in a clip." He is no longer in his body, hence can no longer receive sensory input.

Snopek also shows some knowledge here of UFO lore. The aliens' arrival is prefaced by "telephones ... all ringing loudly," a reference to some of the incidents John Keel witnessed in West Virginia and documented in *The Mothman Prophecies*. (Keel's visitors could make phones ring *ad libitum*). But most of all, "Waukesha Windows" inaugurates Snopek's interest in musical regionalism, the matter of Wisconsin he will foreground in later works such as *WisconsInsane* and *Beer*. Just like no one thought about writing about Oxford, Mississippi, till William Faulkner, no composer really wrote about my home state (except for fight songs, etc.) till Sigmund Snopek. This is his first (but far from last) example of specific geographic cheesehead referents, in the service of a space opera no less. Combine all this with the beautiful melody, and you have a Wisconsin classic. The energetic piece concludes with another freakout, followed by the sound of a telephone busy signal, (Remember those now that we're in the age of the cellphone?)

"Rhyme Well" opens with a jazzy exploration reminiscent of *Hot Rats* era Zappa. Then it proceeds to a ditty about interplanetary travel using telephones à la John Keel ("running our ship with a tell bell"). Peter Balistreri provides solid drumming throughout. The middle eight "were you dancing?" riff is more romantic Snopek, a piano solo eventually augmented by bass and mellotron.

The next piece, "Interstellar Flight," features a lovely melody and vocal and eventually concludes with synthesizer sounds exactly replicating the explosive bolt warning alarms on the space pod in *2001*. "Arrival Boogie" is exactly that, followed by the jazz of "Arrival Jam." This latter showcases some great trumpet work from Peter Wollenzien and / or Mark Holm. "Bubble Freaks Reply" is loose and funky; "Bubble Man Blues" is not a blues—at least by any terrestrial standards, and maybe that's the musical joke. "Spatial Song" provides a lyrical instrumental interlude marking the Bubble Freaks' departure from Seize, a variation of the haunting theme melody from the science fiction film classic *The Incredible Shrinking Man*. "Star of Seas" has underwater-sounding distorted vocals and a fine flute solo from Snopek.

"Move Very Quickly" is an appropriately fast-tempo number documenting the Bubble Freaks running from the Controllers by departin from the Seas star. Snopek is again featured on flute, and Jack Grassel provides a big rock guitar sound. The next piece, "Flying Free," has an unabashedly retro and conventional rock vocal from David Wadsworth. "Leaving Seas" offers a nice instrumental break on synthesizer; "Infinite Song Word" brings in more mellotron. "6 Years 1000 Eyes" inaugurates the Freaks' arrival on Sees with a jaunty tune. Then we have the climax of Act I with "Hypnotic Eye," an intense rock aria from the head eyeball on Sees. The original vocalist for Cheap Trick, Xeno, gives it all he's got with real rock star *sprezzatura*, augmented by Scott Finch's lead guitar.

The second compact disk contains the two remaining acts of the space opera. Act II ("Consequences") is almost entirely instrumental program music: only the last track ("Whistle Song") contains any lyrics beyond chanting the names of the Controllers. This is the score for the climactic battle between the Controllers and the Bubble Freaks. "Ockar Thrinking" recalls Zappa's work for his science fiction opera *Hunchentoot* (which showed up on *Sleep Dirt*). "The Dry People" is also very close in spirit to Zappa, with some nods to *The Grand Wazoo* and / or "The Black Page" instrumentals.

"First Attack of Free Spirits" is carnival jazz, suitably loose and blowing. The "Cry of the Frees (after Losing)" which follows has some great jazz vocalese from Annie Denison. "War and Carnage," depite its ominous title, is more trippy than bloody synthesizer music, with square waves on the synth standing in for destruction. "Counter Attack and Dimension Warp" begins in a more martial vein with militant rock guitars. This cut is the dramatic climax of the space opera as a whole. We have electronic sound effects simulating battle, great drumming from Mike Lucas, a prog rock blowout and a sudden dramatic conclusion. The second act closes with the only song with lyrics, the irresistibly catchy "Whistle Song" ditty. Try to listen without joining in! The production notes inform us that Thacher Schmid, the chief whistler, "annoys people by whistling wherever he goes" (Snopek, *Trinity*). He's clearly the right man for the job here.

Act III ("Aftermath") concerns the fallout from the war between the Controllers and the Bubble Freaks (including our narrator amongst this latter). As a result of the "Dimension Warp," "time and space are torn and the few survivors are tossed through dimensions, catching glimpses of other times and other worlds" (Snopek, *Trinity*). At this moment, the space opera resembles the cosmic science fiction of British writer Olaf Stapledon (especially see his novel *Star Maker* for a dizzying profusion of worlds). Snopek can only convey this instrumentally, but he does a good job. Case in point: the "Hall of Godcar," where the narrator lands and meets all the deities of the universe. This syncretist vision is conveyed musically by means of a mix of sitar music, Gregorian chant and Islamic prayer calls. It is a long, patient, meditative piece that leads to the narrator's encounter with "The Goddess." Irene Mitkus provides the Lithuanian admonition to our semi-hero. (Snopek wanted to use Sanskrit, but couldn't find a speaker; Lithuanian is the Indo-European language closest to it. There are also some backwards vocals here [phone].) Brian Ritchie of the Violent Femmes plays Japanese *shakuhachi* flute to incorporate Buddhism in the Hall. (He is now a *shakuhachi* master [Big Interview]).

Then "Square of Air" documents his return to things terrestrial:

> so long long tell
> bell
> back to well
> begin where you end
> end where you begin

The "tell bell" reference recalls his initial transport means to Seize; now he is heading back to Earth. Form fits function in "The Twelve Keys," a bass solo from Brian Ritchie of the Violent Femmes. The low playing echoes the narrator's becoming re-grounded.

The following "Symphony of Man" is Snopek's "Ode to Joy," with lyrics by the late poet Jim Spencer. The classically inflected piece alternates between the operatic lead vocals of Leslie Fitzwater and the more raggedy but intriguing choral vocals of Spencer's daughters Lisa and Heidi (this latter augmented by Snopek's mellotron). Sigmund Snopek also takes an ample piano solo in this piece, before the final lyrics combine all the choruses (sort of like a villanelle in poetry).

"Return of the Spirit" establishes that our protagonist has completely returned to Earth, emphasized by descending pitches in the melody. Mike Lucas contributes some apt work on woodblocks. The opera concludes with "The SandKing," a song recorded in the 1973 sessions, but never released on the first vinyl version of the opera. The title refers to sandcastles (where a SandKing would rule)—and hence mutability and mortality. Our main character is older, wiser, sadder after the cosmic journey he has undergone. Susan Thomas on vocals describes an outsider's perspective on what he has become:

> so hopeless this man as he walked in
> his shadow
> giving his reasons for feeling so down
> that he didn't notice the sand
> and the sea
> that he didn't notice what had happened to me ...
> I had lived for the freedom I was poor
> but not lost
> and when we had died at the end of
> our lives
> I spoke to him clearly I opened up wide
> all I had dreamed of all I had tried
> nobody listened but everybody died
>
> oh the SandKing

The abstract lyrics leave one wondering what her back story is: is she a sixties survivor hippie like Robin Wright Penn's character in *Forrest Gump*, and/or is this a tale of repressed, undeclared love in the spirit of Henry James's "The Beast in the Jungle"? Snopek saith not, but we have a sense of our protagonist's diminished life as a returned Earthling. The final triumph of Thanatos ("nobody listened but everybody died") anticipates the death-obsessed quality of Sigmund Snopek's next progressive work, *Nobody to Dream*.

Nobody to Dream

Nobody to Dream is an even messier composition with regard to chronology. Sigmund Snopek first wrote it when he was 16 and 17 (in 1968 and 1969). Thus it predates *Virginia Woolf* and *Trinity Seas Seize Sees* in terms of actual writing. The premiere performance was at Saint Williams Church in Waukesha, Wisconsin, with Snopek's post-Bloomsbury People group called Integrated Light and Sound. (Parts were played previously at the Atlanta Pop Festival by Bloomsbury People on the same stage with Jimi Hendrix, Procol Harum, Ravi Shankar, Poco and the like.) ILS consisted of a light show run by Scott and Susy Marshall and a band featuring Greg Janick (from the Bloomsbury People), Michael Campbell on Hammond organ, Sigmund Snopek on piano and Paul Spencer on vocals. They were accompanied by a string quartet for the occasion: Katie Brooks, first violin; Mel Margolis, second violin; Laura Zodrodnik, viola; and Marilyn Runge, cello. ILS toured in Wisconsin and at colleges in the Southeastern United States subsequently. Their last performance was on October 29,

1971 at the Performing Arts Center in Milwaukee for the orchestral version of "Orange / Blue" (with different personnel including James Gorton on vocals).

Nobody to Dream has been recorded four times in the studio, but only two of these recordings have ever been released: a 1976 Couth Youth album and a 1997 German CD. My discussion will refer to the 1997 CD, both because it is the more readily available version and because Snopek believes "[t]his time it's right"—in other words, this CD offers the best realization of the piece for him (Snopek, *Nobody*). If you can obtain the Couth Youth lp, however, comparisons are interesting.

I would submit that *Nobody to Dream* is Snopek's most achieved prog rock composition, his masterpiece. The fact that it was the earliest one he wrote only shows what a *wunderkind* he was! It combines the compositional lyricism of "Orange / Blue" with the programmatic rigor of *Trinity Seas Seize Sees*. There is really no filler in this composition, unlike his first two solo projects. Every note seems wonderful and essential. As such, this is a great place to start listening to progressive Snopek: it's as good as he gets in this vein. No wonder he laments in the liner notes when thinking "about the record business—how cold, calculating and money-oriented it was in 1970 and how [his] managers and agents in the early seventies slowly steered [him] away from this kind of music" (Snopek, *Nobody*). Nobody did it better.

After re-recording *Nobody to Dream* in the mid-nineties, he "finally realize[d] that this piece is about reincarnation," appropriately enough given its many recorded incarnations (Snopek, *Nobody*). And also true enough, although the sublime angst of the piece dominates the joyous conclusion for most listeners. *Nobody to Dream* is about the dream state and where it leads us to as we dream ever more deeply into Freudian and Jungian realms: yet another oblique commentary on the sixties, which was certainly a collective dream (and occasional nightmare) for many of my generation.

The cover art of both versions sets the tone. The 1976 album has a painting of a somber-visaged Snopek in semi-lotus position sitting on a bare mattress, one of many (the rest vacant) stretching out to infinity on a two-lane highway marked only by the center lines. It's a highway in space, with some suggestion of a planet on the left side: could it be Earth? The 1997 CD also conveys infinity on its cover through a photograph of rows of women seated at grand pianos for a "monster concert' (American composer Louis Gottschalk's term). This image is a still from a Busby Berekeley musical number in *Gold Diggers of 1935*. This latter cover art also brings to mind the extremely surreal fifties dream film, *The 5,000 Fingers of Doctor T* (written by Dr. Seuss!), with its piano keyboard stretching into infinity.

The piece certainly lives up to the expectations created by these visuals. The 1997 CD opens with "Dream Song of the River," a string quartet overture that introduces various leitmotifs from the song cycle (e.g., the theme from

"Dream with Me"). This is the only part of the composition not on the vinyl as well, which begins with the more rock-oriented material (the second track on the CD). The CD version is superior, creating a meditative mood through the straight classical portion—a kind of trance induction for the listener. The first rock track, "Dream with Me," invites us to do that very thing "if you're not afraid." The overall approach is not only psychoanalytic, but Joycean—and it is no accident that Sigmund Snopek's classical *ouevre* includes musical settings of texts from both *Ulysses* and *Finnegans Wake*. In this song cycle, ontogeny will recapitulate phylogeny: we will replay not only our individual lifespan, but the history of the race *à la Finnegans Wake*. Our dreamer / narrator is an Everyman like Joyce's Humphrey Chimpden Earwicker. Here comes everybody!

Snopek's lyrics advise us that we "need a Key, ... a door, a way" into this dream world. In good sixties fashion, the key that opens the door to dreams is love. The lush romantic melody of "Everyday" reminds us that we do need love and dreams everyday. "Softly" continues the hippie idealism with its equally wonderful melody, reminding us "the touch means so very much" (an echo of the rare Lennon-McCartney *Help!*-era song "That Means a Lot" with its line "a touch can mean so much"?). But the end of "Softly" abruptly shifts the mood to a far darker register with its final admonitory lines: "in happiness I am sad / you see the key can drive you mad." In other words, love can drive one insane (a recurrent observation in Snopek's music borne of failed relationships).

Snopek dispels the darkness as quickly as he invoked it in "Coral Dream," a wonderful instrumental excursion for his flute, eventually joined by his piano and the string quartet. But we don't get off that easily: "Night Terror" reintroduces the scary side of dreaming, bringing on "sorrow" and "terror." The loping musical riff adds to the malaise of the lyrics, a technique reminiscent of both Who bassist John Entwistle's scary song "Nightmare" off *Whistle Rymes* and standard Disney spooky music (like "Pink Elephants on Parade" from *Dumbo*, especially as Sun Ra covered it).

Again, though, the descent is gradual. After "Night Terror," we have another upbeat instrumental melody, "Dancing," which replicates various dance tempos (e.g. the waltz). The mood darkens again with the instrumental "Black Horse" featuring exquisite and lost flute touches. The title no doubt refers to a nightmare. (Hey, he wrote this luscious stuff when he was sixteen!) Thematically, this worked well on the album as an end to side one; the second half of the composition is far more gothic.

The next piece, "Night Dream," shows this more melancholy mood well. The music is an intriguing combination of gothic melancholy and jazzy riffing, with neat piano flourishes and solid backing from the string quartet. The lyrics concern the dreamer's fears about the fate of the wife he is presumably sleeping with:

> Be still oh my wife
> I saw you, I saw you in the night dream ... .
> I saw you there, you should really care
> for your death scene was my night dream
> The story was told how you grow old
> I saw it, I saw it in the night dream
> Before my eyes a horror did I behold
> You suddenly grew cold in the night dream
> your hair turned white
> your skin turned yellow
> You walked with a fellow who wore a gray beard
> in the night dream
>
> (Byron Wiemann helped with the editing of all these lyrics on *Nobody to Dream* [Big Interview]).

These lyrics offer a Freudian feast; indeed, the very title reflects Freud's terminology for the dream state in his *Interpretation of Dreams*. The narrator's original invocation of his wife's death ("you should really care / for your death scene was my night dream") has an unmistakable tone of resentful menace to it, almost as if he's implying the "death scene" might be a murder. Of course, the imagery actually refers to the aging process, here rendered as a gothic "horror" rather than a natural cyclic event. The words capture the young person's potential revulsion for the elderly behind the veneer of respect: I'm so beautiful, and they're so ugly. Even worse, she "walked with a fellow who wore a gray beard." The narrator himself will age—something he can apparently only consider obliquely. He does not seem to recognize that this "fellow" is probably himself! The melodrama of the lyrics is fortunately mitigated by the beauty of the music.

"Walking" is an obvious instrumental counterpart to "Dancing." It lacks the latter's grace, content to be merely jazzy and percussive in a manner reminiscent of parts of the "Blue" section from "Orange / Blue" off *Virginia Woolf*. Then we really hit the abyss with "Death," Snopek's version of It's A Beautiful Day's song "Time Is." In fact, on the original vinyl release the song was titled "Death Is," underscoring the parallel. The album version has lyrics which I suspect the more mature Snopek deemed too sophomoric; the CD version is purely instrumental, with a fine use of Arabic tabla by Michael Kashou. This gives the piece a middle-eastern flavor with broad strokes, at times even reminiscent of the soundtrack music from *Lawrence of Arabia*.

This atmospheric composition is followed by "Sunrise Falling," one of Sigmund's greatest *liede* in the German romantic vein. The lyrics ooze world-weariness, *weltschmerz* and despair, almost to the point of suicide (here passively willed rather than actively achieved):

> I watch the sun rise today—behind it the sky blue
> I wonder what you will say—when I tell you
> I'll never see the sun again—never come and touch your hand
> Please understand love
> gonna leave this land love
> move along up to the sky
> gonna give up gonna die
> Morning is ending now—yes and so am I
> I'll never see you again— never look into your eyes

Snopek's haunting delivery somehow makes this moving rather than merely self-indulgent. We are in far deeper waters here than with his first two solo efforts, although the death wishes and alienation carry over from the earlier works.

The following "Hope" instrumental offers a little of same, building up to the crescendo of a lightning strike which Snopek had recorded. The title piece moves from personal mortality to a contemplation of the death of our species:

> Soon, the time is coming soon
> when there'll be no moon
> no one to see the sky
> no one to wonder why
> and when this day comes ...
> what will we say when there's
> Nobody to dream?
> Soon the year is coming soon
> when there'll be no year
> cause nobody will hear
> If you can think of that
> If you can think at all
> Why don't you talk to your friends
> maybe they'll answer
> and if you have no friends, I'll be one to you
> try to make you see if you know what I mean
> Nobody to Dream

This is nothing less than a vision of human (and even cosmic?) extinction: is it the "heat death of the universe" that scared the Victorians? Jonathan Schell's "second death" of the species after nuclear war? We can read in our own fears, but it's an ultimate contemplation of oblivion, a dream of there being "nobody to dream." If you can think of that, if you can think at all ... . The music reinforces the message with its resigned melody, tentative piano gestures and drum working as a heartbeat gradually slowing and ceasing. If this is the product of a sixteen-year-old mind, it's a brilliant one. Sigmund Snopek was an old soul from day one!

As Snopek decided later, the piece is about reincarnation. It ends not with the oblivion of the title track, but with "Morning Child." This final song is a message of hope:

> Morning Child you are truth
> Standing there in golden youth
> You have no face, you're every race
> Your eyes are stars
> Morning Child you are you
> I am me and I see
> Through myself is where I can find you.

This final vision of the child bears a lot of symbolic weight, almost like the Star Child at the end of *2001: A Space Odyssey*. The last line seems to imply this is also an inner child one can get in touch with beyond all the angst which preceded his (her?) arrival. The child offers us the hope of youth and morning, an ending that becomes a beginning. The simple melody conveys this new innocence until the piece ends with soft bells ringing in the new. Hokey? Yes, in the same way that high German romantics like Novalis or Goethe can be hokey. On its own terms, though, the song cycle beguiles and convinces. *Nobody to Dream* remains a neglected prog-rock masterwork with far greater staying power than the more commercially successful material released during the same era.

Roy Rogers Meets Albert Einstein

But, as Sigmund Snopek ruefully acknowledges, his managers and agents were steering him away from these kinds of productions. He was to release only one more progressive rock recording, *Roy Rogers Meets Albert Einstein* (1982) after two released attempts at a more commercial sound (to be discussed below). (Even though I placed this album previously in a trilogy with his other stand-alone compositions for pipe organ [*Miasma Fragments*] and piano [*Jade*], I will consider it here because of its musical affinities to the other three prog rock efforts.) This recording featured three separate and unrelated works by Snopek, ranging in length from 29 minutes to 7 minutes and composed over the course of six years (from 1974 to 1980). The first side of the album (and this complete release is also available on CD from the French Musea label) is devoted to "Ride in the Dark," the second movement of a "rock ballet" written in 1979 (Levitan). (There are three other movements of this never-performed work for the Milwaukee Ballet [Big Interview].) "Ride in the Dark" is an instrumental, except for one section with vocals. As its title implies, this is road music meant to convey the feel of relentless travel. Perhaps this work springs from the same inspiration as Snopek's "Highway Ghosts" rock anthem off *First Band On the Moon*. Its opening movement, "Zully's Truck," begins with appropriate sound effects before morphing into progressive synthesizer jazz. The work's next highlight is "Backpocket Fugue" (the 4th movement), Snopek's version of a fugue using a toy piano among other keyboards. The next section, "Song and Word Dream," features poetry from longtime Snopek guitarist Byron Wiemann III (!) set to music. At this point, Byron was gradually shifting his residence to Europe. His lyrics reflect a frenzy of European travel and a certain sophisticated jadedness:

> Must be Cologne
> I can tell by the sky
> Yes, I'm drinking, swaying
> On a chair that might break ... .
>
> And the Riviera desert fuss
> Crams either side
> Of the coastal road
> Spaghetti fat bathers
> Hot balls in the sand / glass
> You roll by

This lyrical travelogue segues into "Robotiko," a lovelier version of what the German group Kraftwerk was writing at the time—synth music for the autobahn!

"Meanwhile In LA" shifts to a cool jazz sound, creating a surreal transition from what seemed to be a European setting to an American west coast locale. This road music can readily hop oceans. "The Mountains" reprises the theme from "Robotiko, even as the subsequent "Death Valley Vortex" repeats some of the music from "Zully's Truck." "Worldless" gives us a kind of climax to the piece. Its intricate and energized melody both suggests some of Zappa's late seventies work (think *Sheik Yerbouti*) and seventies King Crimson, especially workouts like "Starless" and "Fracture" off *Starless and Bible Black*). Again, the title may even be meant to evoke "Starless," although this is an oblique allusion at best. "Worldless" also reprises the "Robotiko" theme. "Beam Bang" concludes the ballet with an electronic crescendo somewhat reminiscent of the climax of Emerson, Lake and Palmer's "Karn Evil 9." As these glosses suggest, "Ride in the Dark" is both innovative and solidly in the prog rock tradition.

The title piece (composed in 1980) is easily the most eccentric work of the three. "Roy Rogers Meets Albert Einstein" is a postmodern blurring of high art effects and pop culture gutbucket both musically and lyrically. (The back cover photograph of Snopek standing between two people in appropriate costume reinforces the joke.) The composition is a musical setting of two poems: one, by Cynthia Dahlke, is about Albert Einstein and the post-relativistic view of the universe as a curved time-space continuum; the second, again by Byron Wiemann III, is about Roy Rogers and a rather transgressive feast. The first poem is ethereal and even precious, the second vulgar and gross. This piece has the range! The music is equally diverse. The first movement begins with xylophone and violin—eventually joined by saxophone, bass and woodblocks. At one point, Sigmund Snopek takes a piano solo. The feel is close to musical minimalism (there are a significant number of repeated musical phrases as the movement develops), but a little more complex: Phillip Glass's *Einstein on the Beach* trumped.

The second briefer section of the composition, on the other hand, is country and western parody music (the way Frank Zappa does country). This part quotes Roy Rogers' signature tune "Happy Trails" on violins and sax in sundry demented permutations. All this to showcase transgressive, grotesque food and sex imagery—like that which Mikhail Bakhtin associates with popular festive humor in his book *Rabelais and His World*, an early historical example of high / low cultural blurring and uncrowning in the Middle Ages. See for yourself what Byron Wiemann's cooked up for us:

> Friday's mainline dinner featuring:
> Bug-fed collie,
> Rag made moist,
> I never made it to the main course.
> A well tumored horse
> Rumored of course to be Trigger ...
> Hey Roy! It's a hoof down,
> It's a feast at least.
> I'm saving my manhood for Dale, she whacks the whale
> As Betty and Bud look sadly on.

Like many intellectuals from the land of beer, Sigmund Snopek has both an ethereal German romantic side (in his case, also by way of Irish culture and background) and a wacky side. "Roy Rogers Meets Albert Einstein" showcases both of these tendencies, undoubtedly to the detriment of our image-repertoire of Dale Evans. (And is Lassie the "bug-fed collie" in question? One fears so.)

The last composition on the recording, "Song Sing to the Doldrum King," is also the earliest (1974) and the briefest. "Song Sing" is a piece for solo flute, here played dexterously by Llena de la Magdrula from the Wisconsin Conservatory of Music. The work intersperses mouth and flute sounds, often interacting, with vocalese. As it progresses, the music gets slower and quieter—sounding tired and bored in a manner befitting the "Doldrum King" of the title. Eventually it gets so quiet that the tape hiss almost overpowers the music. This ultimate silence ends Sigmund Snopek's last prog rock recording from 31 years ago. There would be more music to come, some touching bases with these most ambitious of works, but Sigmund Snopek had (albeit ruefully) moved on. Undoubtedly, these are his foundational works.[2]

"We're Setting Sights upon the Eighties"

In the later seventies, Snopek's managers and agents encouraged him to abandon prog rock for a more commercial sound that seemed to straddle his older style and some of the more pop-oriented new wave bands. In concert with his new band called Snopek, Sigmund would become more of an entertainer *à la* Zappa: he would joke more with the audience and invite participatory action. In some ways, this was a good thing. After all, letting down one's hair is always refreshing. But this was ultimately a troubled phase of his career, comparable to the Geffen years for Neil Young. His new label, Mountain Railroad records, refused to release two of his studio recordings and delayed putting out *Roy Rogers Meets Albert Einstein* for several years after it was completed.[3] The switch from cover art to photographs of the band on *Thinking Out Loud* and *First band On The Moon* suggests an attempt to traffic in image, however unsuccessfully.

Thinking Out Loud

Having said all that, there is some musical merit in these two hard-to-obtain releases (most readily available via Snopek's website (<www.sigmundsnopek.com>). *Thinking Out Loud* (1978) was his first non-concept album using shorter discrete song formats. Perhaps this development in his career might be most readily compared to the British band Jethro Tull: they began the seventies doing concept albums like *Thick as a Brick* and *Passion Play*, but eventually went more radio-friendly with loosely unified albums such as *War Child* and *Songs from the Wood*. Their 45 rpm single releases, like Snopek's (as we shall see), tended towards novelty songs ("Bungle in the Jungle" off *War Child*).

Thinking Out Loud is loosely unified by a sense that Snopek is taking stock with regard to his diminished situation—and that of the counterculture at large. That seems to be what the band is "thinking out loud" about. The album opens with a pop bid entitled "Kathleen" (who was Byron's wife; Snopek wrote the original lyric and Byron revised it [Big Interview]). A tribute to a follower of the band, it has a slight sense of place (following "Waukesha Windows" and anticipating the later career): she is observed "dancing around in the empty bars / like a ghost in white." A more haunting middle section is bookended by the pop hook of the main melody. "Radio Hearts," which follows, raises the ante by being a meta-commentary on the state of affairs that produced the previous song. The somewhat acerbic lyrics discuss the music business from the position of relative outsiders in the culture industry (Milwaukeeans trying to crack it). The "loyal subjects" of the "mastersinger" have "RADIO HEARTS"; all they care about receiving is "hit after hit after hit me again"—a gibe at the "hit after hit" classic rock format that replaced progressive programming at this time.

The next song, "Shining in Here," gets even nastier with its dissection of a seventies coke orgy. The lyrics, written by Byron Wiemann, have a cynicism (and even misogyny) largely absent from earlier Snopek:

> Face in every hallway
> sign on every door
> stranger needs a party
> party needs a whore

The narrator worries that this latter individual "may never give [him] head." The only redemptive aspect of this song is that it is satirical. The chorus observes "[t]here must be a full moon and it's shining in here." In other words, this scene is insane.

The protagonist's "restless appetite / for a taste of something with a bite" in "Shining In Here" anticipates the more banal fast-food gluttonous lust of "Hamburger Holocaust," the closing song for side one (music by Snopek, lyrics by Wiemann [Big Interview]). A big number in performance, "Hamburger Holocaust" is a novelty song like Jethro Tull's "Bungle in the Jungle." It is also a satire on fast food, reminiscent of the Violent Femmes and Eugene Chadbourne's later attack on McDonald's in *Songs of Peace and Protest* called "Better Going Out Than Coming In":

> Hamburger holocaust
> fries on the side
> counterfeit chicken
> nowhere to hide
> it's a plate full of weakness
> or a mouth full of sweet
> fix it quick—Mr. Sick!
> man's gotta eat

The guitar work pays parodic homage to Heart (appropriately enough, given the subject) before a jazzy wrap-up.

The movement of side one is a gradual descent into triviality and disgust, not a way to make a pop record. From the lingering romanticism of "Kathleen," the songs move on to a corrupt music industry, a decadent party scene and a "hamburger holocaust" of unhealthy food. Not a happy story. If the listener persists, there are some rewards on side two, where things begin to look up a little (in a weird way, cf. *Nobody to Dream*).

The side-opener, "God Is A Big Wheel," also addresses show business in a slightly more positive manner. The song is basically about the wheel of fortune—or, since God is involved, the wheel of providence? More specifically, Byron Wiemann derived the concept from Carl Jung's notion of God as a wheel [Big Interview]. Like "Kathleen," this song is radio-friendly and has a good hook. So does the next song, "New York Jumpers," which finds Snopek in both his morbid and comic vein (cf. "If You Love Me Kill Yourself" from 1980). The lyric is inspired by a *New York Times* story about a man who fell on a Volkswagen after a suicide plunge and killed the man inside the car [Big Interview]. The track has a jazzy feel reminiscent of vintage Steely Dan and zany lyrics about suicide ("King Kong can't be wrong"). Sigmund Snopek also notes that it's a musical tribute to Lambert, Hendricks and Ross [Big interview]. It was fairly tasteless when it came out; after 9/11, it's almost unendurable. People jumping out of New York skyscrapers just isn't much of a laughing matter anymore, is it?

"San Francisco Radio," on the other hand, is the absolute highlight of the album and a taste of the old progressive Snopek. At 9:35, the band finally has time to stretch out and strut their stuff. Sigmund Snopek's lyrics are more thinking out loud about the music business, emphasizing Snopek's self-imposed isolation in Milwaukee and his inability to be a hitmaker:

> San Francisco radio doesn't play on my radio
> don't tell me about Japan and Tokyo
> they're not the places I want to go
> that's not the thing I wanna do

There are references to specific Milwaukee locations ("don't want to be the old rag man on Third and State / it wouldn't be too great") and Snopek's occasional forays into music pedagogy ("don't want to be the teacher man / working just as hard as he can"). Instead, the band offers "some weird show / it's the only show we know": a mixture of "the Grecian islands and Idaho." This last reference seems to allude to the band's endless touring ("Idaho") and some time spent in Greece. The Greek allusions in this phase of his career stem primarily from band member and collaborator Byron Wiemann's interest in the culture (Snopek, Phone message).

The music for this piece is quite lovely, highlighted by fine synthesizer work and a great extended flute solo that seems very close in melody to the James

Gang's song "Collage" off *Yer Album*. The song ends with an out-chorus similar in feel to Brian Wilson psychedelia like "Surf's Up." This more exuberant mood is sustained in the genuinely happy conclusion to the album, "Kali Kala," a tribute to the laidback life on Greek islands: "We're gonna have a forever weekend / celebrate a moment at random." After some of the earlier *sturm und drang* of the record, this is a nice way to close it. All told, *Thinking Out Loud* is a very listenable record, but only "San Francisco Radio" hits the heights of his earlier efforts.

The undated CD reissue of this album on One Way Records adds five bonus tracks: three previously unreleased songs and two alternate takes. Of the latter, the other version of "Shining In Here" is of some slight interest because it's less sexually explicit. Even the band knew they were pushing the envelope with the lyrics; although tellingly, the more transgressive version made the album in 1978.

The former three compositions all have something to recommend them as well. "Hymn" is a broad-gauged jeremiad state of the union address from the band decrying the"[s]lag heaps of America" and "madmen selling children for a fix." "6 Pak Heaven" presents a strange amalgamation of Snopek's lyrical interests past, present and future. There are visions of wizards and unicorns that go back to his progressive rock Tolkienisms, but also an out of the blue nuclear reference: "[a]tom bomb wind still blows she still knows"—and the sudsy brew of the title anticipates later efforts on *WisconsInsane*, *Elephant* and *Beer*. One suspects the former track was shelved for being both too unfocused and too much of a downer for even a Snopek album; the latter is also too diffuse (and strange).

Which brings us to the jewel in the crown of the bonus tracks: "Unknown Performer," a portrait of the artist whose unflinching accuracy anticipates *WisconsInsane* and *Elephant*:

> Four long days and
> Four long nights and
> Four years ago
> I was waiting for an unknown woman
> To come to my room
> In a town I never heard of
> In a place I couldn't know
> For a reason I was unsure of
> I thought up this song forgot it
> Just remembered it now ... .
>
> I'm just an unknown performer singing these
> strange songs
> Maybe I'm some kind of reformer but I better check

out of my motel right now

The simple melancholy piano accompaniment accentuates the bittersweet position of being "an unknown performer singing in / strange towns." As Frank Zappa observed, "touring can make you crazy." This piece is as good or better than anything on the original album (perhaps excepting "San Francisco Radio"). So why was it left off? Not exactly rocket science: an admission of failure is a bad lyrical move on a release intended to get a band a New Wave following. Confessions of popular defeat are intrinsically not very commercial. Fortunately for us (but not always for him), the artist in Sigmund Snopek almost always gets the last word.[4]

First Band On The Moon

First Band On The Moon (1980) offers a similarly mixed bag. In fact, this is an even less unified project only held together by the very loose concept of Snopek as "first band on the moon." Given the achievements of bands like Pink Floyd, their boast seems more prog-rock bravado than anything else. They're spacey and talented, but not at the top of the heap. The brief title track does feature good synthesizer work, however. And who knows? The whole claim may be more of an ironic joke about remote touring than serious pretension (which seems to be how the p. r. men took it [Levitan]).

"Doktor Alles" ("Doctor Everything" in English), the next track, is an eighties cold war song for the Reagan era comparable to gestures from Neil Young we've seen previously. It urges us to "ban the bomb dropped yesterday" and offers us "SEASON'S GREETINGS FROM THE UKRAINE" (caps in the lyrics). (Byron's lyric was originally intended to be about Adolf Hitler, whom he was obsessed with. The song can profitably be read this way as well with its references to Hitler's bunker, cyanide, the Nazi A-bomb program and the Russian front [Big Interview].) The sound is completely new wave, with eighties drum machine effects and a jagged sound reminiscent of vintage Devo. The following track, "Living Out Loud," is this record's highlight. A seeming follow-up to the concerns of the previous album based on its title, "Living Out Loud" is also a great apocalyptic love song sung with conviction by Snopek, Wiemann, and Gorton. It begins by describing a woman who "once in a while ... makes [him] crazy" that he likes to travel with:

> Some big excitement at the airport
> It's fun to vanish in a cloud
> to a land where natives aren't immune to
> living out loud, living out loud (Byron's lyrics)

Other references in the song—"katsika heaven," "I'm Captain Eros never coming back / I'll worship Helen till she dies"—suggest that this is our Greek locale again. Then the music surges to the climactic epiphany:

> We're setting sights upon the eighties
> and if it ends up in a cloud
> we'll raise a glass and have a drink to
> living out loud, living out loud

In this second reference, the cloud has changed from stratocumulus to mushroom. This genial if resigned apocalypticism will recur in *WisconsInsane*. Always interested in personal suicide, Snopek here (as in the title track of *Nobody to Dream*) contemplates larger collective suicides. The fine vocal harmonies and driving rhythm of the song make it all work better than anything else here.

"Controller's Reply" is a funkier synth reworking of a song from *Trinity Seas Seize Sees*, here puzzlingly out of context. Side one closes with a big rock road anthem, "Highway Ghosts." This song is sort of Snopek's version of Golden Earring's "Radar Love." "Highway Ghosts" is an archetypal and engaging sort of song: it's got the road, cars, drugs ("just a few more lines") and even an implied car crash at the end (given the final sound effects). The band has become the ghosts it sings about ... . If the track risks being cheesy, one can always invoke the redemptive irony of the group.

The second side of the record continues the travel theme with a few more numbers: "Avenue Motion" (about Los Angeles, New York, and London) and "Let's Take A Trip" (which proposes many destinations, including "Idaho" and Greece ["we'll fly away to Minos"]). Then "The Armpit Shuffle" offers more Snopek zaniness; it's a dance song where all you have to do is "just lift your hands up in the air" ("it's a new dance that you don't dance at all"). Crowd recordings reveal that, like "Hamburger Holocaust," "The Armpit Shuffle" is essentially a performance event.

"Crazy, Crazy Angel" is another rock anthem. According to Snopek, the song "juxtaposes a lonely 'crazy' performer against the paranoid trip down the avenue of the Illuminati [Robert Anton Wilson's series of conspiracy theory novels] who really control the music business [with] a dose of comic anarchy supplied by the Marx Brothers and the pain of several of [his] dead girlfriends" (e-mail). The angel in question has "got those middle age blues / she feels like no one wants to use her anymore." Sigmund Snopek sings with real sympathy here (after all, his career is not in the best of shapes at the moment); an odd reference to Harpo Marx leads to a harp solo by Ann Labotzke. The album closes with another decontextualized excerpt from a longer work, a rock version of "Robotiko" from "Ride in the Dark" (a sneak preview for the release of *Roy Rogers Meets Albert Einstein*?).

When *First Band On The Moon* first came out, there was also a bonus single. The A side was more morbid / zany Snopek ("If You Love Me Kill Yourself"), a sardonic stab (pun intended) at punk attitudes comparable to Zappa's *Sheik Yerbouti* material such as "I'm So Cute" or "Broken Hearts Are For Assholes." The lyrics by John Schneider (for his Theater X play "Razor Blades") are clever enough if you want to bungle in the jungle:

> Show me a sign
> Put strychnine in your wine ... .
> I've got those "Whatever Happened to Romeo and Juliet?" blues

But, yes, this is a novelty song—once sung with actor Willem Dafoe, when he was a member of Milwaukee's experimental Theater X troupe (Big Interview). The B side, "Solalex," has aged much better: it's another lovely text on the Greek vacation theme with good synth accents, a cool jazz feel combined with a light reggae beat, and a beguiling flute solo. The lyrical observation that he's "been a peasant all [his] life" anticipates the proletarian move Sigmund Snopek is about to make after the breakup of this band.

That's the package of *First Band On The Moon*: intriguing, but not unified. No doubt this was affected in part by ever-increasing career pressures. Unlike the progressive rock phase, this music was supposed to put Sigmund Snopek on the map. Ultimately, of course, it didn't.

Voodoo Dishes (aka *Feeling American*) (1982, referred to in footnote 2) is available from Snopek's website to complete this trilogy. Access to this material gives some insight into why Mountain Railroad Records didn't release it (too much like the other two releases which had limited commercial legs) and why, of course, the band was disappointed (more good music from this phase). The sound overall is slightly more pop than the other two albums—but only slightly. This may have been a semi-conscious or calculated move on the part of the ensemble. The songs that most revisit familiar territory include "Julia Scarlet" (a homage to a "slow motion dreamer" very much in the spirit of *Thinking Out Loud*'s "Kathleen"); "Kitty in the City," "Dead Weight" and "Stop at Cheops" (more satire of scenesters in the spirit of the aforementioned album); and "Only the Lonely Lie" (a bit of self-criticism which shares a tempo and approach very strongly with "God is a Big Wheel").

But there's plenty more quality material at hand. "Feeling American" digs deeper in its critique of those of us who like "watching television with the sound off." This track features elegant harmonies, a distinctive flute break from Sigmund, and what sound like humpback whale songs in the background (a progressive touch derived from playing a flumpet, a flute with the head taken off and played like a trumpet [Big Interview]). "Marijuana Stereo" is a mellow piano-driven piece for stoners—one of two references to the controversial weed in his entire output. The lyrics suggest the synesthetic properties of psychedelics: "What's that smell I hear? Marijuana stereo." "Girl on a Bike" with its fine synthesizer work and lovely harmonies could pass for a lost Beatles song (lyrics like "I wish she would run me over" suggest late Beatles; Pink Floyd's "Bike" from the Syd Barrett era is also a likely precursor.) "Complex Heart" carries connotations to their ultimate conclusion: "I want to operate on my Norma Jean." "Heavy Enough" is another portrait-of-the-artist lament: "I'm glad you're heavy enough to hold me down / It's never been easy just hangin' around."

I'd submit the album's highlights, very much in the spirit of the 1980s, are "Motors" and "Bony Fingers" (written by Byron Wiemann). The former sounds like Snopek doing Gary Numan's Tube Army with a dash of Devo. Car horn effects on synthesizer increase the paranoia of the lyrics ("cruise [close] the borders / we have orders"). "Bony Fingers" is very jazzy (in the wheelhouse of Steely Dan). Its lyrics are also travel-themed, reflecting the band's touring and seeing "trees with bony fingers from a distance." A synthesizer solo soars and the band cooks. It's good to have this missing piece of the puzzle from Snopek's New Wave era.

By the mid-eighties, this band was defunct. Snopek was making a living with his classical compositions and as a touring keyboardist with the Violent Femmes, Milwaukee's own new wave band. Snopek was part of the Horns of Dilemma on the Femmes's 1986 release *The Blind Leading The Naked*; he also contributed trumpet and hunting horn to a funky cover of Sun Ra's "Nuclear War" on bassist Brian Ritchie's 1987 solo project *The Blend*. There is some rare video footage of him playing flute (on "Confessions"), keyboards (on "Faith") and melodica (on "Kiss off") available on *No, Let's Start Over*, a DVD from Universal Studios which documents the 1984 London Lyceum gig with the Violent Femmes on Snopek's birthday (alluded to in the interview below). A later unplugged live document from 1998 that showcases an all-Wisconsin venues tour of the Violent Femmes with Snopek, *Viva Wisconsin*, also gives an indication of the subtle flavors Sigmund Snopek brought to their live shows. His piano work enhances "Sweet Worlds of Angels"; his flute adds fire to the sassy "Black Girls." And Snopek's trombone (as part of the Horns of Dilemma) paired with Brian Ritchie's theremin provides a rousing climax for "Kiss Off."

Snopek was additionally a part of a loose Milwaukee club assemblage called The Noisemakers From Hell, where he would join members of the Femmes and other miscellaneous Milwaukee musicians. This latter would prove to be a showcase for his next avant-pop development: populist musical regionalism intensely focused on the great state of Wisconsin.

WisconsInsane

After seeing a Noisemakers From Hell gig in the mid-eighties, I lost track of Snopek and his career for a few years. Embarassingly enough, so did my old landlord and friend Jan in Durham, North Carolina: when Snopek called in the late eighties on tour with the Violent Femmes looking for a party and / or a place to crash, Jan had forgotten about his existence. I reconnected with him in a most unlikely place: at a conference in Atlanta, Georgia, I skipped out to a big mall and browsed the vinyl bins (not yet having acquired a CD player). There to my surprise was *WisconsInsane*, a 1987 Snopek release on Dali records by way of Chameleon Music Group out of California. When I played it all through that fall and winter in Kirksville, Missouri, I was astonished at what he had accomplished. Beyond even no-depression acts like Uncle Tupelo and spinoffs, Snopek had captured a supreme sense of place. This was his letter to the world that never wrote to him, to quote Emily Dickinson—and his best work since the early seventies.

His core band here (not really a group per se) was himself and two members of the Violent Femmes (Brian Ritchie and drummer Victor DeLorenzo). These three were augmented by a veritable who's who of the Milwaukee music scene at the time. Fine bands like the R & B Cadets and Bad Boy, known in Suds City but obscure elsewhere, showed up to pay tribute to the Badger State. The big discovery Snopek made with the project, anticipated previously as noted but only completely exfoliated here, is that he needn't have run from being a cheesehead. (Think back to the *Bloomsbury People* billing themselves in Milwaukee as being from Chicago or San Francisco.) He could write and play about his region, just as in literature Thomas Hardy worked up Wessex and William Faulkner covered Oxford, Mississippi. Sigmund Snopek's regionalist phase is not only intrinsically important as a Baedeker to Wisconsin folkways; it offers an implicit model to bands from all over to work with their locale as a source for art rather than to ignore it in favor of universal and bland pop statements (a lesson that goes back to the Beatles' "Penny Lane" and "Strawberry Fields Forever" as well as many Kinks' songs such as "Waterloo Sunset"). More than anyone else with a regional sensibility, Sigmund Snopek shows us all a potential way to proceed.[5]

The album is framed by the "Wisconsin Waltz," a comparatively unconventional musical genre for Snopek to work in—but appropriately indigenous to the German-settled state. Then "Shake the Fruit" contributes the first lyrics, a lament about aging and feeling that life has passed one by ("now you're feeling older"). It's Snopek, not the Crazy Angel, who now has the middle age blues. "Slip Away" maintains the mood of regret and loss juxtaposed with a longing to escape. Bad Boy's Xeno (also original lead singer for Cheap Trick) duets with Robin Pluer of the R & B Cadets on lead vocals; Snopek contributes a fine piano solo. At the end, Pluer breaks into Yoko Ono style vocalese, thereby complicating the mood and taking us into deeper waters (the insane part of *WisconsInsane*?).

"On the Way to Oconto" gets us back to the Wisconsin theme: it consists of "domestic ramblings" from Snopek's parents on a car trip, hinting that cheeseheads do have a separate dialect (a point he reinforces at this phase of the career). This field recording leads to the first major works on the album. "The Rose of Wisconsin" is a tribute to the beautiful women who live in strange comparative isolation all over the small towns of the state. Tourists and travelers walk by them and wonder before mostly moving on ... . Backed by a lovely melody and some apt flute, Snopek chants one obscure Wisconsin town after another where he might have met the Rose in question. The result is a kind of Whitmanesque catalogue of enchanted Wisconsin spaces—a reminder of the rich rural abundance that gets obscured in our tendency to remember primarily big cities. If you know the referents (admittedly a big if), Proustian vibes are possible.

"Sing for Me" provides a one-two musical punch with its haunting consideration of urban loneliness, isolation and lost love (a recurrent sub-theme on the album). In this very personal song, Snopek looks back on the good old days of the late sixties and early seventies and wonders what happened to an old girlfriend who used to follow the band:

> Picked up an old copy of the *Milwaukee Journal*
> Saw you in a photo from Summerfest
> I tried to call you, but you don't live there anymore
> Sure hope you didn't disappear like all the rest

Summerfest is an annual recreational event held on the shores of Lake Michigan in Milwaukee; Snopek played there on numerous occasions with diverse bands. He also muses about his paradoxical career as a Milwaukee-based musician ("sometimes I don't know why I stay here"). In the middle eight, he observes to harpsichord backing that "sometimes" he can "see the lover's ghost." The song's wintry setting contrasts nicely with the memories of summer; its specific references pack more wallop than the vaguer settings of the prog rock phase, especially if you catch the allusions. But because of their detail, I think they work even if you don't know the referents (an opinion tested and confirmed anecdotally by playing this record for non-Wisconsinites). Funny how being extremely particular can have universal appeal: the great regionalist discovery.

The side ends with a few musical jokes: "Plainfield," a short saxophone solo paying tribute to the Wisconsin hometown of notorious serial killer Ed Gein; "One Hand Washes the Other," some dissonant noodling with the Femmes sidemen that leads to Victor De Lorenzo's comment "You realize this is the end of your career"; and a cover of the state theme song "On Wisconsin." This last culminates with another wry remark: "McCartney, I'll get you for this." This cryptic allusion refers to the fact that, yes, Sir Paul bought the rights to the Wisconsin state theme song (around the same time he picked up other items such as "Happy Birthday"). The joke was ultimately on him when Michael Jackson picked up on his idea and bought the rights to the Beatles catalogue!

Side two remains initially in the comic vein with "Aina Hey," a dumb archetypal cheesehead chant, and "Thank God This Isn't Cleveland." This last tune offers a backhanded praise of Milwaukee by cheerfully mocking Cleveland: in 1987, a more plausible move than now perhaps. Milwaukeeans still remembered the story of Cleveland's Cuyahoga river being on fire. Harry Reed's bagpipes at the end of the song provide a suitably martial air.

Then Sigmund Snopek provides a welcome change of mood with "Summer Guest," a haunting piano instrumental that recreates the feel of a Wisconsin summer. After that palate-cleanser, we return to the melancholy that characterizes most of the best offerings from this session. "I'm So Tired of Singing about the Sky" features a gorgeous vocal from Robin Pluer and attacks on "sycophantic ghouls who think they know you." "Sometimes I just want to lay down and die," the narrator opines. "I'm so tired of singing about the sky." The sky might be a reference to the aerial nature of Snopek's progressive rock phase: space kidnappings and the like (*Trinity Seas Seize Sees*). He doesn't want to be the first band on the moon anymore; Wisconsin earth is just dandy. The harmonies on this song remind me of vintage Beatles; it would have been a great single in a more just universe.

"8th and Oklahoma" is a brief instrumental referring to a south side of Milwaukee street corner (and the address of the recording studio where the album was made [Big Interview]). The piece opens with the clicking of an old-fashioned manual typewriter—created by pushing down on the saxophone keys—to invite us into the noirish world of the next track, "Movie Songs." This last features fine sax work from Steve MacKay (who also worked with Iggy Pop) and vocals from Victor DeLorenzo about old movies like *Doctor No*, *Born Free* and *Casablanca*. The song offers a Walter Mitty style fantasy that contrasts nicely with the deep melancholy that ensues with the following "Call Me in Wisconsin (before the war)." This thematic juxtaposition parallels his previous transition from "The Rose of Wisconsin" to "Sing for Me" on side one. Like "Sing for Me, "Call Me in Wisconsin (before the war)" reflects on lost sixties loves and being left behind by former contacts: "I'm sick of TV and the AOR" [album-oriented rock radio stations] ... . I'm wacked out in the midwest ... wonder where everyone else has been." In the middle eight, Snopek laments that "[i]t's strange when a voice is voiceless." The party's definitely over for him and his career. His final advice to the listener: call him—and "it would be best to do it before the war / 'cause I'll still be here." Even near the end of the cold war, Sigmund still feared a hard rain was going to fall.

The English horn solo of Laurie Kunde adds to the exquisite melancholy of the song. "Call Me in Wisconsin" sounds like the neo-psychedelia of the Dream Academy, especially their single "Life in a Northern Town." Listening to these two songs back to back before a roaring fire on a cold wintry night proved to be a sublime experience for this listener. And yeah, I waited for that phone to ring right along with Snopek.

Unable to top these heights, the album modestly concludes with a reprise of "Wisconsin Waltz." We've laughed, we've cried, we've been mental travelers in the land of cheese and beer. An amazing album well worth the hunt ... .

Elephant

It would be a decade before Sigmund Snopek put out another release—after touring with the Violent Femmes and cadging together whatever gigs he could get. *Elephant* (copyrighted 1989) is the missing middle of the trilogy formed by *WisconsInsane* and *Beer*: it's the Great Lost Sigmund Snopek album, finally available via his website. Like its counterparts, it fuses extreme pessimism about life and the planet with good-natured resignation and humor. It thoroughly engages the local habitat of the Dairy State. And it is confessional in nature; we learn about Sigmund's lost loves and his almost unavoidable fondness for drinking. (Wisconsin is a tough state for teetotalers.) He gives us a Portrait of the Artist as a Middle-aged Cheesehead. And the world is a richer place for it, just like we owe James Joyce a debt for his indelible depictions of Dublin. An honest look at what's around you can inspire great art. Furthermore, *Elephant* contains "Under the Trees," one of Sigmund Snopek's masterpieces on a par with "Orange / Blue," "Waukesha Windows," *Nobody to Dream*, "San Francisco Radio," the best tracks on *WisconsInsane*, and "North Avenue" on *Beer*.

The CD opens with "I Slept Late with Chairman Mao," a synth-driven synopsis of what's wrong with late 80's America (featuring tried and true targets like televangelists). A Chinese voice reciting a Mao poem adds a mysterious flair to the proceedings. "Florida Sky" follows with its idyllic flute stylings, lovely harmonies, and zany lyrics that cover beach bars, Ponce de Leon's quest for the fountain of youth and geographic theories that Florida "used to be right next to Wisconsin." "Turnaround" gives us another somber self-portrait: "I'm trying not to cry my way to hell ... / There's someone sleeping next to me / But she doesn't love me anymore." "Turnaround" features guest vocals from Jerry Harrison of Talking Heads, Gordon Gano of the Violent Femmes, and Sam Llanas from the BoDeans (Big Interview). These are all fabulous songs!

Then we get a brilliant curveball with the meta-song appropriately entitled "The Most Incredible Song." It's about the quest for a song with the ultimate commercial hook that eludes its channeler (think of Paul McCartney dreaming "Yesterday"). According to Sigmund, he had one of those inspirations, then forgot it, then remembered it again. Needless to say, this song contains that insidious hook! The magic trick here is that we are sucked into the hook while the lyrics mock its cretinous simplicity:

> it was a simple chord progression
> that no one had ever heard
> it wasn't "Louie, Louie"
> it wasn't "The Bird is the Word" [i.e., "Surfin' Bird" by Minnesota's Trashmen].

At one stroke, Sigmund Snopek gets revenge on all those record company jerks who wanted him to be a commercial success on their ever-mutating terms. You want a hit single? Choke on this! And by now, dear reader, you may be beginning to suspect why no record label would release *Elephant*. And he's just getting started ... .

"And They Talk About The Moon" dials it down with rich synthesizer textures. The melody reminds me a bit of Mike Oldfield's "Tubular Bells," which is not a bad thing. Snopek, like Sun Ra in concert, is working with contrasts on this album. He'll challenge and provoke the listener, then beguile them with his lovely romantic melodies. (*Elephant* should not be put on shuffle play!) "We Drove West Flying North with the Rainbow" is another great, haunting travel song (from Wisconsin to St. Louis, Kansas, and Texas). It comes from the same mental place as "I'm So Tired of Singing About the Sky," but it has its own special sauce.

"Taverns and Bars," which follows, changes the mood and proves to be a prophetic microcosm of *Beer*. The narrator "just sit[s] at the bar" and invites us to "join the beautiful losers." Musically, we get a chorus and polka effects to provide a suitable atmosphere—lessons that will not be forgotten on the next Snopek project. The deep Milwaukee vibe continues with "Baseball in Outer Space," a tribute to Hank Aaron, Warren Spahn, and the 1957 National League pennant win by the (then) Milwaukee Braves. Just as "Taverns and Bars" anticipates *Beer*, this song is a preview of Snopek's double CD *Baseball* project (2006). It's an extraterrestrial version of *Field of Dreams*, replete with ray-gun sound effects and a witty mutation of Simon and Garfunkel: "Where have you gone, Jackie Robinson?" Get it?

"1,000,000,000 Ghosts" is a piano and harmonica jazz ballad augmented by spooky synthesizer effects and elephant cries. The subject matter, reminiscent of a fair amount of *WisconsInsane*, is the contrast between Snopek's rich past and a humble present where he's sitting around "eating cheese and drinking wine." So why was this release entitled *Elephant*? Because, like Sigmund, these animals legendarily never forget? Or because his avant-pop career is the elephant in the room of American popular music that almost nobody noticed? This track appropriately segues into "Stranger than Life," a Latin-inflected meditation on friendship.

Then we move into the abyss as only Snopek can push us. "Civilization" uses a distorted vocal and sampling technology to caution us that "[e]verything is dying out / That's what the twentieth century is all about." (Ah, and what of the new millennium?) "Sweet Dreams" is a compensatory musical fantasia of diverse sound textures also deploying sampling. Its lyrics are a wish list: "I'd make the leaders the followers / I'd make the followers the leaders."

Enter "Under the Trees," a Sigmund Snopek masterpiece that perfectly balances his pop proclivities with his skills as a classical composer. Spoiler alert: it would be best if you listened to this composition before you read what I have to say about it. It bears up well to repeated listens, but the first time has the additional impact (bad pun) of surprise. Okay?

This 9:20 hallucination begins with a vision viewed "from the St. Moritz" hotel off New York's Central Park of ghosts flying about "who had somehow died in Central Park"—all to lush musical accompaniment. The narrative abruptly shifts to a view on television of "a baby with a black eye" that survived "a corporate jet crash" in Iowa (United Airlines Flight 232 on July 19, 1989, in Sioux City, to be exact). The narrator muses that "corporate minds should be buried under the trees in Central Park": a return to the initial observations of the lyric and a bit of free association that could have ended the song after a few minutes as a snapshot of postmodern social observation.

But no: the bulk of the song is a musical recreation of the plane flight and crash with the captain's reassuring voice on the runway, a lyrical ascent, and cruising altitude with trademark soothing flute, then a dissonant crash reminiscent of the Beatles' "A Day in the Life" and a coda also in the spirit of that piece—although Snopek's coda consists of voices making statements about the crash derived from actual quotations in *Life* magazine (September, 1989) about the incident ("Death never crossed my mind ... . [It was like] a scary ride at the amusement park ... . We were running through the cornfield"). The effect is sublime and overwhelming.

So what does this composition do? What is it about? I can only give you my take on it. It owes an obvious if modest debt to "A Day in the Life" as noted, but it makes the bold move from automobile crashes (long a staple of pop and rock capable of hitting the highway safety film heights [depths?] of Bloodrock's "D.O.A.") to air disasters. There are far fewer texts on this subject and the handling is often oblique (Pink Floyd's plane crash staged during "On the Run" in the *Dark Side of the Moon* stage show). It's a risky if sublime subject:

consider audience ambivalences about a film like *United 93*.

But this is not mere exploitation. I think the piece is really about how via the media we can imaginatively participate in and be haunted by—even possessed by—the misfortunes of others. "Under the Trees" is a pointed and persuasive rejoinder to the idea that the media deaden our sympathies (a claim made lyrically in Bob Dylan's "Black Diamond Bay" off *Desire* where he contrasts human suffering with the news story about the incident). I think both positions are defensible: different people respond in different ways. But Snopek's response is more typical; he won that debate twelve years later on September 11, 2001. (And indeed this work is haunted retroactively by that future.)

We've seen the move he makes here before in literature. Walt Whitman's "Song of Myself" imaginatively enters into other catastrophic lives until the poet can endure it no more. And lest we make it an American thing, recall John Donne's apt sermon that "no man is an island" or King Lear's injunction to "Expose thyself to feel what wretches feel." I can't trace the trope back any earlier than that: it seems to begin with Renaissance (now Early Modern) Humanism. "Under the Trees" is an astonishing contribution to this chorus using all the technological resources he had at his disposal. Is it any wonder that cowardly record executives demurred on this offering? On the brighter side, this work cements Snopek's legitimacy as an artist and silences naysayers who think I'm hyping a local hero. This can stand on its own with anything else I'm discussing in these pages.

But unlike *Sergeant Pepper*, *Elephant* doesn't end here with this apocalyptic climax and coda (although it certainly could have; but hey, that was done before). There are two more tracks which offer further closure: "Jackie's Melody" and "Three Species a Day." Both return us to the night thoughts of the solitary artist. In the former, he's watching commuters go by, "eating potato chips" and lamenting lovers who've moved on ("I think I see you / I know that you're not there")—all to a gorgeous melody. (The lyrics were added after the melody by John Kruth; they're about a woman Sigmund Snopek lived with for eight years [Big Interview].) The latter continues these melancholy observations ("People don't stay together very long / They walk out of the door and look for the next thing"), but pairs them with far greater disappearances. As the title of the cut indicates, the Earth loses "three species a day" (in 1989). Thus we return to the larger contexts that opened the song cycle. Sigmund Snopek finds cause for melancholy on all levels here—personal, professional and planetary. It's a hot mess his art can illuminate and partially redeem (to the extent that speaking truth to power pleases the cosmos). *Elephant* is not a happy album, but it is a great one well worth seeking out.

Beer

Beer (1998) was worth the wait after *WisconsInsane* while *Elephant* languished. An extension of *WisconsInsane*, *Beer* goes even deeper into the culture at hand. Co-starring vocalist Andrea Terek, the CD on Charm School records also utilizes the Wisconsin Tavernacle Choir, a chorus of drunks captured on field recordings at live venues. Instead of a CD booklet, the CD contains an actual coaster—so you have a place to set your drink, ideally beer, while you listen! And with 23 tracks of excitement, this is a generous pour.

Beer begins with "Fish Fry," a heartfelt tribute to the indigenous Wisconsin custom, initiated shortly after World War II (as the lyrics helpfully inform us), of having a fish fry in many restaurants and bars on Friday night. At the time, the Catholic Church asked its members to abstain from meat on Fridays; this was an example of German Catholics taking lemons and making lemonade. The musical feel of most of this record is, well, quasi-polka (and often straight-up polka). This 2/4 time Bohemian dance, along with the waltz and the lesser-known schodish (spelling uncertain; I've only heard the pronunciation of the dance), are the favored public dances of Wisconsin's German, Polish and Czech / Slovakian communities. A musician of Snopek's ability trafficking in this indigenous (if imported) idiom recalls nineteenth and twentieth century composers such as Dvorak, Sibelius, Mahler, and Bartok using folk materials in their work. Perhaps even more germane an intertext would be Johann Strauss's *Gypsy Baron*, a waltz-opera! *Beer* is real avant-pop fun, a recording that thoroughly blurs high and low culture distinctions. Not only does this music appeal to the few diehard Snopek fans like myself; I can imagine—and eventually actually saw at the Old German Beer Hall in Milwaukee— a very mixed group at a bar dancing and listening to this stuff with only an occasional suspicion that the players were closer in spirit to Pink Floyd or Leonard Bernstein (as composer) than to polka king Frankie Yankovic. This music is pastiche, not parody (cf. Frank Zappa's *Cruising with Ruben and the Jets*).

The next song, "Fug a Muskie," maintains the piscatorial theme with a nod to Norman Mailer and the Fugs (the New York-based rock band that borrowed Mailer's euphemism for "fuck" from his novel *The Naked and the Dead*). Fug a muskie here as in Fug A Muskie, Wisconsin, a mythical town "outside Stevens Point" (a real place) that stands in for hundreds of small towns in northern Wisconsin. "Muskie," by the way, is short for muskellunge, the largest fish in the pike family in Wisconsin (author Mark Spitzer would remind us that the alligator gar is bigger than a muskie) and Wisconsin's greatest sport fishing challenge (our equivalent of the blue marlin). "Fug A Muskie" name checks classic cheesehead bar food like Tombstone pizza (a bar treat before it made your grocer's freezer) and ends with a grizzled local yelling "Where's my brandy?" (the favored hard liquor of this domain).

The party continues with "I Wanna Be Loved by You," a sprightly torch song written and sung by co-conspirator Andrea Terek (her only composition on the CD). Then we have the first of several overt polkas, the "Frozen Lake Polka." This features some interaction with the boozers, including a lesson in "sausageonics" (Wisonsin-speak). For instance, sausageonics for "living room" would be "front room." It's true! Next, we have a group chant for "Free Beer" and a homage to the drinking fountain at the Mitchell Park Conservatory (three geodesic Buckminster Fuller domes in South Milwaukee containing a desert climate, a tropical climate and a seasonal floral display). The title of the piece? Good sausageonics: "Bubbler in the Dome."

"Porta Pottie Porka Polka" is the first but not the last example of Snopek's bawdy side on this recording, a tribute to the dubious pleasures of sex in a porta pottie: "get down on your knees / pass me all your cheese please ... . I'm going to shove some cheese up your butt." (We're a long way from "Orange / Blue"; well, maybe not so far from the "Blue" part.) This polka also name checks the highly addictive Wisconsin card game of Sheepshead / *Shapskopf*.

Always one to know when he's pushing the envelope too far, Sigmund Snopek transitions to an instrumental, "Brady Street Shuffle." Jim Liban contributes some bluesy harmonica to this tribute to "the days." (The corner of Brady Street and Farwell Avenue in the late sixties to early seventies was Milwaukee's equivalent of Haight-Ashbury.) Continuing with the flashbacks, "Ballad of Walter Busterkeys" offers a thinly veiled encomium to the other great keyboardist born and raised in the greater Milwaukee area: Liberace! (His first name actually was Walter.) Snopek's ballad imitates his style; the lyrics by John Kruth recall how some called him "glitter queen," others "Mister Showmanship": "Walter was an original / Now Busterkeys is dead." Despite their great musical differences, both Snopek and Liberace were classically trained cheesehead pianists. This ballad raises the interesting sense of Liberace as Snopek's secret sharer—another guy who had to beat the odds in a culturally challenged environment.

"Locust Street Blues" offers a great foot-stomping piano blues with vocal chorus that does for this hip locale what Mississippi traditional pianist David Thomas Roberts does for New Orleans streets in his work: a jaunty sense of place is evoked just by the music.

Then it's back to the silliness again with another audience chant:

> Goodbye Pabst
> My memory has lapsed
> My lips are really chapped
> I think I'll take a nap ("Goodbye Pabst")

"Shellack My Whacker" provides more bawdy. Snopek offers to possibly "kiss your heinie" in exchange for the shellacking in question; circumstances are only slightly ameliorated by the final revelation that the whacker referred to is a weed whacker! The song even has a dope reference ("doobies"), rare enough in the Snopek oeuvre.

The mayhem continues with an extended reworking of "Thank God This Isn't Cleveland" off *WisconsInsane*. There's a new verse referring to the temporary contamination of the Milwaukee water supply back then by bacteria found in cow feces: "and when you drink our water / it comes right out your ass" (admittedly a concession to Cleveland). Additionally, there's shtick about Snopek's campaign to run for governor on the "Free Beer" ticket. If Wisconsinites taxed visitors from Illinois (payback for all those Illinois toll roads), we could add a third faucet to every tap: "hot water, cold water, BEER." The only way to top this is with a cover of the Polish polka classic "Who Stole the Keeshka?" So that's just what we get.

Followed by "Virgin Sturgeon," an obscenely memorable quasi-polka in tribute to the big lake fish that gives us caviar:

> I got me an urgin'
> To catch a virgin sturgeon
> So how about splurging
> And going up to Sturgeon Bay [yes, on the map]

Ouch. In the live schtick, Snopek argues that this song ought to be the new state anthem, since "On Wisconsin" is now owned by Michael Jackson! (Obviously another follow-up on the music publishing collections of Sir Paul and the King of Pop.)

We get even further into the brew with an "Irish Segment": sing-along covers of "My Wild Irish Rose," "When Irish Eyes Are Smiling," "Tooraloora," and "Whiskey in the Jar." Sigmund Snopek meets the Clancy Brothers. His Irish mother Shirley Behan Snopek does lead vocals on all but the last of these—and yes, the family is related to the great I. R. A. poet/playwright Brendan Behan (Big Interview). Then—just when we're about to fall into the gutter—Snopek hits us with "North Avenue," a taste of the old prog rocker! This interlude features some jazzy riffs and a haunting melody, tastefully accompanied by a more subdued performance from the Wisconsin Tavernacle Choir. Like all this later Snopek in a serious vein, it's nostalgic: a tribute to the great road in Milwaukee that starts on the lakefront by the water reservoir and goes all the way to Waukesha (at one time a classic route for car cruising). It turns into a reflection on personal mortality: "when I'm gone, it'll still be there." The choir chimes in "North Avenue was a friend of mine." This song has the same spirit as the "Ride in the Dark" rock ballet, yet it's deeper, sadder and more succinct a statement. As happens with a serious drunk, we've gone from festive to very sad in a few minutes.

The ingenious "UFO Polka" lightens things up quite a bit with its appropriation of the theme from *Close Encounters of the Third Kind* as a basis for a polka melody. The lyrics refer to alien abductions and butt probes: "the next thing I knew / they took down my pants." Radio personality Art Bell is also suitably invoked.

The CD winds down with a series of fabulous "Beer Quotes" recited by Art Kumbalek (who also plays tenor sax on the cut). I don't want to deny you the pleasure of hearing them for yourself, so I will reveal only one highly appropriate for this book: "You can't be a real country until you have a beer and an airline."—Frank Zappa. The CD ends with "Last Call," another chant, and "Waiting for Godot." This last, sung with brother Shaun, is another progressively tinged number, a transcendence of the folly that has (mostly) preceded it: "rememberrememberremember." A gentle ending for a generous pour of Wisconsin bar culture.

Sigmund Snopek pushes the envelope of exploring the local even further with *Baseball* (2006). This obsessive tour de force actually raises some interesting philosophical questions about art that take us back to my discussion of Andy Warhol's Brillo boxes in the introduction.

First, let's consider the packaging which builds on the *Beer* coaster for that CD. *Baseball* consists of two compact disks, each of which carries the graphic of a baseball. Since they are both image size outward in the casing, the compact disks look like a flattened baseball. He also includes a set of "baseball cards" depicting the musicians who play on the recording and a few other friends (including his cat Angel). And just like a real package of baseball cards, he also includes some chewing gum. (We're somewhere in the territory of John and Yoko's *Wedding Album* with all its goodies!)

The music itself, after some introductory activities, is grouped into nine "innings." Except for the fourth inning, each begins with non-commercial pieces by Sigmund Snopek or guest composers. In addition to these diverse compositions about baseball, there are a series of minimalist works which consist of intoning the name of a famous baseball player (e.g., Satchel Paige and Roger Maris) over varying musical backdrops. (Sigmund Snopek refers to these pieces as "baseball cards" and eventually wants to compose one hundred and one of them [Second phone conversation]). There are also mood-setting instrumentals ("The Spirit of the Diamond"), polkas, blues, and waltzes. And most remarkably, there are forty-one commercials for various Wisconsin businesses, mostly bars and restaurants.

What is the listener to make of all this, especially the commercials? We should start there, I think. Commercials by bands are the most problematic kind of musical release, a notch down from Christmas albums (which Snopek also likes to do a lot). But they are undeniably part of a group's oeuvre: you will find them included on box sets of Neil Young, the Jefferson Airplane and the Grateful Dead (to name but a few examples). Electronic composer Jon Appleton manipulated a Chef Boy-Ar-Dee pizza ad's audio track on his "Chef D'oeuvre" piece. Or consider *The Who Sell Out release*, which had faux ads on the album cover and musical commercials scattered throughout the record in emulation of a pop radio station. So what he's doing here isn't new—except for the lengths to which he carries the gesture. And Snopek's commercials are as well thought-out musically as anything he's done. He fits the setting to the theme: for instance "The Nomad" gets an oriental exotica backing while "Palermo Villa" has an Italian inflection.

These works are in an interesting aesthetic limbo. He clearly made them for the composition. Their inclusion makes *Baseball* resemble a radio broadcast of a baseball game, which would include lots of commercials. (And indeed they largely come before a new "inning" starts.) They serve as Proustian nostalgic triggers for anyone who's been to Milwaukee and/or Wisconsin. But they also work as real commercials. I'm sure at least some businesses picked up on them for radio ads.

Are they art? After Andy Warhol's Brillo boxes, I think we have to answer in the affirmative. Probably an even more germane moment would be when Michael Jackson let Nike use the Beatles song "Revolution" in an ad in the late eighties. That usage did not suddenly turn "Revolution" into an ad jingle, did it? No in this writer's opinion. In like manner, these forty-one pieces are fine Snopek compositions—and advertisements.

These observations lead me into even deeper waters. Baseball itself is a deeply commercial affair, as more than one "real" song on this suite attests. So the inclusion of that element is highly appropriate thematically. Even more interestingly, any celebration of the urban local will eventually necessitate references to business establishments. My recent book of poetry called *Kirksville* mentions a number of local bars and restaurants (and like Snopek, I reference Usinger's Sausage in Milwaukee). Think of all the product placement and name-dropping of pubs and restaurants in Joyce's *Ulysses* and even *Finnegans Wake*.

The bigger truth is that Western art has been inextricably entangled with economic dimensions. And not just as a matter of patronage for the artist. Portraits "advertise" nobility. Hudson River School landscape painters such as Thomas Cole, Frederick Church, George Innes and Albert Bierstadt advertised westward expansion and manifest destiny. Andy Warhol's grand gesture consisted of making this state of affairs the overt cornerstone of his art (befitting his experience in commercial art). Sigmund Snopek is in this tradition as well. This is an artistic move, not just product placement for cash like we get in a James Bond film. (Although some of the businesses later bought these pieces to be played as radio ads.)

And the commercials fit well into the total concept of the piece, which I think should be listened to actively (not as background filler) in one sitting for overwhelming full effect. I'll only mention a few highlights here; after all, the whole is much greater than the sum of its musical parts. After the national anthem (sung by Snopek's brother Jay), we flashback to Snopek's eighties career on "Powder River," a prog rock suite that narrates a game where the Milwaukee Brewers play the Yankees. The lyrics are by Byron Wiemann from that incarnation of the Snopek band. "Diamonds on Fire" is a passionate and angelic power ballad from guest composer and vocalist Keedy (who was in Snopek's later well-named outfit Angel Breath). Comparisons like these are invidious, but think of Sheryl Crow on steroids as a descriptor for Keedy's voice. Next in the first inning we have "Angels in the Outfield," instant classic rock from Xeno (original vocalist for Cheap Trick and sporadic Snopek collaborator).

In the fourth inning, we get Terry Vitone's witty folk song "Traded to the Angels" (i.e., in heaven). In the fifth, we have a jazzy piano and sax instrumental with actual recordings of a baseball game on the radio, including the actual coverage by commentator Ernie Harwell of Sigmund Snopek catching a ball in the stands ("The Old Stadium")! Gordon Gano of the Violent Femmes sings "La Vida en el Diamante" in Spanish backed by acoustic guitar and string quartet.

The next inning opens with Richard Pinney's "We Need a New Baseball Song" (because "Take Me Out to the Ball Game" has worn out its welcome). This is also a witty folk song which directly addresses the bad economics of baseball. Pinney mentions (without naming obvious names) how teams and managers blackmail their constituencies into building new stadiums by threatening to move the franchise, leaving "dumb bunnies to tax themselves" to build it. And yes, the games are quite expensive if you go on a family outing. Optimism is restored in the seventh inning with the soaring melody and harmony of "The New Brewers." In the eighth, "Baseball in Outer Space" from *Elephant* reappears ("they got diamonds on the moon / they got a world series on Mars"). The game ends with one last minimalist tribute to Jackie Robinson and "Try Until You Win," a final blast of uplift and encouragement for those who play on and support teams who have to really work for those victories. Then it's off to the virtual parking lot.[6]

Sigmund Snopek Meets Santa Claus

An equally pop gesture on the avant-pop continuum would be Sigmund Snopek's releasing a whopping three Christmas-themed CDs (his latest trilogy). That sheer volume of product makes him stand out from the other artists I've considered, but it's telling that of the other six only Frank Zappa avoided contributing to the genre. Yoko with John and the Plastic Ono band got on the charts for "Happy Christmas (War is Over)"; Neil penned the little gem "Star of Bethlehem" for a duet with Emmylou Harris; Joni's oh so melancholy "River" has become a standard on hipper holiday anthologies; the Arkestra covered holiday favorites in concert on occasion; and James Brown put out some singles and a memorable Christmas album showcasing "Santa Claus Go Straight to the Ghetto." What you can expect is for avant-pop artists to subvert the genre, however gently, and Snopek is certainly no exception to this rule.

His first holiday offering, *Christmas* (2001) begins with the original "Christmas Cookies," a homage to the ritual baking activity. Mom Shirley recites the recipe while a chorus advises us: "Gotta make 'em, gotta make 'em, gotta eat 'em, take a lookie!" "And boy, are they good," Shirley Snopek assures us. This song definitely fills a neglected thematic niche.

Several traditional instrumentals on synthesizer ("The Little Drummer Boy") and electric piano ("Have Yourself a Merry Little Christmas") ensue before the next original, much in the spirit of *Beer*: "Pumpkin Pie Polka." This witty ditty observes that "dad drinks a little too much beer" at Thanksgiving, gives thanks for the growing pumpkins and reminds us "hey, heavy on the whipped cream"—all to a driving western swing jazz guitar accompaniment from Royce Hall. "Carol of the Bells" gets a jazzy reading on piano; "God Rest Ye Merry Gentlemen" is rendered the way Tom Waits would do it (Weimar cabaret jazz); the flourishes on "I'll Be Home for Christmas" show how well Sigmund can channel Liberace when he wants to.

"Turk the Turkey" is another Thanksgiving original with lyrics by Snopek's daughter Beulah Peters. Given that the turkey has a name, you know he's going to be spared, at least until Christmas: "I guess by gosh / We'll just eat squash / And have some more beef jerky." His final original, "Christmas Lights," features a haunting melody that captures the beauty of the song's subject.

The final cover versions provide the musical highlights for this very respectable contribution to holiday music. "Greensleeves" is nothing short of epic with its wild synthesizer soloing; he lets the prog rock beast out of its cage for a bit. With his classical training, naturally Snopek nails Tchaikovsky's "Dance of the Sugar Plum Fairies" from *The Nutcracker*. He leaves us with an unusual and memorable take on "Silent Night," which has atmospheric electronic background textures and country violin from Eric Segnitz of Milwaukee's Present Music.

Ornaments (aka *Christmas 2010* on the website, although the date of completion is listed as 2008 on the CD) is a somewhat tamer affair, closer in spirit overall to Mannheim Steamroller (although much better musically; Snopek really knows his way around a synthesizer). Only one of the fourteen tracks is an original, and that does give us the most subversive moment. "It's Christmas Again" isn't afraid to get topical: "There are twenty wars on the Earth today / So come on, Santa, get out your peace sleigh." Musical highlights include an extended "We Three Kings," Snopek singing in German on "O Christmas Tree" and "The Little Drummer Boy" and a fine synthesizer backbeat on "Joy to the World." "Deck the Halls" offers both Anna Snopek (Sigmund's niece) on guest vocal and wacky sampling sounds that evoke a chorus of Christmas elves. The more obscure "Pat-A-Pan" gets a jazzy reading to mix things up, since it is preceded by "Away in a Manger" (which has a somewhat similar melody; the latter also has some trademark flute work). Sigmund Snopek plays all the instruments here on this Yuletide offering.

On the other hand, *The Easter Bunny's Christmas* (2011) provides a wacky conclusion to Sigmund Snopek's holiday trilogy. Not that all is fun and games. The opener, "December Dreams," sets up a complex holiday scene with "two cats in the bed / a brother and a sister" and a returning daughter but a father "in heaven"—losses and gains. "December Dreams" is one of six original compositions on the CD. Other Snopek contributions include "Winter Solstice," a mood piece; "Every Family," a celebration of same; and "Christmas on the Mississippi" "On the Wisconsin side" ("And the river flows / As it silently grows").

The highlights here are arguably the more zany offerings, "Santa's Cookies" and the title track. The former describes the preparation of a suitable gift for the bringer of presents:

> He doesn't need whiskey
> He doesn't need stolen jewels
> He doesn't care for
> some unusual health food

Just cookies and milk and "hay for the reindeer." The title track is a mash-up of the two holidays with speeded-up vocals for the bunny in question: "I'm Santa's friend / And I want to help."

In addition to these treats, there are the usual cover versions, the best of which are "Mary's Little Boy Child" (which features funky saxophone work from Michael Woods) and "'Twas in the Moon of Wintertime," a Huron nation carol that lets Snopek pay tribute to Native American music with indigenous flute warbles and shaker percussion. (He comes by it honestly: Snopek's ancestry is Ojibwa as well as Irish, French and Polish [Big Interview].) The set—and the trilogy—ends appropriately with the (literally) ultimate holiday song: "Auld Lang Syne." As of this writing, here Sigmund Snopek abides in his long journey from the avant to the pop end of the avant-pop continuum. But who knows what's next?

Besides his immense intrinsic merits, let Sigmund Snopek represent the host of neglected practitioners of avant-pop, musicians who blur high culture and low culture in a liberating and transformative way. They hearken back to what Mikhail Bakhtin referred to as "the laughing people," the freer popular-festive tradition of medieval culture whose broad laughter has been muted into delicate modern irony. These are very tough times for artists and intellectuals of all sorts. Rupert Murdoch has poisoned the media well with a fascist station, the Fox News Channel, which mirrors back to the hoi polloi their basest assumptions—an appeal to our inner brownshirt. Dubya's administration recalled the most dubious aspects of the Roman Empire in decline. Hunter S. Thompson, always a keen observer, aptly dubbed 21st century America "the Kingdom of Fear." How can we turn this mess around?

A big question for another book, one maybe I tried to write three decades ago called *The Riddle of the Painful Earth*. This project has been more modest, a hunkering-down which acknowledges that in these troubled times art, music, literature do give us solace and hope. For starters, they give us beauty and sublimity—and that nurtures the human spirit beyond measure in a way that most products of the culture industry do not. I hope these words will encourage you to seek these musicians out and enjoy their generosity to us. Avant-pop, let alone music and art itself, are surviving if not thriving these days. You have to search a little harder than you might have had to in the late sixties. But, then again, the internet has made that search easier in some respects. I assure you the quest is worth it. And there's a lot at stake in making these discoveries. If we don't know what we've inherited as a culture, we stumble in our ignorance. If we absorb the legacy of these great individuals, maybe some day we can refute Frank Zappa's wistful observation that "you can't do that on stage anymore."

Works Cited

Borden, Robert. "Bloomsbury People: 'Modishly Obscure.'" *Bugle American* November 5, 1975 (Volume 6, No. 38 [no. 223]). (A Milwaukee semi-underground newspaper.) Pp. 146-7.
Levitan, Stuart. "Snopek in Concert: Escape Velocity." Publicity release, 1982.
Ritchie, Brian. *The Blend*. SST Records SST-141. 1987.
Snopek, Russell. *My Science Fiction Autobiography*. No place of publication listed: Lulu, Inc., 2005.
Snopek, Sigmund. *Beer*. Charm School 004. 1997.
—— Big Interview. 11 / 17 / 2012.
—— E-mail. 2/18/2013.
——. *First Band On The Moon*. Mountain Railroad Records MR 52795. 1981. May be available on cassette from the website.
——. "If You Love Me Kill Yourself" b/w "Solalex." Mountain Railroad Records. MR - 107. 1981. May be available on cassette from the website.
——. *Nobody To Dream*. Music Is Intelligence WMMS 074. 1997.
——. Phone message for the author. September 10, 2012.

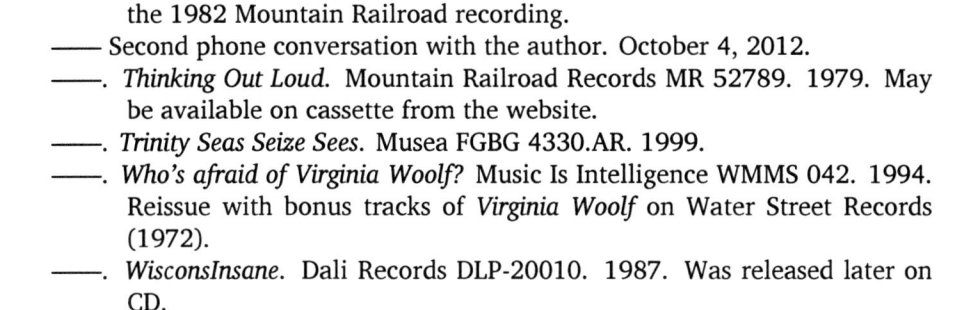

———. *Roy Rogers Meets Albert Einstein*. Musea FGBG 4410.AR. 2001 reissue of the 1982 Mountain Railroad recording.
——— Second phone conversation with the author. October 4, 2012.
———. *Thinking Out Loud*. Mountain Railroad Records MR 52789. 1979. May be available on cassette from the website.
———. *Trinity Seas Seize Sees*. Musea FGBG 4330.AR. 1999.
———. *Who's afraid of Virginia Woolf?* Music Is Intelligence WMMS 042. 1994. Reissue with bonus tracks of *Virginia Woolf* on Water Street Records (1972).
———. *WisconsInsane*. Dali Records DLP-20010. 1987. Was released later on CD.
———. <www.sigmundsnopek.com>. The official website.
Violent Femmes. *The Blind Leading The Naked*. Slash Records 25340-1. 1986.

There are a number of reviews of Snopek works at <www.progarchives.com> by someone named "Bob Moore." (He goes by the name ClemofNazareth.)

Appendix: the Sigmund Snopek Interview

On the sunny and clear morning of Friday, November 16, 2012, Naciketas publisher Neal Delmonico and I drove up to Milwaukee, Wisconsin to meet the man you have been reading about in this last chapter. He invited us to hear a few shows he was doing Friday night and Saturday at the Old German Beer Hall on Third street and State (an address prophetically alluded to on "San Francisco Radio"). From six o'clock Friday evening until 2 am Sunday morning, we spent virtually every waking minute with Sigmund Snopek III. We heard his music; we wound down at his favorite Milwaukee night spots over beer, Irish whiskey, popcorn and pizza; we visited his incredible apartment. And on Saturday afternoon I interviewed him and got his helpful corrections for this chapter (the latter cited as "Big Interview" in the body of the chapter but not transcribed below).

First, a bit on the shows we saw—which were highly suited to the venue. Snopek can be a chameleon in this respect: he reads an audience with extraordinary acumen. The six o'clock show was targeted at the happy hour beer drinkers (and indeed, for a while the Old German Beer Hall gives away free beer). His music consisted of a few originals, German drinking songs, polkas, Christmas songs—the lights were already up in Milwaukee pre-Thanksgiving—and some classical works (Mozart here; he would also do some Beethoven at the later show under the title "Barthoven"). The performance highlight was a musical promenade around the bar with a huge alpenhorn (you see them on those Swiss cough drop commercials). Sigmund would play various fanfares and classical bits to a taped keyboard rhythm backup track while the drinkers used their smart phones for photo ops. He also played flute and an expected bank of electronic keyboards.

The ambience of the place is worth noting. After walking through the bar in the front, you get to the actual beer hall: rows of benches where one enjoys beer and food. In the very back was the small raised stage where he played when he was not working the crowd in the grand tradition of Sun Ra's Arkestra. To the left if you're facing the stage there was a giant chunk of wood, a circular subsection of a tree trunk. Throughout the evening, patrons would play a German drinking game there involving hammering thin-headed nails into the wood with a hammer. (The person with the last nail not hammered in had to buy a round.) Although such activity during a concert would bother most of the musicians in this book, Snopek regards it as a "multi-media experience." The other event of anthropological interest was the ordering and consumption of Killepitsch, a German herbal cordial served in tiny airline bottles. The proper technique for imbibing them is to clamp one's teeth on the neck of the bottle, tilt one's head back and swallow it all at one go. All this, plus Snopek's music!

The two sets of the 9:30 show were much more of a tour de force. Sigmund played with multi-instrumentalist and longtime collaborator Michael Woods (who has a fine jazz-inflected CD called *Burning Trees* out which features Snopek on several tracks). In addition to all of the genres alluded to above, they performed numerous tracks from *Beer*, "Florida Sky" from *Elephant* and a few new and unreleased originals from a project tentatively titled *Remnants of Poets*. I even got to get up onstage and recite a few poems from memory in this highly interactive show. Another guy named Bob, a retired Broadway singer, made an even more spectacular contribution with show tunes "Edelweiss" and "Cabaret." Michael trotted out a fine Louis Armstrong impersonation for "What a Wonderful World."

For me, the absolute surprises were several sixties covers: the one-hit wonder "Everyone's Gone to the Moon" (which led to Snopek singing every song with "moon" in it he knew: "Moon River," "How High the Moon," "Fly Me to the Moon" etc.), the Monkees' "Daydream Believer," "Strawberry Fields Forever" and Procol Harum's "A Whiter Shade of Pale." You haven't lived until you've heard a roomful of beer drinkers singing along note for note on "Strawberry Fields"—Milwaukee's version of the sublime and well worth a trip to the beer hall. He also paid homage to his touring buddies and local heroes the Violent Femmes with a smoking cover of their hit "Blister in the Sun."

On Saturday we visited Sigmund Snopek's lovely and spacious apartment overlooking Lake Michigan on Milwaukee's East Side. It used to be a grand hotel; its lobby has Moroccan lighting and ceiling designs that reminded me of my trip to Marrakech. The first thing you notice upon entering his abode is an abundance of keyboards of every variety, some stacked up in concert

Appendix: the Sigmund Snopek Interview

configuration on stands that can hold more than several at a time. The walls abound with memorabilia: original cover art from his albums, touring posters, photographs from shows, even a proclamation from the mayor of Milwaukee for "Violent Femmes Day."

And as one might guess from his multiple holiday CDs, the dude is seriously into holiday decoration. Neal and I caught the tail end of his Halloween display—soon to convert to a Christmas setup with Dickens village goodies and the like. The Halloween display had everything imaginable, from Bart Simpson to the Green River killer to a train of the dead (it couldn't run) with a sleeping car for Count Dracula, a multitude of flying ghosts in motion and a bevy of lights that grew in beauty as the afternoon waned. Plus the massive Angel and Duchess, two 10 year old cats lucky to share the space with him. Despite all these wonderful distractions, we had work to do. I turned on my tape recorder ... .

Bob Mielke: The inevitable question, a little bit clichéd perhaps: when did you know you wanted to get seriously into performing music and/or composing? Which came first, composing or performing?

Sigmund Snopek III: Performing. Composing came shortly thereafter. We started screwing around with songs, writing them ... .

BM: About when was that?

SS: Writing lyrics? That was about when I was fourteen. And not much happened with it. In the high school years I was in a Top 40 band. As a senior in high school, that's when we started really getting into the songwriting aspects. And the Bloomsbury People, of course, started in my first year of college. But I already had a bunch of music written.

I met the saxophone player and organist Greg Janick and said I want you to come to my house. I got some stuff I want to play for you. And I played him "Virginia Woolf" and "Orange / Blue" and several other songs. That's how it got started. Once we had the platform of the band ... . It wasn't easy to get the band. There were three different versions of it until we finally settled on the final version. And little did I know actually that band would then again morph this time.

BM: Remind me where you went to college.

SS: I went to UW Waukesha, Wisconsin, for the first two years. My favorite music instructor there was Don Stimpert. And he actually plays on the *Jade* CD. We recorded that CD at his house. He has a beautiful Mason-Hamlin nine foot grand piano and a beautiful dual manual harpsichord in a climate-controlled room. He's in his eighties; he's still playing. I still go out and see him and play him my piano compositions. We discuss music. I still take piano lessons from him. He still takes piano lessons! Because it's an unending journey, music. You're never done: if you're done, then you're done. I don't know if that makes any sense. You have to keep exploring, and of course you have to keep practicing. He would show me—on this one piece on *Jade*, I kept going like this all the time [gestures with hands bent at an angle]. I said my wrists are getting tired. He said "go like this [gestures with hands floating above the keys] while you're playing and it takes the pressure off your wrists." By golly, it works. It's a physical thing, especially with a totally acoustic piano. It's way physical.

So that was the rap: between the ages of fourteen and sixteen, and performing came first.

BM: And you never looked back. On you went.

SS: I never looked back. It was "away we go"!

BM: A very broad question. Feel free to narrow it to just one or two things. Whom do you consider to be influences on you? And since you cover many genres, it might be in classical, it might be in rock, it might be in jazz.

SS: Definitely it's a long list.

BM: What pops up first?

SS: The jazz classics we heard on the radio station out of Little Rock, Arkansas. I don't know if you remember that station. We would hear Stanley Turrentine, Sonny Rollins. They all ended up playing at Teddy's [a 1970s nightclub on Farwell Avenue in Milwaukee].

BM: Yeah, I saw a lot of those ... .

SS: John Coltrane, of course.

BM: Rahsaan Roland Kirk played at Teddy's.

SS: And of course Miles Davis. I saw him at the Scene with his *Bitches Brew* band. Dave Brubeck. The Cool Jazz scene. I was playing "Blue Rondo a la Turk" in high school, and we still do "Take Five." We get requests for that and we perform that.

Composers? There's tons of them. Edgard Varese. Without Edgard Varese there wouldn't be any Frank Zappa. People tell me "your music sounds like Zappa." I say "no, it sounds like Edgard Varese." Because of the use of the xylophone and the percussion. He wrote the first piece for all percussion called "Ionisation."

The other composers? George Crumb, great composer; the composer I studied with, John Downey, had a major impact on me; also Yehuda Yannay, he was a composer here at the university; Vince McDermott, he teaches gamelan now. He was my boss when I taught at the Conservatory for four years. And Burt Levy, another composer who passed away a couple of years ago. Stravinsky, Bela Bartok—all the usual suspects! The Impressionists. Claude Debussy. The big one for me was Erik Satie. I actually have a show where I am Erik Satie. I used to do that on Bastille Day for ten years, and that was a lot of fun—because he was quite a character.

Rock groups? The Kinks, of course the Beatles, Procol Harum (which is Latin for "beyond these things"), Buffalo Springfield. I thoroughly enjoyed

Appendix: the Sigmund Snopek Interview 497

Randy Newman. I had the same manager as Randy Newman when I was with the Bloomsbury People. Tom Waits.

Getting back to the groups. A lot of the local groups: the Robbs. They were signed and they played on *Where the Action Is*, that afternoon TV show. Plus I loved the Monkees. Everybody hated the Monkees in the sixties. But they were actually great performers.

BM: I loved the Monkees!

SS: And the people that gave them their sound were some of the greatest musicians on the West Coast. And the songwriters also.

BM: Including Neil Young and Stephen Stills, who played for them.

SS: Yeah. We played at the Atlanta Pop Festival and Jimi Hendrix was there. Actually, Procol Harum played at one in the morning. There were half a million naked people there. There was Lee Michaels screwing some girl underneath the stage. And there were people walking around naked. Procol Harum was performing "A Salty Dog": [sings] " 'All hands on deck / We've run afloat' / I heard the Captain cry." They were singing that at one in the morning. It was a starlit night. And then when they finished, Hendrix came on. That was about three months before he died. And that was amazing. My brother and I were just ... . We got up the next morning and came back to see more music—and played that afternoon. Ravi Shankar played a six-hour set in the morning from six until noon to wake everybody up on Sunday morning. And then we played right after him.

Other groups? You can go on and on. I'd have to go through my record collection. Of course Jethro Tull. I now am irritated with Jethro Tull because when you pick up a flute that's all anybody says: "Jethro Tull." That's all they know, They don't know other [flautists like] James Galway or Herbie Mann. And there's many other great flute players. But it's maddening, actually. It never fails. I feel like we're out there educating people. There's other flute players. What about me?

BM: This next question I had to revise after last night. In your recorded output you don't have any what I would call "serious" covers as opposed to standards and traditional. Last night you played "Strawberry Fields Forever" and "Everybody's Gone to the Moon" and some Louis Armstrong—and all that stuff was, I think, very serious covers. Procul Harum. Would you like to record some of those at some point?

SS: First of all, you have to pay mechanicals on the product. But yeah, it would be fun. I'd like to do a project called *Techno Beatles*. That particular version of "Strawberry Fields" is in that genre. I'd like to make a recording of Beatles tunes. Or you could take the best covers and do them. But I have so much of my own material that's not recorded that sometimes it seems like it would be a waste of time. And so many other people have covered the Beatles. And let's not forget the Beatles themselves.

Or consider their partners: all the Mersey Beat. The Dave Clark Five. The Animals. And then the psychedelic bands. The Femmes did a great cover of "Children of the Revolution."

BM: T. Rex!

SS: Yeah, T. Rex song. In the old days it used to be the record company wanted you to do one or two covers that would go on the album—just to get people into it. We usually covered the Beatles; we did some David Bowie covers. Of course, Procol Harum.

We did tons of covers in the sixties. [1967] was a great summer. I was touring beer bars in Wisconsin. In those days it was an eighteen year old drinking age for teenagers, and we spent the whole summer touring. That was the summer "A Whiter Shade of Pale" came out at the beginning of the summer; in the middle of the summer *Sergeant Pepper* came out. It was the summer of love. I was sixteen. That summer I started really getting into writing. It was just a lovely summer. At the end of that summer, we all cried. Because the band, called "Music Incorporated," had to break up. Some of the guys were going on to college; I was entering my senior year in high school. That was a cover-laden year.

When I worked with Andrea Terek about five years ago—but I performed with her for about twelve years—she was all covers. She wouldn't do anything else. When I did my stuff, that's when I developed the wacky polkas, being a counterpart to her seriousness with the covers. Also the wacky polkas were developed during the Noisemakers from Hell, where we would do anything.

BM: Yeah, I saw one of their shows. Great show.

SS: That was anarchy. That was an anarchist band.

BM: Aptly named.

SS: Yes.

BM: What do you see as the relationship, if any, between your rock and pop work and your classical composing and playing? Is there a synergy?

SS: There are times when it comes together, when it's actually a piece for orchestra and rock band. When you add the two together, it becomes progressive rock. In the late sixties, it was funny; they didn't want to use the term "progressive rock." My record company that put out *Virginia Woolf* said "we need some way to package this." I said "it's progressive rock." They said, "well, that's not good enough." And I would say, "no, you're wrong, it's a great name for the genre." I like the genre you picked for the title of your book: avant-pop. It's fabulous.

Later now in my composing, when it's more mature, you might find that rock influences are much subtler in the classical music and vice versa. So yeah, they do reflect upon each other and are related to each other. But then there are moments that are totally unrelated. I guess that's an ambiguous answer.

BM: That's good. I thought that was a hard question. That was very helpful.

SS: You might see it in a piano composition that's using rock and roll chord progressions, but I'm playing minimally. I'm doing repetitive things. That's a subtle intrusion of the rock genre, harmonic language, into the classical format. One of the things that always has disappointed me about new music is that people are not developing the harmonic language. They're using the same chord progressions over and over. You can take a chord progression and sing five songs to it. One of my theories is that there are really only four pop songs: there's the one chord, the two chord, the three chord and the four chord. Some groups that venture around harmonically usually tend to be less popular because people want to hear the same thing over and over.

BM: Another can of worms: what do you think of the music business then—when you began—and now? How has it changed? What's your sense of that?

SS: When I got into it, it was very expensive to make an album. Not anybody could make an album. You would need twenty thousand dollars. And you'd have to have distribution. And you'd have to have somebody organize all these events—and that's the record company. In many cases, they were dishonest. They ripped off many, many great artists who didn't understand how the business worked. Especially the black artists, many of whom were illiterate. Basically, they'd take them to the cleaners.

So the business was much wilder then and people didn't know very much about it. I remember seeing for the first time a book called *This Business of Music*. I had already been in the business for ten years when I saw this and then came to understand what mechanical rights were, what licensing was, what total ownership was, sharing royalties, performance royalties. All that jargon and all that stuff was used to mystify people in the late sixties and early seventies.

Now, of course, you can have your own record company. I have my own record company. You just put up a website and you advertise it. Let people know where it is. Of course, it does help to have people that go to work every day at nine in the morning on the phones for your product while you're at home sleeping off last night's inspirational binge. So you have to be more disciplined in this day and age. In those days, the only thing I did was that I was a songwriter and I was the guy performing the songs. Maybe we were the road manager too. Nowadays you're the publisher, the songwriter, you're the recording engineer.

I didn't even know how to run a board. The first mixing boards came into existence in the late fifties, I believe. In my day when I first started they were so expensive. Now you can get a tremendous board for three hundred dollars. So your hardware costs are down and you're wearing more hats: you're mixing. Like last night. Normally in the old days, you'd have a guy mixing. And you still do when you do bigger shows. But when you make a living the way I do, you find yourself doing everything. You're the road manager, you're the truck driver, you're the guy who wrote the song.

Then it eats away into your creative time. One of the things I enjoyed about touring with the Violent Femmes was that I was just a side man. Another job I had was that I had to go out with Brian Ritchie to restaurants and museums. Those were my two obligations. And once in a while drive a Cadillac. I wrote music on the road. I wrote pieces. I took outside jobs with various people and was able to be making a couple of hundred dollars a day from writing while I was on the road.

So you have to diversify in this day and age. In the old days it was just "I'm the artist. And I play the piano." I think even the bands that have made it now and have the road managers and the road crew, they did go through that phase. Probably some of them still do odd jobs. There was always the ongoing dispute: should Sig take down his equipment or should the roadies take it down? Brian Ritchie put his foot down and said "He's in the band. You have to deal with his equipment." The roadies didn't like that.

So yeah, there's all these aspects of the music business. The greatest aspect is the exposure and the control of the radio stations. Now I think they're controlled by three major corporations. One station plays only this kind of music; another station only plays that kind of music. In the old days your top forty list had country and western on it, it had pop music. All those genres were mixed together. So people got exposed to different things. Now the person goes to just what they like. I always urge people that are into music to broaden your horizons. Listen to fado, Portuguese music, listen to what's happening in jazz. Some musicians I know just like this one genre and I think they're just cheating themselves out of the rich and varied tapestry of the musical language that now exists. We have the whole world at our fingertips.

In the early seventies my friend Bob Patrick and I were talking. We had been imbibing some pot. "You know, in the future houses are going to be all connected. And there's going to be computers in every house. And people won't have to go out." This was in 1970 that I said this. We called it "House-ism." "It would be like a religion: people would just stay in and nobody would go out. And there'll be houses." We were predicting the internet, which is the bane of many things and the savior. It's a miracle.

Also it's a miracle for me to be able to say "You want a CD? I can go in there and I can burn it, put the label on it." In the old days you waited a year for your album to come out. When you finally got it, you looked at it and went "Wow. It's here."

BM: I think you're sort of answered the next question as well. I don't know if you want to add anything. How has technology impacted upon your career? You've pretty well covered that.

SS: Yeah, I've covered that.

BM: What do you like to read and how does that creep into your art? I'm especially curious about what science fiction you read, because I get a sense that there's a lot of science fiction themes in your work.

SS: I read a lot of science fiction. Like most people, I don't do a lot of reading now. There's not much time for it. But what I do choose to read? The last book I read was a book about the silence on Christmas Eve between the sides in World War I. A fabulous book. I was thinking about turning that into a piece of music. I forget the title of it. [Perhaps *Truce: The Day the Soldiers Stopped Fighting* by Jim Murphy.]

BM: Why should Benjamin Britten have all the fun? [Referring to his *War Requiem*].

SS: Yeah, that's right.

BM: Do you remember what sci fi authors you liked to read when you did read them?

SS: I liked Ursula Le Guin, who's my favorite. Plus Robert Heinlein, Ray Bradbury—all the usual suspects. And then the odd ones: the people that wrote the UFO encounter books.

BM: George Adamski!

SS: And the ringing phone guy, *The Mothman Prophecies* [John Keel].

BM: Good. I refer to that [in discussing "Waukesha Windows" above].

SS: That's true. What's the name of that movie that's out? *The Mothman Prophecies*. I've been enjoying too seeing books being made into wonderful movies. In the sixties people tried, but now they're doing a pretty good job. Tolkien's books, everybody read those in the late sixties and early seventies. There were many attempts ... .

BM: Animation. Ralph Bakshi..

SS: I'm looking forward to *The Hobbit*. That's going to be out in a couple of days, I think. Other reading books? Of course Herman Hesse, philosophy, and English literature. We're going to be plowing through that big thick English lit book for *Remnants of Poets*..

BM: This is a hideously broad question. Maybe narrow it down to one or two. Favorite gigs?

SS: I have a top ten list of favorite gigs. [Reads.] "Top ten stage moments or musical experiences you participated in?"

- Playing the same day, same stage as Jimi Hendrix, [Atlanta] Pop Festival, 1970.

- Spending two weeks in the presence of John Cage, 1971, UW-Milwaukee.

- On stage at the Performing Arts Center with the Milwaukee Symphony playing my first symphony *Orange / Blue*.

- Doing a concert at UW-Baraboo in 1971. I played solo, then Muddy Waters played solo. We shared the same dressing room and had a nice visit.

- 1972, doing a concert at South Campus, Waukesha, my high school alma mater, with my five-piece band and 1000 kids. [This is the basis for the forthcoming live CD.]
- Playing every day, twice a day, at Summerfest [in Milwaukee]. from 1975 to the year 2000.
- Performing my second symphony with the Milwaukee Symphony in 1975, *The Talking Symphony.*
- Playing a show with the Femmes, October 1984, in London on my birthday at the end of my first European tour with the band.
- Playing "Thank God This Isn't Cleveland" in Cleveland at the Agora Ballroom.

BM: I got to ask: how did they respond?
SS: Well first of all, we're backstage and Vic [Victor De Lorenzo] is going "C'mon Sig. We're going to do 'Thank God This Isn't Cleveland.'" I said, "Vic, this IS Cleveland." He said, "I don't care. Do it or you're fired." I said, "Okay. You want to play it? C'mon, let's go."

So we went on stage and the first reaction was [shows jaw dropping] and the next reaction was [shows the middle finger salute] from 3,000 people. And then the next reaction was everybody started laughing. I don't know if anybody taped that, but probably somebody has.

BM: I hope so.
SS: I'm not done yet. There's two more, I think.

- A jam session one night at the Blue River Cafe with myself, James Lee Stanley, John Hiatt and Corky Siegel.

BM: Oh yeah, of Siegel-Schwall [a Chicago-based blues band].
SS: Beware of guys named Corky. The next day he yelled at us. He didn't like the jam. It was too wild for him.

- A concert my four-piece band "Snopek" did in a barn on Washington Island in 1980.

Top ten [sic]. There were many others, though. Those are mainly rock moments..

BM: Corollary: Worst gigs?.
SS: I think one of the second gigs I did in my life we were pelted with stuff by my classmates. You know how high school students can be mean. They threw panties and crap at us. Other than that, I've enjoyed them all.

BM: Knowing your music, I thought you might have said that.

This goes right back to last night and Art Bell [whom we listened to on the ride back to our hotel]. A number of your songs are about UFOs and witches, and Russell [Snopek] has you seeing ghosts at one point in his science fiction memoir. Have you had any paranormal experiences you'd be willing to talk about?.

SS: I have, yeah. Our house in Waukesha was haunted. It was over a hundred years old. I was babysitting one night. When my brothers and sisters were all sleeping on the floor, I'm sitting in a chair watching a scary movie. All of a sudden this thing came around the corner and had its hands around my neck. I'm going "Aaaah!" It was one of those black things with the top they talk about on Art Bell. It's a ghost with a tall, open-ended hat. And we would hear huge banging noises in the basement. And the night that I wrote "Virginia Woolf" somebody tapped me on the shoulder. I ran upstairs.

That's why I sleep in a loft bed—because I still have bad feelings about people under my bed. And for a while I was convinced that there was a creature that was following me around.

BM: So you sleep on the top bunk?

SS: Yeah. Ever since that, it's not a problem. And the cats. The cats chase stuff like that away.

BM: I'm in good shape [with five cats].

SS: I can tell you a story about the dimes too, if you want. When I was a little kid, I was on my way to school and like most kids I used to look for any kind of diversions. I started digging in the ground and I dug up a dime. I didn't think anything of it at the time.

Years later I had this girlfriend. Her name was Rebecca Schuster. We broke up in the summer and she was sad about it. When I saw her that fall—that was the fall that "Brown-Eyed Girl" [by Van Morrison] came out—I saw her at a CYO dance [Catholic Youth Organization], St. Mary's CYO. I bent down to the ground. It had been her birthday the day before. I looked down to the ground and there was a dime. I said "Hey, here's a dime. You can have it for your birthday." As a joke. "Happy birthday!" She was laughing. In those days, of course, a dime was worth a lot more.

Then a couple of weeks later, on Friday the thirteenth, October, we were rehearsing in the basement of the lead singer's girlfriend's house. During the rehearsal I bend down to the ground—and there's a dime! I said "Hey look, I found a dime. Does it belong to anybody?" "No." In those days everybody was broke. "No, it's not my dime." I went over to UW-Waukesha, which is right across the street from this house.

I have to backtrack a little bit. A couple of weeks before I found a dime on the floor. I had a dream that my brother and my two best friends, Steve Smart and Bill Butchart, were playing football in the road. Somebody dropped the football and there was a screaming crash. There was a car crash and somebody was screaming.

Now going back to walking across the street with the dime from the band rehearsal. I found out that there had been a terrible car crash. I immediately knew that my brother had been involved in it. I thought my brother was dead. Because I had the dime. The thing about the dimes went all the way back to when I was a little kid. I thought that all that night.

I went downtown to find out what had happened. My brother was in the car with these two guys I had the dream with. He got out of the car and she got in, Rebecca, the girl I gave the dime to. The night I gave her the dime for her birthday, she said she'd give me a dime for mine. (We're getting the dimes all mixed up.) She got in the car and three minutes later she was beheaded by a car going ninety miles an hour. It was at the same time I picked up the dime in the basement at the band rehearsal. That was when she died. It was the very same time.

I still find dimes all the time. That's my dime story.

BM: It's quite a story.

SS: Yeah, I think that I'm a bit fey. I know I am..

BM: [Nods and moves on.] This came up a little bit last night in some of the songs. What do you see as the political aspects of your work, if any? How should music and politics intersect?.

SS: I have overtly political songs like "I Slept Late with Chairman Mao." There's another one called "The World is in a Dream":

> There are no leaders
> Only people who like to holler
> And the truth is whispering
> And held enslaved by the dollar
> And the world is in a dream
>
> Rich people murder
> Poor people can't
> I guess it doesn't matter
> You can rave and you can rant
> The world is in a dream

That's one of my overtly political songs. *Trinity Seas* is political. That's world politics. That speech at the end is in Lithuanian and backwards English. Actually, nobody's ever come to me and said "I've figured it out." It's a secret. I still have it written down somewhere. I have to pull it out and check it out. But it's a paragraph about world politics that's spoken by the Goddess in the Hall of Godcar. The "car" is political..

BM: And there's a lot of environmentalism in your work, too..

SS: Yeah. There's a song called "Green Milwaukee" where everybody lives underground and Milwaukee is totally like a huge park. Which would be unrealistic, because Milwaukee's built on a swamp! There is no underground. The whole downtown was swamp.

BM: Which compositions are you proudest of? Fondest of? And that might be two separate aspects. You can be proud of some and you can be fond of some ... ..

SS: I like my first two symphonies. There are eight of them now. There's the "Baby Symphony." I'll play some of them for you. My song cycles. (I'm talking mainly about my classical music at this point. I'll get into the rock music shortly thereafter.) The first one, which is called "The Desert Songs"— poetry by Paul Spencer. I think there's like seven or eight song cycles. The ones with the Portuguese poet (Fernando Pessoa) I love.. I also really enjoy "Love Songs of Woman D'Este" which was done by Present Music. (I can give you a copy of that on CD.) .And my piano music.Those are some of my favorites.

As far as the rock stuff goes, I like the prog rock. You know, it's funny that you had picked out *Nobody to Dream*. Because about a year ago, I thought "I must be crazy, because I think that *Nobody to Dream* is my favorite piece of the prog rock days." And then you confirmed that.

BM: And it's evolved. It isn't like you can say "well, I was washed up at age seventeen." Because you revised it and the latest version is brilliant, although that live one is killer too.

SS: The live one is killer. There are two, three [other versions]. There's an initial demo *Nobody to Dream* that was just keyboards and voices and sound effects. I should get that one out too. Then there's the definitive recording that we made. We were supposed to finish *Trinity Seas* back then, but our record company decided to release a really horrible version of *Nobody to Dream* that we just really disliked. So we made our own version as good as we could. So that makes three versions.

BM: So there's the Couth Youth [vinyl], and there's the CD, and then there was a missing one.

SS: There was a Water Street Records [version]—that same label that put out *Virginia Woolf* wanted to release this version of *Nobody to Dream*. The vocals were awful. We never got to redo the vocals. The sound we didn't like. So there's those three; then the fourth one is the German one. [He's counting the demo, the Water Street, and Couth Youth recordings. I refer to the German version above as "the CD."] And the fifth one will be the live one, which actually existed before any of them.

And then I would like to make one more version sung in German. I use a string quartet with a full rock band. And I'll use a better string quartet [than on the German CD]. That string quartet is good, but now I work with the guys that are on the *Baseball* CD, the guy that plays on Gordon's song ["La Vide en el

Diamante" by Gordon Gano]. It's Eric Segnitz. He's the guy who plays violin on "Silent Night." I think that that piece is destined to be sung in German: [sings] "Traum mit mir ... .".

BM: It's kind of a lieder cycle.

SS: Yeah. So I'd like to do it with the best heavy rock musicians I can find and a top-notch string quartet.

BM: What is your sense of your fan base? Who do you think listens to you? What kinds of people?.

SS: It varies, because a lot of times the people who listen to the *Beer* CD are not going to want to hear the pipe organ music. So there's different places. Like I was mentioning before about the diversification. You used to hear the music all in one place: the rock festival. It was the music festival. You can still hear that at Summerfest. But even at Summerfest now they don't have jazz. There is no jazz..

BM: That's sad.

SS: They call themselves the world's largest music festival. Sorry, no jazz!

BM: I heard Gato Barbieri [Latin American saxophone player] there in the day.

SS: Yeah.

BM: And Bonnaroo is like that too. Very diverse, but no jazz. [Except for traditional New Orleans.]

SS: No jazz. Poor jazz. It gets kicked around. So what was that question?

BM: I think you've answered this. There wasn't a monolithic fan base. You've got all ... .

SS: The fan base: different faces, different places. Some people transverse the whole geography of music, you could call it. I'll see them at the Beer Hall, then I'll see them watching us play Irish music. I like to parade a lot. We're in parades. Then a lot of people see you.

BM: If I lived here, I'd be that guy. To me, I like Snopek music—whatever you do.

SS: And we mix it up. There are some covers, some of our own music that I would do at the Beer Hall, that I would do at Paddy's [an Irish pub].

BM: We loved the range last night. You can clearly get away with a lot.

SS: I stretched it for you last night.

BM: Oh good! Normally you don't quite go that far?

SS: It depends, yeah. We don't do as much original material as I did last night.

BM: Well, thank you for that..

SS: We do the obvious ones like "Brady Street Shuffle." That's the Milwaukee New Orleans thing.

BM: I gave Neal [publisher Neal Delmonico] a little history about Brady and Farwell [Milwaukee's Haight-Ashbury district in the late sixties and early seventies].

Speaking of which, how would you describe your relationship with Milwaukee? And how has that affected your music? Very broad question.

SS: It's a love/hate relationship. I mean there are people here who do hate me. Some who think "Snopek? I thought he died." Sure. I can remember playing with Andrea Terek and people coming up to me and saying "You look just like Sigmund Snopek." Odd, man. The audience, the Milwaukee audience.

And there are the diehards and the people who are really into the classical music. They won't come to the bars. Just not their cup of tea. Having a classical piece performed is like a piano recital. You have seven hundred people in there. Although Present Music really has done a tremendous job. Usually there'd be two or three people in the old days at the avant-garde concerts. But now there's close to a thousand at these performances. I'll play you a song cycle. I also want to play you a sequence of my last orchestral work.

BM: What are a few of your favorite Milwaukee and/or Wisconsin places and activities? Just a few, and why? What do you like best?

SS: I love Door County. I love going for the Swedish pancakes. I love performing music up there. That's an area of Wisconsin where they expect you to play original music. I helped nurture that feeling in the early seventies. We were one of the first bands up there playing all original tunes.

BM: It's kind of an artist's colony.

SS: So going up there and performing in all the different venues has always been fun. That barn concert on Washington Island, that was a four-day festival, underground festival. We had to know. It wasn't advertised in the paper or anything.

In Milwaukee, especially in this day and age, there's an endless list of new clubs and new places to go. I like to prowl around at night unless I have a project with a deadline. Then, of course, you're working all the time. The Circle A is a great place to go. Every night is a surprise. The deejay is different every night. Sometimes there's two of them. [pauses.] Some nights the music's intolerable—and then you just split and go somewhere else.

BM: Anyone can deejay if they ask?

SS: Yeah. If you wanted to deejay the next time you came up again, we could arrange that. Are you a deejay?

BM: Yeah, I am. For decades. For college radio. Bring your own vinyl, eh?

SS: Yeah, you bring your own stuff. Paddy's Irish Pub. We should go there. It's beautiful. Do you remember Kalt's restaurant on Oakland [Avenue]? The German place that had all this stuff hanging from the ceiling? Bottles everywhere.

BM: I only got into German restaurants after I left Milwaukee. Craziest thing. I think my parents thought they were too expensive, which they're not.

SS: The Paddy's place went and got a lot of their antiques and they're in Paddy's. If you go upstairs, there's tubular bells and you can play them on a little keyboard that's behind the bar. And there's all kinds of things hanging from the ceiling. There's whiskey barrels. It's hard to describe. It's upstairs—it's a bit of a hike. We should probably go there tonight. You want to go to a couple of places tonight? I can give you a good tour. [He did!]

I love Milwaukee,, I love Madison, I love Door County. I have two brothers who live up on the Mississippi—and that's another area of surprise. Not only people that vote Democratic, but [that] are into original music. From La Crosse, all the way up. My brother lives sixty miles north of La Crosse at the backwaters of the Mississippi. Beautiful area. He's a taxidermist, a karaoke star, and the water commissioner for this small town. When he had to take down his Christmas decorations, I went downtown. He said, "We haven't changed these, traded them out. We've had the same decorations since 1947." And they only had three strands. I said "Where the fuck's Opie [from *The Andy Griffith Show*], man?" It was a fun little town: Nelson, Wisconsin.

And of course, touring with the Femmes, London was a tremendous place. I always loved playing in Manhattan, playing Carnegie Hall. I'll give you one of my more famous lines. I'm one of the few people that's played Carnegie Hall and a bowling alley in West Bend in the same month! Talk about culture shock. One night it's vichyssoise and limousines, the next night it's a '65 Ford van and Tombstone pizza—burnt.

BM: That variety goes into your show, too. How in your opinion did Milwaukee embrace the 1960s?

SS: Better than Waukesha did! I can remember coming here in the sixties to see concerts. There was a place right here: the Avant Garde. That's the first time I ever saw Jim Liban play harmonica. He was in a band called the New Blues.

It was fairly underground and it was really oppressed by the straight people, by Harold Breier [chief of the Milwaukee police] and Mayor Maier. We had the rock festivals. Bloomsbury People played at the Washington Park one.

BM: And [there was] the Alternate Site, down by the lake.

SS: We got our connection with MGM [Records] at the Midwest Rock Festival that was held at State Fair Park. There was a guy there whose name was Bud Carr. He saw the Bloomsbury People play and wanted to sign us. So we signed on. They were our managers. It was Budd Carr and Eliot Abbot. [Carr] went on to manage Kansas. Eliot Abbot went on to manage Randy Newman and Karen Carpenter, Sam Kinison. Do you see a pattern here? These people are all dead [except for Newman]. One of the reasons I got away from him [Abbot] was that I heard he was taking out huge insurance policies on artists. In fact I did an interview once before Kinison died. Kinison accused him of it in the *Rolling Stone*. I mentioned this to the interviewer and she was freaked

Appendix: the Sigmund Snopek Interview 509

out. I said, "Yeah, Sam is being managed by him right now." And then two months later he died. She came to me. She had goose bumps.

BM: Maybe he loved your lyrics for *Bloomsbury People* and thought you'd be a good investment! For a payday.

SS: We kind of stepped away from those managers. Going back to the management in Milwaukee in the sixties, there were a fair number of crooks and booking agents and managers who kind of tainted the sixties for me, the Milwaukee sixties.

We actually, living in Waukesha, did most of our recording and rehearsing, a lot of it, in Chicago. So we got to have a kind of dislike for Milwaukee. We preferred Chicago, actually, in those days. Milwaukee, of course, returned the favor to us and didn't really care for us. It wasn't until the mid-seventies that the Bloomsbury People got a really decent write-up. We had already been broken up for five years.

And then cracking Milwaukee, that was a rough one. Because they're just stuck in their ways. Stubborn Germans.

BM: Any regrets, things you wish you had done differently?

SS: Yeah, I wish that I had kept the band together, the Bloomsbury People. But if I stayed with that guy, then I'd be dead now! The guitar player just passed away and the lead singer's in jail. I won't go into that.

BM: Even the [Buffalo] Springfield. Bruce Palmer and Dewey Martin both passed. It was just Furay, Stills and Young [at Bonnaroo]. And new people.

SS: My four piece band is playing without me next Friday at Linneman's [another Milwaukee venue]. And they're playing a bunch of my stuff.

BM: Oh great.

SS: Byron does that once a year.

BM: What's next? A very broad question, but give us a few teasers.

SS: I'd like to get that live album out, the live CD thing out. And I have *Extra Innings* [a sequel to *Baseball*] which is halfway done. Then I'd like to do the *Remnants of Poets* as far as recordings go. And *Pugsley, King of the Barnyard*. Along with this book, I'd like to muscle out three CDs and the live one—just to make a big splash. Just to make things really happen. Just to remind people that I'm still alive.

BM: Speaking of which, if you could play with any musician or group of musicians, alive or dead, that you haven't, who would it be and why?

SS: That's an interesting question. I'd say the Beatles. Because they were the most creative and it seemed that they were having the most fun. And I liked the way that they lived their lives.

Notes

[1] To complicate the neatness of these categories, there are Wisconsin references in the earlier phases of the career as well ("Waukesha Windows" on *Trinity Seas Seize Sees* and "San Francisco Radio" on *Thinking Out Loud* ["Don't want to be the old rag man on Third and State"]).

[2] There may soon be an addition to these recordings. Sigmund Snopek intends to issue a three CD live album *Live at South* commemorating three sets performed at South Campus Waukesha High School in May or June of 1973. This is a huge development because, for starters, Snopek has never put out a live concert recording (the few bar field recordings on *Beer* don't really count). And as anyone who's seen him in concert can attest, he's every bit as good in live performance as in the studio. In addition, this particular event captures the last show with a particular five-piece line-up: Snopek on keyboards and vocals, Byron Wiemann III on guitar and vocals, James Gorton on lead vocals and guitar, Michael "Ding" Lorenz on percussion and drums and James Paolo on electric bass. And finally, the sheer length of the show indicates that Snopek can really stretch it out right up there with Bruce Springsteen and the Grateful Dead.

Thanks to Sigmund Snopek, I had the privilege of hearing an advance copy of this music. The audio quality of Jim Duwel's tape is quite good for the time and the audience is both enthusiastic and respectful: once they prematurely clap at the end of "Orange / Blue" when the music has a false ending (*à la* Haydn's "Surprise Symphony"), but overall they seem to actually know the way these challenging compositions play out.

The first disk—and the first set—of this long, tuneful evening begins with "Soothsayer's Dove," the hit single from *Virginia Woolf* in a better parallel universe. Several never-released compositions follow, increasing the value of this concert. "Songs from Beneath the River" continues the water imagery of *Bloomsbury People* and *Virginia Woolf* (not surprisingly, since the first song, "Golden Lion," also appears on the former album). It has three sections including the aforementioned "Golden Lion," which features tight bass work from Paolo, and the celestial harmonies and guitar explorations of "Faceless Angel." Then the band does two other pieces introduced as "new." "Change by Change by" is an unabashed tribute to English Renaissance song (well before Sting got around to it!) that illuminates just how deep Sigmund Snopek's classical proclivities run. Despite its title, "Cauliflower Suite" is quite brief, but dense with compositional twists and turns—a lot of audio information.

The first set concludes with a quintessential reading of "Orange / Blue," which Snopek introduces as a "standard" for the group "since 1969" and one that has been performed with orchestras as well, most recently (then) with the venerable Milwaukee Symphony. He also solves some of the mysteries regarding the piece's synesthetic implications by noting that it was written to be accompanied by a light show. After these preliminaries, we have the lovely work itself. There are enough differences from the studio versions to make things interesting. The "Orange" section has some more extended guitar soloing; the opening of "Blue" has slightly more discordant keyboard work. And there are somewhat different melodic arrangements in the "Blue" section as well—variations on the soaring theme.

The second set is devoted exclusively to an energetic reading of *Nobody to Dream*. The vinyl version begins right off with "Dream With Me" and the CD starts out with the string quartet "Dream Song of the River." This live rendition begins with an extended blazing and driving rock bolero, thus making a fabulous piece even better. This introduction concludes with thunderous synthesizer washes which persist into "Dream With Me": the snoring of the gods?

As with "Orange / Blue," the live delivery here is exceptional. James Gorton's vocals on "Everyday" and "Softly" are particularly haunting; "Coral Dream" delicately shimmers before it builds; the band stretches out and jams on "Night Terror." By the time we get to the rollicking version of "Dancing," I'm prepared to argue that this is the best version of *Nobody to Dream* I've heard—and that's really saying something. For this suite holds its own with any prog rock masterpiece (yeah, even that one with the prism on the cover). Such a work coming out of Milwaukee seems almost miraculous.

But I digress. Other highlights include the additional guitar filigree work on "Night Dream," a mellow extended version of "Walking," an intensely rhythmic "Death" and an exquisite rendering of "Sunrise Falling." The studio versions end with a subdued "Morning Child" as a coda; here we get a big climax after it worthy of the Who, followed by an appropriate amount of applause.

The third and final set opens with a revelatory "Ciudad." On the studio version, we only get a few excerpts of this larger piece. In concert, one can see that this was intended to be every bit as ambitious a work as "Orange / Blue" and "Virginia Woolf." "Ciudad" has an extended electronic introduction, a few spacey interludes and a ratcheted-up tension between slow and fast tempos. This extended compositional length gives more room to develop the urban paranoia themes only glimpsed in miniature on *Virginia Woolf*. "Demian" off *Bloomsbury People* changes the pace and gives the band a chance to relax after their workout on "Ciudad." This song, whose title and lyrics refer to the Herman Hesse novel of the same name, is just for piano and voice; the audience is so quiet that you could have heard a pin drop in the auditorium of the high school.

A stripped-down and jazzy "Virginia Woolf" provides the finale to the event. Ding Lorenz gives us the expected brilliant drum solo as the Nazi war drums threaten. More unexpectedly, there are some comic interludes including the use of whistles, horns and xylophone (this last quoting from *Also Sprach Zarathustra* and the *William Tell Overture*); the audience laughs appreciatively at the tour de force showmanship before erupting in thunderous applause. Then they clap along during the final "Virginia walked into the sea" section. Sigmund introduces the band and they play a modest encore, "Pioneer Saint of Death" from *Bloomsbury People*. An epic evening and an important document: according to the program notes, "the next day the group broke up." Thanks to Jim Duwel's recordings we can hear their splendid swan song.

[3] The two unreleased Mountain Railroad sessions were *Voodoo Dishes* (AKA *Feeling American* (1982) and *Modern Heaven* (1983). I obtained this information from the Sigmund Snopek website. *Voodoo Dishes* is now available on CD from the website.

[4] Sigmund Snopek fares much better in the alternate universe his cousin Russell Snopek describes in his novel *My Science Fiction Autobiography*. In that world, he's an incredibly rich businessman, actor and (of course) musician who owns real estate, theme parks, and the publishing rights to all the Beatles songs (continuing the family joke) (110). The younger version of Russell marvels about Siggy's luck:

> "Basically, everyone's life turned out close to what I imagined except yours, which is unlike anything I imagined. Not that I didn't think you could be famous. I just never thought that musicians could be so rich and influential. You are more of an industrialist, politician and corporate figurehead than an entertainer." (272)

To which Sigmund concedes "[t]here were times when I wondered how much longer I could hang on" (272). The author explains elsewhere why he believed in this alternate universe:

> I realized that just a little tweaking of the past events might have resulted in the fulfillment of my childhood dreams. For instance my cousin, Sigmund Snopek III, who began touring nationally in 1969 at age nineteen, has had a successful musical career that now reaches international audiences. A break here or there might have catapulted him to superstar status. Why not? He possessed the drive, talent, and originality. It all boiled down to being in the right place at the right time. Science fiction's resurgence and Sigmund's frequent use of it in his compositions could have combined in making him the space-rock icon I envisioned. (292-3)

Obviously, I more or less agree with this assessment—it's the whole point of this chapter!

[5]Reading over the Zappa chapter, I realized that I made similar claims for him as a regionalist. I think the reason why my praise of Snopek is stronger in this regard has to do with his total commitment to regional representations in *WisconsInsane* and *Beer*. Zappa, by contrast, provides extensive regional data about Southern California throughout his project / object. But he never focused complete albums on it (vs. individual songs). The aficionado in this latter case has to gather up the more scattered material to get a deeper picture of what Zappa's up to. In Snopek's case, you can't ignore the intensely regional quality of the later pop material.

[6]Perhaps this is the time to discuss briefly Sigmund Snopek's stand-alone trilogy of quasi-classical compositions. I have already considered *Roy Rogers Meets Albert Einstein* (1982). *Miasma Fragments: New Music for Pipe Organ* (Spiritone Records, 2001) offers a generous sampling of a decade's worth of works composed for pipe organ by Snopek and performed by David Bohn on a Kimball and Company organ in the Immaculate Heart of Mary Catholic church in Chilton, Wisconsin. It's a lovely instrument for showcasing these pieces. The anthology begins with the programmatic "Sidereal Storm." Its thunderous opening segues into quiet rainfall (augmented by rain stick percussion); the calming "Tacit Rainbow" is a suitable follow-up. "A Gift of Light Will Turn into Sound" thoroughly explores the sonic resources of this instrument. "Magical Concatenations" goes for a shimmering ambience. "Eight Nighttimes" is a series of brief minimalist dreamscapes, quick sonic sketches.

Then we come to the three concluding master works. "For the Cherub Cat is a Term of the Angel Tiger" is the earliest composition here (1990); its success no doubt inspired Sigmund Snopek to pen more. You have to love a piece that derives its title from a work by the great mad eighteenth-century poet Christopher Smart. And the title is an apt clue as to the intentions of this programmatic work. Just as Smart's *Jubilate Agno* idolizes his cat Jeoffrey, this piece celebrates and captures the grace and unpredictability of feline motion. There are some very nice effects afoot here (ouch), including birdsong to tempt the cat—duly appreciated and responded to by my furry co-auditors—followed by slow stalking notes and the dramatic capture replete with celebratory climax. A feast for the ears of any cat lover!

The title piece is the longest work here and one of the latest (1998). It perfectly illustrates how David Bohn's liner notes describe the composer: "Snopek's classical music presents a very personal voice, a singular synthesis of disparate elements into a unified style." In this assemblage of "fragments" you can readily hear both the diffuse musical interests and their ultimate emergence as a unified compositional fingerprint.

The virtual recital concludes dramatically with the (again) helpfully named—by poet Cynthia d'Este—"Foghorns Call Lowly O'er Ambivalent Seas."

Initial deep bass resonances give us the foghorns in question sounding off; then we transition to muted higher notes and a gentle reprise of the bass over them. The synesthesia of this highly visual music pairs nicely with *Foghorns*, an Arthur Dove painting I have seen over the years at the Whitney Museum, a painting that travels in the other direction by painting the sound of the horns in question.

Jade (2003) compiles Sigmund Snopek's solo piano works performed on a Mason-Hamlin grand piano by Snopek and pianist Don Stimpert. This collection proves Sigmund Snopek's essential grounding in classical romanticism and impressionism; the only foray into more recent schools of composition can be detected in the dash of minimalist repetition appropriately discernible in "The Afternoon Slips By." But if you're looking for the dissonances of Ives, Schenberg or Ligeti's piano writing, you won't find them here. And that's okay: this is a lovely CD on the composer's terms.

Highlights for me include the sprightly "Daughter's Dance," a piano-only resetting of the lovely "Jackie's Melody" off *Elephant* and "A Song for Penelope" (an exquisite and shimmering re-visitation of Grecian interests). "The Poet" is a driving yet succinct programmatic portrait; "Sleeping Cat" pays suitable tribute to the feline in repose; "Miniature Chorale" certainly lives up to its name at a length of twenty five seconds!

"Sixties in Blue" is a nostalgic time capsule that evokes Milwaukee's Autumn of Love (the season I associate with the arrival of our counterculture). We get a new reading of *WisconsInsane*'s "Summer Guest," even more nuanced than the original. The quasi-title track "Mama Jade" flashes intense note clusters; "Mobil Eyes" is yet another travel-themed instrumental that offers a soundtrack for the endless highway. It's all beautiful work. If it isn't Ives or Ligeti, neither is it Paul McCartney or Billy Joel! Sigmund Snopek is a gifted classical composer, not a cultural tourist. And these collections just scratch the surface of his many classical writings.

Index

A Clockwork Orange, 29
Abbey, Edward
   The Monkey Wrench Gang, 216
Abraham, Alton
   on secret codes, 321
Adamski, George, 333
Adorno, Teodor, ix, xvii, 59
Age of Manifestos, xv, xvi
album packaging, 487
Allison Krauss and Union Station, 256
Allman, Gregg, 259
American Catholicism, xii
American Foundations, xi
American Woodmen Junior Division, 329
Ammer, Christine
   Unsung: A History of Women In American Music, 43
Ann Arbor Blues Festival, xx
Antheil, George
   Ballet Mecanique, xvii
anti-Japanese sentiment, 9
Antony (of Antony and the Johnsons)
   on *Yes, I'm a Witch*, 39
Anzaldua, Gloria, 37
Arcade Fire, 256
Arkestra
   Sun Ra and his
      blending theater and music, 44
   A Song for the Sun, 385
   at the Paradox Music Club in 2008, 386
   Music for the 21st Century, 385
Arkestra, Sun Ra and his, 313, 315, 317, 318
Armstrong, Craig
   on *Yes, I'm a Witch*, 39
Armstrong, Louis
   Secret Order, 326
Art Ensemble of Chicago, 10, 44, 315, 321, 369
Artaud, Antonin, 12
Atlanta Pop Festival
   Sigmund Snopek III at, 451, 461
Au Pairs, 19
Aunt Mimi, 13
Ayler, Albert, 11

B-52s, 11
Babes in Toyland, 19
Bakhtin, Mikhail, 468, 491
   Rabelais and His World, xii
Ballard, J. G.
   Crash, 21
Bangs, Lester, x
Baraka, Amiri
   Dutchman, 16
Bartok, Bela, 95, 129

Baudrillard, Jean, 302
Baxter, Les
   crucial link, 329
Beatles, 8, 72, 73, 80, 130
   Rubber Soul, 314
Beirut, 259
Bela Fleck and the Flecktones, 255
Bell, Norma Jean, 86
Beneath the Planet of the Apes, 147
Benjamin, Walter, ix
   "The Work of Art in the Age of Mechanical Reproduction", 250
Berg, Alban, 10
Berkeley, Busby
   Stars Over Broadway, 262
Berry, Chuck, 14
Bertolucci, Bernardo
   1900, xi
   The Last Emperor, xi
Black Mountain College, xiii
Blake, William
   Songs of Innocence and Experience, 140
      "The Chimney Sweeper", 142
Bloomsbury People, 495
Blow Up
   on *Yes, I'm a Witch*, 38
Blues Project, 323
Boulez, Pierre, 89
Bovee, Greg, 318
Bowie, David, xii, 97
   use of masks, 176
Bowie, Lester, xii
   Avant-Pop, xviii
Bozzio, Terry, 76, 79, 82, 85, 86, 88, 104
Bradbury, Ray
   The October Country, 134
   Something Wicked This Way Comes, 134

Brecker brothers, 88
Breton, Andre
   Surrealist manifestos, xv
Brock, Napoleon, 71, 72, 77, 79, 85, 86, 88, 100, 101
Bronstein, Stan, 28, 29
Brown, James, xx
   a child at his aunt's bordello, 425
   Afrocentric polyrhythms, 418
   album cover of *I Can't Stand Myself When You Touch*, 421
   amazing contributions to world music, 440
   arrival of funk full-blown on "Papa's Got a Brand New Bag", 430
   brought Africa to America, 440
   cameo appearance in the movie *Ski Party*, 435
   catalized soul and rap, 417
   cavalier treatment by record labels, 419
   "Choo-Choo (Locomotion)"
      his first rap recording, 434
   complex ethnicity, 423
   consummate outsider, 418
   contributor to rap, not an originator, 434
   dealings with the IRS, 418
   double consciousness as African-American, 422
   earliest funk sermon on "Money Won't Change You", 431
   funk's influence on jazz and fusion, 430
   fusion of gospel, R & B, and jazz, 426
   "Get Up, I Feel like Being a Sex Machine", 432

Gravity
"How Do You Stop", 440
"Hot Pants", 432
huge supporter of M. C. Hammer, 435
"I Got the Feelin'", 432
"I Got You (I Feel Good)", 431
in his powerful screaming and shouting soul mode, 425
indication of true soul is elasticity, 426
"It's a Man's Man's Man's World", 428
I'm Real, 439
"Let a Man Come In and Do the Popcorn", 436
"Let Yourself Go", 432
Live at the Apollo, 427
Live at the Apollo, Volume II, 432
more melisma in soul, 427
Motherlode, 442
no organized archival access, 420
on being pressured to record "I Won't Plead No More", 419
on his first incarceration, 418
on his identity, 424
on Polydor, 419
on the transition from soul to funk, 429
on *Live at the Apollo*, 427
paradoxical status as insider/outsider, 422
polyrhythm, 429
precursor to the rap genre, 434
public icon of otherness, 438
Revolution of the Mind, 440
Revolution of the Mind, 433
Road Runner of Soul, 439
semiotics of his album covers, 421
Sex Machine, 432
skepticism about the "soul" genre, 425
Soul on Top, 443
Star Time 4-CD box set, 420
stream-of-consciousness sermons, 438
surreal libidinal economy, 437
surrealist element in his style, 435
T. A. M. I. Show, 425
"Take a Look at Those Cakes", 437
taped applause on original vinyl releases, 421
the Mashed Potatoes, 436
The Next Step, 442
the Popcorn, 436
Bubble Freaks, 457
Buffalo Springfield, 257
Burke, Edmund, 18
Burroughs, William, 55
  The Nova Convention: A William Burroughs Tribute, 120
Bush, George W.
  Dubya, x
Bush, Kate, xii
Byrd, Donald
  Ethiopian Knights, 430
Byrd, William
  History of the Dividing Line
  iconography of the rural in, 173
Byrne, David, xii, 16

Cage, John, 10, 74, 75, 390, 501
  4'33", xviii
  A Chance Operation: The John Cage Tribute, 120
Caldwell, Erskine

iconography of the rural, 173
Cale, John, xii, 10
Cameron, James, 14
Campbell, Joseph
   Hero with a Thousand Faces, 423
Cantor, Eddie
   "Makin' Whoopee", 32
Capp, Al
   iconography of the rural, 173
Captain Beefheart, xii, 57, 78, 79
   Grows Fins, 118
   Trout Mask Replica, 115
Caruso, Enrico, xvii
Carver, Lisa
   Reaching Out with No Hands: Reconsidering Yoko Ono, 45
Cashbox, 15
Celine, Louis-Ferdinand, 12
Christmas music, 489
Cixous, Helene, 19
Clapton, Eric, 14, 17
Clayson, Alan (with Barb Jungr and Robb Johnson)
   Woman: The Incredible Life of Yoko Ono, xii
Clinton, Bill, x
Close Encounters of the Third Kind, 341
Colaiuta, Vinnie, 101
Coleman, Ornette, 10, 16
   free jazz movement, 319
Collins, Bootsy: "free your ass and your mind will follow", 41
Collins, Ray, 92
commercialism, 447--448, 454, 470, 489
commercials, 487--489
Conrad, Joseph, xvi
Corbett, John
   Extended Play, 388

Cordwainer, Smith, 333
Crane, Stephen, xvi, 391
Crnkovich, James, xi
Crosby, Bing, xvii
Crow, Sheryl, 19
CSN & Y
   American Dream, 201
Cucurullo, Warren, 101

Danto, Arthur
   After the End of Art: Contemporary Art and the Pale of History, xv
Davis, Miles
   On the Corner (1972), 430
   Pangea, 368
   Sketches of Spain, 383
De Lorenzo, Victor, 502
de Saussure, Ferdinand
   the semiotics of cultural placement is a system constructed on differences, 283
Debussey, Claude, xvi
Delany, Samuel R.
   cities, 345
Demme, Jonathan
   Heart of Gold
      culmination of the *Prairie Wind* CD and DVD, 218
   Journeys
      Declan Quinn Director of Photography on, 248
      "Leia", 249
      "You Never Call", 249
   Journeys, third in a documentary trilogy on Neil Young, 248
   Trunk Show, unreleased second film in Demme's documentary trilogy on Neil Young, 248

Diamanda Galas, 11
Dickerson, Walt (jazz vibist), 323
Dickinson, Emily
    "Because I Could Not Stop For Death", 21
Diddley, Bo, 13
DiFranco, Ani, 19
Douglas, Mike, 17
Dragon Lady, 8
Dream Academy, 480
Duchamp, Marcel
    "Fountain", xvi
Duchamp, Marcel (Fluxus), 44
"Duke of Earl", xxi
Duke, George, 71, 77, 83, 88, 350
Dunbar, Aynsley
    drummer, 84
Dylan, Bob, 8, 130
    analogue of Neil Young, 173
    confessional turn begins with, 273

Earth, Wind and Fire, 430
Eisenstein, Sergei
    October, 223
El Saturn
    Sun Ra's home record label, 313
Elephant's Memory Band, 18
Eliot, T. S.
    Four Quartets, 296
    "Tradition and the Individual Talent", 14
Emerson, Ralph Waldo
    as teacher, 316
Eminem, 259
Eno, Brian, xii
Ensemble Ambrosius
    The Zappa Album, 115
Ensemble Modern, 99
    Ensemble Modern Plays Frank Zappa: Greggery Peccary and Other Persuasions, 116
Enslinger, Hillary, 89
Estrada, Roy, 85, 86, 103
Explosions in the Sky, 259

Felix Da Housecat
    on *Open Your Box*, 40
Fillmore East, xx
Fischer, Larry
    An Evening With Wild Man Fischer, 117
Fish, Stanley
    meaning is neither fixed nor arbitrary, 149
Fisk University Jubilee Choir on "When God Made Me", 234
Fitzgerald, F. Scott
    James Gatz as self-reinventor, 424
Fleetword Mac
    "Don't Stop (Thinking About Tommorrow)", x
Florence and the Machine, 255
Fluxus, 17
Fluxus neo-dada movement, 10
Fowler, Tom, 71
Franklin, Aretha, 427
    "Respect", 50
"free jazz", 10
Freelance Whales, 254
Friedan, Betty, 63
Friedlander, Erik (cellist), 42
Fripp, Robert, xii
    Frippertronics, 239
Frith, Simon and Howard Horne
    Art Into Pop
        demonstrated the significance of art school, 267--268
Fry, Roger
    Bloomsbury Group, xv

Futurebirds, 254

Gabriel, Wayne, 29
Gates, Henry Louis, Jr.
   The Signifying Monkey, 395
George, Lowell, 103
Gershwin, George, 15
Gibson, William
   Neuromancer, 150
Gillespie, Dizzy, 318
Ginsberg, Allen, xiii
Girard, Rene
   Things Hidden Since the Beginning of Time, 335
Glass, Phillip, 390
Goebbels, Joseph, x
Goldman, Albert, 7, 30
Gordon, Kim
   Yokokimthurston, 44
Gore, Al
   An Inconvenient Truth, 222
Gorton, James, 511
Grand Funk Railroad
   Good Singin' Good Playin', 118
Grand Wazoo, 99
Grateful Dead, xii
Greenberg, Clement, xv
GTO (Girls Together Outrageously)
   Permanent Damage, 119
Guardian (June 20, 2005) on Ono's London concert, 43
Guliano, Geoffrey, 7
Gurdjieff, 334
Gyoto Monks, 10

Haden, Charles, 10, 16
Hancock, Herbie, 350
   River: The Joni Letters, 307
Hare, Pat (bluesman)
   "I'm Gonna Murder My Baby", 134
Harris, Bob, 75

Harris, Eddie (mellow jazz), 324
Harris, Sugar Cane, 98
Harris, Thana, 76, 97
Harrison, George, 15, 17
Harvey, Polly Jean, xii, 19
Havadtoy, Sam, 35, 42
Hazard to Ya Booty, 431
Hells Angels, xiii
Henderson, Fletcher, 319
   influence on Sun Ra, 327
   other innovations, 328
Henderson, Joe
   Multiple, 430
Hendrix, Jimi
   Electric Ladyland
      "Moon, Turn The Tide ... gently gently away", 17
Herman, Judith
   Trauma and Recovery, 33
Hesse, Herman, 511
hetai, 10
Hines, Earl, 360
Hirsch, Jerry, 160
Hoch, Studebaker, 85
Hole, 19
Honegger, Arthur, 15
Hornsby, Bruce, 259
Howells, William Dean
   The Riddle of the Painful Earth, xi
Hughes, Sarah
   2002 Winter Olympics gold-medal performance, 427
Hume, David, xviii
Hurvitz, Sandy, 120

Indica Gallery, London, 9
International Harvesters
   Young's country band, 199
Ippolito, Adam, 27
Irigiray, Luce, 22
Iron Butterfly, 96

Index 525

Ives, Charles, xvii, 293
I'm Your Man, 39

Jackson, Wanda, 255
Jacson, James
    the infinity drum, 317
Jameson, Frederic
    "Transformations of the Image in Postmodernity", 18
Janov, Arthur
    primal scream, 13
Jarmusch, Jim
    Year of the Horse, 154
Jarrett, Michael, xvii, 15
Jaynes, Julian
    The Origin of Consciousness in the Breakdown of the Bicameral Mind, 333
Jefferson Airplane
    Jefferson Airplane Loves You, 118
Jethro Tull, 469
Jobson, Eddie, 82
Joe Jones and the Tone Deaf Music Company, 16
Joplin, Janis, 19
Joshua, ix
Joyce, James, 12

kabuki, 10
Kahn, Herman, xi
Kandinsky (painter)
    synaesthetic effects, 270
katu-tugai, 7
Kaylan, Howard, 17, 83
Keats, John
    "On First Looking into Chapman's Homer", 232
Keel, John
    on UFOs, 332
Kennedy, Jackie, 21
Kenny's Castaways, 19

Kesey, Ken
    Merry Pranksters, xiii
Keys, Boddy, 17
Khan, Nusrat Fateh Ali, 10
Kieslowski, Krystof
    Decalogue, 32
King Crimson, 467
Kipnis, Laura
    scholarship on *Hustler* magazine, 173
Klein, Allen, 29
Kristeva, Julia
    abjection, 9
    Abjection, Powers of Horror, 12
Kubrick, Stanley, 59, 63, 109, 128, 130
    2001: A Space Odyssey, 410
Kundera, Milan
    The Book of Laughter and Forgetting, xvii
Kuras, Ellen, Director of Photography for *Heart of Gold*, 234
Kusama, Yayoi, 9
Kyoko, 15

L7, 19
Lacan, Jacques
    Mirror Stage, 45
Lady Mitchell Hall, 11
Laing, K. D., 8
Lange, Art (critic), 319
Langley, Johnny, 159
Larson, Nicolette
    backing vocals on Young's "Goin' Back", 174
Le Concert Impromptu and Bossini
    Prophetic Attitude, 120
Le Tigre
    on *Yes, I'm a Witch*, 38
Led Zeppelin, 455
LeMay, Curtis, 13
Lennon and Ono

Unfinished Music No. 1: Two Virgins, 10
Double Fantasy, 30, 31
Milk and Honey, 31
Sometime in New York City, 17
    "Don't Worry Kyoko", 17
Two Virgins, 8
Unfinished Music No. 2: Life With The Lions, 11
    "Cambridge 1969", 11
Wedding Album, 8, 15
White Album, 10, 14
    "Revolution 9", 11
Lennon, John, xx, 72, 90
    Heart Play, 31
    John Lennon/Plastic Ono Band, 15
    Skywriting By Word of Mouth, 50
    "lost weekend", 18
Lennon, Julia, 13
Lennon, Sean Ono, 29
Levi-Strauss, Claude, 56
Levine, Lawrence W.
    Highbrow/Lowbrow: The Emergence of Cultural Hierarchy in America, xii
Lewis, Andre, 85, 86
Lewis, Jerry Lee, 13
Liberace, Walter, 485
Lifton, Robert Jay
    "nuclearism", 147
Ligeti, Gyorgy (Hungarian composer)
    sound track of *2001: A Space Odyssey*, 314
Lil' Wayne, 256
Lincoln Center, xiv
Lind, Jenny, xiii
Little Richard, 14
Lock, Graham
    liner notes to *Live in London 1990*, 395
Longinus on hyperbaton, 158
Loyola, St. Ignatius, x
Lunch, Lydia, 19
Lynn, Loretta, 257
Lynyrd Skynyrd
    response to Neil Young in "Sweet Home Alabama", 159

MacDowell, Edward, 293
Marinetti
    Futurist manifesto, xv
Mars, Tommy, 75
Marsh, Dave
    on funk, 430
Marshall Allen Arkestra
    Points on a Space Age, 387
Maxfield, Richard, 10
McCartney, Linda, 8
McCartney, Sir Paul
    Memory Almost Full, 42
Metheny, Pat (guitarist), 300
Michael Ray and the Cosmic Krewe, 372, 388
Miles, Barry, 86
Mingus, Charles
    as avant-pop artist, 299
Mitchell, Joni, xx, 19, 42
    alternate tunings, 270, 271
    parallels and influences, 271
    approach to sound deeply shaped by love of visual, 269
    at the Alberta College of Art in 1963, 268
    avant-pop claim to fame is *Blue*, 266
    Blue, 273--279
    "A Case of You", 278

begins with a few songs about her relationship with James Taylor, 276
"Blue", 277
"California", 277
"Carey", 276
devasting emotional power of "Little Green", 276
easier now to see foci of the album, 275
"Little Green", 276
masterpiece of concentrated beauty and pain, 279
"The Last Time I Saw Richard", 278
"This Flight Tonight", 277
both famous and unknown, 308
contracted polio in 1952, 265
Court and Spark
a radio-friendly confection of pop and light jazz, 279
disillusionment with her audience, 274
Dog Eat Dog, 300--305
"Dog Eat Dog", 304
"Ethiopia", 304
"Fiction", 302
"Good Friends", 301
her most political album, 301
"Impossible Dreamer", 304
"Lucky Girl", 305
"Shiny Toys", 304
"Smokin' (Empty, Try Another)", 303
"Tax Free", 303
"The Three Great Stimulants", 302
Don Juan's Reckless Daughter, 291--296
album's structure, 292
"Cotton Avenue", 292
difficulties with the project, 291
"Don Juan's Reckless Daughter", 295
"Dreamland", 294
her only double studio album, 291
"Jericho", 292
"Off Night Backstreet", 295
"Otis and Marlena", 294
"Paprika Plains", 293
"The Silky Veils of Ardor", 295
"Talk To Me", 292
"The Tenth World", 294
gender issues, 271
Hejira, 284--291
"A Strange Boy", 288
"Amelia", 286
"Black Crow", 290
"Blue Motel Room", 290
"Coyote", 286
double recorded her guitar sound, 285
"Furry Sings The Blues", 287
"Hejira", 288
lyrics exemplify new approach to writing, 285
"Refuge of the Roads", 290
"Song for Sharon", 289
the greatest album of her illustrious career, 285
her own description of her sound, 271
journeys through the ditch, 279
justifiably included in roster of practitioners of avant-pop, 267
Miles of Aisles
her first live album, 280

Mingus, 296--300
  "A Chair in the Sky", 297
  "God Must Be A Boogie Man", 296
  "Goodbye Pork Pie Hat", 299
  "Sweet Sucker Dance", 299
  "The Dry Cleaner From Des Moines", 299
  "The Wolf That Lives in Lindsey", 298
"Music is my sorrow, painting is my joy", 268
Night Ride Home (1991), 306
on Reagan presidency, 301
on the Isle of Wight festival, 274
on the '80s, 300
on *Dog Eat Dog*, 305
open-tuned bass strings resemble a "wash" in visual arts, 270
painterly eye in her lyrics, 269
paradoxes of, 308
parallels with Neil Young, 265
  effect on their music, 265
patriarchal music industry kept her music off the air, 272
resistance to easy genre categorization, 271
Shadows and Light (album and video), 300
Shine (2007), 307
  "Night of the Iguana", 307
synaesthetic effects, both musically and lyrically, 270
The Hissing of Summer Lawns, 279--284
  "Don't Interrupt The Sorrow", 281
  "Edith and the Kingpin", 281
  "Harry's House—Centerpiece", 283
  "Shadows and Light", 284
  social observation rather than personal confessions, 280
  "Sweet Bird", 284
  "The Boho Dance", 283
  "The Hissing of Summer Lawns", 282
  "The Jungle Line", 280
Travelogue (2002), 307
Turbulent Indigo (1994), 306
  won two Grammy awards, 306
unique position of *Blue* in her career, 275
Wild Things Run Fast, 300
wonderfully productive forays into the ditch, 266
Mohawk, Essra
  see Sandy Hurvitz, 122
Monk, Thelonious, 317, 318
Monroe, Marilyn, 22
Moody Blues, 15
Moon, Keith, 17
Moore, Thurston
  Sonic Youth, 17
  Yokokimthurston, 44
Morisette, Alanis, 19
Morton, Jelly Roll, 360
Mothers of Invention, xx, 17
Mozart, 103
Music
  autobiographical, 272
  mass media, 273
  the veil of a persona, 273
My Morning Jacket, 256

Nancarrow, Conlon, 94, 104

Index

Naomi Shelton and the Gospel Queens, 256
NASCAR, xiv
New Orleans Allstars, 254
Nirvana
    grunge, 447
Noel, Dan
    Approaching Earth, 410
Nyro, Laura, 19

O'Connor, Sinead, 19
O'Hearn, Patrick, 86
Oates, Joyce Carol
    "Where Are You Going, Where Hare You Been?", 21
Odin, Bianca, 82
Old Crow Medicine Show, 256
Ono, Isoko, 13
Ono, Yoko, xii, xx, 90
    feminism in, 18
    A Story, 19, 30
    Approximately Infinite Universe, 18
        "Catman (The Rosies Are Coming)", 29
        "Death of Samantha", 29
        "I Felt Like Smashing My Face in a Clear Glass Window", 28
        "I Have a Woman Inside My Soul", 28
        "Looking Over From My Hotel Window", 29
        "Move On Fast", 29
        "Waiting for the Sunrise", 29
        "What a Bastard the World Is", 27
        "Yangyang", 29
    Between My Head and the Sky, 41, 43
    Blueprint For a Sunrise, 36
    "Don't Worry Kyoko", 14
    Feeling the Space, 18, 20, 25, 29
        "Coffin Car", 21
    "The Feminization of Society" in the *New York Times* (1971), 26
    Fly, 12, 16
    Grapefruit
        "City Piece", 50
    It's Alright (I See Rainbows), 35
    "John, John (Let's Hope For Peace)", 14
    "Joseijoi Bansai", 30
    "Mirror Mirror"
        psychomachia in, 45
    Onobox, 15, 19, 25, 27
    Open Your Box, 37, 40
    Rising, 17, 36
    Rising Mixes, 36
    Season of Glass, 50
    Season of Glass, 9
        "No, No, No", 34
    Starpeace, 35
    subversive approach to the fine arts, 268
    Unfinished Paintings and Objects, 9
    "Woman of Salem", 22
    YES, 36
    "Yes, I'm a Witch.", 22
    Yes, I'm A Witch, 37, 40
    Yoko Ono/Plastic Ono Band, 15
        "Greenfield Morning I Pushed An Empty Baby Carriage All Over The City", 15
    Yokokimthurston, 43
        "Early in the Morning", 45
Orange Factory
    on *Open Your Box*, 40
Orpheus, ix
Ouspensky, 334

Paglia, Camille
   Sexual Personae, 428
Palermo, Ed
   Take Your Clothes Off When You Dance, 119
Palmer, Robert, 13
   on *Onobox*, 35
Parents' Music Resource Center (PMRC), ix, 114
Parker, Charlie, 318
Parliament / Funkadelic, 430
Partch, Harry, 17, 347
Peaches
   on *Yes, I'm a Witch*, 38
Peck, Abe
   Uncovering the Sixties, ix
Peel, David, 18
Pennebaker, D. A.
   Sweet Toronto, 13
Perkins, Carl
   "Blue Suede Shoes", 14
Permanent Midnight, xviii
Persuasions, 84
Persuasions, The
   Frankly A Cappella: The Persuasions Sing Zappa, 119
Pet Shop Boys
   on *Open Your Box*, 40
Phair, Liz, 19
Phlorescent Leech, 17
Picasso, xvii
Pickett, Wilson, 427
Pierce, Jason (of the neo-psychedelic British band Spiritualized)
   on *Yes, I'm a Witch*, 39
Pink Floyd, 97
   Meddle
      "Echoes", 45
Plastic Ono Band, 14
Plath, Sylvia, 9, 20
   juvenilia, 20
   "Poem for a Birthday", 21

Plato
   The Republic, ix
Pluer, Robin
   vocalist, 479
politics, 492
Ponty, Jean-Luc, 91, 101
   King Kong, 117
Popeil, Lisa, 75, 91
Porcupine Tree
   on *Yes, I'm a Witch*, 38
Postmodernism
   as double-edged coding, 146
Preston, Billy, 17
Preston, Don, 17, 61, 82, 83, 88
Prince/The Artist, xii, 430
psychomachia (in Ono), 44
Pythagoras, 334

Rabelais, Francois
   Gargantua and Pantagruel, xii
Radio Pacifica, 313
Ravel, Maurice, xvi
Record Mirror, 15
Redding, Otis, 427
Reed, Lou, xii
   Magic and Loss, 9, 34
regionalism, 477
REM, xiv
Rennie, Michael
   The Day the Earth Stood Still, 358
Restless
   Neil Young and the, 202
Reynolda House Museum of American Art, xi
Rhapsody Films
   Mystery, Mr. Ra, 361
   Sun Ra: A Joyful Noise, 361
Rich, Adrienne, 9, 20
   "Transcendental Étude", 26
   "Twenty-one Love Poems", 27
Rock and Roll Circus, 425

Index 531

Rodgers, Jeffrey Pepper (musicologist)
    bass "wash" in Mitchell's "Chelsea Morning", 270
Rolling Stone
    cover story on Sun Ra, 314
    dubbed Joni Mitchel "Old Lady of the Year", 272
Rose, Cynthia, 431
Rousseau, Henri, 382
    The Dream, 346
Ruben and the Jets
    For Real, 120

Sainte-Beuve, Charles-Augustin, 7
Sapphirecut
    on *Open Your Box*, 40
Sarah Lawrence, 10
Saunders, Red, 319
Scheler, Max
    Der Formalismus in der Ethik und die Materiale Wertethik, 393
Schoenberg, Arnold, xvii
School of Seven Bells, 254
Scriabin (musician)
    synaesthetic effects, 270
Seven Sisters, 20
Sexton, Anne, 9, 20
    "Her Kind", 23
    "The Addict", 23
    "The Play", 24
    "Wanting to Die", 23
Shankar
    Touch Me There, 116
Shankar, L, 101
Shepp, Archie, 91
Sherman, Cindy
    photographer, 203
Sherwood, Motorhead, xx
Shitake Monkey
    on *Yes, I'm a Witch*, 38

Shocklee, Hank
    on *Yes, I'm a Witch*, 39
Shpongletron Experience, 256
Shute, Nevil
    evoked by Young's *On the Beach*, 184
Silva, Alan
    Celestial Communication Orchestra
    "Seasons", 320
Simmons, Jeff
    Lucille Has Messed My Mind Up, 117
Sinatra, Frank, xvii
Sinister side of rap, 435
Slick, Grace, 118
Slits, 19
Smith, Patti, xii, 19
Snopek III, Sigmund, xii
    Abbot, Eliot as manager, 508
    apocalypticism, 474, 480
    Baseball, 481, 487--489
    baseball cards, 487
    bawdy, 485--486
    Beer, 449, 481, 484--487
    biographical, 495
    Bloomsbury People, 450--451, 508--509
    Bloomsbury People, 511
    Bloomsbury People, 450, 509
    Carr, Bud as manager, 508
    categories of musical output, 449
    Christmas, 490
    classicism, 452, 453, 510, 513
    commercialism, 454, 462, 469, 481
    commercials, 487--489
    comparison with Frank Zappa, 451, 452, 459
    Couth Youth, 505
    covers, 497--498

death obsession, 455, 465, 466
"Desert Songs", 505
disaster as genre, 482--483
dream interpretation, 462--466
dream vision, 453, 454
Easter Bunny's Christmas, 491
Elephant, 480--483
environmentalism, 457, 483, 504
favorite gigs, 501--502
First Band On The Moon, 473--475
future plans, 509
German CD, 506
Germanic cultures, 484, 493--494
holiday music, 449, 490--491
influences on, 496--497
Integrated Light and Sound, 461
Irish influences, 486
James Joyce, 463
language syncretism, 460
Miasma Fragments: New Music for Pipe Organ, 513
Miasma Fragments: New Music for Pipe Organ, 489
middle-aged cheesehead, 480, 482
Milwaukee scene, 507--509
missing jazz, 506
music as business, 499--500
new wave, 449, 473
Nine Women, 452
Nobody to Dream, 511
Nobody to Dream, 461--466, 505
Noisemakers From Hell, 477
Orange / Blue, 501
"Orange / Blue", 453--454, 510

Ornaments, 490--491
paranormal, 503--504
parodist, 468, 470--471, 474--475, 491
politics, 453, 455, 472, 473, 504
postmodernism, 468
progressive rock, 449--469, 510
Remnants of Poets, 501
road music, 467, 481
Roy Rogers Meets Alberet Einstein, 466
satire, 470
science fiction, 456--457, 500--501, 512
song cycles, 505
space rock opera, 456--461
stoners, 475
Summerfest, 478, 502
symphonies, 505
syncretism, 491, 498--500, 506--507
Talking Symphony, The, 502
technology, 500
televangelists, 480
Thinking Out Loud, 469--473
Trinity Seas, 505
Trinity Seas Seize Sees, 456--461
UFO lore, 457, 458
Violent Femmes, 448, 476--477, 480
Virginia Woolf, 511
Virginia Woolf, 450--456
Voodoo Dishes, 475--476
weekend with author, 493--495
Wisconsin regionalism, 449, 458, 471, 477--481, 484--508

Index

Wisconsin tavern culture, 484--487
WisconsInsane, 477--480
worst gig, 502
Snopek, Russell
    fictional version of Sigmund, 512
Snopek, Shirley, 490
Society for Values in Higher Education, x
Sonic Youth, 11, 44
Spaceways Incorporated: Thirteen Cosmic Standards by Sun Ra and Funkadelic
    Sun Ra tribute album, 388
Spicoli (Sean Penn)
    Fast Times at Ridgemont High, 154
Spinozza, David, 20
Spitzer, Mark, 484
    Age of the Demon Tools, 217
    Bottom Feeder, 217
Stable Gallery, xvi
Stapledon, Olaf, 460
Staples, Mavis, 259
Starr, Ringo, 15
Steiger, Rod, 303
Stein, Gertrude
    Geographical History of America, 392
Stevens, John, 11
Stevens, Samantha
    Bewitched, 29
Stimpert, Don
    Snopek's teacher, 495
Sting, 77
Stockhausen, Karlheinz (electronic composer), 10, 44
Stravinsky, Igor, 56
    Rite of Spring, xvii, 93, 96
    Soldier's Tale, 95
Streiber, Whitley, 332

Sun Ra, xx, 95
    A Fireside Chat with Lucifer, 368
    A Night in East Berlin, 370
    A Quiet Place in the Universe, 360
    A Space Odyssey: From Birmingham to the Big Apple—The Quest Begins, 384
    A Tribute to Stuff Smith, 372
    African-American paradox, 336
    alien abduction account, 331--332
    ambivalence about black folks, 337
    and The Nu Sounds and The Cosmic Rays, 322
    and Yochanan, 322
    angels and demons at play, 317
    Art Forms of Dimensions Tomorrow, 342
    as a lounge act, 329
    as consummate showman, 321
    as teacher, 315
    at Toronto's Horseshoe Tavern
    10 CD box set on the Transparency label, 363
    Atlantis, 348
    Aurora Borealis, 366
    aware of fifties trend in Euro-American music, 328
    Batman and Robin, 323
    became his myth, 330
    Beyond the Purple Star Zone, 367
    A Black Mass
    in collaboration with Amiri Baraka, 414
    A Black Mass, 380
    Black Myth / Out in Space, 351
    Blue Delight, 371, 394

born Herman Poole Blount in 1914, 319
called "Lucifer", 410
Celestial Love, 368
central doctrine of birth and death, 333
Chicago years, 340--341
circularity of his classic show, 339
College Tour Volume I: The Complete Nothing Is, 346
Cosmos, 360
course taught at UC Berkeley 1971, 381
critiques of black ethnicity, 337
Crystal Spheres, 356
cycles in his career, 339
Cymbals, 356
Dance of Innocent Passion, 366
Destination Unknown, 372
Discipline 27-II, 355
Disco 3000, 362
dismissal of Christianity, 334
esoteric doctrine and pedagogy behind the music, 338
etymology and punning, 334
Fate in a Pleasant Mood, 341
favored repetition and circularity, 339
Friendly Galaxy, 372
God Is More than Love Can Ever Be, 366
hidden angels and demons among us, 335
Hidden Fire, 373
Hidden Fire 2, 370
his alien abduction like a conversion experience, 333
his first recorded work, 321
his music is space music, 320
his records, audio souvenirs of live musical events, 340
his two-sided dialectical coin, 337
Holiday for Soul Dance, 341
Horizon, 353
in Helsinki, October 1971, 352
in Milan, Italy, January 23, 1978, 362
jazz as a generic mask, 320
Lanquidity, 362
  a serious bid for a larger audience, 324
Life Is Splendid, 353
Live at Montreux, 360
Live at Praxis, 370
Live at Slug's Saloon, 354
Live in Cleveland, 358
Live in London 1990, 371
Live in Rome, 366
live solo piano recital in Venice, 1977, 362
Love in Outer Space, 370
Mayan Temples, 371
Media Dreams, 363
Monorails and Satellites, 360
My Brother the Wind, 350
My Brother the Wind, Volume 2, 350
New Steps, 362
New York years, 342--349
Night of the Purple Moon, 350
Nothing Is, 346
"Nuclear War", 324
Nuits de la Fondation Maeght, Volume 1, 351
Oblique Parallax, 367
on angels and demons, 336
on avant-garde music, 320
on free jazz, 319
on his being a failure, 394
On Jupiter, 364

Index 535

on Louis Armstrong's playful relationship to melody and rhythm, 327
on the Carolina Cotton Pickers, 326
on the diaspora, 336
On The Other Side of the Sun, 364
other pop projects, 322
Philadelphia: 1968-1970, 349--351
"Pink Elephants on Parade" on *Stay Awake,* 325, 370
plausible lineage for his sounds, 329
poetry
  "In Some Far Place", 392
  "Nature's Laws", 391
  "The Foolish Foe", 390
practitioner of free jazz, 319
pure pop songs, 322
Ra to the Rescue, 367
resistant to labeling, 318
resonances with Joyce, Derrida, and Cage, 335
saw musical opportunities in the disco craze, 323
Second Star to the Right (Salute to Walt Disney), 325, 370
Secrets of the Sun, 342
significance of the crucifixion, 334
Sleeping Beauty, 365
Solo Piano Volume I, 360
Some Blues but Not the Kind That's Blue, 361
Somewhere over the Rainbow, 361
Sound Sun Pleasure, 340
space chants, 315
Space Is The Place, 354
Space Is The Place (1974 film), 325, 393
space key or space chord, 315
Spaceship Lullaby, 363
St. Louis Blues, 360
Stardust From Tomorrow, 371
Stars That Shine Darkly (Volumes 1 and 2), 369
Strange Strings, 347
Sub Underground Series, 358
Sun Ra Featuring Pharaoh Sanders and Black Harold, 344
Sun Ra live in Paris at the "Gibus", 356
Sun Ra Visits Planet Earth / Interstellar Low Ways, 341
Sunrise in Different Dimensions, 366
synaesthetic effects, 270
The Antique Blacks, 356
the Arkestra as ark, 338
the Arkestra, a musical family and body of disciples, 337
The Complete Detroit Jazz Center Residency, 367, 398--410
The Futuristic Sounds of Sun Ra, 342
The Great Lost Sun Ra Albums, 356
The Heliocentric Worlds of Sun Ra (Volumes 1 and 2), 346
The Lost Reel Collection
  Volume 1: *The Creator of the Universe,* 380
  Volume 2: *Intergalactic Research,* 381
  Volume 3: *The Shadows Took Shape,* 382
  Volume 4: *Dance of the Living Image,* 382
  Volume 5: *The Universe Sent*

Me, 383
Volume 6: *The Road to Destiny*, 384
The Magic City, 345
the Man from Saturn, 330
the many standards played by, 325
The Paris Tapes, 353
"The Sensational Guitars of Dan and Dale", 323
The Singles, 322
The Solar-Myth Approach
Volume 2, 315
Volumes 1 and 2, 350
The Soul Vibrations of Man, 361
The Sound Mirror, 363
The Sun Ra All Stars, 412
The Sun Ra Arkestra Meets Salah Ragab in Egypt, 368
Transparency's 6 live DVDs, 373
Volume 1: *Sun Ra Arkestra Live at the Palomino*, 374
Volume 2, 374
Volume 3, 375
Volume 4, 375
Volume 5, 376
Volume 6, 377
Transparency's *Untitled Recordings*, 379
Transparency's "Audio Series,"
Volume 1, 378
Volume 2, 378
two potential chart-toppers, 322
Unity, 360
used a Solovox on "Deep Purple", 315
When Angels Speak of Love, 344
When Sun Comes Out, 343
Sun Ra All Stars, 374, 412, 414
Sun Tzu, xi

Swedenborg, Emmanuel, 335
Szwed, John F.
on Sun Ra, 316
on the elements in the music of Sun Ra, 329

Taylor, Cecil, 360
Tchicai, John, 11
Temple, Julien
"This Note's For You"
video MTV initially refused to air, 200
Tenaglia, Danny
on *Open Your Box*, 41
Terek, Andrea, 498
The Apples in Stereo
on *Yes, I'm a Witch*, 38
The Bluenotes
Young's ten-piece blues band, 200
The Flaming Lips
on *Yes, I'm a Witch*, 39
The Grandmothers, 102
The Osbournes, xiv
The Polyphonic Spree
on *Yes, I'm a Witch*, 39
The Sleepy Jackson
on *Yes, I'm a Witch*, 39
The Thin Red Line
animals in response to war, 169
Thompson, Chester, 71
Thompson, Hunter S., xiii
Thompson, Robert Farris
on food imagery in James Brown, 437
Three Kings
animals in response to war, 169
Tickling the Dragon's Tail: American Nuclear Culture, xi
Toronto Rock 'n Roll Revival, 13

Index 537

Toscanini, Arturo, xvii
Travers, Joe, 81, 84, 86, 102, 111, 112
Tudor, David, xviii
Turrentine, Stanley (mellow jazz), 324
Turtles, 83
Twain, Mark
   Adventures of Huckleberry Finn, xiii
Tyson, June
   vocalist for Sun Ra, 317

U2, xiv
Uncle Skeleton, 254
underground and internet, 448
Underwood, Ian, 98, 99, 103, 121
Underwood, Ruth, 71, 78, 81, 88, 99

Vai, Steve, 75, 91, 97, 100, 103, 106
Van Vogt, A. E., 333
Varese, Edgard, 81, 94, 102, 103, 122, 342, 390
Velvet Underground, 16
   blending theater and music, 44
VH1
   Behind the Music, 7
Violent Femmes, 495
   Ritchie, Brian, 460
Vliet, Don, 57
Volman, Mark, 17, 83
Von Clausewitz, xi
von Daniken, Erich
   Young borrows from, 147
Voorman, Klaus, 14, 17

Wackerman, Chad, 96
Wag the Dog, 302
Wagner, Richard, 56
Waits, Tom, 8

Wake Forest, *see* Reynolda House Museum of American Art
Walker Art Museum, xvi
Warhol, Andy, xvi, 8, 487--488
Washington Jr., Grover (mellow jazz), 324
Watson, Ben, 56--58, 61, 62, 64--67, 86, 87, 93, 104
   Negative Dialectics of Poodle Play, 53
Watson, Johnny, 87
Wavelength Infinity
   Sun Ra tribute album, 388
Wesley, Fred
   on James Brown, 417
White Light / White Heat, 390
White Stripes, xiv
White, Alan, 14
White, Ray, 88
Whitely, Sheila, 73, 130
Whitman, Walt, xiii, 8, 483
   "Song of Myself", 395
Who
   "Won't Get Fooled Again", x
Wiemann, Byron, 467, 469, 471
Wild Man Fischer, 107
Wilson, Brian
   Smile, 39
Wilson, Owen, xviii
Wisconsin Tavernacle Choir, 484, 486
Wolfe, Tom
   Electric Kool-Aid Acid Test, xiii
Wong, Suzy, 8
Woods, Michael, 491, 494
Woolf, Virginia
   suicide, 452, 455
WWF, xiv

xenchronicity, 97
Xeno, 459
xenochronicity, 79, 81

Yates, William Butler
   like Young switching between masks, 176
Yo La Tengo
   Nuclear War, Or How I Learned to Stop Worrying and Love the Bomb
      Sun Ra tribute album, 389
Young, La Monte, 10
Young, Neil, xx
   alienation of most of his fan base, 183
   Americana, 245
      "Oh Susannah", 246
   apocalyptic mood in *On the Beach*, 184
   approach as a filmmaker in *Journey Through The Past*, 178
   Arc, 204
   Archives, Volume One (2009), 236
      DVD/Blu-Rays discs set up as a file cabinet, 236
      each song has a whimsical, minimalist film, 236
      hidden "Easter eggs", 236
      leather-bound booklet, 237
      "Unparalleled Access to Neil's History", 236
      virtual intimacy between performer and his public, 237
   Why does this matter?, 237
   Are You Passionate?
      "Are You Passionate", 209
      "Be With You", 211
      "Differently", 208
      "Goin' Home", 210
      "Quit", 208
      role of neglect in, 208
      "She's A Healer", 212

      structure of the album, 207
      "Two Old Friends", 211
      "When I Hold You In My Arms", 211
      Young's first concept album, 206
      "You're My Girl", 207
   autobiography
      "Don't Be Denied" on *Time Fades Away*, 180
   Backstage at the Bridge School Benefit Concert, 244
   bands, 135
   benefits for Walden Woods, 170
   Berlin
      (video) shows the Transband cooked in concert, 197
   best claims to avant-pop in 1990s, 204
   biker mask, 174
      "Live to Ride" (unreleased), 174
      "Motorcycle Mama" from *Comes A Time*, 174
      "Unknown Legend" from *Harvest Moon*, 174
      "Westy" in the film *'68*, 260
   Bridge School Concerts
      "Country Feedback", 243
      "Déjà Vu", 243
      Fleet Foxes, 245
      "Love and Only Love", 243
   Bridge School Concerts (2 CDs and 3 DVDs), 243
   Bridge School Network Interviews, 244
   "Broken Arrow", 144
      second verse of, 148
   Buffalo Springfield, 138--139

Index

Buffalo Springfield at Bonnaroo (2011), 240
  didn't blaze like they used to, 241
  Richard Furay as a balancing force, 241
  what does Neil have planned for the band?, 241
career, 135
childlike, innocent mask, 140
Chrome Dreams, xx
Chrome Dreams
  never released original, 230
Chrome Dreams II, 229
commemoration of Flight 93 in "Let's Roll", 168
"Cortez the Killer", 144
Crazy Horse, 140
  the yang to the yin of Neil's acoustic voice, 140
cri de coeur, 206
critique of stoner persona
  "Hitchhiker", 156
  "Too Far Gone", 156
CSNY/*Déjà Vu*, 220
  band resurrected "Ohio", 229
  dissension in the band, 229
  documents walkout of the Atlanta audience when "Let's Impeach The President" was played there, 226
  favors the larger story of the tour, 228
  looks like the work of a professional film director, 228
  sad story of Karen Meredith, 229
  ultimate CSN & Y gesture, 218

death knell for the sixties on *Time Fades Away*, 181
dialectic between burning out and fading out, 183
"Don't Let It Bring You Down", 151
doomsayer penning apocalyptic jeremiads, 174--175
  "Goin' Back" on *Comes A Time*, 174
  "L. A." on *Time Fades Away*, 174
  "Trans Am" from *Sleeps With Angels*, 175
"Dreamin' Man", 153
Eldorado
  import EP with the Restless, 202
environmentalism
  "Mother Earth (Natural Anthem)" on *Ragged Glory*, 169
  "Natural Beauty" on *Harvest Moon*, 169
Everybody's Rockin'
  doomed leader of the Shocking Pinks, 197
Fork In The Road, 230
  "Cough Up The Bucks", 230
  "Fork In The Road", 230
  seven out of ten songs about cars., 230
  slight falling off of powers, 220
Freedom, 202
"Freedom of Speech" tour, 221
Geffin's attempt to sue him, 176
gentleman farmer, country boy, agrarian persona, 171--174
  "Are You Ready For the

Country?", 171
"Don't Spook The Horse", 172
Greendale
  "Be The Rain", 216
  "Carmichael", 215
  charm is in Young's laid-back approach, 217
  "Falling From Above", 214
  genesis of the project, 212
  "Grandpa's Interview", 214, 215
  "Leave The Driving", 215
  shock of the new, 213
  songs given chapter numbers in film, 217
  songs performed in order written, 214
  "Sun Green", 216
  the film, 217
  the show, 213
grim artwork on *Time Fades Away*, 181
Gulf War and environmentalism
  "War of Man" on *Harvest Moon*, 169
  Weld, 169
Hawks and Doves
  a transitional album, 192
headed for the ditch, 136
Heart of Gold
  filmed at historic Ryman Auditorium in Nashville, 234
"Helpless", 142
how he works, 220
Human Highway, 146
  premiered on August 16, 1982, 193
  Young's second narrative film project, 191
"I Am A Child", 141

instruments, 134
journey through the ditch on *Time Fades Away*, 179
Journey Through The Past, 136, 154, 160
journeys through the ditch, 177--203
Landing On Water
  modified synthesizer sound, 199
Le Noise, 238
  "Hitchhiker", 240
  "It's an Angry World", 240
  "Love and War", 239
  "Peaceful Valley Boulevard", 240
  "Rumblin'", 240
  "Sign of Love", 239
  "Someone's Going to Rescue You", 239
  "Walk With Me", 239
"Let's Impeach The President"
  a hand grenade thrown by Young into the mediascape, 227
Life
  "Inca Queen", 147
  return to Crazy Horse, 199
Lincvolt project, 230
Live On Air: The Lost Tapes Volume 2, 243
Living With War
  "After The Garden", 221
  an astonishing populist statement, 228
  each song has as many as five forms, 220
  "Families", 223
  "Flags Of Freedom", 224
  "Let's Impeach The President", 225
  "Living With War", 222

"Lookin' For A Leader", 227
most ambitious political statement on, 219
"The Restless Consumer", 222
"Roger And Out", 227
"Shock And Awe", 223
many masks, 134
masks, 140--176
"Misfits", 152
most obvious examples of his vatic and surreal troubadour mask, 149
"My Heart", 143
Native American mask, 144
new rock sound on *Everybody Knows This Is Nowhere*, 137
new sound courtesy of Daniel Lanois, 238
new sound in 2010 and 2011, 238
Old Ways
  as avant-country, 198
  country album, 197
  "Misfits", 198
Omemee, childhood home, 142
On the Beach
  "Ambulence Blues", 187
  best album?, 185
  interesting lineup of players on, 184
  "On the Beach", 187
  one of his best train songs in "See The Sky About To Rain", 185
  "Revolution Blues", 186
  "Vampire Blues", 187
  "Walk On", 185
oscillation between gentle county/folk rock and passionate and raw electric work in 1990s, 204
phenomenology, 133
"Philadelphia" from the soundtrack of the movie *Philadelphia*, 143
played at the Grand Old Opry, 173
"Pocahontas", 145
political activism
  "Are You Ready For the Country?" on *Harvest*, 160
  "Campaigner", 162
  "Comin' Apart At Every Nail" on *Hawks and Doves*, 162
  "Ohio", 157
  "Southern Man" on *After The Gold Rush*, 159
  "War Song, 161
political activist mask, 157--171
political views
  "Berlin", 164
  "Hawks and Doves" on *Hawks and Doves*, 162
  "Long Walk Home" on *Life*, 166
  "Mideast Vacation" on *Life*, 164
  "Rockin' in the Free World", 167
  "Southern Pacific" on *Re.Ac.Tor*, 163
  "This Old House", 167
  "Union Man" on *Hawks and Doves*, 163
poor critical reception for soundtrack of *Journey Through The Past*, 178
"Powderfinger", 143
Prairie Wind, 218

another concept album, 218
"It's A Dream", 218
Prairie Wind / Heart of Gold
  encore highlighting his previous work, 235
  "Fallin' Off The Face Of The Earth", 232
  "Far From Home", 232
  "He Was The King", 234
  "Here For You", 233
  "It's A Dream", 233
  memory theme in encore, 235
  "No Wonder", 232
  "The Old Laughing Lady", 235
  "One Of These Days", 235
  "The Painter", 231
  "Prairie Wind", 233
  "This Old Guitar", 233
  "When God Made Me", 234
Prairie Wind / Heart of Gold project, 231
proto-gothic gloom rocker mask, 150--154
Psychedelic Pill, 250
  "Born in Ontario", 251
  "Driftin' Back", 250
  "For the Love of Man", 251
  "Psychedelic Pill", 250
  "Ramada Inn", 251
  "Twisted Road", 251
  "Walk Like a Giant", 251
psychodrama as inoculation, 183
Ragged Glory
  Young out of the ditch, 202
Re.Ac.Tor
  least accessible work with Crazy Horse, 193
  "Shots", 193
  "Southern Pacific", 15, 193
renunciation of drugs and hippiedom
  Landing On Water, 156
  "No More" from *Freedom*, 157
  Old Ways, 156
Reprise's reluctance to and delay in releasing *Tonight's The Night*, 182
reunited and toured with Buffalo Springfield, 238
Rust Never Sleeps
  Young's third film, 191
second (actually third) ditch album *On the Beach*, 184
second journey into the ditch an avant-gard gesture?, 202
second son Ben diagnosed with cerebral palsy, 192
second, longer trip into the ditch, 192
separation and subsequent divorce of his parents, 140
shift to the right
  Hawks and Doves, 162
  Re.Ac.Tor, 162
SIR sessions on *Tonight's The Night*, 181
Sleeps With Angels, 205
"Soldier", 142
soundtrack for Jim Jarmusch's *Dead Man*, 205
speaking to *Melody Maker*, 182
Squires, 138
stoner persona
  "After the Gold Rush", 154
  "Albuquerque", 155
  "Homegrown" on *American Stars 'N Bars*, 155
  The Last Waltz, 155
  Tonight's the Night, 155

Index

stoner persona (mask), 154--157
"Sugar Mountain", 140
The Bridge School Story, 244
"The Great Divide", 153
"The Loner", 150
"The Old Laughing Lady", 150
"There's A World", 142
This Note's For You
  with the Bluenotes, 200
Tonight's The Night, 189
  "Come On Baby Let's Go Downtown", 190
  drunken / stoned musings on, 190
  on the release of, 188
  "Tired Eyes", 190
"Touch the Night", 152
tour with the Santa Monica Flyers, 182
Trans
  "Computer Age", 195
  "Computer Cowboy (AKA Syscrusher)", 196
  distinctive voice concealed, 194
  "Like an Inca", 146
  "Sample and Hold", 196
  "Transformer Man", 196
  two types of songs (with one exception), 195
  "We R In Control", 196
A Treasure, 241
  "Amber Jean", 242
  "Are You Ready For The Country?", 242
  "Flying On The Ground Is Wrong", 242
  "Grey Riders", 242
  "It Might Have Been", 242
  "Let Your Fingers Do The Walking", 242

"Motor City", 242
"Soul of a Woman", 242
"Southern Pacific", 242
trilogy of confessional albums, 179
tRockets, 139
trouble in paradise (1972), 177
ultimate outlaw, 173
underemphasis of some of his best work, 137
"unstuck in time", 241
urban homelessness
  "Life in the City" on *This Note's For You*, 168
  "People on the Street" on *Landing On Water*, 168
vatic and surreal troubadour mask, 147
"Violent Side", 152
virtual intimacy, 249
Waging Heavy Peace: A Hippie Dream, 247
What's next?, 252
"The Will to Love", 142
willingness to explore during disappointing periods, 179
with the Ducks, 136
Year of the Horse, 56
Zuma
  beginning of a second commercial run in the 1970s, 191
Young, Pegi
  Bracing for Impact
    Neil made some contributions to, 245
Yvega, Todd, 94, 116

Zappa, Dweezil, 97, 100
Zappa, Francesco

(baroque composer), 109
Zappa, Frank, xx, 17, 492
   200 Motels, 63, 83, 84, 89, 100, 109
   Absolutely Free, 61, 76
   absurdist, 92
   Ahead Of Their Time, 108
   Anyway The Wind Blows, 113
   Apostrophe, 110
   As An Am, 113
   as editor, 107
   as sociologist, 56, 58, 83, 89, 102, 106, 130
   At The Circus, 101
   Baby Snakes, 104
   Baby Snakes (film), 58, 86, 91
   "Billy the Mountain", 85, 90
   Bongo Fury, 65, 79
   Boulez Conducts Zappa: The Perfect Stranger, 89
   Broadway the Hard Way, 77
   "Brown Shoes Don't Make It", 64, 76, 78, 127
   Buffalo, 106
   Burnt Weeny Sandwich, 98
   capitalism, 68
   Carnegie Hall, 83, 102
   censorship, 114--115
   Chunga's Revenge, 83, 110
   Civilization Phaze III, 93, 94
   classical, 67, 89
   classical albums ranked, 126--127
   commercialism, 69, 73, 108, 115
   Conceptual Continuity, 107
   Congress Shall Make No Law. . ., 113
   contract dispute, 87
   country, 127--128
   Cruising With Ruben And The Jets, 56, 59, 92
   dental hygiene, 128
   digital dust, 89
   Disconnected Synapses, 84, 88
   documentary, 80
   Does Humor Belong In Music?, 100
   "Duke of Prunes", 76
   Electric Aunt Jemima, 113
   Everything Is Healing Nicely, 88
   Feeding the Monkies at Ma Maison, 94
   feminism, 61--68, 77, 90, 118
   Fillmore East, 83
   Fillmore East, June 1971, 110
   film, 89
   Finer Moments, 101, 102
   Flo and Eddie, 90
   for lovers, 127
   Francesco Zappa, 94, 109
   Frank Zappa Meets The Mothers Of Prevention, 98
   Frank Zappa Plays The Music of Frank Zappa: A Memorial Tribute, 70
   Freak Out, 54, 57, 59, 61
   FZ:OZ, 85
   genres and techniques, 59, 80, 101, 116, 117
   Grank Wazoo (band), 106
   Greasy Love Songs, 91
   groupies, 63, 119
   Guitar, 96
   Halloween, 100
   Hammersmith Odeon, 86
   his project/object, 55--61
   hocketing, 88
   Hot Rats, 105
   Hot Rats: Waka / Jawaka, 83
   Hunchentoot, 77, 97
   Imaginary Diseases, 105
   "Inca Roads", 71, 78, 111
   jail, 66, 78, 113

jazz albums ranked, 126
Jazz From Hell, 104
Joe's Corsage, 112
Joe's Domage, 111
Joe's Garage, 78
Joe's Menage, 85
Joe's Xmasage, 113
"Jumbo Go Away", 66
Just Another Band From L.A., 64, 83, 90
Lather, 87, 105
London Symphony Orchestra, 99
Lumpy Gravy, 57, 59, 73--74, 106
Lumpy Money, 106
Lumpy Money: an FZ audio documentary project / object, 73
Make A Jazz Noise Here, 95
"Merely a Blues in A", 71
Mothermania: The Best of the Mothers, 75, 76
Mothers of Invention, 58--59, 75, 76, 81, 83, 86, 88, 92, 98, 102, 103
Mystery Disc, 112
New Age religion, 112
on gender, 61--68, 116
one shot deal, 104
One Size Fits All, 77, 108
Orchestral Favorites, 105
Our Man In Nirvana, 107
Over-Nite Sensation, 130
Over-Nite Sensation, 55, 59, 83, 97, 110
parody, 108, 109
perfectionism, 112, 122
Petit Wazoo, 105
Philly, 82
"Pick Me, I'm Clean", 66
Piquantique, 91
Playground Psychotics, 17, 90

poodle play, 128
posthumous release, 84
productions, 115--122
project/object, 65, 91
QuAUDIOPHILIAc, 82
Rare Meat: Early Productions of Frank Zappa, 115
regionalism, 513
Road Tapes Venue, 102
Road Tapes Venue . . . Vancouver . . . 1968, 81
rock albums ranked, 124--126
rock opera, 78, 90, 110
Roxy & Elsewhere, 71, 77
Ruben and the Jets, 91
Saarbrucken, 113
Sheik Yerbouti, 66, 79
Shut Up 'N Play Yer Guitar, 101
Sleep Dirt, 76, 87
sociologist, 98, 130
Studio Tan, 105
subversive approach to the fine arts, 268
Sun Ra, 80
surrealism, 59
synclavier, 94, 127
television special, 100
Tenga Na Minchia Tanta, 108
The Ark, 111
The Best Band You Never Heard In Your Life, 108
"A Few Moments With Brother A. West", 303
"The Black Page", 77, 87, 91, 100
The Ensemble Modern, 93
The Grand Wazoo, 106
"The Illinois Enema Bandit", 64--66, 86, 87
The Lost Episodes, 111
The Man From Utopia, 103
The Real Frank Zappa Book, 67

The Torture Never Stops, 100
The World's Greatest Sinner, 56
The Yellow Shark, 129
The Yellow Shark, 88
Them Or Us: The Book, 68, 77, 97, 128
thematic mix tapes, 127--128
Thing-Fish, 59, 67, 77, 109
Tinseltown Rebellion, 78
'Tis The Season To Be Jelly, 111
Too Late To Save A Drowning Witch, 75
Trance-Fusion, 95
transgressive, 64--68, 73, 75, 76, 90, 91, 97, 109, 113
Uncle Meat, 61, 72, 98, 102, 103
Unmitigated Audacity, 88
Video from Hell, 94
Waka / Jawaka, 99

"Watermelon in Easter Hay", 71, 78
Wazoo, 99
Weasels Ripped My Flesh, 98
We're Only In It For the Money, 56, 59, 60, 62--63, 72, 73, 75, 85, 88, 98
Yoko Ono, 80
You Are What You Is, 69, 79, 100
You Can't Do That On Stage Anymore, 90, 91, 101, 106, 108
You Can't Do That On Stage Anymore, Volume 2: The Helsinki Concert, 71
Zappa in New York, 87
Zoot Allures, 65, 81
Zappa, Gail, 65, 74, 94, 116
Zappa, Moon Unit, 75, 93

CPSIA information can be obtained at www.ICGtesting.com
Printed in the USA
LVOW11*2044231213

366626LV00001B/1/P